# INCLUSIVE EDUCATION IN THE EARLY YEARS

***Dedication:***

*This book is dedicated to all the children, families, students and early years professionals who have shared the journey with me.*

# INCLUSIVE EDUCATION IN THE EARLY YEARS

## RIGHT FROM THE START

*Edited by*
KATHY COLOGON

OXFORD
UNIVERSITY PRESS

Oxford University Press is a department of the University of Oxford.

It furthers the University's objective of excellence in research, scholarship, and education by publishing worldwide. Oxford is a registered trademark of Oxford University Press in the UK and in certain other countries.

Published in Australia by
Oxford University Press
253 Normanby Road, South Melbourne, Victoria 3205, Australia





First published 2014





National Library of Australia Cataloguing-in-Publication data

Title: Inclusive education in the early years / Kathy Cologon, editor.
ISBN: 9780195524123 (paperback)
Notes: Includes index.
Subjects: Inclusive education–Australia.
Early childhood special education–Australia.
Early childhood education–Australia.
Educational equalization–Australia.
Children with disabilities–Education–Australia.
Other Authors/Contributors: Cologon, Kathy, editor.
Dewey Number: 371.90460994





Cover design by Ana Cosma
Text design by Ana Cosma
Typeset by diacriTech
Proofread by Liz Filleul
Indexed by Julie King
Printed by Markono Print Media Pte Ltd, Singapore

# Contents

# Expanded Contents

# List of Figures

# Preface

Inclusive education is the right of every child—it is not an 'added extra' or a charitable 'special effort'. A common misunderstanding is that inclusive education is simply about the placement of children who experience disability in settings alongside peers who do not experience disability. On the contrary, inclusive education *is about everyone*.

Nonetheless, some of us are at greater risk of being excluded. When a person or group of people are excluded, conscious efforts are required to challenge and address this exclusion and bring about greater inclusion.

Inclusive education is based on the premise that no child is 'broken' and that children do not need to be 'fixed' or 'cured'. There are no 'special' children and 'regular' or 'normal' children—there are just children. Inclusive education requires rejecting the notion of the mythical 'normal child'. Rather than denying difference, or associating difference with deficit, inclusive education involves embracing all human diversity and responding to it in a way that supports children in positive engagements with each other and the world.

Like many governments across the world, the Australian Government has expressed its commitment to uphold the right to inclusive education. Through its ratification of international covenants and in an array of documents and policies, including the *National Disability Strategy*, the *Australian Curriculum*, the *Australian Professional Standards for Teachers*, the *National Quality Framework* and the *Early Years Learning Framework for Australia*, it recognises the importance of responding to student diversity and ensuring the inclusion of all children. However, in reality, many children continue to be denied equal access to inclusive education.

There are many barriers to inclusive education identified through research. Such barriers include stigma and negative attitudes around 'difference' and 'disability', inadequate education and professional development for early years professionals, and systemic barriers. Yet, despite these challenges, research evidence supports inclusive education. Not only does it provide evidence of positive outcomes for social justice and sense of community and belonging, it shows that inclusive education benefits social, academic, cognitive and physical development in *all* children—regardless of labels of 'difference' or 'disability'.

Education of all children *together* is an important prerequisite for inclusion. However, it isn't enough on its own. Inclusive education is *much more* than this. Inclusive education doesn't just require all children being present—it requires their full participation and belonging as equal members of any given education community. Inclusive education demands more than replacing the term 'special education' with the term 'inclusive education'—instead, it involves transforming educational systems, processes and practices. Understanding inclusive education is a key starting point for this process.

The concept of inclusive education and what this means as a philosophy, as a process and in practice is explored in this book. Throughout the book, the authors draw on a range of theoretical perspectives to inform everyday inclusive practices. Underpinning the book is engagement with a strengths-based and rights-based approach informed by a social relational understanding of 'difference' and 'disability'. Such an understanding incorporates all forms of diversity, including diversity in relation to culture, ability, gender, age, belief/non-belief, background and experiences. This social relational understanding forms the theoretical framework of the book.

Many early years professionals come to a book like this one thinking that in order to support the education of all children, they need to obtain detailed information regarding diagnostic categories of difference—or characteristics of 'disabilities'. However, what they find when they approach inclusive education *in practice* is that this information is of little assistance. In fact, research is increasingly showing that diagnosis-specific knowledge can be a problem for inclusive education: early years professionals easily become focused on the label and not the child, thus they implement inappropriate strategies that do not suit the child. Instead, in contrast to common assumptions, research shows that it is beliefs about, and attitudes towards, inclusive education that create spaces to make inclusion possible—or to prevent it. This necessitates an ongoing cycle of *reflection and action* involving openness to reconsidering current attitudes and practices and a willingness to *genuinely* listen to people who are excluded—including children.

This is not to say that technical knowledge regarding inclusive practice isn't important—it is, but it is only useful when informed by a genuine commitment to inclusive education as a fundamental right of every child. At the same time, early years professionals require support in developing practical everyday strategies for bringing about inclusion in practice. Consequently, this book approaches inclusive education as both philosophy and practice—and as a process of ongoing engagement in critical reflection and action. The issues explored within this book are complex and therefore require consideration beyond 'simple answers'. Reflecting the diversity of the children we teach and the complexity of the issues, the chapters take a variety of approaches in order to illuminate their content. For example, in Chapter 8 Sue Atkinson and Prasanna Srinivasan engage in dialogic discussions considering the complexities of practising Aboriginal identities in current postcolonial societies, and how such complexities are reflected within the early years. In Chapter 5 I focus on the voices of families as parents share their experiences of, and perspectives on, inclusive education. In Chapter 17 Melanie Nind, Rosie Flewitt and Fani Theodorou draw on ethnographic research with young children in early years settings to illuminate the importance of play for children's inclusion and the role of early years professionals in facilitating inclusive play. Each of the 26 chapters approaches the content with the intention of creating a space to engage with the complexity of inclusion in the context of everyday practices.

Inclusive education is a 'big idea', but it is lived out in individual moments. To bring about inclusive education, we need to create situations where all children can be valued, experience a sense of belonging, and be supported to flourish.

The implications of inclusive education reach beyond the classroom. If the right to inclusive education were to become a reality for all children, this would provide the ideal conditions for creating a more inclusive society as a whole. Early years professionals have a daunting responsibility—and yet an exciting challenge—to make a major contribution to this transformation and, in doing so, to contribute positively to the lives of each child and family with whom they engage. This book is intended to support early years professionals in these efforts.

# About the Editor

**KATHY COLOGON**, PhD, lectures in Inclusive Early Childhood Education at the Institute of Early Childhood, Macquarie University. Through her teaching and research Kathy seeks to contribute to knowledge and understanding about how early childhood professionals can ensure all children flourish as valued community members. Prior to entering academia, Kathy worked in mainstream preschool and school settings and developed and implemented early intervention and inclusive early childhood programs. In her research, Kathy continues to work closely with children, early years professionals, families and policy makers across the Asia-Pacific region and beyond. Kathy has conducted research into effective supports for language, literacy and numeracy development; disability studies in education, including child, parent and teacher perspectives on and attitudes towards inclusive education and children's rights; inclusive approaches to disaster risk reduction; and inclusive community development.

# About the Contributors

**KATE ALEXANDER** completed a Bachelor of Early Childhood Studies (Hons.) in 2004 and a Master of Education (Research) in 2007. In her Master's thesis, she explored children's understandings of gender-neutral characters in children's picture books. In 2006 she began working at the Centre for Equity and Innovation in Early Childhood as a research assistant, and has assisted in several research projects. Kate is currently a Senior Administrator in the University of Melbourne's Graduate School of Education.

**SUE ATKINSON** is an Aboriginal Victorian, a Yorta Yorta woman who has worked in the early childhood field for over thirty years. Her 2008 PhD thesis, *Indigenous self-determination and early childhood education and care in Victoria*, positions postcolonial discourse around self-determination. In her research she explores the movement to decolonisation in early childhood settings as the Indigenous early childhood community, in both concert and conflict with the wider early childhood community, deal with the effects of colonisation by accessing and exercising power as a community and as individuals. Sue has recently retired due to ill health but continues to contribute to academia as Honorary Research Fellow at the University of Melbourne's Graduate School of Education, Youth Research Centre. She also remains active at a community level as a member of various committees.

**PETER CLOUGH** is Honorary Professor of Education at the University of Sheffield. In the 1970s Peter taught English and Drama in London and later in a number of special schools. His research interests include the use of narrative and fictional writing in research and research reports. Peter has taught Inclusive Education and Early Childhood Education at the University of Sheffield, has been Professor of Inclusive Education at Queen's University Belfast and at Liverpool Hope University, and Research Fellow at the University of Chester. Now at the University of Sheffield, Peter teaches Masters and Doctoral students. His more than fifty publications, including several books, focus on equality, inclusion, difference, and teachers' lives. Key titles are: *Narratives and Fictions in Educational Research* (OUP, 2002), *A Student's Guide to Methodology* (Sage, 2012), *Early Childhood Education: History, Philosophy and Research* (Sage, 2008), and *Inclusion in the Early Years: Critical Analysis and Enabling Narratives* (Sage, 2013; with Cathy Nutbrown).

**DINAH COCKSEDGE** has worked in a variety of education contexts, specialising in Early Childhood from birth to five years, for 20 years. For the past 12 years, she has worked in a regional community-based child care centre with a strong and active philosophy of inclusion and social justice. Dinah's academic career started at Macquarie University, with a BA in Ancient History. This background still colours the way she understands the world: she has been known to talk about 2000-year-old rag dolls and wooden horse toys when she documents the play of the twenty-first century children she works with. Subsequent Master of Education and Master of Teaching (birth to five years) degrees, also at Macquarie University, have inspired and supported Dinah's current work in both early childhood and adult education.

**LISA DETERS** is an early childhood development specialist, a certified early childhood and elementary educator in the USA, and an experienced humanitarian. Lisa has recently completed her doctorate focused on early childhood development (ECD) in Emergencies; she also holds a Master's degree in International Educational Development. Her research draws on her experience as an emergency responder assessing, designing and implementing emergency education and ECD responses. Her practitioner and research experiences have deployed her to diverse post-disaster and post-conflict contexts, most recently with Save the Children in Tunisia, Libya, Ivory Coast, Haiti, Kenya, Somalia, South Sudan and the Philippines.

**AUDREY D'SOUZA JUMA** is Director at Notre Dame Institute of Education and Honorary Research Fellow at the Youth Research Centre at the University of Melbourne. Her doctorate is in the area of early childhood and gender. She has worked as a faculty member and coordinator of early childhood programs at the Institute for Educational Development, Aga Khan University. She has also been a member of the advisory committee for the review of the Pakistan National Curriculum for early childhood. She has extensive teaching and teacher education experience in varied settings in Pakistan and Australia. Her research interests include gender, play, early childhood curriculum and pedagogy, ethnic diversity and identities.

**RHONDA FARAGHER** is Head of Education and Senior Lecturer in Mathematics Education on the Canberra campus of Australian Catholic University. Her doctorate investigated numeracy in the context of Down syndrome. Research interests have centred on helping all learners experience success with mathematics, particularly those with Down syndrome. She serves on a number of international committees including the Board of the Academy of the International Association of Scientific Study for Intellectual and Developmental Disability (IASSIDD). She has received a number of awards for her work, including a Vice-Chancellor's Award for Teaching Excellence and a Commonwealth of Australia, Endeavour Executive Award.

**ROSIE FLEWITT** is Senior Lecturer in Early Years and Primary Education at the Institute of Education, University of London, and a member of the London Knowledge Lab. Her research focuses on the complementary areas of young children's communication, language and literacy development in a multimedia age and on inclusive practices in early education. Rosie has spent many years developing ethnographic and multimodal approaches to the study of early learning and how children use combinations of modes, such as spoken and written language, gesture, images, sounds and layout, as they engage with written, oral, visual and digital texts. Recent research includes an evaluation of Vivian Gussin Paley's Helicopter Technique for storytelling and story acting in early education;the multimodal potential of the iPad for early literacy learning; and Multimodal Literacies in the Early Years (see Websites at the end of Chapter 17 for more details).

**LORAINE FORDHAM** is a lecturer and researcher in the field of Early Childhood. Loraine has a PhD in Early Childhood from Macquarie University and has worked as an academic, researcher and speech pathologist in a range of early childhood, academic, health and community organisations. Loraine's research interests include early childhood intervention and working with families and young children, particularly those who experience disability, disadvantage or marginalisation. Loraine is especially concerned with using strengths-based approaches in intervention, education, evaluation and research practice.

**CAMILLA GORDON** is a lecturer in early childhood science at Macquarie University. She has extensive experience in teaching science to children labelled as gifted in informal settings. For her Master's (Hons.) degree she researched family learning in the Starwatcher Programme—an astronomy opportunity for families with children of early childhood age. Her PhD used the results of that research to focus on astronomy learning for children in the year before formal school. She is currently seeking research grants to apply the fruits of both research theses in the early years of school, and with Indigenous preschool children and their families in far western New South Wales.

**LINDA J. GRAHAM** is Associate Professor and Principal Research Fellow in the Faculty of Education at Queensland University of Technology. Linda's work focuses on institutional contributions to disruptive behaviour and the improvement of responses to children who are difficult to teach. Her chapter (24) draws on data produced through a research fellowship funded by the Australian Research Council Discovery scheme, which investigated the increase in diagnosis of special educational needs in New South Wales government schools. In 2011, findings from this program of research led to her receiving the Academy of Social Sciences in Australia Paul Bourke Award and the Australian Association for Research in Education (AARE) Early Career Researcher Award.

**LEANNE HALLOWELL** is a lecturer at Australian Catholic University, Melbourne. Her career in early childhood has included working in a variety of mainstream early childhood services in local government, and for the Free Kindergarten Association and Anglican Free Kindergartens, before she became the Head of Educational Play Therapy at the Royal Children's Hospital, Melbourne (RCH). While at the RCH, Leanne lectured, published and worked in national and international projects that supported better psychosocial outcomes for children in paediatric health care and their families. Leanne's particular interest is children in health care and related discourses. Her Master's thesis reviewed the effect of educational play therapy interventions in Medical Resonance Imaging. In her PhD thesis she is investigating the engagement between children and doctors when doctors explain medical procedures to them.

**JACQUELINE HAYDEN** is Foundation Professor of Social Inclusion at Macquarie University, where she heads a research team specialising in young children and fragile contexts. In previous positions Jacqueline has worked as an early childhood program manager, policy analyst and government director, and has consulted to, and/or directed emergency and development programs for young children around the globe including in Rwanda, Cambodia, Namibia, Eastern Europe and the Asia-Pacific Region.

Jacqueline is widely published on topics relating to conflict, emergency and disaster risk reduction and young children.

**KATE HIGHFIELD** is a teacher educator from the Institute of Early Childhood, Macquarie University. Having taught for many years, Kate now works with educators, student teachers, children and families, with a focus on how technology can be used as a tool to enhance learning and engagement. Kate's PhD focused on the use of simple robotics in mathematics learning and examined how effective technology integration can be used to enable metacognition. The focus of her current research and teaching is the use of technologies for learning and play.

**KERRY HODGE** is an Honorary Associate in the Institute of Early Childhood at Macquarie University and a member of its Children and Families Research Centre. With experience as a preschool teacher and consultant, Kerry's PhD and subsequent research and publications have focused on identifying giftedness in young children and on teachers' perspectives regarding gifted children in early childhood settings. She has lectured at undergraduate and postgraduate level on the educational needs of young gifted children. Kerry is also the Research and Development Manager of the STaR Association, a Sydney charity supporting children with special learning needs—including those with advanced development—and their parents and teachers. She was awarded the 2009 Nancy Fairfax Churchill Fellowship to investigate overseas programs for gifted preschoolers and teacher training in early gifted education.

**TERESA IACONO** is Professor of Rural and Regional Allied Health at La Trobe University, Bendigo. She earned her doctorate in Special Education and Communication Disorders at the University of Nebraska–Lincoln. She is a speech-language pathologist, with clinical, teaching and research interests in assessment and intervention for people with severe intellectual and other developmental disabilities across the lifespan, and the role of augmentative and alternative communication (AAC) in enhancing their communication. She has published widely on these topics, with 90 journal papers, eight book chapters and a co-edited book on AAC and Autism Spectrum Disorders. She is a previous editor of *Augmentative and Alternative Communication*. In 2007, she received the inaugural National Health and Medical Research Council (Australia) Ethics Award for her work into ethical concerns of including people with developmental disabilities in research. She is a member of the La Trobe University Living with Disabilities research group, continuing her work in severe intellectual disabilities, including addressing the needs of those in rural communities.

**CHRISTINE JOHNSTON** is Associate Professor and Director, Engagement and International in the School of Education, University of Western Sydney. She researches and teaches primarily in the areas of early childhood intervention and evidence-based practice. Christine maintains a strong involvement in the early childhood intervention field both nationally and internationally through her teaching, her work with professional groups and her research.

**HANAPI MOHAMAD** is a lecturer in Psychology Studies and Human Development Department in the Sultan Hassanal Bolkiah Institute of Education at Universiti Brunei Darussalam. He obtained his PhD from the University of Western Australia and received the Cameron Prize in Education for Best Piece of Research in Education in May 2007; in August that year he also received a Forgarty Postgraduate Research Award from the Western Australia Institute of Educational Research (WAIER). He has been Head of the Early Childhood Department and of the Educational Technology Centre. He also served as a member of the University Strategic Quality and Assurance Management Unit and the Faculty of Education Senior Management Committee. He was actively engaged with the Ministry of Education Brunei as a member of the Core Committee in the development of a new education system for Brunei Darussalam. His other work has included a Consultancy Project for the National Study on Youth Perceptions of the Arts of Brunei Darussalam and research on day care and nursery settings for the Ministry of Education. He is now a local research consultant for the International Child Resource Institute, USA.

**MELANIE NIND** is Professor of Education at the University of Southampton. While she is best known for her work on Intensive Interaction as a way of working with people of all ages with profound intellectual impairments, her research interests lie in interactive and inclusive pedagogy more broadly. Recently she has also been exploring inclusive research methods. Melanie began her teaching career in special schools as a teacher of students with severe and complex learning difficulties and autism. Since moving to higher education she has spent three decades researching and teaching in special and inclusive education, including early years education. She is currently a co-director of the National Centre for Research Methods and co-editor of the *International Journal of Research and Method in Education*.

**CATHY NUTBROWN** is Professor and Head of the School of Education at the University of Sheffield, where she teaches and researches in the field of Early Childhood Education. Cathy began her career as a teacher of young children and has since worked in a range of settings and roles with children, parents, teachers and other early childhood educators. Cathy is committed to finding ways of working 'with respect' with young children. She sees the concept of quality in the context of what it means to develop curriculum and pedagogy in the early years, with the ambition of working in a climate of 'respectful education'. She established the University of Sheffield MA in Early Childhood Education in 1998 and a Doctoral Programme in Early Childhood Education in 2008. In 2010 she contributed to the Tickell Review of the Early Years Foundation, and in June 2012 she reported on her year-long independent review for government on early years and childcare qualifications (The Nutbrown Review). She is Editor-in-Chief of the *Sage Journal of Early Childhood Research* and author of over fifty publications on aspects of early childhood education. She is author (with Peter Clough) of *Inclusion in the early years: Critical analysis and enabling narratives* (Sage, 2013).

**PAUL PAGLIANO** has extensive experience working with children with sense impairments and, in recognition of this work, in January 2013 he was made a life member of the South Pacific Educators in Vision Impairment. Paul is Associate Professor of Education at James Cook University, where he is Director of Academic and Accreditations overseeing course design and the accreditation of the Bachelor of Education (Early Childhood Education). He is also Course Coordinator of the Master of Guidance and Counselling and the Graduate Certificate of Career Development. Paul's principal research interest is multisensory stimulation and he has authored three books on this topic, his latest being *The multisensory handbook*. Paul is on the editorial boards of eight professional journals and an associate editor of the *International Journal of Disability, Development and Education*.

**EMMA PEARSON** works with the Psychological Studies and Human Development Department in the Sultan Hassanal Bolkiah Institute of Education at Brunei Darussalam. Her research activities reflect a commitment to understanding and promoting the importance of diverse belief and value systems in early childhood theory, policy and practice. Through consultancies with UNICEF and UNESCO in East Asia and the Pacific, she has worked with many colleagues across the region, from North Korea to Vanuatu, and endeavours to build on these experiences in her teaching and research.

**ANNE PETRIWSKYJ** is Adjunct Associate Professor in the School of Early Childhood, Queensland University of Technology, where she lectures on diversity and inclusion in the early years. Her teaching background in rural, remote and Aboriginal communities, in early intervention and in inclusive early years education, frames her research in inclusive pedagogies, transition to school of children with diverse abilities and backgrounds, and effective professional preparation of early years educators.

**MARGARET SIMS** is Professor of Early Childhood at the University of New England. Before joining academia she worked for many years with children with disabilities and their families in early intervention and inclusion services. Her research interests focus around high quality community-based services for children and families, including those with a range of diverse needs such as children who have experienced trauma, children with disabilities, infants and toddlers, and children and families from migrant and/or Indigenous backgrounds. She developed and is teaching in the first Australian graduate programme in integrated early childhood service delivery. She is currently the Editor of the *Australasian Journal of Early Childhood*.

**KYLIE SMITH** is a Research Fellow and Senior Lecturer in the Melbourne Graduate School of Education at the University of Melbourne. Kylie's research examines how theory and practice can challenge equity in the early childhood classroom and she has worked with children, parents and teachers to build safe and respectful communities. Kylie's research is also informed by 25 years' experience working in early childhood services.

**ILEKTRA SPANDAGOU** is Senior Lecturer at the Faculty of Education and Social Work, University of Sydney. She has a teaching background in early years inclusive education settings, and has been involved in teacher education in special and inclusive education both in Greece and Australia. She has experience working with general and special education teachers in the area of theories of inclusive education, and the nexus of policy and school practice. Ilekra's research interests include inclusion, disability, comparative education and classroom diversity. Her publications include the book *Inclusive education: International policy and practice* (co-authored with A.C. Armstrong and D. Armstrong, Sage, 2010).

**PRASANNA SRINIVASAN** is a research fellow in the Equity and Childhood Program, Youth Research Centre at the Melbourne Graduate School of Education. She has also worked in the early childhood field for over twelve years in varied early childhood settings in Melbourne. Srinivasan's doctoral research,

*Contesting identities in othered voices*, looks into how cultures are enacted in early childhood settings. Using participatory action research methodology, she highlights the challenges faced in current Australian multicultural society through the voices of children, families, staff and self. In particular, she outlines some of the key assumptions of early childhood educational leaders that hinder the equitable practices of all cultures in educational settings.

**FANI THEODOROU** is a physical education teacher in a Greek preliminary school for children with disability. She has worked extensively in a wide range of school and clinical settings in Greece, Belgium and the UK. In Greece, she worked for two years on a one-to-one basis with a child with autism in a preliminary school, while in her Master's degree in Belgium she volunteered in a clinical setting, supporting psychomotor interventions for children with autism and intellectual impairment. In the UK, she volunteered for two years in an inclusive school setting; at the same time, she undertook her doctorate degree, which employed more naturalistic and ethnographic ways to understand how children with autism express themselves through play, and their teachers' roles in encouraging this.

**CAROL THOMAS** is Professor of Sociology at Lancaster University, based in the Faculty of Health and Medicine. She is best known for her publications in Disability Studies, including her books *Female Forms: Experiencing and understanding disability* (1997, Open University Press) and *Sociologies of disability and illness. Contested ideas in disability studies and medical sociology* (2007, Palgrave Macmillan). She has also researched and published widely on patients' and carers' experiences of living with cancer, and has developed an interest in illness narratives. Publications on narrative analysis have followed, notably in debate context in *Sociology of Health and Illness, 32 (4)*. Carol is currently Director of the Centre for Disability Research (CeDR) at Lancaster University.

**SANDIE WONG** is Assistant Director of the Research Institute for Professional Practice, Learning and Education (RIPPLE) at Charles Sturt University. Sandie's research focuses broadly on the role early childhood education and intervention have in ameliorating disadvantage and reducing marginalisation, from both a contemporary and historical perspective. Her current research examines integrated early childhood services, collaborative practices and inter-professional working relationships. She is particularly concerned with using collaborative, strengths-based approaches to build and support research capacity in the academy and the early childhood field.

**HJH ZURIYATINI HJ ZAINAL** works as a tutor under the Psychological Studies and Human Development Academic Group in the Sultan Hassanal Bolkiah Institute of Education, Universiti Brunei Darussalam. She is pursuing her MPhil/PhD at the Institute of Education, University of London. Her interest mainly plays around the theories and beliefs of parents and also of teachers in young children's early reading development.

# Acknowledgments

I would like to acknowledge the traditional owners of the lands upon which this book was written, and their elders past and present. In particular I want to recognise the Darug people, the traditional owners of the land at Macquarie University, Sydney, on which many of the chapters were written.

I would like to thank the authors for their valuable contributions to this book and to the field. It has been a pleasure and privilege to work with each of you.

To the reviewers Sue Atkinson, Sue Buckley, Simona D'Alessio, Lisa Deters, Carl Dunst, Alma Fleet, Jacqueline Hayden, Chiharu Kondo, Amanda Niland, Roger Slee, Prasanna Srinivasan, Shirley Wyver, and the anonymous reviewers for OUP, many thanks for generously sharing your time. Your willingness to provide peer-review and your expertise and helpful comments have been very valuable in developing and refining this book.

Thank you to Cameron, Charlie, Emma, Grace, Joshua, Kaitlyn and Lucas for creating and sharing your art to illustrate the book.

Thank you to all the children in the photographs and to the children, their families and educational settings for permission to use these images. Thank you also to the photographers: 'Anita', S. Beadle, 'Danielle', Viki Demetriou, Lisa Deters, Kerry Hodge, Sarah Mann, Alison Wilson, Kerrie Dietz, Brunei Child Development Rising Star School, Rimba II Primary School Brunei, and my particular thanks to Dinah Cocksedge.

Katie Ridsdale, without your invitation to write this book, and your enthusiasm for the project, it would not have happened—thank you. To Debra James, thank you for your ongoing guidance and untiring interest in the book. My thanks to Zinnia Mevawalla and Ruth Cortejos for their assistance. And to Jennifer Butler, thank you for your thoughtful support, careful attention to detail and helpful suggestions in bringing this book to publication.

I would like to thank each of the research participants who have participated in the various projects that are reported in this book. Your time and generosity in sharing of yourselves enriches not only this book, but also our developing understanding of inclusion, and of the human story. My thanks also to Danny Dickson for sharing his speech.

To my students, thank you for the ongoing challenges and inspiration through shared learning.

My thanks to all the children, families and early years professionals with whom I have been privileged to work over many years.

I would like to thank my family for showing me the true meaning of inclusion.

Last, but not certainly not least, my deepest thanks to Adam and Finbar. Thank you for the encouragement, patience and ongoing interest as this book has filled our lives.

---

The author and the publisher wish to thank the following copyright holders for reproduction of their material.

*Images*

**Disability Council of NSW**/Kerry Millard, fig 1.2, 1.3, 3.3; **iStockphoto**/Claudiad, fig 9.2/jo unruh, fig 20.2/ KatarzynaBialasiewicz, fig 17.2/MichaelDeLeon, fig 21.2/NI QIN, fig 5.4; **Peytral publications inc**/ Absurdities and Realities of Special Education, fig 2.3.

*Text*

Centre for Studies on Inclusive Education and Tony Booth for extract from *Index for inclusion* by T. Booth and M. Ainscow (2011); Disability Council NSW for extract from *Interactions with school personnel, More than getting through the gate: The involvement of parents who have a disability in their children's school education in NSW*, Robinson, S. and Hickson, F; Early Childhood Intervention Australia for extract from *Mixed Feelings: A Parental Perspective on Early Intervention*. Presented at the National Conference of Early Childhood Intervention Australia, Brisbane by L. Bridle and G. Mann (2000); Elsevier for extract from journal of *Social Science & Medicine*; Inclusive Solutions for extract from Mason, M. (2000). *Incurably human*; John Wiley & Sons Inc for extract from *Journal of Research in Special Educational Needs*; Palgrave MacMillan for extracts from *My sister Stevie* by Tyrie, B. In T. Curran and K. Runswick-Cole (Eds.), *Disabled children's childhood studies: Critical approaches in a global context/ Sociologies of disability and illness: Contested ideas in disability studies and medical sociology* by C. Thomas (2007); Routledge Taylor and Francis for extracts from *Community, Work & Family* journal/*Assessment of young children with special needs: a context-based approach* (2nd edn). New York by S. Benner & J. Grim (2013)/*Journal of Loss and Trauma: International Perspectives on Stress & Coping*; The Disability Archive, University of Leeds for extract from *Phase 2: Discovering the person in 'disability' and 'rehabilitation'*, Magic Carpet, 27, V. Finkelstein.

Every effort has been made to trace the original source of copyright material contained in this book. The publisher will be pleased to hear from copyright holders to rectify any errors or omissions.

# Publisher's Note

Oxford University Press Australia and New Zealand takes pride in delivering quality teaching and learning resources that lecturers, students and researchers can refer to in the practice of their profession. The publication, *Inclusive Education in the Early Years: Right from the Start*, reflects the commitment to the advancement of scholarly knowledge and its impact on professional learning. Oxford University Press, the editor and the authors involved in this book would like to thank the reviewers involved in the anonymous peer review process, which provided valuable guidance in developing and finalising the book. These reviewers were a range of academics with expertise in specific areas relevant to this book.

The book is grounded in the authors' understandings of the work of early years professionals. It reflects the authors' skills in bringing theory and practice together, and is based on their research and teaching expertise. In addition to containing new insights on contemporary inclusive education literature, the book presents original findings from research on inclusive education in the early years. We believe that the book will assist readers as they work to become ever more inclusive in their practice and expect they will discover creative and critical ways of thinking about inclusion and inclusive education.

SECTION 1

# Understanding Inclusion in the Early Years

# 1 Better Together: Inclusive Education in the Early Years

*Kathy Cologon*

CHAPTER OVERVIEW

This chapter unpacks the concept of inclusive education and explores the implications of inclusion for the early years.

Learning goals for this chapter include:

- Considering the process of stigmatisation and the implications for exclusion;
- Developing an understanding of inclusion, including recognising misunderstandings of inclusion and why they are problematic;
- Identifying the history of inclusive education;
- Recognising macro- and micro-exclusion;
- Developing an understanding of key issues to consider when approaching inclusive early years education.

KEY TERMS AND CONCEPTS

agency
courtesy stigma
early years
early years professional
enacted stigma
felt stigma
inclusive education
integration
macro- and micro-exclusion in education
mainstreaming

# Introduction

As Freire (1970) argued, education is never neutral—it is a political act that is informed by individual and collective values. Inclusive education involves embracing human diversity and valuing and supporting the belonging and full participation of all people together (Cologon, 2013a). This includes upholding the rights of all children and providing education free from discriminatory beliefs and attitudes. To do this requires developing and putting into action inclusive values, policies and practices. This follows the call from writers, such as Freire (1970) and Dewey (1916), to engage in education for social justice and democracy, with a focus on reducing or removing oppression within and beyond education experiences and systems.

**Early years professional:** Throughout this book, this term refers to all professionals involved in early years education and care in a range of roles and settings, including teachers and allied health professionals, for example.

**Early years:** Throughout this book, this term is used to encompass early childhood (prior-to-school) and primary school settings.

Every great **early years professional** is inclusive. As Nutbrown and Clough (2009, p.192) argue, 'respectful educators will include all children'. However, inclusion is frequently misunderstood, and many early years professionals are unsure about what being inclusive involves. Throughout this book, the notion of inclusion will be explored with particular attention to what it means for everyday practice in **early years** settings.

As will be discussed later in the chapter, research provides evidence that inclusive education is better for everyone. Education outcomes are more positive and children learn and grow in ways that do not occur when they are segregated. Early years professionals are more flexible, skilled, confident and competent when they are inclusive. Inclusive early years education has the potential for positive social change—even transformation. However, inclusion is a complex and ongoing process, thus it takes time and commitment to develop a clear understanding of inclusion and to implement this in practice. Ongoing critical reflection, through a process of examining views and practices, is vital in engaging with inclusion—and a key responsibility of every early years professional.

Early years professionals play a powerful role in bringing about genuine inclusion. This book is intended to support early years professionals and researchers as they develop confidence and understanding and undertake the ongoing journey of *becoming inclusive*.

Bringing about inclusive education requires an ongoing commitment to removing barriers to the valued full participation and belonging of all children (Connor & Goldmansour, 2012; Curcic, 2009; Frankel, Gold & Ajodhia-Andrews, 2010; Theodorou & Nind, 2010; Vakil, Welton, O'Connor & Kline, 2009). Inclusion is not the domain of charitable 'do-gooders', but rather an essential component of a functioning society. Inclusion is not about granting 'special favours', nor about changing someone to fit the elusive 'norm' so they can be 'granted access' to the community. Rather, it is about acknowledging our shared humanity and moving beyond false notions of entitlement to recognise that for *any of us* to flourish as members of society, we need to be included. As Prosser and Loxley (2007, p.57) write, inclusion 'is a philosophy of acceptance and about providing a framework within which all children, regardless of ability, gender, language or cultural origin, can be valued equally with respect and provided with equal opportunities'.

Inclusion is a rights-based approach, and as such creates an opportunity to progress beyond a charity perspective, towards social justice. Cultural and educational transformation is needed to fight against discrimination and prejudice in all its forms (Armstrong & Barton, 2008). Inclusive education is a process that occurs within the everyday moments in any education setting and, as noted above, requires ongoing commitment and reflection on the part of early years professionals.

## Barriers to inclusion

One question that arises in relation to inclusion is inclusion of whom and in what? In addressing this question it is important to reflect on underlying philosophies evident in education policy and practice. Embracing our shared humanity requires going beyond a 'them' and 'us'—beyond the idea that there is one 'desirable' group into which all 'others' should be included—to instead recognise and acknowledge that people are all equally human: we are all 'us'. Perhaps surprisingly, social realities suggest that this is harder than it seems.

### STIGMA AND DEHUMANISATION

It is unlikely that anyone would set out intentionally to dehumanise people. However, racism, sexism, genderism, classism, homophobia, transphobia, ableism (see Chapter 2) and ageism all, at their core, involve a process of dehumanisation. Consequently, to work towards inclusion, it is necessary to understand the dehumanising process of exclusion.

Dehumanisation occurs when we make people 'other' to ourselves—that process of creating a 'them' and 'us' in which 'us' is viewed as more desirable or 'better'. This then forms the justification for discrimination. For example, racial segregation in the past was justified on the basis that it was better for the 'them' (the oppressed), while simultaneously maintaining the superiority of the 'us' (the oppressors). Similarly, segregation based on impairment or 'disability' in Australia (and elsewhere) today often stems from the belief that it is better for 'them'.

Dehumanisation, which is often subconscious, unintentional and enculturated, occurs through a process of stigmatisation. In his classic book exploring this notion, Erving Goffman defined stigma as 'the situation of the individual who is disqualified from full social acceptance' (Goffman, 1963, p.9). Goffman outlined the dehumanising process of stigmatisation and the justification that stigma provides for discrimination, explaining that stigma is 'an undesired differentness from what we had anticipated ... By definition, of course, we believe the person with a stigma is not quite human. On this assumption we exercise varieties of discrimination through which we effectively, if often unthinkingly, reduce his [or her] life chances' (Goffman, 1963, p.15).

Consider for a moment one of the most stigmatised groups in Australia at present: asylum seekers. By the process of stigmatisation, asylum seekers have become dehumanised—viewed by many as less than human—and thus even extreme discrimination has been justified (see Chapter 15).

Goffman (1963) identified three different aspects or experiences of stigma: enacted, felt and courtesy stigma.

**Enacted stigma:** The experience of discrimination (Goffman, 1963).

**Enacted stigma** is the most blatant form of stigma and involves active discrimination. For example, discrimination in enrolment processes to prevent a stigmatised person from attending or participating in an education setting would be considered enacted stigma (Lilley, 2013).

**Felt stigma:** The fear of enacted stigma and feelings of shame on account of being stigmatised (Goffman, 1963).

**Felt stigma** involves awareness and fear of stigma and feelings of shame due to being stigmatised. The notion of felt stigma relates to 'stigma consciousness' or 'stereotype threat'. Felt stigma can involve the playing out of the effects of stigma on account of these fears. For example, Link and Phelan (2001) in research in North America found that African–American students had lower test scores when told that they were being tested for intelligence compared with when given the same test but told it was for another purpose.

**Courtesy stigma:** Stigma felt by those around the stigmatised person (Goffman, 1963).

**Courtesy stigma** involves the feeling of stigma by those around a stigmatised person. For example, a family of a person who experiences disability, or the family of a person who identifies as homosexual in a highly conservative community, may experience courtesy stigma. Courtesy stigma may result in strong advocacy against discrimination or, by contrast, in trying to cover up 'difference' or encourage the stigmatised person to 'pass' for 'normal' in order to avoid stigma. Tongue shortening operations and plastic surgery for children who have Down syndrome (Goeke, 2003) are an example of courtesy stigma.

Experiencing disability (disablement), a socially constructed and imposed social process (as explored in Chapter 2), is, in itself, a process of stigmatisation. As Shapiro (1993, p.30) writes, people who experience disability are constantly described or represented as 'either an object of pity or a source of inspiration. These images are internalized ... build social stereotypes, create artificial limitations, and contribute to discrimination and minority status'.

Building on Goffman's seminal work, Link and Phelan (2001, p.367) argue that the following process is involved in the playing out of stigma:

1 In the first component, people distinguish and label human differences;
2 In the second, dominant cultural beliefs link labelled persons to undesirable characteristics—to negative stereotypes;
3 In the third, labelled persons are placed in distinct categories so as to accomplish some degree of separation of 'us' from 'them';
4 In the fourth, labelled persons experience status loss and discrimination that lead to unequal outcomes;
5 Finally, stigmatisation is entirely contingent on access to social, economic and political power that allows the identification of 'differentness', the construction of stereotypes, the separation of labelled persons into distinct categories, and the full execution of disapproval, rejection, exclusion and discrimination.

As Link and Phelan (2001, p.375) note, 'it takes power to stigmatize ... However, the role of power in stigma is frequently overlooked because in many instances power differences are so taken for granted as to seem unproblematic'.

The structures, systems and processes of early years education and care are one such source of power. They hold the potential for the production of stigma, or by contrast—if there is critical engagement with the notion of stigma and a rejection of dehumanisation—for inclusion. Stigma is the basis of segregation and exclusion. Inclusion, on the other hand, is free of stigma. Early years professionals thus need to consider stigma and the process of dehumanisation in their everyday practices.

**CRITICAL REFLECTION QUESTIONS**

1. Have you ever experienced stigmatisation? If you have, what did this feel like? How did you respond? What might it be like to experience this every day?
2. Consider the power early years professionals might hold. Could this power lead to stigmatisation or dehumanisation of children? How might this be addressed in everyday practice?

## MISUNDERSTANDING INCLUSION

One common barrier to inclusion is the misunderstanding of inclusion as assimilation—the idea that people can only be included if they can be 'the same enough', or learn to 'fit' within existing structures and systems. In effect, this is a belief that people can be included if they can alter or hide their characteristics that are linked to stigma, and 'pass' for 'normal'.

In regards to early years settings, this idea leads to an emphasis on changing the child (who is being 'included') to 'fit' within a setting, rather than on changing the setting to include the child (Armstrong, Armstrong & Spandagou, 2011; Avramidis & Norwich, 2002; Curcic, 2009; Lalvani, 2013; Rietveld, 2010). When inclusion is understood as assimilation, a stigmatised child carries a perpetual 'question mark' over his/her right to be 'included' (Bridle, 2005; Cologon, 2013b). Rietveld (2010) describes this dehumanising approach as a demeaning understanding of inclusion, in contrast to a facilitative understanding of inclusion in which all children are valued and recognised as rights-holders and equal human beings.

Another misunderstanding of inclusive education occurs when it is viewed as a 'special effort' or 'added (optional) extra' born out of 'charity', or 'kindness'. This stigmatisation is perhaps more subtle, but the patronising creation of a 'them' and 'us' is clear.

Common to these misunderstandings is the underlying idea that inclusive education gives children permission to be present, rather than valuing the participation of all children and ensuring all children belong. In addition to the negative impact this has on the child and family, this attitude also disempowers early years professionals to a point where they may feel they have little to offer the child. By contrast, as explored throughout this book, early years professionals have a critical role to play in adapting the environment and making changes to teaching approaches and materials in order to include every child, rather than seeking to change them (Avramidis & Norwich, 2002; Biklen, 2000; Cologon, 2010, 2013a). An important question to consider is how these misunderstandings of inclusion developed and how barriers to inclusion can be broken down.

## The journey towards inclusion

'Inclusive education' is one of the most contested terms in education (Graham & Slee, 2008) and is a contentious issue (Barton, 1997). Understandings of inclusive education have changed over time, with the gradual move from extreme levels of segregation towards greater inclusion.

**Macro-exclusion in education:** When children are denied education or excluded from general education settings and segregated into 'special' schools, classes or units for all or some of the time (Cologon, 2013a).

### EXCLUSION AND SEGREGATION

**Macro-exclusion** involves the dehumanising process of stigmatisation as a 'lesser' or 'inferior' person, which is then played out in the form of exclusion from education. At its most extreme, this means a child is not provided with access to any formal education opportunities. Segregation is a form of macro-exclusion that involves the provision of formal education, but within separate settings or activities. This exclusion occurs when a child is barred from a setting, for example on the basis of impairment, or when a child is excluded from particular activities or experiences within a setting. For example, in the past, the exclusion of 'black children' from 'white schools' in the United States, or in Australia until 1972, the exclusion of Aboriginal children from schools if parents of non-Aboriginal children objected to their attendance (Australian Human Rights Commission, 2001). In addition to segregated settings, segregation may occur within general education settings, for example, a 'special' class. As Connor and Goldmansour write, 'with segregation comes devaluation, a loss in cultural capital for individuals. This form of disempowerment actively disadvantages students' (Connor & Goldmansour, 2012, p.31).

When asked about the sensory overstimulation present in everyday classrooms as an argument for segregated education, Jamie Burke—a man labelled with autism—shared that in his experience of education, 'segregation equals a distinction of lesser ability' (Biklen & Burke, 2006, p.172). He goes on to ask: 'Am I lesser because I get nervous about an exam? Am I deemed less intelligent because my feelings only make passing a higher stakes? I again ask you to think of who is it that has placed this way of evaluating worthiness? Have they placed their feet in my shoes? I would enjoin them to try' (Biklen & Burke, 2006, p.172).

## MAINSTREAMING

In the 1960s, strong criticisms of segregated education began to emerge. Questions were raised regarding whether 'special' schools had positive or negative outcomes. Consequently, **mainstreaming**, where all children are educated within the same setting, became more common. This led to research, including meta-analyses, identifying no benefits of segregated education compared with education of all children together (Calberg & Kavale, 1980; Dunn, 1968; Wang & Baker, 1985).

**Mainstreaming:** The placement of children together within the same setting, but without making adjustments or adaptations to facilitate inclusion.

While it is a rejection of extreme segregation and exclusion, mainstreaming is based on the understanding that all children can and should assimilate to 'fit' the existing setting, rather than that education approaches and environments should be developed to include children. Mainstreaming involves attendance, but not inclusion. It is now widely recognised that 'being there is not enough; it is no guarantee of respect for difference or access to the material, social, cultural and educational capital that people expect' (Komesaroff & McLean, 2006, p.97).

**Note**

It is important to distinguish between the terms 'mainstreaming' and 'mainstream'. Settings intended for the 'general population', be that a childcare centre, school, library, swimming pool or any other setting or activity, are often referred to as 'mainstream settings'. For example, a 'mainstream school' would be one that is not targeted at a specific minority group, but rather all children of school age in that locality. As a result, people sometimes talk of inclusion within a 'mainstream' school or centre (as opposed to mainstreaming).

## INTEGRATION

In an effort to address the many issues with mainstreaming, in the 1970s, the increasing focus within policy and practice in Australia (and elsewhere) became **integration** (Doneau, 1984). Integration involves making adaptations or accommodations to enable participation within a mainstream experience or setting.

Integration: Involves attendance at a 'mainstream' setting, part-time or full-time, with needs-based practical accommodations to facilitate participation, but without change to the setting.

Many education settings incorporate segregated 'special' classes or units in which children labelled 'disabled' or 'disordered' are educated. Many of these units have a segregated, fenced off, playground. Children who attend these segregated settings are often integrated into some whole-setting activities. In school settings, for example, the whole school may come together for school assemblies, music or some sport activities. Individual children may also attend part of the day in a mainstream class with age-matched peers. Some children will also join together during outside playtime. Children who attend 'special' settings (for example, 'special' schools) may be integrated for a day or more per week at a mainstream setting.

While the focus on accommodations is critical, integration has been criticised for being tokenistic. Many children who are integrated actually spend little time participating in the centre or school community and most of their time in segregated activities, classes or settings. A major criticism of integration is the implication that someone who is 'different' needs to be 'fitted in', rather than working to include, value and meet the needs of all children within the setting. In this sense, integration is often little more than moving 'special' education from a segregated setting into a mainstream one—the perpetuation of exclusionary practices in the guise of integration. Armstrong and Barton (2008, p.10) argue that 'integration makes no requirement for the school to effect radical change in its culture and organisation because the expectation is that the child is accommodated to existing structures and practices or—at best, if organisational and pedagogical adjustments *are* implemented, they take place *around* the individual child or group of children identified as in need'.

**Note**

This notion of integration is different to the notion of 'an integrated unit of work', which involves integrating different subject areas within one experience, activity or lesson; for example, an experience that is focused simultaneously on teaching literacy, science and mathematics.

### *Micro-exclusion*

Due to the lack of understanding of inclusive education, exclusion and segregation often occur in the name of inclusion. Segregation can occur socially within so-called 'inclusive' settings when children are not given the opportunity to participate, learn and grow together. Like for integration, this can involve moving 'special' education from a segregated setting into a mainstream setting, but without any genuine efforts to bring about inclusion. Children therefore remain segregated and excluded within a so-called inclusive setting. This is what D'Alessio (2011) has termed '**micro-exclusion**'. For example this is evident when a child attends a general education setting, but is excluded from the activities of the rest of the children, as illustrated by McLeskey and Waldron:

**Micro-exclusion in education:** When physical presence or placement alone is misunderstood as inclusion.

> The general education teacher had just completed taking roll and handling the daily chores that are necessary to start the day. As reading was beginning, the special education teacher entered the classroom. She went to a table in the back of the room, and four students with disabilities joined her. The general education teacher gathered the remaining 20 students in the front of the room. The special education teacher began working on a phonics lesson with 'her' students, while the general education teacher was discussing a book she had been reading to the rest of the class for the past week (2007, p.162).

Micro-exclusion occurs when adaptations or accommodations to the environment, curriculum or pedagogy that are required to include a child are not made (for example, refusing to install a handrail in the toilets) (Purdue, Ballard & MacArthur, 2001). Or, it might occur where a child is only permitted to attend a setting under certain conditions (for example, only when a parent or assistant is present, or only for part of the day) (Purdue et al., 2001). Inclusive education, on the other hand, is 'a way of looking at the world that enacts the fundamental meaning of education for all children: full participation, full membership, valued citizenship' (Kliewer, 1998, p.320).

## INCLUSIVE EDUCATION

**Inclusive education:** Involves embracing human diversity and valuing and supporting the belonging and full participation of all people together (Cologon, 2013a).

In response to criticisms of integration, alongside greater recognition of the human rights of all children in legislation and policy (see Chapter 4), there has been a growing move towards **inclusive education**. Beyond mainstreaming and integration, inclusive education involves ensuring the valued full participation and belonging of all children within any given education setting. Inclusive education involves both social and academic inclusion, free from discrimination in any form.

The term 'inclusion' often brings to mind minority groups and people who experience disability in particular, but in reality, inclusion is about everyone (Armstrong & Barton, 2008). However, people from minority groups are often excluded and thus particular emphasis is placed on inclusion to address this issue.

Petriwskyj (2010a) argues that understandings of inclusion reflect beliefs about diversity in any given context. Graham and Spandagou (2011, p.225) found that '[t]he contextual characteristics of a school and its community inform discussions of diversity and define what inclusive education means in specific schools'. Consequently, greater diversity in a school results in a broader understanding of inclusive education (Graham & Spandagou, 2011).

People who experience disability are the largest minority group in the world today (World Health Organization [WHO], 2011) and are among the most marginalised and excluded people in Australia and throughout the world (Hobson, 2010; United Nations Children's Fund [UNICEF], 2013). Therefore, while this book focuses on inclusion of *all*, particular emphasis is placed on inclusion of children labelled 'disabled'. However, as one teacher in some of my research argues, 'Inclusion is really (when you think about it) what teaching is: Meet each child where they are at, build on their strengths and interests to move them along, and adapt your teaching style, resources and pace to each of them. Thus it puzzles me when words such as "disability"/"special needs" throw people off' (Cologon, 2010, p.47).

**FIGURE 1.1** DIVERSITY

*Artwork by Kaitlyn*

### *Confusion between inclusion and integration/mainstreaming*

Confusion sometimes occurs between the terms 'integration'/'mainstreaming' and 'inclusion'. Foreman (2011, p.16) argues that integration and mainstreaming involve asking *'Can we* provide for the needs of this student?', while inclusion involves asking '*How will we* provide for the needs of this student?' The difference between these concepts is important to reflect upon and is illustrated in Figures 1.4 and 1.5.

**FIGURE 1.2** INTEGRATION

*(From 'One of the Kids', published by the Disability Council of NSW, written by Wendy Stroeve and illustrated by Kerry Millard, reproduced with permission.)*

**FIGURE 1.3** INCLUSION

*(From 'One of the Kids', published by the Disability Council of NSW, written by Wendy Stroeve and illustrated by Kerry Millard, reproduced with permission.)*

# Why is inclusion important?

Though Foreman's question 'How we will provide for the needs of this student?' seems a simple one, inclusive education is not always easy to implement (Barton, 2008). So, why would early years professionals commit to bringing about inclusion in reality?

Montaigne, an influential sixteenth-century French philosopher, wrote extensively on the question of 'how should we live?'. Writing of his many and varied experiences of life and observations of what it is to be human, Montaigne explored questions about how one can make honourable choices, live ethically and flourish as a human being.

After meeting conjoined twins, Montaigne (1580) reflected on the human tendency to wonder at what seems uncommon due to lack of understanding and yet not to wonder at what seems common *even when we do not understand that either*. Montaigne argued that this apparent 'novelty' of something that seems less common leads to a perception of strangeness, but that it is in fact this sense of novelty or 'astonishment' (which leads to stigmatisation) that needs correcting. Within this, it could be argued, is recognition of a fundamental aspect of inclusion—the need to embrace human diversity so that it is no longer 'astonishing'. This is a challenge for every early years professional.

While Montaigne did not explore what the experience of *being* 'astonishing' might be like for the children he met, research demonstrates that experiences of exclusion are likely to lead children 'to internalise the messages that they are inferior, incompetent and undesirable peer group members, which in turn is likely to negatively impact on their motivation to seek inclusion' (Rietveld, 2010, p.27). Exclusion results in marginalisation, stigmatisation and often bullying and abuse (Biklen & Burke, 2006; Curcic, 2009; Department of Education, Employment and Workplace Relations [DEEWR], 2012). On the other hand, inclusion results in greater self-esteem (Diamond & Huang, 2005; Fitch, 2003).

Building on Montaigne's essential question 'how should we live?', there is a subtle yet fundamental shift in thinking when we ask 'how should we live *together*?'. This question opens the frame to thinking about all humans living together, rather than bringing into existing settings those of us who are currently left outside. In this sense, 'inclusion goes to the heart of how we as communities of human beings wish to live with one another' (Cologon, 2010, p.47).

## INCLUSION AS A HUMAN RIGHT

Adressing the ways in which humans live together, there is a long history of people from across the world working together to articulate and support the recognition of human rights. As discussed in Chapter 4, inclusion and education are rights of all people. This is outlined in conventions and declarations including the *Convention on the Rights of Persons with Disabilities* (United Nations, 2006), the *Convention on the Rights of the Child* (United Nations, 1989), the *Salamanca Declaration* (United Nations Educational Scientific and Cultural Organization [UNESCO], 1994) and the *United Nations Guidelines on Intercultural Education* (UNESCO, 2006), as well as in the global commitment to *Education for All* (UNESCO, 1990).

## POLICY AND LEGISLATION

Partly on account of these international covenants and declarations, policy and legislation across much of the world outlines a commitment to inclusive education. For example, in Australia the *Australian Early Years Learning Framework* (DEEWR, 2009), *Framework for School Age Care* (DEEWR, 2009) and the *Australian Curriculum* (Australian Curriculum, Assessment and Reporting Authority [ACARA], 2011) describe a clear commitment to inclusive education. (See Chapter 4 for details of policy and legislation.)

## OUTCOMES OF INCLUSION

In addition to the human rights and social justice arguments for inclusive education, changes in policy and legislation have been informed by research, particularly in relation to children who experience disability. There are a number of challenges when considering research into inclusive education. Discriminatory attitudes are present not only in practice, but also in research. Many studies, while intending or claiming to examine inclusive education, are actually based on practices of micro- (and sometimes macro-) exclusion. However, despite these challenges, research provides evidence of benefits of inclusive education for children who do and do not experience disability in terms of social, academic, cognitive and physical development (Cologon, 2013a). This includes research involving children with a diverse range of labels, such as children labelled with 'mild' to 'severe' intellectual, sensory and physical impairments and multiple impairments (Cologon, 2013a).

Overall, research provides evidence that inclusive education results in improved quality of education for all, and education which is more sensitive to children's needs (Jordan, Schwartz & McGhie-Richmond, 2009; Jordan, Glenn & McGhie-Richmond, 2010; Purdue et al., 2001). This contrasts with the absence of evidence to suggest any benefit of segregated ('special') education over inclusive education (Jackson, Chalmers & Wills, 2004; Jackson, 2008).

### *Academic outcomes*

Despite the higher adult to child ratios in 'special' education, inclusive education facilitates greater academic outcomes compared with segregated education, including in the areas of reading, writing and mathematics (de Graaf, van Hove & Haveman, 2013; Finke, McNaughton & Drager, 2009; Giangreco, 2009; Kliewer, 1998, 2008; Myklebust, 2006; Peetsma, Vergeer, Karsten & Roeleveld, 2001; Stahmer & Ingersoll, 2004; Tanti Burlo, 2010; Vakil, et al., 2009; Vianello & Lanfranchi, 2009). Inclusive education creates more opportunities for engaging academically and, consequently, results in outcomes that otherwise may not be possible (Finke et al., 2009; Fox, Farrell & Davis, 2004; Jordan et al., 2009; Jordan et al., 2010).

Early years professionals and parents often report concerns that the inclusion of children who experience disability will impact negatively on the academic outcomes of children who do not experience disability. However, research demonstrates that this concern is unfounded, and children who do not experience disability benefit from inclusive education and demonstrate equal or better academic outcomes than children educated in non-inclusive settings (Dessemontet & Bless, 2013; Farrell, Dyson, Polat, Hutcheson & Gallannaugh, 2007; Kalambouka, Farrell, Dyson & Kaplan, 2007; Kliewer, 1998, 2008; McGregor & Vogelsberg, 1998; Odom & Diamond, 1998; Odom, Buysse & Soukakou, 2011; Purdue et al., 2001).

### *Inclusion and behaviour*

Children's behaviour is reported to be one of the greatest concerns for early years professionals (Cologon, 2012). Research provides evidence that inclusive education facilitates positive behaviour development, including development of greater independence, patience, trust, acceptance of diversity, and responsiveness to the needs of others (Baker-Ericzén, Mueggenborg & Shea, 2009; Diamond & Huang, 2005; Finke et al., 2009; Hanline & Correa-Torres, 2012; Hollingsworth, Boone & Crais, 2009; Kliewer, 2008; Mogharreban & Bruns, 2009; Nikolaraizi et al., 2005; Palmer, Fuller, Arora & Nelson, 2001; Stahmer, Carter, Baker & Miwa, 2003; Stahmer, Akshoomoff & Cunningham, 2011).

### *Communication, language and physical development*

Communication and language development is enriched through inclusive education (Baker-Ericzén et al., 2009; Finke et al., 2009; Fisher & Shogren, 2012; Hart & Whalon, 2011; Johnston, McDonnell, Nelson & Magnavito, 2003; Kliewer, 1998, 2008; Peetsma et al., 2001; Stahmer et al., 2003; Stahmer et al., 2011). Inclusive education has also been found to stimulate physical development (Fox et al., 2004; Qi & Ha, 2012; Stahmer, et al., 2003; Theodorou & Nind, 2010).

### *Inclusion and bullying*

A common assumption regarding segregated education is that in 'special' settings children will not experience bullying or teasing. However, research indicates that all forms of bullying occur in 'special' settings (Davis & Watson, 2000; Rose, Monda-Amaya & Espelage, 2011; Torrance, 2000). While there is variation in studies (Hebron & Humphrey, 2013; Woods & Wolke, 2004), a growing body of research provides evidence that children who attend segregated settings are more likely to experience bullying, with inclusive education being a key strategy for reducing bullying (Rose et al., 2011). In fact, inclusive education has been found to promote positive social development; facilitate friendships that may not otherwise occur; and support the development of a sense of belonging (Baker-Ericzén et al., 2009; Finke et al., 2009; Hanline & Correa-Torres, 2012; Jordan et al., 2009; Kliewer, 1998; Odom et al., 2011; Petriwskyj, 2010b; Stahmer & Ingersoll, 2004; Stahmer et al., 2003; Stahmer et al., 2011).

### INCLUSION AND BELONGING

Belonging is critical to inclusion. In fact it is argued in the *Early Years Learning Framework* that belonging is 'integral to human existence' (DEEWR, 2009, p.7). A sense of belonging leads to a sense of identity and positive self-esteem (DEEWR, 2009; Jones, 2002), which are two of the most essential goals to be addressed through early years education (Nutbrown & Clough, 2009). However, belonging does not occur without participation (Dockett & Perry, 2005). To bring about a genuine sense of belonging, 'there needs to be a strong commitment to inclusive education that expects student **agency**, where the participation of the student in the heart of the classroom is a given, not an experiment, and not conditional, and where participation amounts to more than mere physical presence' (Biklen & Burke, 2006, p.172).

**Agency:** 'being able to make choices and decisions, to influence events and to have an impact on one's world' (DEEWR, 2009, p.45).

In sum, inclusive education is important when we consider 'how we should live *together*'. 'Inclusion is what we make it, and what we make it is what we wish our culture to be' (Kliewer, 1998, p.320).

## Inclusive early years professionals

Dempsey (2011, p.64) writes, 'The argument over whether inclusion works has ended. Inclusion does work when key components of the classroom and the school environment are in place, and legislation and policy now demand that teachers and schools ensure that these components are enacted.' Early years professionals can expect that they will be required to include a diverse range of children—this is the right of every child. However, many early years professionals are concerned about how and whether they can do this.

> Two concerns are commonly voiced among professionals who express resistance to inclusion. The first is that the needs of children will not be met amid the complex dynamics of a general education setting. The second is that the needs of children with disabilities will require an excessive amount of directed resources that take away from the educational experiences of children without disabilities ... neither concern is valid in a thoughtfully structured, well-resourced early childhood classroom (Kliewer, 2008, p.135).

Research provides evidence that early years professionals develop positive attitudes towards inclusion and build confidence in their ability to be inclusive, through experience and support (Avramidis & Norwich, 2002; Cologon, 2012; Jordan & Stanovich, 2001; Jordan et al., 2010; McGregor & Vogelsberg, 1998; Purdue et al., 2001). Early years professionals report increased personal satisfaction and professional growth through the experience of inclusive education (Finke et al., 2009) and become more confident and 'better' teachers of all children (Cologon, 2012; Jordan & Stanovich, 2001; Jordan et al., 2010). With this knowledge in mind, the question then becomes *how* to bring about inclusive education. This question is addressed throughout this book.

Research with parents and early years professionals in New Zealand has identified that inclusion is experienced when (Purdue et al., 2001):

- Children and families are welcomed as valued members of the community and belong;
- Inclusion is viewed as 'ordinary', 'part of life';
- Peer acceptance is fostered;
- Parent collaboration is welcomed;
- Conditions are not placed on attendance and the child is welcome all of the time;
- Adaptations are made;
- Early years professionals work to advocate with parents;
- Resources are created or funding is sought where required;
- All staff within the setting are involved with all children (for example paraprofessional support is used across the setting and visiting therapists work with teachers to support inclusion).

The attitudes of early years professionals are fundamental to the realisation of inclusion (Carlson, Hemmings, Wurf & Reupert, 2012). Ainscow writes that

> The development of more inclusive approaches does not arise from a mechanical process in which any one specific organisational restructuring, or the introduction of a particular set of techniques, generates increased levels of participation. Rather, the development of inclusive practices requires processes of social learning ... becoming more inclusive is a matter of thinking and talking, reviewing and refining practice, and making attempts to develop a more inclusive culture (2007, p.5).

Bringing about inclusive education 'requires the abandonment of special educational stances which focus on compensatory approaches to individual "needs", to embrace a pedagogy of inclusion and a commitment to the rights of all to belong' (D'Alessio, 2011, p.141). This involves abandoning the idea of 'special children', 'special teachers' and of 'making children normal' (Baglieri, Bejoian, Broderick, Connor & Valle, 2011; Barton, 1997; Connor & Goldmansour, 2012; Goodley & Runswick-Cole, 2011) and instead embracing our shared humanity. To do this, it is essential to examine the underlying beliefs and attitudes that we bring to the early years and to our interactions with children and families.

## DEVELOPING INCLUSIVE ATTITUDES

'Children are not born with prejudices ... but acquire them from adults, the media, and the general way in which society is organized' (Rieser & Mason, 1990 cited in Beckett, 2009, p.320). As young as three years of age, children internalise dominant cultural preferences or prejudices, for example identifying people as 'good' or 'bad' on the basis of cultural (stigma) markers (Connolly, Smith & Kelly, 2002). By the age of six, children will make spontaneous biased or prejudiced statements consistent with the dominant cultural preferences of the context (Connolly et al., 2002). Early years professionals play a role in the process of enculturating children and thus have a responsibility to avoid perpetuating stigmatising and discriminatory beliefs and attitudes. The beliefs and attitudes of early years professionals impact on the developing beliefs of the children with whom they work, and are critical to the development of an inclusive culture (Berlach & Chambers, 2011; Carlson et al., 2012).

The environment and culture of a setting influences not only children, but also adults (Kasa-Hendrickson & Kluth, 2005). 'Challenging widely accepted beliefs and practices in education is a difficult and unpopular task' (Slee, 2011, p.14), thus leadership is essential to bring about inclusion (Ainscow, 2007). One important aspect of accepting this challenge is to acknowledge that the beliefs and attitudes we hold are not necessarily the ones we desire to hold or have set out to develop; and, until we examine our beliefs and attitudes, we may often be unaware that we hold them. We all exist within our context and time and are enculturated into the dominant beliefs and attitudes of our society. Nonetheless, early years professionals have an ethical responsibility to uncover our beliefs and attitudes, and to examine and challenge them with a view to unpacking the impact they may have on the children and families we work with. In doing so, early years professionals can contribute to ongoing social change and transformation towards greater inclusion.

**CRITICAL REFLECTION QUESTIONS**

In Chapter 2 we will explore further, deeply held social views that lead to discrimination and exclusion. Before we do this, it is important to consider these questions:

1. What are your own beliefs about who has a right to inclusive education?
2. Who do you think can be educated?

When a person is stigmatised, the beliefs of that person and those around them about their capacity to learn are negatively influenced. When a person is not stigmatised, they are generally presumed to be competent (Biklen, 2000; Biklen & Burke, 2006). Presuming competence 'casts the teachers, parents, and others in the role of finding ways to support the person to demonstrate his or her agency... The notion of presuming competence implies that educators must assume students can and will change and, that through engagement with the world, will demonstrate complexities of thought and action that could not necessarily be anticipated' (Biklen & Burke, 2006, pp.167–168).

In the words of Jamie Burke, 'why do all those who have said they are educated in ways of teaching not know that hope and desire must be moved into place as the pillars of strength first before the floors can be built?' (Biklen & Burke, 2006, p.171).

## Becoming inclusive

In a speech entitled 'In Our Hands' delivered on the tenth anniversary of the Universal Declaration of Human Rights in 1958, Eleanor Roosevelt argued,

> Where, after all, do universal human rights begin? In small places, close to home—so close and so small that they cannot be seen on any maps of the world. Yet they are the world of the individual person; the neighbourhood he [or she] lives in; the school or college he [or she] attends; the factory, farm or office where he [or she] works. Such are the places where every man, woman and child seeks equal justice, equal opportunity, equal dignity without discrimination. Unless these rights have meaning there, they have little meaning anywhere. Without concerned citizen action to uphold them close to home, we shall look in vain for progress in the larger world.

Inclusive education is a human right for all children. Inclusive education is a 'big idea', however, as Eleanor Roosevelt argued, human rights are realised every day, when we live our lives in interaction with others. Inclusive education 'is about providing the best possible education for all' (Armstrong & Barton, 2008, p.11). We *all* need to be included in order to flourish in our lives—and for this to occur we all need to include each other. Early years professionals have identified that respectful engagement with all children and families, taking a rights-based approach and listening to children, embracing diversity and providing equitable access to education are all critical for quality education—and for inclusion (Cologon, 2010).

As noted earlier in this chapter, early years professionals play a powerful role in bringing about (or preventing) inclusion and need to be supported to challenge unquestioned ways of being and doing, thus 'enlarging their capacity to imagine what might be achieved' (Ainscow, 2007, p.6). A key part of this is

**FIGURE 1.4** AUSLAN SIGN FOR *BIG*

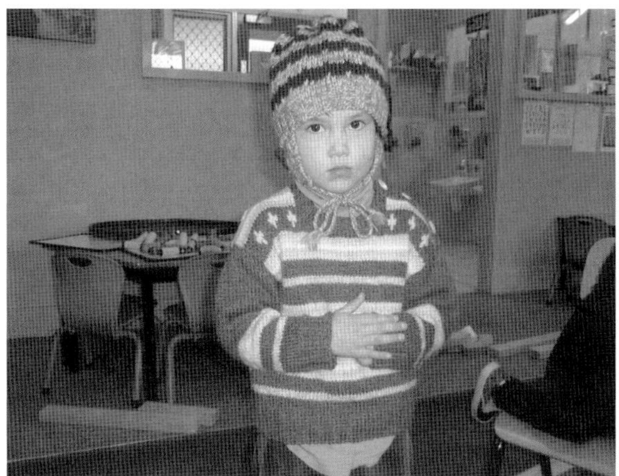

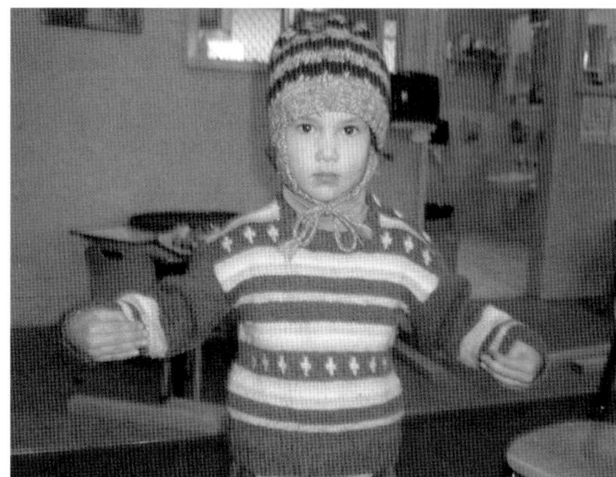

*Photos: Dinah Cocksedge*

challenging false assumptions and low expectations regarding the capabilities and behaviours of certain children or groups of children (Ainscow, 2007).

## Conclusion

In writing about education and inequality Beckett reminds us of the place of education in our society:

> The relationship between "education" and "inequality" has been, and continues to be much debated ... Within this wider debate there is a long history of theorising that supports the idea that the education system has the *potential* to rise above the inequalities of society, and even play a part in reducing those inequalities (Beckett, 2009, p.317, emphasis original).

Inclusive early years professionals can play an important role in bringing this *potential* to a *reality*. If inclusion is embracing our shared humanity, then bringing about inclusive education in reality involves an active and lived *expression* of our shared humanity. This requires putting inclusive values into action.

## FOR FURTHER REFLECTION

1. What do you understand education to mean?
2. What do you understand inclusive education to mean?
3. What do you understand difference and disability to mean?
4. Reflect on the notion of 'curing' or 'fixing' children as a precursor or condition for inclusion. Do children need to be 'the same enough' to be included?
5. Why is inclusion important for bringing about genuine education for all?
6. Consider an early years setting that you are familiar with. Who is included in this setting? Who is excluded? Why and how are inclusion and exclusion determined?
7. What do you consider to be the role(s) of early years professionals in facilitating inclusion? What do you see as a starting point for becoming more inclusive?

## WEBSITES

www.eenet.org.uk/what_is_ie.php
The Enabling Education Network: Provides information regarding inclusive education from a global perspective.

www.csie.org.uk
Centre for Studies on Inclusive Education: Provides information regarding inclusive education.

## REFERENCES


Ainscow, M. (2007). Taking an inclusive turn. *Journal of Research in Special Educational Needs, 7*(1), 3–7. doi:10.1111/j.1471-3802.2007.00075.x

Armstrong, D., Armstrong, A.C. & Spandagou, I. (2011). Inclusion: By choice or by chance? *International Journal of Inclusive Education, 15*(1), 29–39. doi:10.1080/13603116.2010.496192

Armstrong, F. & Barton, L. (2008). Policy, experience and change and the challenge of inclusive education: The case of England. In L. Barton and F. Armstrong (Eds) *Policy, experience and change: Cross-cultural reflections on inclusive education*. UK: Springer Science.

Australian Curriculum, Assessment and Reporting Authority (ACARA). (2012). *Australian Curriculum.* Sydney: ACARA. Retrieved from www.australiancurriculum.edu.au

Australian Human Rights Commission. (2001). Rural and remote education inquiry briefing paper. Retrieved from www.humanrights.gov.au/publications/rural-and-remote-education-inquiry-briefing-paper-26

Avramidis, E. & Norwich, B. (2002). Teachers' attitudes towards integration/inclusion: A review of the literature. *European Journal of Special Needs Education, 17*(2), 129–147. doi:10.1080/08856250210129056

Baglieri, S., Bejoian, L.M., Broderick, A.A., Connor, D.J. & Valle, J. (2011). [Re]claiming 'inclusive education' toward cohesion in educational reform: Disability studies unravels the myth of the normal child. *Teachers College Record, 113*(10), 2122–2154. Retrieved from www.tcrecord.org

Baker-Ericzén, M.J., Mueggenborg, M.G. & Shea, M.M. (2009). Impact of trainings on child care providers' attitudes and perceived competence toward inclusion: What factors are associated with change? *Topics in Early Childhood Special Education, 28*(4), 196–208. doi:10.1177/0271121408323273

Barton, L. (1997). Inclusive education: Romantic, subversive or realistic? *International Journal of Inclusive Education, 1*(3), 231–242. doi:10.1080/1360311970010301

Barton, L. (2008). Social justice, human rights and inclusive education. In G. Richards & F. Armstrong (Eds), *Key issues for teaching assistants: Working in diverse and inclusive classrooms* (pp.152–158). London and New York: Routledge.

Beckett, A.E. (2009). 'Challenging disabling attitudes, building an inclusive society': Considering the role of education in encouraging non-disabled children to develop positive attitudes towards disabled people. *British Journal of Sociology of Education, 30*(3), 317–329. doi:10.1080/01425690902812596

Berlach, R.G. & Chambers, D.J. (2011). Interpreting inclusivity: An endeavour of great proportions. *International Journal of Inclusive Education, 15*(5), 529–539. doi:10.1080/13603110903159300

Biklen, D. (2000). Constructing inclusion: Lessons from critical, disability narratives. *International Journal of Inclusive Education, 4*(4), 337–353. doi:10.1080/13603110050168032

Biklen, D. & Burke, J. (2006). Presuming competence. *Equity & Excellence in Education, 39*(2), 166–175. doi:10.1080/10665680500540376

Bridle, L. (2005). Why does it have to be so hard! A mother's reflection on the journey of 'inclusive education'. In C. Newell and T. Parmenter (Eds), *Disability in education: Context, curriculum and culture* (pp.1–12). Canberra: Australian College of Educators.

Calberg, C. & Kavale, K. (1980). The efficacy of special versus regular placement for exceptional children: A meta analysis. *The Journal of Special Education, 14*(3), 295–309. doi:10.1177/002246698001400304

Carlson, L., Hemmings, B., Wurf, G. & Reupert, A. (2012). The instructional strategies and attitudes of effective inclusive teachers. *Special Education Perspectives, 21*(1), 7–20. Retrieved from www.aase.edu.au/about-us/publications/perspectives

Cologon, K. (2010). Inclusion is really what teaching is. *ARNEC Connections, 3,* 45–48. Retrieved from www.arnec.net/ntuc/slot/u2323/connection/ARNEC%20Connections%202010_FINALfixed.pdf

Cologon, K. (2012). Confidence in their own ability: Postgraduate early childhood students examining their attitudes towards inclusive education. *International Journal of Inclusive Education, 16*(11), 1155–1173. doi:10.1080/13603116.2010.548106

Cologon, K. (2013a). *Inclusion in education: Towards equality for students with disability.* Children with Disability Australia, Issues Papers. Retrieved from www.cda.org.au/_literature_159457/Issues_Paper_on_Inclusion_-_PDF

Cologon, K. (2013b). Recognising our shared humanity: Human rights and inclusive education in Italy and Australia. *Italian Journal of Disability Studies, 1*(1), 151–169. Retrieved from www.edizionianicia.it/docs/Rivista_Vol1_N1.pdf#page=151.

Connolly, P., Smith, A. & Kelly, B. (2002) *Too young to notice? The cultural and political awareness of 3–6 year olds in Northern Ireland.* Belfast: Community Relations Council. Retrieved from http://arrts.gtcni.org.uk/gtcni/bitstream/2428/5586/1/too_young_to_notice.pdf

Connor, D. & Goldmansour, K. (2012). Doing the civil right thing: Supporting children with disabilities in inclusive classes. *Bankstreet Occasional Papers, 28.* Retrieved from www.bankstreet.edu/occasional-papers/occasional-papers-28/doing-the-civil-right-thing/

Curcic, S. (2009). Inclusion in PK–12: An international perspective. *International Journal of Inclusive Education, 13*(5), 517–538. doi:10.1080/13603110801899585

D'Alessio, S. (2011). *Inclusive education in Italy: A critical analysis of the policy of integrazione scolastica.* Rotterdam, Netherlands: Sense Publishers.

Davis, J. & Watson, N. (2000). Disabled children's rights in everyday life: Problematising notions of competency and promoting self-empowerment. *The International Journal of Children's Rights, 8*(3), 211–228. doi:10.1163/15718180020494622

DEEWR, *see* Department of Education, Employment and Workplace Relations

de Graaf, G., van Hove, G. & Haveman, M. (2013). More academics in regular schools? The effect of regular versus special school placement on academic skills in Dutch primary school students with Down syndrome. *Journal of Intellectual Disability Research, 57*(1), 21–38. doi:10.1111/j.1365-2788.2011.01512.x

Dempsey, I. (2011). Legislation, policies and inclusive practices. In P. Foreman (Ed.), *Inclusion in action (3rd edn.)* (pp.42–68). Melbourne: Cengage Learning.

Department of Education, Employment and Workplace Relations (DEEWR). (2009). *Belonging, being and becoming: The early years learning framework for Australia.* ACT: DEEWR. Retrieved from www.coag.gov.au/sites/default/files/early_years_learning_framework.pdf

Department of Education, Employment and Workplace Relations [DEEWR]. (2012). *Report on the review of the Disability Standards for Education 2005.* Canberra: Commonwealth of Australia. Retrieved from http://education.gov.au/disability-standards-education

Dessemontet, R.S. & Bless, G. (2013). The impact of including children with intellectual disability in general education classrooms on the academic achievement of their low-, average-, and high-achieving peers. *Journal of Intellectual & Developmental Disability, 38*(1), 23–30. doi:10.3109/13668250.2012.757589

Dewey, J. (1916). *Democracy and education.* New York: Macmillan.

Diamond, K.E. & Huang, H-H. (2005). Preschoolers' ideas about disabilities. *Infants & Young Children, 18*(1), 37–46. Retrieved from http://journals.lww.com/iycjournal/pages/default.aspx

Dockett, S. & Perry, B. (2005). 'You need to know how to play safe': Children's experiences of starting school. *Contemporary Issues in Early Childhood, 6*(1), 4–18. doi:10.2304/ciec.2005.6.1.7

Doneau, S. (1984). *Edging for Integration: The Australian experience.* Pennant Hills, NSW: Edvance Publications.

Dunn, I.M. (1968). Special education for the mildly retarded—Is much of it justifiable? *Exceptional Children, 35,* 5–22. Retrieved from http://journals.cec.sped.org/ec/

Farrell, P., Dyson, A., Polat, F., Hutcheson, G. & Gallannaugh, F. (2007). SEN inclusion and pupil achievement in English schools. *Journal of Research in Special Education Needs, 7(3)*,172–178. doi:10.1111/j.1471-3802.2007.00094.x

Finke, E.H., McNaughton, D.B. & Drager, K.D.R. (2009). 'All children can and should have the opportunity to learn': General education teachers' perspectives on including children with autism spectrum disorder who require AAC. *Augmentative and Alternative Communication, 25*(2), 110–122. doi:10.1080/07434610902886206

Fisher, K.W. & Shogren, K.A. (2011). Integrating Augmentative and Alternative Communication and peer support for students with disabilities: A social-ecological perspective. *Journal of Special Education Technology, 27*(2), 23–39. Retrieved from www.tamcec.org/jset/index/

Fitch, F. (2003). Inclusion, exclusion, and ideology: Special education students' changing sense of self. *Urban Review 35*(3), 233–252. Retrieved from http://link.springer.com/journal/11256

Foreman, P. (2011). Introducing inclusion in education. In P. Foreman (Ed). *Inclusion in action* (3rd edn.), (pp.2–41). Melbourne: Cengage Learning.

Fox, S., Farrell, P. & Davis, P. (2004). Factors associated with the effective inclusion of primary-aged pupils with Down's syndrome. *British Journal of Special Education, 31*(4), 184–190. Retrieved from http://onlinelibrary.wiley.com/journal/10.1111/(ISSN)1467-8578

Frankel, E.B., Gold, S. & Ajodhia-Andrews, A. (2010). International preschool inclusion: Bridging the gap between vision and practices. *Young Exceptional Children, 13*(5), 2–16. doi:10.1177/1096250610379983

Freire, P. (1970). *Pedagogy of the oppressed*. New York: Continuum International.

Giangreco, M. (2009). Opportunities for children and youth with intellectual developmental disabilities: Beyond genetics. *Life Span and Disability, 12*(2), 129–139. Retrieved from www.lifespan.it

Goeke, J. (2003). Parents speak out: Facial plastic surgery for children with Down syndrome. *Education and Training in Developmental Disabilities, 38*(3), 323–333. Retrieved from http://daddcec.org/Publications/ETADDJournal.aspx

Goffman, E. (1963). *Stigma: Notes on the management of spoiled identity*. New Jersey: Prentice Hall.

Goodley, D. & Runswick-Cole, K. (2011). Problematising policy: Conceptions of 'child', 'disabled' and 'parents' in social policy in England. *International Journal of Inclusive Education, 15*(1), 71–85. doi:10.1080/13603116.2010.496197

Graham, L.J. & Slee, R. (2008). An illusory interiority: Interrogating the discourse/s of inclusion. *Educational Philosophy and Theory, 40*(2), 247–260. doi:10.1111/j.1469-5812.2007.00331.x

Graham, L.J. & Spandagou, I. (2011). From vision to reality: Views of primary school principals on inclusive education in New South Wales, Australia. *Disability and Society, 26*(2), 223–237. doi:10.1080/09687599.2011.544062

Hanline, M.F. & Correa-Torres, S.M. (2012). Experiences of preschoolers with severe disabilities in an inclusive early education setting: A qualitative study. *Education and Training in Autism and Developmental Disabilities, 47*(1), 109–121. Retrieved from http://daddcec.org/Publications/ETADDJournal.aspx

Hart, J.E. & Whalon, K.J. (2011). Creating social opportunities for students with autism spectrum disorder in inclusive settings. *Intervention in School & Clinic, 46*(5), 273–279. doi:10.1177/1053451210395382

Hebron, J. & Humphrey, N. (2013). Exposure to bullying among students with autism spectrum conditions: A multi-informant analysis of risk and protective factors. *Autism (iFirst)*, doi:10.1177/1362361313495965

Hobson, L. (2010). *'How is Australia faring': Social inclusion and people with disability*. Melbourne: Australian Federation of Disability Organisations.

Hollingsworth, H.L., Boone, H.A. & Crais, E.R. (2009). Individualized inclusion plans work in early childhood classrooms. *Young Exceptional Children, 13*(1), 19–35. doi:10.1177/1096250609347259

Jackson, R.L., Chalmers, R. & Wills, D. (2004). Should schools include children with disabilities? *Interaction, 17*, 24–30. Retrieved from http://search.informit.com.au/fullText;dn=138303;res=AEIPT

Jackson, R. (2008). *Inclusion or segregation for children with an intellectual impairment: What does the research say?* Queensland Parents for People with a Disability. www.qppd.org

Johnston, S., McDonnell, A., Nelson, C. & Magnavito, A. (2003). Teaching functional communication skills using augmentative and alternative communication in inclusive settings. *Journal of Early Intervention, 25*(4), 263–280. doi:10.1177/105381510302500403

Jones, L. (2002). Derrida goes to nursery school: Deconstructing young children's stories. *Contemporary Issues in Early Childhood, 3*(1), 139–146. Retrieved from http://www.wwwords.co.uk/ciec/

Jordan, A. & Stanovich, P. (2001). Patterns of teacher-student interaction in inclusive elementary classrooms and correlates with student self-concept. *International Journal of Disability, Development and Education, 48*(1), 33–52. doi:10.1080/10349120120036297

Jordan, A., Glenn, C. & McGhie-Richmond, D. (2010). The Supporting Effective Teaching (SET) project: The relationship of inclusive teaching practices to teachers' beliefs about disability and ability, and about their roles as teachers. *Teaching & Teacher Education, 26*(2), 259–266. doi:10.1016/j.tate.2009.03.005

Jordan, A., Schwartz, E. & McGhie-Richmond, D. (2009). Preparing teachers for inclusive classrooms. *Teaching and Teacher Education, 25*(4), 535–542. doi:10.1016/j.tate.2009.02.101

Kalambouka, A., Farrell, P., Dyson, A. & Kaplan, I. (2007). The impact of placing pupils with special educational needs in mainstream schools on the achievement of their peers. *Educational Research, 49*(4), 365–382. doi:10.1080/00131880701717222

Kasa-Hendrickson, C. & Kluth, P. (2005). 'We have to start with inclusion and work it out as we go': Purposeful inclusion for non-verbal students with autism. *International Journal of Whole Schooling, 2*(1), 2–14. Retrieved from http://www.wholeschooling.net/Journal_of_Whole_Schooling/IJWSIndex.html

Kliewer, C. (1998). The meaning of inclusion. *Mental Retardation, 36*(4), 317–322. doi:10.1352/0047-6765(1998)036<0317:TMOI>2.0.CO;2

Kliewer, C. (2008). *Seeing all kids as readers: A new vision for literacy in the inclusive early childhood classroom.* Baltimore: Paul H. Brookes Publishing Co.

Komesaroff, L. & McLean, M. (2006). Being there is not enough: Inclusion is both deaf and hearing. *Deafness and Education International, 8*(2), 88–100. doi:10.1002/dei.192

Lalvani, P. (2013). Privilege, compromise, or social justice: Teachers' conceptualizations of inclusive education. *Disability & Society, 28*(1), 14–27. doi:10.1080/09687599.2012.692028

Lilley, R. (2013). It's an absolute nightmare: Maternal experiences of enrolling children diagnosed with autism in primary school in Sydney, Australia. *Disability and Society 28*(4), 514–526. doi:10.1080/09687599.2012.717882

Link, B.G. & Phelan, J.C. (2001). Conceptualizing stigma. *Annual Review of Sociology, 27*, 363–385. doi:0360-0572/01/0811-0363

McGregor, G. & Vogelsberg, R.T. (1998). *Inclusive schooling practices: Pedagogical and research foundations.* Baltimore: Paul H. Brookes Publishing Co.

McLeskey, J. & Waldron, N.L. (2007). Making differences ordinary in inclusive classrooms. *Intervention in School and Clinic, 42*(3), 162–168. doi:10.1177/10534512070420030501

Mogharreban, C. & Bruns, D. (2009). Moving to inclusive pre-kindergarten classrooms: Lessons from the field. *Early Childhood Education Journal, 36*(5), 407–414. doi:10.1007/s10643-008-0301-0

Montaigne, M. (1580). Translated by M.A. Screech (2003). Of a monster-child. In M.de Montaigne, *Michel de Montaigne: The complete essays* (pp.807–808). London: Penguin.

Myklebust, J.O. (2006). Class placement and competence attainment among students with special needs. *British Journal of Special Education 33*(2), 76–81. Retrieved from http://onlinelibrary.wiley.com/journal/10.1111/(ISSN)1467-8578

Nikolaraizi, M., Kumar, P., Favazza, P., Sideridis, G., Koulousiou, D. & Raill, A. (2005). A cross-cultural examination of typically developing children's attitudes toward individuals with special needs. *International Journal of Disability, Development and Education, 52*(2), 101–119. doi:10.1080/10349120500086348

Nutbrown, C. & Clough, P. (2009). Citizenship and inclusion in the early years: Understanding and responding to children's perspectives on 'belonging'. *International Journal of Early Years Education, 17*(3), 191–206. doi:10.1080/09669760903424523

Odom, S.L. & Diamond, K. (1998). Inclusion of young children with special needs in early childhood education: The research base. *Early Childhood Research Quarterly, 13*(1), 3–25. doi:10.1016/S0885-2006(99)80023-4

Odom, S.L., Buysse, V. & Soukakou, E. (2011). Inclusion for young children with disabilities: A quarter century of research perspectives. *Journal of Early Intervention, 33*(4), 344–356. doi:10.1177/1053815111430094

Palmer, D.S., Fuller, K., Arora, T. & Nelson, M. (2001). Taking sides: Parent views on inclusion for their children with severe disabilities. *Exceptional Children 67*(4), 467–484. Retrieved from http://journals.cec.sped.org/ec/

Peetsma, T., Vergeer, M., Karsten, S. & Roeleveld, J. (2001). Inclusion in education: Comparing pupils' development in special and regular education. *Educational Review 53*(2), 125–35. doi:10.1080/00131910125044

Petriwskyj, A. (2010a). Diversity and inclusion in the early years. *International Journal of Inclusive Education, 14*(2), 195–212. doi:10.1080/13603110802504515

Petriwskyj, A. (2010b). Who has rights to what? Inclusion in Australian early childhood programs. *Contemporary Issues in Early Childhood, 11*(4), 342–352. doi:10.2304/ciec.2010.11.4.342

Prosser, J. & Loxley, A. (2007). Enhancing the contribution of visual methods to inclusive education. *Journal of Research in Special Education Needs, 7(1),* 55–68. doi:10.1111/j.1471-3802.2007.00081.x

Purdue, K., Ballard, K. & MacArthur, J. (2001). Exclusion and inclusion in New Zealand early childhood education: Disability, discourses and contexts. *International Journal of Early Years Education, 9*(1), 37–49. doi:10.1080/0966976012004417 8

Qi, J. & Ha, A.S. (2012). Inclusion in physical education: A review of literature. *International Journal of Disability, Development and Education, 59*(3), 257–281. doi:10.1080/1034912X.2012.697737

Rietveld, C. (2010). Early childhood inclusion: The hidden curriculum of peer relationships, *New Zealand Journal of Educational Studies, 45*(1), 17–32. Retrieved from http://hdl.handle.net/10092/5223

Rose, C.A., Monda-Amaya, L.E. & Espelage, D.L. (2011). Bullying perpetration and victimization in special education: A review of the literature. *Remedial and Special Education, 32*(2), 114–130. doi:10.1177/0741932510361247

Shapiro, J.P. (1993). *No pity: People with disabilities forging a new civil rights movement.* New York: Three Rivers Press.

Slee, R. (2011). *The irregular school: Exclusion, schooling and inclusive education.* Abingdon, Oxon: Routledge.

Stahmer, A.C., Carter, C., Baker, M. & Miwa, K. (2003). Parent perspectives on their toddlers' development: Comparison of regular and inclusion childcare. *Early Child Development and Care, 173*(5), 477–488. doi:10.1080/0300443032000088267

Stahmer, A.C. & Ingersoll, B. (2004). Inclusive programming for toddlers with autism spectrum disorders: Outcomes from the children's toddler school. *Journal of Positive Behavior Interventions, 6*(2), 67–82. doi:10.1177/10983007040060020201

Stahmer, A.C., Akshoomoff, N. & Cunningham, A.B. (2011). Inclusion for toddlers with autism spectrum disorders. *The International Journal of Research & Practice, 15*(5), 625–641. doi:10.1177/1362361310392253

Stroeve, W. (1998). *One of the kids*. Sydney: Disability Council of NSW.

Tanti Burlo, E. (2010). Inclusive education: A qualitative leap. *Life Span and Disability, 13*(2), 203–221. Retrieved from http://www.lifespan.it

Theodorou, F. & Nind, M. (2010). Inclusion in play: A case study of a child with autism in an inclusive nursery. *Journal of Research in Special Educational Needs, 10*(2), 99–106. doi:10.1111/j.1471-3802.2010.01152.x

Torrance, D.A. (2000). Qualitative studies into bullying in special schools. *British Journal of Special Education, 27*(1), 16–21. Retrieved from http://onlinelibrary.wiley.com/journal/10.1111/(ISSN)1467-8578

United Nations. (1989). *Convention on the rights of the child.* New York: United Nations General Assembly. Retrieved from http://www.ohchr.org/en/professionalinterest/pages/crc.aspx

United Nations. (2006). *Convention of the rights of persons with disabilities*. Retrieved from: http://www.un.org/disabilities/convention/conventionfull.shtml

United Nations Children's Fund (UNICEF). (2013). The state of the world's children: Children with disabilities. New York: United Nations. Retrieved from: www.unicef.org/sowc2013/

United Nations Educational Scientific and Cultural Organization (UNESCO). (1990). *World Declaration on Education for All: Meeting basic learning needs*. Retrieved from www.unesco.org/education/wef/en-conf/Jomtien%20Declaration%20eng.shtm

UNESCO. (1994). *The Salamanca statement and framework for action on special needs education*. Retrieved from www.unesco.org/education/pdf/SALAMA_E.PDF

UNESCO. (2006). *Guidelines on intercultural education*. Retrieved from http://unesdoc.unesco.org/images/0014/001478/147878e.pdf

Vakil, S., Welton, E., O'Connor, B. & Kline, L.S. (2009). Inclusion means everyone! The role of the early childhood educator when including young children with autism in the classroom. *Early Childhood Education Journal, 36*(4), 321–326. doi:10.1007/s10643-008-0289-5

Vianello, R. & Lanfranchi, S. (2009). Genetic syndromes causing mental retardation: Deficit and surplus in school performance and social adaptability compared to cognitive functioning. *Life Span and Disability, 12*(1), 41–52. Retrieved from www.lifespan.it

Wang, M.C. & Baker, E.T. (1985). Mainstreaming programs: Design features and effects. *The Journal of Special Education, 19*(4), 503–521. doi:10.1177/002246698501900412

World Health Organization (WHO). (2011). *World report on disability.* Geneva: World Health Organization.

Woods, S. & Wolke, D. (2004). Direct and relational bullying among primary school children and academic achievement. *Journal of School Psychology, 42*(2), 135–155. doi:10.1016/j.jsp.2003.12.002

# 2 Ableism, Disablism and the Early Years

*Kathy Cologon and Carol Thomas*

CHAPTER OVERVIEW

In seeking to support early years professionals in embracing diversity, this chapter will explore the concept of disability by considering the social construction of disability. This is fundamental in developing an understanding of the role that early years professionals can play in disestablishing all forms of discrimination, including ableist, racist, classist, homophobic, transphobic, ageist, sexist and gendered beliefs and practices, to pave the way for genuine inclusion. The importance of changing early years practices, rather than changing children, will be discussed.

Learning goals for this chapter include:

- Understanding the social construction of disability;
- Examining the key elements of, and differences between, medical and social models of disability;
- Considering the social relational aspects of disability and developing a social relational understanding;
- Recognising barriers that impose the experience of disability upon individuals;
- Understanding what ableism and disablism are and why these are a problem for inclusion;
- Exploring children's views on experiencing disability;
- Identifying ways to reduce or remove barriers to inclusion for children experiencing all forms of social oppression.

KEY TERMS AND CONCEPTS

ableism

disablism

medical model of disability

social model of disability

social relational understanding of disability

# Introduction

As individuals and as a society we rarely stop and critically engage with common assumptions about, or understandings of, disability. 'Disability' is a concept that most people think they understand, having absorbed general social views throughout life. In this chapter, we are going to unpack this social construct and consider what 'disability' actually means. An important consideration in relation to this is the question of whether disability is a biological difference that exists within a person (which is a common assumption), or whether disability is something much more complex.

The World Health Organization (WHO) states that disability is '[A] complex phenomenon, reflecting the interaction between features of a person's body and features of the society in which he or she lives. Overcoming the difficulties faced by people with disabilities requires interventions to remove environmental and social barriers' (WHO, 2013, n.p.).

In this chapter we will examine different understandings of disability, and the barriers that impose restrictions on the life chances of individuals with designated impairments. We will also draw attention to the social imposition of barriers imposed not only through what has been termed 'ableism' (Campbell, 2009), but also those resulting from racism, sexism, genderism, classism, homophobia, transphobia, ageism and discrimination in relation to religious belief/non-belief. These social justice issues are at the core of everyday early years practice and are therefore of critical concern to early years professionals. Consequently, this chapter addresses key issues that underpin inclusion or exclusion in education and society, and in doing so forms the theoretical framework for this book.

# Medical and social model understandings of disability

**medical model of disability:** Holds that disability exists within a person, that it is impairment or is caused by impairment, that it is a tragedy, and that the person needs to be 'fixed' and 'cured' (Cologon, 2013; Thomas 2004; WHO, 2002).

Understandings of disability can be roughly divided into two categories:

- Medical models;
- Social models.

In this section, we will explore these models of disability.

## THE MEDICAL MODEL OF DISABILITY

The **medical model of disability** holds that disability is impairment, or at least that disability is caused by impairment (Thomas, 2004). The medical model, with its underlying view of people who experience disability[1] as tragic and in need of charity and pity, is also referred to as a 'tragedy model' or a 'charity model'. At its most fundamental, a medical model view of disability considers disability to be something 'broken' inside a person. From this perspective, the required response is therefore to 'fix' the person, to try to change the person in ways that make it easier for the person to 'fit in' with society. Another response is seeking to eliminate the 'disability'. This can include the termination of pregnancy on the basis of 'risk' of impairment, or the withholding of medical treatment on the basis of impairment. Extreme examples include the killing of approximately 200,000 people who experienced disability, who were deemed 'lives unworthy of life', in Nazi Germany prior to the Holocaust (Foth, 2013).

In understanding disability as impairment, the medical model does not consider that society plays any role in disabling people, other than exposing them to biological or environmental 'risks' (for example lead, rubella, alcohol during pregnancy, hazards resulting in injury). As such, the medical model fails to take into account individuals' social context and the very real impact of society and social relationships. By ignoring society and social context, the medical model operates as though individuals live as isolated and separated beings, rather than as part of a complex and multi-layered relational social context.

When we consider the discipline and practice of medicine, it becomes possible to see how the medical model of disability formed and has been articulated. For example, when there are concerns regarding a child's behaviour and a medical practitioner prescribes medication for that child, that specialist is working to 'fix' a 'problem' within the individual, just as one might take antibiotics for an infection—this is a medical model view. However, stepping back from this medical interventionist view, it is important to consider the question raised above: Is being disabled something that exists within a person, or is it something much more complex than that? The medical model places disability, and being disabled, solely within the person. Continuing with the example of medicating children to address concerns about behaviour (leaving aside questions around whether or not medication can be helpful to children labelled with 'behaviour disorders'—see Chapter 24 for an exploration of children and behaviour), medicating a child doesn't address the environmental and relational factors influencing behaviour. It also leaves the early years professional no role in supporting the child.

A medical model view of disability as caused by impairment results in the conclusion that all activity limitations and participation restrictions occur directly as a result of the person themselves, and that society is separate from this. But is this even possible? Can we isolate the experience of life from context, people and interactions? The old adage from John Donne's 1623 poem 'no man [or woman or child] is an island' has currency here.

## THE SOCIAL MODEL

**social model of disability:** Holds that disability is a socially created problem, not a problem within an individual, and that it demands a political response.

In stark contrast to the medical model, a **social model** view suggests that disability is imposed upon a person by society (people, structures, institutions). Therefore, from a social model perspective, it is the society that needs to be fixed—not the person. Society needs to change to accommodate the diversity of people who live within it, rather than expecting all individuals to change to fit society. This is not at all to deny people who experience disability access to health care for medical treatments that are health enhancing—indeed, non-disablist health care is a key human right.

In the 1960s a 'challenge to dominant social perceptions of disability as personal tragedy' (Campbell & Oliver 1996, p.20) 'turned our understanding of disability completely on its head' (Oliver 2004, p.7). This accompanied the realisation that rather than impairments, the main cause of problems for people who experience disability is the way society responds to this oppressed minority (Oliver, 2004). This alternative understanding holds that disability 'is the social response to impairment that prevents the person from participating as a valued member of society' (Cologon, 2013, p.102). This shift in thinking has disrupted the medical model view and enabled people to recognise how environments can be unnecessarily disabling (Campbell & Oliver 1996). From a social model understanding, impairment is not considered the same as disability—they are two different things.

Importantly, the social model takes account of the social context in which we live and the impact of society on individuals. '[A] person is disabled when he or she is socially prevented from full participation by the way society is arranged' (Finkelstein,1975, p.34). As such, the social model recognises the interconnectedness and interdependence of all humans (that no one is an island!).

Viewed from the perspective of the social model, disablement occurs as a result of society, rather than the individual.

> In the broadest sense, the social model of disability is about nothing more complicated than a clear focus on the economic, environmental and cultural barriers encountered by people who are viewed by others as having some form of impairment—whether physical, mental or intellectual. The barriers [people who experience disability] encounter include inaccessible education systems, working environments, inadequate disability

> benefits, discriminatory health and social support services, inaccessible transport, houses and public buildings and amenities, and the devaluing of [people who experience disability] through negative images in the media—films, television, and newspapers (Oliver, 2004, p.21).

Thus, from a social model perspective, it is the lack of accommodations within the environment or curriculum that result in disability for a child, rather than a child's impairment or other form of diversity.

## Deconstructing disability

In deconstructing the commonly accepted, generally unquestioned and unexamined understanding of disability (the medical model), it is important to recognise that an individual may have a designated impairment, but not experience disability. For example, an individual in Australia today who has a vision impairment that is addressed through the use of glasses does have a designated impairment, but is unlikely to experience disability.

However, society often imposes limitations and restrictions on individuals who have particular types of impairment. For example, when a person has a designated impairment that results in a noticeable or visible difference, those around may stare, ask inappropriate questions and make a raft of assumptions that result in disabling the person.

Another example would be an individual who is labelled as having an intellectual impairment and encounters socially imposed restrictions on the basis of the assumption that the person is incapable of parenting—regardless of his/her abilities (see Chapter 5), or a person who uses a wheelchair, walker, or other mobility aid, who experiences socially imposed limitations and restrictions when access to, and within, buildings is not provided. As Finkelstein (1975, p.34) argues, when a person cannot get into a building due to access limitations, this disabling experience 'is *caused* by having steps into buildings and not by the inability to walk'. If there is a ramp or lift, or level entry, the person is able to access the building.

Finkelstein (1975), illustrating the social construction of disability, developed a story about a village in which everyone used wheelchairs (similar to Het Dorp, a village set up in the Netherlands in the 1960s [Zola, 1982]). In this story, a group of people who use wheelchairs created a fully accessible village. The villagers built buildings that were appropriate for this society, for example, buildings with ramps and wide doorways. Over time the villagers also introduced low ceilings and low doors, as they realised no one in the village needed high ceilings or doors.

**FIGURE 2.1** DISABILITY

*Artwork by Cameron*

**FIGURE 2.2** ACCESSIBILITY

*Artwork by Cameron*

Finkelstein (1975, p.34) writes: 'Now everyone is happy in this village, all the physical difficulties in the environment have been overcome and this little society has changed according to the physical character of its members.'

Some time later, a few people who did not use wheelchairs moved to this village. 'Naturally, one of the first things they noticed was the height of the doors and ceilings. They noticed this directly, by constantly knocking their heads on the door lintels. Soon all the able-bodied members of the village were also marked by the dark bruises they carried on their foreheads' (Finkelstein, 1975, p.34).

These 'able-bodied' villagers eventually sought assistance from the village doctors (doctors who used wheelchairs of course). The village doctors wrote 'learned reports' and the other villagers (who used wheelchairs) took pity on the 'able-bodied' villagers and provided helmets and braces to enable them to fit into the buildings. These supports were provided for free, but were to be worn at all times. Gradually the 'able-bodied' villagers were pathologised, stigmatised and constructed as disabled.

> But one day, when the able-bodied were sitting together and discussing their problems they realised that they were never consulted by the wheelchair-users about their problems in this little society. In fact they realised that there may be solutions to their problems which had never occurred to the wheelchair-users simply because they never looked at the problems in the same way as those who had the problem. In fact, it occurred to these able-bodied disabled people that perhaps the *cause* of their problems was not at all in themselves because they were physically abnormal (by being too tall) in this village, but because the society took no account of their physical condition in its social organisation. They began to see a social cause to their problems and a social solution—they suggested that the door and ceiling heights be changed! Of course some of the village wheelchair-users thought the able-bodied disabled were failing to accept their disabilities and had chips on their shoulders because they argued so strongly for social change and a change in attitude by the wheelchair-users. The able-bodied disabled even argued that perhaps their disabilities could be overcome (and disappear!) with changes in society (Finkelstein, 1975, p.35).

Finkelstein's story highlights the unnecessary nature of disabling attitudes and disabling environmental barriers. When the starting point is accessibility, rather than impairment, the question becomes: Who is disabled? How? Why? The pathologisation of social issues as individual deficits or 'disability' and a focus on pity and charity, not recognition of social oppression and the need for social change, is the process through which disablement occurs. As Finkelstein explores through this story, in order to reduce or remove disablement, we need to challenge the misperception of 'denial' as a personal characteristic rather than a social issue.

Critically reflecting on the medical and social models and comparing their underlying tenets brings to light the question of whether an individual who experiences disability is 'whole' or 'broken'.

- Within a medical model a person is viewed as broken and needing to be fixed.
- Within a social model a person is viewed as whole and, in a sense, society is viewed as broken and needing to be fixed.

**CRITICAL REFLECTION QUESTIONS**

1. Thinking about your own view of yourself and those close to you, how might you feel about being constructed as a 'whole person', or a 'broken person'?
2. Perhaps the question then becomes, is it okay to be different?

When applying this thinking to early years settings, it is important to consider carefully the motivation behind approaches to early intervention and education. Understanding education or early intervention as being about 'fixing' a 'broken' child is a medical model view and while it is a common—though often subconscious—understanding, it is one that needs to be challenged.

Considering whether an individual who has a designated impairment is constructed as 'whole' or 'broken' underlies the necessity of the rejection of the medical model of disability. This is something that the disability movement has been advocating for quite some time now. However (as you may know from personal experience), the medical model still holds considerable currency in our society today.

**REFLECTION**

It is important to pause and note that for you, the reader, deconstructing disability may be a new experience. And, given the pervasive and insidious nature of the medical model, you may have subconsciously developed a medical model view of disability, in which disability is seen as existing entirely inside a person and in which a person who experiences disability is seen as 'broken' or 'lesser' and needing to be 'fixed'. You are unlikely to have developed this view deliberately, but rather, you may have absorbed unquestioned dominant social views through the process of enculturation. Contemplating a social model of disability may therefore make you feel uncomfortable—and each of us come to these ideas from different experiences and backgrounds. But don't be alarmed—hang in there! The challenge is to think and reflect deeply on these ideas and consider why a move towards a social model perspective is important—for early years professionals, for everyday early years practice, and for society as a whole.

# Towards a social relational understanding of disability

The social model has grown and developed over time and there are now a number of approaches that have the social model at their core. One development is Thomas' '**social relational**' understanding of disability. A social relational understanding acknowledges the individual lived experience and the social relational nature of how disability is constructed and experienced. Thus, 'disability is a form of social oppression involving the social imposition of restrictions of activity on people with impairments and the socially engendered undermining of their psycho-emotional wellbeing' (Thomas, 1999, p.60).

**social relational understanding of disability:** Suggests that disability is always socially situated, and arises from social interaction between people with ascribed impairments and people without, with the former being constructed as 'second rate'.

Thomas (1999, 2001) has proposed that a social relational understanding explains disability as being:

- Defined through lived experience or through the lived body;
- Existing within an unequal social relationship;
- Like racism or sexism in that disabling restrictions are imposed through social relationships upon individuals who have designated impairments.

As such, a social relational understanding acknowledges the humanity of, and individual experience of, disability for every person.

Thomas argues that we need to understand the importance of 'taking account of the personal experience of disability' and 'acknowledging the personal experience of living with impairment' (Thomas, 2001, p.57). In taking these perspectives into account, while in no way supporting medical model thinking (Thomas, 2001), a social relational understanding further develops the social model.

A social relational understanding can help early years professionals recognise the ways in which early years practice can impose the experience of disability. In developing this understanding, a social relational model may support early years professionals to reduce barriers that impose disability, therefore creating more inclusive communities. Consequently, it is important to explore the components that make up a social relational understanding of disability.

Drawing on the combination of factors resulting in disability for an individual, Thomas has identified some major components of disability within the social relational model. These components of the lived experience of disability have been referred to as 'barriers to doing' and 'barriers to being'. Additionally, Thomas (1999) identifies bio-social 'impairment effects', which form the medium through which disability is imposed (Thomas, 2007).

## BARRIERS TO DOING

Barriers to doing involve socially imposed restrictions in the form of environmental and economic barriers such as access issues, be that building access (as illustrated through Finkelstein's story discussed above) or access to the curriculum, for example. These barriers to doing impose restrictions or prevent people from participating in certain activities. Some examples of barriers to doing that may exist within an early years setting include:

- Barriers preventing use of a building or environment:
- Barriers to communication, when alternative forms of communication are not provided;
- Barriers to participation, when modified equipment or pace is not provided;
- Barriers to participation, when translation is not provided.

**CRITICAL REFLECTION QUESTIONS**

1. Consider your everyday environments and interactions. What barriers to access are present within them? What changes could be made to remove these barriers?
2. Consider your pedagogical approach and the learning environments you have witnessed in early years contexts. What barriers to doing are present in such environments and pedagogical approaches? How can this be addressed?

## IMPAIRMENT EFFECTS

Impairment effects are a more complex concept than barriers to doing as they are bio-social, meaning they are both biological and socially constructed. Thomas writes that impairment effects are 'the *direct and unavoidable* impacts that "impairments" (physical, sensory, intellectual, emotional) have on individuals' embodied functioning in the social world. Impairments and impairment effects are always bio-social and culturally constructed in character, and may occur at any stage in the life course' (Thomas, 2010, p.37, emphasis original).

Illustrating the intersection between impairment effects and disability (the process of disablism), Thomas shares the following personal story:

> [C]onsider a young woman missing a hand. Her absent hand is a 'real' phenomenon, representing a marked variation in human morphology—in any time or place. In *contemporary* society, she cannot hold a boiled kettle in one hand while lifting a jug or saucepan in the other to receive the boiled water. This restriction of activity is an immediate *impairment effect*. If, however, other people in positions of power or authority (parents, doctors, social workers) were to decide that she is unfit to be a paid care worker, or to become a parent, *because* she cannot pour boiling water from a kettle into a

> hand-held container—or perform other commonplace 'two-handed' actions—then the restrictions of activity that follow (becoming a parent, obtaining employment in the care sector, and so forth), premised on the impairment effect, constitute disablism. In such circumstances an impairment effect intermeshes with the effects of disablism to shape lived experience (Thomas, 2007, p.136, emphasis original).

In understanding the bio-social construction of impairment, it is important to consider that 'bodily variations only carry the "impairment" label in particular socio-cultural times and places ... In a capitalist society, a missing hand at birth is constructed by medicine as a biological "abnormality", and this, in the wider view, is socially variable and conditional. In previous eras, and in some contemporary non-Western cultures, a missing hand at birth may be explained and responded to through spiritual or other cosmologies ... the bio-material intersects with the socio-cultural' (Thomas, 2007, p.137). Similarly, in Deaf culture, being deaf is not viewed as an impairment, but rather as a cultural marker. Indeed, Deaf children of Deaf parents (see Chapter 3 for discussion of this terminology) are viewed as 'royalty'—that is, highly desired and valued—within many Deaf communities. By contrast, outside of Deaf culture, being deaf is generally viewed as an impairment and this view leads to the imposition of disability, including the devaluing of any form of communication other than speech (Komesaroff, 2008). Again, this highlights the bio-social construction of impairment.

**FIGURE 2.3** SHIFTING SNOW AND SHIFTING MINDSET

REFLECTION

Now that you have been introduced to the bio-social construction of impairment effects, pause to consider the senses, physical actions, knowledge and skills that you use differently in day-to-day activities. What is important to, or valued in, each of these processes? Think about whether there may be more than one way to go about completing different tasks, and whether different approaches may be valued more and less by different people in different contexts. For example, consider the fact that 'intelligence' is something that is defined and measured in a way deemed to be important by a particular group of people in a particular context and time. In Australia (and elsewhere) performance on an IQ test is used to determine intellectual ability or impairment. However, an IQ score simply means that a person performed at X level on X tasks (with X cultural significance) on X day—nothing more. A person is considered more or less 'intelligent' depending on what skills or knowledge is valued in a particular context and his/her performance against this measure.

## BARRIERS TO BEING

Barriers to being can occur at individual or personal, as well as at systematic or institutional levels. Barriers to being involve inappropriate, hurtful or hostile behaviour that has a negative impact on an individual's sense of self, thus affecting who or what an individual feels s/he can *be*. Thomas has referred to this process as *psycho-emotional disablism* (Thomas, 2007). Psycho-emotional disablism

> involves the intended or unintended 'hurtful' words and social actions of [people who do not experience disability] (parents, professionals, complete strangers, others) in inter-personal engagements with people with impairments. It also involves the creation, placement and use of denigrating images of 'people with impairments' in public spaces by [people who do not experience disability] ... The effects of psycho-emotional disablism are often profound: the damage inflicted works along psychological and emotional pathways, impacting negatively on self-esteem, personal confidence and ontological security ... Moreover, impairments may themselves be affected in problematic ways by the impact of psycho-emotional disablism (Thomas, 2007, p.72).

Barriers to being involve the living out of stigmatisation (see Chapter 1) on account of impairment. It is very important to reflect on barriers to being when considering the role of an early years professional (we will explore examples of barriers to being from the perspective of children who experience disability in the section below).

Taken together, barriers to doing and being and impairment effects constitute disability, but these are social relational in nature—they do not occur all by

**FIGURE 2.4** EXCLUSION

*Artwork by Emma*

themselves. Disability occurs through the mechanisms and processes of society at many different levels and through the people who make up society in a process that has been termed 'disablism'. Psycho-emotional disablism, while very harmful, is only one form of disablism. **Disablism**, and ableism (which is discussed below), are present in everyday early years practices and in the attitudes of early years professionals. Consequently, examining and eliminating ableist and disablist views and practices are a practical day-to-day concern for early years professionals.

**Disablism:** 'The social imposition of avoidable restrictions on the life activities, aspirations and psycho-emotional well-being of people categorised as "impaired" by those deemed "normal"' (Thomas, 2012, p.211).

## Ableism

**Ableism** and disablism are sometimes used interchangeably, but their emphases are somewhat different. Fiona Kumari Campbell, an Australian Disability Studies scholar, argues that '[d]isablism relates to the production of disability and fits well into a social constructionist understanding of disability' (Campbell, 2009, p.152). Ableism, on the other hand, is 'a network of beliefs, processes and practices that produces a particular kind of self and body (the corporeal standard) that is projected as the perfect, species-typical and therefore essential and fully human. Disability then is cast as a diminished state of being human' (Campbell, 2009, p.9).

**Ableism:** 'Discriminatory and exclusionary practices that result from the perception that being able-bodied is superior to being disabled' (McLean, 2008, p.607).

A medical model understanding of disability is, in and of itself, ableist. Ableism and ableist beliefs are expressed through actions at both individual and collective or systemic levels, but also through the words we use. There are two features that produce ableism within interactions and relationships:

1 The idea of *normal* (normative individual);
2 A *constitutional divide* – a division enforced between the 'normal' = human, and the aberrant (sometimes pathological) = subhuman (Campbell, 2012, p.215).

The problem with the socially constructed myth of the 'normal child' is explored further in Chapter 3.

As noted above, a medical model understanding of disability operates through ableist beliefs and practices. 'A chief feature of an ableist viewpoint is a belief that impairment (irrespective of "type") is inherently negative which should, if the opportunity presents itself, be ameliorated, cured or indeed eliminated' (Campbell, 2009, pp.154–155).

Major social movements such as the civil rights movement (centred around anti-racism) the feminist/women's rights movement, the lesbian, gay, bisexual, and transgender (LGBT) rights movement, and the disability rights movement are examples of collective human efforts towards greater inclusion. In Australia we have travelled much further down the road towards equality and equity on the basis of gender, sexuality and cultural background, for example, than we have towards the disestablishment of ableism. However, in all areas we have further work to do. Discrimination and oppression of minority groups creates considerable barriers to inclusion. 'Ableism is deeply and subliminally embedded within ... culture' (Campbell, 2009, p.153). In effect our current society is conditioned towards ableism, resulting in exclusion, discrimination and segregation of people on the basis of 'disability' within and outside of the education system/s—and even to death, for example the acceptance of impairment as a reason for abortion and past examples, such as the example noted earlier in the chapter, in Nazi Germany. Therefore, to bring about inclusive education, we need—individually and as a society—to examine and resist ableist thinking and practices.

Ableist understandings of inclusive education are underpinned by deficit understandings of diversity in which some people are positioned as 'normal' while others are constructed as 'subnormal' and in need of 'fixing' or 'curing'. This attitude towards diversity creates barriers to inclusive education on many levels. A medical, 'special education model of disability is also likely to result in discrimination, inequity and injustice for children with disabilities and their families' (Purdue, 2009, p.135). Many exclusionary and discriminatory practices identified in a range of research studies can be understood as ableist views and practices. For example:

- Providing separate classes or separate activities for children who do and do not experience disability (Hurley & Horn, 2010), including segregating a child from activities in which they do not 'fit in' rather than making adjustments and accommodations to practice or environment to facilitate inclusion (Macartney & Morton, 2013);
- Thinking that interactions are 'abnormal' if they fall outside of what is typically expected (Komesaroff, 2007; Purdue, Gordon-Burns, Gunn, Madden & Surtees, 2009; Wong & Cumming, 2010), therefore, stereotyping and considering children who experience disability to be 'abnormal' (Kalyva & Avramidis, 2005; Kasa-Hendrickson, 2005; Purdue, 2009);
- Locating 'problems' within the child (Baglieri, 2008; Macartney & Morton, 2013; Orsati & Causton-Theoharis, 2013; Rietveld, 2010; Theodorou & Nind, 2010) and therefore considering that inclusion is conditional on disability category or severity (Huang & Diamond, 2009; Hurley & Horn, 2010; Kasa-Hendrickson, 2005; Purdue, 2009);
- Requiring children to meet specific criteria before permitting them to participate (Hurley & Horn, 2010);
- Believing that 'special teachers' are required for 'special children', including believing that a teacher can educate all children *except* those labelled disabled (Recchia & Puig, 2011);
- Thinking that including children who experience disability will disrupt or interfere with the learning of other children in the setting/classroom (Finke, McNaughton & Drager, 2009; Purdue, 2009; Warming, 2011; Wong & Cumming, 2010). This includes concerns that children who experience disability will 'take up time, money or attention from the deserving, "normal" children' (Purdue, 2009, p.135) or that the presence of children who experience disability will in some way pose a risk to the development of children not labelled disabled (Jordan & Stanovich, 2001; Stahmer, Carter, Baker & Miwa, 2003);
- Requiring that children prove that they are 'worthy of inclusion' (Biklen, 2000). An example is circular criteria for inclusion in which it is assumed that children who are labelled disabled will not benefit from inclusion and yet simultaneously (without addressing the impact of this assumption on attitudes and practices) children must prove that they *are* benefiting from inclusion in order to be permitted to participate (Biklen & Burke, 2006);
- Having a set view of expectations or limitations associated with a specific disability label (Biklen, 2000; Kasa-Hendrickson, 2005);

- Making 'assumptions of *in*competence', for example, assuming that someone is less competent if they do not talk or move in ways that are considered 'normal' (Biklen, 2000);
- Viewing inclusion as an optional policy that schools/teachers can choose to accept or ignore, rather than recognising the shared human right to inclusive education for all children (Kliewer, 1998);
- 'The uncritical general acceptance within a school of the exclusion of children because they have an impairment or are categorised as "having learning difficulties"' (Booth & Ainscow, 2011, p.43).

Addressing these barriers through inclusive education in the early years has the potential to break the intergenerational cycle of enculturation into oppressive beliefs and practices. This is essential 'if the struggle for a society fit for all is to be achieved' (Oliver & Barnes, 2012, p.176).

**CRITICAL REFLECTION QUESTIONS**

Consider the above examples of ableism in practice.

1. What ableist views can you identify in your own beliefs?
2. What impact do these have on your practices?
3. How can you challenge yourself to identify and disestablish ableist views and practices in your everyday role as an early years professional?

## Children's experiences of disability

For early years professionals, resisting ableist thinking and practices involves careful reflection on children and childhoods. As it is easy to imagine, conducting research to find out about children's understandings and thoughts around experiencing disability is very sensitive and brings to light many ethical considerations. Perhaps as a consequence of this, there is a great deal more research looking at the views and experiences of adults, families or professionals who work with children who experience disability, than there is exploring the views and experiences of children themselves. However, children have a right to be heard (United Nations, 1989) and, as encapsulated in the slogan of the Disability Rights Movement, 'nothing about us without us' (Charlton, 1998), it is inappropriate to consider the experience of disability for children without consulting children directly. While further research is needed, some work has been done exploring children's experiences and understandings. This research helps us as adults to understand the different ways that children who experience disability experience barriers to being, barriers to doing and impairment effects.

In this section we draw on UK research from Kirsten Stalker and Clare Connors (Connors & Stalker, 2003, 2007; Stalker & Connors, 2003, 2005). In this research, Connors and Stalker explored the experiences and understandings of disability of 26 children, using Thomas' social relational understanding of disability as an analytical framework. They also explored the perspectives and experiences of each child's family.

An important aspect of Connors and Stalker's research was the inclusion of children as 'research advisors'. The research advisors provided advice regarding the design, wording and suitability of information and consent forms, interview materials and questions. Augmentative and alternative communication methods were critical to making this study possible.

Connors and Stalker did not want to ask children directly about disability or impairment. Rather they asked questions to see what the children expressed about these things when talking about their daily lives. However, they also included a question in which they asked the children 'If you had a magic wand and you could wish for something to happen, what would you wish?' If the children did not mention impairment or disability in responding to this question, the researchers asked a follow up question: 'What about your disability? Would you change anything about that?'

To this question, only three of the children mentioned anything relating to their impairment: one child said they would like to see better; two children said they would like to be able to walk. One of the participants, a nine-year-old boy, responded with this comment: 'That's it, I'm in a wheelchair so just get on with it ... just get on with what you're doing' (Connors and Stalker, 2007, p.25). Perhaps this reflects another aspect of Connors' and Stalker's findings. They reported that, while children shared both positive and negative views and experiences, children's views of themselves and their experiences of disability were much more positive than the views of parents and professionals commonly reported in research.

Connors and Stalker (2007) found that the children experienced barriers to doing in terms of physical or material barriers. Significant areas of restriction reported by the children related to issues with:

- Lack of access to leisure facilities;
- Transport difficulties;
- Paucity of after-school activities;
- Lack of support with communication.

They also found that children in this study experienced some negative impairment effects including:

- Repeated health problems;
- Tiring easily;

- Being in pain;
- Difficulty completing schoolwork.

While the children in this study shared impairment effects, they viewed impairment as 'not a big deal', not a 'tragedy' and made no reference to loss or being 'hard done by'.

However, Connors and Stalker found that barriers to being were the most influential negative experience for children. Children in their study reported experiencing barriers to being such as

- Being stared at;
- People 'talking down' or being patronising;
- People making inappropriate comments;
- People engaging in inappropriate behaviour;
- Overt sympathy.

It was reported that for many children, their schools and those around them responded positively and they had positive views of themselves, but they also reported that 'where difference was badly managed children could feel hurt and excluded resulting in the barriers to being that Thomas (1999) identified' (Connors & Stalker, 2007, p.27). For example, one child in the study who attended a 'special' unit in a mainstream school 'asked his mother what he had done "wrong" to be placed in a "special" class' (p.27). Connors and Stalker (2007, p.27) concluded from this that '[l]ack of information and explanation had led [this child] to equate difference with badness or naughtiness'.

Considering the views and experiences shared by the children in this research, Connors and Stalker (2007) reported that

- Very few children mentioned their label/diagnosis—the children's focus was on sameness not difference in relation to peers.
- Children reported they were happy 'most of the time' and saw themselves as good friends and helpful classmates.
- Most children reported a sense of achievement in relation to school or sport.
- Most children expressed that they had a sense of autonomy and 'say in their lives', although some teenagers wanted greater independence from their parents (as Connors and Stalkers point out, this is not an unusual sentiment for a teenager!).
- The children reported 'typical' age-related aspirations.

It is essential to remember the impact of society in creating barriers to doing and barriers to being, which can significantly influence children's attitudes towards and concepts about themselves. Children do experience the negative impacts of disablism. However, this research leads to the conclusion that children do not view impairment or the experience of disability as a tragedy, nor as their defining characteristic.

**CRITICAL REFLECTION QUESTIONS**

1. What barriers to being can you identify in your own experiences—as an individual, as a member of your family and community, as well as within the early years experiences you have engaged with to date?
2. Reflect on the notion of barriers to being and barriers to doing in relation to racism, sexism, genderism, classism, homophobia, transphobia, ableism, ageism and discrimination in relation to religious belief/non-belief.
3. Recall the personal experiences of children shared in the research from Connors and Stalker. Using what you now know about models of disability, consider:
   a. Who needs to change—the individual or society?
   b. What does this mean for the role of the early years professional?
4. Why is understanding a social model view of disability important for early years practice?
5. What is the role of the early years professional in reducing or eliminating barriers to being and doing?

# Conclusion

A social relational understanding of the oppression that results in and is sustained by racism, sexism, genderism, classism, homophobia, transphobia, ableism, ageism and discrimination in relation to religious belief/non-belief can be a powerful tool in working towards greater inclusion. From an inclusive perspective, educational 'difficulties' do not belong to, or stem from, a child. Children who experience disability or 'difference' are not 'lesser', 'lacking' or 'broken'. 'Difference' is not inherently negative. A child exists in context and each early years professional can make changes to that context that can completely alter the situation for a child or group of children. Developing the ability to recognise and challenge medical model, deficit views of difference that consider a child is 'broken' or 'lacking' in some way is essential to achieving inclusive practice and meeting the needs of every child. This can require recognising deeply entrenched deficit views of difference—any difference—including ableist views of children who experience disability. In applying a social relational understanding to early years practice, the challenge is to consider what barriers to doing and barriers to being impose restrictions on belonging, being and becoming for any child—regardless of the presence or absence of labels related to social oppression—and what you, as an early years professional, can do to reduce or remove these barriers.

# FOR FURTHER REFLECTION

1. Before reading this chapter, what did you understand the term 'disability' to mean? Consider your reflections following Chapter 1 and compare those with your understanding now. In what ways has the information in this chapter challenged your previous understandings of disability?
2. Why might it be important to reflect on the meaning of the term 'disability'?
3. What are the dangers of a medical model understanding of disability?
4. Who needs to change—the individual or (the disabling) society?
5. Is a child who experiences disability whole or broken?
6. Why is understanding the social construction of disability important for inclusive education?
7. In exploring the concepts of disability and ableism, what implications are there for inclusion in regards to removing barriers that oppress all minority groups? For example, consider the parallels between ableism, disablism and racism.

## NOTE

1 In writing this chapter, we acknowledge that 'disabled person' is the commonly used term within a social model understanding (Shakespeare, 2004). However, in many contexts, including Australia, common use of the term 'disabled person' involves a negation of personhood, or a denial of agency, rather than an acknowledgment of the social construction and imposition of disability. Consequently, the term 'person who experiences disability' is used throughout the chapter to both acknowledge personhood and agency, as well as to highlight the social construction and lived experience of disability (rather than confusing disability and impairment). Further discussion of terminology is contained in Chapter 3.

## WEBSITES

http://dsq-sds.org

*Disability Studies Quarterly* is a scholarly journal dedicated to disability studies. All articles are available freely online.

www.lancaster.ac.uk/fass/centres/cedr/index.php

The Centre for Disability Research at the University of Lancaster is an interdisciplinary research centre with a focus on disability and disablism. The website contains information regarding current research, conferences and other resources.

http://disability-studies.leeds.ac.uk

The Centre for Disability Studies is an interdisciplinary research centre at the University of Leeds. The website contains information regarding current Disability Studies research and a wide range of publications.

www.chapmandisabilitystudies.com

This website developed at Chapman University provides an overview of Disability Studies in Education and discussion of a range of relevant topics.

## REFERENCES

Baglieri, S. (2008). 'I connected': Reflection and biography in teacher learning toward inclusion. *International Journal of Inclusive Education, 12*(5), 585–604. doi:10.1080/13603110802377631

Biklen, D. (2000). Constructing inclusion: Lessons from critical, disability narratives. *International Journal of Inclusive Education, 4*(4), 337–353. doi:10.1080/13603110050168032

Biklen, D. & Burke, J. (2006). Presuming competence. *Equity & Excellence in Education, 39*(2), 166–175. doi:10.1080/10665680500540376

Booth, T. & Ainscow, M. (2011). *Index for inclusion.* Bristol, UK: Centre for Studies on Inclusive Education.

Campbell, F.K. (2009). *Contours of ableism: The production of disability and abledness.* Basingstoke: Palgrave Macmillan.

Campbell, F.K. (2012). Stalking ableism: Using disability to expose 'abled' narcissism. In D. Goodley, B. Hughes, & L. Davis (Eds), *Disability and social theory: New developments and directions* (pp.212–231). Basingstoke: Palgrave Macmillan.

Campbell, J. & Oliver, M. (1996). *Disability politics: Understanding our past, changing our future.* London: Routledge.

Charlton, J.I. (1998). *Nothing about us without us: Disability oppression and empowerment.* California: University of California Press.

Connors, C. & Stalker, K. (2003). *The views and experiences of disabled children and their siblings: A positive outlook.* London: Jessica Kingsley.

Connors, C. & Stalker, K. (2007). Children's experiences of disability: Pointers to a social model of childhood disability. *Disability & Society, 22*(1), 19–33. doi:10.1080/09687590601056162

Cologon, K. (2013). Growing up with 'difference': Inclusive education and the portrayal of characters who experience disability in children's literature. *Write4Children: The International Journal for the Practice and Theories of Writing for Children and Children's Literature, 4*(2), 100–120. Retrieved from www.winchester.ac.uk/academicdepartments/EnglishCreativeWritingandAmericanStudies/Documents/w4cJune2013Diversity.pdf

Finke, E.H., McNaughton, D.B. & Drager, K.D.R. (2009). 'All children can and should have the opportunity to learn': General education teachers' perspectives on including children with autism spectrum disorder who require AAC. *Augmentative and Alternative Communication, 25*(2), 110–122. doi:10.1080/07434610902886206

Finkelstein, V. (1975). Phase 2: Discovering the person in 'disability' and 'rehabilitation', *Magic Carpet, 27*(1), 31–38. Retrieved from http://disability-studies.leeds.ac.uk/files/library/finkelstein-finkelstein4.pdf

Foth, T. (2013). *Caring and killing: Nursing and psychiatric practice in Germany, 1931–1943.* Birkach, Germany: V&R Unipress.

Huang, H.-H. & Diamond, K.E. (2009). Early childhood teachers' ideas about including children with disabilities in programmes designed for typically developing children. *International Journal of Disability, Development and Education, 56*(2), 169–182. doi:10.1080/10349120902868632

Hurley, J.J. & Horn, E.M. (2010). Family and professional priorities for inclusive early childhood settings. *Journal of Early Intervention, 32*(5), 335–350. doi:10.1177/1053815110385650

Jordan, A. & Stanovich, P. (2001). Patterns of teacher–student interaction in inclusive elementary classrooms and correlates with student self-concept. *International Journal of Disability, Development and Education, 48*(1), 33–52. doi:10.1080/10349120120036297

Kalyva, E. & Avramidis, E. (2005). Improving communication between children with autism and their peers through the 'circle of friends': A small-scale intervention study. *Journal of Applied Research in Intellectual Disabilities, 18*(3), 253–261. doi:10.1111/j.1468-3148.2005.00232.x

Kasa-Hendrickson, C. (2005). 'There's no way this kid's retarded': Teachers' optimistic constructions of students' ability. *International Journal of Inclusive Education, 9*(1), 55–69. doi:10.1080/1360311042000253591

Kliewer, C. (1998). The meaning of inclusion. *Mental Retardation, 36*(4), 317–322. doi:10.1352/0047-6765(1998)036<0317:TMOI>2.0.CO;2

Komesaroff, L. (2007). Denying claims of discrimination in the federal court of Australia: Arguments against the use of native sign language in education. *Sign Language Studies 7*(4), 360–386. doi:10.1353/sls.2007.0024

Komesaroff, L. (2008). *Disabling pedagogy: Power, politics, and deaf education.* Washington DC: Gallaudet University Press.

Macartney, B. & Morton, M. (2013). Kinds of participation: Teacher and special education perceptions and practices of 'inclusion' in early childhood and primary school settings. *International Journal of Inclusive Education, 17*(8), 776–792. doi:10.1080/13603116.2011.602529

McLean, M.A. (2008). Teaching about disability: An ethical responsibility? *International Journal of Inclusive Education, 12*(5), 605–619. doi:10.1080/13603110802377649

Oliver, M. (2004). If I had a hammer: The social model in action. In J. Swain, S. French, C. Barnes & C. Thomas (Eds), *Disabling barriers—enabling environments* (2nd ed.) (pp.7–12). London: Sage.

Oliver, M. & Barnes, C. (2012). *The new politics of disablement.* London: Palgrave Macmillan.

Orsati, F.T. & Causton-Theoharis, J. (2013). Challenging control: Inclusive teachers' and teaching assistants' discourse on students with challenging behavior. *International Journal of Inclusive Education, 17*(5), 507–525. doi:10.1080/13603116.2012.689016

Purdue, K. (2009). Barriers to and facilitators of inclusion for children with disabilities in early childhood education.

*Contemporary Issues in Early Childhood, 10*(2), 133–143. doi:10.2304/ciec.2009.10.2.133

Purdue, K., Gordon-Burns, D., Gunn, A., Madden, B. & Surtees, N. (2009). Supporting inclusion in early childhood settings: Some possibilities and problems for teacher education. *International Journal of Inclusive Education, 13*(8), 805–815. doi:10.1080/13603110802110743

Recchia, S.L. & Puig, V.I. (2011). Challenges and inspirations: Student teachers' experiences in early childhood special education classrooms. *Teacher Education and Special Education, 34*(2), 133–151. doi:10.1177/0888406410387444

Rietveld, C. (2010). Early childhood inclusion: The hidden curriculum of peer relationships *New Zealand Journal of Educational Studies, 45*(1), 17–32. Retrieved from http://hdl.handle.net/10092/5223

Shakespeare, T. (2004). Social models of disability and other life strategies. *Scandinavian Journal of Disability Research, 6*(1), 8–21. doi:10.1080/15017410409512636

Stahmer, A.C., Carter, C., Baker, M. & Miwa, K. (2003). Parent perspectives on their toddlers' development: Comparison of regular and inclusion childcare. *Early Child Development and Care, 173*(5), 477–488. doi:10.1080/0300443032000088267

Stalker, K. & Connors, C. (2003). Communicating with disabled children. *Adoption & Fostering, 27*(1), 26–35. doi:10.1177/030857590302700105

Stalker, K. & Connors, C. (2005). Children with learning disabilities talking about their everyday lives. In G. Grant, P. Goward, M. Richardson & P. Ramcharan (Eds). *Learning disability: A life cycle approach to valuing people* (pp.105–118). Maidenhead, UK: Open University Press.

Theodorou, F. & Nind, M. (2010). Inclusion in play: A case study of a child with autism in an inclusive nursery. *Journal of Research in Special Educational Needs, 10*(2), 99–106. doi:10.1111/j.1471-3802.2010.01152.x

Thomas, C. (1999). *Female forms: Experiencing and understanding disability.* Buckingham: Open University Press.

Thomas, C. (2001). Feminism and disability: The theoretical and political significance of the persona and the experiential. In L. Barton (Ed), *Disability, politics and the struggle for change* (pp.48–58). London: David Fulton.

Thomas, C. (2004). Disability and impairment. In J. Swain, S. French, C. Barnes & C. Thomas (Eds), *Disabling barriers—enabling environments* (2nd ed.) (pp.21–27). London: SAGE Publications.

Thomas, C. (2007). *Sociologies of disability and illness: Contested ideas in disability studies and medical sociology.* Hampshire: Palgrave Macmillan.

Thomas, C. (2010). Medical sociology and disability theory. In G. Scambler & S. Scambler (Eds), *New directions in the sociology of chronic and disabling conditions: Assaults on the lifeworld* (pp.37–56). Basingstoke: Palgrave Macmillan.

Thomas, C. (2012). Theorising disability and chronic illness: Where next for perspectives in medical sociology? *Social Theory and Health, 10*(3), 209–227. doi:10.1057/sth.2012.7

United Nations. (1989). *Convention on the rights of the child.* New York: United Nations General Assembly. Retrieved from www.ohchr.org/en/professionalinterest/pages/crc.aspx

Warming, H. (2011). Inclusive discources in early childhood education? *International Journal of Inclusive Education, 15*(2), 233–247. doi:10.1080/13603110902783365

Wong, S. & Cumming, T. (2010). Family day care is for normal kids: Facilitators and barriers to the inclusion of children with disabilities in family day care. *Australasian Journal of Early Childhood, 35*(3), 4–12. Retrieved from www.earlychildhoodaustralia.org.au/australian_journal_of_early_childhood.html

World Health Organization (WHO). (2002). *Towards a common language for functioning, disability and health.* WHO, Geneva. Retrieved from www.who.int/classifications/icf/training/icfbeginnersguide.pdf

WHO. (2013). *Disabilities.* Retrieved from www.who.int/topics/disabiities/en

Zola, I.K. (1982). *Missing pieces: A chronicle of living with a disability.* Philadelphia: Temple University Press.

# 3 More than a Label? The Power of Language

*Kathy Cologon*

CHAPTER OVERVIEW

This chapter will focus on language and labelling in relation to 'difference' and 'disability', with a view to moving beyond deficit assumptions.

Learning goals for this chapter include:

- Developing an understanding of respectful language use;
- Reflecting on the power of language and the role of the early years professional;
- Recognising that language changes over time and that ongoing reflection is required;
- Understanding person-first language;
- Considering the myth of 'normal';
- Examining the role of stigma in labelling;
- Critically engaging with the notion of 'denial'.

KEY TERMS AND CONCEPTS

euphemisms

othering

person-first language

# Introduction

Ainscow (2007, pp.4–5) writes of the harsh reality that:

> It is easy for educational difficulties to be pathologised as difficulties inherent within students. This is true not only of students with disabilities and those defined as 'having special educational needs', but also of those whose socioeconomic status, race, language and gender renders them problematic to particular teachers in particular schools. Consequently, it is necessary to explore ways of developing the capacity of those within schools to reveal and challenge deeply entrenched deficit views of 'difference', which define certain types of students as 'lacking something' (Trent, Artiles & Englert, 1998). This involves being vigilant in scrutinising how deficit assumptions may be influencing perceptions of certain students.

In Chapter 2, the construct of disability and the playing out of stigmatising beliefs through ableism, racism, sexism, genderism, classism, homophobia, transphobia, ageism and discrimination in relation to religious belief/non-belief was explored. These beliefs are expressed through actions at both individual and collective or systemic levels, but also through the words we use. In this chapter language and labelling in relation to 'difference' and 'disability' will be considered.

Language and labelling are areas of frequent confusion and misunderstanding, particularly in relation to the construct of disability. This chapter will de-mystify relevant terminology, while highlighting the contested framing of disability. The importance of recognising ableist (and other stigma-based) assumptions inherent within language use is also considered. Thoughtful consideration and understanding of respectful language use is essential to respectful early years practice. Therefore, acceptable and respectful language use in Australia will be discussed in this chapter, with attention to the relationship between labels, beliefs and practices.

# Respectful language use and 'disability'

Our understandings are strongly reflected in the language we use. As early years professionals, the words we use also influence and impact on the children and families we interact with.

The late novelist Angela Carter (1983, p.77) provides food for thought about language. She says, 'Language is power, life and the instrument of culture, the instrument of domination and liberation'. Early years professionals play powerful roles in the lives of children and families. The language that we use is one aspect of this power and requires careful and ongoing reflection.

Like with our underpinning beliefs and attitudes, we don't often set out with the intention of using disrespectful, dehumanising or derogatory language. In fact, despite the entrenched ableist views and frequent discrimination that still occurs today, many people try hard to use language that is not derogatory, de-valuing or all-encompassing of an individual's identity. Over time, and through critical reflection and much discussion, we now have a greater understanding of the different intentions and meanings read into various different words.

However, language is living and growing and changes with time, and what language is acceptable can also depend on who and where you are. It is therefore critical to think deeply and respectfully about the language we use, the meanings this conveys (and reproduces) and the impact that this has on others with whom we converse or to whom we write. We may not always 'get it right' with the language we use, but if we take seriously the responsibility to examine our language use, we are engaging respectfully and our language is far less likely to have a negative impact on the children, families and colleagues we work with.

Thoughtful consideration of language use often gets a bad rap as 'political correctness' or even 'political correctness gone-too-far'. However, as noted above, the language we use reflects and shapes our understandings and influences those around us. Through language and labelling we stigmatise or include. This is much more than tokenistic 'political correctness', it is about the way we view each other and ourselves. It is about the way that the words we use impact on the self-concept of each other and ourselves and serve to impose

**FIGURE 3.1** ASYLUM SEEKERS, 'BOAT PEOPLE' OR 'ILLEGALS'

*Artwork by Cameron*

or remove barriers to being (see Chapter 2). It is about the way that the language that we use influences our actions.

### *Variations in 'disability' terminology*

You will notice that so far in this book, we have used the term 'children who experience disability'. As noted in Chapter 2, the term 'disabled person' is often used, particularly in UK literature relating to the social model of disability (Shakespeare, 2004). From a social model perspective, the term 'disabled person' identifies the social imposition of disability—thus a person is disabled through society and the environment, rather than disability being a personal characteristic. However, in many contexts, including Australia, use of the term 'disabled person' commonly involves a negation of personhood, or a denial of agency, rather than an acknowledgment of the social construction and imposition of disability:

> A student who was having difficulties in learning becomes a mentally retarded student, a learning disabled student, an emotionally disturbed student. The disability, once a suspected characteristic, then an identified quality, now becomes *the* defining factor of the student. With the label and placement to go with it, disability achieves what sociologists call 'master status.' Those who interact with or observe the labelled person have trouble seeing a person; they see instead a disabled person and all of the stereotypes associated with that status (Biklen, 1989, p.13, emphasis original).

While the term 'mental retardation' is no longer used in Australia (and all forms of this term are considered extremely offensive and derogatory), the process of a person *becoming* the label is just as current today as when Biklen was writing about it in the late 1980s. I hope that in the future there will be widespread recognition of the social construction of disability and significant inroads into combating and disestablishing disablism and ableism. However, presently in Australia the term 'disabled child' usually indicates that its user considers the child to *be* 'disability', rather than indicating that they recognise the social oppression faced by people who experience disability.

In seeking to recognise personhood and agency, while also acknowledging the social construction and lived experience of disability—that people are disabled by society—I use the term 'person who experiences disability'. In doing so, I recognise the person first, and that disability is socially constructed—that it is something that a person experiences, rather than something inside of them.

You will notice some authors in this book use terms such as 'child/person with disability' or 'child/person with disabilities'. These are 'person-first' terms (see below). I also use 'person with', 'or person labelled with' in relation to impairment labels because impairment (while still socially constructed—see Chapter 2) is not the same as disability. For example, I have microtia, which impacts on my hearing and the appearance of one of my ears. So I am a 'person with microtia'. While I always have microtia, I only experience disability if people impose barriers to being or doing (see Chapter 2). Alternatively, I use 'person labelled with autism' (rather than 'person with autism'), for example, as autism is a subjectively applied label that describes a set of human characteristics that can alternatively be viewed as neurodiversity (Broderick & Ne'eman, 2008).

Another variation I would like to mention, before unpacking person-first language, relates to the terminology around being 'd/Deaf'. People who belong to the Deaf community in Australia (or elsewhere) identify as being culturally Deaf just as some people identify as being French, Indian or Irish, for example. Deaf (with a capital D) refers to cultural identity, while deaf (with a small d) is used when talking about hearing/deafness. People who identify as being culturally Deaf do not consider deafness to be an impairment, are proud of Deaf culture and language and usually prefer to be called a 'Deaf person', while people who don't identify as being culturally Deaf generally prefer person-first language such as 'person who is hard of hearing', 'person who is deaf' or 'person with a hearing impairment'. Similarly, although less frequently, some people who are labelled with autism have adopted the term 'autistic person' as a proud identity marker, recognising autism as an aspect of human neurodiversity, rather than as an impairment (Broderick & Ne'eman, 2008). However, autism is more commonly viewed as an impairment and thus it is important not to assume this use of language unless people use it themselves as a chosen identity marker. If you are unsure about which terminology to use, simply ask the person you are talking to what they prefer.

## PERSON-FIRST LANGUAGE

To avoid dehumanising language use, **person-first language** is used throughout this book. Person-first, or people-first, language simply involves placing the person before the label. This is intended to emphasise the whole person, rather than to subsume the person under the label (Baglieri & Shapiro, 2012). Using terms such as 'the disabled' inadvertently summarises people as *being* disability. On the other hand, placing the person first recognises personhood (Baglieri & Shapiro, 2012).

**person-first language:** Naming the person before the use of a label. For example, a person with chronic illness.

Consider the examples of person-first language in Table 3.1. These are examples of language or terminology that is generally accepted in Australia at present. By contrast, using the label before the person—as in *non* person-first language—does not recognise the social construction of 'difference' or 'disability', but rather suggests that the child *is* the label. For example to use the term 'Down syndrome child' or 'Down syndrome' (without child), or 'the autistic' suggests that there is no child, only a diagnostic category. This process dehumanises and does not acknowledge personhood.

**TABLE 3.1** EXAMPLES OF PERSON-FIRST LANGUAGE

| Person-first language | | Disrespectful language |
|---|---|---|
| 'A child with cerebral palsy' | NOT: | 'A cerebral palsy sufferer' |
| 'People living with disability' | NOT: | 'The disabled' |
| 'Children with and without autism' | NOT: | 'Autistic children and normal children' |
| 'A child with Down syndrome' | NOT: | 'A Down's syndrome child' |
| 'A person who has epilepsy' | NOT: | 'An epileptic' |
| 'A child who is identified as gifted' | NOT: | 'A gifted child' |
| 'Children living in foster care' | NOT: | 'Foster child' |

As discussed above, the intention of person-first language is to be respectful and to acknowledge the person first, recognising that the label identifies only one characteristic of the person. In addition to placing the word 'child', 'person' or 'people' before the label (person-first), there are a number of other considerations in the examples in Table 3.1, which we will now explore.

**CRITICAL REFLECTION QUESTIONS**

1. Review the list of disrespectful language examples in Table 3.1. For each example identify why it might be disrespectful.
2. The term 'gifted child' is frequently used and seen as non-problematic. Why might this be the case? What does this tell you about labelling and why is person-first language still important in relation to the label of 'gifted'?

## *Suffering or living?*

Stemming from the ableist views dominant in society, language often incorporates value judgments connected with a medical model, tragedy view of disability. Jamie Burke, a man labelled with autism whom we heard from in Chapter 1, argues that the 'use of the term "suffer" implies that autism is a kind of wound' (Biklen & Burke, 2006, p.167). While many people with labels may suffer when they experience pain or stigma, it is not for someone else to determine whether someone is 'suffering'—and of course most of the time people are *living*, not suffering. Many people labelled with autism do not consider their 'autistic characteristics' to be negative or to be the basis of 'suffering'. Not only in relation to autism but in relation to all labels, it is essential to carefully examine the assumptions inherent in the language we use. Using the word 'suffer' or 'suffering' demonstrates tragedy-based assumptions about that person.

Beliefs about disability are reflected in the choice of language we use. 'A medical model assumes that [a person who experiences disability] is deficient but, it is hoped, alterable; whereas society is fixed, with limited capacity for, or willingness to, change' (Runswick-Cole, 2008, p.176). Viewing a person from a medical model considers disability to be a 'personal tragedy'. Language such as 'poor things' or people 'suffering from' and the like, comes from a medical model (tragedy) view.

The language we use impacts on society and specifically on the lived experiences of the children and families we work with. In research with children who experience disability (see Chapter 2), Connors and Stalker (2007, p.27) explored children's views on language use. In a 'special' school where some of the participants attended, the teachers 'referred to pupils as "wheelchairs" and "walkers"'. One of the child participants, who uses a wheelchair, noted, 'It's sad because we're just the same. We just can't walk, that's all the difference.' Another participant attending the same school said, 'I'm happy being a cerebral palsy.' The first child resisted being defined as his wheelchair. The second child internalised the dehumanising language use. In both cases, the language used sends the message to the children that they are viewed as, or have *become* their label.

**FIGURE 3.2** PLAYING

*Artwork by Emma*

A fundamental consideration here is the way in which the language we use—as early years professionals and as citizens—influences the language children use and, importantly, their developing understanding of the world and those within it. As Beckett (2009, p.320) states, children 'internalise the attitudes that they encounter within the disabling society, through the process of socialisation.' This underlines the importance of each of us considering very carefully the language that we use and making sure that we work hard to always use respectful language that acknowledges the full personhood of every human being.

**FIGURE 3.3** A PERSON, NOT A WHEELCHAIR

*(From 'One of the Kids', published by the Disability Council of NSW, written by Wendy Stroeve and illustrated by Kerry Millard, reproduced with permission.)*

## *The myth of 'normal'*

Another issue flagged in Table 3.1 is the use of the term 'normal'. There is a common tendency to refer to people from the dominant group (for example, people who do not experience disability) as 'normal' people and, in doing so, directly stating or indirectly implying that a person who has an impairment and/or experiences difference or disability is *not* normal.

As discussed in Chapter 2, ableism, and other forms of stigma, are expressed not only through actions, but also through language. Key to the production of ableism is the idea of a 'normal person', which then creates a 'subnormal' or 'abnormal' person (Campbell, 2012).

The notion of a 'normal child' is at the core of exclusionary approaches to education. When children are compared to the mythical 'normal child', they are frequently deemed lacking (Baglieri, Bejoian, Broderick, Connor & Valle, 2011). Consequently, the focus becomes 'fixing' or 'curing' the child, rather than embracing impairment simply as one element of human diversity (Cologon, 2013a, 2013b). Connor and Goldmansour argue that:

> [S]tudents should learn with, and from, each other—coming to know true diversity in terms of physical, cognitive, sensory, and emotional differences. In this way, artificial notions of 'normalcy' that have served to diminish and devalue children [who experience disability] for so long can begin to change. As microcosms of society, classrooms must come to reflect, exemplify, and engage with actual diversity (2012, p.31).

The idea of 'normal' is a social construction. Think for a moment about what would be a 'normal day', a 'normal week', a 'normal evening', or a 'normal dinner' for you. What is 'normal' to you is likely to be different to what is 'normal' to anyone else reading this chapter. No matter how many labels you might have, the common everyday experiences of life will be 'normal' to you—and different to everyone else. For a person with cerebral palsy, for example, having cerebral palsy would be part of what is 'normal' to that person. Having microtia is 'normal' to me.

**CASE STUDY 3.1**

## Be my (normal) Valentine

In research with Baglieri (2008), a pre-service teacher recollected an activity from a guided experience placement. In this activity, the class made Valentine's Day cards for each other. The pre-service teacher observed that

> Gina's card was very sweet and referred to Emily as one of her best friends in the class. However, it also said 'Even though you are in a wheelchair you are like a normal person'. I knew that Gina had meant no offense by this comment for the two were close friends. However, I wasn't sure how to approach this issue with Gina (p.595).

**CRITICAL REFLECTION QUESTIONS**

1. What does Gina mean by the word 'normal' in her card? Why is this problematic?
2. What might be shaping Gina's views?
3. If you were Gina's teacher, how would you respond in this situation?

### *Is the label even necessary?*

Having examined examples of person-first language, I would like to point out the importance of considering whether it is necessary to use a label at all.

Clearly there are times when this information may be important. However, if I was to tell you that I am going out to dinner on the weekend with a friend, and this friend happens to be someone who has Down syndrome, I would not say 'I am going out for dinner with my friend who has Down syndrome', much in the same way that I would not say, 'I am going out for dinner with my friend who has brown hair'. In both cases this *would* be person-first language, but why would it be relevant to mention that my friend does or does not experience disability, or to mention my friend's hair colour? I would simply say 'I am going out for dinner with my friend'.

However, if a label was an important piece of information to provide for a particular reason, then I would use person-first language. For example, if I were taking a child to hospital because they were having a seizure, I would mention that 'this is Henry and he has epilepsy' as this would be relevant information for the hospital staff. Reflecting on the relevance of the information we seek or share is an important responsibility of early years professionals.

### *Irregular settings*

The language we use also extends to labels for settings. Ableist views play out in practices of segregation and labelling, wherein

> The term, *the regular school*, is frequently offered as the counterpoint to the term: *special school*. It is also code for the implied *normal school*. It follows that there must be *normal or regular students* for whom these schools exist. And, as the logic proceeds, there are *other* children who are not normal, regular or valid—they are our in-valid population (Slee, 2011, p.12, emphasis original).

Slee (2011) makes the tongue-in-cheek suggestion that we therefore should create 'irregular schools'. The same issues are relevant to early years settings. We need to be thoughtful in the language we use, not only when referring to people directly, but also indirectly through the labels that we give to education settings and programs—and *to whom we consider belongs in which settings*. Of course if we eliminated segregation then this issue would be resolved and perhaps then we would only have 'schools' or 'centres' without the need for demarcation by population.

## Euphemisms

When trying to move beyond negative language use related to disability, people often enthusiastically embrace a range of alternative terms that, at first glance, appear more positive. For example:

- Exceptional children;
- Special children;

- Children with special needs;
- Children with additional needs;
- Children with special rights;
- Handi-capable;
- Differently abled;
- Physically challenged;
- Mentally different;
- Able-disabled.

The terms 'exceptional children' and 'special children' are *non*-person-first. Additionally, as Smart explains:

> '[S]pecial' and 'exceptional' are words that many people with disabilities dislike because these words invoke a history of segregation. There are many stories of parents being told that their child was going to be placed in a 'special' classroom or a 'special program.' The words 'special' and 'exceptional' also have a euphemistic quality. 'Special' and 'exceptional' are labels that people with disabilities instantly recognize as meaning segregated and inferior (2001, p.59).

In addition to the socio-historical connotations of 'exceptional' and 'special', terms like 'children with special rights' and 'children with additional needs' imply that some children want more than their basic needs and rights. Of course in reality, people who experience disability are fighting for their basic human rights and needs to be met—not for anything extra. Booth and Ainscow argue that

> Labelling children as 'having special educational needs' can lead to lowered expectations. When linked with the categorisation of children as 'gifted and talented', it can be part of the creation of a hierarchy of value of children seen as 'less than normal', 'normal' and 'supernormal' learners. In practice some children are categorised both as 'having special educational needs' and as 'being gifted and talented'. Many schools work hard to value all children equally despite labels, but they are working against wider perceptions that their categorisation also helps to foster. We should reflect carefully, therefore, before we label someone as 'having special educational needs' (2011, p.41).

Terms like 'differently abled', 'physically challenged', 'mentally different', 'handi-capable' and 'able-disabled', while intended to refute common stereotypes, may actually reinforce stereotypes as they are patronising and imply that impairment is too tragic and negative to be discussed openly (Linton, 1998; Smart, 2001). Simultaneously, these terms make light of the genuine barriers faced by people who experience disability (Linton, 1998; Smart, 2001). Importantly, these **euphemisms** maintain a medical model focus on a 'problem' within a person, rather than focusing on the barriers within society and the

**euphemisms:** Words that are used with the intention of being less blunt or direct when a topic or term is considered embarrassing, rude or unpleasant.

environment that produce disability (Linton, 1998). These terms also maintain a 'them' and 'us', thus perpetuating a process of othering. For example, consider terms such as 'differently coloured' or 'gender challenged'.

Consequently, euphemisms are generally considered to be insulting, condescending and patronising (Linton, 1998; Smart, 2001), although for some they provide an alternative to the negative connotations of 'disabled' (Stone, 2013). For example, if the term 'differently abled' was used to apply to everyone—as in, we are *all* differently abled (thus there is no group of people termed 'differently abled') this could avoid **othering** and stigmatisation. However, as these terms are overwhelmingly used to label one group as compared to another, they remain problematic.

**othering:** The process of creating a 'them' and 'us' so that a person, or group of people, are made 'other' to 'ourselves'—not 'one of us'.

## Recognising 'difference' or stigmatising?

The process of stigmatisation associated with labelling is dangerous and highly problematic. Ho (2004, p.90) argues that '[t]he problem with our educational and social systems is not that we recognize differences. Rather, the problem is that we often make *erroneous* assumptions about the *causes* of differences and difficulties, and we either *ignore* differences or *stigmatize* those who are considered different' (emphasis original). If we are to embrace our shared humanity in all our diversity, as is essential to inclusive practice, then recognising (rather than ignoring) difference is important. However, this needs to occur without deeming difference to be inherently negative.

Recall from Chapter 1 that stigmatising is a process whereby people label human differences, link labelled persons to negative stereotypes and place people into label-based categories in order to separate 'us' from the (now less desirable) 'them' (Link & Phelan, 2001). People who are labelled then experience status loss and discrimination leading to unequal outcomes and, finally, stigmatisation allows the full execution of disapproval, rejection, discrimination and exclusion of people who are labelled (Link & Phelan, 2001).

Labelling, and the associated stigmatisation, is particularly problematic in relation to people who experience disability. As Baglieri and Shapiro (2012, p.42) discuss,

> Labels are often derived from what seem to be neutral descriptions of impairment. However, they frequently work against children and adults with disabilities. They may conjure distorted or diminished expectations and stereotyped images of what particular individuals are like. Labels can take on an encompassing quality...The label takes the place of the person's individuality, and invites others to define the essence of the person with the disability (2012, p.42).

**CASE STUDY 3.2**

## Labels or a person?

This child has hydrocephalus. Hydrocephalus means that a person has an excess of cerebral spinal fluid collecting in the head that—for a range of reasons, depending on the type of hydrocephalus—cannot drain. Consequently the brain is compressed and, if left untreated, hydrocephalus can be life threatening. Hydrocephalus is treated by inserting a shunt into the head to enable the cerebral spinal fluid to drain, thus the person doesn't die and the head does not continue to expand.

When this child was born the doctor reported that he saw very little evidence of brain tissue, as the child's brain was so severely compressed that brain tissue was hard to detect. Doctors concluded that if he survived he would have severe intellectual and physical impairments and would never develop beyond the level of a nine-month-old baby.

When he was born a shunt was inserted into the back of his head. He will always have a shunt to allow the cerebral spinal fluid to drain from his head at regular intervals.

After the shunt was inserted he contracted meningitis and was dangerously ill as a result. He survived, but as a consequence of the meningitis he developed ongoing epilepsy and has regular uncontrollable seizures. These seizures often last for considerable periods of time and it is thought that they may continue to cause brain damage.

As a further result of the meningitis and his hydrocephalus, he developed a cerebral palsy-like syndrome that impacts on his physical development. Learning to walk has been an ongoing struggle. He falls often and always walks with an uneven gait. He has only limited control of his hands. When he was younger he was unable to isolate one arm from the other, so all movements with one would simultaneously occur with the other. His physical movements are clumsy and atypical and this impacts on all physical activities.

He also has a rare chromosomal disorder involving the deletion of part of one of his chromosomes. This is associated with intellectual impairment and a range of developmental delays or difficulties.

He is frequently labelled with autism due to the many differences in his social and language development and behaviour, including the fact that he hits himself in the head—often very hard—both when he is excited and happy and when he is frustrated, sad or angry. He is viewed as having social, behavioural, language, cognitive and physical impairments.

**CRITICAL REFLECTION QUESTIONS**

1. What does this tell you about this child?
2. What image do you have of this child after reading this description?
3. As an early years professional, how would this information inform planning and support for this child in his education?
4. Can you identify this child's strengths and learning styles from this description?
5. What *doesn't* this information tell you about this child?

*Kathy Cologon*

To illustrate, let me tell you about a 12-year-old boy who has many diagnostic labels. Let me start by telling you his labels and what these mean from a medico-diagnostic perspective.

If we stop and think about it, each of us has labels—it might be sister, brother, daughter, son, friend, early years professional, researcher, teacher, colleague, writer, partner, parent, and so on. However, none of these labels encompasses our whole being—they each describe only one aspect of who we are or the roles we play. We all have multiple identities and our entire being cannot be captured or defined in a label—and nor would we wish it to be (Smart, 2001). This is no different for this child; so now let me tell you about him from the perspective of lived experience, rather than from a medical model perspective. Firstly let me give him a name. I am going to call him Anthony (a pseudonym).

## CASE STUDY 3.3

### Meet Anthony

Anthony loves music, painting, running, books, swimming, horse riding, flowers, leaves and in fact all plants. He enjoys engaging with people and is affectionate to those around him, but this cannot be taken for granted. He is affectionate as and when he chooses to be. He frequently hugs his family members and tells them that he loves them. On the other hand he gets cranky with his siblings and his nephews and tells them off or gets grouchy sometimes when he doesn't want to do something he is told to do.

Sometimes Anthony can be affectionate to a stranger. For example, on meeting a person who was homeless and begging on the street (who seemed unhappy), Anthony sat down next to him and put his arm around him to comfort him. On the other hand, Anthony might meet another stranger or even a family friend and be very wary and not wish to be touched by them or to touch them, sometimes getting upset at uninvited touch or voicing his fears and reassuring himself—'She won't hurt me, will she?'

Anthony's favourite activity at the moment is painting. He will paint for hours, talking all the time about the colours and showing the paintings to those around him with great pride: 'Look at my painting, do you like my painting, it is so beautiful.' He will also compliment those around him on their paintings: 'I like your painting! Your painting is so beautiful.'

Anthony has a remarkable memory. He remembers things from long ago and also has a great memory for words and tunes of songs and for stories. If he hears a story or song a couple of times then he will remember it entirely.

Anthony learns language through frequent repetition and through making patterns of language and social processes. As he learns a new pattern he wants those around him to follow the pattern correctly. He will help them to do so, prompting them for the correct response when needed. For example, when he was first figuring out social greetings he identified the pattern: you ask someone how they are; they say they are good and ask you how you are; then you respond that you are good too. While Anthony was figuring this out, if he asked 'How are you?' and you didn't respond with something to the effect of 'Good thanks, how are you?', he would prompt you so that you would: 'Are you good? You are good aren't you?' As Anthony becomes comfortable with each pattern of language he becomes more flexible with it and even enjoys disrupting it or mucking around with nonsensical responses.

Anthony feels things deeply and is developing ways of expressing his thoughts and emotions so that those around him can understand and respond. Anthony has hypersensitivity to sensory input and has worked hard at being able to talk about what he is feeling. For example on hearing a loud noise he will now say 'That was loud' and often identify or ask what it was, whereas he used to be frightened and respond by hurting himself.

Anthony has developed awareness of the signs that his body is entering a seizure and will call out for help if he knows this is happening. He will try to get himself into recovery position if he has control of his body for long enough to do so. Anthony often stays conscious during a seizure and will talk for as long as he has the control to do so. He sometimes expresses being annoyed about the seizure, but also appears to recognise the fear of others and is very loving to those around him when this is happening.

Anthony often shares that when he grows up he wants to be a rock star, but sometimes he says that he just wants to grow up to be a man.

Anthony has been learning to read and write for a long time. He has superb phonological awareness and can make a word out of any combination of sounds (phonemes). He enjoys playing with the sounds of language. He recognises many words and is learning to put these together to read passages. Writing is difficult for Anthony, but the more he works towards drawing and writing the better his hand control is getting. Through engaging in many experiences using his hands, Anthony is now able to use his hands independently of each other.

Drawing and painting, as well as playing on the piano, are important processes for supporting Anthony in developing his capacity to write. So is storytelling, and Anthony loves to tell stories and put on shows for those around him. His storytelling is growing more sophisticated with time and he has developed a clear understanding of the components of a story; he enjoys adding absurd elements to make his stories funny.

Anthony gets frustrated at things he can't do and is hurt when others assume he can't do things. He is also very proud of the things that he can do and loves to share these with those around him. Sometimes these are different to the triumphs of his family and friends—it is a victory for Anthony to dress himself and he will share with great pride if he managed to get his clothes on himself. Likewise he will share when he successfully hits the cricket ball when playing with his Dad and big brother.

Anthony is determined and self-motivated. If he sees the value of something then just about nothing will stop him. When he was first learning to walk, one of the most difficult things for him to do was climb stairs, but he wanted to climb stairs so he would climb every set of stairs he could find—anywhere, anytime. He wanted to learn to run and no number of falls was going to stop him. The opportunity to do these things is critical for Anthony.

Anthony has a great sense of humour. He loves to laugh and make others laugh. He sees the funny side of so many things and often uses humour to conquer his fears.

Anthony needs lots of support in many different ways and this support needs to be provided to him as part of living his life. Anthony has learnt to, often, ask for help when he needs it, rather than getting frustrated or stuck. He also offers support to those around him in many different ways.

In all this, Anthony still has his long list of diagnostic labels. Acknowledging these labels and the ways in which Anthony engages with the world is not necessarily a problem and some of his medical information is important to know. Those around him need to be prepared if he has a seizure and know that someone needs to check his shunt if he falls and hurts his head. However, Anthony's *labels* don't provide any insight into *who he is* as a person. The picture you might have had in your head after I listed his labels is probably very different to the picture you have now.

Anthony is not his labels. He is a vibrant and spirited individual living his life. It isn't necessary to know about hydrocephalus, cerebral palsy, epilepsy, chromosomal deletions or even autism (which is a label Anthony and his family do not use) to get to know Anthony. What is necessary is to take the time to recognise and get to know the person that he is. Labels don't identify Anthony's strengths and the ways in which he can engage in learning and developing. However, getting to know Anthony and building a relationship with him does.

**CRITICAL REFLECTION QUESTIONS**

1. What have you learnt about Anthony? Write a list of Anthony's strengths. How would this inform your planning as an early years professional?
2. Reflecting on the two stories of Anthony, can you identify some of the potential dangers of an emphasis on labels? What might be useful to know about Anthony's labels? How could focusing on his labels be detrimental to his education? Aside from diagnostic/medical labels, what other labels does Anthony have? What labels do you and Anthony share?
3. Why is getting to know an individual child, regardless of labels—and *presuming competence*, as discussed in Chapter 1—important for effective education planning?

### *In denial?*

'[L]abelled people are not passive recipients of oppression. They are active and resilient social members' (Goodley, 2000, p.72). Research in Canada and the UK with adults labelled with multiple sclerosis, physical impairments or intellectual impairments has found that many people do not choose to identify as 'disabled' and reject their labels on account of the stigma attached to being labelled (Finlay & Lyons, 2005; Goodley, 2000; Stone, 2013). Reflecting on the processes of stigma, the dominance of the medical, tragedy model perspective and widespread ableist attitudes, it is unsurprising that many people do not claim or share their labels. When parents do not wish to have their child labelled, when they do not wish to use or share the label, or when they do not view their child as needing to be fixed, those around them often assume the parents are unable to accept their child and are grieving or 'in denial'; in short, they make assumptions regarding the person and their psychological processing or status. These assumptions are common in the early years and require critical examination.

An important point is that denying or rejecting a label is different to denying support needs (Finlay & Lyons, 2005). 'Many studies have shown that even when people deny or do not claim the label, they are quite willing to talk about specific difficulties and needs they have as well as the oppressive situations they find themselves in' (Finlay & Lyons, 2005, p.121). Additionally, adjusting to impairment for the individual and the family is not the same as adjusting to the attitudes of others towards impairment and disability (Finlay & Lyons, 2005; Goodley, 2000).

Finlay and Lyons (2005) explore the notion of 'denial' in relation to labelling and present three different concepts of denial:

- *Denial as repression*—the person is aware of the label and the impairment effects, but they suppress this to some extent from themselves and others. This is generally based on a medical model understanding of disability as personal tragedy and undesirable;
- *Denial as passing*—the person accepts the label and is aware of any associated challenges, but will try to conceal this from others to 'pass as normal' in order to avoid stigma (perpetuated through ableism);
- *Denial as the rejection of the usefulness of the concept or the rejection of others' definitions*—the person is aware that other people label them (and is aware of their own support needs, strengths and limitations), but they do not find the label useful and may find that it does not fit well with their experiences. The person rejects the social assumptions that come with the label and therefore prefers not to be labelled.

It is important to recognise here that labels are social constructs. 'The label or category does not represent a natural or biological distinction but is, rather, an administrative category' (Finlay & Lyons, 2005, p.123). Labels do not represent a 'truth' or 'reality' about someone, but rather labelling is process of grouping and categorising people on the basis of 'difference' (Goodley, 2000). These categories are often poorly understood and negatively associated (Finlay & Lyons, 2005; Goodley, 2000). However, people who experience disability and their families may choose to use labels *when they consider them to be useful* (for example in order to obtain a 'disability parking permit' where needed, or for funding to access required support), but *not to adopt the label as their identity,* thus being cast as 'in denial' by some (Craig, Craig, Withers, Hatton & Limb, 2002; Finlay & Lyons, 2005; Stone, 2013). Unless a label serves a useful purpose, free of stigma, then it is easy to understand why many people reject labels.

**CRITICAL REFLECTION QUESTIONS**

Imagine you have just commenced work in an early years setting. You are focused on getting to know the children and families and building relationships in order to enable you to effectively fulfil your role. One of your colleagues (who is not qualified to make a diagnosis) is very concerned that a family in the setting are 'in denial' about their child. The child does not have a label (although the family do see a paediatrician), but your colleague is sure the child 'has autism'. The family are very supportive of the child and keen to assist in any way possible to ensure their child's genuine inclusion, but are not interested in labelling their child.

1. Consider the notion of 'denial' presented by your colleague. What does your colleague mean by 'in denial'?
2. Compare this with the notions of denial outlined by Finlay and Lyons. Why might the family not wish to have their child labelled?
3. Where does the difficulty lie in this situation? What are the issues with your colleague deciding to label the child?
4. How would you approach the situation going forward? Specifically:
   a. What information would you seek from your colleague and the family?
   b. How would you ensure that you do not pass judgments on the family, but that you do provide appropriate support for the child in the setting?

# Conclusion

'In education, the medical model positions students labelled with disabilities as abnormal, unfortunate patients in need of expert remediation. If we perceive students labelled with disabilities as qualitatively not like other students, even the most frequently recommended education supports—adaptations or modifications—take on an exclusionary tone' (Baglieri, 2008, p.587). Research investigating the impact of teachers' attitudes on children's engagement in their learning, child and teacher interactions, and child self-concept finds that teachers who take on a medical model view of children who experience disability do so to the detriment of their students (Jordan & Stanovich, 2001; Jordan, Schwartz & McGhie-Richmond, 2009). The language that we use reflects, shapes and reproduces our understandings and beliefs about difference and disability. It also influences the beliefs and attitudes of those around us—including the children, families and colleagues with whom we work.

An early years professional has power and influence, and there are many different and important aspects to this. One of these is language use, which informs and is informed by beliefs and attitudes. This is significant, because language use, beliefs and attitudes work together to direct our choices and actions. In considering language and labelling, the idea is not to be alarmed but to reflect and think deeply. To you, is a child who experiences difference or disability 'whole', or 'broken'? Is difference and diversity an everyday part of humanity, or 'a problem'? The language you use will reflect your conscious or subconscious answer to these questions.

## FOR FURTHER REFLECTION

1. View the following five-minute talk by Stephen Fry on the power of language: www.upworthy.com/stephen-fry-somehow-makes-sense-of-racism.
2. Drawing on this talk (and the discussion of dehumanisation in Chapter 1), reflect on the process of dehumanisation and consider the role of language in this process. Think about Fry's comments regarding using 'special language' for 'special people'. Fry explores these issues as they relate to racism. Consider the implications also in regards to ableism and other forms of discrimination.
3. Reflect on the language used to label children in the early years. What might be the implications of early years language use?
4. What about insults/derogatory language?
    a. Consider the words that you use to express negative sentiments—write down a list and reflect on the origin and meaning of these words. Is racism, ableism or other forms of stigmatisation evident in any of these words?
    b. What steps do you need to take to examine your own language use?

## REFERENCES

Ainscow, M. (2007). Taking an inclusive turn. *Journal of Research in Special Educational Needs, 7*(1), 3–7. doi:10.1111/j.1471-3802.2007.00075.x

Baglieri, S. (2008). 'I connected': Reflection and biography in teacher learning toward inclusion. *International Journal of Inclusive Education, 12*(5), 585–604. doi:10.1080/13603110802377631

Baglieri, S., Bejoian, L.M., Broderick, A.A., Connor, D.J. & Valle, J. (2011). [Re]claiming inclusive education toward cohesion in educational reform: Disability studies unravels the myth of the normal child. *Teachers College Record, 113*(10), 2122–2154. Retrieved from www.tcrecord.org

Baglieri, S. & Shapiro, A. (2012). *Disability studies and the inclusive classroom: Critical practices for creating least restrictive attitudes.* New York: Routledge.

Beckett, A.E. (2009). 'Challenging disabling attitudes, building an inclusive society': Considering the role of education in encouraging non-disabled children to develop positive attitudes towards disabled people. *British Journal of Sociology of Education, 30*(3), 317–329. doi:10.1080/01425690902812596

Biklen, D. (1989). Redefining schools. In D. Biklen, D. Ferguson & A. Ford (Eds). *Schooling and disability* (pp. 1–24). Chicago, IL: National Society for the Study of Education.

Biklen, D. & Burke, J. (2006). Presuming competence. *Equity & Excellence in Education, 39*(2), 166–175. doi: 10.1080/10665680500540376

Booth, T. & Ainscow, M. (2011). *Index for inclusion.* Bristol, UK: Centre for Studies on Inclusive Education.

Broderick, A.A. & Ne'eman, A. (2008). Autism as metaphor: Narrative and counter-narrative. *International Journal of Inclusive Education, 12*(5), 459–476. doi:10.1080/13603110812377490

Carter, A. (1983). Notes from the front line. In M. Wandor (Ed.), *On gender and writing* (pp. 69–77). London: Pandora Press.

Campbell, F.K. (2012). Stalking ableism: Using disability to expose 'abled' narcissism. In D. Goodley, B. Hughes & L. Davis (Eds), *Disability and social theory. New developments and directions* (pp. 212–230). Basingstoke: Palgrave Macmillan.

Cologon, K. (2013a). Recognising our shared humanity: Human rights and inclusive education in Italy and Australia. *Italian Journal of Disability Studies, 1*(1). 151–169. Retrieved from www.edizionianicia.it/docs/Rivista_Vol1_N1.pdf#page=151.

Cologon, K. (2013b). Growing up with 'difference': Inclusive education and the portrayal of characters who experience disability in children's literature. *Write4Children: The International Journal for the Practice and Theories of Writing for Children and Children's Literature, 4*(2), 100–120. Retrieved from www.winchester.ac.uk/academicdepartments/EnglishCreativeWritingandAmericanStudies/Documents/w4cJune2013Diversity.pdf

Connor, D. & Goldmansour, K. (2012). Doing the civil right thing: Supporting children with disabilities in inclusive classes. *Bankstreet Occasional Papers, 28.* Retrieved from www.bankstreet.edu/occasional-papers/occasional-papers-28/doing-the-civil-right-thing

Connors, C. & Stalker, K. (2007). Children's experiences of disability: Pointers to a social model of childhood disability. *Disability & Society, 22*(1), 19–33. doi:10.1080/09687590601056162

Craig, J., Craig, F., Withers, P., Hatton, C. & Limb, K. (2002). Identity conflict in people with intellectual disabilities: What role do service-providers play in mediating stigma? *Journal of Applied Research in Intellectual Disabilities, 15*(1), 61–72. doi:10.1046/j.1360-2322.2002.00101.x

Finlay, W.M.L. & Lyons, E. (2005). Rejecting the label: A social constructionist analysis. *Mental Retardation, 43*(2), 120–134. doi:10.1352/0047-6765(2005)43<120:RTLASC>2.0.CO;2

Goodley, D. (2000). *Self-advocacy in the lives of people with learning difficulties*. Buckingham: Open University Press.

Ho, A. (2004). To be labelled, or not to be labelled: That is the question. *British Journal of Learning Disabilities, 32*(2), 86–92. doi:10.1111/j.1468-3156.2004.00284.x

Jordan, A. & Stanovich, P. (2001). Patterns of teacher-student interaction in inclusive elementary classrooms and correlates with student self-concept. *International Journal of Disability, Development and Education, 48*(1), 33–52. doi:10.1080/10349120120036297

Jordan, A., Schwartz, E. & McGhie-Richmond, D. (2009). Preparing teachers for inclusive classrooms. *Teaching and Teacher Education, 25*(4), 535–542. doi:10.1016/j.tate.2009.02.101

Link, B.G. & Phelan, J.C. (2001). Conceptualizing stigma. *Annual Review of Sociology, 27*, 363–385. doi:0360-0572/01/0811-0363

Linton, S. (1998). *Claiming disability: knowledge and identity.* New York: New York University Press.

Runswick-Cole, K. (2008). Between a rock and a hard place: Parents' attitudes to the inclusion of children with special educational needs in mainstream and special schools. *British Journal of Special Education, 35*(3), 173–180. Retrieved from http://onlinelibrary.wiley.com/journal/10.1111/(ISSN)1467-8578

Shakespeare, T. (2004). Social models of disability and other life strategies. *Scandinavian Journal of Disability Research, 6*(1), 8–21. doi:10.1080/15017410409512636

Slee, R. (2011). *The irregular school: Exclusion, schooling and inclusive education*. Abingdon, Oxon: Routledge.

Smart, J. (2001). *Disability, society, and the individual.* Austin, TX: ProEd.

Stone, S.D. (2013). The situated nature of disability. In M.P. Cutchin & V.A. Dickie (Eds), *Transactional perspectives on occupation* (pp. 95–106). New York and London: Springer.

Stroeve, W. (1998). *One of the kids*. Sydney: Disability Council of NSW.

# 4 Legislation and Policy in Early Years Inclusion

*Anne Petriwskyj*

CHAPTER OVERVIEW

This chapter will focus on national and state legislation and policy in Australia related to inclusion in the early years.

Learning goals for this chapter include:

- Understanding contemporary perspectives on diversity and inclusion represented in early years policy settings;
- Identifying legislation and policy relevant to specific early years settings, jurisdictions and diversity categories;
- Linking current legislation and education policy to expectations of inclusive practice in ECEC services and the early years of school;
- Recognising the implications of national curriculum frameworks for inclusive early years practice.

KEY TERMS AND CONCEPTS

intercultural education

international convention

reasonable adjustment

shadow assistant

unreasonable or unjustifiable hardship

# Introduction

Inclusion in early years programs takes into account equitable provision for diversity across both early childhood education and care (ECEC) and the early school years. Adherence to relevant legislative and policy settings is crucial for early years professionals, yet it demands an understanding of the specific provisions that apply in each situation. Some legislative and policy provisions cater broadly for diversity and support inclusion in education services (e.g. national anti-discrimination legislation). Other legislation and policy settings in Australia may be state-based rather than national (e.g. Queensland anti-discrimination legislation), may focus on a specific sub-group of diversity (e.g. disability), or may be intended only for ECEC or for school education. Australia is also a signatory to international conventions on human rights and disability and is guided by United Nations international position statements on inclusion. Therefore, discussion of these legislative and policy frameworks in this chapter is organised in broad groupings of international conventions, national overarching or universal documents, target category documents and state documents. This chapter will identify some implications for practice and indicates where further practical implications are addressed within other chapters of this book.

### Note: Staying up to date with changes

It is important to note that regular changes occur in legislation, policy, sources of information and the naming of programs or support organisations. These changes occur in response to shifts in education expectations, international trends and changes of government. Regular changes in links to web-based resources and other policy publications also occur in response to changes in education structures and support organisations or shifts in policy positioning or legislation. It is, therefore, vital for educators to remain aware of changes through ongoing professional learning in order to ensure they are adhering to current legislative and policy provisions at all times.

## CONTEMPORARY PERSPECTIVES ON INCLUSION

As discussed in Chapters 1 and 2, inclusion moves away from a deficit or medical model perspective within which differences were seen as an individual problem requiring remediation, to a social model that recognises that differences are socially constructed through disabling or discriminatory practices. Contemporary inclusive approaches attend to a wide range of variations among children and focus positively on the ways provision is made possible for all children.

**FIGURE 4.1** DIVERSITY

*Artwork by Emma*

The current definition of inclusion in *Belonging, Being and Becoming: The Early Years Learning Framework for Australia*, which applies in ECEC services prior-to-school entry, incorporates both an indication of diversity (who) and a statement of the intent of inclusion (what).

> Inclusion involves taking into account all children's social, cultural and linguistic diversity (including learning styles, abilities, disabilities, gender, family circumstances and geographic location) in curriculum decision-making processes. The intent is to ensure that all children's experiences are recognised and valued … all children have equitable access to resources and participation, and opportunities to demonstrate their learning and to value difference (Department of Education, Employment and Workplace Relations [DEEWR], 2009a, p.24).

Thus diversity is defined broadly as variations in children's:

- Characteristics (e.g. gender, learning style);
- Abilities (e.g. giftedness, impairment, learning difficulty);
- Background (socio-economic and other family circumstances, cultural and linguistic experience, geographic location).

The term *diverse learners* may be used in schools, although it is not person-first language (see Chapter 3 for discussion of person-first language).

The *Framework for School Age Care* presents a similar national position on inclusion in outside-school-hours care to that in ECEC. In school education, definitions indicate generally consistent perspectives yet vary by state jurisdiction and school auspice (e.g. church, community group, state government). For example: 'Inclusion means that all students, regardless of their differences, are part of the school community and can feel that they belong. The mandate to ensure access, participation and achievement for every student is taken as a given' (Department of Education Tasmania, 2006, p.3).

The *Australian Curriculum* for schools (Australian Curriculum, Assessment and Reporting Authority [ACARA], n.d.) contains statements on principles of equity and personalised learning. Universal Design for Learning and curriculum differentiation is important for enacting these principles in practice Universal Design for Learning caters pro-actively for diversity through:

- Multiple types of learning opportunities or tasks;
- Multiple teaching strategies for supporting learning;
- Multiple means of assessment for and of learning (Van Kraayenoord, 2007).

Further differentiation in school education takes into account the individual learning pattern, ability and style of each child. In addition, support services (e.g. advisory teachers for vision impairment, learning support teachers, English as a second language teachers, cultural assistant teachers) may assist students and teachers in ensuring children participate in learning and the life of the school.

Legislation, policy and funding regimes in contemporary Australia indicate not only the diversity groups whose concerns are currently foregrounded, but also the specific perspectives on inclusion that are privileged. While these positions are framed by changing national and regional priorities and pressures, they are also influenced by international policy developments.

## INTERNATIONAL POSITION STATEMENTS AND CONVENTIONS

Australia's response to diversity is broadly framed by its being a signatory to **international conventions** such as the *United Nations Convention on the Rights of the Child 1989*, the *Salamanca Declaration 1994* and the *United Nations Convention on the Rights of Persons with Disabilities 2006*. National policy development is further informed by international position statements on education such as the United Nations *Guidelines on Intercultural Education 2006*.

**international convention:** An international human rights document which, unlike a declaration, is legally binding. Conventions are supported by protocols to facilitate their implementation by signatory countries.

The principles of the United Nations *Convention on the Rights of the Child* include the rights of children to education, and advocacy for their development, including

- The best interests of the child being the primary consideration in all actions concerning children;

- Protection of children from all forms of discrimination;
- The right of all children to education;
- Education that develops each child's personality and talents to the full.

The United Nations Educational Scientific and Cultural Organization (UNESCO) *Guidelines on Intercultural Education* indicate the value of

**intercultural education** goes beyond education *about* cultural and linguistic diversity to engage educators and children in challenging stereotypes and racism in order to develop more culturally inclusive attitudes and behaviours.

- Respect for the cultural identity of children through the provision of culturally appropriate and responsive quality education for all;
- Provision for every child of cultural knowledge, attitudes and skills necessary to achieve active and full participation in society;
- Enabling children to contribute to respect, understanding and solidarity among individuals, ethnic, social, cultural and religious groups;
- Provision for the heterogeneity of learners and for learning in children's home languages.

The *United Nations Convention on the Rights of Persons with Disabilities* (UNCRPD) (2006) includes recognition that

- Disability arises from an interaction between impairments and the attitudinal and environmental barriers that impede equal participation in society;
- Discrimination 'on the basis of disability is a violation of the inherent dignity ... of the human person' (n.p).

The rights-based approach embedded in these documents has established a frame for the development of complementary legislation and policy in Australia.

# National universal legislation and policy

This section considers overarching national documents. Initially, these national documents attended to prevention of discrimination, particularly that related to race or disability. Recent legislation and policy takes a broader view of diversity, and focuses on the quality of teachers and of education provision.

**unreasonable or unjustifiable hardship:** Demonstrated when catering for a child's needs would require extraordinary and unmanageable changes to facilities, staffing or education services that are beyond reasonable service resources or available funding sources.

## DISCRIMINATION LEGISLATION AND NATIONAL STANDARDS

Anti-discrimination legislation such as the *Australian Disability Discrimination Act 1992* and the *Racial Discrimination Act 1975* protect the rights of all children to participate in education, regardless of their race, ability, sexuality or gender. However, a clause in the disability discrimination legislation permits rare cases of exclusion on the grounds of **unreasonable or unjustifiable hardship**.

Demonstration of unreasonable hardship should take into account Australia's ratification of the UNCRPD and should be understood as a serious legal discrimination matter. Legal decisions based on this clause are dependent on interpretation of legal precedent as contained in case law, and an application by the education service justifying their decisions to exclude a child.

The *Disability Standards for Education 2005* supplement the *Disability Discrimination Act 1992* and apply to all education settings. They support the development of practices that comply with the anti-discrimination legislation with respect to children with a disability. Under the standards, such practices might include:

- Participation support such as flexibility in provision, alternative activities and access to assistance to support achievement of learning outcomes;
- Reasonable adjustment of classroom practices, including changes in the complexity of the curriculum. This includes adaptations to assessment strategies in the early years of school such that children with disabilities can demonstrate learning without standards being compromised.

These standards were reviewed in 2012 (Australian Government Department of Education, 2012). Some key outcomes include plans for consolidation of anti-discrimination legislation into a single law, clarification of terms such as unreasonable hardship, a requirement to offer individual education plans in schools and the extension of the Standards to child care.

The *Melbourne Declaration on Educational Goals for Young Australians 2008* (Ministerial Council for Education, Early Childhood Development and Youth Affairs [MCEECDYA], 2008) established two principles relevant to inclusive early education, framed mainly in relation to schools, but also aimed at strengthening early years education and partnerships with families. These are that

- Australian education promotes equity and excellence, including freedom from discrimination and respect for cultural (e.g. Aboriginal) knowledge;
- Young Australians become successful learners, confident, creative, active and informed citizens (e.g. appreciating cultural diversity and contributing to reconciliation between Aboriginal and non-Aboriginal Australians).

The *National Professional Standards for Teachers* (Australian Institute for Teaching and School Leadership [AITSL], 2011) include teachers' knowledge of students with diverse backgrounds and those with disabilities, and an understanding of how to differentiate teaching to cater for diverse abilities (see box below).

### EXCERPTS FROM THE AITSL STANDARDS FOR TEACHERS

Demonstrate knowledge and understanding of:

- Teaching strategies that are responsive to the learning strengths and needs of students from diverse linguistic, cultural, religious and socioeconomic backgrounds (p.1);
- The impact of culture, cultural identity and linguistic background on the education of students from Aboriginal and Torres Strait Islander backgrounds (p.2);
- Strategies for differentiating teaching to meet the specific learning needs of students across the full range of abilities (p.2).

*(AITSL, 2011)*

# Sector-specific national legislation and policy

Early years education is concerned with both prior-to-school early years and the early years of school. These sectors have separate legislations and policies, including separate curriculum frameworks, related to the age groups of children involved. However, they share an emphasis on equity and excellence, and pay attention to the avoidance of discrimination as outlined above.

## ECEC NATIONAL LEGISLATION AND POLICY

Legislation and policy for ECEC applies to long day care, family day care, school age care and preschool (sometimes called kindergarten, depending on the state jurisdiction) and is directed at strengthening the quality of ECEC programs.

The *National Quality Framework* (NQF) was established under the *Education and Care Services National Law 2010* and accompanying *Education and Care Services National Regulations 2011* (Australian Children's Education and Care Quality Authority [ACECQA], 2010). The NQF comprises a number of elements including the National Quality Standards, the *Early Years Learning Framework*, the *Framework for School Age Care* and a quality assessment and ratings process. Inclusion is explicitly addressed in the NQF. For example, in the National Quality Standards inclusion is evident in quality areas pertaining to education program and practice, physical environment, relationships with children, and collaborative partnerships with families and communities (see box below).

## EXCERPTS FROM THE *NATIONAL QUALITY STANDARDS* INDICATORS

1.1.2 Each child's current knowledge, ideas, culture, abilities and interests are the foundation of the program (p.28).

1.1.5 Each child is supported to participate in the program (p.34).

5.1.3 Each child is supported to feel secure, confident and included (p.132).

5.2.3 The dignity and rights of every child are maintained at all times (p.141).

6.2.1 The expertise of families is recognised and they share in decision making (p.156).

6.3.1 Links with relevant community and support agencies are established (p.161).

6.3.3 Access to inclusion and support assistance is facilitated (p.165).

*(ACECQA, 2011)*

An Inclusion and Professional Support Program supports the maintenance of high quality and inclusive ECEC services. The funding model provides for Inclusion Support Agencies, service subsidies and Professional Support Coordination and Indigenous Professional Support programs (DEEWR, 2009b). The focus of this program is enhancement of the skills, knowledge and attitudes of professionals and service management through professional learning programs and the development of Service Support Plans (see Chapter 11). It is not directed towards the provision of direct services for individual children.

Bicultural support is available for children from culturally and linguistically diverse backgrounds and Indigenous children in an ECEC service. The Inclusion Support Subsidy is available for ECEC services to include children with significant support requirements such as children with diagnosed disabilities and children who are refugees. It may be used to employ an additional educator to improve adult to child ratios, but is not intended to offer one-on-one support for children or to fund building changes or provision of medical or therapy services. Support processes are designed to encourage inclusive practices across a service, rather than the provision of a **shadow assistant**.

**shadow assistant:** A support educator who focuses on one child (e.g. a child with a disability) to offer substantial individual assistance throughout the day.

Purdue (2009) notes negative impacts on ECEC program quality if children with disabilities interact only with shadow assistants, as productive social interactions with peers offer learning opportunities and a sense of belonging. Shadow assistance has also been identified as a potential barrier to the social participation of school students with disabilities (McArthur, Higgins & Quinlivan, 2013).

*Early Childhood Australia* (ECA), the key professional organisation for ECEC, issued a position statement in 2005 indicating the current view on

CASE STUDY 4.1

## Inclusion support in practice

There was some debate about whether the local ECEC centre could accept Damien's enrolment, as he used a wheelchair and required a lot of physical assistance, including for feeding and toileting. Since his requirements did not constitute unreasonable hardship under the Disability Discrimination legislation, his enrolment was accepted. With the assistance of an Inclusion Support Agency, the centre developed procedures, applied for funding for an additional educator, linked with his parents and other agencies working with Damien and his family, and engaged in staff professional learning to ensure quality standards could be met.

CRITICAL REFLECTION QUESTIONS

1. How might one-on-one or shadow assistant support of Damien by the additional educator impede his social inclusion? What alternative approaches might facilitate Damien's inclusion?
2. What education might the professionals who work with Damien require to support effective and equitable provision for his education and care?

quality, social justice and inclusion in the education and care of children from birth to eight years of age. This position statement was updated and expanded in 2012 to include a position statement on children of asylum seekers and a statement of regret and commitment to Aboriginal and Torres Strait Islander children and families. A joint position statement with *Early Childhood Intervention Australia* (ECIA) on the inclusion in ECEC of children with a disability (ECA, 2012), which emphasises children's rights and collaboration between children, families, educators and support professionals, was also issued (see box below). The ECA and ECIA codes of ethics inform these position statements.

### EXCERPTS FROM THE ECA/ECIA JOINT POSITION STATEMENTS ON INCLUSION

Every child has the right to access and participate in ECEC programs in which they are recognised as active agents in their own learning (p.2).

Diversity and difference are valuable in their own right, as are commonalities amongst people (p.3).

Equity requires that each child receive the support and resources needed to participate, engage and succeed (p.3).

Inclusion of children with a disability requires ... strengthening the contribution made by all members ... [including] support for parents' advocacy ... and cooperation between early childhood educators, support professionals ... and families (p.5).

*(ECA, 2012)*

## EARLY YEARS OF SCHOOL NATIONAL LEGISLATION AND POLICY

In the early years of school, emphasis is placed on enhancing academic outcomes for all children and towards accountability. As discussed in Chapter 1, inclusive education is beneficial to this goal. Curricular differentiation, support processes for target groups, and **reasonable adjustments** to statutory assessment are mechanisms for enacting inclusive policy in this context (see section on target groups for group-specific policy settings).

**reasonable adjustment:** An adaptation to assist a child with disability to participate in education, while balancing the interests of others and ensuring the validity of assessment outcomes.

Assessment in the context of the *National Assessment Program* (NAP) (ACARA, 2011a), particularly the *National Assessment Program—Literacy and Numeracy* (NAPLAN) (ACARA, 2011b) may present challenges for children whose performances differ from that anticipated for their age group. NAPLAN supplementary information indicates that children with disabilities or children who do not speak English may be excluded from testing, yet it offers no explicit direction on reasonable adjustments if such children undertake the tests. Therefore, test outcomes for some children may be meaningless or inaccurate. Parents may request that their child undertake tests regardless of disability or English language proficiency, so reasonable adjustments demand careful professional decision-making, planning and documentation.

Publication from 2010 of NAPLAN data on the *My School* website, which allows comparison of data from all schools in Australia, has placed further pressure on schools to exclude from testing children with disabilities, learning

**CASE STUDY 4.2**

### NAPLAN and inclusion

Aidan was progressing well in mathematics and science, and managed many literacy tasks when a computer was available. The school staff, however, requested that he stay home during NAPLAN testing, because of behaviours associated with autism spectrum disorder. His parents insisted that he should be included in the tests. He was then provided with a computer and individual supervision by a teaching assistant in a quiet room, as reasonable adjustments for the testing process.

**CRITICAL REFLECTION QUESTIONS**

1. What emotional and social impact might exclusion from high-stakes testing have on a child?
2. What support provisions might form reasonable adjustments, while still making sure that Aiden's literacy and numeracy ability is being accurately assessed?

*Anne Petriwskyj*

difficulties or limited English, in order to show higher scores than comparable schools (Conway, 2010). In this high-stakes testing context, a narrowing of teaching content and exclusions from assessment may detract from inclusive policy intentions.

## NATIONAL CURRICULUM DOCUMENTS

The national curriculum documents for the early years contain explicit attention to inclusion. However, as noted earlier in this chapter, there are separate documents for ECEC, school and school age care related to the differing focus of each service type. These are:

- *Early Years Learning Framework* (DEEWR, 2009a) for ECEC services;
- *Framework for School Age Care* (DEEWR, 2009a) for young children in outside-school-hours care;
- *Australian Curriculum* (ACARA, n.d.) for children in school.

In the *Early Years Learning Framework* and *Framework for School Age Care,* inclusion is a key component. This is consistent with the overarching NQF and is visible across both the content of these documents and the supporting materials such as the Educators' Guide.

- A view of children's lives as characterised by belonging, being and becoming;
- Principles (including partnerships with families and support professionals, high expectations and equity, and respect for diversity);
- Practices (including continuity of learning between home and ECEC, and educators' demonstration of cultural competence);
- Learning outcomes (including children's sense of identity demonstrated through their use of home languages and engagement with their cultural heritage, awareness of fairness, and responding to diversity with respect).

The Educators' Guide support resources address cultural competency through discussion of its meaning and examples in practice, particularly in relation to Aboriginal and Torres Strait Islander children, families and communities. These documents embed inclusion within high quality universal provision of ECEC.

Although the original draft principles underpinning the *Australian Curriculum* addressed inclusion more broadly, later versions and outcomes statements incorporate cultural diversity yet demonstrate limited evidence of inclusive provision for disability or for advanced ability (Berlach & Chambers, 2010). The academic learning outcomes are level-based (e.g. Foundation, Year 1), and must be interpreted in relation to individual children in order to address differentiation of the curriculum for each child. The accompanying materials contain statements on personalised learning and support provision for children with disability, children identified as gifted and children with English as an additional language or dialect (ACARA, n.d.).

Inclusive content with a social and cultural emphasis in the *Australian Curriculum* considers both learning about cultures and engaging in socially inclusive behaviours:

- General capabilities (Personal social capability, Ethical behaviour, and Intercultural understanding);
- Cross-curricular priorities (Aboriginal and Torres Strait Islander histories and cultures; and Asia and Australia's engagement with Asia).

**CRITICAL REFLECTION QUESTIONS**

1. Reflect on the commonalities in the national curriculum documents with respect to inclusion. What similarities and differences do you identify in the wording of the documents related to diversity?
2. How might differences between the *Australian Curriculum, Early Years Learning Framework* and *Framework for School Age Care* impact on children and families?
3. What similarities are possible in inclusive principles and practices among ECEC, school age care, and the early years of school? How might this impact on smooth processes of transition to school?

# National policy for target groups

The historical division between inclusive policy regarding disability and cultural background remains evident in the fact that there are separate policy settings for these two broad target groups. Some policies are directed explicitly towards improvement in the outcomes of Aboriginal and Torres Strait Islander children, and others are targeted towards children with disability as key priority areas in contemporary Australia. Targeted policies reflect the reality of funding restrictions, as each policy has resourcing implications. For example, a policy directed at a specific group may require the provision of additional or specialised staff, specialised teaching materials, new community partnerships, and changes in pre-service or in-service professional education.

## POLICIES FOR DISABILITY GROUPS

The *Better Start for Children with Disability* (Australian Government Department of Social Services, n.d.) initiative was intended to offer early intervention (e.g. health services, therapy, resources, specialist teachers) for children up to six years with diagnosed disabilities such as Down syndrome, Fragile X syndrome, cerebral palsy and hearing or vision impairment. Family registration for early intervention funding from the Department of Social Services is managed through a registration and information service operated by Carers Australia. The *Helping Children with Autism* version of this early intervention initiative also links families of children on the autism spectrum to autism-specific playgroups or early learning and care centres in major centres, and to parent workshops and websites providing information on autism spectrum disorder.

The *National Disability Insurance Scheme* (Australian Government, 2013) is being introduced as a combined national and state program to provide improved lifetime support for people with disability. National Disability Insurance Agencies and local coordinators assist families to access relevant community services and to be involved in the development of participant plans. There is an emphasis on early intervention funding, but there will also be a school interface.

## POLICIES TO ADDRESS DISADVANTAGE

Efforts in Australia to provide more effectively for children whose life circumstances are considered to constitute educational and social disadvantage have focused on programs offered before school to children, families, or the community. Direct provisions for children have included extending access to early years programs, funding childcare benefits, and expanding universal access to preschool education. Programs for families include the *Home Interaction Program for Parents and Youngsters* (HIPPY) through which families are offered home tutoring by trained community members in strategies to engage their preschool children in learning activities. The aim of this program is improved parent–child relationships as well as enhanced child confidence and learning capacity (Dean & Leung, 2010). Community interventions include the use of the *Australian Early Development Index* (AEDI) to identify communities characterised by disadvantage, so that additional services might be offered in those communities (Agbenyega, 2009). Despite the potential of such tools to better target support, there is concern that children may be stigmatised if the data are misunderstood (e.g. misinterpretation of data as implying deficit in a child or family may lower expectations of the child and hamper productive relationships with the family). Further policy directions include integrated service provision (e.g. early years settings, child and family centres) and programs designed to sustain social inclusion and strengthen protective factors while minimising risk factors (e.g. *Brighter Futures* New South Wales).

## POLICIES FOR CULTURAL GROUPS

The *National Statement for Culturally Inclusive Schooling in the 21st Century* (Ministerial Council for Education, Early Childhood Development and Youth

Affairs [MCEECDYA], 2000) builds on the social justice principles adopted in the earlier *Adelaide Declaration on National Goals for Schooling in the 21st Century*. It emphasises the rights of Indigenous children to high quality education and the role of Indigenous parents and caregivers as a first educators of their children, and is supported in the *Melbourne Declaration on Educational Goals for Young Australians 2008* (MCEECDYA, 2008). This was followed by an *Aboriginal and Torres Strait Islander Policy and Action Plan 2010–2014* (MCEECDYA, 2010), which includes provision for children's participation in culturally inclusive, high quality ECEC programs, and support during their transition to school, as well as partnership with families and communities; the policy also provides for children to learn Standard Australian English while being recognised as multilingual learners.

The *Closing the Gap* national strategy to improve the lives and outcomes of Aboriginal and Torres Strait Islander Australians includes provisions for improved child health, access to preschool education for four year olds and enhanced school education (Australian Government Department of Social Services, 2013). The strategy is enacted through state-based processes focused on improvements in literacy and numeracy outcomes in the early years of school, school attendance and retention, as well as the funding of Child and Family centres, Multifunctional Aboriginal Children's Services (MACS) and Indigenous preschool education to improve transitions between ECEC and school. It incorporates Aboriginal and Torres Strait Islander community engagements through consultative committees.

The *Cultural Support Program (Childcare)* (Multicultural Development Association, n.d.) is offered through the Multicultural Development Association (MDA) and regional bicultural support services. It assists ECEC services by providing cultural information and a cultural support educator to assist with the social inclusion of children and families from culturally and linguistically diverse backgrounds. The intention is that the cultural educator works across the group, rather than working only with an individual child, as this would be exclusionary.

**CRITICAL REFLECTION QUESTIONS**

1. Some cultural support assistants in ECEC continue to work solely with an individual child, rather than across the group, although this runs counter to the policy intentions for cultural support and inclusion (Miller, Knowles & Grieshaber, 2011). Why do you think this practice persists?
2. Whose interests are served by this strategy?
3. What could ECEC services do to change their support strategy to make it more inclusive?

# Targeted state-based policy

Each state education system has developed separate policies on inclusion and has specified categories of school students who are eligible to access Australian Government funding for support services. Eligibility for support service funding depends on formal documentation of evidence that children require support additional to that otherwise provided in classrooms. Educators must ensure they understand the current policies, including eligibility criteria and access processes, relevant to their specific location and setting.

Support funding often requires a formal diagnosis of a specific form of impairment, such as cognitive, sensory or physical impairment or autism spectrum disorder. This policy is sometimes extended to ensure provision for children with learning difficulties, particularly those with literacy difficulties. For example, Western Australia has policies on children at education risk, while Victoria has general policies on support for children with disabilities, and targeted policies for children with autism spectrum disorders (Victorian Department of Education & Early Childhood Development [DEECD], 2012; Western Australian Department of Education, 2001). In some states, policy extends to supported transition to school for children with disabilities; for example, the Education Queensland supplementary guidelines (Education Queensland, n.d.).

**CRITICAL REFLECTION QUESTIONS**

1. Why might funding be so narrowly targeted?
2. How might the targeting of funding for support impact on children's inclusion?
3. What might be the negative consequences of deficit-focused targeting?

School funding is also available for supporting children with English as an additional language, providing literacy support for Aboriginal and Torres Strait Islander children, and for programs for refugee children in the initial phases of resettlement in Australia. The criteria for targeted provisions vary by state jurisdiction. In South Australia, a New Arrivals Program caters for children of refugee families and has prompted structural changes within schools to ensure successful implementation (Pugh, Every & Hattam, 2012).

Documents to address the invisibility of giftedness as a diversity consideration in Australian education focus on schools and are state-based. The *Gifted and Talented Education Quality Teaching Framework 2008* (New

South Wales Department of Education and Training [NSW DET], 2008) in New South Wales outlines the differentiation of the curriculum in content, process and skills to offer additional challenge in school. In the Northern Territory, the *Gifted Education Guidelines 2006* support identification, curriculum differentiation, and implementation of policies such as early entry to school. See Chapter 25 for discussion on the implications of policy for the education of children identified as gifted.

## Conclusion

Australia's inclusive policy settings have been framed to some degree by international conventions and position statements. National issues such as the progress of Aboriginal and Torres Strait Islander children also establish key priorities. National legislation and policy reflect expectations of both equity and excellence and address overarching concerns related to a range of diversity categories. However, some legislation and policy is directed to a specific early childhood sector in recognition of the varying expectations in ECEC, school age care and the early years of school. Additional policies target specific groups of children, reflecting current concerns, historical policy settings and funding restrictions. The specific context (e.g. ECEC, school), location (e.g. state) and circumstance (e.g. cultural background, disability) should be taken into account in enacting legislation and policy.

## FOR FURTHER REFLECTION

1. Compare legislation and policy in ECEC, school age care and school settings to clarify which requirements are shared and which are context-specific. Discuss how this would impact on cross-sectoral professional discussions about provision for children.
2. Attention to broader diversity groups, including those from culturally and linguistically diverse backgrounds, represents a major policy shift away from a sole focus on disability. Might this divert resources from children with disabilities, or does it assist educators in appreciating the complexity of individuals and inclusion?
3. Enacting support policies in a manner that avoids stigmatising target groups is a key challenge in inclusive early years programs. Consider the strategies that would help professionals address this challenge.

## WEBSITES

www.coag.gov.au/sites/default/files/early_years_learning_framework.pdf
Belonging, being and becoming: The early years learning framework for Australia

http://acecqa.gov.au/national-quality-framework/legislation/
Education and care services Australian national law and national quality framework

www.australiancurriculum.edu.au/StudentDiversity/Student-diversity-advice
Australian Curriculum v 5.1: Student diversity

http://ccccnsw.org.au/wp-content/uploads/guide-to-the-national-quality-standard.pdf
Guide to the Australian national quality standard for early childhood care and education and school age care

www.teacherstandards.aitsl.edu.au/Standards/Standards/AllStandards
The Australian National Professional Standards for Teachers

www.earlychildhoodaustralia.org.au/position_statements.html
Early Childhood Australia and Early Childhood Intervention Australia Position statement on Inclusion

www.curriculum.edu.au/verve/_resources/National_Declaration_on_the_Educational_Goals_for_Young_Australians.pdf
Melbourne Declaration on Educational Goals for Young Australians

https://education.gov.au/aboriginal-and-torres-strait-islander-education-action-plan-2010-2014-0
Aboriginal and Torres Strait Islander action plan 2010–2014

www.mdainc.org.au/
Multicultural Development Association Cultural Support Program

www.ohchr.org/en/professionalinterest/pages/crc.aspx
United Nations Convention on the Rights of the Child

www.un.org/disabilities/convention/conventionfull.shtml

www.dss.gov.au/the-united-nations-convention-on-the-rights-of-persons-with-disabilities-uncrpd-in-auslan-australian-sign-language
United Nations Convention on the Rights of Persons with Disabilities

www.unesco.org/education/pdf/SALAMA_E.PDF
The Salamanca Statement and Framework for Action on Special Needs Education

http://unesdoc.unesco.org/images/0014/001478/147878e.pdf
UNESCO Guidelines on Intercultural Education

## REFERENCES


Agbenyega, J. (2009). The Australian Early Development Index. Who does it measure: Piaget or Vygotsky's child? *Australian Journal of Early Childhood, 34*(2), 31–38. Retrieved from www.earlychildhoodaustralia.org.au/australian_journal_of_early_childhood.html

ACARA, *see* Australian Curriculum, Assessment and Reporting Authority

ACECQA, *see* Australian Children's Education and Care Quality Authority

Australian Children's Education and Care Quality Authority (ACECQA). (2010). *Education and care services national law and national quality framework*. Retrieved from http://acecqa.gov.au/national-quality-framework/legislation/

Australian Children's Education and Care Quality Authority (ACECQA). (2011). *Guide to the national quality standard*. Sydney, NSW: ACECQA. Retrieved from http://ccccnsw.org.au/wp-content/uploads/guide-to-the-national-quality-standard.pdf

Australian Curriculum, Assessment and Reporting Authority (ACARA). (n.d.). *Australian Curriculum v 5.1: Student diversity*. Retrieved from www.australiancurriculum.edu.au/StudentDiversity

Australian Curriculum, Assessment and Reporting Authority (ACARA). (2011a). National assessment program. Retrieved from www.nap.edu.au

Australian Curriculum, Assessment and Reporting Authority (ACARA). (2011b). National assessment program – literacy and numeracy. Retrieved from http://www.nap.edu.au/naplan/naplan.html

Australian Government. (2013). *National Disability Insurance Scheme—Children*. Retrieved from www.ndis.gov.au/document/301

Australian Government Department of Education. (2012). *Review of the Disability Standards for Education 2005*. Retrieved from http://education.gov.au/disability-standards-education

Australian Government Department of Social Services. (2013). *Closing the gap*. Retrieved from www.dss.gov.au/our-responsibilities/indigenous-australians/programs-services/closing-the-gap/

Australian Government Department of Social Services. (n.d.). *Better start for children with disability*. Retrieved from www.dss.gov.au/our-responsibilities/disability-and-carers/program-services/for-people-with-disability/better-start-for-children-with-disability-initiative

Australian Human Rights Commission. (n.d.). *Legislation*. Retrieved from www.humanrights.gov.au/our-work/legal/legislation

Australian Institute for Teaching and School Leadership (AITSL). (2011). *The national professional standards for teachers*. Retrieved from www.teacherstandards.aitsl.edu.au/Standards/Standards/AllStandards

Berlach, R. & Chambers, D. (2010). Inclusivity imperatives and the national curriculum. *The Education Forum, 75*(1), 52–65. doi:10.1080/00131725.2010.528550

Conway, R. (2010). Australian schools, policy and legislation in perspective. In M. Hyde, L. Carpenter & R. Conway (Eds), *Diversity and inclusion in Australian schools*. (pp.14–33). South Melbourne: Oxford University Press.

Dean, S. & Leung, C. (2010). Nine years of early intervention research: The effectiveness of the HIPPY program in Australia. *Learning Difficulties Australia Bulletin, 42*(1), 14–16. Retrieved from www.hippyaustralia.org.au/file/1975

Department of Education, Employment and Workplace Relations (DEEWR). (2009). *Belonging, being and becoming: The early years learning framework for Australia*. ACT: DEEWR. Retrieved from www.coag.gov.au/sites/default/files/early_years_learning_framework.pdf

Department of Education, Employment and Workplace Relations (DEEWR). (2009b). *Inclusion and professional support program*. Retrieved from www.deewr.gov.au/earlychildhood/programs/childcareforservices/supportfamilyccs/pages/inclusionsupportprogram.aspx

Department of Education Tasmania. (2006). *Inclusive education*. Retrieved from www.education.tas.gov.au/curriculum/archived/needs/inclusive

Early Childhood Australia (ECA). (2012). *Position statements*. Retrieved from www.earlychildhoodaustralia.org.au/position_statements.html

Education Queensland. (n.d.). *Supplementary guidelines: Students with disabilities of prep eligible age with significant educational support needs*. Retrieved from http://education.qld.gov.au/studentservices/learning/docs/suppguidelines.pdf

MCEECDYA, *see* Ministerial Council for Education, Early Childhood Development and Youth Affairs (MCEECDYA)

McArthur, J., Higgins, N. & Quinlivan, K. (2013). Children's and young people's social participation. In S. Carrington & J. Macarthur (Eds), *Teaching in inclusive school communities* (pp.237–265). Milton: John Wiley.

Miller, M., Knowles, M. & Grieshaber, S. (2011). Cultural support workers and long day care services. *Australian Educational Researcher, 38*(3), 275–291. doi:10.1007/s13384-011-0032-x

Ministerial Council for Education, Early Childhood Development and Youth Affairs (MCEECDYA). (2000). *National statement of principles and standards for more culturally inclusive schooling for 21st century*. Retrieved from www.mceecdya.edu.au/verve/_resources/principl_file.pdf

Ministerial Council for Education, Early Childhood Development and Youth Affairs (MCEECDYA). (2008). *Melbourne declaration on educational goals for young Australians*. Retrieved from www.mceetya.edu.au/verve/_resources/

National_Declaration_on_the_Educational_Goals_for_Young_Australians.pdf

MCEECDYA. (2010). *Aboriginal and Torres Strait Islander action plan 2010–2014*. Retrieved from www.mceecdya.edu.au/verve/_resources/A10-0945_IEAP_web_version_final2.pdf

Multicultural Development Association. (n.d.). *Cultural support program*. Retrieved from www.mdainc.org.au/

New South Wales Department of Education and Training (NSW DET). (2008). *Gifted and talented education: Quality teaching and curriculum planning*. Retrieved from www.curriculumsupport.education.nsw.gov.au/policies/gats/assets/docs/qt_curricplan.doc

Northern Territory Department of Education and Children's Services. (2006). *Gifted education guidelines*. Retrieved from www.education.nt.gov.au

Pugh, K., Every, D. & Hattam, R. (2012). Inclusive education for students with refugee experience: Whole school reform in a South Australian primary school. *Australian Educational Researcher, 39*(2), 125–141. doi:10.1070/s13384-011-0048-2

Purdue, K. (2009). Barriers and facilitators of inclusion for children with disabilities in early childhood education. *Contemporary Issues in Early Childhood, 10*(2), 133–143. doi:10.2304/ciec.2009.10.2.133

UNESCO, *see* United Nations Educational Scientific and Cultural Organization

United Nations. (1989). *Convention on the rights of the child*. New York: United Nations General Assembly. Retrieved from www.ohchr.org/en/professionalinterest/pages/crc.aspx

United Nations. (2006). *Convention of the rights of persons with disabilities*. Retrieved from www.un.org/disabilities/convention/conventionfull.shtml

United Nations Educational Scientific and Cultural Organization (UNESCO). (1994). *The Salamanca statement and framework for action on special needs education*. Retrieved from www.unesco.org/education/pdf/SALAMA_E.PDF

United Nations Educational Scientific and Cultural Organization (UNESCO). (2006). *Guidelines on intercultural education*. Retrieved from http://unesdoc.unesco.org/images/0014/001478/147878e.pdf

Van Kraayenoord, C. (2007). School and classroom practices in inclusive education in Australia. *Childhood Education, 83*(6), 390–394. doi:10.1080/00094056.2007.10522957

Victorian Department of Education and Early Childhood Development (DEECD). (2012). *Strengthening support for students with autism spectrum disorders*. Retrieved from www.education.vic.gov.au/healthwellbeing/wellbeing/disability/handbook/autism.htm

Western Australian Department of Education. (2001). *Making the difference*. Retrieved from http://det.wa.edu.au/policies/detcms/policy-planning-and-accountability/policies-framework/policies/students-at-educational-risk

SECTION 2

# Diversity and Inclusion in the Early Years

# 5 *'Not just being Accepted, but Embraced'*: Family Perspectives on Inclusion

*Kathy Cologon*

CHAPTER OVERVIEW

By developing an understanding of the lived experiences of families, early years professionals can understand more deeply what it means to be included. This chapter will consider the implications of child and family experience for early years professionals.

Learning goals for this chapter include:

- Considering the importance of inclusion and inclusive education to families;
- Understanding family perspectives on what inclusion means;
- Recognising barriers to inclusion for families who experience disability;
- Reflecting on the role of early years professionals in working with families, resisting stigma, disestablishing ableism and, ultimately, facilitating inclusion.

KEY TERMS AND CONCEPTS

belonging

opportunity

participation

recognised contribution

# Introduction

There are many challenges that families report regarding inclusion, exclusion and the experience of disability. However, these challenges are often different to the *assumed* challenges that dictate the broader social narrative. The tragedy model of disability is pervasive and leads to many assumptions regarding families who experience disability. In particular the assumption that being labelled as having an impairment, or having a child labelled with an impairment, is necessarily a negative experience (Green, 2003, 2007; Haraldsdóttir, 2013; Skitteral, 2013).

It is now commonly acknowledged that family understandings are embedded within a socio-cultural, socio-historical context. This means that family perspectives and experiences change over time. However, it is less commonly acknowledged that the ways in which researchers and early years professionals interpret and engage with families is also informed by socio-cultural and socio-historical contexts (Ferguson, 2002). This underlines the importance of genuinely listening to families, rather than mistakenly falling back on stereotypes or assumptions about family experiences.

There are many stressors on families, including families who experience disability—particularly in relation to the social construction of disability. However, as Ferguson (2002) argues, the most important thing that happens when a child who experiences disability is born is that *a child is born* and the parents become parents of that child. While it may be an unexpected initial shock, for most families the experience of tragedy in parenting a child who experiences disability (or in experiencing disability oneself) is in the response of society, not the child (Derbyshire, 2013; Ferguson, 2002; Green, 2007; Haraldsdóttir, 2013). While not in any way making light of the challenges and barriers families encounter, listening to families, rather than making assumptions, uncovers the many positive aspects of living life as a family with a member who experiences disability (Derbyshire, 2013; Ferguson, 2002; Green, 2007; Haraldsdóttir, 2013). We also learn that support assists families to adapt and to resist a tragedy understanding of disability and of themselves and the life of their family (Ferguson, 2002; Green, 2007).

In this chapter I will draw on family views about inclusion. This is important in developing an understanding of family perspectives that moves beyond research that has been directed by assumptions and stereotypes (Ferguson, 2002). As Green (2007, p.151) argues, 'Parents of children with disabilities must raise their children within the context of powerful societal discourse that devalues adults with disabilities and, therefore, holds low expectations for the ultimate "success" of parenting children with disabilities.' Similarly, adults who experience disability face many barriers and stigma around parenting

(Kilkey & Clarke, 2010; McConnell & Llewellyn, 2002; Robinson, Hickson & Strike, 2001; Russell & Norwich, 2012). Given the importance of family-centred practice (see Chapter 9), seeking to understand family perspectives is essential in the everyday practice of the early years professional. Consequently, this chapter draws on research with families in Australia, the USA, Iceland and the UK, including from 114 Australian families who have participated in a larger research study with me (with 121 participants, including families with older children), exploring experiences of inclusion and exclusion in the early years.

The families in my research are a diverse group. They come from a range of cultural backgrounds and live in urban and remote locations. Family makeup is also diverse. Each of these families have in common that at least one child in the family is labelled disabled. Diagnoses include: autism spectrum disorder (ASD), Down syndrome, Attention Deficit Hyperactivity Disorder, cerebral palsy, intellectual impairment, sensory processing disorder, language disorder, hydrocephalus, Beckwith–Wiedemann syndrome and global development delay. Many of the children in the research have multiple labels. The focus of my research was on the early years experiences of these children. The children were aged between 1–12 years. Slightly more than half of the children were boys (53 per cent). The formal education backgrounds of the parents ranged from Year 10 through to postgraduate university studies. Throughout the chapter I will seek to allow the families to speak for themselves and for their voices to come through.

**FIGURE 5.1** FAMILY

*Artwork by Emma*

## Importance of inclusion

I would like to begin with considering the importance of inclusion to the families in my research. Of the 114 participants, only one family reported that inclusion was not important to them. For this family, their comments reflect a response to experiences of exclusion leading to the view that inclusion is not possible for their family:

> Obviously it [inclusion] is important for those who have the intellectual and emotional capacity to participate in normal social and educational situations ... My Autistic child is unable to keep up with the social and academic demands of a normal classroom. He is not even toilet-trained at the age of 9, so most schools simply will not have the facilities to look after his physical needs through the day. Anywhere that he goes, he has to be accompanied and controlled by a carer. Although we take him to cafés and restaurants and beaches, he is unable to integrate in a normal way. On the other hand, we do try to include him wherever possible—as in attending church and Sunday school—but unless he develops normal communication ability and stops running away into danger, inclusion in most circumstances is simply not practical ... Even the supported class at a local school would not take him in, because he was not as advanced as the other children, and needed too much physical care (being incontinent). (Family #13)

The other families in this research reported that inclusion was highly important to them. These families focused on the importance of inclusion 'because it is fair' (Family #6) and because it is a basic human right; for acceptance, living of life, to increase life opportunities, acceptance and tolerance; for happiness, friendship and community (and to avoid isolation); for education and development of the child, peers, family and society; to ensure every person can contribute and be valued for their contributions; and as a fundamental aspect of belonging. For example:

> To be included in any setting is a fundamental desire of any human being. To be accepted for who we are is something we all want as adults, to be included and accepted as a person with a disability even more so, as that person already knows that they are different to the majority, they only require people to look past the obvious and see the person that they are. (Family #8)

> People are more like each other than they are different and society is better if we value each person who is a part of that society—we are interdependent beings and every person has something to offer every other person if we take the time to notice. (Family #77)

> Everyone wants to be welcome, to have friends, to have a place. (Family #109)

Consistent with the research evidence explored in Chapter 1, families suggested that inclusion is important, not only for themselves and their children, but for society:

> We believe it is our daughter's right to be included in all aspects of society. We believe that our daughter benefits greatly from being included for example developing friendships and learning skills. We also believe that others benefit from her inclusion for example from learning to accept others. (Family #85)

> Inclusion is important for all human beings, it provides a feeling of safety and being valued by those around you. (Family #105)

> Inclusion is important to allow all members of my family the ability to participate in society with the same equality and opportunities. And to educate all of society about the strengths and abilities of people who have a disability. (Family #107)

For some families the importance of inclusion was emphasised on account of the negatives of exclusion:

> Exclusion is hateful. It stops us from achieving our potential. It limits our abilities. It takes joy and achievement from life. (Family #86)

> It is only real-life that offers real, ordinary development for children. Brothers and sisters should be together as other families are. Segregated, congregated education teaches how to be disabled intellectually and socially thereby increasing a person's impairment. (Family #69)

> I have two wonderful boys who have much to experience and to give, they can only do that to the extent to which those around them allow it. When they are excluded in any way they learn that they are 'disabled'. (Family #119)

Families reported that experiences of inclusion led to happiness, a positive outlook on life, progress and development for the family, feelings of pride and of being valued and simply that inclusion was a wonderful experience. The desire for respect for every child, for inclusion to be 'ordinary', and for children to be viewed simply as children, was important to the families in this research:

> Nothing less, nothing more, nothing extraordinary, just the same. (Family #75)

Similarly, in writing of her own experiences growing up with impairment in Iceland, Haraldsdóttir (2013, p.21) shares that critical to her developing identity was her parents' view of her as simply a child, 'Nothing more. Nothing less'. Haraldsdóttir argues that her family's focus on inclusion as an ordinary part of life was essential to her amid many challenges in a disabling society.

## The meaning of inclusion

> Every child should have total acceptance, and feel equal as well as unique. (Family #83)

To understand the importance of inclusion for families and to consider what this means for everyday early years practice, we also need to understand what families view inclusion to mean. In analysing the family responses in this research, four themes emerged that explained the meaning of inclusion to these families:

- Inclusion is belonging;
- Inclusion is participation;
- Inclusion is opportunity;
- Inclusion is recognised contribution.

## INCLUSION IS BELONGING

**belonging:** 'Knowing where and with whom you belong ... Belonging acknowledges children's interdependence with others and the basis of relationships in defining identities' (DEEWR, 2009, p.7)

**Belonging** emerged as a key aspect of inclusion for families in this research:

> Belonging is a fundamental right—in that it is value, respect, acceptance of people. Inclusion to me is like belonging—the ability of my children to join in with any activity reinforces their rights to belong, have a go, to fail, succeed, to be cared for regardless of how it goes. (Family #82)

Within the understanding of inclusion as belonging, being valued and welcome were fundamental aspects of inclusion:

> Not just being accepted, but embraced. (Family #73)

> Being supported to live a valued life in the same way as other Australian citizens—through culturally valued settings including school, work and home and through culturally valued activities, events and opportunities. (Family #77)

> No feeling of being left out, behind or unwelcomed. (Family #65)

Inclusion was also viewed by families as requiring each person to be valued as an equal, without conditions placed on belonging:

> Never having anyone think twice about whether or not the person with the disability will participate along with everyone else who does not have a disability. (Family #88)

> An opportunity for the child to be included and their differences respected and accepted. For the child and their family to be accepted in social and educational situations as equal members of the group with other members understanding, respecting and accepting their needs and abilities. (Family #95)

CASE STUDY 5.1

## Fish and friends

In research in the UK, Billie Tyrie (Tyrie, 2013, p.12), who is eight years old, shared this story about her family and her younger sister, Stevie:

> [O]ne day, when we went to the aquarium, my mum, my dad and I were sitting down a little way away from Stevie. Stevie was looking at the fish in the tank and a little girl came over and started talking to her. She asked Stevie's name and told Stevie that she was called Ella. Stevie and Ella talked about the fish and which ones they liked best. Stevie told Ella all about being born too early and explained why she was in a wheelchair. Ella told Stevie she would be her friend. When we got home Stevie said it was the best day ever! It would really make me and Stevie so happy if people treated Stevie like this little girl did.

**CRITICAL REFLECTION QUESTIONS**

1. Consider Billie's story. What might be important in this story for Billie and Stevie?
2. What does this story suggest about the other experiences that Stevie and Billie have had?
3. Reflect on Billie and Stevie's story in light of the views of families about inclusion as belonging.

**FIGURE 5.2** WHALE-SHARKS

*Artwork by Charbel*

## INCLUSION IS PARTICIPATION

**participation:** Being involved and taking part, through action, along with others.

As discussed in Chapter 1, belonging is widely considered to be critical to inclusion and to positive human experiences (DEEWR, 2009; Jones, 2002; Nutbrown & Clough, 2009). However, belonging is based on valued **participation** (Dockett & Perry, 2005). Consistent with these arguments, families in this research viewed participation as integral to inclusion and intertwined with belonging. This suggests that inclusion is

> Being able to fully participate in the community. Having people and organisations make accommodations to enable us to do so. (Family #45)

> Where every effort is made to allow anyone to have the fullest experience possible of an event (school, reading, sport) as a true participant. Inclusion should not be an act of toleration or a token gesture but a genuine belief in the rights of people to belong, have a go and participate to their greatest ability. (Family #82)

## INCLUSION IS OPPORTUNITY

**opportunity:** Circumstances, a situation or an occasion that makes it possible to do something, achieve a goal, or develop.

Participation does not occur without **opportunity** and, likewise, participation and belonging facilitate further opportunities. Access to opportunity emerged as a key aspect of inclusion for the families in this research:

> Opportunities for a person to participate in educational and social activities with other people who have no disability. (Family #13)

> Giving children with disabilities the same level of opportunity all children without disabilities are offered. (Family #67)

> Same opportunities to all. Inclusion in education does not distinguish between 'general education' and 'special education' programs; instead, all students learn together. (Family #118)

## INCLUSION IS RECOGNISED CONTRIBUTION

**recognised contribution:** Contributions made by a person or group that are recognised and valued by those around them.

The final theme that describes the understanding of inclusion shared by the families in this research is inclusion as **recognised contribution**. Families reported that inclusion, which they understood to be dependent on belonging, participation and opportunity, requires being valued for the contribution that you make to the family, community and society:

> Inclusion means all people are able to contribute to their community and have their contribution recognised while fully participating in their society and having their differences and the contribution those differences make, valued. (Family #120)

> When a person is fully included in all aspects of life, and seen as a contributing member of society. (Family #94)

> All people participating fully and being valued members of the community. (Family #121)

These families view their children as valuable, worthwhile human beings who are living their lives and contributing positively to the family and to the world. These families reported that their children could not be truly included without others recognising what their children have to offer.

Taken together, these four themes—belonging, participation, opportunity and recognised contribution—illustrate the meaning of inclusion for the families in this research. For some families, this understanding of inclusion was developed through experiencing inclusion. For others it was through experiencing exclusion. Experiences of inclusion for these families were characterised by acceptance, occurred in mainstream settings and involved appropriate support where required. These perspectives and experiences shared by families provide important insights for inclusive early years practice. However, the families also shared many barriers to inclusion.

## Barriers to inclusion

Ableist social views (see Chapter 2), resulting in stigma (see Chapter 1), formed the dominant barrier to inclusion for families in this study. This included fear, resulting in negative, exclusionary and ignorant attitudes, as well as apathy to change. Lack of valuing the child and lack of recognition of the child's contribution to the setting and community was identified as a major barrier to inclusion:

> [We were] asked to leave day-care [when he was] a two-year-old. Relatives buy presents for other children but not him because he 'doesn't know so it won't matter'. Unable to attend family functions, have to leave public places. (Family #65)

> While walking down the street of a major inland city, my two sons aged four (who has Down syndrome) and 13 were walking behind me. Apparently a couple stared and commented to each other in the hearing of my children 'people like that shouldn't be let out in public'. My eldest son was so devastated he didn't tell me of this event for some years. (Family #86)

Families reported lack of support and education for inclusion, which compounded the fear and stigma. This includes a lack of education on inclusion for early years professionals, families and the community and an unwillingness or lack of knowledge regarding making pedagogical adaptations. For example:

> Lack of knowledge. People not wanting to be out of their comfort zone, wanting to do things the way it's always been done. Not enough training done when people are going through university as to what true inclusion is for children going through the school system. Special schools and support units are not where you will find real inclusion, but this is where teaching students are shown about disability. (Family # 72)

> Maths lessons in grade 4 with my twins with intellectual disability and mild cerebral palsy sitting in the corner 'playing' with calculators while the rest of the class did maths. (Family #64)

> Our daughter was seated at the side of the class by herself for most of the first term. There was no reason for this as she is well liked by her peers and as she has Down syndrome she is a social learner and learns best by being with her peers. (Family #85)

Families reported encountering frequent misunderstandings of inclusion where inclusion was viewed as presence, but not as participation and belonging, or where inclusion was misunderstood as assimilation. Families also identified common exclusionary education practices, including:

- Lack of respect for the child;
- Lack of openness to embracing diversity;
- Lack of communication;
- Stereotyped views, assumptions and unexamined preconceptions;
- Failure to get to know and build a relationship with the child;
- Lack of knowledge of and respect for the child and family's goals;
- Rigidity/lack of openness and flexibility;
- Seeing the label, not the child.

Stigma playing out in the form of low expectations, or a presumption of *in*competence (Biklen & Burke, 2006), was a common barrier encountered by families in this research. This was exacerbated by a focus on competitiveness and outcomes at any cost, coupled with the assumption that the child poses a threat to this:

> When a group of mums got a soccer team going we weren't asked as they wanted to be competitive and felt it may be too difficult for [son]. (Family #83)

> Rejection from a dance school that claimed to be 'relaxed and friendly'—said no without even asking about my daughter specifically after I gave them the label of her disability. Also she is excluded at school when she is withdrawn to work with an aide. (Family #115)

> She was placed in a 'unit' within a primary school. This teacher refused to integrate her into mainstream. They shut the door and I think watched DVDs most of the day. (Family #92)

Similarly, Derbyshire (2013, p.33), writing of her life in the UK with her daughter who is labelled with intellectual disability, shares that 'it wasn't Hannah's additional needs that would be detrimental to her, but other people's ill-informed and low expectations of her'.

As for the families in this research, other research in Australia, with mothers of children labelled with ASD, has found evidence of stigmatisation in relation to enrolment processes (Lilley, 2013). 'When a parent mentions the word "autism", the process of enrolment is often entirely redefined' (Lilley, 2013, p.523). One mother in Lilley's research encountered the following response when seeking to enrol her son at the local school:

> She said straight up to me, 'No, we don't take special needs children.' I said, 'But you haven't seen my child; you haven't asked what the special need is.' She said, 'No, we don't do that'... I was just dumbfounded that they can just say 'no' without even looking at the child or even asking. Just a straight out 'no' (2013, p.10).

Led by 'a sense of social justice', this mother returned and had another discussion with the Acting Principal:

> When I began I said, 'I don't agree with what's been said here.' I said, 'I would like my child to come to this school.' She was saying, 'No, we're not having them because it will bring our score down in the school.' And that's when I got really angry. I said, 'How dare you! You don't even know my son. He might bring the score up for you. How do you know he's going to bring the score down?' Then I still put my enrolment forms in and just left it (Lilley, 2013, p.523).

Families in this current research also reported that a barrier to inclusion was their own exhaustion in the face of continued experiences of exclusion. For some families this led to them 'giving up the fight' and to a lack of hope. In regards to inclusion in the early years, families shared that the fight began early and continued year after year:

> Unfortunately some people still like to remind me of the GREAT EFFORT and EXTRA things that need to be done to maximise my daughter's participation at school. This disclosure of effort is the barrier. This is what teaching is—being responsive, finding what works for students, modifying curriculum to meet levels of ability. The reminders are subtle ways to keep reminding me this is still possibly a 'privilege' to have my child placed at the school and not her right. (Family #82)

This is echoed in the words of Bridle (2005, pp.2–3): 'Nowhere ... are we entirely insulated from social views that we are "lucky" to be so included, that the school is commendable for taking Sean and that perhaps his right to be there should be considered provisional.'

For some families the experience of enacted stigma includes blame for the fact that their child has an impairment or even for the very existence of the child. For example:

> I had to overcome a lot of anger ... people would say to me: 'Did you know he was going to be Downs before you had him?' Like I would have changed my mind if I had known and I used to just want to cry right in public. I would be thinking: 'What a mean thing to say.' 'How could you say that?' (mother in Green, 2003, pp.1366–1367)

Some parents shared their experiences of coming to the defence of their child or themselves:

> I was in the supermarket and Danny was playing up. I told him that if he wasn't to walk nicely then he could sit in the pushchair. So in he goes and he's kicking and fidgeting and testing all the boundaries. Suddenly, this man came over to him and said 'now you just stop that' and points his finger into Danny's chest. I went berserk (mother in Goodley, 2007, p.151).

But for some, even knowing where to begin when responding to such comments remains a constant challenge:

> At the shops people will come up to me and say 'oh, the poor little thing, you must be so wonderful to look after him', or 'oh, they are such little angels aren't they, always so happy'. They seem to think my boys can't hear them or don't understand them. I find it so hard to know how to respond. How to explain that even though they THINK they are being nice actually they are being horrible. These are my boys. They are not 'poor little things' or 'little angels', they are people—and they are listening! (Family #119)

Like this family, Derbyshire (2013, p.32) argues that the most difficult situations to respond to are those where ableism is cased in intended kindness. She relates: 'My earliest memory of this was taking Hannah on a children's train ride, when she was three years old. I handed the man the right money and he gave me 50p back, but when I asked why he smiled at me kindly and said, "don't worry, I never charge for retards"'.

Whether families develop strategies for responding, or whether they feel at a loss for what to say, this process can be exhausting as family members have to constantly deal with ableist views, as well as with regulating their own emotions and those of others (Green, 2003).

CASE STUDY 5.2

## Benefits and dangers of professional support in the early years

Lisa Bridle and Glenys Mann are mothers of two boys, Jack and Sean, who have Down syndrome. They wrote of their experiences of early intervention in Australia, along with the experiences of other mothers in Bridle's research (Bridle & Mann, 2000). Writing of the struggle to have their sons recognised as valuable members of the community, Bridle and Mann highlighted the difficulties with a system that frequently constructs children as 'different, defective, as a patient, a consumer or client' (p.11). They noted that '[a]s mothers we have been challenged by the struggle between *how we see our children* and *how the world sees them*' (p.11, emphasis added).

Bridle and Mann emphasise the importance of genuinely listening to and respecting family perspectives and working to understand and share the family's view of their child. While families do know their children best, they frequently seek advice and look to early years professionals for guidance. Bridle and Mann (2000, p.11) argue:

> It is often suggested, and rightly so, that families need to be involved in decision-making processes and that programs need to be built around what individual families want. What worries me is that at this stage many parents don't know what they want, and are in some way, just 'surviving' day to day ... Even the most well-intentioned therapist has, potentially, a lot of power over the attitudes that will be developing in this painful and sometimes fragile situation.

This creates some important considerations. Firstly, early years professionals have a significant responsibility to provide accurate and unbiased information to families and to seek to support families in working towards family goals and priorities. Simultaneously, early years professionals need to use their own knowledge and skills to support families in developing goals and strategies that are respectful of the families' strengths, culture, priorities and needs. However, sometimes interpretations of family-centred practice can leave early years professionals feeling that they have no role to play, and families feeling that they have all the responsibility to develop strategies. One father shared with me that he has fought many battles for inclusion for his son who is labelled with ASD, and has frequently been left feeling that developing strategies and addressing issues of concern is solely his responsibility:

> I have had hundreds of meetings over the years trying to get a fair go for him, I have been pitted against a room full of (sometimes up to 16) representatives from all facets of the Education Department including consulting doctors and so forth, and was always amazed that in their view, it was I, that had to come up with all the solutions? My standard response to this was that a room full of university-educated professionals require the Grade 10 drop-out to solve the problems. This always got a laugh but that was about it. (Family #8)

CRITICAL REFLECTION QUESTIONS

1. Consider the barriers to inclusion experienced by families. What role could early years professionals inadvertently play in creating or maintaining these barriers?
2. What role could they play in reducing or eliminating these barriers?
3. What would you need to address in your own practice and beliefs in order to support families and facilitate inclusion?

## BARRIERS FOR PARENTS WHO EXPERIENCE DISABILITY

People who experience disability are often stereotyped as asexual beings not capable of parenting (Haraldsdóttir, 2013; McConnell & Llewellyn, 2002; Skitteral, 2013). This ableist view is, of course, incorrect and many people who experience disability are parents—thus making up some of the diverse group of families that early years professionals interact with as part of everyday practice.

Robinson et al. (2001) reported experiences of families in Australia within which at least one parent experiences disability. Parents were vocal in recognising the constraints and pressures experienced by early years professionals. However, for many parents the experience of stigma was a powerful, negative—and unnecessary—component of everyday efforts to support their child's education:

> Especially being in a wheelchair, they think that because your legs don't work your brain doesn't work, so then they palm you off by thinking that 'well, he won't understand any of it anyway'. (Father) 'Isn't it wonderful that even though he's got funny parents he's such a clever child?' And they never think that we had any intelligence, we were pretty well miracles walking. (mother) (Robinson et al., 2001, p.25)

For many parents physical inaccessibility of buildings and lack of willingness of teachers to accommodate for this was a considerable barrier:

> At one stage I needed to see my son's teacher. At that time, I was in a great deal of pain and I spent most of my time at home. But I wanted to go and talk to the teacher. And I sent a written note, because she wasn't listening to my son and she was like 'well, tell your mother when she's better, then I'll see her'. But I didn't want to see her when I was better because it could take me a year—I wanted to see her now. And I believe she could have come down to the hall, or even to the playground and sat with me for five seconds, because I couldn't climb stairs, it was as simple as that. (mother) (Robinson et al., 2001, p.27).

A mother with visual impairment shared that she had been told she was no longer welcome at the school as the Principal felt she was an embarrassment because she sometimes fell over due to unexpected barriers in the way (Robinson et al., 2001).

These challenges—while creating very difficult barriers for the families involved—can generally be easily addressed by the early years settings. For example, one mother shared that the school moved their parent–teacher interviews to the library so that they were accessible without having to single out her or anyone else who uses a wheelchair (Robinson et al., 2001). Another mother shared that the school asked whether sending home notes in large print would be helpful (Robinson et al., 2001).

Mothers feature particularly strongly in research relating to families and disability. However, Kilkey and Clarke (2010) conducted research (in the UK) with fathers who experience disability. This research reveals complex and conflicting experiences and findings. Many fathers emphasise the positive experiences and benefits of having more time with children as an impairment effect (due to less paid employment), but this is complicated by stigma, including in relation to gender stereotypes about the role of mothers and fathers in raising children—coupled with the process of disablement:

> I loved spending time with my son and staying at home but I felt it wasn't the right thing. I just felt I should be the main breadwinner ... My life drastically changed; I wouldn't have even considered being a stay at home dad prior to my accident but I think the fact that there was a possibility it just made me feel less of a, I suppose it sounds really bad against women, but it made me feel less of a man being the person who was provided for instead of providing for. (Kilkey & Clarke, 2010, p.137)

Another father in this study also shared that some of the most difficult challenges related to gender roles and the stigma around what is perceived by some to be non-masculine. Speaking of a lack of acceptance in mother's groups, this father shared that 'one of the hardest things has been not as a disabled dad but as a stay at home dad; it's hard being accepted in some circles' (Kilkey & Clarke, 2010, p.138).

A common societal assumption regarding parents who experience disability is that their children take on the caring role. This stigmatising assumption is difficult for many families:

> It's hard as a blind person to be taken seriously anywhere and in some ways I feel it's hardest when it's in front of your children ... Being a father has been a big part of my identity; for a number of years it was more important for me to look after them than to work full time. I worked part time. I wanted to look after them half the time all those years and it was very important for me. It was hard when that wasn't received by other people. I felt it had another layer of contempt because of my sight, because they didn't quite believe that

> I was looking after them anyway. A common reaction was 'oh I expect they look after you don't they?' assuming that they're your carer rather than I'm a dad doing the caring (Kilkey & Clarke, 2010, p.142).

For many fathers in this study, the most difficult aspect was the felt stigma, with some fathers choosing not to go out or participate in the world for fear of the stigma they experienced.

One of the aspects of being a parent that many parents who experience disability report as being most difficult is the perpetual question mark hanging over their head regarding whether or not they are 'fit to be a parent'. While for most people the general assumption is that adults who have children will be fit to parent (a presumption of competence), when a parent has an impairment—especially an intellectual impairment—this is frequently brought into question. Not necessarily because there are any actual factors of concern, but simply because a person has an impairment and this brings with it a set of societal assumptions or stereotypes. As illustrated in this contribution from a father who has an intellectual disability, parents who experience disability are often placed under much greater scrutiny than any other parents: 'You should be able to wash the pots, watch the kids, hoover-up, cut the grass in the garden and see what the next door's dog is doing all in about five seconds. You've got to have your radar on overdrive ... You have to work harder with being a person with [an intellectual impairment]' (Kilkey & Clarke, 2010, p.142).

Australian researchers McConnell and Llewellyn (2002) have conducted research into the removal of children from parents who experience disability, particularly parents with intellectual impairments. While these researchers argue that for some children—of parents with *and without* impairments—removal is required, they report concerning realities regarding the excessive and inappropriate removal of children from parents who experience disability in Australia and internationally: 'There is unnecessary, unwarranted and all-too-frequent removal of children when their parents have an intellectual disability ... the grounds for such removal are not related to protection of the child, but rather to misguided or prejudicial ideas about parents with intellectual disability' (McConnell & Llewellyn, 2002, p.297–298).

The role of stigma in this process is alarming. McConnell and Llewellyn (2002) have found that:

- Parents face discrimination and thus both enacted and felt stigma;
- Stereotypical assumptions have little basis in truth;
- Extensive research has demonstrated that parenting programs can be effective where required;

- The current rates of removal are disproportionate and point to concerning stereotypical views within the legal and child protection field, as well as within the wider community.

Some of the work of these researchers has included researching the views of judges and other lawyers. It has been found that many such legal professionals have stereotypical or prejudiced views leading to the assumption that the outcome of any such case will always be removal, thus forming the basis of enacted stigma.

**CRITICAL REFLECTION QUESTIONS**

1. What are your assumptions about parents who experience disability?
2. What is the basis for these assumptions?
3. Reflecting on these family stories, what steps can you take to be inclusive of parents who experience disability in terms of your attitudes, practices and the way that you set up the early years environment?

# Resisting stigma and disestablishing ableism

While stigma is a common experience, families are not passive victims. Many families actively fight against or resist stigmatisation, in individual moments and in working towards broader social and systematic change. So can early years professionals—and they often do. There are many such examples, in fact the inclusion movement in itself could be viewed as resistance to stigmatisation.

One step towards resisting stigma and disestablishing ableism is to recognise that 'difference' is an everyday part of life. In reality there is no such thing as 'normal' or 'abnormal' (see Chapter 3). This is a process of acceptance—of the self and each other. As one mother in Goodley (2007, p.150) shared: 'You see, I can't keep chasing the normal. I mean I've done so much to try and make my son normal but I can't keep that up ... I need to accept him in the ways that he is and just enjoy them and him'.

Some family members develop, over time, the capacity to respond to ableism with the assumption that—however offensive the comments or behaviours—the person making them (be they family, early years professionals or perfect strangers) is not intending to be offensive. On this basis families sometimes seek to educate rather than focus on hurt or anger (mothers in Green, 2003, p.1367):

> I say something really positive and I do that right away ... because I know that some people ... don't know what to say.

> I felt like I was constantly educating people ... but by being gentle ... but frank and saying just the right thing ... I broke down a lot of barriers.
>
> ... my heart was healed because I started laughing about it ... I would find funny ways to say something back ... Like 'no I didn't know he would have Down syndrome but I knew he'd have this gorgeous head of blond hair' and I'd laugh. We just started laughing at home about some of the questions that were asked us during the day.

Early years professionals too can resist ableism by recognising stigma, breaking down stereotypes and seeking to engage with every person *as a person*, not as a label or category (McConnell & Llewellyn, 2002). Families in my research shared:

> I was shocked when the local preschool teacher asked me when my son was coming to preschool ... I had no idea he was even permitted to attend the local preschool. I couldn't believe I hadn't realised he could attend a local preschool and it opened my eyes to the future in such a positive way. It was exactly what [son] needed as he was so sociable and just needed to be with others ... Beautiful for the whole family to watch him grow. (Family #83)

> It has been wonderful to have her in educational situations where the organisation hasn't just taken her, but have actively wanted her and rejoiced with us in every little step of progress. Our daughter has had aides and teachers who meet us at the end of each day, excited about our daughter's day and what she achieved. (Family #89)

With resistance to ableism and stigma comes the reclaiming of the person as whole and not-broken—thus the recognition that disability is a socially constructed imposition, rather than a problem within a person that needs to be 'fixed' (see Chapter 2). As disability rights activist Judy Heumann writes: 'Disability only becomes a tragedy for me when society fails to provide the things we need to lead our lives—job opportunities or barrier-free buildings, for example' (cited in Shapiro, 1993, p.20).

**CASE STUDY 5.3**

## Siblings challenging stereotypes

One of the key processes for resisting stigma or disestablishing ableism is recognising and challenging stereotypes and prejudices in order to eliminate, or at least reduce, their negative effects. One common stereotype regarding siblings is that if an older sibling experiences disability then the younger sibling who does not experience disability will assume the role of older sibling.

However, one perspective that is very neglected in the research literature is the perspective of siblings who experience disability themselves. Australian researchers Serdity and Burgman (2012) conducted a study exploring the perspectives of older siblings who experience disability. This research involved 10 older siblings aged between eight and 11 years (five girls and five boys).

While one older sibling appeared to fill the younger sibling role, this was not the case for any of the other participants. A key theme emerging from this study was that older siblings who experience disability do fulfil the older sibling role, including taking on the role of protector, teacher, carer and sometimes a parent-type role.

Protecting his little brother from bullies, 'Rambo' (child-chosen pseudonyms) shared, '... they used to bash him so he bashed them back ... They call him fatty ... So I bash 'em' (Serdity & Burgman, 2012, p.41). 'Groovy Princess' shared 'sometimes Mum gets me to just watch [youngest brother] ... while Mum goes down to the shops' (Serdity & Burgman, 2012, p.41). On taking on the role of parent/teacher, 'Rambo' said: 'I've told her [younger sister] she shouldn't be drawing on herself' (Serdity & Burgman, 2012, p.40).

The older siblings also reported rivalry with their younger siblings, consistent with common expectations of sibling relationships—regardless of disability: '... she normally starts chasing me and when she starts chasing I walk into there, get a pillow and just go whack' (Ian Welsh in Serdity & Burgman, 2012, p.41). 'I beat my sister in drawing, like she does a body, a stick. She does like a whole body and a face altogether in one' (Ian Welsh in Serdity & Burgman, 2012, p.42).

In contrast with most research that reports that siblings who do not experience disability often feel they get less of their parents' time, some participants in this study felt that their younger siblings (who do not experience disability) actually get more of their parents' time and attention. Gender and personality also influenced sibling relationships.

There were only two children in this study for whom impairment appeared to impact on their perceptions or experiences of the sibling role. While this was clearly difficult for one child, this was not an example of the dependency type stereotype commonly assumed: 'Well, I've been wanting to play football, and [older brother] was supposed to play football, and then [younger brother] started playing this year ... that's when I really, really wanted to play, and dad told me I just couldn't' (Brett in Serdity & Burgman, 2012, p.45). Overall, this research suggests that siblings who experience disability can and do fulfil the older-sibling role and have well-developed sibling relationships.

**CRITICAL REFLECTION QUESTIONS**

1. Before reading about the perspectives of the siblings in this study, what were your notions regarding older siblings who experience disability? What do you think these beliefs are based on?
2. Consider your broader views about siblings and disability. In what ways do you need to challenge ableist views and unexamined stereotypes?

Kathy Cologon

**FIGURE 5.3** LITTLE BROTHER'S FIRST DAY OF SCHOOL

*Photo: Alison Wilson*

# Facilitators of inclusion

The families participating in my research recognise many facilitators of inclusion and have many hopes for the future. Positive attitudes towards inclusion on the part of families and early years professionals were identified as a key facilitator of inclusion. This includes valuing the child for who they are, genuinely understanding inclusion and being committed to inclusion and embracing diversity:

> Greater awareness of the value of all people and greater understanding of inclusion and disability. Social change to move away from a tragedy view of disability towards an embracing of human diversity. Equal opportunities. (Family #121)

Inclusive relationships were identified as another key facilitator of inclusion. Families reported that this involves educators building relationships with the child, being open-minded, flexible and creative, seeing the child (not the label) and being willing to get to know and learn how to address the needs of the child:

> For all, to see him as an individual with as much to offer as the next person. That his life can be a good life like everyone else's. Opportunity to be loved, give love, feel happiness and respect. (Family #83)

Families reported that inclusion also requires respect and collaboration between the family and setting and collaborative partnerships with a range of professionals. Families argued that inclusion from an early age facilitates ongoing inclusion. Families shared that supportive community networks and promoting inclusion within the wider community are important for belonging, and thus for inclusion:

> To be included in all aspects of society from the very beginning as is his natural right of passage. (Family #72)

> Acceptance of the wider community. Reversal of current political policy that sees the disabled and needy as a burden to society. (Family #74)

Addressing systemic barriers and providing education for early years professionals to ensure understanding of inclusion and confidence in taking flexible approaches, were identified as key facilitators of inclusion. Families also experienced greater inclusion when educators enjoyed their role:

> Educating the teachers is most important because that will filter through to children and then to future generations. Laws against schools to exclude children from a program because they do not think he/she is able to achieve it. (Family #118)

> Abolition of support units for children with disabilities and education in a mainstream setting with an aide alongside their peers. Achievement would be much higher and prospects would also be greater. (Family #9)

Families emphasised the importance of a strengths (not deficit) based approach with high expectations (presuming competence). Recognising the contribution the child makes to the setting and community was viewed as critical to facilitating inclusion:

> We need to keep focused on her abilities and helping others who know her to see her strengths. She needs to believe in herself and have lots of practice making choices and being successful, like everyone does. She needs the wider support from the community to allow her opportunities (and not assume she can't or shouldn't do ordinary things) and she needs the financial support to make any adaptions needed. (Family #55)

Important practices were identified, including:

- Putting inclusive values into action;
- Thoughtful and reflective inclusive planning;
- Support to make education goals achievable;
- Support for transitions.

Advocacy on the part of families and early years professionals was also identified as a key facilitator of inclusion. Families reported that this requires determination and perseverance, knowledge of rights and anti-discrimination laws, families and early years professionals modelling inclusion, and ongoing leadership.

**FIGURE 5.4** THE WISHING WELL

# Conclusion

> I want my son to be a happy, contributing member of society who is understood, respected and accepted by the people he comes into contact with. I want him to know that we are a family, just as other children and parents are families, and that his differences do not limit him. (Family #95)

There is much to learn from the experiences of families and the understanding of inclusion that families build through these experiences. There are many ups and downs and often an ongoing mixture of pain and joy. In all of this the overwhelming message from families is one of love and joy in experiencing life together. A key message that emerges for early years professionals is the need to challenge stereotypes and to recognise all people as people—whether or not they experience disability.

Early years professionals have an important role to play in reducing the difficult experiences of stigma and ableism that families face. By addressing barriers to inclusion and by welcoming children and families and fostering belonging, we can work together towards inclusion for all.

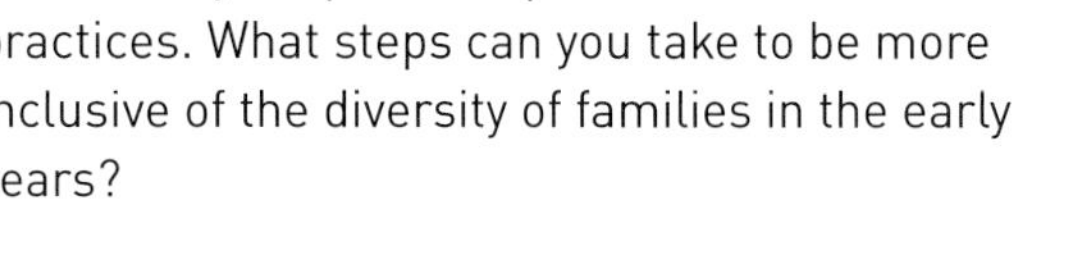

# FOR FURTHER REFLECTION

1. What have you learnt from the family experiences shared in this chapter?
2. Why is it important to consider your views, assumptions and preconceptions about families and the experience of disability?
3. Reflect on your past and present views and practices. What steps can you take to be more inclusive of the diversity of families in the early years?

## WEBSITES

http://www.family-advocacy.com
Family Advocacy (NSW) is an independent advocacy organisation.

www.resourcingfamilies.org.au
Resourcing Families provides information and resources for families, friends and allies of people with disability.

www.cda.org.au
Children with Disability Australia

www.dss.gov.au/our-responsibilities/disability-and-carers/program-services/for-people-with-disability/national-disability-advocacy-program/models-of-disability-advocacy/national-disability-advocacy-agencies-funded-by-the-australian-government-by-state-or-territory
National Government-funded Disability Advocacy Agencies

## REFERENCES

Biklen, D. & Burke, J. (2006). Presuming competence. *Equity & Excellence in Education, 39*(2), 166–175. doi:10.1080/10665680500540376

Bridle, L. (2005). Why does it have to be so hard! A mother's reflection on the journey of 'inclusive education'. In C. Newell, and T. Parmenter, *Disability in education: Context, curriculum and culture* (pp.1–12). Canberra: Australian College of Educators.

Bridle, L. & Mann, G. (June, 2000). Mixed feelings: A parental perspective on early intervention. Presented at the National Conference of Early Childhood Intervention Australia, Brisbane. Retrieved from www.downsyndromensw.org.au/data/Mixed_Feelings_by_Bridle__Mann.pdf

Department of Education, Employment and Workplace Relations (DEEWR). (2009). *Belonging, being and becoming: The early years learning framework for Australia.* ACT: DEEWR. Retrieved from www.coag.gov.au/sites/default/files/early_years_learning_framework.pdf

Derbyshire, L. (2013). A mug or a teacup and saucer? In T. Curran and K. Runswick-Cole, *Disabled children's childhood studies: Critical approaches in a global context* (pp.30–36). New York and London: Palgrave Macmillan.

Dockett, S. & Perry, B. (2005). 'You need to know how to play safe': Children's experiences of starting school. *Contemporary Issues in Early Childhood, 6*(1), 4–18. doi:10.2304/ciec.2005.6.1.7

Ferguson, P.M. (2002). A place in the family: An historical interpretation of research on parental reactions to having a child with a disability. *Journal of Special Education, 36*(3), 124–130. Retrieved from http://sed.sagepub.com

Goodley, D. (2007). Becoming rhizomatic parents: Deleuze, Guattari and disabled babies. *Disability & Society, 22*(2), 145–160. doi:10.1080/09687590601141576

Green, S.E. (2003). What do you mean 'what's wrong with her?': Stigma in the lives of families of children with disabilities. *Social Science & Medicine, 37*, 1361–1374. doi:10.1016/S0277-9536(02)00511-7

Green, S.E. (2007). 'We're tired not sad': Benefits and burdens of mothering a child with a disability. *Social Science & Medicine, 64*, 150–163. doi:10.1016/j.socscimed.2006.08.025

Haraldsdóttir, F. (2013). Simply children. In T. Curran and K. Runswick-Cole (Eds), *Disabled children's childhood studies: Critical approaches in a global context* (pp.13–21). New York and London: Palgrave Macmillan.

Jones, L. (2002). Derrida goes to nursery school: Deconstructing young children's stories. *Contemporary Issues in Early Childhood, 3*(1), 139–146. Retrieved from doi:10.2304/ciec.2002.3.1.4

Kilkey, M. & Clarke, H. (2010). Disabled men and fathering: Opportunities and constraints. *Community, Work & Family, 13*(2), 127–146. doi:10.1080/13668800902923738

Lilley, R. (2013). It's an absolute nightmare: Maternal experiences of enrolling children diagnosed with autism in primary school in Sydney, Australia. *Disability and Society 28*(4), 514–526. doi:10.1080/09687599.2012.717882

McConnell, D. & Llewellyn, G. (2002). Stereotypes, parents with intellectual disability and child protection. *Journal of Social Welfare and Family Law, 24*(3), 297–317. doi:10.1080/09649060210161294

Nutbrown, C. & Clough, P. (2009). Citizenship and inclusion in the early years: Understanding and responding to children's perspectives on 'belonging'. *International Journal of Early Years Education, 17*(3), 191–206. doi:10.1080/09669760903424523

Robinson, S., Hickson, F. & Strike, R. (2001). Interactions with school personnel. In *More than getting through the gate: The involvement of parents who have a disability in their children's school education in NSW* (pp.24–37). Sydney: Disability Council of NSW.

Russell, G. & Norwich, B. (2012). Dilemmas, diagnosis and de-stigmatization: Parental perspectives on the diagnosis of autism spectrum disorders. *Clinical Child Psychology and Psychiatry, 17*(2), 229–245. doi:10.1177/1359104510365203

Serdity, C. & Burgman, I. (2012). Being the older sibling: Self-perceptions of children with disabilities. *Children & Society, 26*, 37–50. doi:10.1111/j.1099-0860.2010.00320.x

Shapiro, J.P. (1993). *No pity: People with disabilities forging a new civil rights movement.* New York: Three Rivers Press.

Skitteral, J. (2013). Transitions? An invitation to think outside y/our problem box, get fire in your belly and put pebbles in the pond. In T. Curran and K. Runswick-Cole (Eds), *Disabled children's childhood studies: Critical approaches in a global context* (pp.22–29). New York and London: Palgrave Macmillan.

Tyrie, B. (2013). My sister Stevie. In T. Curran and K. Runswick-Cole (Eds.), *Disabled children's childhood studies: Critical approaches in a global context* (pp.10–12). New York and London: Palgrave Macmillan.

# 6 Cultural and Linguistic Diversity in the Early Years: Implications for Inclusion and Inclusive Practice

*Emma Pearson, Hanapi Mohamad and Zuryatini Zainal*

CHAPTER OVERVIEW

The purpose of this chapter is to stimulate thinking and discussions around inclusion, specifically in the context of cultural and linguistic diversity.

Learning goals for this chapter include:

- Understanding issues around 'inclusion' in the context of global policy/practice;
- Recognising the importance of 'cultural perspectives' in professional interactions with families from culturally and linguistically diverse (CALD) backgrounds;
- Considering the potential of 'relationship-based' approaches in building caring, mutually respectful and supportive partnerships between families and early years professionals.

KEY TERMS AND CONCEPTS

cultural perspective

culturally and linguistically diverse (CALD)

Education for All (EFA)

multiculturalism

relationship-based approaches

# Introduction

The purpose of this chapter is to highlight some of the ways in which families' experiences of disability are shaped by culture and context, with a specific focus on families whose cultural values systems are not represented in majority, or mainstream, systems and approaches. As discussed in Chapter 1, inclusion, by its very nature, compels systems and professionals to learn about and engage with perspectives held by different groups of people, in order to ensure that no individual or group is excluded from opportunities to participate and be represented. This may be the most challenging, yet critical, aspect of inclusive practice. This chapter draws on research that has documented the experiences of families from **culturally and linguistically diverse (CALD)** backgrounds in Australia and elsewhere to demonstrate that the task of engaging with multiple perspectives, albeit complex, is particularly crucial in drawing on the strengths, and responding to the needs and priorities, of families from CALD backgrounds caring for children with (and without) disabilities.

**culturally and linguistically diverse (CALD):** A term often applied in policy contexts to describe groups of people whose languages, beliefs, customs and daily practices may differ from those of the 'mainstream'.

Note that in applying the term 'culturally and linguistically diverse', it is critically important not to generalise within or across groups of people. Individuals from the same ethnic group, for example, may hold vastly different beliefs if they do not subscribe to the same religious faith. In the same vein, individuals from different ethnic backgrounds may, on the other hand, share fundamental values.

This chapter will begin by briefly summarising some international developments in inclusive practice, to highlight the global concern with inclusion that underpins education developments in most countries around the world currently. The chapter will then reiterate principles of inclusion, using sources that interpret it from a global perspective. Providing a global perspective reminds us that inclusion is a priority not only for Australia but also, as discussed throughout the book, for many other countries around the world. The chapter will then focus more closely on cultural perspectives and how they relate to inclusive practices in the Australian context, highlighting the critical importance of cultural values and beliefs in parenting and child rearing by touching on some experiences of CALD families interacting with early intervention systems in Australia. The chapter concludes with a call to practitioners and professionals working in the early years to think about ways in which they can influence 'systems' to become more responsive, reflective and inclusive in supporting families to achieve what they believe is best for their children.

# 'Inclusion'—the global context

Since this chapter is concerned with cultural diversity, it should be noted that 'inclusion' is important in the provision of early years education and care not

**FIGURE 6.1** CHILDREN'S DAY, BRUNEI

*Photo: Brunei, Child Development Rising Star School*

only for Australia but for most countries around the world, both developed and developing. National education policies in most countries nowadays draw heavily on international perspectives and priorities. To understand the ideas behind national policy and practice, then, we need to be mindful of policies and conventions that influence developments on an international level (see Chapter 4 for discussion of international conventions and national policies).

In theory, an inclusive approach emphasising equity and universality of access has underpinned expansion of most education systems around the world since the early 1990s. The World Conference on **Education for All (EFA)**, held in Jomtien, Thailand in 1990, is noted as an important milestone in international efforts to promote inclusion, because a key focus during discussions was the significant number of children and learners being excluded from education systems worldwide (Miles & Singal, 2010). Since education is viewed by most as a basic human right, this marginalisation of vulnerable groups of learners posed a serious challenge to many countries around the world.

**Education for All (EFA):** A global movement committed to ensuring that *all* citizens in *all* societies can benefit from basic education.

The 1990 World Declaration on Education for All, signed by over 1000 nation leaders (United Nations Educational Scientific & Cultural Organization [UNESCO], 1990) at the conclusion of the World Conference, reaffirmed the principles underpinning inclusive education referred to above. Global acknowledgment of the role that early years education and care can play in equalising early experience, and in laying the foundations for equitable participation in formal education, is also reflected in the very first of six international goals set out in the Dakar Framework for Action: 'Expanding and improving comprehensive early childhood care and education, especially for the most vulnerable and disadvantaged children' (UNESCO, 2000, p.8). Guided by this goal, 'inclusivity' (albeit understood and interpreted in slightly different ways across diverse contexts) is referred to in the early years policies of many countries around the world.

Definitions of 'inclusion' have been provided throughout this book. However, we believe that it is important, given the significant complexities associated with both defining and in carrying out inclusive education, to keep reinforcing definitions and meanings. Getting to know, and working around, multiple perspectives may be one of the most important skills required of early years professionals working with families from CALD backgrounds in Australia to achieve inclusion. In terms of daily practice in early years settings, for example, these skills require ongoing engagement with how 'inclusion' might be perceived by different groups/individuals in any particular setting, as well as a clear understanding of abiding principles of inclusion. Constantly engaging with and reacting to the distressing exclusionary practices that millions of children around the world continue to experience daily in our twenty-first century, globalised world is also important in galvanising society-wide awareness and support for inclusive practice.

As the Enabling Education Network, an international network based in the UK, points out, interpretations of 'inclusive education' can be varied and fluid, largely because its meaning depends on contextual circumstances, which may be constantly evolving (Enabling Education Network, n.d.). However, as discussed throughout the book, there are guiding principles that may be seen to form the basis for inclusive practices in education. Save the Children (2008) lists the following principles as key to international efforts in promoting inclusion:

- Acknowledging that all children are capable of, and have a right to, learning opportunities;
- Acknowledging and respecting differences in children based on age, gender, ethnicity, language, disability, HIV and TB status, etc.;
- Ensuring that education structures, systems and methodologies meet the needs of all children;
- Making inclusive education part of wider, society-based strategies regarding inclusion.

The set of principles laid out above reflects the varied priorities and focuses of countries and regions—ranging from mental and physical impairment to HIV and languages—in working towards inclusive policies and practice. It also provides some insight into the vast extent of conditions that can lead to exclusion, and clearly illustrates the array of challenges faced by countries

**FIGURE 6.2** WORKING TOGETHER

*Photo: Rimba II Primary School, Brunei*

worldwide in fulfilling these complex, yet essential, principles. As Barton (2003, p.14) has suggested, inclusive education is by no means a 'simple' topic or issue, but should be considered crucial by all systems, particularly education: 'Being concerned with an agenda for working towards inclusive thinking and practice is not an optional or light-hearted activity. It is of fundamental importance demanding serious commitment to time, imaginative, creative thought, energy and the development of effective collegial relationships based on trust and respect.'

Despite global rhetoric, therefore, many countries including Australia continue to struggle with inclusion and millions of children continue to experience disadvantage as a result of not having access to learning opportunities. Globally, the most serious and challenging barriers to education access exist among children who experience social isolation resulting from 'double disadvantage'; that is, belonging to minority social/cultural groups *and* experiencing disability or poor health. These children and their families, according to key reports on access to early years education, are at particular risk of discrimination and the impact of stigma (Pearson & Tan, 2013). As discussed in Chapter 1, stigma results from dominant negative social perceptions and assumptions about health conditions, people or attributes (Link & Phelan, 2013). The 'double disadvantage' experienced by children facing stigma and discrimination (enacted stigma—see Chapter 1) can lead to devastating outcomes related to poor health and development, as well as increased vulnerability to abuse and neglect, partly because stigma and social exclusion often lead to reduced access to and uptake of health services (Pulerwitz, Michaelis, Weiss, Brown & Mahendra, 2010).

There is evidence that early years professionals in Australia hold positive attitudes towards inclusive education compared to professionals in some other developed countries (Cologon, 2012; Loreman, Forlin & Sharma, 2007). This suggests that we are doing relatively well in creating an inclusive society. However, there is also evidence that many of the aspects of stigma and exclusion that affect children and families living in other countries are also being experienced by families living in Australia (see Chapter 5). While **multiculturalism** is celebrated by many Australians, and widely espoused by education theory and practice, reports on access to formal services for people with disability portray a somewhat negative set of experiences for families and individuals from CALD backgrounds. A 2008 report published by the National Ethnic Disability Alliance of Australia (NEDA, 2008) estimated that as many as three out of four people from CALD communities in Australia do not access services that are designed to support people with disabilities.

**multiculturalism:** Often used to refer to the Australian Government's Multicultural Policy. 'Multiculturalism' reflects acknowledgment that Australia is made up of, celebrates and embraces, cultural diversity.

A prominent early childhood organisation in Sydney, concerned about the lack of access by families from CALD backgrounds to its early intervention services, supported research designed to shed light on the experiences of CALD families who have children with disabilities. The study sought to understand better the circumstances that might lead to families from CALD backgrounds not knowing about, or being reluctant to access, services for children who could benefit from early intervention. Later in this chapter, we draw on excerpts from this research to illustrate key points.

### CRITICAL REFLECTION QUESTIONS

1. Why is it useful for professionals working within inclusive education systems to have some insight into international policies and priorities?
2. Do you think inclusive education means the same thing to all people/organisations?
3. For you personally, what are the most important and/or challenging aspects of 'inclusion'?
4. What, in your opinion, are the most serous barriers to achieving inclusive practice across systems that cater for children? Do you think these barriers are similar to, or different from, barriers faced in other countries?
5. 'Advocacy' is often associated with government lobbying, or with making public statements on important issues. However, not all people are comfortable with participating in public arenas or agendas and, as Australian artist Paul Kelly once sang, 'From little things, big things grow'. On the basis of your own strengths, context and preferences, in what ways do you think you could contribute to bettering the lives of all children and practising inclusion in your own life?

# Experiences of early intervention services among families from CALD backgrounds living in Australia

Conversations with parents from CALD backgrounds collected as part of a study (brief excerpts from which are provided here) revealed a range of complex issues that could possibly account for problems in accessing early intervention. These ranged from pragmatic concerns, such as transportation to early intervention services (a major challenge for parents living in places with limited public transportation services) to more sensitive issues around feelings of discrimination or cultural misunderstandings.

Culturally grounded values such as those expressed below by Mina, one of the mothers who participated in our study of CALD families in early intervention, provide individuals and groups with identity and purpose, often having a profound influence on children's and families' lifestyles (Nsamenang, 2008). When these values are threatened or belittled, disengagement and confusion are hardly surprising.

**CASE STUDY 6.1**

## The importance of 'listening' to understand better

Mina and Robert were a Tamil couple from South India residing in a Sydney suburb. Born in India, their two-year-old son Aabi had experienced a number of medical complications while he was still in India, due to what was later diagnosed as hydrocephalus. As a result of delayed treatment, he had developed difficulties with swallowing and speech. Mina and Robert's major concern when we first met was their son's reluctance to eat solids. They had decided to visit the mobile early intervention playgroup (operated by the early childhood organisation mentioned earlier) for help with this. In response, staff were providing Mina and Robert with advice on suitable foods and encouraging peer interaction to encourage Aabi to eat with friends during snack times at the playgroup sessions. Mina and Robert's experiences with more formalised services encountered during the process of their son's diagnosis (a formal diagnosis is necessary for families wishing to access state-funded early intervention services in New South Wales) were less than satisfactory, at times traumatic. Robert explained both his deep regard for intervention services in general, but also the family's frustration at having to submit their son to a battery of assessments, when they felt that their own understanding of their son's difficulties was not being considered. It is important to note the value that families in general attach to advice from clinicians and experts. As Robert explained: 'Every time we meet somebody we ask for their advice and just changing ourselves as well ... [when the doctor tells us] "Take the right direction for the child. It would be good for your child" ... that's fine for us ... We take advice if we need knowledge. So we said, "OK, we'll correct something".'

An excerpt from one of our conversations with Robert, presented below, however, shows frustration at not being 'listened to' by medical staff during assessment procedures. These frustrations reflect a similar challenge reported in the literature on culturally diverse families' experiences in interacting with formal service providers (Skinner & Weisner, 2007): 'Instead, they should concentrate on particular children ... So consider what he needs and we'll go to that. That's what they don't do ... They should see children [as having] separate needs. Different problems. But they categorise all in one basket [i.e. formal diagnosis].'

Many Asian families practise shared sleeping arrangements (Nelson & Taylor, 2001). In many homes, the whole family will share the same room for sleeping and, in some cases, the same bed. This practice is considered by these families as most appropriate for ensuring that children are safe at night, as well as for ensuring a level of inter-connectedness among family members. Extended family, including 'uncles', 'aunts', 'sisters' and 'brothers' who may or may not be related by blood, are also an important feature of families from collectivist cultures. At some point in her communications with the family General Practitioner (GP), similar arrangements in Mina and Robert's family were shared. The GP's observations were noted formally in the form of a report, a copy of which was given to the family. Regrettably, Mina felt that the GP had misunderstood and expressed disapproval of the family's customs, resulting in her feeling a sense of marginalisation from formal, medical services. Mina expressed a deep level of hurt at what she felt had been the GP's unjustified focus on family customs and their appropriateness, rather than on discussions around Aabi and his condition: 'Nothing she asked ... She's not interested in him [Aabi]. She all interested in us [family structure], not interested in him. [The report] was all over us, not the child. We went for the child, not us. She even asked Uncle [a family friend who accompanied Mina to the meeting] ... who are you?' Many of the conversations that were held with these families suggested that such misunderstandings could be avoided very simply by greater efforts, on the part of practitioners, to explain why information is being sought and to reassure families that their priorities and needs are valued and respected as part of an inclusive approach to early intervention.

In line with the family-centred practice approach outlined in Chapter 9, 'partnership' between therapists/early intervention practitioners and families of children with disabilities is widely touted as crucial for effective intervention. However, achieving the level of mutual respect and open communication required for genuine 'family-centred' practice is challenging for professionals working with families whose cultural values and practices they are familiar with, let alone professionals who work with families whose life views and child-rearing beliefs may contrast, or even conflict with, deeply held ideals of their own.

Hodge and Runswick-Cole (2008), both academics and parents of children with disabilities, highlight the problematic nature of partnerships between parents of children with disabilities and professionals within the early intervention system. An underlying issue that prevents partnership (particularly between professionals from mainstream, dominant cultural backgrounds and caregivers from diverse socio-cultural groups) is that professionals working within the system are neither ready nor encouraged/enabled to engage with caregivers at the levels required to sustain genuine collaboration based on shared interests/goals. For many busy professionals, engaging with families' values and home practices may be considered too time-consuming, or not relevant to 'diagnosis' and 'treatment' procedures. However, Mina's response to her GP's questions, and to the perceived judgment of her family's customs, demonstrate how important this level of engagement is, in achieving truly inclusive systems.

In order to understand the profound role of belief systems in shaping the customs and experiences of CALD families, it is worth referring briefly to theoretical frameworks developed within the discipline of cultural psychology. Cultural psychologists who work with families view (and seek to promote) the connections between value systems and child-rearing practices not simply as a topic of interest, but as crucial in understanding and 'tuning into' what families see as important or 'good' for their children. Rudolph Schaffer, one of the forefathers of developmental psychology with a particular interest in cultures and contexts of early childhood, once explained: 'the behaviour of individual children is given meaning by the relationships in which the child is embedded, in systems such as families, and [that] these too can only be fully understood within the context of the society of which they form part' (Schaffer, 1996, p.12).

## Insights from cultural psychology

Australia has cultural and linguistic diversity at its very core. According to the Australian Bureau of Statistics (ABS, 2013) as many as 34 per cent of people who live in the five mainland state capitals were born overseas. In one particular city council located in New South Wales, 40 per cent of the population were born overseas, around half of residents report speaking a language other than English at home, and 21 per cent say they either do not speak English, or feel that they do not speak it well. The rich cultural and ethnic diversity that exists across Western Sydney is evident in the various suburbs defined, respectively, by Vietnamese, Cambodian, Sudanese and Lebanese influences. Understanding the impact that this diversity might have on families, and on the daily interactions that we have with families in early years settings, is therefore important. In this chapter, we argue that some of the principles and philosophies underpinning cultural psychology can be applied usefully in developing the kind of understandings that support a deeply 'inclusive', respectful approach to building relationships with families from diverse backgrounds.

Traditionally, psychology and psychologists have been interested in identifying and tracking developmental 'norms' in society. From a psychological perspective, 'difference and diversity' are of interest because they reflect deviation from 'norms'. Cultural psychologists take a somewhat different view of 'diversity'. From a cultural psychology perspective, understanding the characteristics of groups of people whose beliefs, practices (and abilities) may differ is of value largely because it presents opportunities for us to think carefully about our own assumptions of what is considered 'right' or 'wrong'/'appropriate' and 'inappropriate' in human behaviour (Kitayama & Cohen, 2007). This is often described as 'making the strange familiar, or the familiar strange'.

Because of developments in knowledge on culture and value systems, supported to a great extent by research conducted in cultural psychology, ways of thinking about culture and its impact on families and children have changed in recent decades. Those who are interested in studying 'culture' in the context of families' and children's lives have moved away from viewing culture simply as an 'add-on', or something that only influences certain aspects of a child's development such as social competence or academic ability. Culture is now viewed as something that is not only integral to development but also to judgements regarding what is 'appropriate' in development, which might differ across individuals and/or groups.

With relatively few exceptions, all parents want to see their children grow up happy and contented. What this actually means and how they express this differs according to parents' '**cultural perspective**' as well as the circumstances under which they are raising their children. Family values depend on a vast array of complex, sometimes competing values and agendas. Such values and agendas could include whether families value formal education and independence for their children; adherence to strict moral codes and interdependence; inclusion in 'mainstream', regular classrooms or segregation and 'special' attention; or shared or separate sleeping arrangements. What is important, particularly in working with families from CALD backgrounds, is acknowledgment that all cultures value children, but they express this in different ways. It is important to acknowledge that dominant, Westernised beliefs about educating and socialising children do not necessarily match the views of parents from other cultures, or serve the best interests of all children. Contextual factors will determine both what is perceived to be 'best' for children and what actually is.

**cultural perspective:** The set of values, beliefs and practices that characterise the behaviours and priorities of a group of people.

Despite the vast diversity in beliefs about human nature that exists across our globe, human service provision across the world tends to be dominated by Euro-American notions of what is 'right' for individuals and their development. A defining feature of such beliefs is that people are both obliged and entitled to become independent in their lifestyles. This focus on, or assumption of, the need for independence is reflected in historical responses to disability in Western contexts. Many families, for example, were obliged to institutionalise their children with disabilities, in order to avoid perceived threat to others'

**FIGURE 6.3** CHILD DRAWING

*Photo: Rimba II Primary School, Brunei*

(for example, siblings) healthy development and education (Ferguson, 2001). Some accounts of medicalised responses to childhood disability provide a stark account of the historical emphasis on 'damage' related to living with disability in some Western cultures, as reflected in one mother's report on an early conversation with her physician: 'The doctor cleared his throat and spoke very quietly. "I am so sorry to have to tell you this, but I'm afraid that our tests show that it is extremely unlikely that your daughter will ever be educated"' (Copeland, 1973, cited in Ferguson, 2001, p.11).

Descriptions of philosophies underpinning child rearing in other cultural and spiritual contexts, however, suggests that not all cultures view impairment in the same way, as illustrated in this example of ways in which faith-based values might shape perspectives on 'inclusion'.

**CASE STUDY 6.2**

## Diverse perspectives on disability and inclusion: Insights from faith-based cultures

The national philosophy of Brunei Darussalam (where the authors of this chapter are now based) is referred to as grounded in three key elements: Malay (representing our geographical location and dominant cultural group); Islam (reflecting the most widely practised religion in the nation) and Monarchy (reflecting the importance of the Royal Family to the nation).

Islam, as one of the main components of this philosophy, has profoundly influenced the culture and 'mentality' of most Bruneians. Islam as a way of life is intended to give persons with and without disability equal rights and status, with expectations that all individuals carry out the spiritual duties given to them by Allah that comply with their abilities. The faith does not identify people with disabilities as either dependent or a burden on society.

According to Islam, 'children with impairment' are considered not only as a gift from God, but also as a reminder of the virtues that are expected of those who practise the faith. All children, with or without disabilities, are viewed as honoured creations of God. Responsibility for caring for any member of the family, particularly family members who may be vulnerable, falls ultimately on their guardians, with formalised support systems considered largely as an alternative form of care. Parents are seen as the first guardians responsible for the care of their children. In addition, family members are responsible for each other's care. Because family members inherit from each other, shared responsibility for care is considered crucial in fulfilling family duties.

This set of beliefs is strongly embedded in Brunei culture, where families provide the first point of support for each other and capable members of the family make every effort to support relatives in need of support, whether their need is caused by poverty, accident or impairment. Within communities and families, inclusion of and care for family and community members lies at the heart of this body of beliefs. Despite the assimilationist nature of families and communities in this small nation, it is important to note that exclusion can be found at a 'systems' level, where implementation of an inclusive education policy (adopted in 1994) faces challenges due to the naturally exclusionary nature of the formal education system, which is based on British values and approaches.

The values that are central to this faith are also reflected in daily practices described by one of the mothers who participated in our Sydney-based research. Her natural practice of faith in caring for her child reflects the inherent role of values in shaping lives and mentalities that we described earlier.

> [W]hether I come across something that God wants me to come across, or whether it's something I'm looking for yes, that's me reaching out for help. That's just an unconventional place, but it's not a person or it's not some sort of concrete thing ... It probably transcends having heaps of relatives coming and doing my housework or looking after my kids.

> [W]henever I prepare a drink for him I'll say this prayer. It's only a few lines long, but I'll say it either three, five or seven times and just blow on my hand and then put it over the cup of drink. And that's hopefully ... I believe in this and I believe it will help. And it's just part of the other medical and psychological or behavioural treatments he's having. And it's just like an integral part. I don't see it as anything strange or anything.

Shweder, Goodnow, Hatano, LeVine, Markus and Miller (1998) refer to the link between culture (or faith, as outlined in the example above) and child rearing as reflecting an 'intimate association between ... mentality and ... practice' (p.872). In observing this link they adapted Whiting and Child's model of 'custom complexes', which helps in understanding the ways in which daily practices actually reflect deep-seated values (Whiting & Child, 1953, cited in Shweder et al., 1998). By definition, 'custom complexes' highlight the intricate nature of cultural processes. Whiting and Child defined 'customs' as individual habits *which are identifiable as units of culture.* Perhaps the most useful insight offered by the custom complex concept is that some values and beliefs attached to practices are not usually explicitly expressed. These habits might involve the kinds of practices described above, such as blessing food and drink with prayer, or the importance of extended family involvement in caring for children, which may not usually be discussed in parent–professional meetings or discussions, unless a close relationship has been established and there is mutual interest in such practices.

Regular practices that reflect important values might also include seemingly innocuous gestures that involve early years professionals, such as presenting visitors to the home with gifts of fruit or food. Such practices can reflect deeply held beliefs regarding blessings associated with receiving visitors to the home. By refusing such gifts, home visitors might innocently and unwittingly cause discomfort, or offence. Professionals working within the framework of family-centred practice therefore need to be careful, mindful, and respectful of family's daily practices (in addition to priorities more directly related to parenting), in order to avoid discomfort and possible misunderstandings.

Values may not only be implicit but in some cases repressed. As some of our data indicate, cultural values may be particularly vulnerable to suppression when parents are engaging with early intervention 'systems' that strongly promote dominant, 'mainstream' and medicalised philosophies. In response to this, and other challenges associated with 'partnerships' in early intervention that have been outlined in this chapter, Moore (2007) has argued that '**relationship-based' approaches** to provision of supports for families of children with disabilities provide an appropriate model for inclusively engaging families. Moore suggests that referring to the interaction between caregivers and practitioners as 'relationships' implies a more intimate, mutual association than the term 'partnership'. Building relationships requires a greater effort in 'tuning to the other person's world, understanding their perspectives and experience, and establishing a personal connection' (p.5). This approach is of particular value to professionals working with families from CALD backgrounds, some of whom may struggle to express their deep-seated beliefs about what is best for their

**relationship-based approach:** An approach to professional interactions that emphasises a deep concern with mutual understanding and 'interest' in each other's perspectives/ priorities.

children in the face of a system that strongly espouses particular 'appropriate' methods in responding to childhood disability.

**CRITICAL REFLECTION QUESTIONS**

1. Can you think of examples where you have viewed other people's practices as 'strange' because they are unfamiliar to you? Can you think of habits you have that others might consider 'strange', if they did not understand fully why you practise them?
2. What would you consider to be your own 'beliefs' about children and child rearing?
3. Where do you think these beliefs originate?
4. Can you think of ways in which you put these beliefs into practice?
5. How would you feel if you were told that these beliefs were 'bad' for your health and that you should change your practices to reflect a different set of beliefs?
6. Not all societies provide the level of government-funded, formalised supports for children with disabilities that are available in Australia. How do you think families that are not familiar with accessing formal supports might perceive formalised systems? What kinds of challenges do you think families from CALD backgrounds might face in 'navigating' early intervention programs and services?

# Conclusion

Few would argue against the idea that inclusion should be at the heart of everything that early years professionals do. However, it is important not to confuse inclusion with assimilation (as discussed in Chapter 1). This chapter has attempted to describe how cultural and spiritual values are inherent in child rearing. These values naturally apply equally to children with or without disabilities; in many cases, however, the importance of values and faith may be heightened by experiences of childhood disability, as families seek to understand how to best love and care for their children by understanding their needs and capacities. Family-centred practice requires early years professionals to not only accept, but embrace, different ways of understanding children's needs and how best to respond to them (see Chapter 9). As we suggested at the outset, then, the ability to appreciate, engage and work with multiple perspectives in a constructive manner for the best interests of children may be one of the most important skills required of early years professionals.

The excerpts and case studies presented in this chapter are designed to provide insights into possible experiences, perspectives and priorities of

**FIGURE 6.4** CHILDREN AND TEACHER WORKING TOGETHER

*Photo: Rimba II Primary School, Brunei*

families from CALD backgrounds accessing supports within a range of formalised systems that support young children's learning and development. They reflect the importance of both spiritual and cultural practices in caring for children, as well as a level of anxiety felt by families when they feel that these practices are not appreciated, or may be doubted, by professionals working within formal systems. In response, we suggest that relationship-building, particularly between professionals from a mainstream cultural background and families whose beliefs and practices may be quite different, requires reconceptualisation of professional 'responsibility'. As well as being informed about accountability, results and personal safety, professionals and practitioners need to be supported in becoming acquainted with practices that reflect beliefs and values that are 'under the skin, close to the heart and self-relevant' (Shweder et al., 1998, p.727). This is a vital part of understanding the experiences of caregivers from CALD backgrounds caring for children with and without disability.

In essence, inclusion should, by its very nature, 'work' for children from CALD backgrounds, both those with and without impairment. Many of the issues raised in this chapter apply, to greater and lesser extents, to all families who care for and deeply love their children. Throughout this book, the critical role of early years professionals in achieving inclusion has been strongly emphasised. Inclusion is about putting our best efforts into ensuring that *all* children are provided with access to equitable education opportunities, in Australia and internationally, by promoting inclusive practices and by advocating for the needs of children around the world. Most importantly, skilled practitioners and professionals have the capacity to shape the kinds of systems described by Len Barton (2003) as essential for inclusion: systems that are willing to rethink and revise long-established education traditions that may lead to the exclusion of certain groups of children and/or families in society.

# FOR FURTHER REFLECTION

Some organisations that provide early intervention services involving home visiting have policies (such as refusing food when entering family's homes and not removing shoes) designed to protect staff.

1. How might these policies impact on relationship-building with families?
2. How might such policies be modified/acted on in ways that avoid misunderstanding or discomfort for both staff and families?

Genuine relationship-building requires high levels of trust and esteem built on mutual understanding of different points of view. Try to imagine a situation in which your own expectations or beliefs regarding children, families and parenting might be challenged and in which you might react negatively.

1. How could you modify your response to ensure that this would not jeopardise relationship-building?
2. How might you be able to assert your own point of view without causing offence or discomfort?

Based on your own experiences, as well as some of the information provided in this chapter, what initial steps should be taken by professionals and practitioners in building the types of relationships with families described by Moore (2007)? Do you think these steps need to be modified when working with families from CALD backgrounds?

## WEBSITES

www.mdainc.org.au
The Multicultural Development Association of Australia

www.dss.gov.au/our-responsibilities/settlement-and-multicultural-affairs/publications/the-people-of-australia-australias-multicultural-policy
Australia's multicultural policy

www.neda.org.au
The National Ethnic Disability Alliance

www.unesco.org/education/wef/en-conf/Jomtien%20Declaration%20eng.shtm
United Nations Educational Scientific and Cultural Organization World declaration on education for all: Meeting basic learning needs.

http://unesdoc.unesco.org/images/0012/001211/121147e.pdf
The Dakar framework for action: Education for all—meeting our collective commitments.

## REFERENCES

Australia Bureau of Statistics. (ABS). (2013). *Australian social trends*. Retrieved from www.abs.gov.au/AUSSTATS/abs@.nsf/Lookup/4102.0Main+Features30April+2013

Barton, L. (2003). *Inclusive education and teacher education: A basis for hope or a discourse of delusion*. Professorial Lecture, London: Institute of Education, University of London. Retrieved from http://disability-studies.leeds.ac.uk/files/library/Barton-inclusive-education.pdf

Cologon, K. (2012). Confidence in their own ability: Postgraduate early childhood students examining their attitudes towards inclusive education. *International Journal on Inclusive Education*, *16*(11), 1155–1173. doi:10.1080/13603116.2010.548106

Enabling Education Network. (n.d.). What is inclusive education? Retrieved from www.eenet.org.uk/what_is_ie.php

Ferguson, P.M. (2001). Mapping the family: Disability studies and the exploration of parent response to disability. In G.L. Albrecht, K.D. Seelman & M. Bury (Eds). *Handbook of disability*. Thousand Oaks, CA: Sage Publications.

Government of Australia. (2011). *The people of Australia: Australia's multicultural policy.* Retrieved from www.dss.gov.au/our-responsibilities/settlement-and-multicultural-affairs/publications/the-people-of-australia-australias-multicultural-policy

Hodge, N. & Runswick-Cole, K. (2008). Problematising parent-professional partnerships in education. *Disability & Society, 23*(6), 637. doi:10.1080/09687590802328543

Kitayama, S. & Cohen, D. (2007). *Handbook of cultural psychology.* NY: The Guilford Press.

Link, B. & Phelan, J.C. (2013). Labeling and stigma. In C.S. Aneshensel, J.C. Phelan & A. Bierman (Eds). *Handbook of the sociology of mental health* (2nd edn) (pp.525–543). Springer: Dortrecht.

Loreman, T., Forlin, C. & Sharma, U. (2007). An international comparison of pre-service teacher attitudes towards inclusive education. *Disability Studies Quarterly, 27*(4). Retrieved from http://dsq-sds.org/article/view/53/53

Miles, S. & Singal, N. (2010). The Education for All and inclusive education debate: Conflict, contradiction or opportunity? *International Journal of Inclusive Education, 14*(1), 1–15. doi:10.1080/13603110802265125

Moore, T. (2007). The nature and role of relationships in early childhood intervention services. *Second Conference of the International Society on Early Intervention,* Zagreb, Croatia. Retrieved from www.rch.org.au/uploadedFiles/Main/Content/ccch/TM_ISEIConf07_Nature_role_rships.pdf

National Ethnic Disability Alliance (NEDA). (2008). *Refugees and Migrants with Disability and the United Nations Convention on the Rights of Persons with Disabilities.* National Ethnic Disability Alliance. Retrieved from www.neda.org.au/page/publications.html

Nelson, E.A.S. & Taylor, B.J. (2001). International child care practices study: Infant sleeping arrangements. *Early Human Development, 62,* 43–55. doi:10.1016/S0378-3782(01)00116-5

Nsamenang, B. (2008). Constructing cultural identity within families. In L. Booker & M. Woodhead (Eds.), *Early childhood in focus 3—Developing positive identities* (pp.18–20). United Kingdom: The Open University.

Pearson, E. & Tan, J. (2013). *Fulfilling child rights through early childhood development.* South-South Cooperation for Child Rights. Working Paper 3, UNICEF ROSA and UNICEF EAPRO, Kathmandu. Retrieved from http://hlmdelhi2013.org/images/ECD.pdf

Pulerwitz, J., Michaelis, A., Weiss, E., Brown, L. & Mahendra, V. (2010). Reducing HIV-related stigma: Lessons learned from Horizons research and programs. *Public Health Report, 125*(2), 272–81. Retrieved from www.ncbi.nlm.nih.gov/pmc/articles/PMC2821857/

Save the Children. (2008). *Making schools inclusive: How change can happen. UK: Save the Children.* Retrieved from www.savethechildren.org.uk/sites/default/files/docs/making-schools-inclusive_1.pdf

Schaffer, H.R. (1996). *Social development.* Oxford, UK: Blackwell.

Shweder, R.A., Goodnow, J., Hatano, G., LeVine, R.A., Markus, H. & Miller, P. (1998). The cultural psychology of development: One mind, many mentalities. In W. Damon (Series Ed.) & R. M. Lerner (Volume Ed.), *Handbook of child psychology, Volume 1: Theoretical models of human development* (5th ed.). NY: John Wiley.

Skinner, D. & Weisner, T. (2007). Sociocultural studies of families of children with intellectual disabilities. *Mental Retardation and Developmental Disabilities, 13,* 302–312. doi:10.1002/mrdd.20170

United Nations Educational Scientific and Cultural Organization (UNESCO). (1990). *World declaration on education for all: Meeting basic learning needs.* Retrieved from www.unesco.org/education/wef/en-conf/Jomtien%20Declaration%20eng.shtm

UNESCO. (2000). *The Dakar framework for action: Education for all—meeting our collective commitments.* Paper presented at the World Education Forum, Dakar, Senegal. http://unesdoc.unesco.org/images/0012/001211/121147e.pdf

# 7 Gender *Matters* in the Early Years Classroom

*Kylie Smith, Kate Alexander and Audrey D'Souza Juma*

CHAPTER OVERVIEW

This chapter will focus on the importance of gender in early years settings. Current policy documents in Australia and Pakistan that are used by early years professionals are explored in terms of how these documents talk about gender and identity. Three theories of gender construction will be examined; applying these theories in practice will be discussed using examples from early years settings in Australia and Pakistan.

Learning goals for this chapter include:

- Learning about the implications that drawing on diverse theories of gender construction can have for curriculum planning and children's gender identity;
- Exploring the tensions involved in 'doing' gender work with young children;
- Inspiring critical thinking and reflection about gender;
- Exploring understandings of gender in policy documents and the implications these understandings have for children, families, communities and educators.

KEY TERMS AND CONCEPTS

biological theories of gender development

diversity dolls

feminist poststructuralist theories of gender development

hegemony

socialisation theories of gender development

## Introduction

Over fifty years of research has increased awareness and understanding about how gender operates and is 'performed' in early years settings; the research has also established the significance gender plays in a child's development (MacNaughton, 2000; Blaise, 2005). Research evidence supports the argument that gender influences the behaviour of two- and three-year-old children and that by the age of four, children know their gender, and understand the expectations of how family, friends and the other people around them should perform gender (MacNaughton, 2000; Robinson & Jones Diaz, 2006). Everyday early years practices reveal, shape and reinforce gendered identities in young children. This is an area of diversity that presents conflicting challenges and often produces emotive responses from teachers, families and the community. This chapter will explore gender and identity in the early years in relation to children and adults, and understandings of diversity and equality for inclusive early years practice in Australia and Pakistan. The chapter will examine different theories of gender construction and explore how these theories can support teachers to interpret children's experiences in the everyday classroom.

## Policy context

It is important to look at policy when exploring gender matters in the early years, as different areas within the field will draw on and be required to follow different policy documents. This is particularly evident when looking at gender matters across different countries. While the research literature highlights how we understand children's gender identity and development 'matters' in the early years, this research appears not to have filtered into or influenced the recent Australian curriculum documents or the quality standards document that early childhood services in Australia are assessed against. This is not dissimilar in the Pakistani early years policy context, where identity development is acknowledged as important to young children's learning and development, but where, like Australia, there is limited specific discussion about gender identity.

It is interesting for us to compare policy discourses across these two countries, which on the surface appear to be different. The three of us met as colleagues at a research centre at the University of Melbourne in Australia, where we discussed our shared interest in gender. The three of us come from different cultural backgrounds and bring with us diverse lived experiences. As we spoke and wrote about our work around gender in both the Australian and Pakistani contexts we began to see similarities and differences. We have brought our stories together in the hope that they will help illustrate that gender does matter in the early years, and that it matters worldwide.

In 2009 *Belonging, Being and Becoming: The Early Years Learning Framework for Australia* (Department of Education, Employment & Workplace Relations [DEEWR], 2009) was introduced, followed in 2011 by the National Quality Framework (Australian Children's Education & Care Quality Authority [ACECQA], 2011). One of five outcomes for children that these documents advised was that children should develop a strong sense of identity. In reviewing *Belonging, Being and Becoming*, we found there were three instances of the word 'gender', while the words 'she' and 'he' were not used in the document. The first time the word gender occurred was in the Learning Outcomes section in the document where the concept of *Being* is explained:

> *Being* involves children developing an awareness of their social and cultural heritage, of gender and their significance in their world (Outcome 1 in DEEWR, 2009, p.20).

Throughout this document, boxes in different colours appear among the text with definitions of key terms included within. It is in one of these boxes that the word gender appears for the second time, as part of the definition of inclusion:

> Inclusion: involves taking into account all children's social, cultural and linguistic diversity (including learning styles, abilities, disabilities, gender, family circumstances and geographic location) in curriculum decision-making processes (DEEWR, 2009, p.24).

The final time the word gender appears is in the Glossary of Terms, where the above definition for inclusion is repeated (DEEWR, 2009, p.45). The Australian National Quality Standards call for educators to support children to participate in programs as a valued member of a group, and note that this participation should be 'regardless' of gender (ACECQA, 2011). The Oxford dictionary defines 'regardless' as 'without regard or consideration for' (2013, n.p.). Does this mean that gender doesn't matter? Or that gender is not a factor for inclusion or exclusion in play and education? This raises questions about how policy privileges some theories and categories of identity and silences or limits how teachers' attention is drawn to children's gendered identities.

In 2002 the Government of Pakistan's Ministry of Education released a national curriculum framework for early childhood education. Like in Australia, this curriculum framework was developed to support quality early education. It was also a part of an education strategy that was influenced by UNESCO's

Education for All (EFA) movement. While gender identity is not specifically named within this framework there is a statement of objectives, which identifies the purpose of this framework. Three key objectives that link to gender identity and equity are (Government of Pakistan, 2002, pp.8–9):

- To provide for the holistic development of the child, which includes physical, social, emotional, cognitive and moral development.
- To nurture in children a sense of Islamic identity and pride in being Pakistani.
- To nurture tolerance and respect for diversity.

As part of a review of achievements related to EFA and development of a regional plan of action to continue this work, Pakistan, as part of the E-9 countries comprising Bangladesh, Brazil, China, Egypt, India, Indonesia, Mexico, Nigeria and Pakistan, and accounting for more than 50 per cent of the world's population, met in Recife, Brazil from 31 January to 2 February, 2000. At this meeting there was an agreement that one of the goals of the regions was to 'sharpen focus on gender equity' (UNESCO, 2000, p.71).

Australia and Pakistan as signatories of the United Nations Convention on the Rights of the Child have a shared commitment to gender equity as a human right for children. Article 29, on the aims of education, asserts that States Parties (including Australia and Pakistan) agree that the education of the child shall be directed to develop the child's 'personality, talents and mental and physical abilities to their fullest potential' and prepare the child 'for responsible life in a free society, in the spirit of understanding, peace, tolerance, equality of sexes, and friendship among all peoples, ethnic, national and religious groups and persons of indigenous origin' (United Nations Committee on Children's Rights, 1989).

Policy documents are often broad and are written for the reader to interpret and implement. The challenge for us as early years professionals is to identify ways to translate policy into practice and where possible to be able to have a voice in the development of policy. What does this mean for us when gender is not named or has a limited coverage in policy documents? Theory has helped us to explore gender in practice and name how multiple gender discourses are performed in early years settings. Theory has helped us explore ways of documenting how gender identities are performed in early years settings. This has been important in Australia at a time where educators need to document children's strong sense of identity for service assessment in the National Quality Framework.

# Theories of gender construction

There are a number of theories on gender construction that examine how children (and adults) understand themselves and others as girls and boys. To explore gender identity to support equity and inclusion in the classroom, it is important first to understand how different theories help to recognise the diverse ways gender is constructed and how it operates. Theories on gender construction are often discussed in limited ways in undergraduate training and are rarely explored in professional development. Further, there is limited professional literature that brings theories and practices together to make sense of gender identity and how that connects to the Australian framework and National Quality Standards and to the Pakistani framework. This chapter will explore biological, socialisation and feminist post-structural theories to examine ways to make sense of children's performances of gender. We hope that it will cast light on how early years professionals might reflect, examine, document and talk about gender with children, families and colleagues.

## BIOLOGICAL PERSPECTIVES

**Biological theories of gender development** argue that gender differences and inequities are inevitable, unchangeable and natural. This perspective draws on scientific interpretations, where gender identity and development is based on chromosomes and hormones and how these frame and form sexual characteristics and physical development. For example, if a person sees a group of boys playing roughly in the playground they might say, 'boys will be boys' (it's natural). Young children are too young and innocent to understand gender discrimination and need to be sheltered from issues around gender identity and development. Some interpretations of biological theories argue that young children do not have the cognitive capacity to behave in sexist ways so discussing or challenging gender inequity can foster discrimination (Bhana & Farook Brixen, 2006) as it is 'introducing' these ideas and concepts.

**biological theories of gender development:** Based on scientific interpretations, these argue that gender differences and inequities are inevitable, unchangeable and natural.

### *Implications for curriculum development*

If working from a biological perspective, a teacher would not plan specific activities or intervene or challenge behaviours because this is biological and therefore preordained and you cannot change these behaviours. From this perspective, participation in education is 'regardless' of gender as noted in the National Quality Standards.

**FIGURE 7.1** FAMILY

*Artwork by Kaitlyn*

## SOCIALISATION PERSPECTIVE

**socialisation theories of gender development:** Argue that children construct their gender identity through their interactions with their social world.

**Socialisation theories** argue that children construct their gender identity through their interactions with their social world. This means that gender is understood within the cultural context of the child's community. Hughes and MacNaughton (2001) describe these theories of identity construction as a 'sponge model', where children passively absorb what it means to be a boy or a girl through what they see and hear in the classroom, at home, in books, on television, and in the community they live in. Children are modelling and imitating what they see and hear (Blaise, 2005). If we analyse the illustration by Kaitlyn in Figure 7.1 from a socialisation perspective we can interpret this drawing to be of a family with a father, mother, daughter and son. The daughter is wearing a similar outfit to the mother while the son is also wearing a similar outfit to the father. Blaise (2005) notes that the 'most obvious and explicit ways in which children practice their gender and identify themselves as either female or male begins with how they wear their gender and present themselves to others' (p.61). We could interpret the daughter and son in this illustration as modelling and imitating what they see the parent that is the same sex as them wearing to ensure they are doing their gender 'right'.

### *Implications for curriculum development*

If working from a socialisation perspective, a teacher would specifically observe and document how children talked and acted in gendered ways and intervene in sexist or biased behaviours (for information on anti-bias curriculum see Derman-Sparks & ABC Task Force, 1989) by introducing materials and conversations that provide alternative/non stereotypical performances of gender (for example posters, books and encouraging girls to play in the construction area).

## FEMINIST POST-STRUCTURAL PERSPECTIVE

**Feminist poststructuralist theories** argue that identity is multiple, contingent, shifting and political. Identities are changeable, that is they are not fixed or complete and children (and adults) perform their identities in multiple ways attached to their pleasure or desire to be included or accepted as part of a social group (Hughes & MacNaughton, 2001; Davies 2003). Gender, sexuality, culture, 'race', class, ability and religion all intersect and cannot be separated when exploring identities. Feminist poststructuralist theories examine how power is produced and exercised within the local context (e.g. the classroom) to examine how 'the gendered social order is structured and regulated' (Blaise, 2005, p.15). Judith Butler talks about the concept of performativity, where we perform or act out who we are as a category of boy or a category of girl, and that these performances will be different for different groups of people and different in that they will reflect the gendered social order within a specific culture (Butler, 1999). There are diverse ways to perform gender: Connell (2000) argues the 'need to speak of "masculinities", not masculinity' (p.10), highlighting the multiple ways masculinity can be performed, and that 'some masculinities are dominant while others are subordinated or marginalized' (p.10). Blaise (2005) discusses 'emphasized femininity', which is a form of femininity that is 'defined around compliance, subordination, and accommodating the interest and desires of men' (p.58).

**feminist poststructuralist theories of gender development:** Argue that identity is multiple, contingent, shifting and political and that identities are not fixed or complete.

### *Implications for curriculum development*

If working from a feminist poststructuralist perspective, a teacher would examine the multiple ways children perform their gender and critically reflect on and discuss with children and families how these performances support inclusion in the classroom. Teachers could introduce materials to examine with children how power circulates within and through the classroom and the world (for example the children's picture book *The Paper Bag Princess* [Munsch, 1980] portrays a princess navigating power in a variety of ways).

Using two cases studies, one from Australia (Kylie and Kate) and one from Pakistan (Audrey), we will now explore how these perspectives might 'look' or be used to interpret children's gendered identities in everyday classroom events, and how these understandings might support curriculum development. These case studies also show how educators might record and interpret children's sense of gendered identity as outlined specifically within an Australian National Quality Standards policy context (ACECQA, 2011).

## Performances of gender in an Australian early childhood classroom

### CASE STUDY 7.1

### Skirts and sparkly shoes

One morning in a three- to four-year-old preschool room in an inner city long day care centre in Australia, Jasmine, Sarah and Rachel were playing in the book area. They constructed a 'home' community space using small figures, dishes and blocks. During this play the girls swapped shoes with each other (red glittery shoes, silver ballet slippers and sandals with flowers) and were also taking it in turns to wear a pink fluffy cardigan, which belonged to one of the girls. Each of the girls wore a skirt and t-shirt in pink and purple. The girls were being princesses and fairies. Lydia arrived in the room and walked over to the group. She was dressed in a pair of blue jeans and a plain red t-shirt. She said hello to the three girls and sat beside them. The girls looked Lydia up and down and then turned their back on her and continued their play. These four girls had attended the centre for three years together and 'knew' each other. That afternoon I developed a story for a diversity doll named Lilly who I used in the classroom to explore equity issues with the children. The story described a situation where Lilly was told that she couldn't play with a group of girls in her early childhood classroom because she wasn't wearing a skirt. At the end of the story I asked the children what Lilly could do about being excluded from the play. Jasmine said: 'She should wear a skirt the next day.' The other girls in the group all nodded their heads in agreement.

**CRITICAL REFLECTION QUESTIONS**

1. Do you recognise this gender performance episode? Have you seen or experienced similar events or conversations?
2. What gender theories can you or have you drawn on to help you understand children's gender identities?
3. How can or have these understandings influenced your curriculum planning?

**FIGURE 7.2** DIVERSITY DOLLS

*Photo: S. Beadle*

Interpretations of this observation according to different theories of gender development follow.

## INTERPRETING FROM A BIOLOGICAL PERSPECTIVE

These girls are 'typical' girls for their age. They enjoy role-play and are drawing on a popular topic of fairies and princesses.

### *Implications for planning the curriculum*

The teacher could construct a fairy and princess space for the children to further explore their ideas; s/he could also support Lydia to extend her social skills and language skills so that she can be more confident in communicating with the group and gain entry into play.

## INTERPRETING FROM A SOCIALISATION PERSPECTIVE

These girls understand that being a girl is about the 'feminine' clothes you wear—how you look. One of the reasons they understand this is because they have each talked about going to a Disney Princess movie and how 'beautiful' the princess is with her dress and long hair.

### *Implications for planning the curriculum*

The teachers would observe and document children's performances of gender specifically noticing what gendered identities are possible to take up and what is silenced. The teacher could use a **diversity doll** to explore stories of inclusion and exclusion based on gender identity; in doing so, s/he could challenge how Lydia has been excluded based on the clothes she wears and how that is understood in relation to her gender identity. Diversity dolls, adapted from Barbette Brown's work with persona dolls, are specifically designed dolls to be used with children to talk about issues of diversity and inclusion (Brown, 2001). The teacher could also model and place materials and resources in the room to show children that you can be a 'girl' who wears jeans rather than skirts and have important and exciting ideas to contribute to the game.

**diversity dolls:** Adapted from Barbette Brown's work with persona dolls, they are specifically designed dolls used with children to talk about issues of diversity and inclusion (Brown, 2001).

## INTERPRETING FROM A FEMINIST POST-STRUCTURALIST PERSPECTIVE

The current discourse that is operating in the classroom about what it means to be a girl is based on feminised identities, where the girls perform being the docile, delicate female who is desirable. To be included in play means that you need to silence non-feminised identities and engage in the dominant powerful social order.

### *Implications for planning the curriculum*

As above, the teacher could use a diversity doll to explore stories of inclusion and exclusion based on gender identity. S/he could also examine and make visible the multiple ways to perform being a girl and listen to children's understandings of what identities are desirable and why; together, the teacher and children could examine when, where and under what circumstances they perform alternative gender identities. Finally, the teacher and her/his colleagues could critically reflect on themselves as teachers and how they perform their gendered identities in and out of the classroom. They could reflect on the effects for children (and adults) when we ask children to resist dominant stereotypical gender performances, and on how power operates within the classroom.

# Performances of gender in a Pakistani early years setting

In certain contexts, gender can be a contentious topic with emotional overtones, linked to religious interpretations. As early years professionals working with culturally diverse groups of people we need to recognise the effects of gender in the lives of children and how we can then address these with families. This is not always simple since as teachers we need to be culturally sensitive yet at the same time disrupt taken-for-granted ways that marginalise and exclude others based on markers of gender such as dress. Children can be emotionally invested within dominant discourses of gender and therefore it is difficult to disrupt some of these. Within the Pakistani classrooms where Audrey worked, discourses around gender and morality were privileged. The moral way of being, especially for girls and women, was strictly defined and children used regulation to ensure that others did not deviate from the correct way of being, as is evident from the case study below.

**CASE STUDY 7.2**

## Women do not wear pants, it's a sin!

The children have just finished playing in the different learning areas and are sitting on the mat while the teacher passes around the books. It is nearly the end of the school day. A group of girls come and sit next to me. One of them starts a conversation about how she went to Punjab by train for Eid. I join the conversation and ask about the Eid celebrations.

Audrey (to the others): What did you do for Eid?

Heer: I made orange clothes and I bought bangles and shoes.

Tasneem: Me too!

Audrey: What did you wear—a dress, *shalwar kameez, ghagra*?

Heer: I bought an orange pant/shirt

Mirah: Me too.

Audrey: I too wore a pant/shirt.

(They all put their hands on their mouth, say 'Ooooo' and start laughing.)

Audrey: Yes, I too wore a pant/shirt.

Heer: Big girls do not wear pant/shirt.

Audrey: Why?

Heer: Because you will get a sin (Taskeen agrees and says: Yes, sin!)

Audrey: But you also wore a pant/shirt.

Heer: We are little, you know. Small (girls) don't get a sin.

Audrey: So only big (girls) get a sin?

Heer: Yes.

Audrey: Who told you this?

Heer: My father said that if big girls wear pant/shirt they will get a sin.

Tasneem: My father also (told me so).

Mirah: And my brother said that if big (girls) wear pant/shirt they will be sinning.

CRITICAL REFLECTION QUESTIONS

1. What are the values, ideas and beliefs that children in this particular classroom hold about performances of gender?
2. How can you as the teacher, in a culturally sensitive way, disrupt taken-for-granted constructions of gender with children, both girls and boys, in your classrooms?
3. How can you plan your curriculum to ensure gender equity and inclusion of all children?

Interpretations of this observation according to different theories of gender development follow.

## INTERPRETING FROM A BIOLOGICAL PERSPECTIVE

The girls in this classroom enjoy talking about clothes and dressing up, and being a girl means wearing new clothes and bangles. It is 'natural' and 'normal' for this to occur.

### *Implications for planning the curriculum*

The teacher could talk about festivities and have children narrate experiences of celebrating the day; s/he could also set up spaces where children can develop understandings of how other groups celebrate occasions.

## INTERPRETING FROM A SOCIALISATION PERSPECTIVE

These girls have learned from their family, especially their fathers and brothers, that there is certain clothing that is permissible to wear. They have also learned from watching others around them that there are differences in the kinds of clothing worn by adults and children.

### *Implications for planning the curriculum*

The teacher could use books from different cultures to show the diverse range of clothing that is worn in different contexts by both adults and children. S/he could also use clothing from different cultures in the dress up area and have children explore and wear a range of clothing. Another option is to talk with the children about commonalities in clothing with other cultures, for example the *ghagra* is similar to a long skirt worn in other countries.

## INTERPRETING FROM A FEMINIST POST-STRUCTURALIST PERSPECTIVE

The current discourses 'other' people who dress differently and judge them as sinful (see Chapter 3 for a discussion of 'othering'). Children thus produce a 'system of morality' by using the 'officially sanctioned truths' that operate in this society (MacNaughton, 2005). Discourses of morality differentiate between people and normalise the *shalwar kameez* or one's own dress as modest, thus excluding others. Children use the binary 'permissible/sinful' to regulate 'big girls' so they do not wear pants. Regulation is thus used to vocalise a specific 'truth' that circulates in the Pakistani society that women who wear pants are 'sinning'. This is strengthened through the discursive practices of society. Patriarchs, in particular, provide access to religious and moral gendered discourses so that female members of the family can self-regulate themselves and others.

### *Implications for planning the curriculum*

The teacher could use dialogue with children to disrupt the 'othering' taking place and to interrogate the children's constructions of sin. Dialogue can help to bring 'under erasure' children's constructions. The teacher could also provide examples of girls in a variety of clothing to show children that there can be multiple ways of being a girl in other cultures as well as within their own culture. Another option is to think about ways in which we use normalising discourses to regulate ourselves and children and the discourses that we ourselves privilege and invest in. Finally, the teacher could critically reflect on how power operates between men and women in certain cultures and how certain discourses marginalise women through markers of gender such as clothes, the division of labour and tasks that are permissible/impermissible. How do teachers then use this knowledge to disrupt taken-for-granted practices that are embedded within our daily practices?

In the next part of the case study, Audrey outlines how, in this instance, dialoguing with children shifted some of the 'othering' the children engaged in. Reflect on how you would disrupt taken-for-granted notions of gender in a similar situation.

**CASE STUDY 7.3**

## Women do not wear pants, it's a sin!

Continued

Audrey: Haven't you seen on television (Pakistani television) so many women wear pants. Will all of them get a sin?

(Kanwal, who is listening to our conversation, joins in).

Kanwal: I have seen. Girls on television wear pant/shirt.

(Heer and Tasneem giggle again and put their hands on the mouth and say 'Ooooo'.)

Audrey: In other countries too girls wear pant/shirt. Will they too get a sin?

Girls: Yes.

Audrey: But that is their attire (*libas*). Just like we wear *shalwar/kameez* and in India, saris are worn, in some countries pant/shirt is the dress worn. It's not worn as a sin. It is the clothing girls wear.

(The teacher calls the children and the group disperses. After a while Heer comes to me and holds her ears and says, 'Sorry'. I ask for what.)

Heer: Because I said, girls do not wear pants and they do!

Thus, through dialoguing, Heer displayed a slight shift in 'thinking'. She was conscious of the arguments put forward about 'wearing pants' and shifted from the subject position she occupied at the beginning of the conversation.

**CRITICAL REFLECTION QUESTIONS**

1. How might you begin to disrupt markers of gender, for both girls and boys, through dialogue with children?
2. How might you provide alternative truths to children in a culturally sensitive way?
3. Do you recognise how children in this particular classroom use regulation and surveillance? How might children use regulation and surveillance in your classroom?

## And still no one answer: The messiness of engaging with constructions of gender identity

Thus far we have been able to show ways of interpreting performances of gender in the classroom and of observing and documenting how children are developing a strong sense of identity. Further, we have shown ways to use your observations to then plan the curriculum to support equity and inclusion in the early years setting. However, the everyday reality is messy and shifting and contingent. In the same early years setting in Australia an event unfolded that illustrates this complexity.

**FIGURE 7.3** EXCLUSION

*Artwork by Emma*

**CASE STUDY 7.4**

### Cultural capital and My Little Pony

Ella, who was three years of age, had been diagnosed with severe language delays and cognitive processing difficulties. Most of our interpretations of Ella's actions were drawn from developmental theories and our objectives and curriculum plans for her were focused on supporting communication skills to support her inclusion in play with others. Due to her language skills, she was seen and assessed as needing a great deal of support in this. One morning Ella walked into the room wearing a flowing skirt. She twirled in a circle and her skirt flared out and she raised her hand to show a pink, sparkly My Little Pony. My Little Ponies are small toy horses that come in a variety of colours. All the girls converged on her and drew her into their play. At this moment, drawing on a feminist poststructural perspective, I understood Ella as a powerful person who performed her gendered identity with the aid of what Bourdieu (1986) calls cultural capital: that is, resources. Ella used this cultural capital—in this case gendered fashion, popular culture and toys—to gain entry into play and inclusion into the social group. She did not need verbal language as she had cultural capital. But what does that mean for gender equity? How could I challenge or silence feminised stereotypical performances of gender when this was a moment of power for a girl who had been excluded due to her language skills?

**CRITICAL REFLECTION QUESTIONS**

1. Do you recognise this gender performance episode? Have similar events or conversations happened in your experience?
2. How do the children in your experience engage with cultural capital?
3. Can cultural capital be a useful tool for gender equity?

## Challenges and tensions of 'doing' gender work

How do we talk about gender identity with families, co-educators, children and policy makers when there are culturally diverse beliefs and ideas about how children should and can perform who they are as a boy or a girl? This is one of the huge issues and dilemmas in our work in and outside the early years setting. Talking about gender can be a taboo topic. Many people and communities draw heavily on biological perspectives of gender construction. Therefore how children perform their gender is seen as natural and 'natural' is based on dominant **hegemonic** (or stereotypical) masculine and feminine ideologies (or beliefs) (Blaise, 2005; MacNaughton, 2000). Often when children perform different gendered identities, questions and concerns are raised about how children can be changed or taught how to be a 'real' or 'normal' boy or girl. Explicit comments such as 'That boy needs to toughen up', 'I don't want my boy to play with dolls, he'll turn into a sissy' or 'That girl is too rough, she needs to be gentle' reinforce these ideas. Teachers' talk and actions can also reinforce this gendered construction in less explicit ways. For example, what is the reaction and language used when a child falls over? As a teacher do you say to a boy 'Up you hop, you're OK' but to a girl do you go over and say 'Are you OK? Do you need a cuddle?' And how would you work with children who display dominant hegemonic masculinity, particularly from cultures where performances of being a man is fixed and unitary?

**hegemony:** The 'domination of one group over another' (Gramsci, 1971 cited in Blaise, 2005, p.21). In relation to gender this means that there are dominant ways of performing gender that are seen as natural and desirable.

**CASE STUDY 7.5**

## Don't you have shame? Girls listening to music

In an early childhood classroom in Pakistan, Wasif refused to work with any of the girls in the classroom. He came from a conservative setting, from a province in Pakistan where hegemonic displays of masculinity operate and are the correct way for men to perform gender. During an interview with one of the teachers, I carried a small tape recorder in my hand. Wasif watched us from outside the window and when he saw the tape recorder in my hand, he called out to us, 'Don't you have shame, being girls you are listening to music'. To his teacher, this was quite a contradiction since she had observed that at the Eid party, when one of the boys sang a song, Wasif really liked and appreciated it. For her, this posed an issue: 'Look at this that he dislikes girls (singing or listening to music) but when a boy is singing he shows a liking for that.'

**CRITICAL REFLECTION QUESTIONS**

1. Reflect on how Wasif's performance of gender identity marginalises the girls in this particular setting.
2. How could you work with these constructions of masculinity and femininity?
3. How could you plan your curriculum to invite boys like Wasif to be inclusive of others?

# Conclusion

Gender matters in the lives of children; it shapes their identities, beings and becomings. Also evident in this chapter is that gender matters across diverse countries in early years settings. As examined in this chapter and articulated by Bhana and Farook Brixen (2006):

> Young children themselves are actively involved in negotiating their own gender identities ... the particular cultural resources available within the environments are significant in shaping the modes of being male and female and gendered meanings that young children embrace (p.20).

Creating inclusive classrooms where children can position themselves in multiple ways is important. As early years professionals, we can provide children access to multiple and diverse discourses that can challenge the taken-for-granted practices that exclude others. To do so, educators need access to gender theories or discourses. The challenge is working through the uncertainties and messiness of varying ideologies to 'do' gender.

## FOR FURTHER REFLECTION

1. How might you use different theories of gender identity to interpret and document gender identity in your classroom?
2. What are the implications of these different theories of gender identity for how girls and boys can enact (or not enact) their gender identity?
3. How can we change the policy documents to ensure that identity is plural rather than singular, thus supporting children in exploring multiple identities?
4. How can you challenge or silence stereotypical feminised performances of gender when they may present opportunities for power for girls? Should you?
5. How can you challenge stereotypical performances of hegemonic masculinity when they limit or silence other ways of performing how to be a boy?
6. How can you navigate the cultural, social and historical challenges within your context to 'do' gender work?
7. How might the examples shared in this chapter help you to document and report on children's sense of identity development for National Quality Standards?

### EXERCISE

Gender equity work cannot be carried out in isolation from what happens in the home context. Working with families is important if gender equity is to be achieved. To begin a conversation with families about gendered identities you can use some of the following strategies:

- Ask families about what their dreams and wishes are for their child and how they want their child to treat other people—this can help start conversations about caring for others and being respectful.
- Undertake an observation with the family and ask them to interpret what is happening.
- Share your interpretations using a couple of different theoretical lenses.
- Critically reflect on what familes' dominant discourses are, and how these support or silence ways for them to understand gender identity.
- Ask yourself some critical questions such as:
  - What are the risks for families in considering multiple understandings of gender identity?
  - Imagine that a child's extended family, friends and the other families in that child's setting understand gender from a biological perspective. How might the family feel if the child performs multiple gender identities that don't fit in with the 'norm'. Would they be, or feel judged as, 'bad' or 'neglectful' parents who are not teaching their child the 'right' way to be a boy or a girl?

Building partnerships with families takes time and space. It is important to remember this and slow down. Rushing conversations and pushing your own agenda can silence multiple perspectives and can impact families' trust in how you will listen to and respect their ideas.

## WEBSITES

https://extranet.education.unimelb.edu.au/ceiec/DiversityDolls/index.html

http://persona-doll-training.org

These websites provide information on diversity dolls.

www.pinkstinks.co.uk

This website explores products, media and marketing that prescribe heavily stereotyped and limited roles for young girls.

www.amightygirl.com

This website lists books, toys, movies, music and clothing that present positive images of girls.

## REFERENCES


Australian Children's Education and Care Quality Authority (ACECQA). (2011). *Guide to the National Quality Standard*. Retrieved from www.acecqa.gov.au/national-quality-framework

Bhana, D. & Farook, B.F. (with MacNaughton, G., & Zimmermann, R.). (2006). *Young children, HIV/AIDS and gender*. The Hague, The Netherlands: Bernard van Leer Foundation.

Blaise, M. (2005). *Playing it straight: Uncovering gender discourses in the early childhood classroom*. New York: Routledge.

Bourdieu, P. (1986). The forms of capital. In J.G. Richardson (Ed.), *Handbook for theory and research for the sociology of education* (pp.241–258). New York: Greenwood Press.

Brown, B. (2001). *Combating discrimination: Persona Dolls in action*. Stoke on Trent, UK: Trentham Books.

Butler, J. (1999). *Gender trouble*. New York: Routledge.

Connell, R.W. (2000). *The men and the boys*. St Leonards, NSW: Allen & Unwin.

Davies, B. (2003). *Frogs and snails and feminist tales*. Cresskill, USA: Hampton Press, Inc.

Department of Education, Employment and Workplace Relations (DEEWR). (2009). *Belonging, being and becoming: The early years learning framework for Australia*. ACT: DEEWR. Retrieved from www.coag.gov.au/sites/default/files/early_years_learning_framework.pdf

Derman-Sparks, L., & ABC Task Force. (1989). *Anti-bias curriculum: Tools for empowering young children*. Washington, D.C.: National Association for the Education of Young Children.

Government of Pakistan, Ministry of Education. (2002). *National curriculum: Early childhood education*. Islamabad, Pakistan: Government of Pakistan.

Hughes, P. & MacNaughton, G. (2001). Fractured or manufactured: Gendered identities and culture in the early years. In S. Grieshaber & G. Cannella (Eds), *Embracing identities in early childhood education* (pp.114–132). New York: Teachers College Press.

MacNaughton, G. (2000). *Rethinking gender in early childhood education*. St Leonards, NSW: Allen & Unwin.

MacNaughton, G. (2005). *Doing Foucault in early childhood studies: Applying post-structural ideas*. New York: Routledge Falmer.

Munsch, R. (1980). *The paper bag princess*. Toronto: Annick Press Ltd.

Regardless. (2013). In *Oxford Dictionaries*. Retrieved from www.oxforddictionaries.com

Robinson, K. & Jones Diaz, C. (2006). *Diversity and difference in early childhood education*. London: Open University Press.

United Nations Committee on Children's Rights. (1989). *United Nations convention on the rights of the child*. Retrieved from www.ohchr.org/en/professionalinterest/pages/crc.asp

United Nations Educational Scientific and Cultural Organization (UNESCO). (2000). *The Dakar framework for action*. Paris: UNESCO.

# 8 *The Possum Hunt*: A Ghost Story for Preschoolers? Death, Continuity and the Revival of Aboriginality in Melbourne

*Sue Atkinson and Prasanna Srinivasan*

*Sue and Prasanna acknowledge the Wurundjeri people, the traditional owners of the land on which this chapter was written.*

CHAPTER OVERVIEW

This chapter will illustrate the complexities of practising Aboriginal identities in current postcolonial societies, which are still influenced by colonial imageries and representations of such identities. Presented as a robust conversation between Sue and Prasanna, this chapter will highlight how such complexities are reflected within the early years, especially when including Aboriginal perspectives.

Learning goals for this chapter include:

- Positioning social justice and equity as very central to discussions for, about and with Aboriginal identities in early years settings;
- Providing postcolonial language and space to challenge some of the dominant pedagogical practices that aim to include Aboriginal perspectives;
- Highlighting the complexities of using specific terms that create and represent Aboriginal identities in particular ways;
- Enabling early years professionals to go beyond the inclusion of Aboriginal perspectives and thereby work against racism and discrimination.

KEY TERMS AND CONCEPTS

| | |
|---|---|
| Aboriginal Elder | authentic/inauthentic |
| Aboriginal identity | intergenerational skills and knowledges |
| Aboriginal perspectives | postcolonial/ism |

# This chapter: Our postcolonial re-vision

Postcolonial realities present many paradoxical situations and thoughts, which are tangled with our desires to decolonise ourselves, and the inevitability of doing so within the current colonial continuum. Constructs are ideas that are conceived and built through particular concepts. Colonisation is an imposed act that actively engages in not just usurping the cultures and identities of people in lands that the colonisers occupied, it also then (re)constructs identities for the colonised people, cultures and land with an aim to control and dominate. Hence, such (re)constructed identities—that is, the identity constructs that were circulated and articulated for purposes of occupation and control—now become the reality for both the colonised and the coloniser. These colonised spaces are increasingly interrupted and occupied by the voices of the colonised in response to the legacies of colonisation, and are therefore in the era of **postcolonialism**, the period after colonialism.

**postcolonial/ism:** A time and space that represents the end of colonial occupation politically, and yet is traversed by practices that are constantly challenging and challenged by colonial domination (Young, 2001; 2003).

Australia can be seen as a postcolonial space where overt colonisation is politically declared as non-existent, yet we find it difficult to shake off the shackles of identity constructs imposed by the colonisers on us. These identity constructs remain with us even after the demise of explicit colonisation in postcolonial lands. The coloniser and colonised dichotomies, which function as coloniser and colonised, as opposites are fracturing in postcolonial spaces where overt colonial dominance is less evident. But we, as Aboriginal and non-Aboriginal individuals in these spaces, have become reluctantly bound to those identity attributes, as we are subjectified as opposites to and inferior to the 'colonisers'. And, despite the absence of overt colonialism, as postcolonial subjects we think, live and act these colonially (re)constructed categorical identity concepts in our day to day lives. Our postcolonial desire to overthrow the colonial occupation that constrains us by marking identities for us, now becomes tangled with our fear of losing the little bits of culture and identity that colonisation has left us. Thus, the postcolonial space is always ridden with tangles of desires of resistance, and fears of existence.

One such inevitable tangle is in some of the key constructs with which postcolonial identities, especially Aboriginality, is marked and enacted by both Indigenous and Non-Indigenous people. After all, the postcolonial subject is always mindful of the constraints of these constructs and their colonial origin, and yet feels compelled to embrace them in order to reclaim what was lost during colonisation. Hence, in this chapter, we particularly want to challenge and destabilise some of the key constructs such as, **authentic** and **inauthentic** Aboriginality, traditional and ancient skills and knowledges, and colonial/ postcolonial identities. Moreover, we want to engage in this process of

**authentic/inauthentic:** Terms often used to define and contrast types of Aboriginality. They use a colonial framework.

**authentic:** Authentic Aboriginal people can be positioned as living a 'traditional' lifestyle in isolated communities in Central or Northern Australia and are dark skinned.

**inauthentic:** Fair-skinned Aboriginal people living in areas such as Victoria are more likely to be viewed as inauthentic, in being totally assimilated or absent.

**intergenerational skills and knowledges:** Include Aboriginal ways of understanding interactions and relationships not just with human beings, but also with the land, animals and the vast spaces above, below and all around us.

**Aboriginal perspectives:** Aboriginal Perspectives Across the Curriculum (APAC) is a project that aims to broaden and deepen students' and teachers' understanding of Aboriginal cultures and ways of being.

destabilising without simplifying our postcolonial realities. Therefore, we have decided to keep our voices tangled and yet separated by presenting this chapter to the readers as complex dialogues, the type people usually have. I am Sue, an Indigenous Australian, a Yorta Yorta woman whose traditional lands radiate out from the junction of the Goulburn and Murray rivers in north east Victoria. I am Prasanna, from Tamil Nadu within the Indian sub-continent, living as a migrant in Australia.

We believe terms such as, 'authentic/inauthentic Aboriginality' and 'traditional/ancient skills' imposes certain attributes to Aboriginal identities and skills, and restricts the postcolonial realities of these representations. We open our dialogue to challenge how the early childhood field sanctions certain imageries for Aboriginality. Then we continue our conversations to specifically question the terms 'ancient' and 'traditional' that are usually used to refer to Indigenous skills and knowledges, and propose that the term, 'intergenerational skills ' represents the truth more accurately. For us, 'intergenerational skills' reflects the fluidity of these knowledges from the past, to the present and the future. To further illustrate our reluctance in using the term 'traditional', we use a story by the late Aunty Iris Lovett-Gardiner, a Gunditjamara Elder. This story is told in Aboriginal communities to pass on such '**intergenerational skills and knowledges**' and to introduce postcolonial Victorian Aboriginal culture to young non-Indigenous children. We first explain the relevance of having such complex conversations in relation to early years education and postcolonial identities, and then commence our complex dialogues that further highlight our postcolonial paradox.

The inclusion of **Aboriginal perspectives** within the early years curriculum has been strongly recommended by documents that underpin and guide early years practices. The National Quality Framework (NQF) (Australian Children's Education & Care Quality Authority [ACECQA], 2011) and the Early Years Learning Framework (EYLF) (DEEWR, 2009), stipulate the inclusion and respect for Aboriginal perspectives within early years curriculum and practice. However, early years educators largely include Aboriginal perspectives as a dichotomy:'authentic' versus 'inauthentic'. We use three key narratives to elaborate the expectations, and attitudes of such inclusion by early years educators. Using our postcolonial vision, we argue how inclusion based on the dichotomy of authentic versus inauthentic Indigenous identity is problematic.

## LOOKING *AT* OUR POSTCOLONIAL VISION

Before we continue with our narratives, we would like to explore the concept of postcolonialism further and what it means to us: that is, we want to look *at* our postcolonial vision. Postcolonialism is sometimes referred to as the period that comes after the colonial, the end of colonisation of space, peoples and cultures. According to Young (2001; 2003), postcolonialism as a body of theory explores the covert presence of colonial domination and the varied ways through which colonial interests are propagated in decolonised societies. In 'settler colonies' such as Australia, the coloniser has never left, and the 'postcolonial' space continues to be complicated by the continued physical and ideological domination of the coloniser. There is no overt colonial presence, but the coloniser and the colonised constantly challenge each other's presence, thus helping to define their respective identities. Loomba (2005) defines postcolonial subjects (the individuals who perform particular identity practices) as those who challenge cultural domination and discrimination, such as, caste, gender, class, ability and 'race'. Therefore, she adds, postcolonialism can be regarded as a body of knowledge that explores and challenges all forms of cultural domination and discrimination in any given society. According to Fox (1971, cited in Camara, 2008), colonisers create identities for the colonised in particular ways that the colonised begin to see themselves through identity prescriptions created for them by the colonisers. The colonial identity constructs become the postcolonial reality not just for the colonised, but also for the postcolonial subjects who want to engage in the process of decolonisation.

Hence, the movement towards decolonisation for postcolonial subjects occurs within a framework of an often unrecognised survival in spite of massive dislocation and dispossession in the form of a postcolonial reality. We argue that it is the creation of identities that haunts the colonised in postcolonial societies, as the colonised are unable to free themselves from the grips of colonial prescriptions.

We now outline very succinctly Said's work, *Orientalism,* which foregrounded postcolonial thoughts and understandings. This body of work enables us to recognise the operation of colonial thoughts controlling postcolonial identities. According to Said (1978), through the collective notion of 'us' against 'them' (see Chapter 1), a dichotomous relationship is established between one group, the coloniser, against all the rest, the colonised. The coloniser constructs 'Self' as superior, while the 'other', the colonised, as inferior. 'Self' is mature and 'normal', while the 'other' is not only mysterious and exotic, but also volatile and dangerous. The coloniser, 'Self', has institutional force, being in charge of peoples and land due to colonisation, therefore, has the power to dominate, impose and maintain these ideas in varied forms from politics, to education, to everyday realities of 'Self' and the colonised 'other' (Said, 1978). Australia has a colonised past and the very creation of this nation, its identity, and the identity of its people can be argued as colonial creations or 'imageries'. Therefore, our **identities** as Aboriginal Australian and migrant

**Aboriginal identity:** 'An Aboriginal or Torres Strait Islander person is a person of Aboriginal or Torres Strait Islander descent, who identifies as an Aboriginal or Torres Strait Islander and is accepted as such in the community in which he or she lives' (Forrest, 1998 p.101).

Australian are as much the colonial 'imageries', as the image of the Australian, which is also a colonial construction.

## LOOKING *WITH* OUR POSTCOLONIAL VISION

**Aboriginal Elder**: A respected person in the Aboriginal community who has a deep understanding, experience and knowledge of culture.

To illustrate how colonial constructions of Aboriginality permeate early years spaces, this chapter focuses on the story of a much-respected Gunditjamara **Elder**, the late Aunty Iris Lovett-Gardiner. The story is *The Possum Hunt* (Lovett, 1991). Aunty Iris lived in Green Vale in the Western District of Victoria. When she was about nine she used to go hunting for possums in the bush on a Saturday with her younger brother Charlie. This is a gentle but powerful story and the power of her story grows throughout this discussion. Anita,[1] a younger Aboriginal woman, has been sharing Aunty Iris's story for many years as a puppet show, with various props supporting the narrative. Anita feels 'it is vital for children to hear the voices of Victorian Elders as a way of learning about local Aboriginal culture' (conversation with Anita 2013).

Our discussions below analyse the responses of early years professionals to this story and the storyteller. Our dialogue highlights how our Indigenous and migrant identities are intertwined by our colonised past, and yet are untwined within this land. While doing so, we also reflect on our own postcolonial complexities, of how our identities as our realities are imaged and imagined in postcolonial Australia. We struggle with our desire to authenticate our identities in our imaginations in order to break out of the ruins of our colonial past.

# *The Possum Hunt*: A postcolonial telling

The story, which is presented in words and music on audiotape, illustrates the events of one particular Saturday when Aunty Iris plays a trick on Charlie. Aunty Iris Lovett[2] (1991), who in Atkinson, Lovett and Elkner is the narrator of the story, describes Charlie: 'Charlie reckoned he knew a lot about animals ... He did know a lot, too, especially when it came to tracking' (p.11). Next we hear young Charlie voiced by an 'actor': 'there's been an echidna over there, looking for ants. Maybe we can find where he made his burrow in the ground ... And over here, there's emu tracks. Mother emu, maybe looking for water' (p.12).

But it is the scratch marks made by possum claws on a gum tree that lead Charlie into the young Iris's trap: a possum jumps from a hollow in the tree onto his chest. As Iris relates, 'Charlie fell straight down on his back. And the possum got away. We didn't look for any more possums that day. They could stay hiding in their trees till night-time, as far as Charlie was concerned' (p.13).

After making a fire in a clearing Iris and Charlie enjoy the damper and billy tea they brought with them before heading home before nightfall. Later that

**FIGURE 8.1** A SMALL PLAY EXPERIENCE SET UP TO ENABLE CHILDREN TO RETELL THE STORY OF *THE POSSUM HUNT* BY AUNTY IRIS

*Photo: 'Danielle'*

night at home in their tent they wait for their regular visit from a ring-tailed possum that they feed on a mixture of sugar, tea and bread. The story ends with Iris teasing Charlie, 'you better watch out. I think that possum's the same one that pushed you out of the gum tree!' (p.14).

We now share with you the varied responses of early years professionals when this story was presented by Anita, a light-skinned Aboriginal woman. We discuss Anita's recollections of her storytelling experiences, exploring the inherent complexities embedded in the responses of early years professionals, and the influence of these responses on the respectful and equitable position of Aboriginal cultures in Australia. We specifically deconstruct the terms 'ancient', 'authentic' and inauthentic' and how these labels can be strengthening and limiting in expressing postcolonial identities.

## THE 'INAUTHENTIC' ABORIGINAL: IN COLONIAL IMAGERY

Anita was invited in 2012 to share her Aboriginal culture at an early childhood centre. We begin with Anita's recollection of her first visit to that early years setting with Sue, and how her 'cultural story' was received. Anita relates:

> There was a negative atmosphere at the centre from the beginning, as a fair-skinned Aboriginal woman I didn't feel welcome. I shared Aunty Iris's story of the possum hunt with the children and did some face painting.

> After the session I went to see the kindergarten teacher; she said 'The staff thought it would be great if you can do some dance with the children,' I said, 'I had spoken to you about what I would be doing, a contemporary story with traditional aspects.' She replied, 'It would be great if you could play the didgeridoo.' She saw my reaction and said, 'Oh, women aren't allowed to do that are they, do you think you could get a didgeridoo player for tomorrow?' I said, 'So you want a dark-skinned man painted up and playing the didgeridoo?' She said, 'Yes, that's what we want'. I didn't want to go back but I had to as I'd left some materials behind. The next morning when I arrived she just ignored me (Conversation with Anita, 2013).

Sue: For myself as a Yorta Yorta Woman, *The Possum Hunt* highlights the tenacity of Victorian Aboriginal culture. It represents as living a set of ancient skills and knowledges such as tracking and learning about country. It is from being on this country years ago, which Aboriginal children can experience today, years later. Its theme of siblings getting into mischief together is enduring and in its understated way it is about showing how Aboriginal culture has stood the test of time. Despite a devastating dispossession our culture has adapted and survived and remains here, in the land of its origins.

Prasanna: How do you think the story showcases that?

Sue: Although this story is about two young siblings teasing each other and muckin' up as Aunty Iris would have said, it also shows Charlie's skill as a tracker and his knowledge of animals. Iris also shows her knowledge of the bush as she tricks Charlie and both children build their connection to country and care for this country as they spend time together in the bush on Gunditjmara land independent of adults. The way Aboriginal cultural practice has adapted to colonisation may be signified in the damper that Iris and Charlie took with them into the bush and heated up on their campfire. For instance, before colonisation Aboriginal people ground up seeds to make a dough which was cooked on fire. After colonisation white flour was used instead but the tradition of cooking bread on fire continued. Both Aboriginal and non-Aboriginal Australians acknowledge that damper is bush tucker and here in Victoria it is now often made with wattle seeds as we reclaim our cultural traditions. Therefore, for me in many ways the story signifies how we, as Aboriginal Victorians, have kept our identity and adapted to colonisation.

Prasanna: Therefore, for you this storytelling signified not just a hunting experience, but more about intrinsic values and relationship understandings of Aboriginal culture and its morphed presence in postcolonial Australia. But Sue, why 'ancient skills'? Isn't that a colonising term? Didn't our colonisers categorise our knowledges as 'ancient and traditional', and discard these as being less adequate to navigate this modern world? However, against our antiquity, they positioned their 'colonising self' as rational and scientific and therefore more suitable for all individuals and groups to internalise and become 'functional'.

Sue: Yes the term 'ancient' is a vexed one but I feel that this word holds power for me as an Aboriginal person and the claim I have on this place, which has only recently been called Australia. Our antiquities, which are represented in Aunty Iris's story, are skills and knowledges that younger Indigenous people draw on to maintain that continuity with our past. It is this continuity that energises the present and future. Aboriginal people have 'reclaimed' the ancient, as our contemporary cultures can trace this antiquity further back than any other culture. These antiquities are also now becoming a part of Australia's national identity, which draws on the antiquities of Australia along with Europe as the source of that identity, an antiquity that makes it unique.

Prasanna: But Sue, can you notice how the teacher in Anita's experience tried to catch and essentialise the very same 'antiquity' to highlight the inauthenticity of Anita's Aboriginality and the story's too? This is why I feel for me these terms are colonising, as we begin to assert our own identity through the gaze of our coloniser. After all it is colonisation that created Aboriginality and Aboriginal identity for all individuals and groups living in this land when it was colonised. Therefore, what we think of now as 'ancient' is what it was and still is. Because, how do you end or mark what was Aboriginal, because it is both what it was, and as it is now. Tracing the past that was marked with unwarranted violation of Aboriginal space, bodies and identities would necessitate the acknowledgement of 'colonial ugliness'. Most of all, how this ugliness impregnated what was here, and created these 'authentic/inauthentic' dichotomies for Aboriginal identities.

Sue: Yet in a colonial framework this continuity of place and our claim to this place are disavowed. That is the reason why it becomes critical to essentialise our identity as it was with what it is. Aunty Iris's story can be seen as a deep narrative, as it is based on her own experiences, but it is backgrounded by unstated and unacknowledged events around dispossession that had led her to this space. But its depth cannot be seen from a colonial gaze and the continuity of the past into the present. The echoes of a devastating dispossession marked by massacre, sexual exploitation and forced assimilation can be seen in the form of Anita the fair-skinned story teller. She is the survivor whose resistance and defiance of extinction is expressed in her endeavours to keep Aboriginality alive and in place by telling and retelling the story of one of her Elders. In Victoria due to colonial ugliness of the past, there are no surviving people who are 'full bloods', to use the colonial term. Fair-skinned Aboriginal storytellers may be seen as 'inauthentic' but they are also 'ghosts' of their dark-skinned ancestors, an authentic representation of both the colonial ugliness and the postcolonial reality. Because this is what has become of us, we embody the colonial infliction whether we like it or not.

Prasanna: What would you recommend then to move out of that colonial ugliness with the postcolonial reality?

Sue: It is about decolonisation. Decolonisation is about connecting with the ancient in ways that recognise dispossession and destruction and the living power of Aboriginal Elders as teachers of the ancient in a contemporary context. The ancient is slowly becoming visible in Melbourne but in a voice that is often unrecognisable through a colonial lens. But, *The Possum Hunt* was positioned as a potential ghost story when early years professionals placed Aunty Iris's narrative within the framework of the colonial. In such colonial spaces where children learn about Aboriginal identity and culture, an urban Aboriginality is seen to be dead, assimilated into the mainstream, an invisible presence unseen and unheard. Aunty Iris's story demonstrates continuity with an ancient culture alive in Victoria today despite a devastating dispossession. Yet, in the learning space of the colonial her voice is muted. Her voice was rejected as inauthentic by the non-Aboriginal listener, who had the power to construct an authentic Aboriginality solely around dark skins, didgeridoos and dance. In these spaces also lurks the spectre of authentic Aboriginality as the primitive, exotic other with the capacity to elicit fear, discomfort and disconnection in young children. In these colonial spaces Aboriginality is twice the ghost, as 'authentic Aboriginality' and 'inauthentic Aboriginality' are beyond the reach of the child in the 'reality' of their everyday lives: one Aboriginality is dead, at best an evanescent form of distant ancestors, one is too remote to reach, frozen in time in remote Australia.

Prasanna: Precisely; this is why I feel decolonisation is an impossible space for me. How do I decolonise or remove the colonial from the postcolonial reality without acknowledging the 'colonial ugliness' of the past? I would subscribe to colonial discourse if I did that, but we need to move out of the colonial and move with it. That is why our reality is a colonial continuum, and therefore postcolonial reality is complex. I want to keep the past and yet move with it together in the present for the future. Rather than categorising Aboriginality as 'ancient', 'authentic/inauthentic', how do we legitimise this as our current 'reality' as you say? It hurts me when Aboriginality is questioned like that, and for me the question is how do we bring the past to the present and to the future, and not lose it by boxing it in particular ways. I want to move away from 'ancient skills' and call it 'intergenerational skills and knowledges', in order to legitimise its presence and sharing in today's world, just like how our coloniser's skills and knowledges are propagated for all of us to internalise.

Sue: That is not so easy, as when we present our contemporary selves, we are discarded as being less representational of our Aboriginality. As I see it, this 'boxing in' of ancient skills is also a call to reclaim and enclose what has been stolen and almost destroyed. But, I do like your use of the term 'intergenerational skills'. This term raises issues, such as the impact of the restrictions placed on Aboriginal people around the passing on of such skills when they were held in missions. And the impact of the stolen generations on the passing of our 'intergenerational skills' has been huge. I feel it is also an articulation of resistance from an Aboriginality that is complex and fluid and resists being essentialised but still retains some boundaries around identity. As Anderson (1995, p.38), an Aboriginal academic, states, 'our ability to manage change is contingent on being able to project ourselves as coherent entities. This is one of the fundamental paradoxes of being human'. This continued compelling challenge is still faced by Aboriginal people, who negotiate this tension often in order to demystify colonial perceptions.

**FIGURE 8.2** ANOTHER SMALL PLAY EXPERIENCE FOR RETELLING *THE POSSUM HUNT*

*Photo: 'Anita'*

## THE AUTHENTICATED ABORIGINAL: IN COLONIAL IMAGINATION

Below is another act of silencing an Aboriginal voice that Anita shared with Sue some years ago and revisited recently. The manner in which it echoes the reaction to Aunty Iris's story in the first example is striking. The first example occurred six years later than the following one, yet both demonstrate the tenacity of colonial constructions of Aboriginality:

> In 2006, Belle[3] a young Aboriginal woman who was working with me went out to a kindergarten to share Aunty Iris's story. That particular kinder was booked for five sessions, I had a long conversation with the kindergarten teacher before the first session about how we introduce young children to Aboriginal people and culture by talking about 'How we live today'. After Belle had done the session, the kindergarten teacher rang me and said she wanted to cancel the other sessions. When I asked her why, she said because it wasn't what they were expecting and it wasn't what they wanted. They were expecting the children to learn more about culture and I said to her 'I explained to you how contemporary stories like Aunty Iris's reflect culture' ... And she said that they would have liked someone to have played the didgeridoo and taught the children a dance. Then she made a remark about Belle not being very dark ... and it was really confronting for both Belle and myself (Conversation with Anita 2013).

Sue: Anita and I as light-skinned Aboriginal people, often talk about how the authenticity of our Aboriginality is almost always questioned. In the reflection above the colonial 'authority' confronting postcolonial Aboriginality not only denies the postcolonial subjectivity of the storyteller but shapes that subjectivity. Anita recently told me that in the last two years, she not only tells early years professionals before her visit how she will be sharing contemporary Victorian Aboriginal culture but that she has light skin and hair. Anita now feels compelled to explicitly prepare early years professionals for a postcolonial Aboriginality. Our postcolonial Aboriginality not only 'sounds' but also looks 'white'. This is our postcolonial reality.

Prasanna: The colonial grasp on Aboriginal identity still prevails, as they clamp down the definitions of Aboriginality repeatedly within their colonial imageries. Can we ever overcome this and how do we put forth postcolonial Aboriginality with all its past darkness and the present whiteness?

Sue: Anita also talks about the possibility for early years spaces to be disrupted by a postcolonial Aboriginality. Here, Anita talks about taking Aunty Iris's story after some years to the same kindergarten and about how the kindergarten teacher's response had shifted.

> One teacher didn't want me to come back and do Aunty Iris's story for a second year because I think she wanted something more traditional, like someone playing the didgeridoo. But I noted later that this teacher had a change of heart and had grown in the way she saw things. When I returned to the centre two years later I got great feedback. I feel the teacher may have been influenced by a staff member new to the centre who was proactive around reconciliation (Conversation with Anita, 2013).

Sue: This 'change of heart' may have come when reflecting on Anita's voice with a new, non-Aboriginal colleague in a dialogic space where the new staff member challenged the discourse of the colonial and allowed the colonised to be heard in its contemporary form. Although the presence of the 'ghosts' of colonisation may have had the potential to influence the heart and mind of the initially resistant teacher, it may have been the lens offered by the new staff member that helped her see these 'ghosts' with more clarity. Therefore the non-Indigenous authority that initially stilled the voice of the colonised retained the power in this dialogic space.

Prasanna: The colonised still do not have the power and space to disrupt the colonial imagery. It had to come from non-Indigenous practitioners in positions of authority for postcolonial Aboriginality to be authenticated. Colonisation as a process creates and maintains the identities of and for the colonised. Therefore, authentic/inauthentic are both in the grasp of the coloniser. For me my presence here in Australia is even more complex. Whether I speak against 'colonial ugliness' or postcolonial Aboriginality, I will only be speaking *about* Aboriginal experiences of the past and the present, and never *as*. As a migrant from the Indian sub-continent, I share histories of colonisation with you. And yet, I feel by being here in Australia and speaking for and about postcolonial Aboriginality, I am propagating and doing as much damage as my coloniser did to Aboriginal identities. When and how do you think we, as colonised people, should move together with our coloniser?

Sue: As colleagues and friends we *speak together* about our mutual experiences and understandings of colonisation and I believe this is a powerful part of the decolonisation process. You recognise the power of colonisation and its ugly legacy here in Australia and you understand how the Aboriginal Australian experience both overlaps and is yet distinct from your own. Your voice also challenges colonisation and strengthens mine. The project of decolonisation cannot come from Aboriginal Australians alone, it must come from us as a community of decolonisers including early years professionals and the children they teach. At the same time recognising the authority of the Aboriginal voice is a process, which we both know can never be complete.

## THE AUTHENTIC/INAUTHENTIC REALITIES: POSTCOLONIAL TRANSLATIONS

In early years settings teaching should happen from a dialogical position. Such a position can create spaces for dialogues and power sharing that recognise a living Aboriginality and destabilise colonial understandings of deceased

Aboriginalities. In these spaces a place is created with moral intent for Aboriginal voices to be heard and to explore what has been silenced or hidden. In one such setting, Anita has been telling the story of *The Possum Hunt* for about eight years. The teacher, through a postcolonial lens, supported Anita's broad engagement with social justice. In the following scenario the teacher Danielle[4] describes her reaction to Aunty Iris's story as shared by Anita:

> This story is fantastic, it's a story of Victoria, a story of this place. It's a story of people I might meet in the street today. I like the fact that it is not tokenistic, it's about two children being at home in the bush environment and looking after it, it's real. It is local knowledge and the children and I can relate to it. The children may not have experienced the bush in this way but they understand it from the perspective of a brother and sister, there is that love and being cheeky. The voice and the presence of the Elder, Aunty Iris, really comes across. Many children here are from diverse cultural backgrounds, for example Vietnamese, South Sudanese and Elders are respected in their cultures too. We also see the story in its context with Anita talking about the Aboriginal flag and the diversity of skin colours Aboriginal people in Victoria can have (Conversation with Danielle, 2013).

Sue: I think Danielle's reading of the story is a postcolonial one in that she positions the story in a way that recognises the place of 'intergenerational knowledges' that animate Aboriginality here, now and in the 'everyday'. In placing Aboriginal culture in the realm of local knowledge that is here in 'this place', Danielle has moved beyond colonial constructions of Aboriginality as distant or absent representations with momentary excursions into the exotic. Anita tells me that she feels welcome and valued in this setting, as she has maintained a respectful dialogue with this teacher for almost a decade. This lies in contrast to the first narrative, where colonial and postcolonial constructions of Aboriginality are positioned in opposition as monologues. There the colonial voice was dominant and disempowering of our postcolonial realities. The fact that Aunty Iris's story has also been translated into Vietnamese in Danielle's centre adds another dimension to the project of decolonisation. It reflects the relationships between multiculturalism and Aboriginal rights and the united struggle for recognition and power of place. Anglo–Celtic Australia does not carry the responsibility for decolonisation alone. Sixth-generation Anglo–Celtic Australians and new arrivals are all living on Aboriginal land.

> When I introduce the story and later when I ask questions of the children it is translated into Vietnamese. Part of the story is also translated but it's so visual it doesn't need a full translation. I visited Aunty Iris before she died and told her that her story had been translated into Vietnamese and she was so happy to hear this (conversation with Anita 2013).

Prasanna: I am still hurt by the racism that many Aboriginal Australians endure in postcolonial Australia. Danielle's action might position the story from the past in the present to move beyond the colonial imageries of Aboriginal identity. However, I am still not convinced that such actions alone can eliminate racism and discrimination. Racism or 'race' construct in Australia operates in two ways. Firstly it constructs dark-skinned people as less, inferior and/or outside the Australian identity. Here, dark-skinned or non-white individuals are regarded as not Australians, and are also 'othered' using discriminatory remarks. Secondly, the very same 'race' construct is used to 'authenticate' Aboriginal identities. Here, one's Aboriginality is questioned as in Anita's case, when the individual is not 'dark' enough in terms of the very same 'race' construct, and is also 'othered' because of the very same 'darkness'. Therefore, as important as it is to respectfully represent Aboriginal identity through acts such as storytelling, it is also important to work against those 'race' constructs. These 'race' constructs are the ruins of our colonial past and we all need to consciously work against these.

Sue: I agree that the telling of such stories alone will not eliminate racism. I doubt that racism can be eliminated altogether. But in order to actively challenge racism and diminish its power, early years educators need to consciously interrogate those colonial concepts of 'othering', which subscribe to colonial imageries of authenticity that still persist in early years spaces. Reconceptualisation of colonial constructions of Aboriginality is a complex undertaking, and it is necessary to deeply reflect upon and critique what is accepted as knowledge in forming an ideological and 'physical' connection to local Aboriginal communities.

## Our postcolonial challenges: Moving beyond translations

In exploring the responses of early years professionals to *The Possum Hunt* it is evident that colonial constructions of Aboriginality have significant consequences for the way Aboriginal perspectives are constructed within the early years curriculum. The challenge for early years professionals is to examine connections between colonisation, dispossession, racism and the silencing of the voices of Aboriginal people. In marginalising these voices through questioning their authenticity, the very authenticity of the inclusion of Aboriginal perspectives in the early years curriculum is not only undermined but helps perpetuate the Aboriginal peoples' dispossession. Aunty Iris's story of *The Possum Hunt* will continue to be told and simply refusing to hear her will not silence her voice and the narrative of colonisation and survival that it represents. Early years professionals need to position stories such as *The Possum Hunt* in ways that challenge racism and the colonial constructions of Aboriginality. Only by doing so, can we create movements towards a more 'just' and 'equitable' inclusion of Aboriginal perspectives in the early years curriculum.

Finding those paths that enable us to move together will always remain a challenge until we stop and ask ourselves, 'How do we hold each other's hands and move together in search of justice and equity?' We present the following questions and particularly encourage current early years professionals to reflect on them, as we believe such reflection is one of the paths towards that movement.

# FOR FURTHER REFLECTION

1. How has this chapter helped you to reconceptualise your own perspectives around Aboriginal identity and culture? Has this chapter helped you to reflect on your own position within the current colonial framework, one that that gives you the power to judge and control what is authentic knowledge?
2. With your knowledge of the relationship between the colonised and the coloniser, how do you now read stories such as Aunty Iris's? What role do stories such as Aunty Iris's, which are narratives of contemporary Victorian Aboriginality, play in overturning dominant ways or representing Aboriginality?
3. Thinking about your philosophy and practice around including Aboriginal perspectives in the curriculum, how are you working to challenge concepts of Aboriginal authenticity and inferiority with children? Most of all, how are you working with young children to challenge racism?

## WEBSITES

www.racismnoway.com.au

This website provides resources for educators to enable children and their communities to become aware of and work against racism for better social cohesion and harmony.

www.reconciliation.org.au/home/resources/factsheets/q-a-factsheets/indigenous-perspectives

The website provides an overview of why and how to teach Indigenous perspectives in Australian schools in a manner that acknowledges Indigenous presence and heritage in Australia respectfully.

http://antar.org.au

A website that highlights the importance of working together with and for the rights of Australia's First Peoples, and how we as individuals and groups can mobilise these causes for a socially just present and future.

www.snaicc.org.au

The Secretariat of National Aboriginal and Islander Child Care (SNAICC) represents the interests of Aboriginal and Torres Strait Islander children and their families across Australia. Their website contains a wealth of resources and information for Aboriginal and Torres Strait Islander people and the broader community around health, education and care.

www.det.wa.edu.au/aboriginaleducation/apac/detcms/navigation/apac/?oid=MultiPartArticle-id-9193776

Developed by the Department of Education, Western Australia, this website is a valuable resource that aims to deepen students' and teachers' understandings of Aboriginal culture and identity. It has resources and lesson plans that teachers can access to include Aboriginal perspectives in their daily pedagogical practices and curriculum.

## NOTES

1 Anita is a pseudonym

2 Aunty Iris was known as Aunty Iris Lovett in the earlier part of her life.

3 Belle is a pseudonym

4 Danielle is a pseudonym

## REFERENCES

Anderson, I. (1995). Reclaiming Tru-ger-nan-ner: De-colonising the symbol. In P. Van Toorn & D.L. English (Eds). *Speaking positions: Aboriginality, gender and ethnicity in Australian cultural studies* (pp.31–42). Melbourne: Victorian University of Technology.

Australian Children's Education & Care Quality Authority (ACECQA). (2011). *National quality framework*. Retrieved from www.acecqa.gov.au/Quality-Areas

Camara, B. (2008). *Marxist theory, Black/African specificities, and racism*. New York: Lexington Books.

Department of Education, Employment and Workplace Relations (DEEWR). (2009). *Early years learning framework: Belonging, being, becoming*. ACT: DEEWR. Retrieved from http://foi.deewr.gov.au/system/files/doc/other/belonging_being_and_becoming_the_early_years_learning_framework_for_australia.pdf

Forrest, S. (1998). 'That's my mob': Aboriginal identity. In G. Partington (Ed), *Perspectives on Aboriginal and Torres Strait Islander education* (pp.96–105). Katoomba, NSW: Social Science Press.

Government of Western Australia. (2010). *Aboriginal Perspectives Across the Curriculum (APAC)*. Retrieved from www.det.wa.edu.au/aboriginaleducation/detcms/navigation/category.jsp?categoryID=7059845

Loomba, A. (2005). *Colonialism/postcolonialism*. New York: Routledge.

Lovett, I. (1991). The possum hunt—Script of Aunty Iris's story. In S. Atkinson, I. Lovett, & B. Elkner (Eds). *Story music and movement: Aboriginal child care support materials* (pp.11–14). Fitzroy: Victorian Aboriginal Child Care Agency.

Said, E.W. (1978). *Orientalism*. New York: Vintage Books.

Young, R.J.C. (2001). *Postcolonialism: An historical introduction*. Oxford: Blackwell .

Young, R.J.C. (2003). *Postcolonialism: A very short introduction*. Oxford: Oxford University Press.

SECTION 3

# Working Together for Inclusion

# 9 Family-Centred Practice for Inclusive Early Years Education

*Loraine Fordham and Christine Johnston*

CHAPTER OVERVIEW

The focus of this chapter is describing family-centred practice and explaining how it can be successfully integrated into the work of early years professionals in all inclusive early years settings.

Learning goals for this chapter include:

- Defining family-centred practice;
- Understanding the fundamental components of family-centred practice;
- Examining the effect of family-centred practice on families;
- Determining the place of family-centred practice in the Early Years Learning Framework;
- Considering what it means to be family-centred early years professionals.

KEY TERMS AND CONCEPTS

effective help-giving

family-centred practice

family–professional partnership

individualised practice

social support

# Introduction

Since the publication of the seminal work *Enabling and Empowering Families* (Dunst, Trivette & Deal, 1988) family-centred practice has been considered 'best practice' in the field of early childhood intervention for young children with disabilities and their families. In this chapter we will make clear how family-centred practice can be an integral part of inclusive early years settings for all children and their families. In order to do this we will first describe what is meant by family-centred practice, outlining its fundamental components and practices; in doing so we will refer to key international and Australian research with children and families.

In the second section we will focus on how we do family-centred practice, by outlining what inclusive family-centred early years education means for families, by explaining how being family-centred relates to the national curriculum, *The Early Years Learning Framework* (EYLF) (Department of Education, Employment & Workplace Relations [DEEWR], 2009a), and, finally, by describing what it is to be a family-centred early years professional. We will use examples of children and families in inclusive early years settings to illuminate our key points.

# Family-centred practice

**family-centred practice:** A set of values, attitudes and approaches to providing services for children with disabilities and their families.

The term **family-centred practice** arose in the 1980s from early intervention programs in the United States and gradually spread to Australia. It refers to both the 'what' and the 'how' of service delivery and specifically it encompasses a 'particular set of beliefs, principles, values and practices for supporting and strengthening family capacity to enhance and promote child development and learning' (Dunst, 2002, p.139).

Family-centred practice is the hallmark of family support programs as it implies that families have the ultimate control over decisions about their children (Allen & Petr, 1996; King, King, Rosenbaum, & Goffin, 1999). It recognises the family as constant in the child's life, expert on their child's abilities and needs, and as a unique and capable unit (Dunst et al., 1988: Rosenbaum, et al., 1998).

In his review of the conceptual and empirical foundations of family-centred practice, Carl Dunst (1997) identified ten 'core practices most often described as key features of a family-centred approach to practice' (p.78). Intrinsic to these practices is the notion that services are provided to families in ways that are individualised, flexible, supportive, sensitive and respectful (Palisano et al., 2012). In sum, they specify the 'what' of family-centred practice. These practices are summarised in Table 9.1.

**TABLE 9.1** TEN CORE PRACTICES OF FAMILY-CENTRED PRACTICE

| Family-centred practice |
|---|
| Treat families with respect |
| Work in partnership and collaboration |
| Share information completely and in an unbiased manner |
| Be sensitive and responsive to family diversity |
| Promote family choices and family decision-making |
| Base intervention on family-identified desires and needs |
| Provide individualised support and resources |
| Utilise a broad range of formal and informal supports and resources |
| Employ competency enhancing help-giving styles |
| Enhance family strengths and capabilities |

*(Source: adapted from Dunst, 1997)*

## Fundamental components of family-centred practice

Family-centred practice comprises a number of fundamental and unique components. The four described in detail below are those we believe to be most relevant for inclusive early years education. They are *the family–professional partnership*; *the nature of help-giving*; *individualised practice*; and *mobilising community supports and resources.*

### *The family–professional partnership*

At the heart of family-centred practice is the partnership between the family and the professional. The collaborative nature of this partnership reflects the mutual, respectful and goal-driven cooperation between all people undertaking the specific task.

**family–professional partnership:** Professionals working respectfully alongside parents and other family members, helping families achieve their goals for their child and/or family.

The fundamental component of cooperative, collaborative interactions between families and professionals is effective communication (Blue-Banning, Summers, Frankland, Nelson & Beegle, 2004). In their qualitative study with 200 family members and professionals, examining the components of **family–professional partnerships**, Blue-Banning et al., (2004) identified six dimensions of family–professional partnerships: communication, respect, trust, commitment, equality and skills. Of the six dimensions, study participants identified communication as a vehicle that facilitates the other five dimensions. Specifically, high quality communication was described as being positive, understandable and respectful to all members. Communication also needed to be at a level that enabled coordination and understanding. Indicators of good communication skills were identified as 'sharing resources, being clear, being honest communicating positively, being tactful, being open, listening, communicating frequently and coordinating information' (p.174).

The notion that early years professionals should have effective communication skills is not a new one. However, in family-centred practice one aspect of the communicative relationship is fundamentally different: the key difference is a change in the power balance. It requires a shift from a communicative interaction where the professional has the power over the family member(s) to an interaction *between* parents and professionals built on equality, mutual regard and shared decision-making (Dunst & Dempsey, 2007; Winton & DiVenere, 1995).

**FIGURE 9.1** LISTENING TO EACH OTHER?

*Artwork by Kaitlyn*

However, it seems that too frequently partnerships between families and professionals fall short of the recommended practice (Summers et al., 2005). Issues can arise with building trusting relationships, delineating roles and responsibilities and providing the right type and level of support (Winton & DiVenere, 1995). In addition, family members and professionals come from diverse cultural backgrounds that have shaped their respective values, beliefs, attitudes and communication styles (Bailey, 1991). A necessary requirement of each professional is to truly believe that parents are equal partners, that they are the experts on their child, that they can make the best decisions for their child and family and that they have the right to do so (Dunst & Trivette, 1996; Viscardis, 1998).

Forming parent–professional relationships is difficult, as Janice Fialka (2001), the mother of a child with developmental disabilities, attested. She described the forming of such partnerships as more challenging than parenting her son, and identified five dimensions that inevitably creep into 'the dance of partnership' (p.21). These are dimensions that parents and early years professionals should recognise, discuss and address together. The first of these is choice—choosing to dance in the first place. Fialka stated that professionals come to the dance ready to partner up with children and families but parents do not; they did not plan this and they did not choose it. Choosing to join the partnership dance requires that parents acknowledge (often again and again) that their child has a disability. The second step is one of forced intimacy—parents are 'often forced into an instant closeness' with strangers and find themselves revealing their pain, guilt, shame and tears 'in front of people whose last names we don't know' (p.23). The third step in the dance is the identification of partners: Fialka stated that early intervention professionals enter the disability field trained to partner up with children but since it is the parents' lives that have been changed the most, the primary partnership should be with them. The fourth step relates to role expectations and deals with the lack of clarity around who leads the partnership. Here Fialka encouraged the notion of 'unique contributions' to the partnership rather than expert ones (p.25). The final dimension in the dance of partnership deals with the different priorities often held by parents and professionals. Fialka urged professionals to enquire about and actively listen to the perspectives of parents so that 'recommendations can be relevant, practical and manageable' (p.26).

**CRITICAL REFLECTION QUESTIONS**

1. Think of a situation that you have been in where parents and professionals worked together. How successful was the partnership? What made it successful/unsuccessful?
2. What would have made it more effective?

## *The nature of help-giving*

**effective help-giving:** Having good technical knowledge and skills, positive attitudes and behaviours, the ability to share decisions and actions with families, and a willingness to collaborate to ensure that goals are achieved.

A second requirement central to the implementation of a family-centred approach is for early years professionals to employ skills that are both **help-giving** and empowering to families (Dempsey & Dunst, 2004; Dunst & Trivette, 1996; Dunst et al., 1988).

On the basis of their studies into the nature of help-giving professional skills, Dunst and Trivette (1996) identified three elements of help-giving. The first of these is the early years professional's specialist knowledge and skill, which assists in the implementation of appropriate intervention. The other two elements are known as the relational and participatory components of family-centred practice. The relational component comprises having good professional skills such as being an active listener, having compassion, empathy and respect, and being non-judgmental, as well as having positive professional beliefs and attitudes towards families, specifically those that support family strengths and capabilities.

While these relational skills can positively influence family wellbeing, on their own they are not sufficient to enhance family capabilities and develop new competencies (Moore, 2001): participatory skills are also needed. These comprise practices that are tailored to family concerns and priorities and that also facilitate family choice, decision-making, collaboration and action in order to achieve desired goals and outcomes. Dunst (2002) confirmed that it is the simultaneous use of both types of skills (relational and participatory) that 'distinguishes the family-centred approach from other approaches to working with families' (p.139).

## *Individualised practice*

The participatory elements of family-centred practice include practices that are tailored to each family's needs and priorities. Contemporary Australian families are couples with children, sole parents, step families, blended families, same-sex families and extended kinship families. It is important for early years professionals to be aware of family diversity to enable a focus on **individualised practice**. Individualised practice is realised by way of the creation of a unique Individual Family Service Plan (IFSP) for every child and family. Individualised planning is paramount if services are to be relevant and effective for children and their families. Ideally, the IFSP process sees the enactment of the help-giving, collaborative, family–professional partnership. In creating an IFSP, early years professionals support and enable the family to firstly identify their child's and family's strengths and needs, and subsequently to ascertain the goals they wish to work towards, over a chosen time period (see Chapter 11 for exploration of the IFSP process).

**individualised practice:** Treating every child and family member as a unique individual and using help-giving practices that are customised to meet each family's needs and priorities.

### *Mobilising community supports and resources*

It is now very well known that providing **social support** to families with children with disabilities is critical to the success of early intervention, that it helps families develop coping strategies and that it directly influences children's wellbeing as well as that of their families (Dunst et al., 1997; Guralnick, 2004).

**social support:** Any type of assistance provided by a member of someone's close personal network that positively helps the recipient.

An extensive review of the research into the influences of social support by Dunst, Trivette and Jodry in 1997 revealed the following related findings:

1 Support provided by informal networks has the greatest positive effect on child and family functioning;
2 Social support functions as intervention;
3 Support is most effective when it is given in response to an indicated need;
4 Support from personal networks has a more positive effect when it is characterised by closeness, caring and capacity building; and
5 When professional help-giving mirrors the features of informal support networks there is greater impact on parental self-efficacy and empowerment (Trivette, Dunst, Boyd & Hamby, 1995).

Another unique component of family-centred practice is the notion of mobilising community resources. Essentially this means that helping children and families to connect with their local community resources enhances communication, interaction and support among community members. This in turn assists families to form strong, interdependent, capacity-building connections in their local environment (Dunst & Trivette, 1994).

Recent research examined the extent to which capacity-building family-centred practices (namely effective help-giving, addressing individual family needs and strengths, and mobilising supports and resources) influenced parent–child interactions and child development (Dunst, Trivette & Hamby, 2007; Trivette, Dunst & Hamby, 2010). The research found that help-giving directly affected parent self-efficacy beliefs and wellbeing and indirectly affected parent–child interactions and child development.

**CRITICAL REFLECTION QUESTIONS**

1. In their already busy days, how do early years professionals find the time to work with families and set up meaningful partnerships with them? What processes can be put into place to ensure that families are engaged in their children's learning and are involved in goal setting?
2. What can early years professionals do to assist families to build strong connections within their local community? How might we work with families from socio-economically disadvantaged, refugee or non-English speaking backgrounds to forge strong community support networks?

**FIGURE 9.2** FAMILIES

## What family-centred practice means for families

At this point, having looked at the 'what' of family-centred practice, it is useful to pause and think about 'why' those working in the early years have concluded that a family-centred approach is best practice. The rationale that can be offered is both philosophical and practical. Hanson and Lynch (1995) argue that, as the most important people in the child's life, parents have both the moral and legal right to make decisions about their child, including those related to the child's education: this is a philosophical argument. On a practical level, they also note that parental input and carry-over in the home—that is, consistency—is essential if optimal effects are to be achieved.

An Australian study by SCOPE in 2004 found that families prefer family-centred services and support over professional-centred services because they see them as having clear benefits for their whole family. These benefits are: i) Increased satisfaction with their parenting role; ii) feelings of empowerment; and iii) enhanced parental and family wellbeing.

Why this might be so is perhaps best understood by considering the ecocultural approach adapted by Bernheimer and colleagues from Bronfenbrenner's (1992) model of social-ecology (see for example Bernheimer, Gallimore & Weisner, 1990; Bernheimer & Weisner, 2007; Gallimore, Weisner, Kaufman & Bernheimer, 1989; Weisner, 2002). In this approach, families are seen as 'actively and proactively responding to the circumstances in which they live, and building and organising environments that give meaning and direction to their lives' (Bernheimer & Weisner, 2007, p.193). Their approach arose from the remark of a parent panellist at a conference on disability who said:

> Professionals kept asking me what my 'needs' were. I didn't know what to say, I finally told them, 'Look, I'm not sure what you're talking about. So let me just tell you what happens from the time I get up in the morning until I go to sleep at night. Maybe that will help?' (Bernheimer & Weisner, 2007, p.192).

By talking with families about their daily routines such as how they manage mealtimes and bath times, we can begin to understand the impact that a child's disability or impairment might have, not just on the child but on the family as a whole.

When professionals work in respectful partnerships with families (including families whose children have a disability and families wherein the parents have a disability), they are doing two key things. Firstly they are acknowledging families' capacities to manage the challenges that arise from raising a child with a disability. And, secondly, they are demonstrating a willingness to learn from the families about how best to meet the child's needs while maintaining the daily routines that are central to the life of the family as well as to the early years setting. Working together with families, we can identify where blocks to daily routines are occurring and jointly decide how to get around them. Bernheimer and Keogh (1995, p.430) perhaps put it best when they said that our task as professionals is to 'reinforce, rather than fray, the fabric of everyday life.' Our aim, then, must be to help families to adjust their daily routines, but not to change them altogether.

**CRITICAL REFLECTION QUESTION**

The discussion so far has tended to suggest that all parents and families want to take an active role in deciding what goals should be set for their child. But what if this is not the case? What if the parents want to leave it to the early childhood educator to make the decisions?

**CASE STUDY 9.1**

## Samir's Story

Samir is four years old and came to Australia with his family two years ago as part of Australia's Humanitarian Program. Originally from the Sudan, his family lived in a refugee camp in Ethiopia for seven years. Samir has two surviving older brothers, Mohammed (now 10 years old) and

David (now eight). All were born while their parents were living in the refugee camp. Since coming to Australia they have had another child, Grace, who is now 18 months old.

Formerly farm workers with little formal education, the parents found what work they could selling produce within the camp. On arriving in Australia they were fluent in Arabic and Dinka but spoke no English. They have since learnt to speak English quite well but have difficulty reading it. Samir's father has a job at a local supermarket and is studying at TAFE to improve his spoken and written English. They are part of a strong Sudanese community in the area where they live and are supported by its members.

Life in the camp had little structure and there was no opportunity for the two older boys to attend school. Mohammed and David found the structure of school difficult initially and needed support within the classroom for the first 12 months. They are now progressing well.

Samir's mother has been attending a supported playgroup for members of their community with Samir and Grace for the past 12 months. Samir has started attending preschool three days per week and is enjoying the experience. His mother drops him off and picks him up every day. He is generally a happy and outgoing child and has made some friends with whom he plays lots of physical games. He is not interested in books or quiet play and finds it difficult to sit still during circle or story time.

The early years professionals decide that they need to find ways of engaging Samir to increase his attention span and ability to participate in these group activities. They would like to get Samir's mother involved in their discussions about what to do but have found her very shy. They know she is eager for her children to succeed educationally but wonder whether she would find it threatening to be asked to talk about Samir's development and would prefer to leave the decisions to them.

**CRITICAL REFLECTION QUESTION**

How should the early years professionals proceed? Set out an action plan that will enable the staff to engage Samir's family in his preschool experience.

### *Family-centred practice and the Early Years Learning Framework*

The EYLF (DEEWR, 2009a), as discussed throughout the book, is centred on three themes: Belonging, Being and Becoming. These place the child firmly within the family and the community as is evidenced by the five outcomes, which are:

1. Children have a strong sense of identity;
2. Children are connected with and contribute to their world;
3. Children have a strong sense of wellbeing;
4. Children are confident and involved learners; and
5. Children are effective communicators.

Furthermore, the EYLF places considerable emphasis on the role of the family and the ways in which parents and carers should be involved in the children's early education experiences, as partners, not spectators. Indeed, the *Information for Families* guide that was developed to accompany the EYLF states, '[educators] will use the Framework in partnership with families, children's first and most influential educators, to develop learning programs responsive to children's ideas, interests, strengths and abilities' (DEEWR, 2009b, p.1).

It goes on to state that '[e]ducators will work with you in order to get to know your child well. They will create a learning program that builds on your child's interests, abilities, and keep you in touch with your child's progress' (DEEWR, 2009b, p.2).

The intent to involve families in a meaningful way in their young children's learning is clear. However, here, too, there is the danger that in its implementation early years professionals may (like their early intervention colleagues) find themselves sometimes simply 'talking the talk' and not 'walking the walk'. The key phrases in these two quotes above are *partnership with families* and *educators will work with you (families)*. Early years professionals need to ensure that their interactions with parents are those of partners in the learning enterprise. We argue that this approach is important for all early years professionals, whether they are working in prior-to-school early years settings or in the early years of school.

## What it means to be a family-centred professional

To embrace both the relational and participatory components of family-centred practice, early years professionals need to do much more than listen to parents. They need to be *led* by them. At its best, family-centred practice means accepting and acknowledging families as equal partners in the education of their child. As we have discussed throughout this chapter, this is not always an easy thing to do. It could be suggested that teachers (and doctors and allied health professionals) have difficulty in being truly family-centred because they see the approach as a negation of their expertise. After all, they have been educated for a considerable number of years; they have the knowledge, skills and experience to make well-considered decisions about what the child needs at a particular point in time. This may well be so. But, it is equally true that families are the experts about their child and their family, and families have insights into how their family functions to which early years professionals are not privy. As educators, our practice can only be improved by working closely with families in meaningful partnerships. Family-centred practice is not about professionals giving up their power or expertise, but about sharing power; most importantly it is about *not* taking power away from families.

So, how do we do this? Sharing power requires skills that are not always part of our training as early years professionals. As Hanson and Lynch (1995) have noted, much of the education we undertake is around working with children, yet in doing this we also need to interact with families and other professionals. Early years professionals do, indeed, need those relational skills discussed earlier, along with many others. Following are some suggestions for how to become a family-centred professional.

1 *Begin as you mean to continue.*

When discussing this issue at university, one of our students recounted that the teachers at her children's school wrote to each of the children and their families before the school year started, to ask what they wanted to achieve in the coming year and to find out what their goals and hopes were. This is such a positive and effective way to start to know children and their families. It sets up the expectation that the child, family and teacher will work together to ensure that the learning journey is engaging and affirming. The letter clearly set the tone for the year, and shaped the classroom interactions as well as the relationships between teacher, parents and children.

In prior-to-school early years settings initial contacts with families could also be through a letter or they could be part of a general conversation about parents' goals for their children. There is also the opportunity to begin a conversation with parents about whether they have any concerns about their child's development. A scale such as the *Parental Evaluation of Developmental Status* (PEDS) (Glascoe, 2000) has only 10 items and could easily be completed by parents as a matter of routine at the beginning of the year. It could provide the basis for positively discussing children's growth and development and together parents and early years professionals could identify mutual goals for the coming year.

2 *Be available to families.*

An advantage for educators in prior-to-school early years settings and in the early years of primary school (compared to their education colleagues in upper primary and secondary schools) is that parents tend to bring their children to the settings in the morning and collect them in the afternoon. While this is likely to be a busy time, it is possible to roster staff to be available to talk with families briefly and informally at this time. This is not to suggest that serious issues should be raised but simply that this provides an opportunity to develop ongoing, professional relationships with parents.

It also helps make you more approachable when they do want to discuss a serious issue with you. Rotating the staff available at these times will mean that parents will be able to interact with all those working with their child.

3 *Schedule regular opportunities for discussion, planning and goal setting with families.*

If families are to be partners in their child's education, early years professionals must do more than report their child's achievements to them. As we have argued throughout this chapter, goals for the child must be driven by parental priorities and collaborative discussions, as well as take into account the child's interests, strengths and priorities. Such meetings need not be onerous, and they are less likely to be time-consuming if they are regular and ongoing.

4 *Develop and enhance your skills.*

The importance of ongoing professional development cannot be overstated. This could be attendance at training courses around, for example, reflective listening or collaboration. Attendance at conferences and workshops where issues in the field are discussed is also a possibility. Keeping up to date with current research is critical to best practice.

5 *Reflect on your practice.*

Schön (1987) wrote extensively about the reflective practitioner and of the importance of reflecting in and on practice. He argued that it was important that we reflect while we are acting (formative evaluation) and modify our behaviour as we proceed, to make it more responsive and effective. He also argued that we should then reflect on our practice when the interaction is completed (summative evaluation). This helps us to identify what is effective and should be repeated in the future, as well as what is less effective and needs to be changed. We suggest that early years professionals reflect not only on our teaching but also on our interactions with families.

6 *Evaluate your practice.*

The reflection discussed above is part of this process but evaluations of our practice should also include feedback from parents. To ensure that they feel able to be honest and not coerced, such feedback should be anonymous. A useful tool for gathering such feedback is the Measure of Processes of Care (MPOC-20) (King, Rosenbaum & King, 1995). This scale measures parents' perceptions of how family-centred they have found their interactions with professionals to be. While designed for families with a child with a disability, it has relevance for those in the early years generally.

**CASE STUDY 9.2**

## Ivy's Story

Ivy is four years old and has spina bifida. She began attending your preschool this year and is settling in well. She can walk short distances with the aid of a walker and leg braces but generally prefers to use a wheelchair. Ivy has had a shunt inserted because of her hydrocephaly. She has also been identified as having a mild level of intellectual disability. Ivy relates well to the other children but is often left alone, particularly when the children are playing outdoors. At these times she just sits watching the others. She has difficulty with matching and puzzles but enjoys story time. She is toilet-timed but has occasional accidents.

Ivy has one older sister who is eight and a keen soccer player. Ivy usually goes along to watch her. Her father works full-time in a demanding job and her mother works at home caring for Ivy and her sister. Her maternal grandparents live close by and Ivy talks constantly about her Nan and Grandad and the things they do together.

Her family have been involved with a local early intervention service since Ivy was discharged from hospital when she was three months old. She has regular input from an occupational therapist, physiotherapist, paediatrician and a neurologist.

During one of your regular meetings with Ivy's mother, she seems stressed and says that she is worried that, in their efforts to do the best they can for Ivy, they are putting too much pressure on her. They are also worried that Ivy's sister is missing out and that most of the attention is on Ivy because of her needs. She asks for your advice.

**CRITICAL REFLECTION QUESTIONS**

1. What are the concerns and priorities for Ivy and her family?
2. How could you work with the family to achieve outcomes that are family-centred?

# Conclusion

This chapter has defined family-centred practice, and described its fundamental components. It has explored the positive effects of employing family-centred practices with families and located the place of these practices within the EYLF. Finally, it has addressed what it means to be a family-centred early childhood professional and provided some practical examples of how to go about this.

Family-centred practice is by no means the easy option, but it is the one most likely to result in the best outcomes for children, their families and, indeed, the professionals working with them.

Through enabling and empowering families, early years professionals have the opportunity to build community capacity and have a positive effect on children's learning long after they have left the early years setting. We encourage you to talk *with* not *to* families, to acknowledge that parents are the experts on their family, and to continue to develop your own skills and expertise.

Despite being staunch advocates for family-centred practice in inclusive early years settings, as well as in the early years of school, we acknowledge that as early years professionals we rarely work in isolation with children and their families. Often children have diverse needs and consequently they and their families can be interacting with several other professionals. Therefore, we also need to know how to work effectively with a range of other professionals, such as speech pathologists, occupational therapists, physiotherapists, psychologists, social workers and nurses. How we collaborate with these other professionals is addressed in the following chapter.

## FOR FURTHER REFLECTION

The introduction of individualised funding models for those with disabilities (such as that which would flow from the proposed National Disability Insurance Scheme—NDIS) is an acknowledgment of individuals' rights to choose what is best for them and, in the case of families who have a young child with a disability, for their child and family. It gives them control and, as such, embodies in many ways family-centred or individual-centred practice. But, it is not without its challenges. It demands that families be able to advocate effectively for children and make informed choices about services and support. This has two main implications for effective family-centred practice.

The first is that families may be asked to make these choices very soon after learning that their child has additional needs. Some families, at least, may need support to do this.

1. What role should early years professionals have in such situations? (They may be the professionals with whom families have most contact and therefore feel most comfortable.)
2. How can families be empowered to deal with this process?

   The second implication is that individualised funding may result in families 'buying' services from individual therapists or other service providers.

3. Can a family-centred approach be maintained in such an environment?

## WEBSITES

www.earlychildhoodaustralia.org.au/position_statements/inclusion-of-children-with-a-disability-in-early-childhood-education-and-care.html

The joint position statement by Early Childhood Australia (ECA) and Early Childhood Intervention Australia (ECIA) sets out a shared commitment to inclusion in early childhood education and care (ECEC). Available at:

www.earlychildhoodaustralia.org.au

The Early Childhood Australia (ECA) website has various resources, including the *Every Child Magazine, Research in Practice Series* and *Everyday Learning Series*.

http://docs.education.gov.au/system/files/doc/other/eylf_in_action_-_educators_stories_and_models_for_practice.pdf

The EYLF: Belonging, being and becoming: Educators' guide to the Early Years Learning Framework for Australia

http://docs.education.gov.au/node/2632

The EYLF: The Early Years Learning Framework in Action: Educators' stories and models for practice

http://ecii.org.au/

Participating and Belonging: Inclusion in practice. Inclusion resources for early childhood educators and consultants

www.rch.org.au/ccch/resources_and_publications/Monitoring_Child_Development/#purchasing_peds

PEDS: Parents' Evaluation of Developmental Status. PEDS is an accurate, reliable tool for providing developmental and behavioural screening and ongoing surveillance in children from birth through to eight years of age.

www.canchild.ca

This website for the Canadian Centre for Childhood Disability Research has an extensive range of excellent information on family-centred principles and practices for early childhood professionals and families. The Fact Sheets (located in the Children and Families section) together with the Resources and Measures sections are particularly useful for early childhood professionals.

http://raisingchildren.net.au/

Raising children network: This website is the complete Australian resource for parenting newborns to teens. It includes up-to-date information and resources for early childhood professionals and families, and has two excellent sections on children with autism and children with disabilities.

www.noahsarkinc.org.au

A not-for-profit Australian organisation that values children and families in all their diversity. The website provides information, resources and supports for early childhood professionals as well as for children and their families.

## REFERENCES

Allen, R.I. & Petr, C.G. (1996). Toward developing standards and measurements for family-centered practice in family support programs. In G.H.S. Singer, L. Powers & A.L. Olson (Eds), *Redefining family support: Innovations in public-private partnerships*, (pp.58–84). Baltimore, MD: Paul H. Brookes.

Bailey, D.B. (1991). Building positive relationships between professionals and families. In M.J. McGonigel, R.K. Kaufmann & B.H. Johnson (Eds), *Guidelines and recommended practices for the individualized family service plan* (pp.29–38). Bethesda, MD: ACCH.

Bernheimer, L.P. & Keogh, B.K. (1995). Weaving interventions into the fabric of everyday life: An approach to family assessment. *Topics in Early Childhood Special Education, 15*(4), 415–433. doi:10.1177/027112149501500402

Bernheimer, L.P. & Weisner, T.S. (2007). 'Let me just tell you what I do all day...': The family story at the center of intervention research and practice. *Infants & Young Children 20*(3), 192–201. doi:10.1097/01.IYC.0000277751.62819.9b

Bernheimer, L.P., Gallimore, R. & Weisner, T.S. (1990). Ecocultural theory as a context for the individual family service plan. *Journal of Early Intervention, 14*(3), 219–233. doi:10.1177/105381519001400304.

Blue-Banning, M., Summers, J.A., Frankland, H.C., Nelson, L.L. & Beegle, G. (2004). Dimensions of family and professional partnerships: Constructive guidelines for collaboration. *Exceptional Children, 70*(2), 167–184. Retrieved from http://journals.cec.sped.org/ec/

Bronfenbrenner, U. (1992). Ecological systems theory. In R. Vasta (Ed.), *Six theories of child development: Revised formulations and current issues* (pp.187–248). Philadelphia: Jessica Kingsley.

Dempsey, I. & Dunst, C.J. (2004). Help-giving styles and parent empowerment in families with a young child with a disability. *Journal of Intellectual and Developmental Disability, 29*(1), 40–51. Retrieved from http://informahealthcare.com/journal/jid

Department of Education, Employment and Workplace Relations (DEEWR). (2009a). *Belonging, being and becoming, The early years learning framework*. ACT: DEEWR. Retrieved from: http://foi.deewr.gov.au/system/files/doc/other/belonging_being_and_becoming_the_early_years_learning_framework_for_australia.pdf

Department of Education, Employment and Workplace Relations (DEEWR). (2009b). *Belonging, being and becoming, The Early Years Learning Framework: Information for families.* ACT: DEEWR. Retrieved from: http://foi.deewr.gov.au/system/files/doc/other/belonging_being_and_becoming_the_early_years_learning_framework_for_australia_information_for_families.pdf

Dunst, C.J. (1997). Conceptual and empirical foundations of family-centered practice. In R.J. Illback, C.T. Cobb & H.M. Joseph (Eds), *Integrated services for children and families* (pp.75–93). Washington, DC: American Psychological Association.

Dunst, C.J. (2002). Family-centered practices: Birth through high school. *The Journal of Special Education, 36*(3), 139–147. doi:10.1177/00224669020360030401

Dunst, C.J. & Dempsey, I. (2007). Family–professional partnerships and parenting competence, confidence, and enjoyment. *International Journal of Disability, Development and Education, 54*(3), 305–318. doi:10.1080/10349120701488772

Dunst, C.J. & Trivette, C.M. (1994). Aims and principles of family support programs. In C.J. Dunst, C.M. Trivette, & A.G. Deal (Eds), *Supporting and strengthening families, Vol 1: Methods, strategies and practices* (pp.30–48). Cambridge, MA: Brookline Books.

Dunst, C.J. & Trivette, C.M. (1996). Empowerment, effective help-giving practices and family-centered care. *Pediatric Nursing, 22*(4), 334–337. Retrieved from www.ajj.com/services/pblshng/pnj/

Dunst, C.J., Trivette, C.M. & Deal, A.G. (1988). *Enabling and empowering families*. Cambridge, MA: Brookline Books.

Dunst, C.J., Trivette, C.M & Hamby, D.W. (2007). Meta-analysis of family-centered helpgiving practices research. *Mental Retardation and Developmental Disabilities Research Reviews, 13*, 370–378. doi:10.1002/mrdd.20176

Dunst, C.J., Trivette, C.M. & Jodry, W. (1997). Influences of social support on children with disabilities and their families. In M.J. Guralnick (Ed.), *The effectiveness of early intervention* (pp.499–522). Baltimore, MD: Paul H. Brookes.

Fialka, J. (2001). The dance of partnership: Why do my feet hurt? *Young Exceptional Children, 4*(2), 21–27. doi:10.1177/109625060100400204

Gallimore, R., Weisner, T.S., Kaufman, S.Z. & Bernheimer, L.P. (1989). The social construction of ecocultural niches: Family accommodation of developmentally delayed children. *American Journal on Mental Retardation, 94*(3), 216–230. Retrieved from www.aaiddjournals.org/loi/ajmr.1

Glascoe, F.P. (2000). *Parents' evaluation of developmental status: Authorized Australian version.* Parkville, Victoria: Centre for Community Child Health. Retrieved from: www.rch.org.au/ccch/resources_and_publications/Monitoring_Child_Development/#purchasing_peds

Guralnick, M.J. (2004). Family investments in response to the developmental challenges of young children with disabilities. In A. Kalil & T. DeLeire (Eds.), *Family investments in children's potential: Resources and parenting behaviors that promote success* (pp.119–137). Mahwah, NJ: Lawrence Erlbaum.

Hanson, M.J. & Lynch, E.W. (1995). *Early intervention: Implementing child and family services for infants and toddlers who are at-risk or disabled* (2nd ed). Austin, Texas: PRO-ED.

King, G., King, S.M., Rosenbaum, P.L. & Goffin, R. (1999). Family-centred caregiving and well-being of parents of children with disabilities: Linking process with outcome. *Journal of Pediatric Psychology, 24*(1) 41–53. Retrieved from http://jpepsy.oxfordjournals.org/

King, S., Rosenbaum, P. & King, G. (1995). *The measure of processes of care: A means to assess family-centred behaviours of health care providers.* Hamilton, ON: McMaster University, Neurodevelopmental Clinical Research Unit.

Moore, T. (2001). *Best start effective intervention programs: Examples of effective interventions programs, and service models.* Melbourne: Department of Human Services, Victoria.

Palisano, R.J., Chiarello, L.A., King, G., Novak, I., Stoner, T. & Fiss, A. (2012). Participation-based therapy for children with physical disabilities. *Disability & Rehabilitation, 34*(12), 1041–1052. doi:10.3109/09638288.2011.628740

Rosenbaum, P., King, S., Law, M., King, G. & Evans, J. (1998). Family-centred service: A conceptual framework and research review. *Physical and Occupational Therapy in Pediatrics, 18*, 1–20. doi:10.1080/J006v18n01_01

Schön, D. (1987). *Educating the reflective practitioner.* San Francisco: Jossey-Bass.

Scope. (2004). More than my child's disability... A study of family-centered practices and family experiences of Scope early childhood intervention services and supports. Victoria, Australia: Scope (Vic) Ltd. Available at: www.scopevic.org.au/index.php/site/resources/morethanmychildsdisability

Summers, J.A., Hoffman, L., Marquis, J., Turnbull, A., Poston, D. & Nelson, L.L. (2005). Measuring the quality of family-professional partnerships in special education services. *Exceptional Children, 72*(1), 65–81. Retrieved from http://journals.cec.sped.org/ec/

Trivette, C.M., Dunst, C.J., Boyd, K. & Hamby, D.W. (1995). Family-oriented program models, help-giving practices, and parental control appraisals. *Exceptional Children, 62*(3), 237–248. Retrieved from http://journals.cec.sped.org/ec/

Trivette, C.M., Dunst, C.J. & Hamby, D.W. (2010). Influences of family-systems intervention practices on parent–child interactions and child development. *Topics in Early Childhood Special Education, 30*(1), 3–19. doi:10.1177/0271121410364250

Viscardis, L. (1998). The family-centered approach to providing services: A parent perspective. *Physical & Occupational Therapy in Pediatrics, 18*(1), 41–53. Retrieved from http://informahealthcare.com/loi/pop

Weisner, T.S. (2002). Ecocultural pathways, family values, and parenting. *Parenting: Science and Practice, 2*(3), 325–334. doi:10.1207/S15327922PAR0203_06

Winton, P.J. & DiVenere, N. (1995). Family–professional partnerships in early intervention personnel preparation: Guidelines and strategies. *Topics in Early Childhood Special Education, 15*(3), 296–313. doi:10.1177/027112149501500304

# 10 Inter-professional Practice to Support Inclusion

*Sandie Wong*

CHAPTER OVERVIEW

This chapter will focus on the development of collaborative relationships between professionals[1].

Learning goals for this chapter include:

- Increasing understanding that working with children and families with complex needs often requires the skills, knowledge and expertise of professionals from diverse disciplinary backgrounds;
- Gaining a greater awareness of the potential benefits for child and family outcomes when professionals work in collaborative inter-professional ways;
- Increasing knowledge of key factors (at policy, service and individual/professional levels) that may assist in the development of collaborative inter-professional ways of working that will support inclusion of all children.

KEY TERMS AND CONCEPTS

multi-disciplinary

inter-disciplinary

trans-disciplinary

# Introduction: Inclusive settings require diverse professional expertise

All children have skills, knowledge and capacities. Likewise, all children have needs. Most will require access to a range of childcare, health, social and/or intervention services. Some children, however, especially those with a disability, and/or those with a parent with a mental or other health issues, and/or from families that are financially, socially and/or culturally marginalised, often have multiple and complex needs that require the skills, knowledge and expertise of professionals from diverse disciplinary backgrounds. These children, such as Sam, the fictional child in the case study below, will likely require the skills of a number of professionals.

**CASE STUDY 10.1**

## Sam's story

Sam is four and a half years old. He was recently enrolled in Lonepine Childcare Centre—a long day care centre in one of Sydney's most disadvantaged suburbs. Sam was temporarily placed in the care of his elderly maternal grandparents (who live in private rental accommodation in the local area) by social services three months ago. His mother, who he lived with up till then, has mental health issues and drug- and alcohol-related problems. She lives in rural New South Wales and is currently on bail awaiting trial for burglary and prostitution—she will likely receive a custodial sentence. His father is unknown.

Sam attends the centre five days a week. His grandparents, who usually drop him off together at about 9.30am, often stay with Sam for an hour or so as he settles into the centre. They usually sit with Sam and other children doing jigsaw puzzles or at the craft table. Sam's grandmother has been teaching origami to the children and often has five or six children, including Sam, sitting with her, deeply engaged in the intricate and complex task of folding paper and making animals and other objects. Sam's grandfather, who has been doing minor maintenance around the centre on a voluntary basis, has promised to work with some of the older children on a woodwork project and has been discussing with the educators how they can do this in a safe and accessible way. Sam's grandparents usually pick him up well before the centre closes and always chat to the educators about Sam's day, asking what he ate, what and who he played with, and if there were any significant events during the day.

The centre's Director, Stacey, a teacher with a four-year university degree, reports that Sam appears to have a very strong, loving relationship with his grandparents—and always smiles and cuddles them when they arrive to pick him up. He is well-nourished and always attends the service in clean, appropriate clothing. In his grandparents' presence Sam engages with craft materials for sustained periods. When his grandparents leave the centre he does not appear overly distressed. He is a mostly quiet child, who often plays alone and seems nervous around unfamiliar adults. While he appears to have settled into the centre quite well, and is frequently able to communicate his needs through gesture (e.g. pointing and facial expression), Stacey is concerned that Sam seldom speaks and when he does it is often in one word utterances. Further, although he complies with instructions this is often only after watching other children and following their lead. In one-to-one interactions he often seems confused or looks away. Given the choice, Sam prefers to play outside in the sandpit where he spends prolonged periods creating elaborate tunnels to drive toy cars through. If other children destroy his tunnels—whether accidently or deliberately—he screams in a high pitched way: on one occasion he hit with a spade and bit a child who stomped on his tunnels. When the carer shouted at him to stop Sam stood still, eyes wide, and wet his pants. During indoor play times Sam builds roadways and tunnels with the blocks. When encouraged he will engage with craft materials but recoils at the touch of paint and paste. At group reading times he sits on the edge of the group and listens attentively but never speaks. Stacey cannot remember a time when she has seen him independently reading a book or using writing implements.

**CRITICAL REFLECTION QUESTIONS**

If you were Sam's teacher how would you go about ensuring that he received the necessary professional expertise?

1. Who would you involve? Think about Sam, his family and community, staff in the service, as well as professionals and services outside the childcare setting.
2. How would you involve them? Think about strategies you could use to ensure multiple voices are heard.
3. What resources might you need and how could you procure them? Think about the resources and expertise that already exists in the service as well as availability of external support (see Wong, Sumsion & Press, 2012a).

From this description of Sam's family history, and Stacey's observations of his behaviour, it is apparent that his family has strengths, but that they and he are also facing a number of challenges. Among the family's strengths is the apparent close, nurturing and supportive relationship between Sam and his grandparents. Sam's grandparents appear comfortable attending the centre and are actively contributing to the centre activities. They are keenly interested in, and are proactive in finding out about, Sam's experiences. In their presence, Sam appears better able to engage in development-enhancing activities than when they are absent. Sam's strengths include his abilities to develop close relationships, to manage others' expectations of his behaviour, and make known and meet his own needs. He also demonstrates capacity to engage in complex tasks and, by and large, to manage well in group social situations. Some of the challenges Sam's family faces are unstable care arrangements; insecure tenancy; and a high likelihood of psychological and financial distress, and mental and physical ill-health. Concerns with Sam's wellbeing include possible speech,

**FIGURE 10.1** PAPER CRAFT

*Photo: Dinah Cocksedge*

cognitive and fine motor developmental delay, and troubling and challenging social behaviours that may indicate abuse.

It will require the expertise and support of a range of professionals to appropriately investigate, identify and build on Sam and his family's strengths, to address the many challenges he and his family face, and to increase the centre's capacity to include Sam and support his development. Some of the professionals that might be called upon to support Sam and his family, for instance, are: educators to facilitate Sam's engagement in development-enhancing learning experiences; family workers to provide advice and support the family in accessing financial and social resources; psychologists to investigate and address behavioural concerns; speech therapists to investigate his language development; and occupational therapists to investigate his tactile sensitivity and fine motor skills and (where necessary) provide appropriate support. Some of these professionals might be employed by the childcare centre. It is more common, however, that they will be employed across multiple external services, requiring families to negotiate a complex and sometimes confusing service delivery system and to tell their stories multiple times, which often results in families receiving diverse and even conflicting advice (Moore, 2008).

Thinking holistically, from an ecological perspective, it is highly likely that many of the challenges and concerns that Sam and his family face are interrelated. For instance, Sam's reluctance to engage with some materials and his poor socialisation skills may be due to his inexperience in group care, or a result of the quality of the care (note, for instance, that the staff member inappropriately shouted at Sam). Or, perhaps they stem from inattentive or chaotic parenting as a result of his mother's mental health and drug-related difficulties, which in turn may have been exacerbated by social isolation from living in a rural area. Likewise, Sam's nervousness around adults and his reluctance to speak may be due to him feeling insecure because of the recent upheavals in his life and ongoing tensions in the family due to his mother's court case, or to his being abused.

The most effective way diverse professionals can support Sam and his family is to work together to develop a holistic care plan. Working together and with his family, these professionals can each draw on their disciplinary expertise to observe and interpret Sam's circumstances and behaviours in a range of domains, carefully identifying areas of strengths, and paying attention to environmental factors (such as the quality of relationships, availability of materials, and engagement strategies used in the centre), to develop mutually agreed goals. In collaborative partnership with Sam and his family they can then jointly plan and implement appropriate, family-centred, cohesive and well-coordinated interventions to reach those goals, evaluating their effectiveness as they go, as well as identifying and addressing issues as they arise. In this way, Sam and his family will experience seamless and consistent care and intervention, tailored to their individual goals and responsive to their emerging needs.

Just as for Sam and his family, many children and families with complex needs and facing multiple challenges require the support and expertise of diverse professionals. The best experiences for these children and families, which are most conducive to positive outcomes, occur when children and families receive intervention that is cohesive, coordinated and integrated (Anning, 2005; Nichols & Jurvansuu, 2008; Siraj-Blatchford & Siraj-Blatchford, 2009; Warmington et al., 2004; Wigfall, 2002; Winkworth & White, 2011). This can only happen when professionals from diverse disciplines work *collaboratively*.

## Defining collaborative inter-professional work

The Macquarie dictionary defines 'collaborate' as 'to work, one with another' (2013, n.p.). Minnis, John-Steiner and Weber (cited in Barnett & Frede, 2001 p.5) state that:

> The principals in a true collaboration represent complementary domains of expertise. As collaborators, they not only plan, decide, and act jointly, they also *think together*, combining independent conceptual schemes to create

> original frameworks. Also, in a true collaboration, there is a commitment to shared resources, power and talent: no individual's point of view dominates, authority for decisions and actions resides in the group, and work products reflect a blending of all participants' contributions.

**multi-disciplinary:** In multi-disciplinary work, professionals from different disciplines work individually, alongside one another, rather than *with* one another.

Collaborative work between professionals in early years settings is referred to in the literature variously and interchangeably as multi-professional (Anning, Cotteral, Frost, Green & Robinson, 2010; Davis & Smith, 2012); inter-professional (Edwards, Daniels, Gallagher, Leadbetter & Warmington, 2009; Trodd & Chivers, 2011); multi-disciplinary (Collin, 2009), and interdisciplinary (Hains et al., 2005). For consistency, the term inter-professional is used in this chapter. However, these terms are also used to refer to the *degree* of collaboration.

**FIGURE 10.2** COLLABORATION

*Artwork by Emma*

**trans-disciplinary:** In trans-disciplinary work, the most recent iteration of inter-professional work in early intervention and also the most collaborative, professionals work across professional boundaries.

**inter-disciplinary:** In inter-disciplinary work, professionals work together (for example, to develop service plans), but maintain professional boundaries.

Collaborative inter-professional work is often placed on a continuum from **multi-disciplinary** to **trans-disciplinary**, depending on the degree of collaboration, with trans-disciplinary indicating the most collaborative working relationships (Briggs, 1997, cited in Moore & Skinner, 2010). Table 10.1 defines and outlines the different characteristics of professionals working at each of three levels of collaborative inter-professional work in early years' settings: multi-disciplinary, **inter-disciplinary**, and trans-disciplinary (McGonigel, Woodruff, Roszmann-Millican, 1994; Moore, 2005; Moore, 2008; Moore & Skinner, 2010) boundaries.

Moore (2005) explains that in the field of early intervention, a shift occurred in the early 1980s from the multi-disciplinary mode to an inter-disciplinary one, motivated by both practice and theoretical considerations. Practitioners recognised the difficulty, stress and alienation that uncoordinated services were causing for families; and research evidence identified that disjointed interventions were not resulting in sustained change. At the same time, the field was influenced by ecological and transactional perspectives relating to

**TABLE 10.1** DIFFERING LEVELS OF COLLABORATION IN INTER-PROFESSIONAL WORK.

| **Multi-disciplinary** work is characterised by professionals who: | **Inter-disciplinary** work is characterised by professionals who: | **Trans-disciplinary** work is characterised by practitioners who: |
|---|---|---|
| ~ View the child and their family according to developmental or other needs, pertaining to their own professional specialisation (e.g. speech; motor; behaviour; social);<br>~ Have limited communication with other professionals supporting the child and family;<br>~ Work with a child independently of other professionals; and<br>~ Report individually to the child's family. | ~ View the child holistically;<br>~ Include and involve families in team discussions;<br>~ Communicate in formal meetings with other professionals regarding assessments and intervention planning;<br>~ Share information and make decisions together with families and other professionals;<br>~ Work within their respective disciplines (e.g. speech/education/family work), to directly deliver services (e.g. therapy/education/ support) to children and families within the context of a coordinated service plan;<br>~ Are jointly accountable for shared goals; and<br>~ Supply information to families according to a case management plan developed by the inter-disciplinary team. | ~ View the child holistically;<br>~ Recognise the importance of relationship skills for working effectively with families, as well as specialist knowledge and practical expertise;<br>~ View their relationship with families and other professionals as a partnership;<br>~ Adopt a shared problem-solving approach drawing on evidence gathered by a range of professionals;<br>~ Work in a coordinated way to ensure service delivery is seamless and consistent for families;<br>~ Work in ways that enable skills and knowledge to be transferred across traditional disciplinary boundaries. That is, they share their disciplinary based knowledge and expertise, teaching others to make specific judgments and perform specific actions. While they may not play a direct service provider role in all cases, they may act as a consultant or coach for families or the trans-disciplinary team member who has the relationship with the family; and<br>~ Encourage generation of new trans-disciplinary skills and knowledge. |

## CASE STUDY 10.2

### The Infants' Home: An integrated early years service

At The Infants' Home Ashfield in Sydney's Inner West, professionals from diverse disciplinary backgrounds work collaboratively to provide a range of education and care and early intervention services. Medical and allied health, social welfare and early years professionals share their specialist knowledge, expertise and understandings about health, nutrition, family support, early intervention and education. They each contribute to the overall program as well as the development of individualised programs and interventions that will best meet the needs of particular children and families. Many work directly with individuals and groups of children in the mainstream setting.

Some of the professionals at The Infants Home work in trans-disciplinary ways. For instance, a speech therapist works within the setting several days a week. Working closely with the educators, the speech therapist uses her expertise to observe children and identify those who might need intensive support. Together, drawing on the teacher's early childhood pedagogical knowledge (e.g. play-based and child's rights perspectives), and her understandings about individual children's temperament, routines, interests and skills, they plan the curriculum. This might include, for example, planning a small language group at an appropriate time and place, and on a topic of interest to the children, targeted at a particular child in the group. The speech therapist also suggests strategies to support the educators' communication with children (e.g. waiting 30 seconds before expecting a reply/repeating back the child's words/using signs and visuals)—strategies that become part of the educators' everyday practice. The speech therapist also models effective communication strategies, carefully explaining their rationale to the educators to ensure fidelity. For instance, the speech therapist might pick up a book with strong alliteration (e.g. *Peter the Parrot*) and explain to the educators that the aim here is to support children's phonological development. Likewise, the teacher might suggest to the speech therapist materials and strategies that the speech therapist can use to respectfully and effectively engage children in both individual and group work (e.g. waiting for an appropriate 'moment' when the child is attentive and not otherwise engaged, using materials that the child/ren have previously expressed interest in, working in a variety of indoor and outdoor spaces and at different times of the day). Through this trans-disciplinary approach the skills, knowledge and expertise of the speech therapist and teacher are combined to provide a setting that supports the inclusion of all children.

early intervention (McGonigel et al., 1994). These perspectives recognised the interrelated nature of human development—that is, children could not be separated out into discrete units requiring individual treatment, but must be treated as integrated individuals with interrelated developmental needs (McGonigel et al., 1994). Further, it was recognised that children's development was connected to other significant relationships in their lives, and by extension, to their family's broader social and community connectedness (as was the case with Sam in Case study 10.1). These new understandings created an imperative for greater coordination and collaboration between diverse early intervention professionals. Two models of work that emerged from this more coordinated approach to practice were the 'team around the child' (Limbrick, 2001 see http://www.teamaroundthechild.com) approach and the 'key worker model' (Drennan, Wagner & Rosenbaum, 2005). In these approaches a multi-disciplinary team of practitioners work together on a 'case' coordinated by one key worker who liaises with the family (see for instance Rural Beginnings, n.d.).

Today, the trans-disciplinary mode of collaborative inter-professional work is often aspired to in early intervention as the 'best practice' (King et al., 2009). As an example of trans-disciplinary work in practice, Case study 10.2 (adapted from Wong & Press, 2012, p.20, and reprinted with permission of The Infants' Home) describes how a speech therapist and educators work together in an early childhood setting. Combining the knowledge and skills from both their disciplines, together they plan and implement the curriculum. The early childhood educators use strategies that support children's language acquisition suggested by the speech therapist in their everyday interactions with children; while the speech therapist works as an integral member of the education team, providing learning experiences for groups and individual children.

A truly trans-disciplinary approach is challenging to achieve, however. It not only requires professional commitment to new ways of working that disrupt traditional disciplinary boundaries, but it also demands supportive organisational and systemic structures. Trans-disciplinary work is made especially difficult when professionals are employed across organisations and service systems—as is most often the case in early years' settings—where structural barriers tend to operate against working in trans-disciplinary ways (Press, Sumsion & Wong, 2010). Rather than see multi-disciplinary, inter-disciplinary and trans-disciplinary ways of working as a strict hierarchy, therefore, it may be more effective for professionals to consider the purpose of working in an inter-professional way for a particular setting, at a particular time. Some of the benefits of working in inter-professional ways in early years' settings are explored below.

# Benefits of inter-professional work in early years settings

The major tenet of collaborative inter-professional relationships in early years' settings is that they allow knowledge and expertise to be shared and distributed across all those working with children to create inclusive environments. In collaborative inter-professional relationships each member is valued for the knowledge and expertise they bring. Diverse ideas and opinions are actively sought and shared openly through mutually respectful exchange: knowledge flows freely among the group, distributing expertise and broadening the understanding and skills repertoire of all team members (Drennan, Wagner & Rosenbaum, 2005; Edwards, 2009). For example, in Case study 10.2 the speech therapist shares her skills and expertise with educators who subsequently integrate this newly acquired knowledge into their everyday professional practice. Likewise, from the teacher, the speech therapist learns about resources, materials and strategies for effectively and respectfully engaging children in individual and group work. The distribution of expertise therefore enhances their respective professional practice in ways that benefit *all* children they work with.

That is not to say that through collaborative inter-professional relationships everybody becomes an 'expert' in all disciplines. As Edwards (2009, p.38) notes, inter-professional work is not about moving towards 'hybrid practice'. Rather, it is about 'developing the capacity to work with the expertise that others offer' (p.38). Disciplinary specialism and expertise continues to be valued and acknowledged.

Collaborative inter-professional relationships enable professionals to respond effectively to the diverse needs of children. Edwards (2009) contends for instance that when professionals see themselves as a part of a collaborative network, where expertise is distributed, they are better able to 'look across the lives of vulnerable children, identify the complex components of risk ... and work together to disrupt trajectories of exclusion' (p.38). For example, collaborative inter-professional relationships heighten awareness of the holistic nature of children's growth and development and its interconnectedness with a range of familial, community, social, cultural, political and historical factors, enabling a more nuanced response. In Sam's case (Case study 10.1), for instance, if educators, family workers, psychologists and speech therapists each bring their professional expertise to bear on his story, multiple and diverse challenges facing him and his family can be made visible and their origins and potential trajectory understood. Once they are bought into the line of sight it then becomes possible to intervene to address those challenges and lessen the severity of any negative outcomes.

Importantly, more than merely distributing existing expertise, collaborative inter-professional work also generates new ways of working. Through respectful and collegial processes of sharing and combining professional expertise, challenging one another's thinking, and engaging in joint problem-solving, alternative ways of practising emerge, and are discussed, implemented and evaluated. Inter-professional collaborations generate new solutions and develop innovative practices (Darlington, Feeney, & Rixon, 2005). In this way, collaborative inter-professional teams have an enhanced ability to respond flexibly to changing circumstances, requirements and emerging needs. In short, in collaborative inter-professional teams the whole is far greater than the sum of its parts.

Research, including numerous evaluations and case studies conducted in Australia (see for instance Brettig & Sims, 2011; Colmer, 2008; Cumming & Wong, 2012; Moore & Skinner, 2010; Press et al., 2010; Wong, Press, Sumsion & Hard, 2012; Wong & Press, 2012), provide compelling evidence of the positive impact of effective and sustained inter-professional and organisational collaborations. Table 10.2 (adapted from Wong et al., 2012a) summarises a number of these potential benefits for children and their families, communities, professionals, the service and service system.

**TABLE 10.2** POTENTIAL BENEFITS OF COLLABORATIVE INTER-PROFESSIONAL PRACTICE

| For children and families: |
| --- |
| ~ Increased awareness of, and understanding about, different disciplines and services;<br>~ Easier referral and access to a range of services through 'soft-entry points';<br>~ Ability to transition simply between services and/or use a range of services simultaneously at the level of intensity required;<br>~ Smoother, more informed transition from early years services to school;<br>~ Families only have to tell their story once;<br>~ More effective identification and response to families' emerging/ongoing needs;<br>~ More timely intervention;<br>~ More holistic service delivery—i.e. families are able to get a range of needs met in one place;<br>~ Families experience increased consistency and continuity across programs/services;<br>~ Reduced family stress due to professionals knowing the whole child within the context of their family and needs;<br>~ Reduced feelings of isolation;<br>~ Children having greater scope for social inclusion;<br>~ Increased parenting confidence and capacity. |

*(Continued)*

**TABLE 10.2** POTENTIAL BENEFITS OF COLLABORATIVE INTER-PROFESSIONAL PRACTICE (*CONTINUED*)

| For communities: |
|---|
| ~ Access to services that meet local needs more effectively;<br>~ A larger pool of skilled and connected professionals. |
| **For professionals:** |
| ~ Increased knowledge and skills;<br>~ Development of collegial and supportive relationships with a range of professionals;<br>~ Career advancement opportunities;<br>~ Advancement of professional standing leading to greater job satisfaction;<br>~ Increased capacity to lead and articulate their practice to families and other professionals;<br>~ Increased satisfaction of contributing to effective service delivery. |
| **For services:** |
| ~ Greater sharing of professional expertise and resources across programs/services;<br>~ More cost-effective service delivery through reduction of duplication within services;<br>~ Greater ability to use funds and resources in innovative ways;<br>~ Increased capacity to respond to families' needs in innovative and creative ways;<br>~ Improved profile and status of services in the community;<br>~ Improved staff retention and an enhanced capacity to attract staff due the service's positive standing and 'marketability'. |
| **For the service system:** |
| ~ Effective referrals resulting in fewer cases of children 'falling through the cracks';<br>~ Greater coherence across services/programs;<br>~ A more comprehensive service system;<br>~ Services are able to reach a broader population;<br>~ Reduced public expenditure through reduced service duplication;<br>~ Prevention of 'problems' becoming entrenched or worsening. |

# Supporting the development of inter-professional collaborative relationships

The process of forming collaborative inter-professional relationships can be challenging. It requires thoughtful, targeted and ongoing action at multiple levels—from legislation and policy, through service delivery, to personal and professional action (Edwards et al., 2009; Horwath & Morrison, 2007; Press et al., 2010; Whalley, 2006). This final section of the chapter outlines some of the key factors for supporting the development of collaborative inter-professional relationships at each of these levels. The discussion is necessarily condensed, so readers are directed to referenced sources that provide expansive discussions (e.g. Mattessich, Murray-Close & Monsey, 2001; Special Edition of *Early Years*, 2013) and to documents that support inter-professional practice (e.g. Prichard, Purdon & Chaplyn, 2010; Wong, Sumsion & Press, 2012b).

## SUPPORTIVE POLICY

Inter-professional collaboration is supported through facilitative policies and practice frameworks. Internationally, inter-professional collaboration has emerged in policy documents as an important way of working in the early years, especially for those working with children and families facing challenging circumstances (Nolan & Nuttal, 2013). In the United Kingdom, for example, greater recognition of the complexity of children's and families' lives have led to shifts, over the last two decades, towards integration between health, welfare and education services. In early years service delivery, in particular, Sure Start Children's Centres were established from the late 1990s to deliver 'joined-up' solutions for 'joined-up problems' (Nichols & Juvansuu, 2008). In these new types of services, diverse professionals work together with the aim of reducing social exclusion and enhancing the life trajectory of disadvantaged children (Lewis, 2010).

Shifts towards inter-professional work are also evident in Australia. In particular, there is increasing interest in the role that integrated early years services, which incorporate a range of professionals from education, care, intervention and family services, can play in ameliorating disadvantage (Press et al., 2010). For example, the Indigenous Early Childhood Development National Partnership Agreement has as one of its three elements, 'integration of early childhood services through the development of children and family centres'. Under this agreement, 35 centres with integrated early learning, childcare and family support services will be established in communities regarded as highly disadvantaged that also have a high proportion of Indigenous children under five years old (DEEWR, 2011). Similar commitments to 'one-stop shops' and collaborative service provision as a way of addressing inequality can be found in state/territory government policies (e.g. Victoria, Western Australia and Queensland) and within local government (e.g. Moonee Valley City Council in Victoria; and the Stronger Families Alliance in New South Wales) (Press et al., 2010; Wong et al, 2012b).

Policies for integrated service delivery require complementary practice frameworks. One such document that acknowledges the importance of collaborative relationships in early years setting is the early years national curriculum *The Early Years Learning Framework* (EYLF) (DEEWR, 2009). In this document, reference is made to the critical role of reflective partnerships between early years educators, educators in the early years of school and other professionals, as well as with children, their families and communities. In particular, such partnerships are recognised as making an important contribution to equitable practice and to inclusion. The EYLF states, for instance, 'by developing their professional knowledge and skills, and *working in partnership* with children, families, communities, other services and agencies, they [educators] continually strive to find equitable and effective ways to ensure that all children have opportunities to achieve learning outcomes (DEEWR, 2009, p.13; emphasis added). Likewise, 'partnerships also involve educators, families and support professionals *working together* to explore the learning potential in every day events, routines and play so that children with additional needs are provided with daily opportunities to learn from active participation and engagement in these experiences in the home and in early childhood or specialist settings' (DEEWR, 2009, p.13; emphasis added).

Yet, despite current Australian policy being supportive of inter-professional relationship development, a number of structural barriers remain. Among factors that have been identified as operating against collaborative relationships are divergent compliance and legislative requirements across and between government departments and service systems (Press et al., 2010). For instance, when professionals operate under multiple jurisdictions they often have to comply with different reporting and acquittal mechanisms requiring the collection of different types of data over different periods. Such procedures can be complex and burdensome for professionals and management alike. Further, competition for government funds can operate against cooperation between organisations. Similarly, while policies are increasingly relying on inter-professional collaboration, there is limited acknowledgement of the additional resources (e.g. time, space, and professional development) required to facilitate this way of working. Moreover, inequitable pay and working conditions between disciplines can compromise collaborative working relationships. Organisations and professionals seeking to work in inter-professional collaborative ways have to negotiate these, and myriad other, challenges—but more than this they have a responsibility to advocate for systemic changes that support new inter-professional ways of working.

## SUPPORTIVE SERVICES

Collaborative inter-professional working relationships are supported in services where there is a clear vision enacted through sound governance and management, an open and trustful organisational climate, and strong, facilitative leadership.

### *Vision, governance and management*

Organisations that support inter-professional ways of working often have a strong vision, grounded in concerns with social justice and human rights that extend well beyond the confines of the organisation (Press et al., 2010). For example, the organisation Vision at The Infants' Home, from where Case study 10.2 is drawn, is for a socially inclusive 'society in which each child is given the opportunity in early childhood to develop the abilities to meet life's challenges and opportunities' (The Infants' Home Annual Report, 2011, cited in Wong & Press, 2012, p.15). Further, work at The Infants' Home is based on a core principle: 'to provide each child with every opportunity' (p.20). Embedded within this larger framework of social justice and equity, The Infants' Home's work is directed to the best interest of their clients. This approach has facilitated inter-agency collaboration and a movement towards inter-professional work. For instance, greater recognition of the holistic needs of children has resulted in information exchange and collaboration with other organisations (such as family support and medical services) to ensure that children get the range of services they require. In addition, the organisation has employed professionals from diverse disciplines to work with early years professionals, to ensure children and families receive the most effective and timely intervention.

Organisational visions can also act as a type of 'social glue' that holds diverse professionals together. They articulate a common goal to which each professional aspires and commits and which orients their practice—fostering what Robinson, Atkinson and Downing (2008) refer to as 'collective ownership'. Having an effective vision is not enough however; the vision needs to be enacted. It has to permeate the practices and procedures of the organisation. Good governance and management, therefore, is critical for supporting collaborative inter-professional work.

Collaborative inter-professional relationships are supported when organisations have sound governance and facilitative management structures that are oriented to this way of working. In particular, organisations must strategically plan the shift towards, or development of, collaborative inter-professional work, recognising the time it can take for such shifts to occur and managing the changes sensitively and effectively. For instance, in regard to personnel, organisations wanting to support inter-professional work need to actively recruit professionals who express a willingness to work in collaborative ways. They need to provide ongoing incentives for those who exemplify this way of working, as well as sensitively support the transition out of those who do not wish to work in that way (Wong & Press, 2013).

Organisational systems, procedures and processes also need to be oriented to supporting collaborative inter-professional ways of working. For instance, Memoranda of Understanding, joint referral processes and staff exchange can expedite inter-professional collaboration across different organisations. Likewise, the provision of adequate resources (e.g. time, space, materials and professional supervision), effective communication strategies (e.g. meetings, documentation and records), and equitable employment conditions, can support inter-professional relationships within organisations (Press et al., 2010). While these structures and procedures are facilitative, collaboration is essentially about relationships, and so workplace culture also plays a critical role in the success or otherwise of inter-professional work.

### *Culture*

Inter-professional relationships are supported where there is an organisational culture and ethos that values and cultivates inter-professional expertise (Edwards, 2009; Horwath & Morrison, 2007; Whalley 2006). For instance, organisations that have been successful in working in inter-professional ways actively operate to build trusting relationships, founded on mutual respect for diverse ability, knowledge and skills (Edwards, 2009). They are often grounded in a commitment to equitable influence where all people's voices are heard. Such relationships are necessary for creating conditions for robust debate in which commonly held 'truths' (such as the centrality of play in early childhood) can be explored; the meaning of language (e.g. child-centred) interrogated; and practices (such as individualised intervention) scrutinised in collegial ways. Organisations that support inter-professional collaboration are also often dynamic and open to change: They encourage risk taking and creativity and take time to celebrate success (Press et al., 2010). Such cultures are often supported by philosophies such as strengths-based approaches and other change-oriented philosophies that assist professionals to reorient interpersonal conflict towards resolution (Press et al., 2010). They also tend to have strong leadership.

### *Leadership*

Strong leadership is a critical factor in the development of collaborative inter-professional teams. Leaders of successful inter-professional teams tend to be committed to this way of working. They are typically described as inspirational, knowledgeable, informed and dynamic (Wong et al., 2012b). They engender the respect of their teams by their openness and willingness to listen to and respond to staff. They are flexible and able to manage change effectively and to negotiate new professional practices (Press et al., 2010). Without such effective leadership, the development of collaborative inter-professional relationships in early years settings will be severely compromised. But even with supportive service conditions, the development of inter-professional relationships depends largely on the willingness, capacities and commitment of individual professionals.

# Personal and professional action

**FIGURE 10.3** WORKING TOGETHER

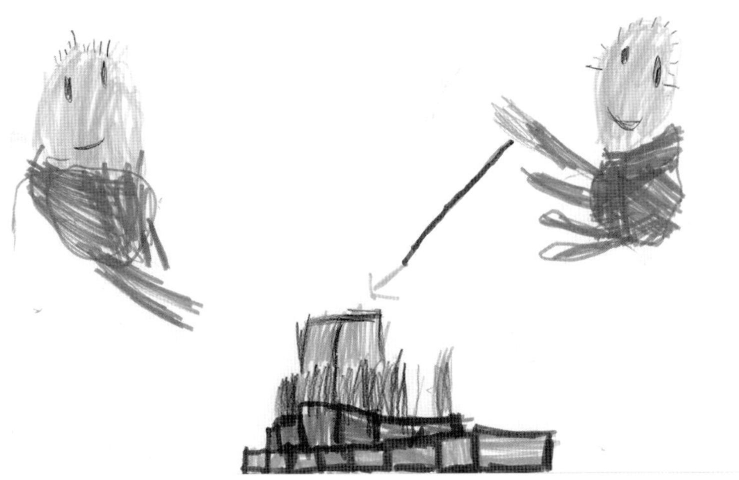

*Artwork by Joshua*

Working towards collaborative inter-professional relationships is a deliberate activity undertaken by professionals with the purpose of improving outcomes for the children in their charge, their families and their communities. To work in inter-professional ways requires personal, philosophical and professional commitment to developing strong relationships and working with others for the purpose of developing shared goals, for which each member of the relationship is responsible. Successful inter-professional relationships also require professionals to have a certain degree of confidence both in their disciplinary knowledge and their competency in their roles. It also requires an ability to articulate that knowledge to others. Those who have been successful in developing inter-professional relationships tend to be highly self-reflexive: They are open and keen to receive new knowledge and experiment with new ways of working, but they are also willing to share their expertise with others and assist and support others' learning (Cumming & Wong, 2012).

While each member of an inter-professional collaboration brings their own disciplinary knowledge, culture and philosophies, inter-professional work, and trans-disciplinary work in particular, requires professionals to not only cross disciplinary boundaries, but also to cede disciplinary control (McGonigel et al., 1994). For some, working in this way can be experienced as a threat to their professional identity (Cumming & Wong, 2012). One way for professionals to develop the skills necessary to engage effectively in inter-professional work with an intact professional identity is to engage in professional development that deepens their disciplinary knowledge as well as that which fosters inter-professional ways of working. Indeed, as collaborative inter-professionalism is increasingly viewed as a key professional competency across many disciplinary domains, a new field of professional development, known as 'inter-professional learning', has emerged. In inter-professional learning, which is common in the United Kingdom but less so in Australia, professionals from a range of disciplines come together to learn around a topic of common interest (Payler, Meyer & Humphris, 2007). Inter-professional learning has the potential to further support inter-disciplinary understandings and foster collaborative relationships. In Australia, several resources have been created to support the development of inter-professional relationships, such as *Moving Forward Together* (Prichard, Purdon & Chaplyn, 2010); *Developing and Sustaining Pedagogical Leadership* (Macfarlane, Cartmel & Nolan, www.ecceleadership.org.au); and *Supporting professional learning in an integrated context: a resource for early childhood leaders* (Wong et al., 2012b).

## Conclusion

This chapter has argued that collaborative inter-professional relationships can support the inclusion of all children, but especially those with complex needs. It has outlined what inter-professional collaboration looks like in practice and its benefits. While acknowledging that working in collaborative ways can be challenging, the chapter has provided information about the conditions at policy and service levels that may assist professionals' work in collaborative inter-professional ways. Ultimately, however, inter-professional work is a personal professional choice. When professionals choose to work in collaborative inter-professional ways, they enable their skills, knowledge and expertise to be pooled with others, through processes of mutual exchange, to create new and innovative ways of working that benefit children, families, the community, services and themselves.

# FOR FURTHER REFLECTION

1. Think about your early years work setting or another place that you are familiar with.
   a. What types of inter-professional work have you seen in action? Think about who was involved; what it looked like in practice; how collaborative it was; and the degree to which multiple voices were heard.
   b. What do you consider some of the benefits and challenges of working in collaborative ways? Think about the children and their families, the local and professional community, the service and the professionals.
2. Minnis, John-Steiner and Weber (cited in Barnett & Frede, 2001, p.5) argue that in a 'true collaboration, there is a commitment to shared resources, power and talent: no individual's point of view dominates, authority for decisions and actions resides in the group, and work products reflect a blending of all participants' contributions'.
   a. What might a collaboration based on these ideals look like in your early years or higher education setting? Think about who would be involved and the ways they would be involved.
   b. What strategies might need to be adopted to ensure a 'true' collaboration? Think about: resources available, processes and practices, the skills, knowledge and expertise of staff, and ways of working.

## WEBSITES

www.tandfonline.com/toc/ceye20/33/4#.U3CgYMbtWlw

For further reading on current and international research and commentary on the provision of integrated early years services and inter-professional work see a Special Edition of *Early Years: An International Research Journal* exploring Integrated Children's Services: Re-thinking Research, Policy and Practice (Volume 33, Issue 4, 2013).

www.ecceleadership.org.au

This website is on 'Developing and sustaining pedagogical leadership'. Authored by Macfarlane, Cartmel, & Nolan, this website provides a number of online learning modules to support leadership capacity, including in integrated services, in the early years sector.

## NOTES

1 This chapter is based on work conducted with my colleagues Jennifer Sumsion, Frances Press, Louise Hard and Tamara Cumming (Cumming & Wong, 2012; Press, Sumsion & Wong, 2010; Wong & Press, 2012; Wong, Sumsion & Press, 2012b; Wong, Press, Sumsion & Hard, 2012).

## REFERENCES

Anning, A. (2005). Investigating the impact of working in multi-agency service delivery settings in the UK on early years practitioners' beliefs and practices. *Journal of Early Childhood Research, 3*(1), 19–50. doi:10.1177/1476718x05051345

Anning, A., Cotteral, D., Frost, N., Green, J. & Robinson, M. (2010). *Developing multi-professional teamwork for integrated children's services* (2nd edn). Maidenhead: Open University Press.

Barnett, W.S. & Frede, E.C. (2001). And so we plough along: The nature and nurture of partnerships for inquiry. *Early Childhood Research Quarterly, 16*(1), 3–17. doi:10.1016/s0885-2006(01)00082-5

Brettig, K. & Sims, M. (Eds). (2011). *Building integrated connections for children, their families and communities*. Cambridge Scholars Publishing: Newcastle upon Tyne.

Collaborate. (2013). *The Macquarie dictionary online* (5th ed.). Retrieved from www.macquarieonline.com.au

Collin, A. (2009). Multidisciplinary, interdisciplinary, and transdisciplinary collaboration: Implications for vocational psychology. *International Journal for Educational and Vocational Guidance, 9*(2), 101–110. doi:10.1007/s10775-009-9155-2

Colmer, K. (2008). Leading a learning organisation: Australian early years centres as learning networks. *European Early Childhood Education Research Journal, 16*(1), 107–115. doi:10.1080/13502930801897111

Cumming, T. & Wong, S. (2012). Professionals don't play: Challenges for early childhood educators working in a transdisciplinary early intervention team. *Australasian Journal of Early Childhood, 37*(1), 127–135. Retrieved from www.earlychildhoodaustralia.org.au/australian_journal_of_early_childhood.html

Darlington, Y., Feeney, J.A. & Rixon, K. (2005). Practice challenges at the intersection of child protection and mental health. *Child & Family Social Work, 10*(3), 239–247. doi:10.1111/j.1365-2206.2005.00373.x

Davis, J.M. & Smith, M. (2012). *Working in multi-professional contexts: A practical guide for professionals in children's services*. London: Sage.

Department of Education, Employment and Workplace Relations (DEEWR). (2009). *Belonging, being & becoming: The Early Years Learning Framework for Australia*. Retrieved from www.deewr.gov.au/EarlyChildhood/Policy_Agenda/Quality/Documents/A09-057%20EYLF%20Framework%20Report%20WEB.pdf.

DEEWR. (2011). *National partnership agreement on indigenous early childhood development*. Retrieved from www.deewr.gov.au/Earlychildhood/PolicyAgenda/IECD/Pages/NationalPartnership.aspx

Drennan, A., Wagner, T. & Rosenbaum, P. (2005). *Keeping current in the 'key worker' model of service delivery*. Retrieved from www.canchild.ca/Default.aspx?tabid=130

Edwards, A. (2009). Relational agency in collaborations for the well-being of children and young people. *Journal of Children's Services, 4*(1), 33–43. doi:10.1108/17466660200900004

Edwards, A., Daniels, H., Gallagher, T., Leadbetter, J. & Warmington, P. (2009). *Improving inter-professional collaborations: Multi-agency working for children's wellbeing*. London: Routledge.

Hains, A., Rhyner, P., McLean, M., Barnekow, K., Johnson, V. & Kennedy, B. (2005). Interdisciplinary teams and diverse families: Practices in early intervention personnel preparation. *Young Exceptional Children, 8*(4), 2–10. doi:10.1177/109625060500800401

Horwath, J. & Morrison, T. (2007). Collaboration, integration and change in children's services: Critical issues and key ingredients. *Child Abuse & Neglect, 31*(1), 55–69. doi:10.1016/j.chiabu.2006.01.007

King, G., Strachan, D., Tucker, T., Duwyn, B., Desserud, S. & Shillington, M. (2009). The application of a transdisciplinary model for early intervention services. *Infants & Young Children, 22*(3), 211–223. doi:10.1097/IYC.0b013e3181abe1c3

Lewis, J. (2010). From Sure Start to Children's Centres: An analysis of policy change in English early years programmes. *Journal of Social Policy, 40*(01), 71–88. doi: 10.1017/s0047279410000280

Limbrick, P. (2001). *The team around the child: Multi-agency service co-ordination for children with complex needs and their families*. United Kingdom: Interconnections.

Mattessich, P.W., Murray-Close, M. & Monsey, B.R. (2001). *Collaboration: What makes it work?: A review of research literature on factors influencing successful collaboration*. (2nd edn). Saint Paul, MN: Wilder Publishing.

McGonigel, M.J., Woodruff, G. & Roszmann-Millican, M. (1994). The transdisciplinary team: A model for family-centered early intervention. In L.J. Johnson, R.J. Gallagher, M.J. LaMontagne, J.B. Jordan, J.J. Gallagher, P.L. Hutinger & M.B. Karnes (Eds). *Meeting early intervention challenges: Issues from birth to three* (2nd ed.)(pp.95–131). Baltimore: Paul H. Brookes Publishing Co.

Moore, T. (2005). Evolution of early childhood intervention practice. Paper presented at *Early Childhood Intervention Australia (Victorian Chapter) Consultative Forum—Moving towards outcomes in early childhood intervention: How do we do this?* 14 October 2005. Retrieved from www.eciavic.org.au

Moore, T. (2008). *Evaluation of Victorian children's centres: Literature review*. Melbourne: The Centre for Community Child Health. Retrieved from www.eduweb.vic.gov.au/edulibrary/public/earlychildhood/integratedservice/childcentrereview.pdf

Moore, T. & Skinner, A. (2010). *An integrated approach to early childhood development: A report prepared for The Benevolent Society*. Melbourne: The Centre for Community Child Health. Retrieved from www.rch.org.au/uploadedFiles/Main/Content/ccch/TM_BenSoc_Project_09.pdf

Nichols, S. & Jurvansuu, S. (2008). Partnership in integrated early childhood services: An analysis of policy framings in education and human services. *Contemporary Issues in Early Childhood, 9*(2), 118–130. doi:10.2304/ciec.2008.9.2.118

Nolan, A. & Nuttal, J. (2013). Integrated children's services: Re-thinking research, policy and practice (Editorial: Special Issue). *Early Years, 33*(4), 337–340. doi:10.1080/09575146.2013.855009

Payler, J., Meyer, E. & Humphris, D. (2007). Theorizing interprofessional pedagogic evaluation: Framework for evaluating the impact of interprofessional development on practice change. *Learning in Health and Social Care, 6*(3), 156–169. doi:10.1111/j.1473-6861.2007.00156.x

Press, F., Sumsion, J. & Wong, S. (2010). *Integrated early years provision in Australia: A research project for the National Professional Support Coordinators' Alliance*: The Professional Support Coordinators' Alliance and Charles Sturt University. Retrieved from www.psctas.org.au/

wp-content/uploads/2010/11/Intergrated-Early-Years-Provision-in-Australia-Report.pdf

Prichard, P., Purdon, S. & Chaplyn, J. (2010). *Moving forward together: A guide to support the integration of service delivery for children and families*. Retrieved from www.rch.org.au/emplibrary/ccch/Moving_Forward_Together.pdf

Robinson, M., Atkinson, M. & Downing, D. (2008). *Supporting theory building in integrated services research*. Slough: National Foundation for Educational Research. Retrieved from www.nfer.ac.uk/nfer/publications/CYL01/CYL01.pdf

Rural Beginnings. (n.d.). *Team around the child: Promising practices profile*. Kurrajong Early Intervention Service. Retrieved from www.aifs.gov.au/cafca/ppp/profiles/pppdocs/itg_rural_beginnings_team.pdf

Siraj-Blatchford, I. & Siraj-Blatchford, J. (2009). *Improving development outcomes for children through effective practice in integrating early years services*. London: Centre for Excellence and Outcomes in Young People's Services.

Trodd, L. & Chivers, L. (Eds). (2011). *Interprofessional working in practice: Learning and working together for children and families*. Maidenhead: McGraw-Hill.

Warmington, P., Daniels, H., Edwards, A., Brown, S., Leadbetter, J., Martin, D. & Middleton, D. (2004). *Interagency collaboration: A review of the literature*. Bath: Learning in and for Interagency Working.

Whalley, M. (2006). Leadership in integrated centres and services for children and families: A community development approach: Engaging with the struggle. *Childrenz Issues, 10*(2), 8–13. Retrieved from www.otago.ac.nz/press/journals/childrenzissues/

Wigfall, V. (2002). 'One-stop' shopping: Meeting diverse family needs in the inner city? *European Early Childhood Education Research Journal, 10*(1), 111–121. doi:10.1080/13502930285208881

Winkworth, G. & White, M. (2011). Australia's children 'safe and well'?: Collaborating with purpose across Commonwealth Family Relationship and State Child Protection systems. *Australian Journal of Public Administration, 70*(1), 1–14. doi:10.1111/j.1467-8500.2010.00706.x

Wong, S. & Press, F. (2012). *The art of integration*. Ashfield: The Infants' Home. Retrieved from www.theinfantshome.org.au/publications/the-art-of-integration/

Wong, S. & Press, F. (2013). *The art of integration: Attracting and retaining staff in integrated early childhood services*. The Infants' Home Ashfield. Retrieved from www.theinfantshome.org.au/site/assets/files/1009/the_art_of_integration_--_may_2013.pdf

Wong, S., Press, F., Sumsion, J. & Hard, L. (2012). *Collaborative practices in Victorian early years services: 10 project sites*. Victorian Government Department of Education and Early Childhood Development. Retrieved from www.eduweb.vic.gov.au/edulibrary/public/earlylearning/collaborativepraceyservices.pdf

Wong, S., Sumsion, J. & Press, F. (2012a). *Supporting professional learning in an integrated context: a resource for early childhood leaders*. Professional Support Coordinators Alliance. Retrieved from www.psctas.org.au/wp-content/uploads/2012/07/supporting-professional-development-in-integrated-context-web-Final.pdf

Wong, S., Sumsion, J. & Press, F. (2012b). Early childhood professionals and inter-professional work in integrated early childhood services in Australia. *Australasian Journal of Early Childhood, 37* (1), 81–88. Retrieved from www.earlychildhoodaustralia.org.au/australian_journal_of_early_childhood.html.

# 11 The A-Z of IFSPs, IEPs and SSPs!: Positive Planning for Inclusion

*Kathy Cologon and Dinah Cocksedge*

CHAPTER OVERVIEW

Ensuring all children can flourish in early years settings requires careful consideration of planning processes and approaches. Individualised Family Service Plans (IFSPs), Individualised Education Plans (IEPs) and Service Support Plans (SSPs) are intended to support the implementation of inclusive practices. These documents and processes will be discussed in this chapter.

Learning goals for this chapter include:

- Developing an understanding of the IFSP and IEP process;
- Reflecting on the importance of a family-centred approach to planning;
- Considering the role of early years professionals in preparing for the IFSP/IEP process;
- Understanding the importance of assessment for inclusion;
- Recognising the importance of a strengths-based approach;
- Engaging in IFSP and IEP planning.

KEY TERMS AND CONCEPTS

assessment for learning

Individual Family Service Plan (IFSP)

Individualised Education Plan (IEP)

Service Support Plan (SSP)

# Introduction

Ensuring all children can flourish in early years settings requires careful consideration of planning processes and approaches. **Individualised Family Service Plans (IFSPs)**, **Individualised Education Plans (IEPs)** and **Service Support Plans (SSPs)** are documents and processes intended to support the development and implementation of inclusive practices that consider the individual child and setting. In some places (for example in the USA) these documents are legal documents.

**Individual Family Service Plan (IFSP):** A planning process and document centred on mobilising resources to support children and families. IFSP outcomes are focused on the child and family.

**Individualised Education Plan (IEP):** A planning process and document focused on supporting a child's education inclusion.

Careful, reflective and collaborative planning is important in ensuring that early years professionals and families are working together and taking seriously the education of every child. However, there are tensions in undertaking explicit planning processes as there is a danger that the focus will become on the label or 'difference', rather than on inclusion of all children together. Awareness of this tension—and a focus on taking an inclusive, strengths-based approach—is an important starting point when engaging with essential planning processes.

**FIGURE 11.1** THE A-Z OF ROAD SIGNS

*Artwork by Cameron*

Individualised planning documents are referred to by various terms in different countries and in different states in Australia. As well as IFSPs and IEPs, they are referred to as 'Family Support Plans', 'Inclusive Support Plans', 'Individual Learning Plans', 'Education Support Plans', 'Negotiated Curriculum Plans', 'Negotiated Education Plans', 'Educational Adjustment Programs', 'Learning Plans' and 'Personalised Intervention Programmes', for example (Allen, Smith, Test, Flowers, & Wood, 2001; Mitchell, Morton & Hornby, 2010; Vakil, Freeman & Swim, 2003). Under all of these names, they are intended to involve a collaborative process and documentation of goals and strategies that

**Service Support Plan (SSP):** A planning process and document centred on staff goals and needs, with a view to enhancing staff capacity to support inclusion.

are then used to inform the planning of educational experiences. In this chapter the terms IFSP and IEP are used as they are the most widely known. SSPs are also briefly explained in this chapter.

These planning processes are predominantly used in relation to children who experience disability. However the fundamental basis of these processes is relevant to all children and families.

In this chapter we will provide sample formats for IFSPs and IEPs. However, many education settings and services have a format of their own (which often reflect variations based on location, including the name) and likewise you may wish to develop your own format. The format is not the important factor, rather the process and the content is key. These processes and documents need to be helpful, but not constraining, and need to be based on a social model (see Chapter 2), strengths-based approach. If the process is undertaken from a deficit-based, medical model approach (see Chapter 2) then it can be detrimental rather than beneficial to the child, the family and to the process of inclusion. This is a serious concern as these planning processes have commonly been approached from a medical model perspective in the past (and, unfortunately, often still are). In this chapter we will work through the process from a strengths-based, social model perspective.

## Service Support Plans

An SSP is a document developed as part of the Inclusion Support Program in Australia (www.cscentral.org.au/Resources/Inclusion_Support_Subsidy_Guidelines.pdf). The SSP is intended to support childcare centres in identifying and addressing barriers to inclusion (KU Children's Services, 2009). For example, an outcome of an SSP might be to hold training in Key Word Sign for all centre staff. Like IFSPs and IEPs, the SSP involves ongoing engagement in reflective practice. The SSP process involves identifying needs, goals and resources to inform the development of an action plan. Ongoing evaluation is key to the SSP process (KU Children's Services, 2009). The SSP is developed with an Inclusion Support Facilitator, who supports the setting step-by-step through the process (KU Children's Services, 2009). At this time it is not yet clear what changes may occur to this process as the National Disability Insurance Scheme unfolds in Australia.

## IFSPs and IEPs

There is limited research on the outcomes of using IFSPs and IEPs. However, they are used across many countries (Mitchell et al., 2010; Shaddock, MacDonald, Hook, Giorcelli & Arthur-Kelly, 2009). Greater emphasis has been placed in the literature on IEPs than IFSPs. However, it has been recognised for some time that there are many lessons that can be learnt for IFSPs through considering the IEP process (Gallagher & Desimone, 1995). The IFSP process also informs the IEP process.

Research in the USA has found that most teachers perceive IEPs to be useful tools for planning and practice (Lee-Tarver, 2006), and that education for teachers on writing goals and objectives is effective (Pretti-Frontczak & Bricker, 2000). However, it has also been found that teachers would like more support in developing their knowledge and confidence (Lee-Tarver, 2006) and that more education is needed to enable teachers to be effective in the process (Rosas, Winterman, Kroeger & Jones, 2009). This chapter provides a starting point for supporting early years professionals in developing this knowledge.

IEPs have been criticised for being used to serve too many purposes simultaneously (Shaddock et al., 2009), and for the lack of clarity regarding their purpose (Mitchell et al., 2010). Key criticisms of IEPs include over-emphasis on behaviourist principles and assumed majority cultural values and practice, the lack of evidence supporting their efficacy, and the isolation of the individual (which can be counter to inclusion) where in fact 'school action plans' and group strategies for differentiating teaching may be more effective (Mitchell et al., 2010).

Another very concerning criticism of IEPs, as mentioned above, is the tendency for the process to be underpinned by a medical model approach, with an emphasis on 'fixing' or 'curing' deficit (Mitchell et al., 2010). However, when these criticisms are addressed, IEPs can be a useful tool for planning and developing curriculum and practice, and for evaluation (Mitchell et al., 2010).

Criticisms of the IEP process can often be applied to the IFSP process. Fundamental to positive engagement with the IFSP and IEP process is taking a social model approach and emphasising child and family strengths and ways in which early years professionals can provide further support and reduce barriers to inclusion.

In an extensive review of the research literature, Mitchell et al (2010) provided recommendations for positive implementation of the IEP process, including

- Ensuring the process is as efficient as possible to reduce the time strain on teachers and families;
- Carefully considering scheduling to ensure all team members (particularly family) can attend;
- Providing release time for early years professionals to attend meetings and to prepare for the process;
- Facilitating active family involvement;

**FIGURE 11.2** 'GIVE WAY'—WORKING TOGETHER

*Artwork by Cameron*

- Wherever possible, involving children in developing their IEPs (this requires careful consideration of preparing children. Older children may lead the IEP process);
- Ensuring that all people involved, particularly children, are given the opportunity to understand the process, and the goals and strategies developed;
- Implementing culturally appropriate approaches.

## Taking a family-centred approach to planning

When approaching the IFSP and IEP process, focus is often placed on the document itself. The document provides a record and is useful for revisiting and for informing planning. However, the process of engaging with families and developing goals and strategies—and then implementing these—is more important than the document itself. One benefit of both the process and the document is that it creates an opportunity for the range of professionals involved in the life of a child and family to come together and develop agreed goals and strategies, thus reducing or removing the conflicting advice that families often receive. However, this only occurs if the process is conducted in a genuinely collaborative manner with mutually agreed and understood goals across the team (Stroggilos & Xanthacou, 2006). Trust and honesty are essential qualities in planning collaboratively.

Essential to the IFSP and IEP process is taking a family-centred approach (see Chapter 9). However, there are a number of barriers that can reduce or prevent family participation. Hornby and Lafaele (2011), identified key barriers, including:

- Family beliefs about their involvement (which differ based on context, experience and culture—see Chapter 6);
- Whether families feel welcome within the setting and perceive the invitation to participate as genuine (for example, whether family input is actively valued and reflected in the process, or whether jargon that families are not familiar with is used, thus positioning the families as 'non-expert');
- The current family context (families face many barriers to the practical process of participation, particularly if the process is not structured flexibly to meet family needs, for example if the meetings are at times when families cannot attend);
- Class, ethnicity and gender (education processes often privilege the dominant values and culture of the context and families from any minority group may be, or feel, excluded);
- The feedback that the child and parents (or other caregivers) are receiving regarding how the child is going within the setting (families may be more willing to participate around positive than negative messages);
- Whether families and early years professionals have shared, or common, goals (goals often differ and this can discourage parent involvement);
- Attitudes of those involved (deficit teacher attitudes are a major barrier. Additionally, an understanding of education as schooling places the teacher as the key driver of education, whereas a broader understanding of education, of which schooling is only one part, recognises the key role of families in education. The same concerns apply in regard to the attitudes of all other professionals involved);
- A mismatch between the language used and the reality of the process (for example, when words like partnership are used, but in reality the process emphasises the power of some over others, or the notion of 'parents and professionals' implying that parents are non-experts);
- Traditional understandings of the role of families that linger in the views of families, teachers and the policies and systemic structures of education settings, including a lack of funding support to facilitate family involvement.

It is essential to listen genuinely to and respect the views and wishes of families, at the same time as recognising the knowledge that early years professionals also bring to the planning process (and not placing the burden of planning onto families). Sometimes this creates a tension and addressing this requires engagement in an ongoing cycle of open and critical reflection and action.

CRITICAL REFLECTION QUESTIONS

1. Reflecting on the importance of family involvement, consider what it might be like to be faced with a large group of professionals in a planning meeting for your child. How might you feel? What are the implications for planning processes?
2. Early years professionals have a significant role to play in working with families. Reflecting on the family perspectives explored in Chapters 5 and 6, consider how you might address the potential tensions between respecting families' views and priorities and contributing to the process in the role of early years professional.

# Preparing for an IFSP and IEP

The IFSP/IEP process brings together a range of people involved in a child and family's lives to develop agreed goals and strategies and to develop or access resources as appropriate to work towards these goals (Treloar, 1997). Through this process, a document is also developed. This document integrates a range of relevant information from all involved and provides a record of the agreed goals and strategies, based on family priorities, which is then revisited in planning and implementing support (Treloar, 1997).

In preparing for an IFSP/IEP, it is essential to provide families with information about the process before holding a meeting. Families need to know what to expect, including:

- Who will be there (and that this is a family choice);
- What role each person (including the family members) will play (including who will run the meeting and who will take notes);
- How long the meeting is likely to last and things the family might like to think about ahead of time (for example, planning questions).

The family also needs to know when they can expect to receive the document, based on the meeting, for review.

IFSPs/IEPs are about supporting children and families and can be used as a way to facilitate greater inclusion through informing inclusive planning. However, as Bridle and Mann (2000, p.13) expressed, there is a risk of 'the unwitting message which we send to our children; that we value them for their "progress" rather than for themselves'. This emphasises the importance of taking a holistic approach to assessment and planning, and includes reassurance that this process is about supporting the child's inclusion and development, *not* about changing the child.

When preparing families, it is important to consider questions that family members may wish to think about. What questions will be appropriate vary widely and need to be based on knowledge of the child, family and setting. However, some planning questions that may be helpful as a starting point to build on include:

- What are your hopes and dreams for your child?
- What does your child enjoy doing at present?
- What is your child doing now that you are really pleased with?
- Do you have any issues or concerns that you would like to discuss?
- Are there any specific strategies or services that have been particularly helpful up to now?
- What would you like to work towards with your child in the next 6–12 months?
- What support or information would be helpful to you at this time?
- When do we need to meet again?

Sometimes starting with broad questions regarding family hopes and dreams for their child, or even what their current goals are can be overwhelming (Bridle, 2005; Bernheimer & Weisner, 2007). Another starting point can be to ask the family to tell you about a day in the life of their family (Bernheimer & Weisner, 2007) or about something that has been working well. Starting with something positive is an important reminder of remaining focused on strengths as a way to build ongoing strategies to support challenges.

Remembering the importance of family involvement, as discussed above, it is critical to consider the family's point of view about the time and location of the meetings. For example, making sure that meetings are arranged for a time and location that the family can attend is vital, as is providing an interpreter, childcare (where a child is not participating in the meeting, or for siblings) or other support for the family where appropriate.

Early years professionals also need to prepare themselves. This includes gathering information such as observations of the child and the setting, preparing a developmental summary and developing ideas for adaptations in the setting to facilitate greater inclusion. It is their role to translate family and child goals into the social as well as temporal life of the classroom, advocating for inclusive practices in the knowledge that these will ultimately best serve everyone involved. For external professionals, the focus may be more on the child and family than the setting. Teachers can assist these professionals in implementing strategies inclusively within the early years setting.

Maintaining confidentiality is an important responsibility of all involved. When requesting information from families, it is also important to consider what information is actually needed and why. Information should only be requested that is essential to the planning process. If families do not wish to share information, this needs to be respected. Through building respectful relationships the basis for open information sharing is created.

## Assessment for inclusion

Considerable emphasis is placed on the assessment of children at younger and younger ages. Early years professionals need to be highly skilled at conducting assessment, as it is important in supporting the participation and inclusion of all children (Watkins & D'Alessio, 2009). Assessment forms an important component of the IFSP/IEP process. However, it is essential to consider carefully the purposes of assessment.

**assessment for learning:** As outlined in the EYLF, this is 'the process of gathering and analysing information as evidence about what children know, can do and understand. (DEEWR, 2009, p.17).

Broadfoot (2007) has developed 10 key principles, in which **assessment for learning:**

1 Forms part of effective planning;
2 Emphasises how a child learns;
3 Is central to education practice;
4 Is a key skill of education professionals;
5 Is responsive (sensitive and constructive);
6 Fosters motivation;
7 Promotes understanding;
8 Assists with learning;
9 Supports the capacity for self-assessment; and
10 Recognises all education achievements.

Assessment sends strong messages to children, families and early years professionals. Assessment influences our concepts of each other and ourselves as learners. This can impact on what children feel they are capable of. It can also influence planning and education practice. It is important to engage in inclusive approaches to assessment that are contextually based, involve children and families as active participants, and that are sensitive to diversity (DEEWR, 2009). From a parent perspective, Bridle and Mann (2000, p.16) write that

> [T]here is a need for all people who are working with a child to see that child as a whole individual and not a sum of deficits. Don't just tell me that my child can only manage a small number of jumps unassisted on the trampoline—tell me of the joy on his face as he tries ... Do not only tell me about the 'problems' but show me, if you can, how much you appreciate my child as he is.

Consider the following two assessment reports of the same child from Benner and Grim (2013, p.95):

1 Seth is a 4-year-old with a severe expressive communication disorder. He is unable to speak in complete sentences, or even put together two-word phrases. His expressive vocabulary consists of fewer than ten words that can be understood consistently. Essentially, he has no effective means of expressive communication other than idiosyncratic sounds and gestures. Developmentally, his expressive communication skills are at the 12- to 15-month level.

2 Seth has a speaking vocabulary of seven words. He uses sounds and gestures to communicate and becomes frustrated when his attempts at communication are not understood. As a 4-year-old, Seth needs to have a functional means of communication that can be used at home or in his preschool setting. He can consistently point to objects and pictures of some objects when their names are called. This skill can be used to establish an alternative means of expressive communication for Seth.

**CRITICAL REFLECTION QUESTIONS**

1. What does the first description of Seth tell you?
2. What does the second description of Seth tell you?
3. To help you think about the difference between these two approaches, make a list for yourself of ten things that you cannot do. Then make a list of ten things that you can do, which could be used as a base from which to build new skills. For example: I can't scuba dive/I can swim.
4. What information would be helpful for planning to include Seth?

Taking a positive, strengths-based approach is essential. As noted above, family participation is at risk when a negative approach is taken. Additionally, deficit-based assessment provides little information to support early years professionals in including children. This does not mean that concerns should not be raised. However, it is essential to emphasise strengths and consider carefully how to approach concerns and support from a strengths-based perspective. Bridle and Mann (2000, p.12) shared that in their experience, early years professionals would sometimes 'notice small steps that perhaps I was too close to see'. Sharing such observations can be affirming for families and can indicate that the professional knows and values the child. This creates a strong basis from which to develop a collaborative relationship and address concerns as they arise.

## CASE STUDY 11.1

### Meet Zoe

Zoe is four and a half She has been attending a childcare centre for two days a week for the past two years. She transitioned between rooms at the centre midway through last year. Focusing on favourite activities like painting and bouncing on the trampoline helped her to ease her way into the new and busier, noisier environment. Zoe uses some Key Word Signs. Her vocabulary is growing and she is keen to use spoken words. An important part of Zoe's day has revolved around her own sleeping and eating routine but it is now becoming possible to merge this routine with the room's routine, enabling Zoe to participate as much as she chooses in all our activities and develop stronger relationships with her peers. Zoe has Down syndrome.

**CRITICAL REFLECTION QUESTION**

Table 11.1 below, contains a developmental summary for Zoe. Read the summary and consider:

- What is the approach?
- What have you learnt about Zoe and about her teachers?
- Write down a list of Zoe's strengths. Building on these strengths, what goals might you suggest working towards with Zoe?

**TABLE 11.1** SAMPLE DEVELOPMENTAL SUMMARY

| |
|---|
| Zoe has been up in the 3–5 room for the last half of 2013. She has settled in and adjusted to the increased hurly-burly of the big room, the adults and the children. |
| *Children have a strong sense of identity.*<br><br>Zoe has a very clear idea of what she wants to do and where she wants to go. She also has curiosity about everything around her and responds warmly and thoughtfully in her social interactions, demonstrating real pleasure in greeting familiar adults. |
| *Children are connected with and contribute to their world.*<br><br>As Zoe becomes more and more engaged with her peers, she is revealing to us the things that really interest her, like play in home corner. When she is busy with something, her attention is very focused and she is deeply engaged. Zoe has just started to be really keen to join us for group times. |
| *Children have a strong sense of wellbeing.*<br><br>Zoe now feels settled and confident in the big room and is starting to go beyond her familiar and comfortable things like painting and the trampoline. She enjoys mealtimes with the other children and eating with them is very motivating. |

*Children are confident and involved learners.*

As children often do in new environments, Zoe started off by watching everything, carefully observing. Now she is starting to step in and participate: she watched a peer build a tower of blocks and when Zoe started to build her own tower, the two girls chatted together as they worked.

*Children are effective communicators.*

Zoe is using more and more words and it is important that we make sure we keep ahead, extending and building her vocabulary, expecting more and drawing other children into the conversation. Zoe is a keen communicator, always responsive but also initiating interaction as well as getting her needs met, coming to get one of the adults by the hand when she needs help.

*Possibilities*

Supporting independence—offering challenges: inviting her to activities that she has not yet attempted.

Meals—think about the timing of Zoe's day so that she can share mealtimes with her peers. Work gradually to support Zoe eating independently. Fitting our routines together generally.

Build specific activities (e.g. vocabulary building, gross and/or fine motor exercises) into the program, developing small group activities.

# Setting goals and developing strategies

Goals for IFSPs/IEPs need to be drawn from child and family priorities, need to be useful for the family and child, and need to be achievable. Goals also need to be written in clear, easy to understand language. When setting goals it is important to carefully consider who can/will support the family, child and setting in working towards the goals.

Locke and colleagues have developed goal-setting theory over a number of decades (see Locke & Latham, 2002). Putting goal-setting theory into action, a commonly used framework is that of SMART goals, in which goals are intended to be **s**pecific, **m**easurable, **a**chievable/attainable, **r**elevant and realistic, and **t**ime-based. The SMART goals framework is generally attributed to Doran (1981), who wrote about developing SMART goals for management. This framework is also used when developing IFSP and IEP goals.

## SETTING GOALS IN PRACTICE

It is important to consider goal-setting carefully. Vague or very broad goals can result in a lack of clear, shared understanding between those involved. Consider the case study of Ally below. The goal 'to increase Ally's inclusion within the setting' is an important goal, but in order to work towards this goal, the goal needs to be far more specific so that it is clear and understood by all and specific strategies can be put in place.

**CASE STUDY 11.2**

## Sharing stories

Ally is five years old and has recently started Foundation Year at Roseberry Primary. Ally frequently engages in imaginative play with peers, developing creative stories by retelling stories and everyday experiences. Following orientation, Ally is growing in confidence in moving independently around the setting and is keen to be involved with all activities alongside peers. Ally enjoys music, art-making, particularly with play-dough, clay or collage; she also enjoys outdoor play, particularly active games that involve counting sets of jumps, claps, steps and hops. Increasingly, Ally will ask for help when needed, for example when moving into an unfamiliar part of the environment. For example, Ally will ask a teacher to act as a guide to assist with orientation to the environment. Ally's peers have also started to offer to act as guides and enjoy describing visual materials and activities to Ally as they are aware that Ally has very low vision. Ally also describes tactile materials and together the children are developing a richer vocabulary due to their greater awareness of touch, sound and visual inputs. Ally enjoys listening to stories and will often create artworks that explore the descriptions of characters and experiences within books.

As identified some time back now by Dunst and colleagues, the phrase 'in order to' can be helpful in working towards a broad goal in more specific ways (Deal, Dunst & Trivette, 1989). So, when working towards the broad goal for Ally to be more included within the education setting, first it is important to identify what barriers are limiting or preventing Ally's inclusion currently. For example, while Ally is very much included in literacy experiences and enjoys listening and responding to stories through retelling and art-making, Ally's inclusion is currently limited in literacy learning experiences focused on developing print literacy, as Braille is required but not provided. Therefore, one specific goal that would work towards the broad goal of greater inclusion could involve the recognition that Braille and other tactile materials need to be provided for Ally in order to achieve inclusion within print literacy activities. For example, a goal could be:

*Building on Ally's interests in books and sharing stories, Braille and tactile materials will be added to storybooks within the classroom. Tactile materials will also be provided for writing experiences to enhance the opportunity for Ally and her peers to create and share stories.*

Initially, in working towards this goal, it would be helpful to identify a number of books or activities per given timeframe in order to increase inclusive practice over time. Another example would be to set a goal around creating consistency of the layout within the environment so that, once oriented, Ally can move around independently alongside peers. A range of strategies would accompany this goal. For example:

*The teacher will work with the children to make a map of the classroom layout. The map will then be embossed using pen on a thin sheet of plastic to make a tactile version.*

*All members of the class will work to keep the layout the same in order to support Ally in independently navigating the classroom environment.*

*When changes are made to the classroom layout the map will be amended and Ally and her peers will move around the classroom together to re-orient themselves.*

## CONSIDERATIONS FOR ACHIEVING GOALS

Motivation has been identified as a key factor in setting and achieving goals (Locke & Latham, 2002). Goal commitment and goal importance or relevance are both important (Locke & Latham, 2002). When developing IFSP and IEP goals, it is therefore important to consider the relevance of and motivation for the goals, for all involved.

As discussed above, family-centred practice is essential to quality early years education. In the context of developing IFSP and IEP goals, families play a key role. This does not mean that families are left with the responsibility for setting goals, but rather that families need to be invited and supported to give as much input as they desire and that goals should be consistent with family priorities and expectations. It is important to ask, is this important and relevant to the child and the family? For IEP goals in particular, as they are child-focused and generally specific to the education setting, it is important to consider the relevance to the setting.

Self-efficacy, which is essential for agency, has been identified as another important moderator for setting and achieving goals (Locke & Latham, 2002). Recognising the importance of self-efficacy does not mean only setting goals that fall within what we feel confident and comfortable in doing (otherwise, we not only risk the child's development, but we also would never progress in our own development). Rather, building on and scaffolding the development of self-efficacy on the part of the child, family and early years professionals is an important part of setting and achieving goals. Take the example of adding Braille to print literacy materials in an early years setting, explored in the continuation of Ally's story below.

**CASE STUDY 11.3**

## Sharing stories

(Case study 11.2 continued)

Ally is very keen to share her knowledge of expressing ideas through tactile materials, touch and sound. Ally is being introduced to Braille in order to develop Braille reading proficiency over time. The incorporation of tactile materials and Braille within print-literacy experiences will support Ally in learning Braille and in further developing her sense of self-efficacy in regard to literacy. These adaptations will also facilitate Ally's inclusion within and beyond literacy experiences.

Ally's family are developing their familiarity with and knowledge of how to incorporate tactile materials and Braille to support Ally's learning and participation. Working together with early years professionals can support Ally's family in gaining confidence in supporting Ally's literacy development. Ally's family have many ideas to share for incorporating tactile materials into everyday experiences. They also have many questions regarding how Ally is being supported in the setting.

The educators are not familiar with Braille, but are open to learning. They had not previously realised the strengths they have in providing tactile experiences to support literacy learning, but upon reflection have realised how naturally and easily tactile materials can be incorporated not only into literacy experiences, but across the experiences within the setting. Through the opportunity to reflect on the use of tactile materials and the support provided to incorporate Braille materials, the educators are developing confidence in how to include Ally more effectively within the setting, including within literacy experiences. The educators are also becoming more flexible and creative in their pedagogical approach and are realising the benefits to Ally, and Ally's peers, of taking a multi-modal approach.

Ally and peers enjoy adding tactile materials to experiences within the setting. They are excited to be learning about Braille and interested in coming to understand what Braille is and how it works. They are developing confidence and a sense of self-efficacy about their capacity to communicate in multiple ways and to value multiple forms of communication, thus expanding their literacy learning.

There are a number of external early years professionals involved in supporting Ally's inclusion. These professionals are familiar with making adaptations to materials to incorporate tactile experiences. They also have expertise in teaching and using Braille. However, these professionals are learning all the time, as they get to know the people involved and the setting. As the family share their knowledge of Ally and the educators share their knowledge of engaging early years experiences, these professionals further develop their knowledge and self-efficacy in supporting inclusion in quality early years education.

Feedback is essential to effective goal setting (Locke & Latham, 2002). A continuous cycle of reflection and action (evaluation) is required to recognise, document and respond to feedback. It is also critical to set regular times to review IFSP/IEP goals, strategies and outcomes.

A willingness to commit to new challenges is key to goal motivation (Locke & Latham, 2002). In turn, success with achieving goals and positive feedback leads to greater willingness to commit to new challenges (Locke & Latham, 2002). Thus a cycle is created that, over time, increases the challenge to which a person is open. This creates space for ongoing professional development and growth in confidence in early years professionals.

## STRATEGIES

Strategies need to be flexible and those involved in the IFSP/IEP process need to be prepared to modify or change the strategies as needed in order to achieve the goals. In order to be successful, strategies need to build on strengths.

Achieving goals requires willingness to commit to new challenges, effort, persistence and the development of appropriate strategies to achieve the goals that have been set (Locke & Latham, 2002). However, careful consideration of both goals and strategies is required. Noting that 'excessive scrutiny of a child's development creates a misleading impression of that child's performance [and] can also lead to very inappropriate intervention' (Bridle & Mann, 2000, p.16). Bridle & Mann (2000) provide the following example of the implementation of strategies aimed at encouraging Sean to make eye contact and greet his peers with sign and voice:

> As time went on it seemed that Sean was actually making less and less effort at greeting people and actively avoided doing so. The worker made greater and greater efforts to engage Sean and eventually was chasing him around the playground, even poking him to get his attention. Her own facial expression and voice were greatly exaggerated and Sean was not at all engaged in the greeting task but very engaged in the avoidance-pursuit game he thought they were playing. The worker's focus on getting him to greet her, had actually led him away from greeting the other children at the centre who were surely the more appropriate focus of this skill development (p.16).

Consequently, Sean's Mum observed the wider group, noticing that:

> [M]any children were highly inconsistent in greeting adults and other children. Some days they would rush up to their teachers and friends and other days they would scarcely acknowledge anyone for a considerable length of time. These children were not however subject to any of the pressure exerted on Sean. Excessive pressure is likely to be counter-productive ... Even if the child with disability does learn a 'skill' which is taught in this way, it does not help them to generalize that skill to relating to their peers (Bridle & Mann, 2000, p.16)

**CRITICAL REFLECTION QUESTIONS**

1. Consider this example of a goal and strategies for Sean. What concerns can you identify with the goal, the strategies and the implementation of the strategies?
2. If you were working towards a goal of encouraging children in their social development, what strategies might you implement to do this in a meaningful and inclusive way? Think about what you would do in setting up the environment and planning experiences for all children in that context, rather than focusing on isolated skill development.

**FIGURE 11.3** 'HELLO'

*Photo: Dinah Cocksedge*

## The IFSP document

One common concern raised by families is that what is promised in an IFSP/IEP meeting doesn't actually occur. A key consideration for avoiding this issue is to ensure that there is agreement not only on goals and strategies, but on *who* will do *what*, *when*. It is essential to make sure that everyone involved does do what they say they will do. This involves implementing the agreed actions, documenting the progress of these actions and maintaining regular communication with families (Treloar, 1997). It is important to remember that this is an ongoing, relationship-based process. Consider the IFSP for David below.

CASE STUDY 11.4

## About David

David is four and a half. He is a confident, sociable child, with a cheeky sense of humour, great determination, a vivid imagination and the best smile. David started walking when he was two and was initially diagnosed with ataxia. He has recently been diagnosed with cerebral palsy, which affects his movement coordination and fine motor control, and speech articulation. Last year he tackled the physical challenges of moving up to the 3–5 room and its big playground with characteristic resolve. His parents' primary concern is that he is happy and safe in a familiar environment. They are also keenly aware of the potential impact David's speech articulation might have on his friendships as his peers become more competent verbally. David attends the centre three days each week and has intensive speech therapy at the centre once a fortnight. We are also using a board with visual cues. David attends physiotherapy sessions and has started playing soccer, which he loves! The team of professionals supporting David and his family includes an Early Childhood Teacher (ECT), Early Intervention Therapist (EIT), Speech Therapist (SpT), Occupational Therapist (OT), Physiotherapist, Paediatrician, and an Inclusion Support Facilitator.

**FIGURE 11.4** DAVID AIMING FOR THE TOP!

*Photo: Dinah Cocksedge*

**TABLE 11.2** DAVID'S IFSP

<table>
<tr><th colspan="4">Individual Family Service Plan<br><br>Name: David      Date of birth: XX/XX/XX<br>Date of meeting: March<br>Location: Centre<br>Present: David's mother, Inclusion Support Facilitator, Physiotherapist, ECT, EIT<br>Apologies: SpT</th></tr>
<tr><th>Issues discussed</th><th>Action</th><th>Who</th><th>When</th></tr>
<tr><td>Update from David's Mum:<br><br>David has made lots of progress in the last three months and has attended several medical appointments (see below). David's parents feel that David is enjoying social confidence and is very happy both at home and at the centre. He continues to attend Playgym, which he loves, and his mum commented that she has noticed great gross motor gains in David's development in the last 6 months. She attributes this to a combination of physiotherapy, Playgym, the centre, David's Theratogs suit and all his incidental therapy work that happens throughout his daily routine.</td><td></td><td></td><td></td></tr>
<tr><td>Occupational Therapy<br><br>David has started seeing an OT once a fortnight. David's mum has asked the OT for a report to determine where David is currently at with his fine motor and general OT skills and abilities and also what direction he is heading in.<br><br>David has intention tremor—this makes it hard for David to handle and manage small items like puzzle pieces and cutlery. David's Mum discussed this with the OT, who has suggested activities with weighted balls in each hand.</td><td>• This OT report will help David's parents decide whether or not David needs to continue with OT at this time.</td><td></td><td></td></tr>
<tr><td>Neurologist<br><br>David had an appointment with the Neurologist 2 months ago. David still doesn't have a definitive diagnosis at this date:<br>• David's lumbar puncture results fell mostly within the accepted range and based on the protein tests, there is no sign of David having a progressive disorder.<br>• Next step for David is to have a follow up MRI scan around August.</td><td>• The Inclusion Support Facilitator will talk to a Cerebral Palsy Alliance (CPA) staff member to see if David would be able to access CPA services before age 5 years, regardless of diagnosis.</td><td>Inclusion Support Facilitator</td><td></td></tr>
</table>

| | | | |
|---|---|---|---|
| **Paediatrician**<br>• David saw the Paediatrician 2 months ago and David's mum felt really comfortable with him becoming David's Paediatrician. He suggested a gluten-free diet (related to David's ataxia) and although David (and his family) tried it for 6 weeks, his mum noticed no discernable difference for David. | • David has his next appointment with the Paediatrician in 2 months. | | |
| **Physiotherapist**<br>The PT has provided some suggestions that we can all use to support David in his mobility—specifically around trunk stability and static (stationary balance).<br>• We discussed the possibility of shoe inserts to help monitor how David's feet are progressing as he has pronated arches—this may change by the age of 6 years but the Physio suggested it would be wise to start supporting this now.<br>• Start with 'off the shelf' inserts and see how these go.<br>• Alternatively, a podiatrist can custom make inserts and this might be an option for Family Assistance Funding (FAF).<br>• The Physio spoke about Hydrotherapy sessions at the hospital and this will help with David's mobility.<br>• David's mum mentioned that one specific area she would like to focus on is David's developing ability to use cutlery—because of his intention tremor, it is hard for him to manage cutlery and this has implications for social interactions at meal times as it can get very messy—finger food is easier. We discussed ensuring David's stability in his chair when at the table for meals. He likes to sit in a big chair, like his big sisters. | • Investigate Birkenstock arches on the internet.<br>• Consider inserts for FAF funding.<br>• Hydrotherapy sessions alternate weeks with speech therapy.<br>• Try using a stool for David to position his feet on when sitting on a big chair at the table at home. (The physio suggested a 'trip trap chair'.)<br>• Support David to use cutlery at mealtimes at the centre. | David's mum<br>EIT<br>Mum<br>Physio<br>Home<br>Physio<br>Centre | ASAP<br>ASAP<br>Ongoing<br>Ongoing<br>Ongoing |
| **Speech Therapist**<br>The SpT was unable to attend today's meeting but sent a summary of what she is working on with David. She has been visiting David at the centre once per fortnight since February and she has made 1 home visit. She is working on the Nuffield Program and 'cued articulation'—these include visual prompts, signs and exercises that David practises at home alongside his sisters at homework time.<br>• David's mum commented that seeing this in action demonstrates how challenging David finds it to make certain sounds with his tongue, lips and general mouth area. | • The SpT is about to send on a report re: David's language and communication.<br>• The EIT to email SpT about strategies around supporting David in his communications and interactions. | SpT<br>EIT SpT<br>Mum | |

(*Continued*)

**TABLE 11.2** DAVID'S IFSP (*CONTINUED*)

| | | | |
|---|---|---|---|
| • The ECT mentioned that it would be great to have some strategies from these programs to help plan and program for David as these strategies can be used with all the centre children and will support inclusion for David.<br>• The Physio discussed the question of 'what strategies should we be using when we cannot understand a word/phrase that David is saying?'<br>• David's Mum said that David remains very tolerant around this but it can be hard for him at the end of the day or when he is tired. Asking him to repeat, point or show what he wants and asking one of his sisters helps! | • Mum is going to bring in the notes she has re: Nuffield speech program and cued articulation to share with staff at the centre. | | |
| **EC Teacher**<br>The ECT reported on how wonderfully well David has made the transition to the 3–5 room at the centre.<br>David is now less dependent on Dinah who came up to the 3–5 room with David—he is relating well and referring to the other adults in the room to interact with and have his needs met.<br>David has increased his social circle and now plays comfortably with a broad group of friends and peers—he enjoys engaging with all aspects of the daily program.<br>The ECT added that David sets himself goals to master e.g. the disc swing in the playground and this is great exercise to help develop his trunk stability. He likes spending a lot of his outdoor playtime on this activity.<br>Re: toilet training—David's preference is to use the 3–5 room toilet with adult support—he rarely has toileting accidents and works hard to be independent in dressing/undressing for the toilet. | | | |
| **Inclusion Support Service**<br>The Inclusion Support Facilitator spoke about the role of inclusion support in supporting staff to include children in centres. This can include extra staff to increase the adult:child ratio and the opportunity to apply for special equipment (via the equipment pool) recommended by therapists.<br>She advised obtaining more documentation would assist their application for inclusion support, which is due in 3 months. | • Inclusion Support Facilitator is meeting with ECT and ECT/Coordinator at centre to discuss funding reviews in 6 weeks. | | |

| | | | |
|---|---|---|---|
| **FAF Funding**<br><br>The FAF (Family Assistance Funding) funding application for a Theratogs suit was successful. YAY!<br><br>Once David's Mum is able to complete the acquittal process by the end of this financial year, she will be able to apply for another FAF in the next financial year. | • David will be fitted with a new Theratogs suit. | Mum | Next week |
| **School Preparation**<br><br>David will start school in 2013 and is on the waiting list for a small independent school. David's parents will consider their local public school although the physical terrain to and from the playground would present challenges for David's mobility skills.<br><br>We plan to start the school transition process from early next year and approach school(s) in case any physical modifications need to be made to accommodate David. | • David's mum is attending the school information morning to start considering school options. | Mum<br><br>Centre | Ongoing |
| **Summary of Goals for David**<br><br>Working on David's trunk stability—e.g. throwing balls while on a large gym ball.<br><br>Working on David's static balance—e.g. stop/go games.<br><br>Encouraging production of language sounds. | • Refer to Physio and Speech Therapy reports. | Home<br><br>Centre | |
| **Review**<br>• David will be away on a family holiday from mid-May til mid-June. Happy hols!<br>• Next meeting planned for early September (springtime!) at 9.30am at the centre. | • EIT to plan itinerant visits around these dates.<br>• EIT to send out reminder emails in August. | EIT | August |

*(Source: The authors acknowledge Connect Child and Family Services as the developer of the IFSP used in this chapter. Used with permission.)*

**CRITICAL REFLECTION QUESTIONS**

1. What did you observe from David's IFSP?
2. Was there anything that surprised you? If so, why?
3. How might you draw on this IFSP in planning inclusively within the setting?

Below is an elaborated IFSP format (Table 11.3). Consider the guidelines provided within.

**TABLE 11.3** AN ELABORATED IFSP FORMAT

| **Individual Family Service Plan**<br><br>**Name:** **Date of birth:**<br><br>**Date of meeting:**<br><br>**Location:** *Often the childcare centre/preschool/school that the child attends (so that care is available for the child)*<br><br>**Participants:** *The parent/s or primary caregivers; other family members. Participants may also include the Family Service Coordinator, ECT, EIT/Special Education Teacher, Therapists (speech pathologist, OT, physiotherapist etc.), Psychologist, Social Worker, Paediatrician, Family Advocate … Families can decide whom they want to participate in an IFSP meeting.*<br><br>**Present:**<br><br>**Apologies:** *It is important to consider who needs to be at the meeting and what this meeting will feel like from the family's point of view. It may be possible for some participants to be represented by a colleague or to send in a report so that the number of participants is reduced.* | | | |
|---|---|---|---|
| *If this is a first meeting ask the family about their hopes and dreams for their child.*<br><br>*If you have had an IFSP meeting before, start by celebrating the child's achievements and successes.*<br><br>*What's working?*<br><br>*Frame your thinking and discussion in positive and achievable ways.* | | | |
| *Consider family resources, priorities, strengths and concerns.* | *Goals must be:*<br>• *expressed in language that the family understands (free from jargon);*<br>• *functional for the child and family;*<br>• *achievable within the time available.* | | |
| *Review and evaluate goals from previous IFSP meetings.* | *Formulate meaningful goals (not too many) with strategies, criteria, timelines and procedures indicated.* | | |
| *Invite contributions/reports/ assessment from each of the participants.* | | Indicate the services that will be involved with each action. | |

| | | | |
|---|---|---|---|
| | | *Indicate where the action will be implemented (always aiming for the most natural environment).* | |
| | | | *Decide dates to start an action and anticipated duration.* |
| | *How will these actions be monitored and evaluated?* | *Who will be responsible for the implementation of each action?* | |

The elaborated IFSP format can be used to assist you to develop a draft IFSP for Tom using the blank format in Table 11.4, and Case study 11.5 below.

**CASE STUDY 11.5**

### Developing an IFSP for Tom

Tom is five. He has amazing language skills and is a brilliant negotiator. He is already reading and responds very positively to written communication strategies. He has a rich and complex imaginative life. Tom is developing social skills and is being supported to share his space with other children, playing cooperatively, negotiating and turn-taking. He has been diagnosed with autism. He attends the centre for three days and a school-based preschool program for two days. Next year he is starting school. He occasionally needs reminding to go to the toilet and when he gets caught up in his play, can have difficulty following the day's routine. His family's goals are that he follows the centre's routine, eats the centre's food and remembers to go to the toilet. The team of professionals supporting Tom and his family includes: ECT and EIT.

## The IEP document

Building on consideration of the IFSP process and document, we will now consider the IEP document. Review the sample IEP format in Table 11.5 below. The format can be repeated as many times as required for multiple long- and short-term goals. However, setting too many goals at any one time may create unrealistic expectations of all involved.

**TABLE 11.4** IFSP FORMAT

| **Individual Family Service Plan**<br>**Name:** **Date of birth:**<br>**Date of meeting:**<br>**Location:**<br>**Participants:**<br>**Present:**<br>**Apologies:** | | | |
|---|---|---|---|
| Issues discussed | Action | Who | When |
| | | | |
| | | | |
| | | | |

**TABLE 11.5** IEP FORMAT

| **Individual Education Plan**<br>**Child's name:** **Date:**<br>**Present at the meeting:**<br>**Long-term goals:** | | | |
|---|---|---|---|
| Agreed short-term goal | Learning experiences:<br>(Implementation strategies and resources) | Who's responsible | Evaluation and reflection |
| *Include links to the EYLF/ Curriculum documents and to long-term goals.* | *Carefully consider inclusive strategies and implementation.*<br>*What will be done, where and when?* | *Consider who will be involved, including peers and family.* | *How will you know if what you are doing is working?*<br>*What strategies will you use to review your learning experiences?* |
| | | | |
| | | | |
| | | | |

The case study below explores the IEP process.

**FIGURE 11.5** DANGER!

*Artwork by Cameron*

**CASE STUDY 11.6**

## Danger! Developing an IEP for Adam

Adam is five years old. He has a quirky sense of humour and a passion for road and danger signs. Adam's social skills are developing and he is discovering the pleasures of friendship and sharing his play and interests with others. He is starting school next year and will attend the transition to school program at his school in the second half of the current year. He is visited at the centre by an OT once a week to work on fine motor and task sequencing skills. His parents are keen to promote his social development and have been concerned about his speech. Adam has been diagnosed with autism. The team of professionals supporting Adam and his family includes: ECT, EIT and OT.

I (Dinah) am struggling to know how to extend and thoughtfully make use of Adam's particular interest in road and danger signs. At the end of some days the rooms are festooned with 'Danger!' signs and Adam's play has apparently revolved entirely around keeping the adults and other children out of places. I know that I should be building on his interests (Kluth & Schwarz, 2008) and I feel it is a failure of imagination on my part that I find it so hard to work with this interest of Adam's. Why not animals? Or even trains?! Partly this is because it seems like a negative interest: about restrictions, doing wrong (when Adam is in his other role as police officer) and keeping out. During one of the OT's visits, she has observed how Adam is able to persuade one or another adult to write a 'Danger!' sign for him. Our part in this is important to consider and we have food for thought about how we could use just the process of creating the signs themselves more creatively and positively with him. But it has also made me consider what this interest, and particularly these signs, mean for Adam. What is his intent (Oken-Wright & Gravett, 2002)? Is it about rules? About limits? About boundaries? Is it about security in an emotional as well as a physical sense?

Some staff are concerned about the 'Danger!' signs, but once I start to consider where Adam usually places them (the laundry door, the storeroom door, the office door, the boundary fence, or wherever he is playing), I wonder if his signs are any different in meaning or intent from the little 'This is not a play space' images that we have on those doors and places? As adults, we cross the boundaries between the children's 'play spaces' and these other spaces many times each day, but the children are asked to remain outside them or only enter these spaces with an adult. They are therefore mostly unknown spaces and perhaps Adam's signs represent this.

Where could we go from here? I am inspired by Kluth's ABC of train terminology (Kluth & Kluth, 2010) to attempt to work with Adam's symbols and extend on them by seeing if I could put together an ABC book using these signs and symbols, as well as finding ways to support Adam socially so that his games could involve rather than exclude other children. The A–Z will include a mix of signs and symbols that I think will mean something to my group and challenge their thinking.

**FIGURE 11.6** DANGER SIGN BY ADAM

*Photo: Dinah Cocksedge*

**FIGURE 11.7** MAKING THE SIGN

*Photo: Dinah Cocksedge*

**TABLE 11.6** ADAM'S IEP

<table>
<tr><td colspan="4">Individual Education Plan<br>Child's Name: Adam Date: October<br>Present at the meeting: Adam's mother, ECT, EIT and OT<br>Long-term goals:<br>To scaffold Adam's developing social competence and friendships.<br>To support Adam's emergent literacy skills.<br>Transition to school.</td></tr>
<tr><td>Short-term goal</td><td>Learning experiences</td><td>Who's responsible</td><td>Evaluation and reflection</td></tr>
<tr><td>Build on Adam's intense interest in road and danger signs in order to specifically support his social connection with his peers.<br>Each of the EYLF learning outcomes relate to this goal, which uses something that is important to Adam as a bridge to his peers, both building new competencies and allowing him to demonstrate and communicate his existing skills and knowledge, enhancing his sense of self and his role within the group of his peers.</td><td>1. I have created an A–Z of road and danger signs, which we can look at together and discuss in group time and also in small groups.<br>2. Encourage support workers to creatively scaffold Adam's play entry skills as well as modelling and supporting responses to other children's bids to enter Adam's play.</td><td>ECT</td><td>1. The A–Z has headed in several directions: Adam is still thinking about signs; his peers incorporate signs into their play. Our discussions have helped the children to understand one another and make connections between their different but clearly related play themes. The children generally are developing an understanding of signs as communicators of meaning.</td></tr>
</table>

| | | | |
|---|---|---|---|
| | 3. We are aiming to go on a sign-finding excursion this fortnight around the town to see and photograph the road signs and the danger signs up at the big building site. (NB. Wednesday when Adam is here). | | October 12: We walked up the street spotting familiar road signs, working out/ decoding unfamiliar ones. We also stopped to watch the building site and saw the big crane (see individual observations and program folder). |
| Increasing Adam's confidence in his own drawing and writing skills in order to support his emergent literacy skills. Scaffolding his persistence at increasingly complex task sequences using materials that are motivating for him.<br><br>*Supporting Adam's communication skills, self-efficacy and sense of agency.* | 1. Working with Adam to help him make his own signs instead of making them for him. Breaking the task down, step-by-step, letter-by-letter, using the A–Z as a guide so that Adam can make his own choices about colour and layout.<br><br>2. Individual pages on the A–Z printed in dotted Foundation script and laminated for tracing and practice.<br><br>3. Getting the children to sign on for themselves everyday, supporting individual children with dotted Foundation Script so that they can trace over the letters. | ECT<br><br>OT<br><br>ECT | Adam has surprised himself now that he has the tools to actualise his idea of what his signs should look like using the A–Z as a guide. Not so many signs, perhaps, but much more satisfying because he has made them and they are just how he wants them.<br><br>October 7: All the children are keen and remind me that they need to sign in (competence/ agency): some are independently thinking about their writing, varying size, becoming confident; others are developing skill and becoming aware of the mysteries of writing. |
| Helping Adam to make a successful transition to school.<br><br>*This is a critical step for all children and connects particularly with their sense of wellbeing and agency, as well as their sense of identity and their role within their wider—and widening—community.* | 1. Weekly visits and sessions at Adam's school in Term 4.<br><br>2. Experiment with using an iPad and explore funding options for this.<br><br>3. Funding may be available to enable the ECT to visit the school and talk to Adam's new teacher, as well as to be at school with Adam in the new year to support his first days at school. | Family<br><br>OT<br><br>ECT | February: The funding did come through and that enabled me to attend school with Adam, observing, supporting and sharing our experience with his new teachers, including simple strategies to help him when he is getting stuck with something. |

# Conclusion

The IFSP and IEP process provides a particularly focused opportunity to reflect on and evaluate practice and put it in the context of what is important for this particular child and family. It also allows participants to benefit from the distinct expertise of others. In this context early years professionals also clearly have a responsibility as advocates:

- For the child and our image of the child as competent and capable;
- For the importance and value of play;
- For inclusive practice; and
- For the role of the child's peers in scaffolding their development.

It is helpful to remind ourselves that we come to these collaborative meetings to share our expertise but also to listen, because the ultimate—and best—outcomes are the fruit of our combined expertise. We always set out on this process—and indeed our day-to-day life in the classroom—as well-prepared as we can be and after that we should be open to serendipity. For example:

> A considerable focus of the minutes of an IFSP meeting for Adam (see IEP case study) concerns his unwillingness to bathe. Everyone present brainstorms imaginative strategies that can be tried to help him accept and even enjoy having a bath. The minutes of a subsequent meeting share the news that Adam has a baby brother; and in a meeting after that, the whole issue of bathing is resolved: Adam loves to have a bath with his brother!

## FOR FURTHER REFLECTION

Research has found that writing an IEP for oneself can be a helpful learning and reflective process for teachers that facilitates the development of effective goal setting and strategy development and enhances understanding of individualised planning (Kamens, 2004). To this end, you are now invited to develop your own IEP (you may wish to use the format in Figure 11.5). To make this process effective, you will need to develop genuine goals and strategies and implement them over the coming weeks and months.

To begin, write down a goal that you have for yourself. Consider whether this is a long or short-term goal. Complete the sample IEP format for your goal, following these steps:

1. Develop short-term goals to achieve your longer-term goal (remember the phrase 'in order to ...' can be helpful);
2. Develop strategies to work towards this goal (include specific consideration of resources that may be needed);
3. Determine the actions that need to be taken to implement these strategies (when, where, what?);
4. Also determine
   a. Who is responsible;
   b. How you will know if the strategies are working.
   c. When you will review the goals and strategies.

## REFERENCES


Allen, S.K., Smith, A.C., Test, D.W., Flowers, C., & Wood W.M. (2001). The effects of 'self-directed IEP' on student participation in IEP meetings. *Career Development for Exceptional Individuals, 4*(Fall), 107–120. doi:10.1177/088572880102400202

Benner, S. & Grim, J. (2013). *Assessment of young children with special needs: A context-based approach* (2nd edn). New York: Routledge.

Bernheimer, L.P. & Weisner, T.S. (2007). 'Let me just tell you what I do all day ...' The family story at the center of intervention research and practice. *Infants & Young Children 20*(3), 192–201. doi:10.1097/01.IYC.0000277751.62819.9b

Bridle, L. (2005). Why does it have to be so hard! A mother's reflection on the journey of 'inclusive education'. In C. Newell & T. Parmenter *Disability in education: Context, curriculum and culture* (pp.1–12). Canberra: Australian College of Educators.

Bridle, L. & Mann, G. (June, 2000). Mixed feelings: A parental perspective on early intervention. Presented at the *National Conference of Early Childhood Intervention Australia*, Brisbane. www.downsyndromensw.org.au/data/Mixed_Feelings_by_Bridle__Mann.pdf

Broadfoot, P. (2007). *An introduction to assessment.* New York: Continuum.

Deal, A.G., Dunst, C.J. & Trivette, C.M. (1989). A flexible approach to developing Individualized Family Support Plans. *Infants and Young Children, 1*(4), 32–43. Retrieved from http://journals.lww.com/iycjournal/pages/default.aspx

Department of Education, Employment and Workplace Relations (DEEWR). (2009). *Belonging, being and becoming: The early years learning framework for Australia.* ACT: DEEWR. Retrieved from www.coag.gov.au/sites/default/files/early_years_learning_framework.pdf

Doran, G.T. (1981). There's a S.M.A.R.T. way to write management's goals and objectives. *Management Review, 70*(11), 35–6.

Gallagher, J. & Desimone, L. (1995). Lessons learned from implementation of the IEP: Applications to the IFSP. *Topics in Early Childhood Special Education, 15*(3), 353–378. doi:10.1177/027112149501500307

Hornby, G. & Lafaele, R. (2011). Barriers to parental involvement in education. *Educational Review, 63*(1), 37–52. doi:10.1080/00131911.2010.488049

Kamens, M.W. (2004). Learning to write IEPs: A personalized, reflective approach for preservice teachers. *Intervention in School and Clinic, 40*(2), 76–80. doi:10.1177/10534512040400020201

Kluth, P. & Kluth, V. (2010). *A is for 'All Aboard!'* Baltimore: Paul H. Brookes Publishing Co.

Kluth, P. & Schwarz, P. (2008). *'Just give him the whale!' 20 ways to use fascinations, areas of expertise, and strengths to support students with Autism.* Baltimore: Paul H. Brookes Publishing Co.

KU Children's Services. (2009). *Introductory guide to the service support plan.* Sydney, Australia www.ku.com.au/resources/other/Introductory%20Guide%20to%20the%20Service%20Support%20Plan%20August%202009%20for%20website.pdf

Lee-Tarver, A. (2006). Are individualized education plans a good thing? A survey of teachers' perceptions of the utility of IEPs in regular education settings. *Journal of Instructional Psychology, 33*(4), 263–272. Retrieved from www.projectinnovation.biz/journal_of_instructional_psychology

Locke, E.A. & Latham, G.P. (2002). Building a practically useful theory of goal setting and task motivation: A 35-year odyssey. *American Psychologist, 57*(9), 705–717. doi:10.1037//0003-066X.57.9.705

Mitchell, D., Morton, M. & Hornby, G. (2010). *Review of the literature on individual education plans: Report to the New Zealand Ministry of Education.* College of Education, University of Canterbury, Christchurch, New Zealand www.educationcounts.govt.nz/__data/assets/pdf_file/0012/102216/Literature-Review-Use-of-the-IEP.pdf

Oken-Wright, P. & Gravett, M. (2002). Big ideas and the essence of intent. In V. Fu, A. Stremmel & L. Hill (Eds). *Teaching and learning: Collaborative explorations of the Reggio Emilia approach* (pp.197–220). Columbus, Ohio: Merrill Prentice Hall.

Pretti-Frontzac, K. & Bricker, D. (2000). Enhancing the quality of Individual Education Plan (IEP): Goals and objectives. *Journal of Early Intervention, 23*(2), 92–105. doi:10.1177/105381510002300204

Rosas, C., Winterman, K.G., Kroeger, S. & Jones, M.M. (2009). Using a rubric to assess individualized education programs. *International Journal of Applied Educational Studies, 4*(1), 47–57. Retrieved from www.questia.com/library/p408829/international-journal-of-applied-educational-studies

Shaddock, A., MacDonald, N., Hook, J., Giorcelli, L. & Arthur-Kelly, M. (2009). *Disability, diversity and tides that lift all boats: Review of special education in the ACT.* Chiswick, NSW: Services Initiatives. Retrieved from www.autismaspergeract.com.au/sites/default/files/Review_of_Special_Education_ACT_2009_Final_Report.pdf

Stroggilos, V. & Xanthacou, Y. (2006). Collaborative IEPs for the education of pupils with profound and multiple learning difficulties. *European Journal of Special Needs Education, 21*(3), 339–349. doi:10.1080/08856250600810872

Treloar, R. (Ed.). (1997). *Recommended practices in family-centered early childhood intervention.* Sydney: NSW Department of Aging, Disability and Homecare/Early Childhood Intervention Coordination Program/Early Childhood Intervention Australia.

Vakil, S., Freeman, R. & Swim, T.J. (2003). The Reggio Emilia Approach and inclusive early childhood programs. *Early Childhood Education Journal, 30*(3), 187–192. doi:1082-3301/03/0300-0187/0

Watkins, A. & D'Alessio, S. (2009). Assessment for learning and pupils with special educational needs. A discussion of the findings emerging from the Assessment in Inclusive Settings project. *RicercAzione Journal, 1*(2), 177–192. Retrieved from www.erickson.it/Riviste/Pagine/Scheda-Rivista.aspx?ItemId=38538

# 12 Adapting the Curriculum in the School Years

*Ilektra Spandagou*

CHAPTER OVERVIEW

This chapter will focus on the upper part of early years education. It starts with a discussion of early years education and implications for inclusion. The chapter will discuss the school years within the context of early years education and implications for inclusion, as well as issues of individualised provision, planning and access to curriculum.

Learning goals for this chapter include:

- Developing an understanding of current issues in the school years as part of early years education;
- Gaining an awareness of relevant curriculum considerations;
- Developing an understanding of the different levels of planning processes for inclusion;
- Becoming familiar with individualised planning and adapting the curriculum in the school years.

KEY TERMS AND CONCEPTS

adaptation of the curriculum
curriculum differentiation
Foundation year
individualised planning
national curriculum
universal design for learning

# Introduction

Learning is what young children do by experiencing the world, interacting with others, playing and so on. During the early years, any environment is a learning environment for children. Social changes in the ways that societies and families are organised, and increased recognition of the significance of early years, have resulted in many countries developing early years education systems and programs, promoting specific learning environments. As discussed elsewhere in this book, many countries aim to increase children's participation in early years education, acknowledging that 'equitable access to quality early childhood education and care can strengthen the foundations of lifelong learning for *all* children and support the broad educational and social needs of families' (Organisation for Economic Co-operation & Development [OECD], 2001, p.7, emphasis added). Thus in modern societies, it is common for children during the early years to experience an increased number of different settings, including family, early childhood education and care, and primary education settings. The coordination of experiences in these settings with appropriate transitions and curricula is essential for children to make the most of their learning. This chapter discusses the upper part of the early years, the school years, and implications for inclusion.

**FIGURE 12.1** WORKING TOGETHER AT SCHOOL

*Photo: Rimba II Primary School, Brunei*

## Starting considerations

A number of considerations should be taken into account in examining inclusion in the school years. Firstly, while inclusion refers to the broader diversity which children bring to and experience at school (as discussed in Chapter 1), this chapter focuses mainly (but not exclusively) on children identified as having a disability. Some children start school having already being identified as 'having a disability' or 'special education needs'. For these children, having access to relevant early years education and care programs is paramount. Accordingly, the United Nations Educational Scientific and Cultural Organization's (UNESCO) (1994) *Salamanca Statement and Framework for Action on Special Needs Education* identifies early years education as a priority area.

For children who have participated in early intervention as part of their prior-to-school experiences, transition to compulsory schooling may be more complex considering the potential different agencies, specialists and settings involved (see Chapter 10 for discussion of inter-professional collaboration for inclusion). However, a clear plan that bridges family-centred early intervention and curriculum-oriented schooling can facilitate this transition.

On the other hand, the early school years are also a period when 'special educational needs' may be first identified. The learning, academic, behavioural and social expectations of school may bring to the fore, exacerbate or even be responsible for learning needs. Identification at this stage aims to provide the necessary support to young learners who are at the start of their school careers. However, for some children this process may be a negative experience, as not only may they struggle with understanding school expectations but they may also resent being 'labelled' and being perceived as different (See Chapter 3 for discussion of labelling). For some children their introduction to schooling may be their first experience of 'failure', of not meeting in an appropriate and timely manner expectations set by others. Again, well-coordinated transition and support systems are needed to minimise early negative experiences. In sum, all children experience the transition to formal schooling as a significant milestone (as discussed in Chapter 13, but this experience varies depending on the types of settings previously experienced. Furthermore, for children labelled with disabilities and/or 'special educational needs' this transition may be differently planned and coordinated, while other children may experience the beginning of identification, assessment and diagnosis at the early stages of compulsory schooling. This chapter addresses issues of transition, planning and adapting the curriculum in early school years.

All states and territories in Australia have a requirement that children must start school by the age of six. However, there is great variation in when children are eligible to start school. There is also great variation on whether the year before **Foundation year** is compulsory. There are significant practical implications for early years settings and educators aiming to promote social justice and equity in the context of inclusive education, as children's early school experiences have the potential to be experiences of both inclusion and exclusion. The extent that children's education experiences are positive, meaningful and inclusive isn't a result of their disability or other personal characteristics, but rather of how early years settings respond to those personal characteristics. The next section outlines some of the factors influencing these experiences.

**Foundation year:** The first year of formal schooling. 'Prep' or 'preparatory' is the title of the school foundation year in some Australian state jurisdictions.

**FIGURE 12.2** ME AND MY TEACHER

*Artwork by Lucas*

# (Dis)continuities of inclusion in early years education

From the above it becomes apparent that continuity and coordination in the transition process between settings during the early years are important to foster positive experiences. Historically, however, in most Western countries early childhood care and education and primary education have been fragmented in terms of administration bodies, funding sources and the existence or not of learning and curriculum frameworks. Policy arrangements are characterised by simultaneous continuities and discontinuities.

Examining the Australian context, an example of such (dis)continuity is the *Disability Standards for Education 2005* (DSE) (Australian Government, 2006), which is a subordinate legislation to the *Disability Discrimination Act 1992* (DDA) (Australian Government, 1992). The purpose of the *DSE* is to guide education providers in meeting their obligations under the *DDA* by clarifying the rights of students with disability. While the *DSE* apply to preschools and schools, they do not apply to childcare programs. As the recent *Report on the Review of the Disability Standards for Education 2005* (Department of Education, Employment & Workplace Relations [DEEWR], 2012) noted, this results in confusion when a setting offers both childcare and part-time preschool programs but the *DSE* covers only the latter. To eliminate this discontinuity the review recommended the inclusion of childcare providers under the *DSE*.

The curriculum is a second example of (dis)continuity. With the introduction of the *Early Years Learning Framework* (EYLF) (DEEWR, 2009) and the school *Australian Curriculum* (Australian Curriculum, Assessment & Reporting Authority [ACARA], 2013a), the full early years period is covered for the first time by **national curricula**. The Joint paper by Early Childhood Australia (ECA) and ACARA entitled *Foundations for Learning: Relationships between the Early Years Learning Framework and the Australian Curriculum* (ECA & ACARA, 2011) argues that there are clear connections between the two frameworks and that the Australian Curriculum builds upon the EYLF. Others have questioned the continuity between the two curriculum frameworks.

**National curriculum (plural curricula):** A common program of learning areas or subjects, skills and capabilities that aims to provide uniformity and consistency of content and standards within a state, regardless of any other differences and variations in the education systems and sectors of different jurisdictions.

For example, Perry, Dockett and Harley (2012) examined the relationship between the EYLF and the Mathematics Australian Curriculum and argued that the two documents have a different focus on learning, with the EYLF taking a more holistic approach with broad learning outcomes in play-based environments, while the Mathematics Australian Curriculum focusing on 'content and proficiency strands, with content descriptions and elaborations' (p.154). They argue that the continuity of content and pedagogy isn't facilitated by these two frameworks and thus continuity of children's learning 'will need to be built by educators as they consider broader issues such as pedagogical continuity, continuity of expectations and experiences, as well as continuity in relationships and support across the prior-to-school and school sectors' (p.157). Educators are central in ensuring continuity for all students, but in particular for those students who may experience difficulties in their transition between prior-to-school and school settings. As we will discuss later, however, this is a process that requires the active involvement of all the significant people and agencies involved in a child's education.

At this point it is also important to acknowledge that increased continuity between the prior-to-school and early school curricula doesn't mean that these curricula should become the same. Indeed the opposite is the case. Increased emphasis in prior-to-school learning on academic elements and specific, narrow cognitive outcomes could result in 'schoolification' (OECD, 2006). Schoolification may lead to children being introduced to content and ways of learning that are not age-appropriate, resulting in what is commonly called 'too much too soon'.

Keeping in mind the distinct histories and traditions of early years education in different states and territories, experiences of implementing the new national curriculum frameworks vary. Petriwskyj, Turunen and O'Gorman (2013) have looked at the pre-existing constructions of pre-Foundation Year in Queensland, NSW and Victoria. Even though in 2012 only Queensland had started the implementation of the Australian Curriculum, it was evident in their policy analysis that there were tensions in the state adaptation of the national curriculum. The authors argued that there is evidence of a shift to constructing pre-Foundation Year based on school-based ideologies. As the introduction of the Australian Curriculum continues, early years professionals need to engage, urgently, in discussion of the purpose of the pedagogy and curriculum in different settings.

Nevertheless, in the last twenty years or so there has been an increased acknowledgement of the potential discontinuities between prior-to-school and school settings. For that reason, strategies have been identified that promote continuity. Continuity can be facilitated by preparing children in advance for change; briefing the primary school; organising common professional development courses; clarifying the expectations of parents, preschool and school teachers about transition; and, preparing the school for young children (OECD, 2006). Central in the success of the above strategies are teachers. By being involved in the transition process, teachers can learn about the prospective children in their class, their strengths and individual needs, and their families' expectations, and this understanding and knowledge results in teachers being able to plan for the diverse strengths and needs of the students in their class.

However, it is important to keep in mind that successful transition requires schools and teachers to see beyond the individual child. Dockett, Perry and Howard (2000, as cited in Dockett and Perry, 2001, para.17) developed ten guidelines for effective transition programs. The last one, which is about accounting for 'contextual aspects of community, and ... individual families and children within that community', reminds us that it is not the child who is responsible for his/her 'readiness', as contextual factors influence the experiences of communities, schools and individual families and children.

## Planning for inclusion in the early school years

The planning process for inclusion takes place at different levels of the education system. As discussed in Chapter 4, the expectation for providing an inclusive education system in Australia stems from international policy and legislation such as the Salamanca Statement (UNESCO, 1994) mentioned above and the *Convention on the Rights of Persons with Disabilities* (United Nations [UN], 2006) and national policy and legislation such as the *Melbourne Declaration* (Ministerial Council for Education, Early Childhood Development & Youth Affairs [MCEECDYA], 2008), the *DDA 1992* and the *DSE 2005*. The above policies and legislations are informed by a discourse of social justice, equity and human rights. They, in turn, inform all aspects of education in terms of enrolment, curricula and extra-curricular activities, funding and support services, examinations and accreditation and so on, which are administered at the federal, state and sector level. However, families and students experience educational inclusion (or exclusion) mainly at the school and classroom level. A number of school characteristics are supportive of inclusion. These include a school being aware of its responsibilities and having the necessary structures, processes and programs in place. Most importantly, inclusion is supported by a school considering inclusion a core principle informing its purpose and practice, and hence inclusion is evident in its overall ethos.

A central structure in promoting inclusive practice at the school level is a designated team that is responsible for designing and promoting school-wide programs that support students' learning and also develop programs for individual students that require them. This team tends to have a core membership responsible for long-term planning and coordination of support programs and personnel, but at the same time its membership is individualised when it comes to individual students. For example, a student with a disability, his or her parents, teacher and other support personnel are part of that student's specific team in addition to the core members. While the *DSE 2005* sketches a framework for working in consultation with students with a disability and their families, how this is implemented in practice differs between states, sectors and schools. The extent and quality of consultation also varies and for that reason the review on the *DSE 2005* recommends a stronger emphasis on ongoing consultation with the family 'about how best to meet the needs of the student with disability, particularly in the early school years' (DEEWR, 2012, p.12).

At the individual student level, it is important to keep in mind that all students are entitled to an education experience that takes into consideration their personal strengths, interests and progress. This means that all students require a level of **individualised planning**. This should take place through the everyday planning processes employed by teachers. However, for some students, a more formalised approach to planning is anticipated. Historically, some groups of students have underperformed due to the lack of appropriate planning and inadequate allocation of resources and support. The introduction of formalised individualised planning aims to ensure that appropriate steps are taken for students to have equitable access to education.

**Individualised planning:** Processes and practices used to develop educational programs for individual students based on their strengths, needs and interests.

As discussed in Chapter 11, internationally, formalised individualised planning is described with different names. For example in the USA, the term Individualised Education Programs (IEPs) is used and IEPs are mandated by the relevant legislation, the *Individuals with Disabilities Education Act 2004* (IDEA). In the UK, where the term Individual Education Plan is more commonly used, they are not mandatory. Thus schools may use Individual Education Plans, Group Education Plans, Provision Mapping, Pupil Profiles, classroom planning and so on. In New Zealand, Individual Education Plans (IEPs) are used only for those students who require differentiation of the curriculum or adaptations to teaching strategies or the environment or are in the process of transition.

**Adaptation of the curriculum:** Changes in the educational environment including the content, delivery and assessment of learning, and the physical and social environment, made to provide equal opportunity of access.

In Australia a specific medium for recording planning for students isn't mandatory but different states, sectors and schools are widely using formalised individualised plans for different purposes. For example, in New South Wales (NSW), the Departments of Education and Communities' (DEC) pilot, the *School Learning Support Program*, refers to learning plans:

> A learning plan is a process to formally tailor learning for a student or a small group of students when their specific learning needs place them at risk of not progressing to their next stage of learning. A learning plan does not have to be a separate document developed for an individual student as, in many instances, a learning plan for a specific student or group of students will be incorporated, maintained and monitored within the classroom program (Department of Education [DET], 2010, p.11).

In NSW DEC schools, individualised or personalised plans are developed for a number of purposes including to support student learning, transition processes to and from school, behaviour and health needs. There is an expectation that personalised education plans are developed for students with a disability who may be working towards different syllabus outcomes from their age/stage peers and for children and young people in statutory out of home care, while personalised learning plans are developed for all students of Aboriginal descent (DEC, 2012). Finally, Individual Learning Plans (ILP) may be developed to improve the literacy and/or numeracy achievement of at-risk students.

There is limited information on the actual use of formalised individualised plans in Australia. In a recent study, Dempsey (2012) conducted a secondary analysis of data collected as part of the Longitudinal Study of Australian Children. The data referred to children aged eight to nine years in 2009. While there was a strong association between having a disability and having an IEP, 53 per cent of school children whose parents identified them as having a disability or medical condition did not have one. Similarly, 64 per cent of students who, according to their teachers, received additional school services did not have an IEP.

Formalised individualised plans have the potential to strengthen the outcomes of consultation process, as they provide a working document and accountability framework ensuring that planning is transparent, easily accessible by all involved and in a format that can support reviewing and further development. On the other hand, formalised individualised plans may also result in additional paperwork, may be completed with no or insufficient consultation with families and students, and be 'written and then never used', until it is time to review them again. As highlighted in Chapter 11, there is another pitfall in the use of individual plans, that they may reinforce an individual and deficit approach to planning for students, detached from the actual context of the class where instruction takes place and the curriculum is taught. This potential discontinuity can be avoided when teachers are actively involved in the development and review of individualised plans and use them as working documents in conjunction with their overall class planning, thus ensuring that all students have access to the curriculum.

**CASE STUDY 12.1**

## Making the IEP an integral part of ongoing planning

Ruth is a very experienced teacher with almost thirty years' teaching experience. She has very strong views about Individual Educational Plans (IEPs) and how they should be used. When she first discusses the role of IEPs with parents, she always starts from her own experience. She explains that she remembers a time that IEPs were unheard of and a regular classroom wasn't seen as a suitable place for students with a disability. She says that most teachers then didn't think that they were trained to teach students with a disability. She thinks that some teachers still struggle with this idea now. She believes that it is a matter of experience and that families or teachers who have experienced living or working with a child with a disability are more positive in their attitudes.

She says to parents that as a teacher who grew up in a different time, her own expectations of herself and her students with a disability have changed over the years of her teaching career. She has learned from others, her students, their parents and families. But as a teacher, most of her working time is spent in class, with her students and sometimes a teacher's aide. The opportunities to work with her students' wider circle of support are limited and that is why she believes so strongly that an IEP is important. An IEP, she stresses, isn't simply a document, it is the process of developing this document and most importantly it is the process of putting it in action, reviewing it, changing it, and at some stage passing this knowledge on to the next people. A good IEP for Ruth puts everybody on the same page. A good IEP isn't just a plan for the student; it is a plan for the community of the student, the class, the teachers and support personnel, the school as a whole, the family, any other agencies and professionals involved.

Ruth emphasises that IEPs can be invaluable but they can also be a wasted opportunity. She has experienced both ends and some in between. She recalls that in her first experience using IEPs, the IEP was developed in advance and it was presented to the parents in a meeting as a finalised document with the expectation that they would sign it after reading it. Most of the time, little attention was paid to it until the next review meeting. She confesses that she thought then that this was good practice. Now she sees IEPs as integral to her planning. Ruth cross-references between her class planning, units of work, daybook and specific students' IEPs. She makes multiple copies of each IEP and annotates them, adding observations, reflections, and attaching the student's work. Even with her younger students she makes schedules or visuals that they can use to check, self-assess and report on their own IEP goals.

### CRITICAL REFLECTION QUESTIONS

1. What are your thoughts on Ruth's journey during her teaching career as far as inclusion is concerned?
2. Reflecting on your own experiences of inclusion, how are they similar/different to those of Ruth?
3. One of the limitations of IEPs, as Shaddock, MacDonald, Hook, Giorcelli and Arthur-Kelly (2009) describe, is that they 'tend to serve multiple roles and this could be part of the problem. For example, the same planning document is expected to serve educational, legal, planning, accountability and resource allocation purposes' (p.69). Reading Ruth's description of the different IEPs she has experienced, what are your thoughts on their purposes?
4. Drawing on Ruth's story, and on Chapter 11, write a short paragraph outlining your own understanding of the purpose(s) of an IEP. How does this understanding affect your actions and practice?

Ilektra Spandagou

**CASE STUDY 12.2**

## Meet Ethan

Ethan is seven years old and was diagnosed with Pervasive Developmental Disorder Not Otherwise Specified (PDD-NOS) the previous year. Ethan experiences expressive language difficulties, has a diagnosis of mild intellectual disability and finds social interactions challenging. He receives Speech Therapy and Occupational Therapy outside school. Following his diagnosis, Ethan was allocated about two hours a week of teacher's aide support in class. However, due to changes in the allocation of funding, this support isn't available anymore. The timing of his diagnosis meant that Ethan had an IEP for only two terms of the previous year.

One of Ethan's IEP goals from the previous year involved him working with his peers. He demonstrated improvement in this with the support of the teacher's aide to facilitate his interactions with his group. Ethan worked well alongside his peers but he was struggling to contribute independently to group work. However, it was evident that the opportunities Ethan has had to work with his peers in class resulted in him being more confident in interacting with them in the playground. Ethan's family is very happy with this outcome, as one of their concerns is Ethan's long-term social inclusion in the school.

**CRITICAL REFLECTION QUESTIONS**

1. On the next page there is an extract from Ethan's IEP. After reading it, consider whether it puts forward a strengths-based approach to learning. Identify specific points that support your answer.
2. Is this IEP accessible and of value to all people involved? How can different people use it?
3. Do a quick Internet search and find two or three IEP templates (there are many available online). Compare them with this one and the one in Chapter 11:
   a. What elements are common?
   b. What elements are different?
4. What elements, in your opinion, are essential for an IEP?
5. Develop another goal for Ethan, identifying the goal, link to the curriculum, potential barriers and strengths related to this goal, strategies and resources, who will enact them, and by when.

**TABLE 12.1** ETHAN'S IEP

<table>
<tr><th colspan="6">Individual Education Plan</th></tr>
<tr><td colspan="2">Student name: Ethan M.</td><td colspan="2">Date of birth: XX/XX/XXXX</td><td colspan="2">Year: 2</td></tr>
<tr><td colspan="2">School: Spring Primary School</td><td colspan="4">School contact person: Principal</td></tr>
<tr><td colspan="2">Date of meeting: 12/11/2012</td><td colspan="2">Interim review date: 10/06/2013</td><td colspan="2">Final Review Date: 09/12/2013</td></tr>
<tr><td colspan="6">Student's team:</td></tr>
<tr><td colspan="2">Student Attended N Report N</td><td colspan="2">Principal Attended Y Report N</td><td colspan="2">School Counsellor Attended Y Report Y</td></tr>
<tr><td colspan="2">Parent(s) Attended Y Report N</td><td colspan="2">Class teacher Attended Y Report Y</td><td colspan="2">Speech Pathologist Attended N Report Y</td></tr>
<tr><td colspan="2">Support person Attended N Report N</td><td colspan="2">Previous teacher Attended N Report Y</td><td colspan="2">Occupational Therapist Attended N Report N</td></tr>
<tr><th colspan="6">Current programs</th></tr>
<tr><th>Program</th><th>Purpose</th><th>School/External</th><th>Contact person</th><th colspan="2">Duration/frequency</th></tr>
<tr><td>Speech Therapy</td><td>Expressive language</td><td>External</td><td>Speech Pathologist</td><td colspan="2">Yearly/1 session per fortnight</td></tr>
<tr><td>Occupational Therapy</td><td>Communication and social skills</td><td>External</td><td>Occupational Therapist</td><td colspan="2">Two terms/ 1 session per week</td></tr>
<tr><th colspan="6">Student's last year snapshot</th></tr>
<tr><th colspan="3">Student's skills and strengths</th><th colspan="3">Student's academic progress based on previous year's IEP</th></tr>
<tr><td colspan="3">Ethan is motivated and persists with his work. He stays on task and he knows how to ask for assistance. He tends to avoid engaging in verbal communication but when he does it is obvious that he uses some of the skills that he has practised in therapy. The level of his comprehension is not always evident due to his expressive language difficulties.</td><td colspan="3">Ethan had an IEP for only part of the year. The teacher and the school set up a program based on the IEP goals. Ethan worked well on all of his goals. While Ethan has made progress in reading, he finds the slow pace of his reading frustrating when reading aloud.</td></tr>
<tr><th colspan="3">Student's engagement and social relationships</th><th colspan="3">Important events</th></tr>
<tr><td colspan="3">Ethan enjoys school and has excellent attendance. He prefers to work on his own or with an adult but he doesn't resist working with peers. He tends not to contribute unless repeatedly prompted. Ethan identifies two of his peers as his friends and this is reciprocal. He socialises with them in the playground but also spends time by himself.</td><td colspan="3">Ethan's diagnosis last year was a significant event for him and his family. He found some of the assessment stressful but he appears to enjoy his therapy sessions. Communication and collaboration between Ethan's family and the school and teacher was ongoing.</td></tr>
</table>

(Continued)

**TABLE 12.1** ETHAN'S IEP (CONTNIUED)

| Education Plan | | | | | |
|---|---|---|---|---|---|
| | **Goals** | **Links to the curriculum** | **Barriers and/or strengths related to goal** | **Strategies/resources** | **Who/When** |
| 1 | Ethan will work cooperatively with peers in small group settings (i.e. set materials, share appropriate roles, share ideas/thoughts) | Understand that language varies when people take on different roles in social and classroom interactions and how the use of key interpersonal language resources varies depending on context (ACELA1461)<br><br>Use interaction skills including initiating topics, making positive statements and voicing disagreement in an appropriate manner, speaking clearly and varying tone, volume and pace appropriately (ACELY1789)<br><br>Compare observations with those of others (ACSIS041) | **Barriers**<br><br>Ethan experiences difficulty in expressing his views verbally.<br><br>Ethan finds it stressful waiting for his turn/ having to contribute in group work.<br><br>**Strengths**<br><br>Ethan's contributions tend to be relevant.<br><br>Ethan's likes and is liked by his classmates. | Structured group work in purposely set groups<br><br>Introduction of group work strategies<br><br>Ethan to be able to use visuals and/or schedules during group work<br><br>Facilitation of group work | Teacher/Relevant units of work during the year<br><br>Teacher/Term 1—reminders in consequent units<br><br>Teacher/Introduction in Term 1 (other students may benefit –avoid singling out)<br><br>Teacher/Other adults present if available (e.g. ESL support teacher) |

# Adapting the curriculum

The principle that *all* children can learn is a powerful driver for education systems, schools and teachers. It is so powerful that it is easy to forget how recent the entitlement to quality education for each and every student is. Historically, pedagogy and instruction in general education was geared towards homogeneity defined by what was perceived as 'normal' development. Students who deviated from this 'norm' were ignored, considered as requiring special education or even as being unable to learn (Armstrong, Armstrong & Spandagou, 2010). Many students with disabilities were taught with age-inappropriate curricula, methods and materials, resulting in a constantly increasing learning gap. Accepting, however, that all children can learn and this should happen in the same classroom, shifted the attention from the child as the problem, to the environments where children learn. Hence, the learning environment, instruction and curriculum (including assessment methods) can—and should—be adapted to provide appropriate adjustments for individuals or groups of students.

**Universal Design for Learning (UDL):** Is structured around three principles that recognise the diverse ways that children learn by providing multiple means of representation, action and expression and engagement. The aim of the UDL is to design a curriculum that is inclusive of all learners.

In the last twenty years a framework of instruction has been developed based on research on the learning sciences. This framework, **Universal Design for Learning (UDL)**, provides three principles that are structured around the questions of *what* we learn, *how* we learn and *why* we learn (see Hall, Meyer & Rose, 2012 and chapters 4 and 6 in this book). UDL promotes the use of technology in the development of curriculum but it is not restricted to it. There are clear intersections between UDL and **curriculum differentiation**, which is a theoretical approach to providing tailored learning experiences within diverse classrooms based on children's individual profiles and learning preferences.

**Curriculum differentiation:** Encompasses different models and approaches aiming to provide teaching and learning experiences to students with diverse abilities in the same class, recognising their background knowledge, interests and preferences in learning.

Education settings and educators are required to provide appropriate adjustments for students with disabilities under the *DSE 2005*. UDL and curriculum differentiation are of assistance in this process, particularly since they are based on the common principle that all students are entitled to an appropriate and meaningful curriculum that recognises their unique characteristics.

The new Australian Curriculum comprises three dimensions: learning areas (English, Maths, History, etc.), seven general capabilities (literacy, numeracy, critical and creative thinking, intercultural understanding, etc.), and three cross-cultural priorities (Aboriginal and Torres Strait Islander histories and cultures, Asia and Australia's engagement with Asia, and Sustainability). According to the curriculum, schools and teachers are expected to use the flexibility provided by these three dimensions to promote personalised learning for *all* students (ACARA, 2013a). This broad understanding of student body diversity is an important, positive underlying principle of the national curriculum. This

**FIGURE 12.3** WORKING ON THE COMPUTER

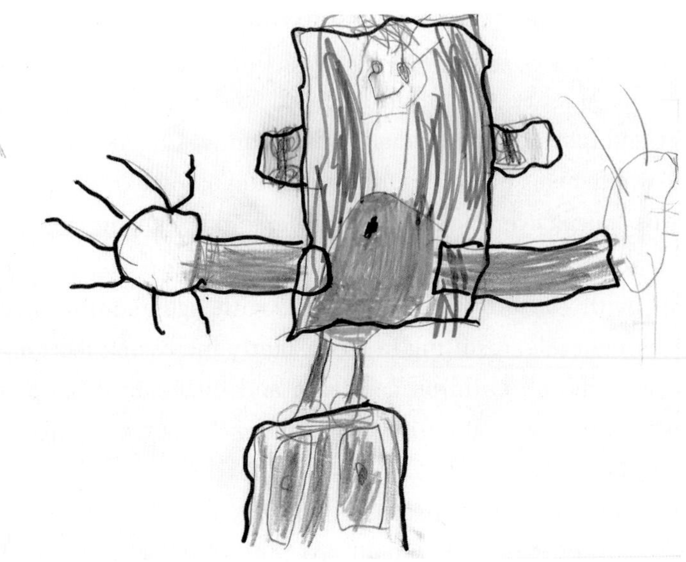

*Artwork by Lucas*

is particularly important as this principle emphasises students' entitlement to age-appropriate curriculum content, as is evident in this statement: 'personalising the teaching and learning program enables teachers to: select age-equivalent content that is meaningful and respects students' individual needs, strengths and interests' (ACARA, 2013a, p.7). In addition to the above expectation for all students, the ACARA's (2013b) document *Student diversity and the Australian curriculum: Advice for principals, schools and teachers* outlines the ways the Australian Curriculum can be used to make curriculum, instructional and environmental adjustments for students who are identified under the umbrella term of diversity; students with disability, students identified as gifted and talented and students for whom English is an additional language or dialect (EAL/D).

**CASE STUDY 12.3**

## Applying differentiated planning

In Ethan's class there are 26 students, 10 of whom are learning English as an Additional Language or Dialect (EAL/D). An English as a Second Language (ESL) support teacher works closely with the class teacher, including regular team teaching sessions. The teacher and the ESL support teacher had discussions about introducing a more structured approach to group work. They looked for models that could accommodate Ethan's specific needs. They decided to introduce a modified version of Collaborative Strategic Reading (CSR).

CSR is usually used with older students (middle years) to develop comprehension (Vaughn & Klingner, 1999). In CSR students are introduced to four strategies, preview (get information about the text before reading it), clink and clunk (identify points that are understood and points/words that are not understood in the text), get the gist (identify central ideas) and wrap-up (after finishing reading). Students are allocated to groups with distinct roles (e.g. leader, clunk expert, gist expert, announcer, encourager, time-keeper). The clunk expert has a set of cards to remind the group of relevant strategies (e.g. reread the sentence without the 'clunk' word). The role of 'clunk expert', using the relevant cards, was seen as a fitting one for Ethan to introduce him to CSR.

The strategy was modified to the extent that the students used the strategy with a variety of texts relating to the Australia Curriculum content description '[u]se comprehension strategies to build literal and inferred meaning and begin to analyse texts by drawing on growing knowledge of context, language and visual features and print and multimodal text structure' (ACARA, 2013a, ACLY1670).

Further, the use of groups was relevant for all students to the 'social management' element of the 'personal and social development' capability, in which 'students learn to negotiate and communicate effectively with others; work in teams, positively contribute to groups and collaboratively make decisions; resolve conflict and reach positive outcomes' (ACARA, 2013c, p.8). Again, this element directly linked to Ethan's IEP goals.

# Conclusion

This chapter discussed issues of inclusion and curriculum in the school years. The chapter is informed by a broad understanding of curriculum: that is, curriculum isn't limited to the content taught in classes, but rather it is enacted within the complex realities of wider socio-political and specific school communities (Luke, 2010). Teachers responsible for enacting the right of all children to quality inclusive education need to negotiate this complexity. Programs and processes of transition, whole-school and formalised individualised plans, curriculum adjustments and evidence-based practices were discussed as available tools in this process, with their potential limitations acknowledged.

# FOR FURTHER REFLECTION

1. After reading this chapter what are three things that made an impression to you? Why? And what are the implications for your actions and/or practice?
2. Are any specific, distinctive characteristics of the school years part of early years education? Justify your answer.
3. What kind of attitudes, knowledge and skills do you think are necessary for early years professionals to adapt the curriculum? How do educators acquire them? What are the implications for your own actions and/or practice?

## WEBSITES

www.australiancurriculum.edu.au
The Australian National Curriculum website

http://seonline.tki.org.nz/IEP
A dedicated website to IEPs by the New Zealand Ministry of Education

www.udlcenter.org
A US website dedicated to Universal Design for Learning (UDL)

## REFERENCES


Armstrong, A.C., Armstrong, D. & Spandagou, I. (2010). *Inclusive education: International policy and practice.* London: Sage.

Australian Curriculum, Assessment and Reporting Authority (ACARA). (2013a). *Australian curriculum.* Retrieved from www.australiancurriculum.edu.au

ACARA. (2013b). *Student diversity and the Australian curriculum: Advice for principals, schools and teachers.* Retrieved from www.australiancurriculum.edu.au/StudentDiversity/Pdf/StudentDiversity

ACARA. (2013c). *General capabilities in the Australian curriculum.* Retrieved from www.australiancurriculum.edu.au/GeneralCapabilities/Overview/General-capabilities-in-the-Australian-Curriculum

Australian Government. (1992). *Commonwealth disability discrimination act (1992).* Canberra: Commonwealth of Australia.

Australian Government. (2006). *Disability standards for education (2005) plus guidance notes.* Canberra: Attorney-General's Department and Department of Education, Science and Training, Commonwealth of Australia. Retrieved from http://education.gov.au/disability-standards-education

DEEWR, *see* Department of Education, Employment and Workplace Relations.

Department of Education (DET). (2010). *School learning support program—Effectively supporting students.* Sydney: Author.

Department of Education and Communities (DEC). (2012). *Report of the program evaluation of Individual Learning Plans.* Sydney: Author.

Department of Education, Employment and Workplace Relations (DEEWR). (2009). *Belonging, being and becoming: The early years learning framework for Australia.* Canberra: Commonwealth of Australia. Retrieved from http://education.gov.au/early-years-learning-framework

Department of Education, Employment and Workplace Relations [DEEWR]. (2012). *Report on the review of the Disability Standards for Education 2005.* Canberra: Commonwealth of Australia. Retrieved from http://education.gov.au/disability-standards-education

Dempsey, I. (2012). The use of individual education programs for children in Australian schools, in *Australasian Journal of Special Education, 36*(1) 21–31. doi:10.1017/jse.2012.5

Dockett, S. & Perry, B. (2001). Starting school: Effective transitions. *Early Childhood Research and Practice, 3*(2). Retrieved from http://ecrp.uiuc.edu/v3n2/dockett.html

Early Childhood Australia (ECA), & ACARA. (2011). *Foundations for learning: Relationships between the early years learning framework and the Australian curriculum.* Retrieved from www.earlychildhoodaustralia.org.au/pdf/ECA_ACARA_Foundations_Paper/ECA_ACARA_Foundations_Paper_FINAL.pdf

Hall, T., Meyer, A. & Rose, D. (2012). (Eds.) *Universal design for learning in the classroom: Practical applications.* New York: Guilford Press.

Luke, A. (2010). Will the Australian national curriculum up the intellectual ante in classrooms? *Curriculum Perspectives, 30*(3), 59–64. Retrieved from www.acsa.edu.au/pages/page503.asp

Ministerial Council for Education, Early Childhood Development and Youth Affairs (MCEECDYA). (2008). *Melbourne Declaration on educational goals for young Australians*. Carlton South Vic: Author. Retrieved from www.mceecdya.edu.au/verve/_resources/national_declaration_on_the_educational_goals_for_young_australians.pdf

Organisation for Economic Co-operation and Development (OECD). (2001). *Starting Strong I: Early childhood education and care*. Paris: Author.

OECD. (2006). *Starting Strong II: Early childhood education and care*. Paris: Author.

Perry, B., Dockett, S. & Harley, E. (2012). The Early Years Learning Framework for Australia and the Australian Curriculum: Mathematics—Lining educators' practice through pedagogical inquiry questions. In B. Atweh, M. Goos, R. Jorgensen, & D. Siemon (Eds.). *Engaging the Australian National Curriculum: Mathematics – Perspectives from the field* (pp.155–174). Online Publication: Mathematics Education Research Group of Australasia.

Petriwskyj, A., Turunen, T. & O'Gorman, L. (2013). The interface of the national Australian curriculum and the pre-Year 1 class in school: Exploring tensions. *Australasian Journal of Early Childhood, 38*(1), 16–22. Retrieved from www.earlychildhoodaustralia.org.au/australian_journal_of_early_childhood.html

Shaddock, A., MacDonald, N., Hook, J., Giorcelli, L. & Arthur-Kelly, M. (2009). *Disability, diversity and tides that lift all boats: Review of special education in the ACT*. Chiswick, NSW: Services Initiatives. Retrieved from www.autismaspergeract.com.au/sites/default/files/Review_of_Special_Education_ACT_2009_Final_Report.pdf

United Nations (UN). (2006). *Convention on the rights of persons with disabilities*. New York, United Nations.

United Nations Educational Scientific and Cultural Organization (UNESCO). (1994). *The Salamanca statement and framework for action on special needs education*. Paris: Author.

Vaughn, S. & Klingner, J. (1999). Teaching reading comprehension through collaborative strategic reading. *Intervention in School and Clinic, 34*(5), 284–292. doi:10.1177/105345129903400505.

SECTION 4

# Transitions and Continuity

# 13 Transitions in the Early Years

*Anne Petriwskyj*

CHAPTER OVERVIEW

This chapter will focus on current approaches to transitions between and within early years programs, including support strategies for children experiencing these transitions.

Learning goals for this chapter include:

- Recognising varied transitions in the early years, and the potential interactions between overlapping transitions;
- Identifying transition possibilities and concerns for children with diverse characteristics, abilities and backgrounds, and making provisions for support;
- Planning ECEC and school educator roles in the transitions undertaken by diverse children and families in the early years;
- Understanding the role partnerships with families, communities and professional colleagues, and dialogue with children all play in transitions.

KEY TERMS AND CONCEPTS

continuity

horizontal transitions

vertical transitions

# Introduction

Transitions in the early years are periods of significant change that present exciting opportunities for children to undertake new experiences, but may be stressful for some children. Although transition to school is widely recognised, other educational transitions also require consideration. Transitions may involve early childhood education and care (ECEC) services, the early years of primary school, school age care, health or therapy services, other specialist services and later school transitions. Transition planning is essential to ensure the change process is supportive for all children and families. It is ideally a long-term process that offers educators, children and families opportunities and time to anticipate change, prepare themselves and feel comfortable about the change. However, for some children, major program or setting transitions require more extensive planning, support and collaboration between stakeholders than that involved in transitions generally. Transitions in the early years include both **vertical and horizontal transitions**, and some children undertake multiple and overlapping transitions.

**vertical and horizontal transitions:** Vertical transitions mark a distinct uni-directional shift from one service to another (e.g. transition into an ECEC service or into school).

Horizontal transitions occur regularly within a day or week (e.g. between an education program and a therapy program), between segments of a program day in the one setting (e.g. mat time to free play) or sometimes within a year (e.g. changing centres or schools for children who are geographically mobile).

Children with complex family circumstances or children who access support services may undertake many horizontal transitions within a short time period. This level of change can be confusing for some children, for example those with cognitive impairment, or those undergoing family separation. Sometimes, the combination of multiple horizontal transitions (e.g. moving between childcare, therapy and preschool programs) and major vertical transitions (e.g. entering an unfamiliar early childhood centre or school program) may be particularly stressful. Collaborative planning that respects the diverse perspectives and rights of children, families and educators is a key strategy for minimising disruption. An inclusive approach to transition incorporates respectful relationships and language, non-stigmatising practices, child and family agency in decision-making, and critical reflection by educators on power dynamics within relationships. Such an approach to transition supports social justice principles of treating all people with dignity and respect, and ensuring all children have an excellent start to their education (Perry, 2013).

In this chapter, transitions involving ECEC services will be discussed initially, followed by an exploration of the transitions involving the early years of school. Specific concerns of some children and families will be identified, together with strategies to address these.

# Transitions and early childhood services

In this section, transitions into ECEC, including those that impact on children and families entering centre-based services such as childcare centres and preschools as well as home-based services such as family day care, will be addressed. Later in this section, horizontal transitions that impact regularly on some children and families will be considered.

## TRANSITIONS INTO ECEC SERVICES

The transition of very young children from home, family and community settings into an ECEC service, particularly a large centre-based service or school, represents three major changes—a change in the range of relationships, a shift in demands, and separation from family members. The relationships formed with educators in the ECEC service are a key aspect of high quality care and underpin the transition process for both children and their families (Recchia, 2012). Families include not only parents, but also siblings and extended family members. In some cultural contexts, the wider community also requires consideration (see the section 'Transition partnerships' on page 276).

The National Quality Framework (NQF) for ECEC identifies the importance of supporting continuity of learning and transitions for each child by sharing information and clarifying responsibilities (Australian Children's Education & Care Quality Authority [ACECQA], 2012). These principles are supported in *The Early Years Learning Framework for Australia* (EYLF) (Department of Education, Employment & Workplace Relations [DEEWR], 2009).

Children's transitions into ECEC environments may be eased through:

- Visits by the family and child prior to commencement in the program, so the child feels secure in the environment and can begin to form relationships;
- Ongoing discussion between educators and family members regarding the child's home routine and their preferred patterns and responses, so that a level of continuity can be maintained;
- Gradual increases in the amount of time spent in the program each day, with a family member present for part of the first few days;
- Careful observation of, and listening to, children, to gain insights into elements of uncertainty and preferences for support strategies;
- Planned strategies for assisting children with separation, including time allocation for educators to offer more sustained soothing during the initial few weeks. Some ECEC services permit transitional objects (e.g. a teddy);
- Sensitivity to the emotional pressures on parents whose children are entering ECEC for the first time. Regular dialogue with parents about child responses shows appreciation of the primacy of parent–child relationships (Dalli, 2002).

In centre-based ECEC environments, particularly larger ECEC centres and preschools, further strategies include:

- Staggered entry (the commencement of small numbers of incoming children each day, rather than an entire incoming group on a single day);

- Use of a primary educator system, in which one educator has primary responsibility for a small number of young children;
- Careful scaffolding of interactions between mixed age groups in shared areas such as playgrounds. Some centres separate babies/toddlers and preschoolers to protect younger children (Dalli, 2002);
- An interpreter or family advocate may be necessary for non-English speaking families to negotiate unfamiliar transition processes and talk with educators.

## FROM EARLY INTERVENTION TO OTHER ECEC SERVICES

For children who access specialist early intervention services, for example services for children with disabilities, additional planning for transition into an inclusive ECEC service may be required. Balaban (2010) recommends that educators:

- Engage with all key stakeholders in a transition planning process that clarifies strategies, roles and responsibilities and ensures that relevant documentation of the child's requirements and progress is shared;
- Organise visits by the child and family to the ECEC service, and educators to the child's early intervention service and home if possible, to form relationships among the child, family and other staff;
- Listen sensitively for the hidden messages within a family's requests for details. They may be worried about unexpected changes in their child, or a loss of control over the intervention process;
- Consider and show concern for the personal wellbeing of the parent, who may be experiencing significant emotional stress about the transition.

Families have a key role in transitions, so sensitive consideration for the demands on their time, resources and feelings is important. During transitions, educators seek to maintain family self-confidence by balancing professional assistance with attention to family agency in decision-making (see Chapter 9). In addition to the above measures, educators may also enquire into family preferences, share holistic, strengths-based assessment information, and discuss support and funding entitlements and processes (see Chapters 5 and 6).

## FROM YOUNGER TO OLDER GROUP IN CENTRE-BASED SERVICES

In many ECEC centre-based programs children move from one group to another on an age-related basis. This may be a smooth change for some children, yet for others each change represents a significant adjustment process. Secure child–educator relationships help support young children's sense of continuity and security as they move between age-based rooms in ECEC centres (Recchia, 2012). However, educators need to be aware that different types of child–educator relationships exist, and that moving between these can pose difficulties. For example, a primary educator model supports attachment in infant and toddler rooms yet may not support transitions into preschool rooms in which this model is not in place (Recchia, 2012). Adjustments to relational practices in preschool rooms, ongoing support from previous primary caregivers and more individual attention to child characteristics offer greater continuity. However, an alternate model of provision involves educators staying with the same group of children for several years, to ensure greater continuity of relationships and planning. Sometimes this constitutes a family mixed age group, so that children from one family may be together. This alternate model assumes stability in enrolments and staffing within the ECEC service.

## TRANSITIONS WITHIN ECEC

This section will consider horizontal transitions including daily home to ECEC transitions and the transitions that occur within an ECEC program day.

### *Daily transitions from home to ECEC program*

The change from home to ECEC, and from ECEC to home each day represents a challenge for some children, particularly those for whom change is stressful or for whom separation from familiar people creates anxiety. However, the reciprocity of parent–child separation behaviours must be considered when planning support for these daily transitions (Jovanovic, 2011). Warm, frequent communication between educators and parents is important because it eases parents' anxiety and assists educators to respond more appropriately to children during daily transition into care. The tendency for educators to encourage children to fit into established ECEC routines and expectations rather than accommodating family patterns and styles to support continuity has been identified as problematic (Dalli, 2002).

**continuity:** Implies that there is a relatively smooth and gradual shift, rather than abrupt major change, as a child and family transition from one setting to another. It does not imply that practices in both settings are necessarily identical.

**Continuity** in care routines between home and centre constitutes a key element of a transition process that respects diverse family child rearing patterns and facilitates daily changes in location and relationships for young children (Kennedy, 2006).

### *Transitions within the ECEC program day*

Transitions within ECEC include those that are relevant to a variety of services including family day care and those that impact only in centre-based services.

**CASE STUDY 13.1**

## Continuity and respect

Joshua, aged sixteen months, is strongly resisting separation from his mother. At home, he has two sleeps a day, is spoon-fed pureed foods, is often carried by his mother, and plays indoors only. His ECEC educators provide one sleep a day, offer finger foods, have lengthy outdoor play, and encourage him to walk. Educators have revised their practices for Joshua to make change more gradual, by offering both spoon and finger foods, being more flexible in sleep schedules, and working with him on the patio while he adjusts to the outdoors. They are engaged in dialogue with his mother to share insights into mutually acceptable ways of encouraging gradual progress in independence and motor skills.

**CRITICAL REFLECTION QUESTIONS**

1. Reflect on Joshua's situation. What challenges to ideals of continuity of care can you identify? . Are Joshua's parents' perspectives balanced with provisions for his enhanced development and learning? What other strategies might best achieve this balance?
2. How do the NQF and EYLF inform your thinking?

1 Daily routine transitions in all ECEC services include

   a Changes in location in separate segments of the program (e.g. between indoor and outdoor play);

   b Routine changes within the day (e.g. rest routine in family day care or long day care; bathroom and lunch routines).

2 Transitions that mark a shift between groups in centre-based services (e.g. for children shifting from one room to another) include

   a Changes in location in segments of the day (e.g. attending an early and late program, and a main group program within a centre);

   b Staffing changes (e.g. when a 'floater' educator relieves during staff rest pauses; when a relief educator is required because of illness).

Ensuring that children retain a sense of security and confidence, and that consistency in pedagogies is maintained presents a challenge for educators in centre-based ECEC programs with regular staff changes. In ECEC centres with long day care programs, attendance numbers and staffing requirements often mean that children are in one mixed group early and late in the day and in their regular group and room for the majority of the day. Some children may resist the routine changes that occur during the day, if change is too abrupt, or they do not understand the change or feel it does not respect their preferences. Children who are unsettled by change may require transitional processes to transfer between educators and locations. These may include offering cues that a change will soon occur, keeping insecure children close to educators during changes in location, using simple transition games and establishing processes for settling children with incoming educators during staff changes. Children should be given some sense of agency in how rapidly the change occurs, a choice regarding the next activity or type of transitory game, and encouragement to develop independence.

# Transitions and the early years of school

In this section, transitions to school will be addressed, including to classrooms and to the broader school context. Later in this section, horizontal transitions that may impact on some children—for example, change of school—will be discussed.

## TRANSITION TO SCHOOL AND OUT-OF-SCHOOL CARE

Transition to school as a shared process of supported change is different from the traditional notion of readiness for school, in which there was an assumption that children would have a specific set of social and academic skills prior to school entry. Such expectations of school-entrant homogeneity are unrealistic. Children with diverse abilities, backgrounds and experiences could be expected to achieve skills at varying times and with differing styles of expression. Inclusive transition processes assume variation in school entrants, and involve a planned sequence of support strategies both before and after school entry. Instead of focusing on stereotypes or deficits, such processes are personalised and affirm children and families through a focus on their strengths and resources.

The introduction of national curriculum documents for ECEC, the school sector of early years education, and out of school care offers opportunities for pedagogic linkages and alignment of curriculum content to enhance continuity during transition to school. However, policy on transition varies by jurisdictions and auspice, so it is important to check the guidelines for each specific context. For example, the Victorian Department of Education and Early Childhood Development (DEECD) (2010) has established a structured process and support resources for transition to school including a teachers' manual. In New South Wales ECEC centres and schools may draw on guidelines for shared transition planning (Dockett & Perry, 2007). The Queensland Studies Authority (QSA) has incorporated a transition planning process into the *Queensland Kindergarten Learning Guideline* for preschool education (QSA, 2010) and there is a state transition policy for children with disabilities (Education Queensland, 2007), which could be relevant to all children (see box, below).

## EXAMPLE OF A TRANSITION POLICY

Transition from one program to another is a process, not a single event. The speed and ease of adjustment for all concerned is facilitated through careful planning and preparation. The establishment of a coordinated, systematic and timely process to guide transition to school is a key priority. Successful transitions are the key to supporting continuity of learning. As with children entering the early years of school, explicit links are made to the teaching and learning practices employed in settings prior to Prep to ensure smooth transitions occur (Education Queensland, 2007).

School-entry processes may include structural provisions (e.g. adjusted timing of school entry), preparation programs, short-term orientation programs and longer-term transitions (see below). Transition processes involve the family, the preschool or ECEC centre, out of school care (where relevant) and the foundation year classroom at a school, and may also involve additional support agencies. It cannot be assumed that all children will have attended an ECEC program, as some may not have access or some families may choose to home-educate prior to (or during) the compulsory school years. Effective transition requires explicit transition planning in both/all settings and effective professional communication between settings. Longer timelines and collaborative planning are vital aspects of a successful transition for all children, but are particularly important in instances where children may experience challenges with school commencement. Transition statements prepared by the child, family and ECEC/early intervention staff may incorporate practical tips such as child friendships, learning preferences and emergency strategies (Conway, 2010).

### *Adjusted timing of school entry*

Children with disabilities and children identified as gifted (who may also have disabilities, see Chapter 25) may have opportunities for changes to the usual timing of school entry. Delayed or accelerated entry is usually dependent on a formal diagnosis and evidence of the needs of the child. Later entry to school, particularly for boys, has been supported by Australian research (Boardman, 2006), yet evidence from the USA indicates that children from challenging home circumstances may be advantaged by earlier school entry if this offers increased cognitive stimulation and learning opportunities. However, adjustments to the timing of school entry alone are not sufficient (Grant, 2013). Children will still require a planned transition process that takes their individual characteristics, background of experiences, family expectations and the capacity of teachers into account.

## TRANSITIONS TO THE CLASSROOM

Transition processes similar to those used during entry to ECEC programs (e.g. gradual increase in day length, staggered intake) may be supplemented by preparation and orientation programs and longer-term transition planning processes, such as:

- Preparation programs—extended whole group sessions (e.g. story) in preschool, more structured learning activities, eating lunch from a lunch box, taking responsibility for personal belongings, talking about school;
- Orientation programs—children's visits to the school, engagement with classroom activities such as drawing, and meetings of parents and teachers to discuss expectations and concerns;
- Transition processes—planning of transitions includes an extended range of relationship-building opportunities over an extended time period. These may include information sharing between teachers, continuity of some preschool-like learning activities and playful pedagogies at the commencement of the school year, visits by teachers to the ECEC program, extended interactions between teachers and prospective families, class allocation that builds on established friendships, organising buddy links with older children at school, and enhancing children's confidence through regular contact with school children e.g. Skype preschool 'visits' to a school foundation class (Glass & Cotman, 2013).

Some groups of children experience difficulties in adjustment that require more comprehensive and personalised transition strategies. These personalised transition plans require thoughtful development and communication so that they take prior experience and characteristics into account without implying deficits in a child or family. Children from Aboriginal and Torres Strait Islander and other culturally and linguistically diverse backgrounds may experience discomfort not only because of variations in English language knowledge, but also because of gaps between family priorities and child-rearing practices and expectations of the school (Sanagavarapu, 2010; Taylor, 2011). Walker et al. (2012) have identified concerns for children with disabilities entering school, if teachers are resistant to accepting some children or feel unprepared. Parents from communities characterised by low socio-economic status have noted the negative impact on children of teachers' low expectations (Raban & Ure, 2000). Coordinated planning is required to personalise shared transition processes (Dockett et al., 2011; Migyanka, 2011). Appreciation by teachers of child and family expectations, together with awareness by families of pressures on schools, supports a reciprocal exchange of insights and shared decision-making.

**FIGURE 13.1** BUILDING ON FRIENDSHIPS

*Artwork by Kaitlyn*

## TRANSITIONS TO THE WHOLE SCHOOL AND PLAYGROUND

Transitions into school must take into account the broader impact of the whole school environment, including the playground environment in which children from varied age groups interact with less structured adult supervision. Playgrounds may be a source of stress when children are not supported to fully understand the structure of play (Smith, 2002). Playgrounds may also cause stress for children with social–emotional difficulties, such as children with autism spectrum disorder and children who are emotionally withdrawn. Periods of the school day and areas of the school in which adult supervision is less intense (e.g. school arrival and departure, toilet areas) may be marred by conflict or bullying, so whole-school planning is important. Discussion with families and children serves to alert teachers to areas of tension and to solutions such as supported play or transitional playgrounds that may assist the child without stigmatisation (Graham & Macartney, 2012). Such discussion may also identify ways to build on friendships and individual preferences.

In schools, children interact regularly with a range of staff other than their classroom teacher (e.g. playground supervision staff, cultural or special education teaching assistants, learning support or extension teachers, guidance psychologists, advisory visiting teachers for disability, English as a Second Language teachers, library and administrative staff and specialist content teachers such as music or physical education teachers). These staff may not all be familiar with children's individual education plans, behaviour support plans, extension plans, or school philosophy and thus may not implement strategies appropriate to individuals. In order to avoid creating difficulties for children, planning for transitions should include whole-school organisation, involvement of specialist and ancillary staff and shared awareness of support goals, strategies and policies. Extension of transition planning processes to educators in out of school care programs, regardless of whether the school and out of school program are in the same location, enhances continuity for children.

**CRITICAL REFLECTION QUESTIONS**

1. In a state system in which children commence school once a year, a family has enrolled their son who only just meets the minimum entry age requirements. His language is limited, he is not yet interacting well with other children, and he requires adult attention. Another teacher has suggested that the family should be asked to enrol him in preschool and commence school a year later. Whose interests are served by taking this perspective?
2. What are the alternative perspectives?
3. Whose voices should be heard in the decision-making?
4. What could the school do to accommodate this child and engage with a personalised transition process?

## TRANSITIONS WITHIN THE EARLY YEARS OF SCHOOL

This section considers daily or regular bi-directional transitions and uni-directional transitions such as those experienced by children who change schools. Some children may experience uncertainty or resistance related to multiple, overlapping transitions, and some may face stress and anxiety related to separation for the first time.

### *Home–school transitions*

The daily transitions between home and school are not necessarily smooth for some children in the early years of school. There may be family stress factors impacting on children's sense of security or school stress factors influencing children's willingness to enter school or school-age-care. Children who experience extreme stress related to daily separation from family or entry into school may exhibit anxiety symptoms (e.g. toilet accidents, social withdrawal) or may engage in truancy or school refusal. A transition process involving the family and the school will ideally also involve the child in decision-making. In some instances, a psychological service provider such as school guidance staff may also be involved.

### *Between school and out of school care*

Shifts between school classrooms and out of school care programs at the beginning and end of each day represent a common experience for Australian children. In some cases these programs are on the same grounds, so that changes in location are minimised, but in others, children must be transported to another facility or locality. Dockett and Perry (2007) identified difficulties in communication between staff groups when children were transported to a separate location for care. This may be of particular concern if a child has experienced a stressful day (e.g. undertaking lengthy statutory assessment). Consideration also needs to be given to negotiating continuity of expectations if children appear confused by differences in behaviour limits in co-located school and care programs (e.g. using resources after school in ways that were forbidden during school time). This may be particularly important to those who experience difficulty adjusting to change (e.g. children with autism spectrum disorder) (Migyanka, 2011).

### *Between general and specialist services*

Some children in the early years of school may resist changes that occur during the day, especially if they feel these are imposed without considering their preferences and involvement in other activities. They may need prior warning that a change is about to occur even for a daily routine such as lunch, or departure, and to be given some sense of agency in how rapidly the change occurs. Children may be assisted by not only verbal cues, but also simple choices, visual planners or a timer to help them prepare for regular daily transitions.

Children who access support services may be offered these services within their general program in the form of in-class assistance (Petriwskyj, 2013), instead of being required to transition from room to room (e.g. classroom to learning support room) or location to location (e.g. ECEC centre to a therapy centre). Change in room or location should be avoided as this constitutes exclusion, creates undue attention to difference and results in loss of learning time. Collaboratively planned processes are required to maintain a coherent approach offering continuity for children.

As discussed in Chapter 16, children with chronic health concerns may also experience regular transition points as they move between hospital services and their centre or school program (Shiu, 2004). Maintaining a sense of educational and relational continuity could involve emails or postcards between the child who is hospitalised and the class, sharing of class work with the absent child (e.g. through a blog), and assisting with re-establishment of friendship links once the child returns to the group or class.

### *Change of school and geographic mobility*

Families dissatisfied with aspects of a school program (e.g. limited intellectual challenge for a child identified as gifted) may relocate their children to an alternative school in an effort to access a more individually relevant program. Children may also transition between schools because their parents move location for employment due to migration, to escape persecution or other emergency situations or for family or personal reasons or due to a range of other circumstances (see Chapters 14 and 15). For some children, particularly those whose families are highly geographically mobile, the disruption of educational continuity and social relationships with peers may impact on their sense of security and confidence (Henderson, 2004). Easing these transitions should include linking and relational strategies such as

- Accessing information from the family and the previous centre or school regarding the children's program content and progress (where possible);
- Setting up a buddy system with children who are established in the group or class, as a regular part of the class peer relationships program;
- Establishing a dialogue with the child and family to share insights into child experiences, resources and preferences. This may need to be by email or phone, as parents may be busy re-establishing a home and work routine.

**CRITICAL REFLECTION QUESTIONS**

1. If a child arrives unexpectedly in a school classroom without school materials, and without prior information sharing by the previous school, how should teachers interpret apparent difficulties in learning and adjustment? Reflect on the feelings of the child and possible responses of other children, likely discontinuities, and the pressures on the family.
2. Critically reflect on the frustration that teachers may feel initially, and on the negative impact of deficit assumptions or low expectations. What are some more child- and family-responsive attitudes and actions that are respectful of the pressures on a family system as a whole?

# Ongoing transitions

The changes that occur later in children's school lives indicate the importance of considering ongoing transitions. Some find the transition from the junior school to middle school difficult as expectations of both classroom social conduct and academic outcomes increase. The shift from primary to secondary school represents a further key transition point for many children, as they enter an environment where there are multiple horizontal transitions during each school day and a less immediate relationship with a classroom teacher (Conway, 2010). For children who have a cognitive or emotional disability, this change in contextual security requires tactful planning that includes the perspectives of the individual student as far as possible. In addition, planning for ongoing support service provision is essential to minimise abrupt discontinuity in forms of assistance on which an older student and their family may have relied.

# Transition partnerships

Children's transitions involve not only the children and their educators but also a range of other stakeholders. Partnerships with these stakeholders, particularly families, are an essential element of a successful transition planning process. In situations involving many professional organisations or community agencies, planned collaborative processes help support transitions.

## PARTNERSHIPS WITH FAMILIES AND COMMUNITIES

Families are key stakeholders who should be consulted regarding transition processes for their children, and their insights are crucial when children are very young or have characteristics or circumstances that may be challenging during transitions (Kennedy, 2006). Some parents may be subject to extended family influence (e.g. from grandparents), may have negative memories of their own education or may have expectations that differ substantially from those of teachers, so sensitivity is required in negotiating shared understandings (Dockett et al, 2011). While in some cultural groups it may not be anticipated that teachers would ask for parental input into educational decisions, Sanagavarapu (2010) identified discussion about expectations and processes as a helpful strategy.

The broader community should also be taken into account, as community support demonstrates a wider valuing of education and a broader network of support relationships available to children and families. Such broader engagement is important in Aboriginal and Torres Strait Islander settings in which Elders and other community members share responsibility for children's wellbeing. See Chapters 5, 6 and 8 for consideration of family and cultural considerations, as well as Chapter 9 for discussion of family-centred practice.

## PARTNERSHIPS WITH COLLEAGUES AND AGENCIES

The establishment of partnerships between early years teachers in prior-to-school, school and school-aged education and care settings offers opportunities to share insights into children's progress and responses, align expectations and strategies to some degree, clarify transition planning and negotiate differences in perspective regarding transitions. If ECEC services link with many different schools or vice versa, this may present logistical problems that could be managed through use of information technologies (e.g. wikis, blogs) or early years sector-wide professional network meetings.

Professional partnerships with specialist services (e.g. paediatricians, psychologists, therapists, advisory visiting teachers, inclusion support facilitators) will also be required for children receiving other support agency assistance (see Chapter 10). Although some support providers may be part of the same organisation as the education service (e.g. occupational therapy provided by a school system), many of these agencies are likely to be separate from the school or centre (e.g. Inclusion Support Agency). Thus, clarification of roles, responsibilities and protocols for sharing information will need to be negotiated, particularly considering the sensitivity of family information (Kochhar-Bryant, 2008). Thoughtful collaborative planning for ongoing service provision is crucial, as discontinuity in support services may result in significant disruption to a child's therapy, English language learning or specialised educational program. Collaborative planning involves negotiating mutually acceptable transition processes.

Transition planning may also involve community agencies that support particular families and children, such as the Gifted and Talented Association, Autism Association, Down Syndrome Association or Multicultural Development Association. The advice and permission of the family should be sought regarding any agency involvement in transition processes. While family privacy must be maintained, some information-sharing may be appreciated by families who do not wish to repeat the same information to separate professional organisations (Colbert, 2010).

# Conclusion

Transitions include not only changes that children and families encounter from year to year, but also the many changes that children and families undertake each day or week. All children require long-term coordinated planning including both the sending settings and the receiving settings, to ensure transitions are relatively smooth. Further negotiation across disciplinary boundaries may also be required for children whose characteristics, abilities and backgrounds differ from the majority of children in their group or class. Partnerships between families, educators and other professionals or agencies that are genuinely respectful and reciprocal provide a supportive context for effective transitions.

# FOR FURTHER REFLECTION

1. A baby commencing at an ECEC centre is from a refugee family in which English is an additional language. What dialogue with the family would be advantageous? What processes should be in place for continuity of care? What support might the educators need to ensure the transition is smooth and secure for the child and family?
2. In the later part of the year, preschool educators and the Director are planning for transition to school. Two children have English as an additional language or dialect, one has autism spectrum disorder, and four have delayed speech and language. Who are the stakeholders whose perspectives should be taken into account? What transition planning will be required for these children in your local education system?
3. In an early years school class, a few children transition from the classroom several times during the week to attend learning support, special education classes, behaviour guidance, extension programs, therapy or English language classes. What alternative strategies for provision of support might be more inclusive and less disruptive?

## WEBSITES

www.education.vic.gov.au/Documents/childhood/professionals/learning/trkall.pdf

This resource is intended to support early years professionals in preparing for transition to school. The kit includes information regarding the research base, strategies and resources available from a range of sources across Australia.

## REFERENCES

Australian Children's Education and Care Quality Authority (ACECQA). (2012). *National Quality Framework*. Retrieved from http://acecqa.gov.au

Balaban, N. (2010). Transition to group care for infants, toddlers and families. In D. Laverick & M. Jalongo (Eds), *Transitions to early care and education: International perspectives on making schools ready for young children* (pp.7–20). Heidelberg: Springer.

Boardman, M. (2006). The impact of age and gender on prep children's academic achievements. *Australian Journal of Early Childhood, 31*(4), 1–6. Retrieved from www.earlychildhoodaustralia.org.au/australian_journal_of_early_childhood.html

Colbert, J. (2010). *Welcoming newcomer children: The settlement of young immigrants and refugees*. Canada: Fairmeadow.

Conway, R. (2010). Accommodating transitions across the years. In M. Hyde, L. Carpenter & R. Conway (Eds), *Diversity and inclusion in Australian schools* (pp.320–335). South Melbourne: Oxford University Press.

Dalli, C. (2002). Constructing identities: Being a mother and being a teacher during the experience of starting childcare. *European Early Childhood Education Research Journal, 10*(2), 85–101. doi:10.1080/13502930285208971

Department of Education, Employment and Workplace Relations (DEEWR). (2009). *Belonging, being, and becoming: An early years learning framework for Australia*. Barton, ACT: DEEWR. Retrieved from http://foi.deewr.gov.au/system/files/doc/other/belonging_being_and_becoming_the_early_years_learning_framework_for_australia.pdf.

Dockett, S. & Perry, B. (2007). *Transitions to school: Perceptions, expectations, experiences*. Sydney: University of New South Wales Press.

Dockett, S., Perry, B., Kearney, E., Hampshire, A., Mason, J. & Schmied, V. (2011). *Facilitating children's transition to school from families with complex support needs*. Albury: Charles Sturt University. Retrieved from: www.csu.edu.au/research/ripple/publications/index.htm

Education Queensland. (2007). *Supplementary guidelines: Children with disabilities of prep eligible age with significant educational support needs*. Retrieved from http://education.qld.gov.au/studentservices/learning/docs/suppguidelines.pdf

Glass, B. & Cotman, M. (2013). Transitions, inclusion and information technology. In B. Perry, S. Dockett, & A. Petriwskyj (Eds.), *Transitions to school: International research, policy and practice* (pp.249–276). Dordrecht: Springer.

Graham, L. & Macartney, B. (2012). Naming or creating a problem? The mis/use of labels in schools. In S. Carrington, & J. Macarthur (Eds), *Teaching in inclusive school communities* (pp.190–208). Milton: Wiley.

Grant, A. (2013). Young gifted children transitioning to school: What matters? *Australasian Journal of Early Childhood, 38*(2), 23–31. Retrieved from www.earlychildhoodaustralia.org.au/australian_journal_of_early_childhood.html

Henderson, R. (2004). Educational issues for the children of itinerant seasonal farm workers: A case study in an Australian context. *International Journal of Inclusive Education, 8*(3), 293–310. doi:10.1080/1360311042000257708

Jovanovic, J. (2011). Saying goodbye: An investigation in parent–child separation behaviours on arrival in childcare. *Childcare in Practice, 17*(3), 247–269. Retrieved from www.childcareinpractice.org/

Kennedy, A. (2006). Continuity in early education: Building sociocultural connections. In M. Fleer, S. Edwards, M. Hammer, A. Kennedy, A. Ridgway, J. Robbins & L. Surman (Eds), *Early childhood learning communities: Sociocultural research in practice* (pp.83–94). Frenchs Forest: Pearson.

Kochhar-Bryant, C. (2008). *Collaboration and system coordination for students with special needs: From early childhood to the post-secondary years*. Upper Saddle River: Pearson.

Migyanka, J. (2011). Supporting and sustaining the transition to formal schooling for children on the autism spectrum. In D. Laverick, & M. Jalongo (Eds), *Transitions to early care and education: International perspectives on making schools ready for young children* (pp.33–44). Heidelberg: Springer.

Perry, B. (2013). Social justice dimensions of starting school. In B. Perry, S. Dockett & A. Petriwskyj (Eds), *Transitions to school: International research, policy and practice* (pp.175–186). Dordrecht: Springer.

Petriwskyj, A. (2013). Pedagogies of inclusive transition to school. *Australasian Journal of Early Childhood, 38*(2), 45–55. Retrieved from www.earlychildhoodaustralia.org.au/australian_journal_of_early_childhood.html

Queensland Studies Authority (QSA). (2010). *Queensland kindergarten learning guideline*. Brisbane: Author. Retrieved from: www.qsa.qld.edu.au/downloads/p_10/qklg.pdf.

Raban, B. & Ure, C. (2000). Continuity for socially disadvantaged school entrants: Perspectives of parents and teachers. *Australian Research in Early Childhood Education, 7*(1), 54–65. Retrieved from www.education.monash.edu.au/research/irecejournal/

Recchia, S. (2012). Caregiver–child relationships as a context for continuity in childcare. *Early Years, 32*(2), 143–157. Retrieved from www.tandfonline.com/loi/ceye20.

Sanagavarapu, P. (2010). Children's transition to school: Voices of Bangladeshi parents in Sydney, Australia. *Australasian Journal of Early Childhood, 35*(4), 21–29. Retrieved from www.earlychildhoodaustralia.org.au/australian_journal_of_early_childhood.html.

Shiu, S. (2004). Maintaining the thread: Including young children with chronic illness in the primary classroom. *Australian Journal of Early Childhood, 29*(1), 33–38. Retrieved from www.earlychildhoodaustralia.org.au/australian_journal_of_early_childhood.html

Smith, N. (2002). Transition to the school playground: An intervention programme for nursery children. *Early Years, 22*(2), 129–145. doi:10.1080/09575140220151477

Taylor, A. (2011). Coming ready or not: Aboriginal children's transition to school in urban Australia and the policy push. *International Journal of Early Years Education, 19*(2), 145–161. Retrieved from www.tandfonline.com/loi/ciey20.

Victorian Department of Education and Early Childhood Development (DEECD). (2010). *Transition: A positive start to school resource kit*. Melbourne: Author. Retrieved from www.education.vic.gov.au/Documents/childhood/professionals/learning/trkall.pdf

Walker, S., Dunbar, S., Meldrum, K., Whiteford, C., Carrington, S., Hand, K., Berthelsen, D. & Nicholson, S. (2012). The transition to school of children with developmental disabilities: Views of parents and teachers. *Australasian Journal of Early Childhood, 37*(3), 22–29. Retrieved from www.earlychildhoodaustralia.org.au/australian_journal_of_early_childhood.html.

# 14 Children in Emergency Contexts: Supporting Transitions and Continuity

*Lisa Deters, Kathy Cologon and Jacqueline Hayden*

CHAPTER OVERVIEW

Disasters are occurring with increasing frequency worldwide, particularly in the Asia-Pacific region. Drawing on research focused on young children's experiences of disaster situations, this chapter will consider the implications of disasters and the role of early years professionals in facilitating successful transitions and continuity for children and families, during and following disaster experiences.

Learning goals for this chapter include:

- Understanding the impact of natural disasters on young children and reviewing supports that can be put in place;
- Recognising the importance of psychosocial support;
- Identifying children's rights in disaster situations and applying a rights-based approach;
- Identifying core concepts of holistic early childhood development in emergencies (as modelled in large-scale international humanitarian contexts);
- Understanding disaster risk reduction, including the role of early years professionals and the role children can play in preparing for and understanding transitions before, during and after disasters.

KEY TERMS AND CONCEPTS

child-led disaster risk reduction (CLDRR)
child rights-based approach
disaster risk reduction (DRR)
early childhood development in emergencies (ECDiE)
natural disaster
psychosocial support

# Introduction

As discussed in the previous chapter, children navigate transitions on a continual basis. Children today are likely to experience varying levels of change in family dynamics, possible relocation, and may face disruptive events during their early years. For many children and families, even the move from home to childcare or preschool and to formal school or from primary school to high school may be a time of stress and anxiety. The way in which these, and all transitions, are handled can recognise children's capacities and resilience, and work to mitigate potentially negative impacts.

Some transitions result in profound contextual and life changes. Natural and manmade disasters are an extreme form of disruption that may create complex transitions for children, families and communities. The occurrence of natural and manmade disasters has risen over the past decades and is expected to increase in the coming years (Ferris, 2011). Millions of children and adults around the world have been affected by floods, fires, tsunamis, cyclones, typhoons and/or by manmade conflicts and wars. These are referred to as emergency contexts. During and post emergencies, very young children have been identified as one of the most affected and vulnerable groups in terms of survival, safety and long-term outcomes (Peek, 2008).

Fortunately, Australia is currently not experiencing war or conflict on its shores, although it has its share of natural disaster emergencies. As a well-resourced nation, emergency services are of the highest quality—and for the most part, Australia experiences less loss of life and destruction, as a result of critical preparedness efforts and response capacities. Nonetheless, early years settings in Australia are likely to support children who have experienced an emergency or disaster in Australia, children who are close to or aware of others who have experienced an emergency or disaster in Australia, children whose families have sought refuge from an emergency to Australia, children who have family members affected by an emergency or disaster overseas and/or children who have been exposed to media coverage of emergencies. The lessons learnt from attending to the needs of children in highly disruptive contexts, including adhering to the rights of all children and applying the principles of holistic early childhood development (ECD) support, are applicable to all early years professionals.

In this chapter, the potential impact of emergencies will be examined through recognising the inherent resilience of children and presenting the key role that early years professionals can play in supporting children and families through difficult and complex transitions.

**FIGURE 14.1** BUSHFIRE EMERGENCY

*Artwork by Joshua*

natural disaster: A natural event or a series of events that disrupts the basic fabric and functioning of a society or community.

**Natural disasters** include both slow and rapid onset emergencies. Examples of rapid onset emergencies that result from a sudden natural event include earthquakes, avalanches, landslides, fires, floods, typhoons, tsunamis, windstorms and volcanic eruptions. A drought impacting a community's water availability, crop and livestock production and prices is an example of a slow onset emergency. Drought may result in long-term chronic food insecurity.

The impact of natural disasters on people's livelihoods and wellbeing depends upon the scope of the disaster and the context. The context refers to the physical, environmental, social, political, economic, historical and cultural landscape of a space. Contextual factors include rural or urban location, stability or conflict and high or low socio-economic status characteristics that impact the likelihood of potential risks. For example, the role of context is reflected in the aftermath of the 2010 earthquake in Port-au-Prince, Haiti that killed more than 220,000 people (Ferris & Ferro-Ribeiro, 2012) and the earthquake in Canterbury, New Zealand the same year that resulted in no deaths (Cubrinovski et al., 2010) (unlike the 2011 New Zealand earthquake). In 2010 Haiti and New Zealand experienced earthquakes of similar magnitudes, 7.0 and 7.1 respectively, and both earthquakes resulted in considerable destruction and devastation to the affected communities. However, Haiti's quake struck a densely populated urban space coping with weak infrastructure and endemic poverty (Pinto, 2010); whereas, New Zealand has a history of investing in earthquake engineering and benefits from social, political and economic stability, thus reducing some of the drastic impacts of disasters.

# Disaster response

Disaster response involves providing assistance, support or intervention during or immediately following a disaster (United Nations International Strategy for Disaster Reduction [UNISDR], 2004). The assistance offered to children and their families can be categorised into the provision of life-saving and life-sustaining activities. Life-saving activities include sustained access to food, water, shelter and health care; life-sustaining activities include education, protection, psychosocial wellbeing and livelihood activities (Sphere Charter, 2004).

A nation state, including national and local governing bodies, is considered the primary duty bearer to first respond and to guarantee that the rights of children are protected, following a disaster. In circumstances where the nation state is unable to meet the needs of the child, the humanitarian community plays a key role in enabling the rights of the child (Penrose & Takaki, 2006). This humanitarian community may include local and international relief and development organisations.

All people have the right to protection and assistance. The international humanitarian community seeks to uphold principles of humanity, neutrality, impartiality, and independence and responds to all children and adults affected (Harvey, 2013). Disaster response and management typically operate with a rescue-relief-rehabilitation model. International organisations then apply a rights-based humanitarian approach. Common approaches to disaster response aimed towards supporting the rights and resilience of young children are explained below.

# Children experiencing disaster

Children experiencing disasters are exposed to disrupted and often harsh environments. They may be at risk of death, injury, illness and malnutrition. A host of child protection issues may also arise due to family separation and the disruption of services such as facilities for health care and education. Early years facilities may face destruction, damage, a loss of materials or a loss or displacement of staff. Risks and hazards may be exacerbated in rural or urban environments or due to pre-existing threats or poverty. A key consideration is that disasters often break up families and interrupt care for young children. Children who experience disability are often forgotten within, or left out of, disaster planning and response efforts (Cologon & Hayden, 2012).

In disaster contexts, children constitute over half the affected population and are particularly vulnerable to the aforementioned risks such as separation from their families, child trafficking and a host of other child protection concerns (Peek, 2008). Specifically, the youngest children are often a disaster's first victims (Martin, 2010).

## CASE STUDY 14.1

### The need for an inclusive approach to disaster planning and response

As discussed in Chapter 2, Connors and Stalker (2007) conducted a study in the UK with children who experience disability, and their families. They shared the following story to illustrate the point that '[r]ules and procedures designed for the majority do not always fit the minority' (Connors & Stalker, 2007, p.27). One mother shared that her son, who uses a wheelchair, had been left alone in the school during a fire drill:

> He was telling me the other day how they did the fire alarm and everybody was screaming out in the playground. Richard was still in the school and everybody was outside. He was saying 'Mum, I was really, really worried about what happens if there's a real fire.' No one came to his assistance at all (Connors & Stalker, 2007, p.27).

If the rights of *all* were taken into account in planning infrastructure, this situation would never have occurred as this boy would simply wheel out of the school. However, tragically, all over the world there are reports of where people who experience disability have been left to perish during emergency or disaster situations—be that intentionally or on account of there being no preparation to enable evacuation.

**CRITICAL REFLECTION QUESTIONS**

Consider an early years setting that you are familiar with:

1. What are the emergency evacuation policies and practices in this setting?
2. Who is consulted and considered in planning for emergencies?
3. Are the rights of all people in the setting considered?
4. Are there any changes that could be made to ensure the emergency policy and practices are inclusive of all people in the setting?

Vulnerability in terms of a disaster means that an individual or group of people experience significant barriers to coping, resisting and recovering from the impact of the disaster (Grotberg, 2001). The vulnerability of children is related to the availability of a caregiver and caring connections, food, shelter, and security. Young children are considered to have unique vulnerabilities due to this dependence on their caregivers for their physical and psychological wellbeing. When a child lacks the care and protection of an adult, concerns increase for the child's safety and wellbeing.

**psychosocial support:** Protecting or promoting psychosocial wellbeing and development for children and their families (Inter-agency Standing Committee [IASC], 2007).

## Psychosocial support

A focus on securing and supporting a child's interpersonal relationships is critical during emergency response. Providing **psychosocial support** to mediate risk and support transition following an emergency is a critical aspect of emergency services for young children and their caregivers (Wessells, 2009). All kinds of support, and especially psychosocial support, need to be culturally appropriate, age appropriate, and safe.

For children, play is an example of psychosocial support. Play is an adaptive mechanism and is fundamental in maintaining and building children's ability to cope (Aguilar & Retamal, 2009). Further, play and learning activities can promote a young child's sense of agency (Grotberg, 1995). A child's strong sense of self and self-efficacy is vital to building resilience (Grotberg). Offering informal or formal play and learning activities is beneficial. When daily routines are continued or established, children gain a sense of stability and continuity as they transition to an altered reality.

Sensitive emergency interventions for young children and their families generally aim to restore or create a sense of stability. This is achieved through programs and activities that promote a sense of safety, calmness, self- and community efficacy, connectedness and hope during the recovery and relief periods (Hobfoll et al., 2007).

## A rights-based approach to protecting children in natural disaster

Children's rights include the rights to survival, development, protection and participation. As discussed throughout this book, the rights of *all* children are articulated in the United Nations *Convention on the Rights of the Child* (CRC) (United Nations [UN], 1989). Rights are applicable to all young children experiencing disasters (Penrose & Takkaki, 2006). This means that no child should be forgotten or overlooked in disaster planning and response. A number of relevant articles from the CRC are listed below (UN, 1989).

> **Children have the right to survival**
>
> States are obligated to ensure the child's survival and development (Article 6).
>
> States are tasked to provide the highest standard of health for children (Article 24).
>
> **Children have the right to support for development**
>
> States are tasked to provide rehabilitative care and appropriate treatment for children's recovery and social integration (Article 39).
>
> Children have a right to develop to their capacities to their full potential (Article 5).
>
> Children have the right to education (Article 28).

Children have the right to rest and leisure and play and recreation (Article 31).

**Children have a right to protection**

States are tasked to protect a child from abuse and neglect (Article s19 and 37).

States are required to protect children without the care of a family (Article 20).

States are required to protect children from sexual exploitation, trafficking and other forms of exploitation (Articles 34, 35 and 36).

**Children have a right to participation**

Children have a right to be involved in decisions affecting them (Article 12).

Children have a right to expression and freedom of thought and religion (Articles 13 and 14).

Children have a right to information (Article 17).

Children have the right to enabling and inclusive environments (Article 23).

Children are commonly seen and treated only as beneficiaries to the services provided in the aftermath of a disaster. Further, in large-scale international disasters, children are often heavily photographed as 'suffering' or passive beneficiaries. In such cases, the rights of children to participate and be consulted in the design of activities, programming and services are overlooked (Nikku, 2013).

**child rights-based approach:** Humanitarian organisations that apply such an approach use the principles of child rights to plan, implement, manage and monitor emergency responses with the goal to strengthen the rights of children (Save the Children, 2002).

A **child rights-based approach** to programming is essential to the work of humanitarian organisations. Basic questions to consider when responding with this approach include: *In what ways have the rights and needs of children been addressed? Have children's rights been mainstreamed into the program designs?*

Suggestions on how to apply a rights-based approach in early years programming are provided in the box below.

---

## APPLYING A RIGHTS-BASED APPROACH TO EARLY YEARS PROGRAMMING

- Place children at the centre, recognising them as rights-holders and social actors;
- Recognise governments as primary duty-bearers, accountable to children and the international community;
- Recognise parents and families as primary caregivers, protectors and guides;
- Prioritise children and create child-friendly environments;
- Be inclusive (of gender, class, ethnicity, caste, religion, ability, etc.) and seek inclusive solutions;

- Hold a holistic vision of the young child and the rights of the child;
- Hold a holistic vision of ECD that requires a multi-sectoral response;
- Use participatory and empowering approaches with children and their caregivers;
- Build partnerships among ECD stakeholders for the promotion of child rights.

*(Adapted from Save the Children, 2002)*

---

# Early Childhood Development in Emergencies: A holistic response

An aim of **early childhood development in emergencies (ECDiE)** is to uphold children's rights and promote holistic child development (United Nations Children's Fund [UNICEF], 2010). ECDiE refers to the specific actions and responses taken to protect and realise the rights of all young children.

Children benefit from ECDiE responses that provide opportunities for play, learning and socialising with peers (Kamel, 2006). Structured ECD activities offer stability and promote daily routines. In addition, caregivers and communities benefit from ECD initiatives that enhance quality of child–caregiver interactions, support families to pursue economic opportunities, and support community involvement and development. Features of early years programs in disrupted environments are described in the box below.

**early childhood development in emergencies (ECDiE):** ECDiE takes on a comprehensive approach that is critical to supporting the holistic wellbeing of young children. It considers the development of the whole child and promotes an integrated response to supporting children in emergencies.

---

## EARLY YEARS PROGRAMS IN DISRUPTED ENVIRONMENTS

In a review of nine early years programs within disrupted environments, Connolly and Hayden (2007) identified reported benefits and outcomes associated with service provision under extreme conditions. These include:

- Early years settings provide a physically safe place even in the midst of devastation and crumbling communities;
- Early years settings provide a psychologically safe environment for children and families where emotions can be dealt with, discussed and worked through, thus they can be a place of healing;
- Early years settings become an entry point for families to access health services, needed resources, and other community supports;
- Early years settings play a role in mobilising families to advocate for children's needs.

---

## ECDiE STANDARD RESPONSES

At the onset of a large-scale emergency, a host of humanitarian actors including national, international and UN agencies rapidly respond to the needs of young children. Leading rights-based children's organisations with mandates to provide relief and development such as Save the Children, Plan International, ChildFund and World Vision work with UN agencies such as UNICEF to promote and protect the rights of children. International humanitarian actors also aim to engage with local governmental bodies and collaborate and coordinate responses with existing national humanitarian actors.

Humanitarian actors seeking to support young children commonly respond with an integrated approach to ECD. A rapid assessment is first conducted to determine the numbers, existing supports and specific needs of young children and their caregivers. A rapid assessment may include informal focus groups and stakeholder discussions with local leadership, government agencies and caregivers to identify immediate needs (Anderson & Woodrow, 1998). Any emergency response should be sensitive to the type and scope of the emergency, to the cultural context, and to the children and families' existing supports and needs (Kostelny, 2006).

Depending upon the severity of the emergency and the characteristics of the affected environment, such as population density or whether the environment is urban or rural, consequences vary from near-total devastation to limited destruction. Responses to support the needs of young children and their families may involve an integrated approach to nutrition, health, water, sanitation and hygiene (WASH), shelter, livelihoods, education, child protection, and psychosocial programming.

During sudden-onset disasters, safe and supervised environments are often established as central spaces to address the needs of young children and their caregivers (Madfis, Martyris & Triplehorn, 2010). The safe spaces may be labelled as baby tents, breastfeeding tents, baby clinics, therapeutic feeding centres, child-friendly spaces (CFS), ECD spaces, ECD centres, early learning spaces, or informal preschools. Regardless of the label, the safe spaces help engage children and families in appropriate and structured activities.

Htwe and Yamano (2010) identified four roles of a CFS: (a) to provide outreach to vulnerable children, (b) referral to basic and specialised services, (c) engagement with community, and (d) advocacy at the government and local authority levels. Typically, an ECD space in emergencies is implemented by education or child protection humanitarian sectors/actors. An adapted version of Htwe and Yamano's model is shown in Figure 14.2 below. The ECD space serves as an entry point for reaching children, making referrals, engaging caregivers, and advocating among local authorities.

**FIGURE 14.2** ROLE OF AN ECD SPACE

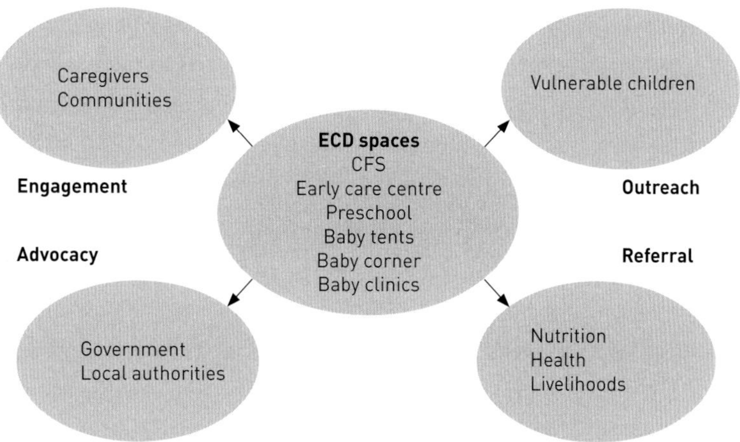


*(Deters, 2014, adapted from Htwe & Yamano, 2010)*

As shown in Figure 14.2, ECDiE activities may focus on nutrition or health interventions targeting prenatal women, breastfeeding, infant and young child feeding (IYCF), or vaccinations. In addition, the activities may be oriented around infant stimulation or early years education.

When implementing learning and recreation activities and psychosocial programming, international agencies often offer a pre-packaged activity kit such as UNICEF's *ECD Kit* or Plan's *Big Blue Bag*. The kit or bag contains an array of learning materials intended to support play and learning activities for a group of young children. Activities can then be offered and structured to meet children's evolving capacities. Case study 14.2 below, about post-earthquake Haiti, provides an example of a baby tent in Haiti programming with a UNICEF ECD Kit.

**CASE STUDY 14.2**

## Providing holistic ECD in emergencies with baby tents

The devastating 2010 Haiti earthquake directly affected over three million people, including over 800,000 children living in temporary settlements, of whom 500,000 were deemed highly vulnerable (UNICEF, 2011). Humanitarian agencies worked to respond to the large number of children in critical need of protection, shelter, water, food, nutrition, and medical care.

A specific example of a response targeting the youngest children was the baby tent. As part of my doctoral research focusing on support for young children in emergencies, I (Deters) examined the use of the baby tent in post-earthquake Haiti (Deters, 2014). The baby tent was a

*Lisa Deters, Kathy Cologon and Jacqueline Hayden*

physical safe space set up initially to support mothers who were breastfeeding. In the Haitian context, a baby tent comprised of a large tent or tarps sourced from international agencies. The baby tent was promoted as a safe space where mothers and caregivers could gather to rest and recuperate. At the tent, mothers, caregivers, and expectant mothers could access water, food, and expertise on nutrition and health. Health workers were available to promote lactation and disseminate information on neonatal concerns and issues related to the care and wellbeing of infants and mothers.

The baby tent benefited all parties involved—the implementing agencies, the mothers and caregivers, and the young children. The international agencies were able to identify and respond to specific needs. The health workers were able to conduct screenings on the nutritional status and health of young children and their caregivers and provide referrals to hospitals and clinics when needed. For the mothers and caregivers, social connections were fostered and in some tents resulted in the establishment of supportive mother groups. Psychosocial wellbeing was addressed. Further, young children were engaged through stimulation, play and access to toys and learning materials.

Toys and learning materials were supplied with the UNICEF ECD kits. Following the earthquake in Haiti, the kits were widely distributed and used in programming for young children in child friendly spaces (CFS), early learning spaces and baby tents. Each kit contained learning and play materials for up to 50 young children such as puzzles, games, counting items, boxes to stack and sort, board books, puppets, art supplies and items to promote hygiene. In the baby tents the kits were used to promote infant–caregiver interaction through modelling infant stimulation and encouraging play.

This case study reflects the benefits of immediately providing access to a contextually appropriate child and family friendly safe space. A baby tent is one approach to meeting the needs of young children and their caregivers. Any support and programming offered in a baby tent requires adaptation to meet the specific context, culture, and identified needs.

The baby tent exemplifies how programming can be developed around a safe space for young children including nutrition, health, water, sanitation and hygiene (WASH), child protection, and early education services. Moreover, the programming was informed and designed by the Haitians utilising the space. The baby tent was identified as an entry point to capture the specific needs of the youngest children, breastfeeding mothers, expectant mothers, and caregivers of young children.

For early years professionals, simple guidelines do exist: 1) identify a safe space, 2) promote access to the safe space for *all* children; 3) identify, design, and offer relevant services; and 4) seek and encourage community participation throughout the process. Early years professionals can contribute to strengthening ECD or strengthening family and community support by providing safe, inclusive and relevant spaces for young children and their caregivers.

During slow-onset natural disasters, the provision of nutritional support for young children is an important focus. When needed, supplementary and therapeutic feeding should be provided to stem severe and moderate acute malnutrition (SAM and MAM). The distribution of water treatment materials and information on sanitation and hygiene practices also supports families with young children.

Regardless of the specifics of the emergency, guiding principles do exist. First and foremost, all interventions should 'do no harm' (Anderson, 1999). Humanitarians operate under a humanitarian imperative to address immediate needs of the most vulnerable in a dignified manner. Further, humanitarians strive to provide relief in a neutral and impartial manner to avoid inadvertently doing any harm by physical presence or by physical assistance.

Guiding principles also exist to uphold the specific rights of children to access protective and respectful support and programming. Parents, caregivers and communities deserve to be involved and supported to care for their children. In addition, children and their caregivers have the right to participate in the decisions around supports and interventions and the right to hold the responding agencies accountable. In Table 14.1 simple recommendations are provided for caregivers and parents supporting children coping with disaster.

It is important to focus on support for and involvement of children in the early years and beyond. Case study 14.3 below explores a community approach to disaster recovery in primary schools in Australia, following the 2009 Black Saturday bushfires in Victoria.

**TABLE 14.1** RECOMMENDED STRATEGIES TO SUPPORT YOUNG CHILDREN COPING WITH DISASTER

| Strategies for caregivers (educators, volunteers) | Strategies for parents/family members |
|---|---|
| ~ Give age-appropriate information; | ~ Reassure your child that you love him/her; |
| ~ Be willing to talk about the incident if the children want to; | ~ Ensure your child's physical needs are met; |
| ~ Do not ask children to talk about the incident if they do not want to; | ~ Explain what happened at an age-appropriate level (may be within a faith/value system); |
| ~ Find out the cultural norms/values for expressing emotions; | ~ Set up a routine for your child as soon as possible; |
| ~ Encourage creative activities; | ~ Involve your child in decisions about the family; |
| ~ Reassure children (that they are safe, that all feelings are OK). | ~ Explain what will happen (when you know). |

*Adapted from World Vision, 2006*

CASE STUDY 14.3

## A creative community approach to disaster recovery

In February 2009 the Australian state of Victoria was hit by a series of bushfires known as the Black Saturday bushfires. In the fires, 173 people lost their lives, more than 414 people were injured, in excess of 1,700 homes destroyed, approximately 7,000 people were made homeless, and the death of animals and destruction of bushland, farmland and forests was widespread (Victorian Bushfire Royal Commission, 2010). Wide-ranging practical and psychosocial supports were put into place to assist children and families affected by the disaster.

One area affected by the Black Saturday fires was the Murrindindi Shire, with 95 lives lost and 40 per cent of the shire burnt. CARTWHEELS (Connecting Community, Art, Resilience, Tribes, Wellbeing, Health, Empathy and Engagement, Education, Learning and Schools) is a community project that was implemented in this shire following the fires. This case example draws from Keating's (2012) evaluation of CARTWHEELS.

CARTWHEELS was developed by Berry Street Victoria—a non-profit child and family welfare organisation—in collaboration with The Royal Children's Hospital Melbourne's Festival for Healthy Living (FHL) program. The aim of the project was to take a strengths-based community capacity building approach to supporting the wellbeing and emotional literacy of children affected by the bushfires, through arts-based weekly workshops. The project involved children from the early years of school onwards from six primary schools and one secondary school working with 24 local artists. Families were invited to participate, although only a small number participated weekly.

The weekly workshops incorporated creative arts projects that explored and addressed mental health concerns. During these workshops, children were involved in music, art and movement activities, including performing in a play, making a CD or film, drumming, singing, writing songs, rock climbing, dancing, drawing, painting, creating mosaics and sculptures, and circus activities such as juggling, pyramids and gymnastics. The program involved an inclusive approach responsive to the diversity of participants and was developed to fit the unique needs of each school community. While initially the workshops were run at individual schools, as the project developed schools also worked together.

Data was collected from children, teachers and other education and health professionals, artists, family and other community members to determine the impact and outcomes of the project. Participants reported positive program outcomes including developing skills in teamwork, performing, social and emotional development, decision-making, and creativity. Children reported experiencing higher self-esteem, an increased sense of resilience, and an enhanced capacity to resolve conflict through talking. Participants reported enjoying the activities, having fun and feeling greater confidence in taking risks, and persevering in the face of challenges. Teachers reported that they observed increased development in participant relationship skills and social awareness.

CARTWHEELS offered strong support for community involvement, which improved relationships between organisations and sectors within the community. It allowed members of the community to work together, offered employment opportunities for artists and encouraged parents and other community members to participate as volunteers. Families, teachers and principals reported beliefs that the program helped bring the school community together, which reverberated into the wider community. The workshops and performances provided all members of the community with an opportunity to come together and celebrate. Furthermore, it encouraged the community to feel a sense of pride and achievement in the local schools. The CARTWHEELS project highlights the potential benefits of implementing whole community approaches and using an arts-based program to promote disaster recovery.

*(Keating, 2012)*

## Children and disaster risk reduction

In responding to disaster issues, there is an opportunity to work towards future **disaster risk reduction (DRR)**. DRR is now a focus for most nations around the world. A global action plan for reducing the risks of disasters, called the *Hyogo Framework for Action,* outlines strategies including ongoing assessment, early warning programs, facilitating a culture of safety, and, notably, focusing on health and care at the community level (UNISDR, 2005).

**disaster risk reduction (DRR):** Working to reduce risks and strengthen supports to mitigate the impact of disasters (Hayden & Cologon, 2011).

According to the Hyogo framework, communities that reflect social cohesion and inclusion have reduced risks in disaster situations (UNISDR, 2005). A strong social network and the availability of social safety nets ensure that all members of a community—including those groups at risk of marginalisation—are able to access support, assistance and services when needed.

Children have the right to receive and be involved in DRR as upheld in the CRC (UN, 1989), the Hyogo Framework for Action (UNISDR, 2005) and the Children's Charter for DRR (Plan International, Save the Children International, United Nations Children's Fund & World Vision International, 2011). Children can be agents—as well as recipients—of reduced disaster risks. **Child-led disaster risk reduction (CLDRR)** refers to programs in which children take an active role in their own safety and wellbeing. CLDRR may include mapping exercises, identifying safety routines, disseminating information within the community, and other risk reduction methods (Lopez, Hayden, Cologon, & Hadley, 2012).

**child-led disaster risk reduction (CLDRR):** A community-based, child-centred approach to DRR that actively supports children in working individually and in groups to bring about positive DRR outcomes (Lopez et al., 2012; Martin 2010; Mitchell, Haynes, Hall, Wei, & Oven, 2008).

A range of materials and activities can be used to include young children in DRR. Song and dance, skits and role-play, storytelling and literacy activities, art, games and puzzles have all been used with children of all ages from childcare to high school. Nonetheless, room for innovation remains, particularly on how to authentically engage young children in CLDRR. School-aged children have charted information, mapped escape routes, and raised awareness via peer-to-peer learning and among their families and communities. Children are competent and influential advocates for spreading messages of safety and preparedness to their peers, siblings, parents and extended families. CLDRR results in a culture of safety within the school classroom, early learning centre or community (Martin, 2010).

Communities are key to DRR and preparedness. In Case study 14.4, below, a recent program directed at enhancing DRR in the Asia-Pacific region is described. The program reflects the relationship between identifying and promoting community support for young children, and strengthening DRR. In the end, strong, inclusive, child-centred communities are communities prepared for disaster outcomes.

**CASE STUDY 14.4**

## Community support for young children and Disaster Risk Reduction

In our review of DRR in the Asia Pacific, adapted and built upon some of the indicators from the UN Hyogo Framework for Action (UNISDR, 2005), we (Hayden and Cologon) developed tools to measure attitudes and behaviour, liaison, coordination, partnership, inclusion, and governance at the community level. Additional items addressed the extent to which a focus on the early years was embedded within the study communities.

The study indicated a relationship between the child centredness of a community and the potential to reduce risks associated with disaster. The very use of the tools, including *Indicators for Assessing Disaster Risk Reduction Readiness for Young Children* was shown to be effective in enhancing community attention to and services for young children (Hayden & Cologon, 2011).

A sample of the indicators, in a range of areas, used to determine the extent of community support and thus preparedness for disruption, is below*:

### Attitudes and behaviour indicators

- There are trusted institutions in this community (Church, NGOs, donor agencies).
- The community has a high level of volunteerism (participation).

- There is a community feeling of responsibility for children.
- There is a sense of calmness (as opposed to constant alertness to or fear of disaster).
- There is a sense of safety within the community.

### Liaison/coordination/partnership indicators

- Organisations and services are well known to *all* groups within the community.
- There is a good pattern of communication: there are effective vehicles for dissemination of information.

### Inclusion indicators

- Decision-making is inclusive: marginalised groups/affected populations have a voice in the development and implementation of policies and processes that relate to their lives.
- Organisations and services are equally accessible to all community members.
- People in this community accept pluralism (multiculturalism).
- All people have a sense of belonging to the community.
- There is a sense of community solidarity: people tend to look after one another.
- Printed or media messages would be accessible and understood by all people in this community.

### Ownership indicators

- Most programs and services for young children at community level are community owned.
- Financial and other resources/supports for young children emanate from the community (as opposed to from external, private, international sources).

### Support for young children indicators

- The community is aware of the needs of young children.
- The community is aware of potential hazards for young children during disasters and emergencies.
- There is awareness about how decision-making affects services and where the experiences of young children take place.
- There is potential for influencing change in the community.
- There is expertise regarding the needs of young children and/or there is ready access to expertise within the community.
- Family participation is a common feature of this community.
- There are identifiable advocates for young children.
- A high percentage of the population takes an active interest in services for young children.
- A high percentage of the population has influence on decision-making around young children.

### ECD programs and services indicators

- There is ECD leadership in this community (people know where to turn for ECD support and advice).
- There are adequate health services for young children.
- There are adequate nutrition services for young children.

*(These indicators were developed by drawing from Hobfoll et al., 2007; Iscoe, 1974; King & Macgregor, 2000; Landau & Saul, 2004; McKnight, 1997; Mercer, Kelman, Lloyd & Suchet-Pearson, 2008.)*

**The full set of tools are available at: www.arnec.net/ntuc/slot/u2323/publication/Disaster%20Risk%20 Reduction3_small.pdf*

# Conclusion

Disaster emergencies create complex situations for children and their families. Following a disaster children urgently need support. However, appropriate support needs to consider children, their capacity and resilience, within the context of families and communities.

Early years professionals play an important role in supporting children during and following disasters. As explored through this chapter, this involves acknowledging the importance of providing a range of practical and psychosocial supports within a community-based approach. Recognising children's agency, it is important to take a rights-based approach to DRR and recovery, including attention to possibilities for CLDRR.

# FOR FURTHER REFLECTION

The Children's Charter for Disaster Risk Reduction (DRR) (Plan International, Save the Children International, UNICEF & World Vision International, 2011) was a result of consultations with children in 21 countries representing children in Africa, Asia and Latin America. More than 600 children were asked about what impact disasters had on their lives. The children identified five priorities:

1. Schools must be safe and education must not be interrupted;
2. Child protection must be a priority before, during and after a disaster;
3. Children have the right to participate and to access the information they need;
4. Community infrastructure must be safe, and relief and reconstruction must help reduce future risk;
5. Disaster risk reduction must reach the most vulnerable.

These five priorities make up the Children's Charter. The priorities are useful for early years professionals to reflect on how children's priorities are being addressed through an early years response both in school, as emphasised in the charter, and in early years settings prior to school.

1. Considering the use of baby tents (an ECD safe space) in post-earthquake Haiti, were children's concerns upheld? In general, how can an early years space be used to consider and address children's priorities?
2. How can an early years space be used to
   a. support a continuation of early learning and education?
   b. promote child protection?
   c. offer children and their families critical information?
3. How can a (potentially temporary) early years space be used to promote (permanently) safe infrastructure?
4. How can an early years space be used to target the most vulnerable and promote DRR and CLDRR?

## WEBSITES

www.tgn.anu.edu.au

The high five model of psychosocial preparedness from the ACTAGLN website links to this website (the trauma and grief network) on support in Australia.

www.redcross.org.au/emergency-resources.aspx and www.redcross.org.au/files/Emergency_services_how_to_talk_to_children_fact_sheet_20110609.pdf

Red Cross resources on supporting children and families in emergency situations.

### Child-friendly spaces

Columbia University Mailman School of Public Health and World Vision. (2012). *Child Friendly Spaces: A structured review of the current evidence-base*. Retrieved from http://reliefweb.int/sites/reliefweb.int/files/resources/CFS_Literature_Review_final_Aug_2012.pdf

Save the Children. (2008). *Child friendly spaces in emergencies: A handbook for Save the Children staff.* Retrieved from http://cpwg.net/wp-content/uploads/2013/08/SC-2008-Child-Friendly-Spaces-in-Emergencies-A-Handbook-for-Save-the-Children-Staff.pdf

UNICEF. (2011). *Guidelines for child friendly spaces in emergencies.* Retrieved from www.unicef.org/protection/Child_Friendly_Spaces_Guidelines_for_Field_Testing.pdf

### Child protection in emergencies

Child Protection Working Group (2011). Provides a child protection rapid assessment (an inter-agency tool). Retrieved from http://cpwg.net

Child Rights Information Network (CRIN). (2013). *Guides for practitioners.* Retrieved from www.crin.org/hrbap/

Save the Children Sweden. (n.d.). *Library: Save the children's resource centre*. Retrieved from http://resourcecentre.savethechildren.se/start/library

### Disasters and DRR

Save the Children. (n.d.). *Child-led disaster risk reduction: A practical guide.* Retrieved from www.preventionweb.net/files/3820_CHLDRR.pdf

Sphere Project Handbook (2004) includes the Humanitarian Charter and Minimum Standards in Disaster Response. Retrieved from www.sphereproject.org/handbook/

UNICEF, Save the Children, Plan & World Vision. (n.d.). *Children's Charter: An action plan for disaster risk reduction for children by children.* Retrieved from www.childreninachangingclimate.org/database/CCC/Publications/children_charter.pdf

UNISDR. (2004). *Living with risk: A global review of disaster reduction initiatives*. Retrieved from www.unisdr.org/we/inform/publications/657

### ECD in emergencies

Asia-Pacific Regional Network for Early Childhood (ARNEC). (2013). *ECD in emergencies focused on the Asia-Pacific region.* Retrieved from www.arnec.net/cos/o.x?ptid=1036089&c=/swt_arnec/articles&func=list&type=theme&value=Emergencies

Consultative Group on ECCD (CGECCD). (2014). *Emergencies: Early childhood in emergencies working group*. Retrieved from www.ccdgroup.com/focus-areas/emergencies/

INEE (International Network for Education in Emergencies). (n.d.). *INEE toolkit: Key thematic issues—early childhood development.* Retrieved from http://toolkit.ineesite.org/toolkit/Toolkit.php?PostID=1058

Mental Health and Psychosocial Support Network (MHPSS). (n.d.). *Early childhood care and development (ECCD) discussion and resource page.* Retrieved from http://mhpss.net/groups/psychosocial-care-protection-of-children/early-childhood-care-development/

Plan International. (2014). *Early childhood care and development in emergencies.* Retrieved from https://plan-international.org/about-plan/resources/publications/emergencies/early-childhood-care-and-development-in-emergencies/

UNICEF. (2013). *Early childhood development in humanitarian action.* Retrieved from www.unicefinemergencies.com/downloads/eresource/ecd.html

UNICEF & World Health Organisation (WHO). *Integrating early childhood development (ECD) activities into nutrition programmes in emergencies: Why, what and how.* Retrieved from www.who.int/mental_health/emergencies/ecd_note.pdf

### Humanitarian response

IASC (Inter-Agency Standing Committee). (2013). *IASC guidelines on mental health and psychosocial support in emergency settings.* Retrieved from http://www.humanitarianinfo.org/iasc/pageloader.aspx

INEE. (n.d.). *INEE minimum standards: Minimum standards for education: Preparedness, response, recovery—a commitment to access, quality and accountability.* Retrieved from www.ineesite.org/en/minimum-standards

International Federation of Red Cross & Red Crescent Societies. (n.d.). *Code of conduct.* Retrieved from www.ifrc.org/en/publications-and-reports/code-of-conduct/

## REFERENCES

Aguilar, P. & Retamal, G. (2009). Protective environments and quality education in humanitarian contexts. *International Journal of Educational Development, 29*, 3–16. doi:10.1016/j.ijedudev.2008.02.002

Anderson, M.B. & Woodrow, P.J. (1998). *Rising from the ashes: Development strategies in times of disaster.* Boulder, CO: Lynne Rienner Publishers.

Anderson, M.B. (1999). *Do no harm: How aid can support peace—or war.* Boulder, CO: Lynne Rienner Publishers.

Cologon, K. & Hayden, J. (2012). Children in emergencies. In J. Bowes, R. Grace & K. Hodge (Eds), *Children, families and communities: Contexts and consequences* (4th edn, pp.271–288). South Melbourne: Oxford University Press.

Connolly, P., Hayden, J. & Levin, D. (2007). *From conflict to peace building: The power of early childhood initiatives lessons from around the world.* Retrieved from www.paulconnolly.net/publications/pdf_files/WF_Peacebook_complete.pdf

Connors, C. & Stalker, K. (2007). Children's experiences of disability: Pointers to a social model of childhood disability. *Disability & Society, 22*(1), 19–33. doi:10.1080/09687590601056162

Cubrinovski, M., Green, R., Allen, J., Ashford, S., Bowman, E., Bradley, B.A., Cox, B., Hutchinson, T., Kavazanjian, E., Orense, R., Pender, M. & Wotherspoon, L. (2010). *Geotechnical reconnaissance of the 2010 Darfield (New Zealand) earthquake.* University of Canterbury. Retrieved from www.geerassociation.org/GEER_Post%20EQ%20Reports/Darfield%20New%20Zealand_2010/GEER_Darfield_2010_11-14-2010.pdf

Deters, L. (2014). *Collective Caregiving: Reconceptualising the role of ECD in emergencies.* (Unpublished doctoral dissertation), Institute of Early Childhood, Macquarie University, Sydney.

Ferris, E. (2011). Megatrends and the future of humanitarian action. *International Review of the Red Cross, 93*, 915–938. doi:10.1017/S181638311200029X

Ferris, E. & Ferro-Ribeiro, S. (2012). Protecting people in cities: The disturbing case of Haiti. *Disasters, 36*(SI), S43-S63. doi:10.111/j.1467-7717.2012.01285.x

Grotberg, E.H. (1995). A guide to promoting resilience in children: Strengthening the human spirit. Bernard van Leer Foundation (Series Eds.). *Early childhood development: Practice and reflections.* Retrieved from http://resilnet.uiuc.edu

Grotberg, E.H. (2001). Resilience programs for children in disaster. *Ambulatory Child Health, 7*, 75–83. doi:10.1046/j.1467-0658.2001.00114.x

Harvey, P. (2013). International humanitarian actors and governments in areas of conflict: Challenges, obligations, and opportunities. *Disasters, 37*, 151–170. doi:10.1111/disa.12019

Hayden, J. & Cologon, K. (2011). *Disaster risk reduction and young children, assessing needs at the community level: A guidebook for the Asia-Pacific Region,* Asia-Pacific Regional Network on Early Childhood (ARNEC), Singapore. Retrieved from www.arnec.net/ntuc/slot/u2323/publication/Disaster%20Risk%20Reduction3_small.pdf

Hobfoll, S.E., Watson, P., Bell, C.C., Bryant, R.A., Brymer, M.J., Friedman, M.J. & Ursano, R.J. (2007). Five essential elements of immediate and mid-term mass trauma intervention: Empirical evidence. *Psychiatry: Interpersonal and Biological Processes, 70*(4), 283–315. doi:10.1521/psyc.2007.70.4.283

Htwe, N.N. & Yamano, M. (2010). Child friendly: The dual function of protection and education in Myanmar. In K.M. Cahill (Ed), *Even in chaos: Education in times of emergency* (pp.261–277). New York: Fordham University Press.

Inter-agency Standing Committee (IASC). (2007). *IASC guidelines on mental health and psychosocial support in emergency settings.* Retrieved from www.who.int/mental_health/emergencies/guidelines_iasc_mental_health_psychosocial_june_2007.pdf

Iscoe, I. (1974). Community psychology and the competent community. *American Psychologist, 29*(8), 607–613. doi:10.1037/h0036925

Kamel, H. (2006). *Strong Foundations: Early childhood care and education* (Background paper prepared for the Education for All Global Monitoring Report 2007). Retrieved from http://unesdoc.unesco.org/images/0014/001477/147794e.pdf

Keating, C. (2012). Evaluation of the CARTWHEELS Cathedral Ranges project. Richmond, Victoria: Berry Street Childhood Institute, 2012. Retrieved from www.berrystreet.org.au/Assets/1888/1/CARTWHEELSEvaluationReport_FINAL.pdf

King, D. & MacGregor, C. (2000). Using social indicators to measure community vulnerability to natural hazards. *Australian Journal of Emergency Management, 15*(3), 52–57. Retrieved from http://search.informit.com.au/documentSummary;dn=369807987774661;res=IELHSS

Kostelny, K. (2006). A culture-based, integrative approach: Helping war-affected children. In N. Boothby, A. Strang & M. Wessells (Eds), *A world turned upside down: Social ecological approaches to children in war zones* (pp.19–37). Bloomfield, CT: Kumarian Press, Inc.

Landau, J., & Saul, J. (2004). Facilitating family and community resilience in response to major disaster. In F. Walsh & M. McGoldrick (Eds), *Living beyond loss* (pp.285–309). New York: Norton.

Lopez, Y., Hayden, J., Cologon, K. & Hadley, F. (2012). Child participation and disaster risk reduction. *International Journal of Early Years Education, 20*(3), 300–308. doi: 10.1080/09669760.2012.716712

Madfis, J., Martyris, D. & Triplehorn, C. (2010). Emergency safe spaces in Haiti and the Solomon Islands. *Disasters, 34*(3), 845–864. doi:10.1111/j.0361-3666.2010.01172.x

Martin, M.L. (2010). Child participation in disaster risk reduction: The case of flood-affected children in Bangladesh. *Third World Quarterly, 31*(8), 1357–1375. doi: 10.1080/01436597.2010.541086

Mitchell, T., Haynes, K., Hall, N., Wei, C. & Oven, K. (2008). The role of children and youth in communicating risk. *Children, Youth and Environments, 18*, 254–279. Retrieved from www.jstor.org/stable/10.7721/chilyoutenvi.18.1.0254

McKnight, J. (1997). *A twenty-first century map for healthy communities and families.* Evanston, IL: Institute for Policy Research.

Mercer, J., Kelman, I., Lloyd, K. & Suchet-Pearson, S. (2008). Reflections on use of participatory research for disaster risk reduction. *Area, 40*(2), 172–183. doi:10.1111/j.1475-4762.2008.00797.x

Nikku, B.R. (2013). Children's rights in disasters: Concerns for social work—insights from South Asia and possible lessons for Africa. *International Social Work, 56*(1), 51–66. doi:10.1177/0020872812459064

Peek, L. (2008). Children and disasters: Understanding vulnerability, developing capacities, and promoting resilience—an introduction. *Children, Youth and Environments, 18*(1), 1–29. doi:10.1017/S0954579411000198

Penrose, A. & Takaki, M. (2006). Children's rights in emergencies and disasters. *Lancet, 367*, 698–699. doi:10.1016/S0140-6736(06)68272-X

Pinto, A.D. (2010). Denaturalizing 'natural' disasters: Haiti's earthquake and the humanitarian impulse. *Open Medicine, 4*(4), E193-E196. Retrieved from www.ncbi.nlm.nih.gov.simsrad.net.ocs.mq.edu.au/pmc/articles/PMC3090106/

Plan International, Save the Children International, United Nations Children's Fund, & World Vision International. (2011). *Children's charter: An action plan for disaster risk reduction for children by children*. Retrieved from http://plan-international.org/files/global/publications/emergencies/Childrens_Charter%20new.pdf

Save the Children. (2002). Child rights programming: How to apply right-based approaches in programming. A handbook for International Save the Children Alliance Members. Retrieved from www.crin.org/docs/PDN%20Ingles%20Final.pdf

Sphere Charter. (2004). *Humanitarian charter and minimum standards in disaster response* Retrieved from http://ocw.jhsph.edu/courses/refugeehealthcare/PDFs/SphereProjectHandbook.pdf

United Nations (UN). (1989). *Convention on the rights of the child*. New York: United Nations General Assembly. Retrieved from www.ohchr.org/en/professionalinterest/pages/crc.aspx.

UNICEF, *see* United Nations Children's Fund

United Nations International Strategy for Disaster Reduction (UNISDR). (2004). *Living with risk: A global review of disaster reduction initiatives*. Retrieved from www.unisdr.org/we/inform/publications/657

UNISDR. (2005). *Hyogo framework for action 2005–2015: Building the resilience of nations and communities to disasters*. World conference on disaster reduction, Kobe, Japan, January 2005. Retrieved from www.unisdr.org/we/inform/publications/1037

United Nations Children's Fund (UNICEF). (2010). *Integrated quality framework for early childhood development in Emergencies*. Unpublished manuscript.

United Nations Children's Fund [UNICEF]. (2011). *Children in Haiti one year after: The long road from relief to recovery*. Retrieved from www.unicef.org/files/Children_in_Haiti_-_One_Year_After_-_The_Long_Road_from_Relief_to_Recovery.pdf

Victorian Bushfire Royal Commission. (2010). *Victorian bushfire royal commission final report*, State of Victoria. Retrieved from www.royalcommission.vic.gov.au/Commission-Reports

Wessells, M. (2009). Do no harm: Toward contextually appropriate psychosocial support in international emergencies. *American Psychologist*, 842–854. doi:10.1037/0003-066X

World Vision. (2006). *Children in emergencies manual*. Retrieved from http://childprotection.wikischolars.columbia.edu/file/view/Children+in+Emergencies+Manual_World+Vision.pdf

# 15 Trauma, Disruption and Displacement

*Margaret Sims*

CHAPTER OVERVIEW

There are many factors that can result in disruption and displacement of young children. This chapter will consider the implications for early years pedagogy of responding to the diverse needs of children who are refugees or live in foster care. Issues such as parent incarceration and detention of asylum seekers will also be discussed.

Learning goals for this chapter include:

- Understanding the neurobiology underpinning trauma/disruption/displacement;
- Appreciating the impact of foster care on young children;
- Reflecting on the impact of the refugee experience on young children;
- Being aware of the impact of parental incarceration on children;
- Knowing about strategies for working with young children who have been traumatised/displaced/experienced disruption, and their families.

KEY TERMS AND CONCEPTS

asylum seeker

coping strategies

epigenetic legacy of disadvantage

refugee

rights framework

# Introduction: A focus on difference

Our use of the terms 'children with additional needs' or 'children with different needs' imply that there are 'regular' children with 'regular' needs and that children with these other labels are different. The issues associated with this assumption were addressed in Chapter 3. However, it is important to emphasise that the use of the term 'needs' prompts deficit thinking. In deficit thinking the 'problem' is located in the child who lacks particular skills, knowledge and/or abilities and the role of the adult is to 'fix' that lack in the child (Sims, 2011a). Deficit thinking focuses on what children don't or can't do, which is in direct contradiction to the principles in the Early Years Learning Framework (EYLF) (Department of Education, Employment & Workplace Relations [DEEWR], 2009). For example, one of the principles in the framework is that of high expectations and equity where educators are expected to '... believe in all children's capacity to succeed, regardless of diverse circumstances and abilities' (p.12). I have previously proposed a **rights framework** that can be used for planning that avoids a deficit approach, honours children's agency, and takes an ecological, strengths-based approach (Sims, 2011a).

**rights framework:** A framework used for observing, interpreting and planning. It focuses on strengths and children's agency, using a strengths-based, ecological approach.

This chapter uses this rights-based philosophy, and acknowledges that we should not categorise children nor make assumptions about individual children based on their category (in the case of this chapter categories associated with trauma, displacement and disruption). In order to build trusting partnerships with families and, through these, provide relevant learning opportunities for children, however, it is useful to have some understanding of general issues associated with particular groups of children and families. This general understanding can then be used to enable us to open our eyes and our minds when we are working with each unique child and family, so that we see the strengths and resilience of each human being. The focus in this chapter is on children and families who have experienced trauma, displacement and disruption in their lives. Those children and families with whom we work are the people who have demonstrated resilience, and who continue to demonstrate resilience every day. Our role is to honour their resilience, their uniqueness, and use our knowledge of the world and our general understanding of the situations that create trauma to work with them to enhance their resilience and create positive and enriching learning experiences.

**refugee:** Someone who 'owing to a well-founded fear of being persecuted for reasons of race, religion, nationality, membership of a particular social group or political opinion, is outside the country of his nationality, and is unable to, or owing to such fear, is unwilling to avail himself of the protection of that country' (UNHCR, 2013, para. 3).

Trauma, displacement and disruption can happen in many different ways, including:

**asylum seeker:** A refugee whose claims have not been formally processed, and therefore whose refugee status has not been officially determined.

1 Through conflict and persecution resulting in **refugee** displacement and **asylum seekers**—the World Bank (2010) estimates there were 43 million forcibly displaced people worldwide at the end of 2009; that is, people forced to leave their homes because of armed conflict and human rights abuses.

**FIGURE 15.1** DREAMING OF FREEDOM—A LIFE IN DETENTION

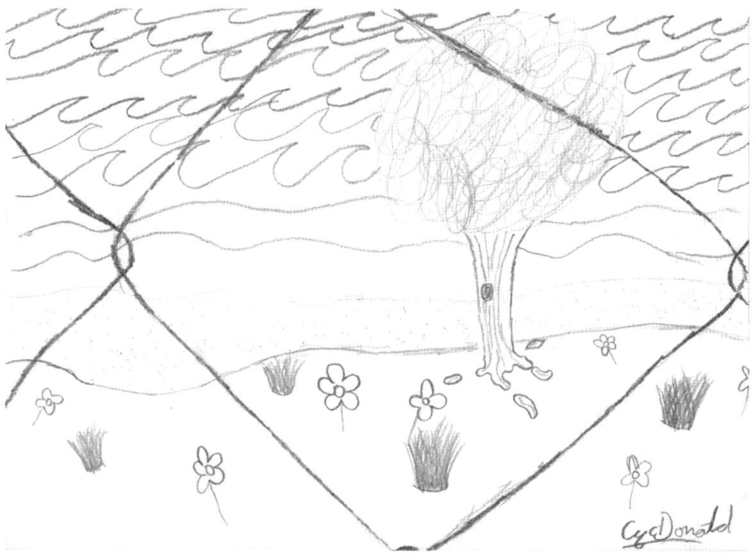

*Artwork by Cameron*

2 Through poverty resulting in economic displacement—economic migrants are those who choose to leave their country in the hope of a better life somewhere else. Both refugees and economic migrants may spend time in refugee camps and/or detention centres as their claims are processed or when they arrive in Australian territory without prior permission.

3 Through familial trauma or parental incarceration resulting in displacement into foster care or kinship care.

In all cases it is essential for educators to build individualised, trusting and caring relationships with each child and family (understanding that families are diverse and may include a range of people beyond those in the nuclear family), and to develop a shared understanding with each family in relation to their experiences, wishes and goals for themselves and their children. The information provided in this chapter is intended to support educators in these processes.

**CASE STUDY 15.1**

## War and refugee camps: A story of survival

Bashir is four years old and attends XYZ Childcare Centre. He was born in Afghanistan and militants killed his parents in front of him when he was eight months old. His older sister, Najeeba, who was five at the time, managed to get to the nearby village where their uncle, aunt

*Margaret Sims*

and cousins lived. The family struggled in poverty for some time but were constantly targeted by the Taliban as they were of the Hazara ethnic minority. When Bashir was two his sister and two cousins were killed and the remaining family were thrown out of their home. They were hidden in a truck and smuggled out of Afghanistan into Pakistan and from there to Indonesia where they were put on a boat by people smugglers. There was not enough food and water in the boat and many of the refugees became very sick. Bashir's uncle died at sea as did another cousin, leaving Bashir, his six-year-old cousin Ahmed and his aunt, who was pregnant. Their boat was intercepted and the refugees were taken to Christmas Island. His aunt gave birth on Christmas Island and was very ill for some time so was not able to support Bashir and Ahmed. They joined a group of other children but this group was torn apart when the family were moved to a facility in Melbourne after six months on Christmas Island. They stayed in the Melbourne facility for a further two months then were released with Temporary Protection Visas. The family now live in a small one-bedroom apartment in a disadvantaged area of the city. Bashir's aunt works at night as a cleaner and Bashir and Ahmed look after the baby while she is at work. Ahmed has just begun at the local state school and Bashir attends the local childcare centre every morning so his aunt can attend English language classes.

Bashir rarely verbalises. The educators work hard to share information with his aunt. He acknowledges his aunt's presence when she arrives with a half smile and then turns his head away. Bashir is watchful, notices what is going on around him all the time, and uses this to quickly fit in with whatever routines are happening. He will copy other children but has not yet responded to a request made to him in English. Educators have learned a few key words from his aunt in his home language (e.g. toilet, eat, drink) and Bashir mostly responds to these words. He prefers to play alone (at some distance from other children) and may mimic other children's play while remaining at a distance. He will stop what he is doing to investigate every unexpected noise or movement, which means that his concentration on any one thing is momentary. One day when the children had built a cubby, Bashir spent most of his time hidden inside and refused to come out for lunch. He shows exaggerated startle reactions to unexpected loud noises and a thunderstorm one morning had him curled in a ball under a blanket in the corner of the room.

Bashir likes to run around outside, and particularly enjoys the bikes. He was not able to ride one when he started at the centre but within the first week had figured it out and now spends a lot of time racing around the bike track. He is still developing the skills to swerve to avoid other children, and will get angry with those who get in his way.

He eats everything that is given to him, and will come back for more whenever he can. He doesn't appear to have any food or drink preferences, and when given a choice does not appear to understand what is required of him; he tends to grab for the first item offered or the one closest to him. He is adept at managing finger foods. He will often give up using cutlery in frustration and revert to finger feeding.

He generally uses the toilet but struggles to manage the taps and will use soap to wash his hands when reminded. He seems to be developing hay fever and presents with a runny nose often. He will wipe his nose when reminded, often on his arm.

CRITICAL REFLECTION QUESTIONS

1. Rights-based thinking works from a strengths perspective. What strengths does Bashir demonstrate?
2. Go through the case study again and include in your list the strengths evident in Bashir's family.

## The underpinning neurobiology of trauma

Displacement, whether caused by societal, community or familial trauma, impacts on children's biology. Recent neurobiological research is beginning to identify the pathways through which these traumatic early life experiences affect neurology and physiology, setting the foundation for poor adult outcomes (Meaney, 2010; Sims, 2011b; Strathearn, 2010). The emerging field of epigenetics shows that such experiences affect genetic make-up and are transmitted to the next generation (Meaney, 2010; Sweatt, 2009). This means that when children experience trauma the impact is not only on them but on their children too. Thus it is important for educators to understand the underpinning neurobiology of trauma because their work with children today will impact not only on the children themselves, but also on future generations.

Our physiological responses to stress can be categorised as positive, tolerable and toxic (Shonkoff, Garner, The Committee on Psychosocial Aspects of Child and Family Health, Committee on Early Childhood Adoption & Dependent Care & Section on Developmental & Behavioural Pediatrics, 2012). *Positive stress* triggers a brief and mild physiological response that quickly returns to baseline when the child is supported by the actions of a caring and responsive adult. These experiences allow children to learn to manage adverse experiences in a healthy and positive manner. *Tolerable stress*, in contrast, arises from greater adversity or threat; often an unusual situation such as a death, illness, natural disaster or act of terrorism. If a responsive and caring adult is available, and able to offer the required support, the risk of excessive activation of the stress system is lessened but if not, the child is at significant risk of system dysregulation (where a child's internal systems do not work as they should) and long-term negative outcomes. *Toxic stress* results from chronic, extreme activation of the stress systems when there is no responsive, caring adult to provide support. The most commonly observed examples of this are in children who have experienced child abuse or neglect. This chronic stress results in dysregulation of the stress systems that ultimately result in learning and behaviour impairments, and stress-related physical and mental ill health (Shonkoff et al., 2012). There is a small amount of evidence suggesting that dysregulation of the stress system may improve if children are exposed to better environments (Flinn, 2009; Gunnar & Quevedo, 2008), but this is not universally accepted and a recent review claims that '... toxic stress in early childhood is not only a risk factor for later risky behaviour but also can be a direct source of biological injury or disruption that may have lifelong consequences independent of whatever circumstances might follow later in life' (Shonkoff et al., 2012, p.e238).

Perry (2009) explains that the earlier in life experiences of stress or trauma occur, the more likely fundamental components of the lower parts of the brain are adversely affected; components that support the development of self-regulation, attention, arousal and impulse control. Later disruption is likely to impact on the limbic areas of the brain, which support the development of relationships. Trauma later in childhood will impact on cortical areas of the brain affecting cognition and language. Because the brain is hierarchical, dysregulation in the lower parts of the brain will impact negatively on upper brain levels and the child will require more global support as a result.

This means that children who have experienced displacement and the trauma associated with displacement are likely to require a range of supports depending on the timing of the trauma and what is available to them in their environment to help them cope. It is clear that adults can mediate the impact of traumatic experiences (Gunnar, Sebanc, Tout, Donzella & Dulmen, 2003). There is considerable evidence now available demonstrating that nurturing, loving relationships are very important in facilitating positive outcomes for children (see Sims & Hutchins, 2011). Unfortunately, in many cases of disruption and displacement, adults themselves are traumatised, which impacts on the support they can provide to their children (Lorek et al., 2009).

**CRITICAL REFLECTION QUESTION**

Why do you think it is helpful for practitioners to understand the neurobiological evidence?

# Refugee children

Over a decade ago, Machel (1996) delivered a report to the United Nations (UN) on the impact of armed conflict on children. Since that time, the UN have had a Special Representative of the Secretary General for Children and Armed Conflict and that representative reports regularly to the UN on progress made in protecting children (see http://childrenandarmedconflict.un.org/) against the key violations identified in the report, such as the killing or maiming of children, recruitment or use of children as soldiers, sexual violence against children, attacks against schools or hospitals, denial of humanitarian access for children and abduction of children.

Machel (2009) reported there were 56 conflicts worldwide in 2005, many of these involving paramilitary and non-state groups such as tribal groups, criminal gangs and groups ideologically opposed to their government. The nature of these conflicts is changing, with children and other civilians more likely to be affected. For example in Sudan, militia groups allied to the government, including Janjaweed, are responsible not only for recruiting child soldiers, but for using rape of children, both boys and girls, as a weapon of intimidation. Children are being used as hostages (for example the 2004 Beslan school hostage-taking in the northern Caucasus) and trained as terrorists (in Afghanistan children are being used as shields for adult terrorists and as suicide bombers).

In her earlier report, Machel (1996) noted that the arrival of peacekeeping forces did not improve the safety of children. Instead, the arrival of peacekeepers resulted in a huge increase in child prostitution in Cambodia and nearly three quarters of these child prostitutes were found to be HIV positive.

Children and families escaping these situations usually spend time in a refugee camp. Commonly in refugee camps, normal law and order is suspended as the camps do not come under the jurisdiction of the state in which they are located (Turner, 2005). How order is enacted is dependent on local conditions—some camps may be heavily influenced by the presence of relief agencies, while others remain lawless and residents may be in more danger in the camp than they were outside it. Some states (such as Tanzania) forbid the growing of crops, as to permit this would imply a permanency to residency that they wish to avoid (Turner, 2005)—this has a major impact on the food available to camp residents. Camps such as Kakuma in Kenya are overfull (over 100,000 people) and continue to grow as refugees (75 per cent of them women and children, and 15 per cent children under 5) from South Sudan, Burundi, Ethiopia, Somalia and the Democratic Republic of the Congo continued to head there in 2013. There are already major concerns around the lack of water (UNHCR, 2012), and only 40% of residents have access to latrines, which poses a major health risk (Australia for UNHCR, n.d.).

The impact on children of living in a refugee camp is profound. Lack of physical safety, exposure to violence, inadequate nutrition and hygiene and limited or no access to education (including lack of opportunity for safe play) all serve to increase the risk of poor physical and mental health outcomes (Fox, Cowell, & Montgomery, 2007). Children are likely to demonstrate Post Traumatic Stress Disorder (PTSD), which may diminish with specialised mental health treatment post resettlement, but often does not (Thabet, Vostanis

& Karim, 2005). Levels of familial anxiety are related to the prevalence of PTSD in children, particularly in communities marked by conflict (Khamis, 2005).

People who are defined by the UNHCR as refugees can apply to come to Australia as humanitarian migrants. Such application requires a demonstration that the person is subject to persecution in their home country. For a number of refugees, formal processing of this claim is not possible because either there are no processing points (people in Afghanistan, Iran, Iraq, Sri Lanka or Burma have no legally accessible processing places so cannot apply), the wait at available points is too long (it can take up to two years in some places), or people are sufficiently desperate to risk everything to get to a place of safety (ChilOut, n.d.). Those who come to Australia without official migrant status are placed in detention until their claim is processed. In detention centres, additional exposure to violence and trauma is high: detention centres have high rates of rioting, hunger strikes, self-harming behaviours and suicides (Lorek et al., 2009). Thus children and families entering detention centres with existing higher rates of mental and physical health problems are likely to be even more negatively impacted. Lorek and colleagues' work in the UK demonstrates that this increasingly negative impact is clearly evident in children, even if their stay in detention is short term. An Australian study (Mares & Jureidini, 2004) found that all children over the age of six who had been in detention for a year or more were clinically diagnosed with both PTSD and major depression with suicidal ideation. Preschool aged children were '… identified with developmental delay, emotional problems, disturbed sleep and feeding routines, as well as delays in language and social development' (Lorek et al., 2009, p.3). Many of the adults in Lorek and colleagues' study found that their anxiety over their status as refugees, the fear of being returned to their country of origin, the loss of friends and family from their former lives and the prison-like aspects of detention which for many triggered memories of past traumatic experiences, impacted negatively on existing poor mental health and wellbeing. Given this level of trauma, the ability of parents to support their children is impaired, and this increases the risk of poor physical and mental health outcomes for children.

**CRITICAL REFLECTION QUESTIONS**

1. Read some of the stories posted by the Refugee Council of Australia at www.refugeecouncil.org.au/r/list-bk.php. What is your reaction?
2. Do you think you can address these issues with young children? Read John Marsden and Matt Ottley's (2008) children's book *Home and Away*. Plan how you would share this with children.
3. Explore the stories of children in detention at www.chilout.org. Think about the experiences these children have written about and how you might support other children with similar experiences.

## Case study 15.1 continued

Following is a rights-based framework that can be used to plan inclusively for how to work with Bashir and his family to ensure that their rights are met. This framework helps you identify what *you* need to do as Bashir's educator, and not on what Bashir lacks.

**TABLE 15.1** USING A RIGHTS-BASED FRAMEWORK—BASHIR

| | **How are the child's rights currently met (from your observations and discussions with parents and others)?** | **Do educators have to do anything to ensure rights are met?** |
|---|---|---|
| *Level 1: The right to food, shelter, warmth (clothing) etc.;* | Family are currently managing on a limited income, with no reserves—it is a struggle but they do meet basic family needs much of the time. | Acknowledge aunt's ability to support her family. Make sure aunt's strengths are affirmed at least several times a week.<br><br>Offer information about low cost local shopping options (e.g. Op Shops, discount food). Check if she would like someone to introduce her to these lower cost shopping options. |
| *Level 2: The right to physical safety—avoiding external dangers and things that might harm: safety, security and protection;* | Family live in an area where it is not safe for children to play outside. The children are able to remain indoors.<br><br>Aunt has a job that requires her to work in the evenings. The children remain in the apartment at night while she is at work.<br><br>Bashir is developing skills at riding the bike and avoiding accidents. | Offer aunt support to build friendships with other Afghani women in the area—potential play visits to local parks, each other's homes etc.<br><br>Provide opportunities for Bashir to manoeuvre the bike through obstacles etc. to enhance his control. |
| *Level 3: The right to love, affection, care, attention, closeness to another person;* | Bashir appears content with his own company—he has not been observed connecting with anyone.<br><br>He is aware of other children and will imitate their play. | Make time to communicate with aunt to build a trusting relationship—experiment with different communication strategies.<br><br>Focus on building positive, caring relationships between Bashir and his aunt, Bashir and a key educator. |

**TABLE 15.1** USING A RIGHTS-BASED FRAMEWORK—BASHIR *(CONTINUED)*

| | **How are the child's rights currently met (from your observations and discussions with parents and others)?** | **Do educators have to do anything to ensure rights are met?** |
|---|---|---|
| | He has experienced multiple losses of loved ones and friends.<br>Bashir is observed to communicate with his aunt using modes other than speech . | Aim for educators to learn a key Afghani word from aunt every day and use Afghani words as often as possible, pairing them with the English equivalent.<br>Encourage all the children to use multi-modal communication in addition to words (English/Afghani pairings where possible. Use of visuals and Key Word Sign—see Chapter 23.<br>Use a buddy system to support Bashir to engage in adult structured play opportunities. |
| *Level 4: The right to feel valued and worthy, to be valued by others, to be accepted, appreciated and have status;* | Bashir and Ahmed take on the responsibility of caring for the baby at nights. | Undertake further observations to determine Bashir's interests. Use these interests to create a valued role for him among peers.<br>Recognise how important his role of carer is to his self-identity and seek ways to support this but make it safer at the same time—see Level 2. |
| *Level 5: The right to realise one's potential. Maslow calls this self-actualisation.* | Nothing yet observed. | Undertake further observations. |

# Children in foster care

Foster care is the primary form of out of home care service-provision for children (up to 18 years of age) in Australia (McHugh, 2007). At 30 June 2010, 35,895 Australian children were living in out of home care, which represents a 97 per cent increase on the numbers from a decade ago. Rate of placement in out of home care currently is seven children per 1000 (Lamont, 2011).

Children are removed from their families and placed into foster care for a range of reasons including child abuse, neglect, family violence, homelessness, and parental drug abuse, mental health issues, death, incarceration, or based on the belief that the foster setting will provide a more positive experience than children's own families (Chipungu & Bent-Goodley, 2004; Lawrence, Carlson & Egeland, 2006; Wilson, 2006). Over 90 per cent of children in foster care in one study were found to have experienced abuse and/or neglect (Osborn & Delfabbro, 2006). As a result of these experiences in the children's early years, they enter foster care needing considerable support to attain long-term positive health and wellbeing outcomes. For example, a study of 52 children ranging in age from four to 11 in long-term foster care in the UK indicated that, at the time of placement, 93 per cent were rated as exhibiting behavioural and emotional difficulties (Schofield & Beek, 2005). Australian research indicates that approximately 15 to 20 per cent of children placed in foster care have significant behavioural and emotional problems, and these problems complicate their adjustment to foster care (Barber & Delfabbro, 2004), and concerns about behaviour are identified for up to 60 per cent of children children placed in foster care (Osborn & Bromfield, 2007).

While children in foster care possess strengths, they often need ongoing support to help them regulate their behaviours, catch up with learning, build relationships, and avoid developing coping skills (with the associated neurobiological underpinnings) that prompt them to engage in various risky behaviours such as delinquency, substance use, and risky sexual behaviours (Schofield & Beek, 2005; Tarren-Sweeney & Hazell, 2006; Wilson, 2006). Occasionally children may need support to manage behaviours such as self-injury and eating disorders (Tarren-Sweeney, 2008). Longitudinal research indicates that traumatic events in early life are significantly related to incarceration as an adolescent (Jonson-Reid & Barth, 2000) and a reduced quality of life in adulthood (Ventegodt, 1999). Such outcomes reflect complex psychopathology that is not easily addressed, and educators must work with foster families to create an appropriately supportive, learning environment.

Children who are in foster care for the long term have opportunities to develop secure relationships with their foster carers and there is evidence that many children do learn to adjust to their new home and their foster carers (Osborn & Bromfield, 2007). Through these relationships they are able to demonstrate improvements in health and wellbeing. However, there remains a small group of children in foster care who do not demonstrate improvements; who continue to exhibit complex support needs to manage conduct disorder, insecure attachments, attention problems, mental health problems, eating problems and inappropriate sexual behaviours (Tarren-Sweeney, 2008). It is ironic that children who have experienced the most trauma prior to entering foster care are also those who are most likely to experience unstable foster placements (Osborn & Delfabbro, 2006), exacerbating the risk of poor outcomes. Educators working with children in foster care and their families need to consider how to best deliver the social, emotional, behavioural, relational and academic supports needed to ensure children have the best possible opportunities to learn and grow. The rights-based approach to planning discussed in Sims (2011a) and outlined in the case studies in this chapter provides a framework that can be used.

## Aboriginal children in out-of-home care

Government policies focusing on assimilation were responsible for the forcible removal of Aboriginal and Torres Strait Islander children from their families and communities and this has left an **epigenetic legacy of disadvantage** that is now played out in the disproportionate number of Indigenous children in foster care (Richardson, Bromfield & Osborn, 2007). In fact, the rate of Indigenous placement in care is nine times that of non-Indigenous children (Boetto, 2010). Indigenous children in care are likely to have experienced more forms of trauma compared to the general foster care population, but appear to be less adversely affected by their experiences (Osborn & Delfabbro, 2006). There has been little research analysing the components of foster care for Indigenous children that best supports their wellbeing but Richardson and colleagues claim that 'the use of concepts such as attachment and bonding to assess the wellbeing of Aboriginal and Torres Strait Islander children in care are inconsistent with Aboriginal and Torres Strait islander values of relatedness and childrearing practices' (2007, p.3). Because we know so little about what works for Indigenous children in foster care, it is even more important for educators to build trusting relationships with children and their foster families and work together to provide the appropriate support to facilitate learning and wellbeing.

**epigenetic legacy of disadvantage:** Adverse experiences impact on the genome in ways that are then inherited by descendants. See the section entitled 'The underpinning neurobiology of trauma'.

### Kinship care

Instead of placement in foster care, many children, particularly Indigenous children, are placed in kinship care (Spence, 2004). Kinship care is care provided by a family member or a close friend or community member, and is the fastest growing form of care in Australia (Boetto, 2010). Kinship care aims to support children to maintain links with their extended family and this is thought to be in the best interests of the child (Dunne & Kettler, 2006). Despite this, children in kinship care demonstrate poor outcomes, similar to those in foster care;

however, it is not possible to identify if those outcomes are associated with the non-parental care itself, or to children's experiences prior to going into care.

Kinship carers are more likely to be sole women, and be economically disadvantaged compared to foster parents (Boetto, 2010). Many kinship carers are grandparents, and many of these are grandmothers on their own. They experience financial stress associated with additional costs and limited avenues of support, social isolation, health problems and physical tiredness. Support for these carers is limited and the legal issues they face can be complex, particularly when they are in conflict with their own children around the custody of grandchildren (Bromfield & Osborn, 2007).

Early years educators working with children in kinship care need to be sensitive to the demands faced by kinship carers. Additional demands (even though they are focused on the wellbeing of the child) may result in additional carer stress and have the unintended consequence of worsening the situation rather than helping. Build relationships with both the children and carers and make sure that planning takes into account the strengths of both the carers and the children. Use the rights-based framework to develop an understanding of the child and carers' lives and where educators can most effectively provide support.

**CASE STUDY 15.2**

## The power of kinship care

Sally attends the local Multifunctional Aboriginal Children's Services (MACS) and you are her educator. She has been attending the MACS since she was six months old and you have known her since then, although you have only just become her key educator. Sally initially lived with her mother (who was 16 when she was born), her grandmother (her mother's mother) and six other of her mother's siblings ranging from one to 14 years of age. Sally's grandmother encouraged her mum to return to school to complete secondary school and Sally spent most of the time with her grandmother and her aunts and uncles. Her mum dropped out of school when Sally was one year old then left the town to go to the city. Sally's family have not heard from her mother for 10 months. Sally's grandmother has six children of her own living with her as well as Sally. She is not in paid work and manages on a sole parent benefit. Sally's grandfather is in prison. When he was with the family he was violent and some of the younger children experienced broken bones from his attacks. He was imprisoned when Sally was six months old.

Sally is very happy at the MACS and transitions into care each day joyfully. She is collected in the MACS bus and sometimes an educator goes into the house to collect her, as she is not ready. The educators all know her grandmother well, as most of Sally's aunts and uncles had, in their turn, attended the MACS. When she arrives at the MACS she has breakfast and usually asks for this immediately on arrival. She is extremely hungry and will eat several pieces of toast, some fruit and drink two cups of water most mornings.

Sally enjoys active games. She loves to ride the bikes and run around outside. She has some trouble on uneven ground and often trips and stumbles but she bounces up to her feet again quickly and carries on. She enjoys playing in the sandpit, and with encouragement can play for 20 minutes without throwing sand or jumping on other children's creations. She is not as enthusiastic with tabletop activities but will occasionally use the painting easel. She holds a large paintbrush in her fist and makes large, colourful swirls on the paper. She prefers to tear paper rather than use scissors, and happily joined with others in tearing and gluing paper to make a shared paper maché creation last term. She can participate in group story-times when she is involved in the story (e.g. when she is manipulating a puppet, or telling the story with gestures). She particularly enjoys Aboriginal stories and songs.

Sally can maintain cooperative play with other children for a short time but struggles to resolve conflict positively. She often attempts to solve conflict by yelling loudly at others, and will occasionally hit out at others. Her grandmother says that at home she bosses the younger children around, and they accept her dominant role without question. She tries to mimic the older children at home, and will use a range of swear words to try to get attention. She expects to have exclusive use of any toy she is using for as long as she wants but once she is finished, is happy for someone else to take it over.

## CRITICAL REFLECTION QUESTIONS

1. Sally's age is not given in the case study. Does this matter? What does knowledge of Sally's age contribute to your understanding of Sally's strengths? Does knowing Sally's age make it more likely you will think about what she lacks in comparison with her age peers?
2. Work through the rights-based planning approach using the case study about Sally:
   a. Write a list of the strengths demonstrated by Sally.
   b. Write a list of the strengths demonstrated by Sally's family.
   c. Complete a planning table for Sally.

**TABLE 15.2** SALLY'S STRENGTHS AND INTERESTS

| Sally's strengths | Sally's interests |
| --- | --- |
| | |

**TABLE 15.3** USING A RIGHTS-BASED FRAMEWORK—SALLY

| | **How are the Sally's rights currently met (from your observations and discussions with parents and others)?** | **Do educators have to do anything to ensure rights are met?** |
|---|---|---|
| *Level 1: The right to food, shelter, warmth (clothing) etc.;* | | |
| *Level 2: The right to physical safety—avoiding external dangers and things that might harm: safety, security and protection;* | | |
| *Level 3: The right to love, affection, care, attention, closeness to another person;* | | |
| *Level 4: The right to feel valued and worthy, to be valued by others, to be accepted, appreciated and have status;* | | |
| *Level 5: The right to realise one's potential. Maslow calls this self-actualisation.* | | |

# Parental incarceration

A large number of children in foster care are placed because their parents are incarcerated (Johnson & Waldfogel, 2002). These children are more likely to experience residential instability and need support to manage the insecure behaviours this creates. Boys seem particularly vulnerable to the impact of this instability (Geller, Garfinkel, Cooper, & Mincy, 2009). Children whose parents are incarcerated are more likely to experience economic stress, and need support to form attachments (Miller, 2006).

Johnson and Waldfogel (2002) estimate that most children of incarcerated parents have been exposed to multiple risk factors throughout their lives, before, during and after parental incarceration. They may have been exposed to parental drug and/or alcohol addiction, family and community violence and poverty (Murray & Murray, 2010). This accumulation of stressors increases the risk that children will cope by developing behaviours that put them at risk of social alienation (Dannerbeck, 2005) and mental health concerns (Murray & Murray, 2010).

However, Johnson (2006) suggests that incarcerated mothers were often not the primary caregivers of their children prior to incarceration, and rarely become so on their release in any form other than transitory care. Despite this, other researchers focus on the attachment issues associated with separation from the mother as the primary caregiver and position this as a core factor in children's psychopathology (Murray & Murray, 2010). Aaron and Dallaire (2010) argue that the impact of parental incarceration can be separated from familial factors, that incarceration is linked to children's subsequent delinquent behaviours, and that recent incarceration is linked to current family conflict and victimisation as well as children's subsequent delinquent behaviours. In other words, there are consequences of parental incarceration that operate independently of any previous family and community risk factors to which children were exposed.

Often mothers who are imprisoned do not have visits from their children, particularly if children have to travel some distance to get to the prison. In some cases parents themselves do not want their children to visit, either through shame, or a wish to protect the children. It is not uncommon for children to not know their parent(s) is/are in prison (Hairston, 2007). Children's alternative caregivers may also restrict contact, either through shame, a wish to punish the parent, or a wish to protect the children.

Some parents are able to maintain contact with their children using the phone and snail mail and some facilities offer video contact. Visits often take place in environments not conducive to children's needs or comfort, though some prisons offer a play area where children and parents can visit. These are more likely to be available for parents in minimum-security prisons where contact visits are allowed. In some circumstances contact may be limited to a hug on greeting and leaving. In some jurisdictions prisoners are allowed overnight visits and the parent and children can stay together in an appropriate facility inside the prison (Hairston, 2007). Some prisons offer mother–baby facilities where very young babies can stay with their mother (Robertson, 2007). This is offered in order to facilitate the mother–baby bond and to support breastfeeding. There is considerable debate as to how old children should be before they are removed from the prison environment and at what age the restrictive prison environment is likely to impact negatively on children. Specialist mother–baby units tend to be built more like regular houses and mothers are supported in their parenting to gain new knowledge and skills.

CRITICAL REFLECTION QUESTIONS

1. Are there mother–baby units in the women's prisons in your state? If so, how long can children stay with their mothers in these?
2. Are there other transition programs in place to help re-integrate parents and their children on release from prison? What are they?

## Working with children and families who have been displaced

**FIGURE 15.2** PLAYING

*Artwork by Emma*

Many years ago Bloom (1995) argued that children who have been traumatised need special support that recognises their inappropriate behaviours as examples of **coping strategies**: behaviours that were adaptive in their traumatic environment but which are not appropriate in different contexts.

**Coping strategies:** Behaviours that were adaptive in a child's traumatic environment but which are not appropriate in different contexts.

For example, children who have lived with fear are more likely to interpret innocent actions as threatening and respond accordingly. If we punish them for their reactions we are simply reinforcing the message that the world is uncaring and unfair, and increasing the risk that they will continue to exhibit these inappropriate behaviours. Bloom (1995) talks about creating a sanctuary, a place where children can feel safe, where they learn that not everything is threatening and where they can be coaxed into trying new behavioural responses.

In many ways the work of Perry (2009; Perry & Hambrick, 2008), beginning from the perspective of neurobiology rather than therapy, reinforces these ideas. Perry (2009, p.248) argues:

> Removing children from abusive homes also may remove them from their familiar and safe social network in school, church and community. And worse, the presence of new and unfamiliar individuals can actually activate the already sensitized stress-response systems in these children, making them more symptomatic and less capable of benefiting from our efforts to comfort and heal. Our well-intended interventions often result in relational impermanence for the child: foster home to foster home, new schools, new case workers, new therapists as if these are interchangeable parts. They are not. Even 'best practice' therapeutic work is ineffective in an environment of relational instability and chronic transition.

While it is important to acknowledge that, for some children, removal from abusive homes is the better option (and may be their only chance of survival), it is also important to recognise that all children experiencing abuse need appropriate support. Behavioural responses (Bloom's coping mechanisms) arise out of physiology and neurobiology, and as such, work with children needs to focus on addressing the impact of the trauma on the appropriate levels of the brain (Perry, 2009; Perry & Hambrick, 2008). Where children have been exposed to trauma very early in life and have poorly developed self-regulation, attention, arousal and impulse control, therapy needs to address components of the lower brain and brainstem. The underpinning assumption in Perry's work is that repetition causes the brain to lay down new pathways to process this regularly occurring input. Activities such as music, movement, yoga, breathing exercises, play and art therapy, drumming and therapeutic massage (Perry, 2009) help reprogram the areas of the brain dealing with these attributes. The rights, strengths-based approach to planning discussed in this chapter (adapted from Sims, 2011a) provides a tool that can be used to scaffold the approaches mooted by Bloom and Perry. I propose a framework based on Maslow's hierarchy of needs (Maslow, 1970) recast as a framework of rights. I ask educators to focus not on what the child lacks, but on what they need to address to ensure the child and family's rights are met at each level of the hierarchy. For example, at Level 1, a child's behaviour may lead us to question the child's feelings of safety, particularly given that we know a child who has experienced trauma is likely to perceive innocent behaviours as threatening, and that such perception may lead to coping behaviours that we are likely to judge as inappropriate in our context. The planning framework focuses not on the child's inappropriate behaviours, but on what we, as educators, need to do to support the child's feelings of safety.

**CRITICAL REFLECTION QUESTIONS**

Think about a child with whom you work. What are the child's strengths? Think about how the child's right to food, clothing, protection, safety and relationships are met. What can you do as an early years professional to support the child and family in ensuring these rights are met?

## Conclusion

It is important that we are aware of the challenges experienced by children who have undergone trauma/displacement and/or disruption. This awareness enables us to be more empathetic as we build relationships with children and their families. In the context of these relationships we are able to plan together how we will work towards ensuring children's rights are met and that the learning opportunities we provide are culturally and contextually relevant. It is important that we see our knowledge of trauma/displacement/disruption as tool to enhance our empathy and do not use it to overlook the uniqueness of each child and each family. While it is common for children in foster care to need emotional support, for example, not all children in foster care will do so, and not all children in foster care will have the same emotional issues. It would be disrespectful of children to categorise them because of their experiences and fail to appreciate their individual strengths. This chapter provides some pointers as to some of the experiences children may have in common. It is the starting point from which early years professionals can undertake a unique journey of personal exploration with every child.

# FOR FURTHER REFLECTION

1. How does the argument in this chapter (and Chapter 3) about deficit thinking resonate with you? How does this link to your thinking about inclusion?
2. Identify the countries from which families attending a local early years service have migrated. Select one country that is/was experiencing conflict. Research the social/political environment of this country. Ask the family if they would be comfortable talking to you about their experiences as migrants—don't insist if they would rather not. Focus on trying to build your understanding of this family's experiences.
3. Search for personal accounts of foster care. There are a number of stories/novels that can give you an insight into what it can be like to be a child in foster care.
4. How can you work with children and encourage them to act inclusively?
5. To what extent should you support children to understand some of the atrocities that take place in our world? Should children understand the issues around child soldiers for example? Should they understand what it is like to live in a detention centre? Should they understand what it is like when your parents hurt you rather than nurture you? Do children learn empathy through trying to understand experiences such as these?

## WEBSITES

www.chilout.org
A website exploring the situation for children in detention in Australia

www.quno.org/resource/2004/6/women-prison-and-children-imprisoned-mothers-preliminary-research-paper
Information on the impact of parental imprisonment on children

www.unicef.org/publications/index_49985.html
A report on children in conflict situations

www.aifs.gov.au/nch/pubs/brief/rb3/rb3.pdf
Research brief on the outcomes for children and young people in out of home care

www.aifs.gov.au/nch/pubs/brief/rb8/rb8.pdf
Research brief addressing cultural considerations in out of home care

www.rch.org.au/uploadedFiles/Main/Content/ccch/CPR_Vol_19_No_3_Epigenetics_and_oral_health_web.pdf
Information about epigenetics

## REFERENCES


Aaron, A. & Dallaire, D. (2010). Parental incarceration and multiple risk experiences: Effects on family dynamics and children's delinquency. *Journal of Youth and Adolescence, 39*(12), 1471–1484. doi:10.1007/s10964-009-9458-0

Australia for UNHCR. (n.d.). *Kakuma water and sanitation appeal*. Retrieved from www.unrefugees.org.au/programs/kakuma

Barber, J., & Delfabbro, P. (2004). *Children in foster care*. London: Routledge.

Bloom, S.L. (1995). Creating sanctuary in the school. *Journal for a Just and Caring Education, 1*(4), 403–433. Retrieved from www.sanctuaryweb.com/PDFs_new/Bloom%20Sanctuary%20in%20the%20Classroom.pdf

Boetto, H. (2010). Kinship care: A review of issues. *Family Matters* (85), 60–67. Retrieved from www.aifs.gov.au/institute/pubs/fm2010/fm85/fm85g.html

Bromfield, L. & Osborn, A. (2007). Kinship care. *National Child Protection Clearinghouse Research Brief, 10*, 1–7. Retrieved from www.aifs.gov.au/nch/pubs/brief/rb10/rb10.pdf.

ChilOut. (n.d.). Children out of immigration detention: Myths and facts. Retrieved from www.chilout.org/myths-and-facts

Chipungu, S. & Bent-Goodley, T. (2004). Meeting the challenges of contemporary foster care. *The Future of Children, 14*, 75–93. doi:10.2307/1602755

Dannerbeck, A. (2005). Differences in parenting attributes, experiences, and behaviours of delinquent youth with and without a parental history of incarceration. *Youth Violence and Juvenile Justice, 3*(3), 199–213. Retrieved from http://yvj.sagepub.com/

Department of Education, Employment and Workplace Relations (DEEWR). (2009). *Belonging, being and becoming. The early years learning framework for Australia.* Canberra, ACT: Commonwealth of Australia. Retrieved from http://docs.education.gov.au/system/files/doc/other/belonging_being_and_becoming_the_early_years_learning_framework_for_australia.pdf

Dunne, E. & Kettler, L. (2006). Social and emotional issues of children in kinship foster care and stressors on kinship carers. *Children Australia, 31*(2), 22–29. Retrieved from www.ozchild.org.au/ozchild/about-ozchild/resources/40-children-australia-journal#.UY7LfiuSDC4

Flinn, M. (2009). Are cortisol profiles a stable trait during child development? *American Journal of Human Biology, 21*, 769–771. doi:10.1002/ajhb.20981

Fox, P., Cowell, J. & Montgomery, A. (2007). The effects of violence on health and adjustment of Southeast Asian refugee children: An integrative review. *Public Health Nursing, 11*(3), 195–201. doi:10.1111/j.1525-1446.1994.tb00401.

Geller, A., Garfinkel, I., Cooper, C. & Mincy, R. (2009). Parental incarceration and child well-being: Implications for urban families. *Social Science Quarterly, 90*(5), 1186–1202. doi:10.1111/j.1540-6237.2009.00653.x

Gunnar, M. & Quevedo, K. (2008). Early care experiences and HPA axis regulation in children: A mechanism for later trauma vulnerability. In E. de Kloet, M. Oitzl & E. Vermetten (Eds), *Stress hormones and post traumatic stress disorder.* (Vol. 167, pp.137–149). Amsterdam: Elsevier.

Gunnar, M., Sebanc, A., Tout, K., Donzella, B. & Dulmen, M. (2003). Peer rejection, temperament and cortisol activity in preschoolers. *Developmental Psychobiology, 43*, 346–358. doi:10.1002/dev.10144

Hairston, C. (2007). *Focus on children with incarcerated parents: An overview of the research literature.* Baltimore, MD: The Annie E. Casey Foundation. Retrieved from www.aecf.org/KnowledgeCenter/Publications.aspx?pubguid=%7BF48C4DF8-BBD9-4915-85D7-53EAFC941189%7D

Johnson, D. (2006). The wrong road: Efforts to understand the effects of parental crime and incarceration. *Criminology and Public Policy, 5*(4), 703–719. Retrieved from http://onlinelibrary.wiley.com/journal/10.1111/(ISSN)1745-9133

Johnson, E. & Waldfogel, J. (2002). Parental incarceration: Recent trends and implications for child welfare. *Social Service Review, 76*(3), 460–479. doi:10.1086/341184

Jonson-Reid, M. & Barth, R. (2000). From placement to prison: The path to adolescent incarceration from child welfare, supervised foster or group care. *Children and Youth Services Review, 22*, 493–516. doi:10.1016/S0190-7409(00)00100-6

Khamis, V. (2005). Post-traumatic stress disorder among school age Palestinian children. *Child Abuse & Neglect, 29*, 81–95. doi:10.1016/j.chiabu.2004.06.013

Lamont, A. (2011). Children in care. *Resource Sheet. National Child Protection Clearinghouse, March*, 1–5. Retrieved from www.aifs.gov.au/cfca/pubs/factsheets/a142092/index.html

Lawrence, C., Carlson, E. & Egeland, B. (2006). The impact of foster care on development. *Development and Psychopathology, 18*, 57–76. doi:10.1017/S0954579406060044

Lorek, A., Ehntholt, K., Nesbitt, A., Wey, E., Githinji, C., Rossor, E. & Wickramasinghe, R. (2009). The mental and physical health difficulties of children held within a British immigration detention center: A pilot study. *Child Abuse & Neglect 33*(9), 573–585 doi:10.1016/j.chiabu.2008.10.005

Machel, G. (1996). Promotion and Protection of the Rights of Children. Impact of armed conflict on children. *Report presented to the Fifty-first session, Item 108 of the provisional agenda of the United Nations.* Retrieved from www.unicef.org/graca/a51-306_en.pdf

Machel, G. (2009). *Machel Study 10-year strategic review. Children and conflict in a changing world.* New York: Office of the Special Representative of the Secretary-General for Children and Armed Conflict, and United Nations Children's Fund. Retrieved from www.unicef.org/publications/index_49985.html

Mares, S. & Jureidini, J. (2004). Psychiatric assessment of children and families in immigration detention—clinical, administrative and ethical issues. *Australian and New Zealand Journal of Public Health, 28*(6), 520–526. doi:10.1111/j.1467-842X.2004.tb00041.x

Marsden, J. & Ottley, M. (2008). *Home and away.* Melbourne: Lothian Children's Books.

Maslow, A. (1970). *Motivation and personality.* New York: Harper and Row.

McHugh, M. (2007). *Costs and consequences: Understanding the impact of fostering on carers.* (Doctor of Philosophy), University of New South Wales. Sydney. Retrieved from http://unsworks.unsw.edu.au/fapi/datastream/unsworks:1607/SOURCE02

Meaney, M. (2010). Epigenetics and the biological definition of gene x environment interactions. *Child Development, 81*(1), 41–79. Retrieved from http://onlinelibrary.wiley.com/journal/10.1111/(ISSN)1467-8624

Miller, K. (2006). The impact of parental incarceration on children: An emerging need for effective interventions. *Child and Adolescent Social Work Journal, 23*(4), 472–486. doi:10.1007/s10560-006-0065-6

Murray, J. & Murray, L. (2010). Parental incarceration, attachment and child psychopathology. *Attachment & Human Development, 12*(4), 289–309. doi:10.1080/14751790903416889

Osborn, A. & Bromfield, L. (2007). Outcomes for children and young people in care. *National child protection clearinghouse research brief, 3*. Retrieved from www.aifs.gov.au/nch/pubs/brief/rb3/rb3.pdf

Osborn, A. & Delfabbro, P. (2006). An analysis of the social background and placement history of children with multiple and complex needs in Australian out-of-home care. *Communities, Families and Children Australia, 1*(1), 33–42. Retrieved from www.aifs.gov.au/cfca/

Perry, B. (2009). Examining child maltreatment through a neurodevelopmental lens: Clinical applications of the neurosequential model of therapeutics. *Journal of Loss and Trauma: International Perspectives on Stress & Coping 14*(4), 240–255. doi:10.1080/15325020903004350

Perry, B. & Hambrick, E. (2008). The neuroseqential model of therapeutics. *Reclaiming Children and Youth, 17*(3), 38–43. doi:10.1080/15325020903004350

Richardson, N., Bromfield, L. & Osborn, A. (2007). Cultural considerations in out-of-home care. *National Child Protection Clearinghouse Research Brief, 8*. Retrieved from www.aifs.gov.au/nch/pubs/brief/rb8/rb8.pdf

Robertson, O. (2007). The impact of parental imprisonment on children. *Women in prison and children of imprisoned mothers series*. Geneva: Quaker United Nations Office. Retrieved from www.quno.org/geneva/pdf/humanrights/women-in-prison/ImpactParentalImprisonment-200704-English.pdf

Schofield, G. & Beek, M. (2005). Providing a secure base: Parenting children in long-term foster family care. *Attachment and Human Development, 7*, 3–25. doi:10.1080/14616730500049019

Shonkoff, J., Garner, A., The Committee on Psychosocial Aspects of Child and Family Health, Committee on Early Childhood Adoption and Dependent Care, & Section on Developmental and Behavioural Pediatrics. (2012). The lifelong effects of early childhood adversity and toxic stress. *Pediatrics, 129*(1), e232–e246 doi:10.1542/peds.2011-2663

Sims, M. (2011a). *Social inclusion and the early years learning framework: A way of working.* Castle Hill, NSW: Pademelon Press.

Sims, M. (2011b). What is epigenetics. *Community Paediatric Review, 19*(3), 1–3. Retrieved from www.rch.org.au/ccch/resources_and_publications/Community_Paediatric_Review/

Sims, M. & Hutchins, T. (2011). *Program planning for infants and toddlers. In search of relationships.* Castle Hill, NSW: Pademelon Press.

Spence, N. (2004). Kinship care in Australia. *Child Abuse Review, 13*, 263–276. doi:10.1002/car.854

Strathearn, L. (2010). *The intergenerational transmission of attachment: What the brain has to say.* Paper presented at the 2nd Biennial International Association for the Study of Attachment Conference, St Johns College, Cambridge UK. Retrieved from www.iasa-dmm.org/images/uploads/Lane-%20intergenerational.pdf

Sweatt, J. (2009). Experience-dependent epigenetic modifications in the central nervous system. *Biological Psychiatry, 65*(3), 191–197. doi:10.1016/j.biopsych.2008.09.002

Tarren-Sweeney, M. (2008). The mental health of children in out-of-home care. *Current Opinion in Psychiatry, 21*(4), 345–349. doi:10.1097/YCO.0b013e32830321fa

Tarren-Sweeney, M. & Hazell, P. (2006). Mental health of children in foster and kinship care in New South Wales, Australia. *Journal of Paediatrics and Child Health, 42*, 89–97. doi:10.1111/j.1440-1754.2006.00804.x

Thabet, A., Vostanis, P. & Karim, K. (2005). Group crisis intervention for children during ongoing war conflict. *European Child and Adolescent Psychiatry, 14*, 262–269. doi:10.1007/s00787-005-0466-7

Turner, S. (2005). Suspended spaces—contesting sovereignty in a refugee camp. In T. Blom Hansen & F. Stepputat (Eds.), *Sovereign bodies: Citizens, migrants, and states in the postcolonial world* (pp.312–332). New Jersey: Princeton University Press.

United Nations High Commissioner for Refugees (UNHCR). (2012). Kakuma camp in Kenya surpasses its 100,000 capacity. Retrieved from www.unhcr.org/501fdb419.html

UNHCR. (2013). Flowing across borders. Retrieved from www.unhcr.org/pages/49c3646c125.html

Ventegodt, S. (1999). A prospective study on quality of life and traumatic events in early life—a 30-year follow-up. *Child: Care, Health, and Development, 25*, 213–221. doi:10.1046/j.1365-2214.1999.00100.x

Wilson, K. (2006). Can foster carers help children resolve their emotional and behavioural difficulties? *Clinical Child Psychology and Psychiatry, 11*, 495–511. doi:10.1177/1359104506067873

World Bank. (2010). 43 million people worldwide forcibly displaced in 2009. Retrieved from http://data.worldbank.org/news/43mil-people-worldwide-displaced-in-2009

# 16 Supporting the Inclusion of Children with Chronic Illness and Health Issues in the Early Years

*Leanne Hallowell*

## CHAPTER OVERVIEW

More children with chronic health conditions are attending early years settings than ever before. Using a multi-disciplinary approach, which includes communication and collaboration between all, inclusion of children with chronic health conditions can be successful and effective.

Learning goals for this chapter include:

- Developing understandings of the individual impacts of chronic health conditions on children and their families, including siblings;
- Critically examining the purpose and value of communication and planning within multi-disciplinary teams to support inclusion in early years services;
- Considering ways in which inclusion of children with chronic health conditions can be supported by understanding their needs and adapting the engagement and environment to support them.

## KEY TERMS AND CONCEPTS

adaptations

chronic health condition

medical play

# Introduction

More children than ever before live with chronic health conditions. In part, this is due to increases in the incidence of conditions such as asthma and type-1 diabetes, and prolonged life expectancies for people with conditions such as cystic fibrosis (Hicks & Davitt, 2009). Many more children are surviving conditions such as leukaemia. Some chronic health conditions are life long. Some have uncertain outcomes. Some previously requiring repeated and long hospitalisations are now often managed with fewer and often shorter hospital stays, although they may require extended and ongoing treatment regimes. Some children have benefited from advances in medical technology and many children with complex ongoing health needs such as tube feeding and ventilation are now, with appropriate support, able to have their health care managed at home and are able to attend early years settings (Shaw & McCabe, 2008).

Some children with chronic health conditions will 'grow out of them', others will require varying degrees of ongoing support, medical and psychosocial, to be able to participate in everyday activities. With this support and with sensitivity to individual and specific needs, children with chronic health conditions can be genuinely included in early years settings (Hicks & Davitt, 2009).

# Defining chronic health conditions

**Chronic health condition:** A health condition that continues for a considerable time, has persistent consequences, requires ongoing hospitalisations, has a poor prognosis and impacts on quality of life.

There is no agreed definition of what constitutes a **chronic health condition**. Thompson and Gustafson (1996) define a condition as chronic if it:

- Lasts for a considerable time. Hicks and Davitt (2009) suggest at least three months, while O'Hallaran, Miller and Britt (2004) suggest longer than six months;
- Has consequences that persist for more than three months in a year;
- Requires hospitalisation for more than a month. Hicks and Davitt (2009) suggest that hospitalisation would be continuous.

O'Hallaran et al. (2004) also suggest that a chronic condition will

- Have a poor prognosis; and
- Impact on quality of life.

Some chronic health conditions are diagnosed at or before birth. For example, cystic fibrosis (CF) is usually diagnosed during post-natal screening. Other chronic health conditions may be acquired and diagnosed in infancy or childhood, such as juvenile diabetes, or be the result of injury or accident.

Not all chronic health conditions will require hospitalisation. Where required, children may be hospitalised at diagnosis to stabilise the condition and then to educate the child and the family about ongoing care. Some children may not require hospitalisation, but may have more regular check ups and outpatient appointments for allied health interventions.

Some chronic health conditions are clearly evident. Other conditions such as diabetes, asthma and food allergies are almost invisible until an episode occurs requiring an intervention. Until then they can be 'out of sight, out of mind', requiring children, parents, carers and educators to establish reminders of their existence to ensure that the child's health is supported.

This chapter will not review chronic health conditions themselves. They are numerous and individual in how they impact on a child and their family. Instead, it will look at what it means to a child and family to live with a chronic health condition, and address some of the concerns early years professionals may have about including a child with a chronic health condition.

When children with chronic health conditions are enrolled in an early years setting, it is suggested that educators focus, in the first instance, on the child and their family and then undertake to learn more about the condition. Learning about the condition and the impact it may have starts with discussions with the family, including the child, about how their lives are impacted and what adaptations have been made or are needed in the setting. Olson, Seidler, Goodman, Gaelic and Nordgen (2004) suggest that open discussions should also occur between medical and educational settings. In some instances it may be possible for educators to attend seminars at major paediatric centres, for in-service professional development (Olson et al., 2004). Professional development may include developing understandings of the impact the condition may have on the child and their family, and how adaptations to programs, curriculum and the environment may support transition and engagement in discussion of the condition (Royal Children's Hospital, 2013). With the permission of the child and family, early years professionals may choose to contact or to talk with health care providers or support groups working with the family to learn more. In some instances there is less professional support available and reports from families are critical to successful engagement.

## Seeing obstacles as hurdles

Hospital admissions and frequent outpatient appointments may result in disruptions to attendance at educational settings (Taras & Potts-Datema, 2005) and disturbances to developing peer relationships and social competence (Shute, McCarthy & Roberts, 2007; Shiu, 2004a). Ongoing absenteeism, some prescribed medications and changed familial contexts can produce behavioural and cognitive changes in children, which may impact adversely on (Ray, 2002), and be seen as an obstacle to, effective inclusion.

Seeing the child through a sympathetic lens, parents, educators and adults may overlook or misunderstand some of these behaviours, giving latitude to the behaviour. Practices usually used to support children to behave in socially accepted ways may not be implemented (Woods, Catroppa, Barnett & Anderson, 2011). Changing the behavioural boundaries for some children may set up situations where children may be seen as favoured (Meijer, Sinnema, Bihstra, Mellenbergh & Walters, 2000).

By the time a child born with a chronic health condition is ready to attend an early years setting, the family has already developed skills of advocacy that they use to ensure that their child's inclusion is well supported. These skills, often learnt to navigate the medical system, result in many families no longer seeing obstacles, but hurdles. Often the family will be the ones who will see a potential issue and will be able to suggest a way forward. Accustomed to maintaining continuity and coordination for the medical care of their child, they can then translate their skills and knowledge into their child's ongoing education. Where knowledge is lacking or answers to the specific needs of a child are missing, parents are often able to provide that information to educators (Miller, Condin, McKellin, Shaw, Klassen & Sheps, 2009).

Inclusion of children with chronic health conditions involves discussing a child's needs and how these may be met. This can occur through communication between the family, educators and the health care team, which results in

- Understanding of the condition and its impact on the child and their family;
- Training for education staff in providing for some health care needs;
- Flexible ways to manage the child's possible frequent and sometimes extended absences (St Leger, 2012);
- Ways to manage and support the needs of siblings.

## Siblings are a part of the family

Research suggests that siblings of children with chronic health conditions may also be vulnerable to difficulties with adaptation. For example, they may experience depression and social isolation, and often also exhibit signs of stress (Hamama, Ronen & Rahaw, 2008), anger, guilt and jealousy (Murray, 2001). Their lives are directly, although not intentionally, affected by changes in family finances and dynamics (Van Riper, 2003). Siblings may fear, often without foundation, they will contract the condition, or that they caused it. Some siblings understand that there will be times when parents need to spend considerable time in hospital or at other appointments, and that their family still loves and cares for them. Other siblings struggle with this and need additional support from other important people in their lives (Murray, 2000).

Siblings require that their particular needs also be met. At some level, they need to have their questions about the condition and treatment answered by someone whom they can trust (Gursky, 2007). The extended time required to attend to the needs of a child with the chronic health condition can limit the capacity of parents and their availability to attend to the needs of well siblings. Without informational support, further fears and anxieties can be realised. Informational support can be provided by a health care professional, but equally it could be a trusted educator. Often siblings don't ask for this support from their parents and parents are reported as feeling uncomfortable in providing it. Newton, Wolgemuth, Gallivan and Wrightson (2010), believe professionals with an understanding of child development may be best placed to provide this knowledge and support. This may be a hospital play specialist or an early years professional who works with the sibling and their family (Gursky, 2007). As much as possible, regular routines need to be maintained. That may include attendance at an early years setting, after school activities and visiting friends and family, and the routines within these structures. It may mean that play, in a variety of forms, be maintained and supported.

## The importance of play

As explored in Chapter 17, play is central to a young child's learning and development. It supports engagement with others. Through play and play based programming children are supported to engage with others, and to explore their environment even when they are in hospital (Armstrong & Aitken, 2000), and when transitioning back home and to the early years setting.

Children thrive on the security and safety offered by predictable routines, including play and playful interactions. Hospital admissions and frequent medical appointments impact these routines. Maintaining opportunities to play can reduce potential negative impacts, such as loneliness, isolation, sadness, decreased self-esteem and anxiety, when interruptions occur (Shiu, 2004b).

### PLAY IN HOSPITAL

When children are hospitalised or unwell, it is important that play is not left behind. Play enhances coping and provides emotional support; it also creates stability and has educational and therapeutic benefits for the child and their family (Parson, 2009). When life experiences such as hospitalisation occur, it is important that participation is maximised and contact with others maintained.

In health care settings, the provision of child-focused play spaces, with appropriate materials and activities and where encouragement can be given to engage in play, is important for child wellbeing and development. Play, in the form of medical play, can also be used as an assessment tool for health professionals to access the child's level of understanding of their medical conditions and treatment options. Play opportunities within health care settings support play between child patients who may have different types of physical and cognitive abilities and are used by children as a way to cope (Salmela, Slalanera, Ruotsalainen, & Aronen, 2010). From the child's perspective, play in hospital may be considered more important than the medical treatment (Parson, 2009).

While recognising the importance of play in hospital, maintaining contact with the early years setting is equally important. Communications between the play staff in the hospital and professionals in the early years setting allows for a flow of information, including details about the activities being undertaken in both. Sharing images of routines, activities and friends helps maintain connections, while distracting the child from the hospital environment and the condition itself.

Contact with an early years setting can provide emotional support, which helps adjustment and supports transitions between education and medical services. Children who are often absent may have difficulties in maintaining friendships with peers or attachments to adults in the early years setting because of their frequent absences (Dockett, 2004; Shiu, 2004a). Each day absent from their early years setting is another day separated from the children they are developing friendships with, which may exacerbate feelings of isolation. Contact while in hospital helps to support re-engagement when transitioning back into the setting.

**FIGURE 16.1** PLAYING WITH CENTRE MATERIALS IN HOSPITAL

*Photo: Sarah Mann*

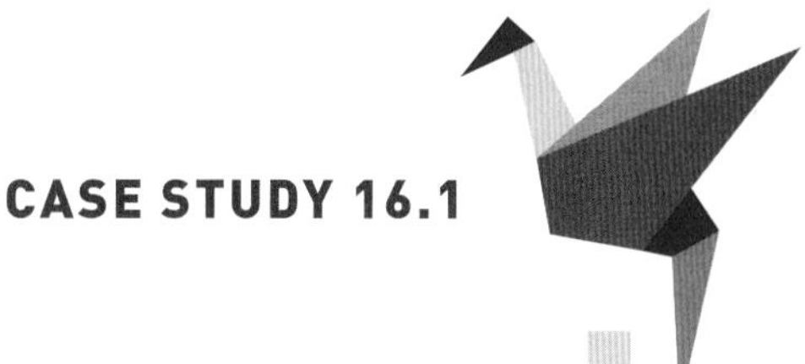

CASE STUDY 16.1

## Kayla really, really wants to paste

Kayla was four years old when her mother, Linda, took her to the emergency department of the local hospital one weekend. Linda was concerned when Kayla became lethargic, was constantly thirsty and seemed to always need to go to the bathroom. Kayla was diagnosed with juvenile diabetes.

Kayla and Linda had to stay in hospital for a number of days while they undertook a series of sessions with diabetic educators and dieticians to learn about diabetes and its management. This included learning about the types and amounts of food required, how to check Kayla's blood sugar levels and how, when required, to inject insulin.

Kayla had started in an early learning centre a few months prior. She thrived in the environment. While in hospital she constantly asked her mother, 'When am I going back to kinder?' She said that she missed playing with her friends and that she really, really wanted to do pasting.

**CRITICAL REFLECTION QUESTION**

Consider how an early years professional may be able to help a child who is hospitalised to maintain a connection to the service and their peers and to support maintenance and development of skills. (Note that it is usually inappropriate for staff to visit children while in hospital; however technology now makes contact much easier and would be worth considering.)

# Transitioning and returning

Hospital admissions may be planned, others may occur due to a sudden exacerbation of the condition and be unplanned. Successful transition back to the early years setting begins when the hospital admission is first known about. Key to ensuring a smooth transition is having appropriate supports in place (Schischka, Rawlinson & Hamilton, 2012). The child, family, the early years setting staff and peers should all be ready for the child's return.

Ways to achieve this include:

- Early and ongoing communication with the child, parents, health care providers (including allied health) and early years professionals, which will help facilitate smooth transition on return (Schischka et al., 2012);
- Sharing of information, allowing for all voices to be heard and to be acted on;
- Preparing peers for the return of a child who has been to hospital or had an extended absence due to poor health;

- Supporting children to re-engage based on possible changes to functioning;
- Engagement with a specific peer or buddy;
- The inclusion of siblings in transition planning. This may also support their inclusion needs;
- Making adaptations to play activities, environment or equipment to facilitate the child's return.

**FIGURE 16.2** THE MAGIC BANDAID

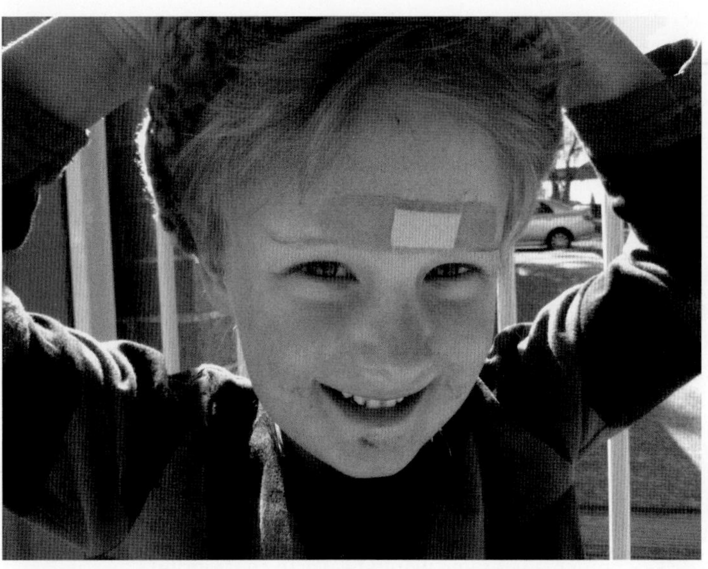

It's a special bandaid. It's a science bandaid. It tells you all about science. Volcano science. Tornadoes too. The world. Animals—the magic is inside the bandaid, so the bandaid tells me: 'Sorry for telling you,' the bandaid tells me. 'Didn't you know?'

Photo: Dinah Cocksedge

Adaptations: Changes to activities or the environment to meet the presenting needs of the child. This may require reviewing and reassessing goals and objectives in consultation with the child, the family and health professionals.

The purpose of an adaptation is to allow children to use their current skills while promoting the acquisition of new skills. **Adaptations** can make the difference between a child merely being present, and a child being included and actively involved in their early years setting (Office of Head Start, 2009).

Developing adaptations and accommodations is a continuous process. It involves the individual child, their family, and education and health care teams. In developing these adaptations and accommodations the child's current abilities need to be assessed first, followed by an assessment of the early years environment where the child will be spending time. Goals and objectives are identified and expectations for the child's participation are jointly established. Adaptations and accommodations are developed to address those needs. Effectiveness should be assessed on an ongoing basis and revised, as needed.

Supporting transition needs to be undertaken with a degree of sensitivity and consideration to individual needs and to confidentiality. Stresses of hospitalisation, treatments or effects of the condition can have an effect on children. Peers are likely to note possible changes to appearance, ability, behaviour and to any management requirements of the returning child. Some children who are returning may be reluctant to approach or engage with their peers, and their peers may experience the same reluctance. For peers the reasons for this are varied and range from knowing how to approach a child with a difference, to concern they may contract the condition. For the child returning it may be that they feel different and are unsure how they will fit again, thus the sense of isolation they felt while absent continues. Some children will show limited effects of hospitalisation, while others may exhibit behaviours that suggest changes to their social functioning (Meijer et al., 2000).

Returning children may not want a fuss made of them or their condition. They simply want to be an active member of the group again. Some, however, are excited and want to tell all about the new knowledge they have. Others may be embarrassed and wish to withhold that knowledge. Discussion needs to take place with the child and the family about what information they are happy to share and what information the early years professional believes the group of children needs to have (Hicks & Davitt, 2009). Planning how this will occur needs to be undertaken in a timely fashion. Peers will need to be helped to understand the information provided to them.

Physical or emotional changes in some children with chronic conditions may make play difficult. For some, the ability to participate in activities may fluctuate depending on the current phase of their treatment. Some treatments cause tiredness, chronic nausea, weakness, decreased mobility, pain, emotional changes and reduced attention span. Other treatments can have a negative impact on learning and still others on communication and information processing skills. It is important that early years professionals discuss with the child, parents and health care providers the impact that treatments may have or be having on the child and their ability to engage in activities (Shiu, 2004a). This will allow for provision of play activities, which will support engagement at a level of comfort and will meet the child's current needs. Some play activities may support development and therapeutic needs in specific areas. An example of this is language games, which can support speech therapy interventions. Children who have withdrawn from social contact and have difficulty engaging with peers, or who have withdrawn from play, may need additional support to engage. Although friendships cannot be contrived, structures and processes should be put in place that allow for an environment where supportive friendships may develop (St Leger, 2012). Quality of life, and a return to routine and stability, is supported by a smooth transition.

CASE STUDY 16.2

## Adaptations during transition

Valerie was returning to her early years setting after breaking her arm. Her arm was now in a plaster cast for six weeks. She would return to the doctors to have her plaster checked in a day or so and would need to have an x-ray in a week to ensure that the bone was setting. Until the plaster was removed it needed to remain dry and nothing was to get between the plaster and her arm—sand, rice and other small objects in between the plaster and skin can rub against and irritate skin.

CRITICAL REFLECTION QUESTION

Considering that tactile and sensory play is an important part of many play activities in the early years, and that the needs of all children in a centre need to be taken into account, in what ways could you support Valerie's engagement in tactile experiences while maintaining the integrity of the plaster cast?

As children transition back into an early years setting, it is likely that they will engage in play and talk about what has happened. This should be facilitated by providing space to allow the play and discussion to occur. Children will talk about the experience as they are ready. The discussion should not be forced or coerced from the child. Educators also need to be able to recognise signs the child has had enough discussion and to give them permission to come back to the discussion if/when they wish. The child's feelings about the hospital admission or condition need validation (Salmela, Aronen & Salentra, 2011).

CASE STUDY 16.3

## 'Are you fixed yet?'

David was either hospitalised or attended an outpatient appointment three times in one month, thus he missed some of his kindergarten sessions. His kindergarten teachers had kept him engaged in the centre by sending activity packs and emailing photos to him.

On the day of return after the third absence, David became upset and yelled at his friend Stevie, 'I don't know! Leave me alone!'.

In discussion with David and Stevie, Eveline, the kindergarten teacher, discovered that Stevie had been asking David when the doctors were going to 'fix' him.

Eveline realised that she needed to support the children in the room to understand more about David's condition and how it is managed, while still having them understand that many illnesses can still be cured. It eventually led her and the children through a journey of understandings of health and wellbeing.

**CRITICAL REFLECTION QUESTION**

It is common for young children to believe that doctors 'fix you up'. With chronic health conditions symptoms are managed rather then 'fixed' or cured. When children are supported to understand the nature of some chronic health conditions, and how they may help to support a child with a chronic health condition, transition becomes easier. Consider ways you may talk with children in an early years setting about chronic health conditions and how conditions may be managed.

Supporting self-esteem development is important during transition. Allow children to engage in activities, adapted when required, where they can succeed and do well. Such activities could include managing their condition, for example a child with cystic fibrosis counting out their enzymes, or a child with diabetes checking their own blood sugar levels. Promoting and celebrating milestones, no matter how small, is important. These can be significant for the child.

The child's self-esteem may have been damaged by actual physical changes to their body due to the chronic condition or medical treatment, or the child may perceive that their body has changed. Body changes may be to function, or to the way a body looks—scars and bruising, or plaster and bandages are examples. Other children in the setting may need to informed about why these changes have occurred, to limit potential teasing or bullying, over-questioning of the child and an unwanted focus on the condition (Shaw & McCabe, 2008).

The re-establishment of routines, rituals and schedules (Gaynard, 2006), including a return to early years settings, is important for the child's wellbeing, allowing for integration of medical treatments into everyday tasks, rather than the medical treatments being a focus. Routines, including medical routines, provide predictability for the child (Gaynard, 2006).

**CASE STUDY 16.4**

## David is ready for preschool. Is preschool ready for David?

David was diagnosed with cystic fibrosis (CF) soon after birth. When he was diagnosed, David's family, who were initially shocked, spent some time with him in hospital learning about CF and how to support him. In the intervening years, David had a couple of hospital admissions to manage lung infections.

David's mother Annie stayed in hospital with David whenever he was admitted. Living far from the hospital made it difficult for David's father, Evan, and his older sister Sasha to visit

Leanne Hallowell

often, but they were able to keep contact using web based technologies. Annie had decided to not return to work after David's diagnosis. Although this placed additional financial stress on the family, David's parents wanted to focus on his health and care at this point.

With support from medical and allied health staff, David had maintained reasonably good health and a positive developmental trajectory. When he turned four, David's family decided that he should attend his local preschool. His name had been put on the waiting list when he was two, anticipating that he would be able to attend. David had attended playgroup and many of the children in his playgroup were going to the local preschool as well.

David's kindergarten teacher, Thea, had recently graduated from university. She knew nothing about CF, and wondered how she would manage a child with a chronic health condition in the centre. She decided to meet with David and his family before the preschool year started, as she did with all children and families new to the setting. Rather than worrying about the condition, at this point she wanted to focus on David.

**CRITICAL REFLECTION QUESTIONS**

Consider an early years setting you work in, or have worked in:

1. Were there any children with a chronic health condition and how much did you know about the child and condition?
2. Were there things about the condition that you would have liked to know and that might have helped you in planning?
3. Where did you go to find out more about the condition and how to support the child and their family? Were there other places you could have gone for support?

Children react to hospitalisations in a variety of ways. Some of those reactions may include crying, withdrawal, regression, separation anxiety, sleep or behavioural disturbances, anger and aggression (Salmela et al., 2010) These behaviours may also be seen in children who are aware they are about to go into hospital, and by children who have recently been discharged from hospital. These reactions need to be managed with sensitivity. Some children are able to articulate their feelings, and some are not. Acknowledging how a child may be feeling and letting them know that their feelings are acceptable is important.

**Medical play:** Play that uses real or pretend medical equipment and supplies to help children understand and express their feelings and fears about hospitals and medical procedures. It also allows them to practise new skills and understandings.

When children have negative experiences with hospitalisation, they may avoid medical health care encounters in adulthood (Justus, Wyles, Wilson, Rode, Walther & Lim-Sulit, 2006). Fear and distress and other impacts of negative experiences may be reduced through sensitive play experiences in childhood (Salmela et al., 2010). For those children who have not had a hospital encounter, **medical play**—a form of non-directed play that uses actual medical equipment—can help familiarise children with the medical equipment they may see in a doctors surgery or hospital and help them to cope with potential hospital admissions (Salmela et al., 2010). For those children who have had a hospital encounter, medical play allows them opportunities to play through and tell some of their story. Providing actual medical equipment such as stethoscopes, blood pressure cuffs, plastic syringes, theatre hats and masks, medicine cups and surgical gowns supports the child in this retelling (Justus et al., 2006; Parson, 2009).

In medical play, just as in all types of play, children create an environment where they are in control, where open self-expression is facilitated and emotional growth leading to positive mental health and wellbeing is supported. Skilled educators can use play to enable clearer, more appropriate, child-centred communication and understandings of the hospital environment, medical staff and medical equipment (Hallowell, 2008). When children engage in medical play they become more open to learning that may empower them throughout their hospital experiences.

**FIGURE 16.3** THE DOCTOR

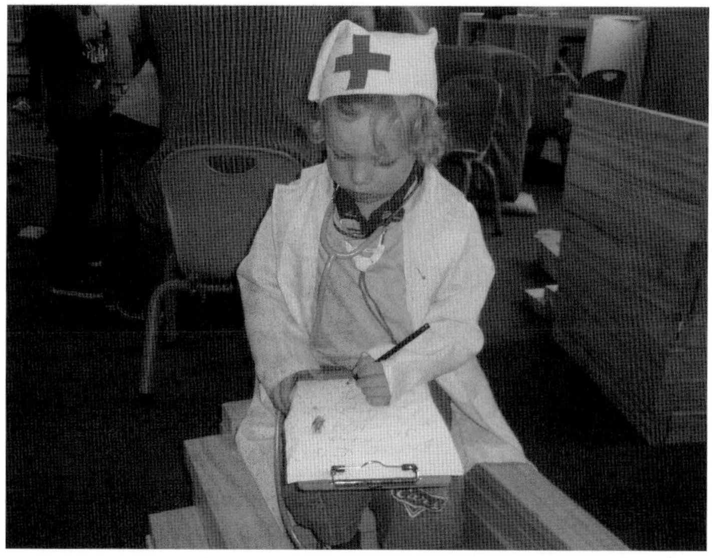

*Photo: Dinah Cocksedge*

Parents of children with chronic health conditions, and others who have close contact with these children, often are reluctant to set boundaries. Low expectations and lack of boundaries create anxiety in children. Children benefit from clear, consistent expectations (Woods et al., 2011), and from knowing the consequences of their actions (Baxter & Fawcett, 2006).

CASE STUDY 16.5

## My medicine makes me busy

Asthma is a condition often treated with steroids. Robyn was prescribed steroids when she was diagnosed with asthma at three years of age. As a result, Robyn became quite active and at times aggressive. These side effects distracted some of the other children in her three-year-old preschool group. Some stopped wanting to play with her, while other children started to mimic her behaviour. Robyn's mother was becoming frustrated with her aggressive behaviour in particular and upset when she noted her child often playing alone.

*(Source: author's clinical experience)*

CRITICAL REFLECTION QUESTIONS

1. Consider how you would support Robyn and her family in this situation. How should expectations of behaviour be managed for all the children in this group?
2. Robyn's mother needs support to understand and develop ways to manage her daughter's behaviour. How would you respond to her needs?

# Conclusion

When children have a chronic health condition, or are hospitalised, connections and re-entry to their early years settings supports stability and familiarity. It allows for what all children are entitled to—opportunities to develop and engage to the fullest of their potential, opportunities to be industrious and develop a sense of self and self-esteem. In this supportive context, skills are redeveloped and mastered, and further developed. Children re-engage with peers and discover new ways to interact with other children and adults, and learn about themselves. Rather than being seen as an obstacle, children's transitions back into early years settings should be seen as opportunities to develop new knowledge and ways of being. Regardless of health care status, all children have a right to inclusive early years experiences that meet their needs.

## FOR FURTHER REFLECTION

1. Often our personal values and beliefs impact on how we see inclusion. Reflective practice is a way to review and to reconsider our values and beliefs. When you reflect on your practice related to inclusion, consider reflecting on the context your pedagogical decisions were made in and how your values and beliefs may have impacted these.
2. The changing demographic of inclusion means that there are many more people and organisations available to support our needs as early years professionals but also the needs of the children and families we work with. Some of these may be specific for the clients we work with. Being aware of what is available is important in supporting our practice and in supporting children and families. Updated resource files, which may include details of support networks and organisations, links to information about specific conditions, adaptations, equipment and ideas, are invaluable.

## WEBSITES

www.rch.org.au/education/educators/

Practical information to support children and young people affected by health conditions from the Royal Children's Hospital.

http://youtu.be/qRfUrjNnxoc

A video from Sydney Children's Hospital explaining hospital play therapy.

## REFERENCES


Armstrong, T.S.H. & Aitken, H.L. (2000). The developing role of play preparation in paediatric nursing. *Paediatric Anaesthesia, 10*(1), 1–4. doi:10.1046/j.1460-9592.2000.00406.x

Baxter, A. & Fawcett, H. (2006). *More than a mom. Living a full and balanced life when your child has special needs.* Bethesda, MD: Woodbine House.

Dockett, S. (2004). 'Everyone was really happy to see me!' The importance of friendships in the return to school of children with chronic illness. *Australasian Journal of Early Childhood, 29*(1), 27–32. Retrieved from www.earlychildhoodaustralia.org.au/australian_journal_of_early_childhood.html

Gaynard, L. (2006). Play as ritual in health care settings. In D.P. Fromberg & D. Bergen (Eds), *Play from birth to twelve: Contexts, perspectives, and meanings* (pp.343–352). New York, New York: Taylor & Francis Group.

Gursky, B. (2007). The effect of educational interventions with siblings of hospitalized children. *Journal of Developmental and Behavioral Pediatrics, 28*(5), 392–398. doi:10.1097/DBP.0b013e318113203e

Hallowell, L.M. (2008). *Practice MRI—analysis of educational play therapy intervention in the practice MRI unit at the Royal Children's Hospital, Melbourne.* Unpublished masters thesis. University of Melbourne: Melbourne, Australia.

Hamama, L., Ronen, T. & Rahav, G. (2008). Self-control, self-efficacy, role overload and stress responses among siblings of children with cancer. *Health and Social Work, 33*(2), 121–131. doi:10.1093/hsw/33.2.121

Hicks, M. & Davitt, K. (2009). Chronic illness and rehabilitation. In R. H. Thompson (Ed.), *The handbook of child life: A guide for pediatric psychosocial care* (pp.257–286). Springfield, Illinois: Charles C. Thomas Publishers.

Justus, R., Wyles, D., Wilson, D., Rode, D., Walther, V. & Lim-Sulit, N. (2006). Preparing children and families for surgery: Mount Sinai's multidisciplinary perspective. *Pediatric Nursing, 32*(1), 35–42. Retrieved from http://www.pediatricnursing.net/

Meijer, S.A., Sinnema, G., Bijstra, J.O., Mellenbergh, G.J. & Wolters, W.H.G. (2000). Social functioning in children with a chronic illness. *Journal of Child Psychology and Psychiatry and Allied Disciplines, 41*(3), 309–317. doi:10.1111/1469-7610.00615

Miller, A.R., Condin, C.J., McKellin, W.H., Shaw, N., Klassen, A.F. & Sheps, S. (2009, December 21). *Continuity of care for children with complex medical conditions: Parents' perspectives.* BMC Health Services. doi:10.1186/1472-6963-9-242

Murray, J.S. (2000). Attachment theory and adjustment difficulties in siblings of children with cancer.

*Issues in Mental Health Nursing 21*(2), 149–169. doi:10.1080/016128400248167

Murray, J.S. (2001). Self-concept of siblings of children with cancer. Issues in Comprehensive Pediatric Nursing, 24(2), 85–94. doi:10.1080/01460860116709

Newton, A.S., Wolgemuth, A., Gallivan, J. & Wrightson, D. (2010). Providing support to siblings of hospitalised children. *Journal of Paediatrics and Child Health, 46*(3), 72–75. doi:10.1111/j.1440-1754.2009.01640.x

Office of Head Start. (2009, update February 1, 2011). *Accommodating all children in the early childhood classroom.* Retrieved from http://eclkc.ohs.acf.hhs.gov/hslc/tta-system/teaching/Disabilities/program%20 planning/accessibility/accommodatingall.htm

O'Hallaran, J., Miller, G.C. & Britt, H. (2004). Defining chronic conditions for primary care with ICPC-2. *Family Practice, 21*(4), 381–386. doi:10.1093/fampra/cmh407

Olson, A.L., Seidler, A.B., Goodman, D., Gaelic, S. & Nordgren, R. (2004). School professionals' perceptions about the impact of chronic illness in the classroom. *Archives of Pediatric and Adolescent Medicine, 158*(1), 53–58. doi:10.1001/archpedi.158.1.53

Parson, J. (2009). Play in the hospital environment. In K. Stagnetti & R. Cooper (Eds.), *Play as therapy: Assessment and therapeutic interventions* (pp.132–144). London: Jessica King Publishers.

Ray, L.D. (2002). Parenting and childhood chronicity: Making visible the invisible work. *Journal of Pediatric Nursing 17*(6), 424–438. doi:10.1053/jpdn.2002.127172

Royal Children's Hospital. (2013). *Education professionals*. Retrieved 1/03/2014, from www.rch.org.au/education/educators/

Salmela, M., Salantera, S. & Aronen, E.T. (2010). Coping with hospital-related fears: Experiences of pre-school-aged children. *Journal of Advanced Nursing, 66*(6), 1222–1231. doi:10.1111/j.1365-2648.2010.05287.x

Salmela, M., Aronen, E.T. & Salantera, S. (2011). The experience of hospital-related fears of 4- to 6-year-old children. *Child: Care, Health and Development, 37*(5), 719–726. doi:10.1111/j.1365-2214.2011.01229.x

Salmela, M., Salantera, S., Ruotsalainen, T. & Aronen, E.T. (2010). Coping strategies for hospital-related fears in pre-school-aged children. *Journal of Paediatrics and Child Health, 46*(3), 108–114. doi:10.1111/j.1440-1754.2009.01640.x

Schischka, J., Rawlinson, C. & Hamilton, R. (2012). Factors affecting the transition to school for young children with disabilities. *Australasian Journal of Early Childhood, 37*(4), 15–23. Retrieved from www.earlychildhoodaustralia.org .au/australian_journal_of_early_childhood.html

Shaw, S.R. & McCabe, P.C. (2008). Hospital-to-school transition for children with chronic illness: Meeting the new challenges of an evolving health care system. *Psychology in the Schools, 45*(1), 74–87. doi:10.1002/pits.20280

Shiu, S. (2004a). Maintaining the thread: Including young children with chronic illness in the primary classroom. *Australian Journal of Early Childhood, 29*(1), 33–38. Retrieved from www.earlychildhoodaustralia.org.au/australian_journal_of_early_childhood.html

Shiu, S. (2004b). Positive interventions for children with chronic illness: Parents' and teachers concerns and recommendations. *Australian Journal of Education, 48*(3), 239–252. doi:10.1177/000494410404800303

Shute, R., McCarthy, K.R. & Roberts, R. (2007). Predictors of social competence in young adolescents with craniofacial anomalies. *International Journal of Clinical and Health Psychology, 7*(3), 595–613. Retrieved from www.aepc.es/ijchp/articulos_pdf/ijchp-240.pdf

St Leger, P. (2012). Practice of supporting young people with chronic health conditions in hospitals and schools. *International Journal of Inclusive Education*, (iFirst), 1–17, doi:10.1080/13603116.2012.679320

Taras, H. & Potts-Datema, W. (2005). Chronic health conditions and student performance at school. *Journal of School Health, 75*(7), 255–266. doi:10.1111/j.1746-1561.2005.00034.x

Thompson, R.J. & Gustafson, K.E. (1996). *Adaptation to chronic childhood illness*. Washington DC: American Psychological Association.

Van Riper, M. (2003). The sibling experience of living with childhood chronic illness and disability. *Annual Review of Nursing Research, 21*, 279–302. Retrieved from www.highbeam.com/Annual+Review+of+Nursing +Research/%20publications.aspx

Woods, D.T., Catroppa, C., Barnett, P. & Anderson, V.A. (2011). Parental disciplinary practices following acquired brain injury in children. *Developmental Neurorehabilitation, 14*(5), 274–282. doi:10.3109/17518423.2011.586371

SECTION 5

# Inclusive Early Years Education

# 17 Play and Inclusion

*Melanie Nind, Rosie Flewitt and Fani Theodorou*

CHAPTER OVERVIEW

This chapter will focus on the importance of play for children's inclusion and how play opportunities can be facilitated.

Learning goals for this chapter include:

- Understanding play as the cornerstone of early childhood development and an entitlement of every child;
- Considering how practitioners can enable children's involvement in play, whatever their challenges;
- Identifying the various roles of practitioners as supporters of play, mediators of play and play partners;
- Exploring the role of play in helping practitioners to know, relate to and assess all children, including those with differences in social, physical and cognitive development.

KEY TERMS AND CONCEPTS

intervention programs

modes of communication

non-directive

play-based assessment

play-based learning

sociocultural context

## Introduction

We begin this chapter on play and inclusion by outlining the premises that underpin our perspective and that have informed our research. Some of these points may seem obvious, but when a child is in an early years setting *and* experiences disability, for example, this child can be presumed to be vulnerable, needy and passive (Davis & Watson, 2002). There is a risk that we see the child as being there for us to manage and do interventions on. This is not our starting point. First, we see all young children as active meaning-makers, who use their personal and social resources to make sense of the world as they experience it. We can help children's sense-making by enriching their personal and social resources through the play opportunities we provide. Children who experience disability also experience barriers to doing and being (see Thomas, 2004 and Chapter 2). In our focus on their agency within the constraints that are acting on them, we address these barriers. As we will illustrate, children's abilities vary greatly according to the social and play opportunities they encounter, and these abilities can be extended through creative and inclusive environments, which we can help to provide.

Second, we recognise the potential to enhance children's competence by identifying and building on their strengths, by joining forces with them, following their lead and, in the process, enabling them to realise their own agency. We can think of this in terms of Goodley's (2001) concept of distributed competence—our abilities lie not just in ourselves but also among those who enable us. We view children's play as empowering, in that it supports children's agency to make choices, which in turn can improve their confidence, self-esteem and self-realisation.

**modes of communication:** Channels of communication such as writing, drawing, using technology, speech, gesture, gaze and posture.

Lastly, we work on the premise that all **modes of communication** and interaction are valuable and important in children's meaning-making and in the complex social and interpersonal processes of children and adults understanding each other (see Chapter 23).

**play-based learning:** A playful context for learning in which children enjoy themselves, and are self-motivated and actively engaged.

In addition to having some working assumptions about children, we have some working assumptions about play and inclusion, and we make these explicit too. Young children are experts at play. It is through playful explorations and endeavours that children learn, and **play-based learning** is at the heart of early education (Booth, Ainscow & Kingston, 2006). Children make sense of what they encounter through playful engagements, enabling them to feel good about it, know it, and begin to feel that they belong (Seach, 2007). To include children in play is to include them in the social worlds of their peers and their education environments. It also enables them to view themselves as active learners and play partners.

**FIGURE 17.1** AUSLAN FOR *PLAY*

*Photo: Dinah Cocksedge*

We want this chapter to be useful to anyone seeking to enable young children to participate in and benefit from play and inclusion. Therefore, we seek to bring to life episodes of play and the role of practitioners in that play. As we do this we draw your attention to the subtle processes at work. We draw our examples largely from our own ethnographic work—that is, when we have spent time immersed in getting to know children's everyday lives and cultures. This includes a case study of two children with autism within inclusive early years settings in the south of England with rather different ethos and practices (Theodorou, 2011; Theodorou & Nind, 2010). We also draw on an ethnographic study of the social experiences of four-year-olds with intellectual impairment negotiating different settings (Flewitt, Nind & Payler, 2009; Nind, Flewitt & Payler, 2010). Additionally, we discuss an action research study involving collaborative efforts to enhance the learning environment of a large early years unit in an area of deprivation (Nind, 2003).

# Learning from naturalistic research

Many of the assumptions that underpin current approaches to play and disability derive from an established tendency in psychological research to use experimental methods of investigation. There is consequently a long history of research into the play of children with disability where their play is intervened with, and compared to that of matched, non-disabled peers. For example, such research has investigated play 'skills' and used what are presented as 'objective' tests of play, and/or structured assessments with quantitative measures (Anderson, Moore, Godfrey & Fletcher-Flinn, 2004; Dominguez, Ziviani & Rodger, 2006; Skaines, Rodger, & Bundy, 2006). Research with children with autism, for instance, has tended to focus on those areas of play that are perceived to be lacking, with a particular focus on joint attention (mutual focus on an object, person or activity) and comprehending pretence (understanding something that is pretending or imaginary). By comparing the behaviour of children who experience disability to the behaviour of their non-disabled peers, these research methods have inevitably been oriented towards identifying children's deficits rather than their strengths. It has been part of 'a dominant discourse of the disabled child as a non-playing object that requires professional therapeutic intervention' (Goodley & Runswick-Cole, 2010, p.499). Therefore, many of the resultant **intervention programs** have been built on the premise that something is 'wrong' with children who experience disabilities, and on the assumption that professionals can do things to make them 'function' better or normally. Such interventions are based on a fundamental understanding that difficulties reside within individuals. (See Chapter 2)

**intervention programs:** Programs that are usually designed to meet specific needs—this may be for children perceived to have difficulties, or they can be concerned with a particular curriculum or behaviour goal.

However, a small but growing body of research conducted over more recent years has begun to look beyond the individual and to consider how a child's context, including their peers, might impact upon that child's abilities. Wolfberg and Schuler's (1993) longitudinal ethnographic case study addressing the impact of a peer play intervention in the play of children with autism is an early and rare example in the literature in which natural play in natural settings is explored as valid. More recently, Theodorou (2011) has shown that adult intervention programs may actually reduce or impoverish children's play with each other. Furthermore, the act of intervening in or removing individual children from naturally occurring peer play can be disruptive, and adult interventions may risk reinforcing perceptions of children as delayed, rather than as making progress (Nind, Flewitt & Payler, 2011). There is a long history of research with children with autism and those who experience disability in different ways that has been conducted mostly in clinical rather than naturalistic settings. Such research doesn't consider the flux, spontaneous and holistic nature of play as it evolves in natural contexts and playful environments among and between children. Therefore, we argue that for research to provide knowledge that is useful to practitioners in early years settings it needs to look at play in context and to consider the opportunities for play offered by the human and physical resources available to children in particular social contexts. As Avgitidou (1997) argues, we need to understand how children play in social and cultural contexts, and how different contexts inevitably define and construct play differently.

This brings us to the core of our theoretical perspective: play is an activity that unfolds in and is shaped by the **sociocultural context** in which it occurs. Our perspective is influenced by the work of Vygotsky (1981), who considered that learning is motivated in the first instance through social interaction. From this perspective, development occurs first on a 'social plane' where two or more individuals interact to make sense of a situation or try out an idea, and this experience may then be internalised on an 'individual plane' (Vygotsky, 1981), with both the social and individual planes essential to learning. Learning, therefore, is shaped not merely by the 'competence' of an individual but also by a complex web of social, historical and cultural beliefs that the individual encounters through everyday practices. There is a dynamic relationship between the individual and how social environments support learning. Vygotsky developed the notion of the 'zone of proximal development' (ZPD) (also sometimes referred to as the 'zone of potential development') to describe how a child's learning occurs most effectively through supportive interaction with a more capable peer or adult. From this sociocultural perspective, play can be seen as providing powerful opportunities for learning, and children experiencing disability can be seen as active and playful meaning-makers, who encounter different social and relational networks, and who can be enabled or disabled by these networks.

**sociocultural context:** The combination of social and cultural factors such as the resources, customs, beliefs and attitudes associated with the individual's social, ethnic, cultural or religious group.

Play is therefore much more than a simple inventory of play behaviour and play skills; it is an individual and social activity that is shaped by the sociocultural contexts within which it unfolds. The nature of play entails understanding, cooperation and mutuality. It is fluid and varied and integrally connected to the everyday settings that children negotiate. Many studies of play in inclusive settings have focused on comparative problems or positioned some children as 'other' to the norm (see e.g. Holmes & Willoughby, 2005). In contrast, in our research we have closely observed children experiencing disability or difference going about their lives at home and in their early years settings. We have been able to develop a 'thick description' (Geertz, 1973) of play episodes that illuminate the ways in which practitioners and family members operate as supporters of play, as mediators of play and/or as active play partners to facilitate children's inclusion in play.

## PRACTITIONERS AS SUPPORTERS OF PLAY

One of the ways in which we can support the play of all children is through the quality of the opportunities we create. 'Planning and resourcing' play is one important way of doing this (Seach, 2007, p.6) and in this respect the Index for Inclusion (Early Years) (Booth et al., 2006) with its criteria for

Orchestrating Play and Learning within the Evolving Inclusive Practices Dimension is helpful. Adults may be proactive in creating situations whereby children can become involved in group play, and consequently understand and include each other. For example, in a study of the inclusive practices of special and mainstream early years settings (Nind et al., 2010; 2011), we followed the play experiences of Mandy, a four-year-old girl with intellectual and physical impairments who spent two mornings each week at a suburban Sure Start Children's Centre, and two mornings at a rural and local preschool playgroup closer to her home. We were able to see the contrasting approaches to physical support and 'therapy' within the different settings and the different opportunities for playful interactions that they offered. The Children's Centre had previously been a setting for special provision and had become a specially resourced inclusive setting supported by the local authority, though it retained a high proportion of children experiencing disability, with special programs and equipment. Here, Mandy was supported to use a walking frame for focused, one-to-one 'interventions'. This was observed, for example, with a practitioner in front of her holding up a 'favourite' toy just out of reach to encourage her to move forwards, or the practitioner behind her using gentle physical and verbal support to encourage her to put one leg in front of the other. The Village Playgroup, in contrast, was a parent-run inclusive setting with a collaborative problem-solving approach to including any children experiencing disability or difference. Here, Mandy did not have a walking frame but practitioners supported her by holding her under her arms to take some of her body weight as she moved from one activity to another in the playroom. These episodes of walking therefore had a purpose for Mandy, and provided communicative opportunities that practitioners seized upon. For example, they chatted with her about the activity they were heading for ('Where are we off to now?'), about her peers ('Peter's over there, isn't he?'), and about the effort and progress she was making ('That's brilliant, well done'). In this supportive environment, Mandy was able to join in outdoor and indoor group physical games, either supported by an adult as she walked or pushed in a pushchair in faster pace activities. Case study 17.1 describes one such occasion, where Mandy enjoyed a music and movement activity with her peers.

**non-directive:** This is about not leading the child directly, not working to prescribed patterns or structures, but being responsive to the child and to emerging possibilities.

What is important about the practitioners' role in this example is that they adopt the least level of intervention they can, which enables children to maintain the natural flow of their playful interactions. Practitioners are at their best when they are **non-directive** and optimally facilitative, and their support is most effective when it follows the child's lead, enabling children to enjoy participating in an activity they show an interest in, and where other children can encourage their active inclusion by imitating the adults' inclusive

CASE STUDY 17.1

## Mandy joins in some physical fun

All the children are gathered on the carpet, with Mandy in her pushchair, and the lead practitioner starts a recorded activity, 'Come on, everybody, let's stamp our feet ...'. As the children stamp their feet, an adult stands in front of Mandy, gently bending her own legs in time with the music, and encouraging Mandy to bend her legs. As new instructions are given by the tape, one of two adults immediately helps Mandy to move the part of her body that other children are moving, always bending to maintain eye contact with lots of smiles as well as joining in the rhythmic actions. These practitioners also encourage Mandy's peers to take part more actively so Mandy is not 'singled out'—she is just another child being encouraged. When the tape changes to 'Can you stretch out very tall ...?' Mandy reaches one arm up high on her own, copying the other children's movements. As the children march around in time to the music, Mandy is pushed by an adult in her pushchair, with several children taking turns to push her around, exchanging smiles with Mandy in their shared excitement. When told to 'clap', two boys stand in front of Mandy, encouraging her to clap along with them, to which Mandy responds by exchanging their gaze, smiling and moving her arms in a clapping motion. When the children are asked to lie still on the carpet, an adult gently strokes Mandy's head as she relaxes in her chair.

behaviours. We know that 'teacherly' styles of interaction, in contrast, can lead to practitioners dominating the interactive space (Hughes & Westgate, 1997) and inhibiting children's opportunities to contribute and develop (Ogilvy, Boath, Cheyne, Jahoda & Schaffer, 1992). We can see this in Case study 17.2, from Honilands nursery (Nind, 2003, p.353). It involves a teacher and Mark, a child who talks at home but rarely in the early years setting, and some miniature play equipment.

Such directive styles can emerge when practitioners are managing large numbers of children or working with children whom they perceive to have 'problems'. Practitioners who understand their role in play can help counter this by fostering the pauses, turns and spaces for children to set their own agendas. Later in the chapter, we discuss how we achieved this together with the educators at Honilands.

## CASE STUDY 17.2

### Mark doesn't join in with teacher-directed talk

Teacher: What goes in there?

[Mark looks at teacher, makes no attempt to answer]

Teacher: Is there a little blue box?

Teacher: You look in there.

Teacher: I'll look in here.

Teacher: I can't see a blue box.

Teacher: Is it in there?

[Mark shrugs shoulders, starts looking through leaflet]

Teacher: We've got the castle one, haven't we?

Teacher: What do you put in a kitchen?

Teacher [points to picture]: It's there so it sits on there.

Teacher [puts blue box on dresser and holds up knife]: What's this?

Teacher: It's a ... [expectant pause]

Nearby child: Knife.

Teacher: Let Mark say it.

Early childhood professionals sometimes offer a commentary to children's activity, especially when children do not themselves give expression to their thoughts through words. In another study, ethnographic observation showed an adult-led activity in an inclusive nursery where the children, including Vicky who was diagnosed with autism, were required to talk about their activities during the day. The context was a familiar playful ritual rather than a situation of instrumental instruction and the teacher facilitated the children's understanding and learning by commentating on their contributions. For example one teacher used a toy car to 'arrive' at different children to prompt their verbal contribution: 'Are you ready? Here it comes: brrm, brrm.' When it was Vicky's turn to say where she had played that day the teacher stopped the car on Vicky's drawing and asked what she had been doing. Vicky hid her face in her arms while her response was awaited. The teacher did not insist but instead described what Vicky had done that day on Vicky's behalf: 'She did some lovely jumping.' In this way Vicky was part of the game without having to speak on cue. On another occasion Vicky joined in more actively, aided by the involvement of a robotic toy, the 'bee-bot'.

**CASE STUDY 17.3**

## Vicky joins in

One of the children, Mary, having discussed her play plans, sends the 'bee-bot' to Vicky and goes on playing without moving away. Mrs Baker looks at Vicky and describes in a loud voice the bee-bot's action—'It is going forward towards Vicky'—and smiles at her—'Where is Vicky going to play today?' Vicky points at some books in the book corner. Mrs Baker explains to the children that Vicky's favourite book is *Night Garden*. Vicky is looking at her very attentively. 'Anything else?' asks the teacher and Vicky says in a soft voice 'painting' while looking downwards. Her key worker leans towards her and asks her 'what colour painting?' Vicky looks at her and replies 'painting' again in a soft voice. Her key worker asks her, 'Where do you want to send your bee-bot?' and, unexpectedly for everyone, Vicky replies 'Mary' and starts pushing the buttons of the bee-bot making it go towards Mary. Mrs Baker thanks her, informs her that she can go and play and goes on with the other children.

In these situations the teacher acts as a commentator for Vicky, and fosters all the children's learning and understanding by creating a playful atmosphere that encourages communication within the safe confines of familiar play rituals. Talk is a supportive tool alongside action, gaze and technology. The interaction is not perfect, but the balance is with playful involvement when teacherly demands are kept to a minimum.

## PRACTITIONERS AS MEDIATORS OF PLAY

By acting as supporters of play, practitioners can help the play along and gently draw children in. When acting as mediators their role is more purposefully interventionist, yet still they intervene no more than is needed. They respond contingently in the face of real or potential misunderstanding or exclusion (Theodorou & Nind, 2010). They might need to repair breakdown in playful exchanges or provide minimal, timely prompts. They can make themselves available to children by being in quiet proximity to their play, ready to be drawn in as a resource if needed (Nind, 2003). The following vignette again features Vicky who has autism and it depicts a teacher/key worker, Mrs Roms (pseudonym), acting as a mediator to offer just enough support through verbal prompts to facilitate the children's play in a discrete and non-directive way.

**CASE STUDY 17.4**

## The teacher makes a timely intervention

Vicky is playing in the garden with a ball. She sees Katia getting on a plastic horse; she follows her, sits behind her and hugs her, full of joy. Katia swings the horse and suddenly shouts, 'Vicky, you need to look the other way!' Vicky starts screwing up her face, showing mild distress, but does not respond. Mrs Roms, who is in the garden, goes towards the two girls, crouches, touches Vicky's back and says, 'Katia thinks you need to look the other way,' Vicky looks at her, smiles and with a loud, happy voice says 'yesss'. The key worker then helps Vicky get off and get on again facing the other way while Vicky starts smiling again even before the key worker asks her 'Is that better now?' When she sees Vicky's face, she says, 'Oh, OK, you are smiling now.' Katia looks ahead smiling happily as the two girls ride the horse.

In Case study 17.5, the teacher takes the role of a mediator and occasionally becomes an active player to enable Vicky to interact naturally with the other children. She is not obviously needed, and does not treat Vicky as a special case, but her gentle involvement eases the episode along.

**CASE STUDY 17.5**

## The teacher joins in

Vicky joins three children and a key worker who are constructing a house with colourful mats. As soon as they finish, Vicky jumps lightly on the mat and smiles as the house falls down. The children exclaim 'Oh no!' and the key worker prompts them: 'What are we going to do?' Vicky repeats the whole phrase in a soft voice and looks at the teacher while the rest of the children volunteer suggestions. 'Shall we do another house then?' suggests the key worker and the children start giving her pieces of mat to build another one. In the meantime, Vicky climbs on a triangle and remarks that 'it is too slippery'. Her teacher looks at me and smiles, seemingly surprised that Vicky is talking. The children and the teacher build the house together and the key worker asks Vicky, who is just watching the other children, 'Could you please bring the square?' Vicky looks at her and without hesitation brings the square to the key worker who puts it on top of the house and the house falls down again. Before the other children react, Vicky remarks, 'Not again', while the key worker prompts the children to build the house once more.

Practitioners who are aware of their potential as mediators of play may have come to that awareness through immersion in training programs where they learn to read children's cues and intentions and repair breakdowns in reciprocity (ability and willingness to respond positively to each other) by addressing their own interactions and avoiding becoming controlling. Video review can also be a highly effective tool for practitioners to reflect on practice and on the complex processes of social interaction. Alternatively, adopting a reciprocal role can be intuitive, as it often is between parents and children, where children's responses can trigger reciprocal playfulness in the adults around them. One of our challenges as practitioners is to act with a combination of spontaneity and reflection to help create opportunities and social contexts for playful exchanges that support children's inclusion in naturally occurring social interactions.

## PRACTITIONERS AS ACTIVE PLAY PARTNERS

Increasingly, researchers are finding that children and peers play in ways that adults find difficult to emulate. Roeyers (1995, cited by Jordan & Jones, 1999), for example, argues that friends make better teachers of play than adults. For Trevarthen, Aitken, Papoudi and Robarts (1996), the way in which friends enjoy mutual interest and pleasure, thus sustaining their play, is critical. On one occasion, we observed children playing around a water trough at Honilands, adapting their playful communications to draw in a less communicative child, Vincent. One child put his face in front of Vincent's and another used physical play until Vincent relaxed into the fun, exclaiming, 'Know what Haydn, know what Ritchie, this is a swimming pool' (Nind, 2003, p.355). If adults attempt to imitate this mutuality as a professional intervention there can be a lack of authenticity that can disrupt the play space: the adult's agenda can destroy the delicate balance of power and opportunity that maintains peer play. By being genuinely playful play partners, however, by having genuine fun and joining in, on as equal a footing as possible, practitioners can 'automatically supply props in an appropriately considerate and cooperative way, or at least ... assure the potential availability of such a supply, and ... make approving noises, joining with appreciative comments into the child's efforts at meaningful action' (Trevarthen et al, 1996, p.89). In a sense, the adult playmate can simultaneously act as a play partner and as a role model for how to play. In this way, skilled practitioners, parents or carers can combine the role of being playmate with that of facilitating children in being playmates for each other. They might even

## CASE STUDY 17.6

### Playing together

The play episode begins with Vicky finding a spoon; prompted by the teacher to think about what she's going to do with it, she also finds some play dough.

Teacher: Can I have some play dough? [extending her hand]

[Vicky gives her some]

Teacher: Share, couldn't we?

Vicky: Yeah [puts some play dough in her teacher's plate instead of her hand]

Teacher: Thank you, Vicky.

Vicky: I like to taste it. [putting some dough in her lips]

Teacher: You like to taste your play dough, do you? [rolling some of the dough]

[Vicky pretends to eat]

Teacher: I make my sausages and beans, more beans I'm gonna break it up and make some small balls.

[Vicky stops eating and rolls some dough]

Teacher: Are you making some food for me, Vicky?

...

Vicky [smiles and with a loud voice]: Weee sausages!

Teacher: You are making sausages too .

Vicky: Rolly polly, rolly polly, rolly polly! [in a playful voice]

Teacher: Oh, I am making some beans, how many sausages will you have for your dinner?

Vicky: Is got one.

Teacher: You got one sausage, I am gonna have one, I can't eat too many sausages. [rolling dough]

Vicky [extends her hand, takes some of her teacher's dough]: That's this one.

Teacher: You can have that one, if you want that one.

Vicky: That one. [taking some more]

Teacher: You can have all of them.

[Vicky takes a spoon and is ready to eat]

manage to move seamlessly between their roles as play providers, partners, supporters and mediators as we saw in one early years setting (Theodorou & Nind, 2010), and as illustrated in Case study 17.6. This is only possible, however, if the adult is not also trying to perform the multiple roles of negotiator and enforcer of rules, manager of resources and so on (Nind, 2003).

The case study shows how the teacher created a relaxed playful atmosphere and by playing alongside and with Vicky, enabled her to become involved in enjoyable playing and talking. You might want to reflect on how the teacher could have been even more facilitative as our responses are never perfect.

## Enabling teachers to enable children

The examples we have included above illustrate how various individual practitioners worked to get children playing and thereby enabled them to be included in the rich social and cultural activity of their peers' lives. It is important, however, to reflect on and analyse what enables practitioners to perform these skilled roles. The data from our different studies suggest clearly that it is difficult for individual practitioners to make an enduring difference to young children's lives unless they are operating in an environment that supports their inclusive practice. In Forest Nursery, for example, where the teachers were very successful in including Vicky in rich and varied play, the institutional environment was characterised by a collaborative approach, a shared ethos and a supportive curriculum framework. Mandy was best supported in the inclusive Village Playgroup environment where children's competence was constructed by practitioners through their sensitive interpretations of the range of verbal and silent modes of communication that the children used in their playfulness: through their movements, smiles and gaze rather than merely their words. In Honilands the staff were keen to reflect systematically on their practice to help create an environment rich in play and communication opportunities for all children.

Our research shows that if practitioners work collaboratively, then they can reap the tangible benefits of their ideas being shared and developed based on the insights of more than one individual. Achievements can be shared and this generates a virtuous cycle in which success breeds success. Early years settings function at their best when children have a supportive network around them and when warm, sensitive and responsive patterns of support combine with inclusive and engaging play interactions. Practitioners working collaboratively can engage in peer supervision, asking questions that prompt each other to reflect and find solutions, and hold a mirror up to each other in order to see their own practices afresh (Wadsworth, 2001; Nind, 2003).

Working within a supportive curriculum framework, such as the HighScope approach (Schweinhart, Barnes & Weikhart, 1993) used at Forest Nursery, can provide practitioners with guiding principles for action. Thus, the people working with Vicky shared an understanding that they needed to foster active learning based on trusting children to act on their desire to explore, and that

**FIGURE 17.2** DISCUSSING PLAY

they had to enable children to transform this action into play (Bennett, Wood & Rogers, 1996). They understood the value of discreet, non-intrusive roles, providing a variety of play materials and allowing children to set their own play agendas. This kind of curriculum framework recognised every child's, and every adult's potential to be both an expert and a learner. Similarly in Mandy's Village Playgroup, the experienced practitioners adhered to the inclusive principles advocated by the Preschool Learning Alliance, but were also guided by their expert knowledge as members of the local community to which the children in their care belonged.

Our examples illustrate the role played by the culture and ethos of the early years setting in terms of enabling (and sometimes not enabling) pervasive playfulness. Working towards building an enabling ethos is a highly productive use of practitioners' energy, which, we would argue, can be more beneficial for all than working to apply or develop specialist interventionist methods. The former approach is inclusive and self-sustaining for all children and adults, while the latter positions individual children as needing something 'extra' beyond the resources of the staff and peers. Rather than drawing on the rich human resources that are available, the latter approach can burden practitioners and children with always being in some way inadequate. At Honilands the decision to improve the learning environment for all the children rather than to address the deficits or needs of particular children reflected the inclusive ethos (Nind, 2003). Nutbrown and Clough (2006, p.1) assert that 'every early years setting represents a *culture* which is created by children, practitioners, parents and others'. Getting the culture right is something that children and adults can do together, but is ultimately the responsibility of the staff team.

The moment-by-moment play interactions constitute micro-cultures and these can come together to create a playful, inclusive learning culture.

## Play-based assessment

Earlier in the chapter we argued that research based in naturalistic contexts is more suitable for understanding children's play as a social phenomenon. Here we argue that assessment of children through play is more suitable as a means for getting to know them holistically and to know not what they can do alone, but what they can do in optimally supportive social situations. **Play-based assessment** puts the emphasis on what children can do rather than what they cannot do, which is, as Lloyd (1997) argues, a central principle of early years education. Play-based assessment follows the child's interests, and uses their playful spontaneous interactions rather than experimentally suggested procedures that aim to 'validate' play-related experiences and abilities (Stagnitti & Cooper, 2009) and decontextualise the real nature of play to create a picture of the children's 'supposed' play skills. A good example of a play-based assessment that tries to capture children's real play abilities is Linder's (1993) trans-disciplinary play-based assessment. This involves a team observing the child in unstructured and structured play, in play with other children and with parents, and in various environments. The focus is on a range of domains and the assessment can inform intervention and curriculum plans. Here play is regarded as the natural context for observing, understanding and facilitating children's development.

Play-based assessment: Involves evaluating children's developmental skills, social interactions, learning approaches and so on in the natural context of play.

Goodley and Runswick-Cole (2010) warn that some assessments (e.g. of playfulness) are used to judge children's play activity as appropriate or lacking. Play-based assessment can be more inclusive. Crucial to this is retaining a perspective in which play is valued for its own sake and not 'eclipsed by a focus on its instrumental value for disabled children and their families ... [and] colonised by adults seeking to support their learning and development at the expense of its intrinsic value' (Goodley & Runswick-Cole, 2010, p.500). Play-based assessment can be used less inclusively, but it can also be used to get to know children as people with preferences and personalities that vary as their play contexts vary. We can resist trying to teach play, or to normalise it in ways that detract from the task-free essence of play. This does not mean we have to value play *either* for its own sake *or* for what it offers for children's social interaction, belonging, and development. Goodley and Runswick-Cole (2010, p.500) are adamant that, based on the new sociology of childhood, play 'is for fun, not for assessment, intervention or therapy', but we maintain that a delicate balance can be reached by practitioners who are sensitive to these issues. Indeed, children's right to play can be brought to life through minimally interventionist assessment and support focused on a child (and not just children experiencing disability or difference) *in context*.

## Conclusion

In this chapter we have considered the value of ethnographic observation of children's play, drawing primarily from our own research. This has illustrated the different skilled roles that practitioners can adopt when they are focused on fostering the play of all children, working within a supportive ethos and curriculum framework. There is a lot that individual practitioners can do to create optimal play environments and even more that they can do when working as a team. The ideal is to create environments that are consistently supportive in providing the multimodal communications, spaces, times and playfulness for children to express and be themselves.

# FOR FURTHER REFLECTION

Consider the following questions:

1. What have I learnt and how can I communicate this to the team where I work and/or will work?
2. How can our curriculum framework promote more playful interactions?
3. How am I going to act more subtly or more proactively in play situations like those featured in this chapter?
4. What actions am I going to pursue, in and with my particular setting, to foster an inclusive play culture?

## WEBSITES

http://touchedbyolivia.com.au/inclusive-playspaces/
Information about inclusive play-spaces across Australia

http://playgroupaustralia.org.au/Home.aspx
Information about playgroups across Australia

www.makebelievearts.co.uk/docs/Helicopter-Technique-Evaluation.pdf
An evaluation of Vivian Gussin Paley's Helicopter Technique for storytelling and story acting in early education

www.open.ac.uk/blogs/multimodalliteracies
Multimodal Literacies in the Early Years: research exploring the range of literacy skills and practices that three- and four-year-old children develop as they engage with diverse printed and electronic texts

## REFERENCES


Anderson, A., Moore, D.W., Godfrey, R. & Fletcher-Flinn, C.M. (2004). Social skills assessment of children with autism in free-play situations. *Autism,8*(4), 369–385. doi:10.177/1362361304045216.

Avgitidou, S. (1997). Children's play: An investigation of children's co-construction of their world within early school settings, *Early Years: An International Journal of Research and Development, 17*, 6–10. doi:10.1080/0957514970170202

Bennett, N., Wood, L. & Rogers, S. (1996). *Teaching through play: Teacher's thinking and classroom practice.* Buckingham: Open University Press.

Booth, T., Ainscow, M. & Kingston, D. (2006). *Index for inclusion: Developing play, learning and participation in early years and childcare.* Bristol: Centre for Studies on Inclusive Education (CSIE).

Davis, J. & Watson, N. (2002). Countering stereotypes of disability: Disabled children and resistance. In M. Corker & T. Shakespeare (Eds) *Disability/postmodernity: Embodying disability theory* (pp.159–174). London: Continuum.

Dominguez, A., Ziviani, J. & Rodger, S. (2006). Play behaviours and play object preferences of young children with autistic disorder in a clinical play environment. *Autism, 10*, 53–69. doi:10.1177/1362361306062010

Flewitt, R.S., Nind, M. & Payler, J. (2009). *'If she's left with books she'll just eat them'*: Considering inclusive multimodal literacy practices. *Journal of Early Childhood Literacy*, 9, 211–233. doi:10.1177/1468798409105587

Geertz, C. (1973). Thick description: Toward an interpretive theory of culture. In C. Geertz (Ed.) *The importance of cultures* (pp.3–30). New York: Basic Books.

Goodley, D. (2001). 'Learning difficulties', the social model of disability and impairment: Challenging epistemologies. *Disability & Society, 16*, 207–31. doi:10.1080/09687590120035816

Goodley, D. & Runswick-Cole, K. (2010). Emancipating play: Dis/abled children, development and deconstruction. *Disability and Society, 25*, 499–512. doi:10.1080/09687591003755914

Holmes, E. & Willoughby, T. (2005). Play behaviour of children with autism spectrum disorders. *Journal of Intellectual and Developmental Disability, 30*, 156–164. doi:10.1080/13668250500204034

Hughes, M. & Westgate, D. (1997). Assistants as talk partners in early years classrooms: Some issues of support and development. *Educational Review, 49*, 5–12. doi:10.1080/0013191970490101

Jordan, R. & Jones, G. (1999). *Meeting the needs of children with autistic spectrum disorders*. London: David Fulton.

Linder, T.W. (1993). *Transdisciplinary play-based assessment: A functional approach to working with young children* (Revised Edn). Baltimore: Paul H. Brookes Publishing Co.

Lloyd, C. (1997). Inclusive education for children with special educational needs in the early years. In S. Wolfendale (Ed.) *Meeting special needs in the early years: Directions in policy and practice*. London: David Fulton.

Nind, M. (2003). Enhancing the communication learning environment of an early years unit through action research. *Educational Action Research, 11*, 347–63. doi:10.1080/09650790300200226

Nind, M., Flewitt, R. & Payler, J. (2010). The social experience of early childhood for children with learning disabilities: Inclusion, competence and agency. *British Journal of Sociology of Education, 31*, 653–70. doi:10.1080/01425692.2010.515113

Nind, M., Flewitt, R.S. & Payler, J. (2011). Social constructions of young children in 'special', 'inclusive' and home environments. *Children & Society, 25*, 359–70. doi:10.1111/j.1099-0860.2009.00281.x

Nutbrown, C. & Clough, P. (2006). *Inclusion in the early years: Critical analyses and enabling narratives*. London: Sage.

Ogilvy, C.M., Boath, E.H., Cheyne, W.M., Jahoda, G. & Schaffer, H.R. (1992). Staff-child interaction styles in multi-ethnic nursery schools. *British Journal of Developmental Psychology, 10* (1), 85–97. doi:10.1111/j.2044-835X.1992.tb00564.x

Schweinhart, J.L., Barnes, V.H. & Weikhart, P.D. (1993). *Significant benefits: The HighScope Perry Preschool study through age 27* (Monographs of the HighScope Educational Research Foundation, 10). Ypsilanti: HighScope Press.

Seach, D. (2007). *Interactive play for children with autism*. London: Routledge.

Skaines, N., Rodger, S. & Bundy, A. (2006). Playfulness in children with autistic disorder and their typically developing peers. *British Journal of Occupational Therapy, 69*(11), 505–512. Retrieved from www.ingentaconnect.com/content/cot/bjot/2006/00000069/00000011/art00004?crawler=true

Stagnitti, K. & Cooper, R. (2009). *Play as therapy: Assessment and therapeutic issues*. London: Jessica Kingsley Publishers.

Theodorou, F. (2011). *Children with autism: Towards an understanding and description of their play in the naturalistic environments of two inclusive preschool settings*. (Unpublished PhD thesis), University of Southampton, UK.

Theodorou, F. & Nind, M. (2010). Inclusion in play: A case study of a child with autism in an inclusive nursery. *Journal of Research in Special Educational Needs, 10*, 99–106. doi:10.1111/j.1471-3802.2010.01152.x

Thomas, C. (2004). Rescuing a social relational understanding of disability. *Scandinavian Journal of Disability Research, 6*, 22–36. doi:10.1080/15017410409512637

Trevarthen, C., Aitken, K., Papoudi, D. & Robarts, J. (1996). *Children with autism: Diagnosis and interventions to meet their needs*. London: David Fulton.

Vygotsky, L.S. (1981). The genesis of higher mental functions. In J.V. Wertsch, (Ed.) *The concept of activity in Soviet psychology*. New York: Sharpe.

Wadsworth, Y. (2001). The mirror, the magnifying glass, the compass and the map: Facilitating participatory action research. In P. Reason & H. Bradbury (Eds), *Handbook of action research: Participative inquiry and practice* (pp.420–432). London: Sage.

Wolfberg, P. & Schuler, A. (1993). A case illustration of the impact of peer play in on symbolic activity in autism. *Biennial Meeting of the Society for Research in Child Development* (SRCD), New Orleans, LA.

# 18 Inclusive Literacy Learning

*Kathy Cologon*

CHAPTER OVERVIEW

Inclusive early literacy experiences will be considered within this chapter, with particular focus on including young children who experience disability. Key issues will be discussed in light of research evidence with a view to creating accessible and inclusive early literacy experiences.

Learning goals for this chapter include:

- Recognising the importance of literacy learning opportunities for all children;
- Identifying key barriers to literacy learning;
- Considering the evidence for a holistic approach to literacy learning;
- Examining the role of expectations and the importance of presuming competence;
- Exploring adaptations to facilitate inclusive literacy learning for all children.

KEY TERMS AND CONCEPTS

individualised teaching

literate citizenship

phonic decoding

phonological awareness

# Introduction

> There can be little doubt that the ability to know, to understand, to engage in conversation, to judge without bias, to think critically, to interpret and to view, to represent, to imagine, to participate meaningfully in society—to live—is enhanced and enriched through the pursuit of higher personal levels of reading literacy ... Access to and engagement with literature in its many forms enables the development of such literacy (Gibson-Langford & Laycock, 2008, p.9).

literate citizenship: Being valued and supported as an active and developing participant in the literate world of any given community (Kliewer, 2008).

In its fullest meaning, literacy encompasses all forms of human communication and therefore **literate citizenship** is crucial for valued participation and inclusion in society (Kliewer, Biklen & Kasa-Hendrickson, 2006; Kliewer, 2008). Literacy learning can be a source not only of choice, opportunity and participation, but also of personal enjoyment and engagement in the shared human story (Cologon, 2013).

The *Early Years Learning Framework for Australia* (Department of Education, Employment & Workplace Relations [DEEWR], 2009) and the Australian Curriculum (Australian Curriculum, Assessment & Reporting Authority [ACARA], 2011) outline the importance of supporting *all* children in their literacy learning. Additionally, as discussed throughout this book, access to education is a basic human right for all children (United Nations Committee on Children's Rights, 1989; United Nations Committee on the Rights of Persons with Disabilities, 2006). This means that early years professionals need to consider how to support *all* children through inclusive literacy practices.

Given the widely accepted importance of literacy learning, this chapter focuses on the potential for enhancing access to inclusive literacy learning opportunities. There is a concerning lack of literacy learning opportunities provided to many children who are labelled 'disabled' (Browder et al., 2009; Cologon, 2008, 2012; Erickson, 2005; Hetzroni, 2004; Katims, 2000; Kliewer & Biklen, 2001; Kliewer, 2008; Mirenda, 2003; Myers, 2007); this chapter, therefore, will focus particularly on literacy learning opportunities that are inclusive of children who experience disability. However, these considerations are important for the many children who are at risk of exclusion from literacy learning for a wide range of reasons.

# Literacy learning and children who experience disability

Children who experience disability have shown, time and time again, the capacity for literacy learning (Cologon, 2008; Cologon, Cupples & Wyver, 2011; Erickson, 2005; Foley & Pollatsek, 1999; Gillon, 2005; Groen, Laws, Nation & Bishop,

**FIGURE 18.1** INTEREST-BASED READING

*Photo: Kathy Cologon*

2006; Iacono & Cupples, 2004; Kliewer, 2008; Light, McNaughton, Weyer & Karg, 2008; Ricci, 2011). Historically this was not considered possible and, as a consequence, opportunities to engage with literacy learning were extremely limited for the majority of children who experience disability. Even today, lack of literacy learning opportunities poses the biggest barrier to literacy learning for individuals who experience disability (Cologon, 2012; Hetzroni, 2004; Kliewer et al., 2006; Light & McNaughton, 2013; Myers, 2007). The continuation of stereotyped and inappropriate negative assumptions about the capacity of children who experience disability for literacy learning leads to this lack of opportunities (Kliewer et al., 2006).

Indeed, there are many unnecessary barriers to literacy development for children who experience disability. These barriers include the paucity of literacy learning opportunities or direct exclusion from literacy experiences (particularly in segregated educational settings), the promotion of narrow concepts of literacy for children who experience disability, a lack of accessible or appropriate literacy materials and experiences, and low expectations (Browder et al., 2009; Buckley, Bird, Sacks & Archer, 2006; Cologon, 2012; Cologon et al., 2011; Erickson, 2005; Gioia, Johnston & Cooper, 2001; Heller & Coleman-Martin, 2007; Katims, 2000; Kliewer & Landis, 1999; Light et al., 2008; Mirenda, 2003; Myers, 2007).

Even when literacy learning opportunities are provided, barriers occur when oral (spoken) language is privileged over other forms of communication

**FIGURE 18.2** THE VICIOUS CYCLE OF LOW EXPECTATIONS

and participation, meaning that some children cannot access or participate in literacy experiences (Hetzroni, 2004; Kliewer, 2008; Light & McNaughton, 2013; Myers, 2007). Another barrier to literacy learning is the inaccessibility of physical materials for children who are still developing fine motor skills or who require adaptations (for example, to turn the pages of a book or hold a paintbrush or pencil) (Cologon & McNaught, 2014; Johnston, McDonnell & Hawken, 2008; Pierce, 2006).

Lack of opportunities are often the consequence of low expectations. The end result, as illustrated in Figure 18.2, is a vicious cycle of low expectations leading to lack of provision of learning opportunities, leading to limited learning outcomes, which in turn reinforces the low expectations—and so the cycle continues. Early years professionals are tasked with the challenge to take seriously their role in the education of *all* children; to do so, they need to work to break this cycle and ensure the provision of literacy learning opportunities for *every* child.

**phonological awareness:** Phonological awareness can be defined as an individual's ability to consciously focus on the sound structure of language. For example, identifying syllables in a spoken word.

**phonic decoding:** Phonics, which builds on phonological awareness, is the process of actively teaching relationships between graphemes (letters) and phonemes (sounds) and how they are used to make up words in reading and spelling.

## Beyond functional literacy: Taking a holistic approach to literacy learning

Literacy learning occurs within social interactions and therefore forms part of social practice (Cologon & McNaught, 2014; Cremin, Mottram, Collins, Powell & Safford, 2009; Kliewer, 2008). In considering diverse perspectives on literacy development, it is important to note that for some the concept of literacy as social practice and literacy as skills-based are opposing and mutually exclusive ideas. However, a balanced, holistic, approach is important for optimal literacy outcomes for young children (Justice & Pullen, 2003). This involves opportunities for storybook reading and creation of stories, development of **phonological awareness**, **phonic decoding**, sight word learning and writing development—all within meaningful experiences.

Engagement in and exposure to a wide range of personally relevant, enjoyable contextualised and meaningful literacy experiences is essential for all children (Buckley, 2001; Evans & Shaw, 2008; Kliewer & Landis, 1999; Mirenda, 2003; Mol & Bus, 2011; Swanson et al., 2011). In fact, research provides evidence that literacy development, including understanding of print concepts, the development of letter–sound knowledge and word reading ability, depends more on exposure to print over time than on cognitive ability (Ricci, 2011).

The role of phonological awareness and phonic decoding skills is arguably the most contested factor related to literacy learning. However, while phonological awareness and phonic decoding skills alone are not sufficient for reading development, and the direction of the relationship between phonological awareness and reading development remains a matter of debate (Evans & Shaw, 2008), a large body of research provides evidence that phonological awareness and phonic decoding skills play a key role in literacy learning (e.g. Hulme & Snowling, 1992; Snow & Juel, 2005; Swan & Goswami, 1997). As a consequence, large evidence-based reports in Australia, the UK and the USA (for example) have recommended the incorporation of activities intended to support the development of phonological awareness and phonic decoding skills into early reading opportunities (Department of Education, Science & Training [DEST], 2005; National Institute of Child Health & Human Development [NICHHD], 2000; Rose, 2006). This is in direct contrast to common recommendations for reading instruction for children who experience disability, which predominantly focus on functional reading skills through sight–word activities (Broun & Oelwin, 2007; Browder et al., 2009; Conners, 2003; Fidler, Most & Guiberson, 2005; Kay-Raining Bird, Cleave, & McConnell, 2000; Mirenda, 2003). This is despite the fact that research evidence clearly demonstrates the ability of children who experience disability—including children with intellectual impairments, speech and language delays and impairments, and physical impairments—to develop phonological awareness and phonic decoding skills (Cologon et al., 2011; Foley & Pollatsek, 1999; Gillon, 2005; Groen et al., 2006; Iacono & Cupples, 2004; Whalon, Al Otaiba & Delano, 2009).

For example, research with children with speech and language impairments provides evidence to suggest that the greater a child's phonological awareness, the greater the likelihood of success with reading development, *regardless of memory, cognitive ability and vocabulary* (Al Otaiba, Puranik, Ziolkowski & Montgomery, 2009). Furthermore, research in Australia and the UK provides evidence of phonological awareness, phonic decoding skills and advanced reading ability in children with Down syndrome (Cologon et al., 2011; Groen et al., 2006). In fact, it has been argued that a focus on phonic decoding skills may be more appropriate than a sight-word focus in general for children with intellectual impairments (Conners, Rosenquist, Sligh, Atwell & Kiser, 2006).

Given the research evidence, it appears that the dominant focus on functional literacy for children who experience disability is—at least to some extent—a remnant of low expectations that have historically limited reading outcomes for children who experience disability. As Mirenda (2003, p.273) writes, 'in the end, the functional curriculum model—as with its predecessor, the readiness model—also serves to prevent many students from acquiring literacy skills, and thus reinforces the belief that they are unable to become readers.' Providing all children with holistic literacy learning opportunities—including supporting the development of phonological awareness and phonic decoding skills—is critical to avoid placing unnecessary limitations on literacy outcomes.

**FIGURE 18.3** ENJOYING A STORY

*Photo: Kathy Cologon*

## Presuming competence for literacy learning

As discussed in Chapter 1, Biklen and Burke (2006, p.166) argue that, when a child is not labelled 'disabled', those around them generally interact with them on the presumption of competence: 'For example, adults routinely gesture, sing, and talk to infants, presuming such children will at some point connect spoken words and visual enactments to things and concepts. Teaching literacy is carried out within the expectation that most, if not all, children are capable of developing literacy skills.' Whereas, when a child is labelled 'disabled', the presumption instead becomes of *in*competence (Biklen & Burke, 2006). The increased likelihood of positive literacy outcomes for a child who experiences disability today is based on changes in social attitudes and subsequent improvements in educational opportunities, rather than changes in the characteristics of impairments (Cologon, 2008, 2012) or changes in the processes of literacy learning. Consequently, it can be argued that a shift to 'presuming competence' for *all* children, irrespective of disability labels, would further advance literacy learning opportunities and outcomes in children who experience disability.

Additionally, literacy ability has been shown to increase perceived competence and enhance acceptance within society, while improving access to education (Erickson, 2005). Literacy levels are also related to health and access to medical care, and employment opportunities in adulthood (Erickson, 2005).

# Supporting inclusive literacy learning

As noted above, the biggest barrier to literacy learning for most children is lack of literacy learning opportunities. However, within this, there are many specific barriers. These include:

- Lack of accommodation for differences in hearing, language and communication:
  - Children who use signed languages, who use augmentative and alternative communication, who are learning English as a second language, and many children with speech and language impairments face barriers due to the emphasis placed on spoken English in literacy learning and may require alternative opportunities to respond and engage through modes of communication other than speech. Children may face considerable disadvantages when forms of communication beyond spoken language are not valued and opportunities to engage visually are not provided.
- Lack of accommodation for differences in vision:
  - Given that written text and visual images are heavily emphasised for literacy learning, children who have low vision or cannot see commonly have very limited early literacy exposure and face many barriers to literacy learning. Children may face considerable disadvantages when opportunities to engage through auditory and tactile experiences are not provided.
- Lack of accommodation for differences in cognitive development:
  - Children who have delayed or uneven development, or intellectual impairment, may require literacy learning opportunities for longer than typically provided within the education curriculum and may also require more repetition and more gradual introduction of new concepts. Often learning experiences need to be broken down into smaller steps. For many children (unless they have low vision), visual prompts may be very helpful

in this process. Children may face considerable disadvantages for literacy learning when these adaptations and accommodations are not made.

- Lack of accommodation for physical differences:
  - Accessing literacy opportunities may require adaptations to materials or alternative opportunities to provide responses. When adaptations to materials are not provided as needed, children may be prevented from participating in literacy learning experiences.
- Lack of accommodation for the varying types of literacy knowledge children bring to early years settings:
  - Children begin literacy learning at very young ages. However, the extent of literacy learning and confidence in literate citizenship varies considerably, based on the child and context. When the assumption is made that all children are the same and require the same approach to learning, some children will be seriously disadvantaged and may 'slip through the cracks'.

**individualised teaching:** Teaching that recognises the individuality, or uniqueness, of every learner and therefore the need to teach children in a way that matches their individual strengths, interests, knowledge and needs.

Adaptations to facilitate participation in literacy learning experiences can be necessary and helpful. However, these adaptations need to be individualised for each child. This **individualised teaching** requires developing a relationship and seeking to assist that child in a positive developmental trajectory. The ORIM framework, incorporating opportunities, recognition, interactions and a model, provides a valuable scaffold for learning and teaching (see Chapter 20). The box below includes a number of suggestions for inclusive literacy teaching.

## SUGGESTIONS FOR GETTING STARTED WITH INCLUSIVE LITERACY APPROACHES

### Planning for inclusive literacy experiences:

- Within group literacy experiences, consider the positioning of children in relation to each other, teachers and materials to maximise engagement.
- Principles of Universal Design for Learning (see Chapter 12) are essential to inclusive literacy practice. This involves providing multiple forms for responding, engaging and participating within literacy experiences.
- Take a multimodal approach including combining auditory, visual and kinaesthetic materials. For example, pair visual information with auditory information in phonological and phonemic awareness and phonic decoding activities.
- For small group activities, pairing children within activities to build on complementary strengths and areas of need can assist with access to literacy learning opportunities and successful and enjoyable participation.
- Break tasks down into small steps. Accompanying small steps with visual and verbal prompts assists with participation and engagement in literacy learning.

- Build in fun and naturalistic repetition. For example, use stories with repeating patterns and multiple modes of revisiting or building on the same concepts and stories.
- Small group engagement with literacy materials, including retelling and recreating stories in multiple forms, can enable each child to take on a role that builds on their strengths and to contribute to the experience while learning and further developing their confidence.
- Incorporate signs, gestures, movements and facial expressions to enhance meaning and participation; for example, signing or making the sign for 'grow' when planting seeds and learning about the life cycle of plants.
- Provide visual and verbal information about the schedule of the day and what activities or choices are available. Adding Braille and sign enhances inclusivity (see Chapters 22 and 23).

## Making adaptations to materials for participation in literacy activities:

- Quick and easy adaptations can be made to any book. For example, craft sticks, elastic bands or Velcro dots can be added to the corner of each page to provide separators that make turning pages easier. Pages of books can be taped together, forming an 'accordion' shape so that the book stands alone without the need for page turning. E-books and electronic tablets (such as iPads), as well as many other supports for augmentative and alternative communication, also provide many options for adaptation for participation.
- Providing supports for sitting or standing, or adjustable chairs and tables may assist with appropriate positioning and making participation possible for some children.
- Velcro strips or nonslip placemats placed underneath books or other materials can prevent slipping, or clamps can be used to stabilise materials.
- Holding a book, or other materials, at an appropriate height can increase visibility. Slanted surfaces or easels are easy adaptations that help children independently engage with literacy materials.
- Enhancing illustrations by adding texture or creating tactile books can facilitate engagement and access for many children.
- Use or record audio books.
- Use large print where helpful.
- Adapt painting, drawing and writing materials to enhance grip and independence. For example, use large crayons and add a ball or extra thickness with string or tape to paintbrushes, pencils and coloured markers.
- Provide soft marking drawing materials (for example, soft crayons or textas, rather than hard crayons or pencils that take considerable pressure to make a mark).

- Contrast paper and table colours to provide greater visual discrimination.
- Use key word sign (see Chapter 23) and add Braille (see Chapter 22) to literacy materials and to the environment to facilitate participation while also raising awareness and demonstrating valuing of multiple forms of communication.

*(adapted from Cologon & McNaught, 2014)*

---

Respecting the child involves providing accessible and meaningful literacy learning opportunities. This includes providing authentic experiences and ensuring that literacy experiences are provided as part of living life. Some children require explicit daily support for literacy learning and ensuring they have this support is essential. This support needs to be provided within meaningful and contextualised experiences in which children participate together in inclusive literacy experiences.

Making individualised stories creates an opportunity to connect with the lived experience of the child, thus helping make literacy experiences meaningful and authentic. This process also provides a scaffold for shared engagement with experiences and activities of interest to a group of children. One way to do this is through the development of photo-based stories, which have been found to be beneficial to literacy learning (Elias, Hay, Hemel & Freiberg, 2006). Photo-based books may include photos from the education setting, from home and from community experiences. Children often enjoy seeing themselves, their family and friends and things they have been doing in photographs, and shared literacy engagement between home and the education setting can be enhanced through shared photo-stories. Particular aspects of literacy development can be targeted and repetition, or extension and enrichment (see Chapter 25) can be incorporated through this experience-based process, to support individual development. Drawings and artefacts from everyday experiences can also be used (see the box below).

---

## MAKING AN 'EXPERIENCE BOOK'

Making an 'experience book' can provide a powerful catalyst for shared literacy engagement.

An experience book is a physical or electronic scrapbook in which everyday experiences are recorded with brief text and tactile materials or illustrations such as photographs, drawings or artefacts (for example a leaf collected on a nature walk, an example of environmental print, a recording or excerpt of a storybook, or a photograph of an experience of the day).

Creating a storybook of everyday experiences facilitates literacy learning, shared engagement with families and across settings, and provides particular opportunities for language development through natural and meaningful engagement and repetition.

In developing an experience book with children in an early years setting, or sharing an experience book of their own, early years professionals can provide modelling for families to emphasise the literacy potentials of everyday life and experiences and the ease with which everyday experiences can facilitate literacy learning.

---

## Taking seriously the literate lives of all children

One complex challenge in working to support children's learning, is ensuring that children are given the support they need for literacy learning, while also being genuinely included in early years settings. Reading books with children is essential. However, communication development and learning to read and write involves more than this. Most children, including many children who experience disability, require carefully planned daily support for reading and writing. Additionally, as discussed in Chapter 1, genuine inclusion is essential for optimal outcomes for all children, including for literacy learning.

In recent reading intervention research I worked with a preschool to support inclusive literacy learning. This preschool caters for children from two to six years and there are 20 children in each preschool class. I attended the preschool for half a day per week for five months. During this time I worked closely with the teacher in relation to the literacy development and inclusion of two children: Jack, who is diagnosed with Down syndrome, and Sara, who is diagnosed with Autism Spectrum Disorder (ASD) (pseudonyms). The focus of the intervention was to support the teacher in her work with the children, rather than working with the children directly.

There were a number of key principles underpinning the intervention. One of these was respect for every child and a belief in the literacy learning capacity of all children. Another of these was ensuring that the intervention did not inadvertently result in micro-exclusion (see Chapter 1). Literacy is a social practice, thus it was important to ensure that Jack and Sara (along with their peers) were fully involved in the life of the classroom as valued community members. Given the well-documented importance of storybook reading and exposure to print, daily engagement with books, and a print-rich environment was another fundamental principle. It was also important to recognise that, like many children, Jack and Sara required individualised daily support. This was important in taking seriously the role of teachers in supporting literacy learning and upholding a genuine belief that each child can learn to read and write—if given the learning opportunities to make this possible. What this daily support looked like was different for the two children (individualised) and the teacher and I had ongoing discussions regarding the tensions between structured individual experiences and genuine inclusion. In providing individualised daily support, it was necessary to be critically aware of the balance between the students' individual experiences and their inclusion within the whole-class setting. Consequently, the teacher actively supported the children in developing the knowledge and understanding needed for their literacy learning, while continually reflecting on how to do this inclusively.

The intervention explored in Case study 18.1 is messy and imperfect in many ways—as everyday practice often is. However, through this case study it is possible to reflect on the challenge to meet the learning support needs of each child while ensuring the child is fully included. Not supporting a child to learn to read, for example, will result in later and ongoing exclusion. However, separating or removing a child from the activities of the setting in order to teach her/him to read is current exclusion. Navigating these complexities are ongoing challenges for educators that are important to continuously reflect on.

**CASE STUDY 18.1**

## Bugs in rugs and mugs! A preschool early reading intervention

Each week the teacher shared what had been happening in the centre, with particular focus on how she was embedding literacy learning opportunities into daily activities. The teacher kept (brief) daily records, and a more in-depth record one day per week. We reviewed these records each week. We would then discuss the next step in the reading intervention and brainstorm ideas for how this could be incorporated around the children's interests—both Jack and Sara's interests, as well as the wider group—and within the themes being explored in the classroom. For example, when the theme was insects we introduced the word family 'ug' and the children had fun with phoneme blending (blending sounds to make words) and word matching for bugs in rugs and mugs!

Making connections with meaning was a consistent consideration. Focus words related directly to interests and happenings within the setting and were accompanied by songs and games that provided repetition in a fun and engaging way. The children enjoyed finding objects in the environment and books and matching written words to them, as well as writing words in the sandpit and experimenting with words and letters during painting and drawing activities. Throughout the activities, the teacher paired visual information (words, letters and pictures, using a wide variety of materials) with auditory information (spoken words and sounds) and encouraged Sara and Jack to say the words and sounds.

## Sara

Sara is five years old and living with her mum and her younger brother, who is also labelled with ASD. Sara's mum and the staff at the preschool are very enthusiastic to support her with her literacy development. Sara enjoys copying words and letters, and requests support by placing an adult's hand on hers while she writes. Sara likes a wide range of books, but a current favourite is a children's dictionary and she will spend considerable periods of time poring over the words and prompting adults around her to assist with sounding out any unfamiliar words (by taking their hand and pointing them to the words). Sara herself ensures daily individualised literacy learning experiences as she constantly asks for help with reading or writing and her teachers are willing and enthusiastic to provide this.

Sara's interest in reading and writing resulted in a planning focus to follow this interest. The teacher provides an ongoing range of table activities with a particular focus on reading and writing, including on books, words, letters, phonemes, experimental writing, and sentences. Sara especially enjoys a table game involving blending words and matching them to corresponding pictures.

Reading is Sara's pathway to spoken language—she does not talk except when reading out letters or words (although she does vocalise to express her emotions, frequently crying when unhappy). This makes reading particularly important for scaffolding peer engagement, as it is a key way to engage Sara in the activities of those around her. Sara commonly chooses to play on her own outside, but frequently gravitates towards small group activities inside, particularly activities that involve reading and writing materials. Sara and her teacher also bring these materials to other activities that Sara is interested in to support Sara's participation. Sara often watches what is happening out of the corner of her eye for some time before moving towards her peers. Her peers appear comfortable with Sara and each other and happily accept Sara's participation, sometimes commenting on what Sara is writing.

Over the intervention period, Sara continued to develop her reading and writing ability (including her word and letter knowledge and her phonological awareness and phonic decoding ability) and to actively incorporate reading and writing into a wide range of activities.

## Jack

Jack is four years old and comes from a complex family background. He has an older brother and a younger sister and lives at home with his mum and dad. Jack's mum and the staff at the preschool are very enthusiastic about supporting him with his literacy development in the preschool setting, particularly his reading development, with a view to encouraging his spoken language development. Jack communicates mainly through his behaviour, and is developing spoken language gradually.

Jack often arrives mid-morning and immediately gets his food from his bag and sits down at the morning tea table. In this setting children can choose when to have morning tea, so often there are already one or two other children having morning tea, or who join Jack soon after. Jack and his peers enjoy comparing the food they have for morning tea, often engaging in wordless jokes and giggles in the process. Jack commonly moves to the play-dough table after morning tea, particularly enjoying play-dough and water play.

Jack often chooses to join small group activities and tends to avoid large groups or boisterous play. Jack has frequent colds and ear infections and these reduce his hearing temporarily. Jack is very capable of understanding spoken language, but speaks very little himself. Unlike Sara, Jack does not initiate daily reading and writing experiences, so his teacher introduces them. Jack is happy to participate in these activities once introduced, particularly when the activities have a humorous element, or when they relate to animals or other creatures—a strong interest of Jack's. Jack and his peers appear comfortable with each other and happily participate alongside each other. He identifies his key friends and likes to focus his daily reading activities around stories that include them.

The daily literacy focus for Jack is directly tied to what is happening in the wider classroom and to Jack's particular interests. It is also carefully planned to gradually support Jack's development with small steps and ongoing repetition.

The teacher is developing a daily 'experience book' (see the box on page 368) with Jack and this provides a natural source of repetition for the letters and words he is learning. It also creates an ongoing record of the reading activities as these are all incorporated into the book in the course of the morning, with a combination of photographs and stories developed together. Words, sounds and associated materials are also written or pasted into the book.

Jack enjoys creating words with word families, and particularly likes making flip-books where he can create words using different initial phonemes, and games that involve clapping and jumping the syllables in words (with a scaffold of the written words). He also enjoys singing and he and his teachers and peers sing many songs related to focus words and sounds. For Jack, making a 'friends and family' book containing photographs and written names is an important connection between home and school and something that he particularly enjoys engaging with daily. Jack also enjoys playing matching games with the names of his family and friends from his book.

Over the intervention period, Jack developed his reading ability (including developing word and letter knowledge, phonological awareness and phonic decoding ability) and continued to develop his spoken language.

### CRITICAL REFLECTION QUESTIONS

1. Why are daily, individualised literacy learning experiences important for many children?
2. Based on the case study, what can you identify as Jack, Sara and their teacher's strengths?
3. What might be some of the tensions between supporting Sara and Jack's literacy learning and ensuring genuine inclusion in the setting? How might you address these tensions?
4. What pedagogical choices described in the case study do you think would facilitate literacy learning and inclusion in this early years setting?
5. Brainstorm additional ways that you might support inclusive literacy learning in this setting.

Following the interests of children while embedding thoughtful and targeted teaching strategies requires careful planning, reflection, not to mention considerable skill. It is not a haphazard process. It requires constant attention to 'teachable moments' (Hyun & Marshall, 2003), knowledge of each individual child and carefully planned daily learning experiences. It also involves an openness to critical reflection and ongoing learning, and to making changes to teaching to better support children.

## Engaging with literacy for pleasure

It has been argued that the current emphasis within education on standardised assessment is having a negative impact on the confidence and ability of teachers to facilitate literacy learning for pleasure (Cremin et al., 2009; O'Sullivan & McGonigle, 2010). However, case study and anecdotal evidence suggests that children who experience disability do engage in, and benefit from, reading for pleasure (Buckley, 2001) and, given the opportunity, children who do and do not experience disability amuse themselves with books and ask to be read to (Ricci, 2011).

Mol and Bus (2011) conducted a large meta-analysis of research to examine the widely held assumption that reading for pleasure and exposure to print 'makes us smarter and helps promote success in life' (p.267). In considering research on reading development from the early years through to adulthood, with readers of diverse abilities, Mol and Bus (2011) found that reading for pleasure has benefits for reading, language and cognitive development.

Research has shown that reading for pleasure is not only a product of reading development, but also forms a reciprocal relationship with literacy development; in particular, it shows strong correlations between literacy outcomes and time spent reading for pleasure (Mol & Bus, 2011; Smith, Smith, Gilmore & Jameson, 2011; Ricci, 2011). Mol and Bus (2011) found that reading for pleasure encourages children to read more frequently, thus resulting in greater print exposure, which leads to further literacy development. Of particular note is the finding that literacy outcomes are more strongly related to print exposure for children who have difficulty with reading development or 'low-ability readers' than for 'higher-ability readers', leading to the argument that reading for pleasure is especially important for children who may struggle with aspects of literacy development (Mol & Bus, 2011, p.287).

Reading books with children, particularly in small groups, enhances language and vocabulary development, phonological and phonemic awareness, understanding of print concepts, and reading comprehension (Swanson et al., 2011). However, in addition to print exposure, motivation is a key to literacy learning (Smith et al., 2011). Smith et al. (2011) argue that for children who do and do not experience disability, motivation for literacy learning is developed through a combination of sense of self-efficacy in respect to literacy experiences, coupled with enjoyment of a genre or particular text.

In longitudinal research O'Sullivan and McGonigle (2010) found that humour or sense of fun, quality illustrations, links with popular culture and play, significant and memorable characters and relevant themes, including affective themes (relating to feelings and emotions), are important factors for pleasurable literacy learning. Accordingly, access to a diverse range of conventional and less conventional texts is important (Cremin et al., 2009; Gibson-Langford & Laycock, 2008; O'Sullivan & McGonigle, 2010; Smith et al., 2011).

To maximise the benefit of print exposure, it is essential that print exposure takes the form of literacy learning opportunities for all children over an extended period of time (Buckley 2001; Gioia et al., 2001; Kliewer, 2008; Kliewer & Landis, 1999; Koppenhaver & Erickson, 2003). Storybook reading is of particular importance to literacy development and may be especially beneficial to facilitating reading for pleasure due to its impact on reading skills development and also enjoyment and positive attitudes towards reading (Mol & Bus, 2011). Paying careful attention to the communicative interactions, interests and motivators for any young child is essential to active participation and, in turn, to literacy learning. Child–adult interactions during storybook reading can facilitate a strong foundation for literacy learning, including supporting children with language and social development and in developing knowledge

**FIGURE 18.4** READING FOR PLEASURE

*Photo: Kathy Cologon*

regarding conventions about print (Colmar, 2011; Elias et al., 2006; Erickson, 2005; Flewitt, Nind & Payler, 2009). Additionally, as explored above, daily structured support for literacy learning is also essential.

With support, early years professionals can develop greater knowledge, confidence and understanding of what are relevant and engaging texts for the children with whom they work; and knowledge of popular culture in order to better engage children in reading for pleasure (Cremin et al., 2009; O'Sullivan & McGonigle, 2010). This not only results in enhanced reading outcomes and greater engagement in reading for pleasure on the part of children and teachers alike, but also in a more inclusive approach to reading instruction (Cremin et al., 2009). In an inclusive approach, reading develops through social practice in which participation and success is valued not only on the basis of individual skill levels, but on the basis of engagement in shared communication through and about literature, while recognising and valuing reader diversity (Cologon & McNaught, 2014; Cremin et al., 2009; Kliewer, 2008). Considering the importance of enjoyment and sense of self-efficacy for literacy development, this demonstrates the importance of taking a holistic approach to literacy learning for all children (Cologon, 2013).

## INCLUSIVE APPROACHES TO STORYBOOK READING: THE FEELIX KIT

Vision Australia provides a library of 'Feelix Kits' that can be borrowed to facilitate shared and independent storybook experiences with young children who have visual impairments or are blind.

These kits include a published storybook with a transparent Braille translation overlay on each page, a tactile book incorporating a tactile version of the story developed to extend on meaningful engagement with the book, an audio CD reading of the story and hands-on tangible objects related to the key message or experience of the story.

(See Vision Australia for more information: www.visionaustralia.org.au)

### QUESTIONS FOR REFLECTION

1. How could a 'Feelix Kit' be used inclusively within early years practice?
2. What aspects of the kit would be engaging for children in the early years?
3. Why is the inclusion of Braille materials important in inclusive literacy practices?
4. What other ways could tactile and auditory materials be incorporated into early years literacy practices to increase inclusion?

## Conclusion

Children who do and do not experience disability can experience success and enjoyment through engagement in literacy learning. However, low expectations and, therefore, inappropriately limited literacy opportunities create the potential for a self-fulfilling prophecy in which a child is not expected to learn to read and therefore 'probably will not' (Mirenda, 2003, p.271). The labelling of children as 'disabled' often leaves early years professionals feeling that they do not have a role to play, or knowledge to offer, in supporting a child's literacy learning. However, early years professionals have much to offer *all* children, including children who experience disability. As with the process of teaching any child, the starting point is building a relationship with the child and working to support the child in a positive forward trajectory through personally meaningful and enjoyable literacy experiences. Openness to flexible, reflective and creative approaches—including adaptations to materials and experiences as required—is essential, as is careful planning for daily literacy experiences.

Presuming competence and seeking to support enjoyable and meaningful literate engagement for all children requires taking a holistic approach to literacy teaching. This requires careful consideration of the ways in which children who experience disability can be supported through ongoing daily literacy learning opportunities within inclusive settings. Developing an understanding and awareness of the child's experiences, interests and abilities,

**FIGURE 18.5** WRITING TOGETHER

*Photo: Dinah Cocksedge*

and using this information to guide daily naturalistic and socially embedded reading experiences, is essential for literacy learning (Buckley, 2001; Cologon & McNaught, 2014; Kliewer, 2008). Early years professionals cannot, and should not, seek to change the child, but rather seek to change teaching approaches and the education environment to facilitate inclusion. When appropriate education supports and a presumption of *competence* are in place, then literacy learning is for everyone!

## FOR FURTHER REFLECTION

Why is literacy important for all children?

1. Consider the ways in which you engage in literate experiences every day. If you had been excluded from literacy learning experiences, how would this impact on your life?
2. Consider the notion of literate citizenship and the implications this has for the role of early years professionals.

Reflecting on this chapter, identify some of the key barriers to literacy learning for children who experience disability:

1. How can these barriers be addressed? List some key strategies for inclusive literacy teaching.
2. What do you understand the notion of 'presuming competence' to mean? Why is this important for early years professionals?

## WEBSITES

www.visionaustralia.org.au
Vision Australia provides information about the Feelix Library and support for literacy learning in children with visual impairment.

http://www.dseinternational.org/en-us/
Information about supporting learning with children who have Down syndrome, including a particular focus on literacy

http://www.everyonecommunicates.org/resources/literacy.html
Resources to support literacy learning in children who use augmentative and alternative communication systems and require a range of other supports

http://www.paulakluth.com/readings/literacy/
Information about literacy learning and children labelled with autism

## REFERENCES


Al Otaiba, S., Puranik, C.S., Ziolkowski, R.A. & Montgomery, T.M. (2009). Effectiveness of phonological awareness interventions for students with speech or language impairments. *Journal of Special Education 43*(2), 107–128. doi:10.1177/0022466908314869

Australian Curriculum, Assessment and Reporting Authority (ACARA). (2011). *Australian Curriculum.* Sydney: ACARA. Retrieved from www.australiancurriculum.edu.au

Biklen, D. & Burke, J. (2006). Presuming competence. *Equity & Excellence in Education, 39*(2), 166–175. doi:10.1080/10665680500540376

Broun, L.T. & Oelwein, P. (2007). *Literacy skill development for students with special learning needs: A strength-based approach.* Port Chester NY: National Professional Resources, Inc.

Browder, D., Gibbs, S., Ahlgrim-Delzell, L., Courtade, G.R., Mraz, M. & Flowers, C. (2009). Literacy for students with severe developmental disabilities: What should we teach and what should we hope to achieve? *Remedial & Special Education, 30*(5), 269–282. doi:10.1177/0741932508315054

Buckley, S.J. (2001). Reading and writing for individuals with Down syndrome—An overview. *Down Syndrome Issues and Information.* doi:10.3104/9781903806098

Buckley, S.J., Bird, G., Sacks, B. & Archer, T. (2006). A comparison of mainstream and special education for teenagers with Down syndrome: Implications for parents and teachers. *Down Syndrome Research and Practice* 9(3), 54–67. doi:10.3104/reports.295

Colmar, S. (2011). A book reading intervention with mothers of children with language difficulties. *Australasian Journal of Early Childhood, 36*(2), 104–112. Retrieved from www.earlychildhoodaustralia.org.au/australian_journal_of_early_childhood.html

Cologon, K. (2008). *Phonological awareness and 'silent reading': the benefits of intervention and early intervention in reading for children who have Down syndrome.* (Unpublished doctoral dissertation). Macquarie University, NSW.

Cologon, K. (2012). Image, access and opportunity: Children with Down syndrome as readers. In S. Wyver & P. Whiteman (Eds), *Children and childhoods 2: Images of childhood* (pp.27–42). Newcastle upon Tyne: Cambridge Scholars Publishing.

Cologon, K. (2013). Debunking myths: Reading development in children with Down syndrome. *Australian Journal of Teacher Education, 38*(3), 130–151. doi:10.14221/ajte.2013v38n3.10

Cologon, K., Cupples, L. & Wyver, S.R. (2011). Effects of targeted reading instruction on phonological awareness, phonic decoding and reading comprehension in children with Down syndrome. *American Journal on Intellectual and Developmental Disabilities, 116*(2), 111–129. doi:10.1352/1944-7558-116.2.111

Cologon, K. & McNaught, M. (2014). Early intervention for literacy learning. In L. Arthur, J. Ashton & B. Beecher (Eds) *Diverse literacies in early childhood: A social justice approach* (pp.146–165). Melbourne: Australian Council for Educational Research.

Conners, F.A. (2003). Reading skills and cognitive abilities of individuals with mental retardation. *International Review of Research in Mental Retardation, 27,* 191–229. doi:10.1016/S0074-7750(03)27006-3

Conners, F.A., Rosenquist, C.J., Sligh, A.C., Atwell, J.A. & Kiser, T. (2006). Phonological reading skills acquisition by children with mental retardation. *Research in Developmental Disabilities, 27*(2), 21–137. doi:10.1016/j.ridd.2004.11.015

Cremin, T., Mottram, M., Collins, F., Powell, S. & Safford, K. (2009). Teachers as readers: Building communities of readers. *Literacy, 43*(1), 11–19. doi:10.1111/j.1741-4369.2009.00515.x

Department of Education, Employment and Workplace Relations (DEEWR). (2009). *Belonging, being and becoming: The early years learning framework for Australia.* ACT: DEEWR. Retrieved from www.coag.gov.au/sites/default/files/early_years_learning_framework.pdf

Department of Education, Science and Training (DEST). (2005). *Teaching reading: Report and recommendations. National inquiry into the teaching of literacy.* Canberra: Commonwealth of Australia. Retrieved from www.dest.gov.au/nitl/documents/report_recommendations.pdf

Elias, G., Hay, L., Hemel, R. & Freiberg, K. (2006). Enhancing parent-child book reading in a disadvantaged community. *Australian Journal of Early Childhood, 31*(1), 20–25. Retrieved from www.earlychildhoodaustralia.org.au/australian_journal_of_early_childhood.html

Erickson, K. (2005). *Literacy for life—literacy and persons with developmental disabilities: Why and how?* Background paper prepared for the Education for All Global Monitoring Report 2006. UNESCO. Retrieved from http://unesdoc.unesco.org/images/0014/001459/145968e.pdf

Evans, M.A. & Shaw, D. (2008). Home grown for reading: Parental contributions to young children's emergent literacy and word recognition. *Canadian Psychology, 49*(2), 89–95. doi:10.1037/0708-5591.49.2.89

Fidler, D.J., Most, D.E. & Guiberson, M.M. (2005). Neuropsychological correlates of word identification in Down syndrome. *Research in Developmental Disabilities, 26*(5), 487–501. doi:10.1016/j.ridd.2004.11.007

Flewitt, R., Nind, M. & Payler, J. (2009). *'If she's left with books she'll just eat them'*: Considering inclusive multimodal literacy practices. *Journal of Early Childhood Literacy, 9*(2), 211–233. doi:10.1177/1468798409105587

Foley, B.E. & Pollatsek, A. (1999). Phonological processing and reading abilities in adolescents and adults with severe congenital speech impairments. *Augmentative and Alternative Communication, 15*(3), 156–173. doi:10.1080/07434619912331278695

Gibson-Langford, L. & Laycock, D. (2008). The archery of reading. *Access, 22*(2), 9–13. Retrieved from www.asla.org.au/publications/access.aspx

Gillon, G. (2005). Facilitating phoneme awareness development in 3- and 4-year-old children with speech impairment. *Language, Speech and Hearing Services in Schools, 36*(4), 308–324. doi:10.1044/0161-1461(2005/031)

Gioia, B., Johnston, P. & Cooper, L.G. (2001). Documenting and developing literacy in deaf children. *Literacy Teaching and Learning, 6*(1), 1–22. Retrieved from www.readingrecovery.org/rrcna/journals/ltl/index.asp

Groen, M.A., Laws, G., Nation, K. & Bishop, D.V. (2006). A case of exceptional reading accuracy in a child with Down syndrome—Underlying skills and the relation to reading comprehension. *Cognitive Neuropsychology, 23*(8), 1190–1214. doi:10.1080/02643290600787721

Hetzroni, O.E. (2004). AAC and literacy. *Disability & Rehabilitation, 26*(21/22), 1305–1312. doi:10.1080/09638280412331280334

Heller, K.W. & Coleman-Martin, M.B. (2007). Strategies for promoting literacy for students who have physical disabilities. *Communication Disorders Quarterly,* 28(2), 69–72. doi:10.1177/15257401070280020701

Hulme, C. & Snowling, M.J. (1992). Deficits in output phonology: A cause of reading failure? *Cognitive Neuropsychology, 9*(1), 47–72. doi:10.1080/02643299208252052

Hyun, E. & Marshall, J.D. (2003). Teachable-moment-oriented curriculum practice in early childhood education. *Journal of Curriculum Studies, 35*(1), 111–127. doi:10.1080/00220270210125583

Iacono, T. & Cupples, L. (2004). Assessment of phonemic awareness and word reading skills of people with complex communication needs. *Journal of Speech, Language and Hearing Research, 47*(2), 437–449. doi:10.1044/1092-4388(2004/035)

Johnston, S.S., McDonnell, A.P. & Hawken, L.S. (2008). Enhancing outcomes in early literacy for young children with disabilities: Strategies for success. *Intervention in School & Clinic, 43*(4), 210–217. doi:10.1177/1053451207310342

Justice, L.M. & Pullen, P.C. (2003). Promising interventions for promoting emergent literacy skills. *Topics in Early Childhood Special Education, 23*(3), 99–113. doi:10.1177/02711214030230030101

Katims, D.S. (2000). Literacy instruction for people with mental retardation: Historical highlights and contemporary analysis. *Education and Training in Mental Retardation and Developmental Disabilities,* 35, 3–15. Retrieved from www.cec.sped.org

Kay-Raining Bird, E.K., Cleave, P.L. & McConnell, L. (2000). Reading and phonological awareness in children with Down syndrome: A longitudinal study. *American Journal of Speech-Language Pathology, 9*(4), 319–330. Retrieved from http://ajslp.asha.org

Kliewer, C. (2008). *Seeing all kids as readers: A new vision for literacy in the inclusive early childhood classroom.* Baltimore: Paul H. Brookes Publishing Co.

Kliewer, C. & Biklen, D. (2001). 'School's not really a place for reading': A research synthesis of the literate lives of students with severe disabilities. *Journal of the Association for Persons with Severe Disabilities, 26*(1), 1–12. doi:10.2511/rpsd.26.1.1

Kliewer, C., Biklen, D. & Kasa-Hendrickson, C. (2006). Who may be literate? Disability and resistance to the cultural denial of competence. *American Educational Research Journal, 43*(2), 163–192. doi:10.3102/00028312043002163

Kliewer, C. & Landis, D. (1999). Individualizing literacy instruction for young children with moderate to severe disabilities. *Exceptional Children, 66*(1), 85–100. Retrieved from http://journals.cec.sped.org/ec/

Koppenhaver, D.A. & Erickson, K.A. (2003). Natural emergent literacy supports for preschoolers with autism and severe communication impairments. *Topics in Language Disorders, 23*(4), 283–292. doi:10.1097/00011363-200310000-00004

Light, J. & McNaughton, D. (2013). Literacy intervention for individuals with complex communication needs. In D.R. Beukelman & P. Mirenda (Eds), *Augmentative and alternative communication: Supporting children and adults with complex communication needs* (4th edn), (pp.309–352). Baltimore: Paul H. Brookes Publishing Co.

Light, J., McNaughton, D., Weyer, M. & Karg, L. (2008). Evidence-based literacy instruction for individuals who require augmentative and alternative communication: A case study of a student with multiple disabilities. *Seminars in Speech & Language, 29*(2), 120–132. doi:10.1055/s-2008-1079126

Mirenda, P. (2003). 'He's not really a reader': Perspectives on supporting literacy development in individuals with autism. *Topics in Language Disorders, 23*(4), 271–282. doi:10.1097/00011363-200310000-00003

Mol, S.E. & Bus, A.G. (2011). To read or not to read: A meta-analysis of print exposure from infancy to early adulthood. *Psychological Bulletin, 137*(2), 267–296. doi:10.1037/a0021890

Myers, C. (2007). 'Please listen, it's my turn': Instructional approaches, curricula and contexts for supporting communication and increasing access to inclusion. *Journal of Intellectual & Developmental Disability, 32*(4), 263–278. doi:10.1080/13668250701693910

National Institute of Child Health and Human Development (NICHHD). (2000). *Report of the National Reading Panel: Teaching children to read.* Retrieved from www.nichd.nih.gov/publications/nrp/smallbook.cfm

O'Sullivan, O. & McGonigle, S. (2010). Transforming readers: Teachers and children in the centre for literacy in primary education power of reading project. *Literacy, 44*(2), 51–59. doi:10.1111/j.1741-4369.2010.00555.x

Pierce, P. (2006). High expectations for language and literacy with infants and toddlers who have significant disabilities. In S. Rosenkoetter & J. Knapp-Philo (Eds), *Learning to read the world: Language and literacy in the first three years* (pp.335–352). Washington, D.C.: Zero to Three.

Ricci, L. (2011). Home literacy environments, interest in reading and emergent literacy skills of children with Down syndrome versus typical children. *Journal of Intellectual Disability Research, 55*(6), 596–609. doi:10.1111/j.1365-2788.2011.01415.x

Rose, J. (2006). *Independent review of the teaching of early reading.* Department for Education and Skills, United Kingdom. Retrieved from www.teachfind.com/national-strategies/independent-review-teaching-early-reading-march-2006

Smith, J.K., Smith, L.F., Gilmore, A. & Jameson, M. (2012). Students' self-perception of reading ability, enjoyment of reading and reading achievement. *Learning and Individual Differences, 22*(2), 202–206. doi:10.1016/j.lindif.2011.04.010

Snow, C.E. & Juel, C. (2005). Teaching children to read: What do we know about how to do it? In M.J. Snowling & C. Hulme (Eds) *The science of reading: A handbook* (pp.501–520). Oxford, United Kingdom: Blackwell.

Swan, D. & Goswami, U. (1997). Phonological awareness deficits in developmental dyslexia and the phonological representations hypothesis. *Journal of Experimental Child Psychology, 66*(1), 18–41. doi:10.1006/jecp.1997.2375

Swanson, E., Vaughn, S., Wanzek, J., Petscher, Y., Heckert, J., Cavanaugh, C., Kraft, G. & Tackett, K. (2011). A synthesis of read-aloud interventions on early reading outcomes among preschool through third graders at risk for reading difficulties. *Journal of Learning Disabilities, 44*(2), 258–275. doi:10.1177/0022219410378444

United Nations Committee on Children's Rights. (1989). *United Nations Convention on the Rights of the Child.* Retrieved from www.ohchr.org/en/professionalinterest/pages/crc.aspx

United Nations Committee on the Rights of Persons with Disabilities. (2006). *United Nations Convention on the Rights of Persons with Disabilities.* Retrieved from www.un.org/disabilities/convention/conventionfull.shtml

Whalon, K.J., Al Otaiba, S. & Delano, M.E. (2009). Evidence-based reading instruction for individuals with autism spectrum disorders. *Focus on Autism & Other Developmental Disabilities 24*(1), 3–16. doi:10.1177/1088357608328515

# 19 Inclusive Early Numeracy Experiences

*Rhonda Faragher*

CHAPTER OVERVIEW

This chapter asserts that mathematics education is fundamental to inclusion in society, and that effective education practice in the early years forms the basis for lifelong access to mathematics.

Learning goals for this chapter include:

- Understanding mathematics for all, taking a rights perspective on access;
- Being aware of some misconceptions that lead to exclusion from mathematics;
- Understanding challenges to learning mathematics;
- Knowing about inclusive mathematics teaching practices;
- Appreciating the implications for professionals and paraprofessionals in early years settings, and for working with families.

KEY TERMS AND CONCEPTS

attribute
enabling prompts
extending prompts
numeracy
subitising

# Introduction

The early years are a time of wonder and delight in the world around us. Mathematics is one of many ways to come to understand and make sense of our world. Consider the activities listed in the box below and reflect on the mathematics involved.

## MATHEMATICS WAITING TO BE EXPLORED

Jigsaw puzzles; water play; measuring; counting beads; dice; stacking cups; singing; books e.g. 'Going on a Bear Hunt' (Rosen & Oxenbury, 1989); leaf pictogram; painting; box construction

Mathematics is more than learning to count, much more than learning tables, even more than calculation. Mathematics is a rich discipline comprising many sub-fields. In Australia, the mathematics curriculum has been organised into three strands: Measurement and Geometry; Number and Algebra; and Probability and Statistics (Australian Curriculum Assessment & Reporting Authority [ACARA], 2010). Children begin their understanding of each of these very early in life. The *Early Years Learning Framework for Australia* (Department of Education Employment & Workplace Relations [DEEWR], 2009) provides an indication of where and how the development of mathematics might be encouraged in the education of young children. As confident and involved learners in a variety of

**FIGURE 19.1** BUILDING TOWERS

*Photo: Dinah Cocksedge*

settings, and especially through play, children establish the patterns for lifelong enjoyment and accomplishment of mathematics.

Common activities from early years settings listed in the box below are full of mathematics and, through play, children develop some of the fundamental concepts of the discipline. In Table 19.1, activities and the mathematics topics they can include are listed. Note that the activities themselves do not teach mathematics. Through awareness of the inherent mathematics, teachers and parents can guide young learners to attend to aspects of the activity that will develop their mathematics understanding. For example, cooking on its own does not teach mathematics. A teacher may teach mathematics through cooking by drawing the attention of children to explicit counting, measuring and geometry (e.g. shapes of biscuits) as they arise in the activity.

**attribute:** A characteristic of an object that can be measured, e.g. length, mass, colour.

**subitising:** The process of recognising the number of objects in a group without counting them. (From the Italian word *subito*, meaning 'suddenly'.)

**TABLE 19.1** EXAMPLES OF MATHEMATICS IN PLAY

| Mathematics Strand | Activity | Topics |
|---|---|---|
| Geometry | Jigsaws | Orientation of objects in space |
| | Stacking cups | **Attribute**, shape, location |
| | Box construction | Properties of three-dimensional shapes |
| | Children's books | Language of location, attributes (e.g. colour) |
| Measurement | Cooking | Using scales, units of measurement, temperature |
| | Water play | Capacity, attribute, conservation of volume |
| | Craft | Identification of attributes such as colour, shape, size, texture |
| Number | Counting songs | Counting forward, backwards, count word sequence |
| | Board games | Counting in ones, skip counting, **subitising** (e.g. recognising the numbers on dice without counting) |
| | Cooking | Fractions, reading scales |
| Algebra | Pattern blocks | Making and extending patterns |

*(Continued)*

**TABLE 19.1** EXAMPLES OF MATHEMATICS IN PLAY (*CONTINUED*)

| Mathematics Strand | Activity | Topics |
|---|---|---|
| | Stamp pads | Making and extending patterns |
| | Bead making | Making and extending patterns |
| Statistics & Probability | Pictograms | Data analysis |
| | Board games | Likelihood of results |

Mathematics is a part of the early years. This chapter will explore issues of inclusion in mathematics and provides strategies to allow access for all learners to the joys of mathematics that can continue throughout the lifespan.

## Mathematics education is a human right!

The sheer joy of doing mathematics—exploring, visualising, conjecturing—is known to many. Far from the routine of exercises some remember from school, mathematics is a dynamic, creative field of human endeavour that has been at the heart of developments of civilisation across cultures and throughout history (Mankiewicz, 2000). The opportunity to learn mathematics enables people to be part of an important human activity and experience enjoyment and fulfilment in the process. In addition, mathematics is essential to inclusion in a society that is increasingly quantitative (Steen, 2001).

More generally, as discussed elsewhere in this book, education is a fundamental human right, recognised in the United Nations *Universal Declaration of Human Rights* (1948) (Article 26) and the United Nations *Convention on the Rights of Persons with Disabilities* (2006) (Article 24). The opportunity to learn mathematics should be part of that education as it underpins the development of numeracy (Council of Australian Governments Human Capital Working Group, 2008), which in turn contributes to a person's quality of life (Faragher & Brown, 2005). **Numeracy** is the application of mathematics in contexts of life. The more mathematics a person has accomplished, the more they will be able to apply in life contexts.

**numeracy:** The *use* of mathematics in the contexts of daily life.

Unfortunately, the study of mathematics beyond basic skills is often neglected for students with disabilities and intellectual impairments in particular. Indeed, it was once believed that some students were incapable of learning mathematics (a position challenged by Rynders & Horrobin, 1990). In more recent times, research evidence is emerging that indicates learners with intellectual impairments can not only be successful at elementary arithmetic but also can achieve success with learning sophisticated mathematics at the secondary school level (Faragher, 2014; Monari Martinez, 1998; Monari Martinez & Benedetti, 2011). As we will see, there is no justification for limiting access to the study of mathematics by learners with disabilities; on the contrary, it is the right of learners to be supported to continue learning mathematics across the lifespan.

**CRITICAL REFLECTION QUESTIONS**

1. Do you agree that mathematics education is a fundamental human right?
2. Does everyone need mathematics? Why?

# Misconceptions of mathematics

Not all learners have access to a rich experience of mathematics education. Exclusion can arise from misconceptions about the nature of mathematics and how it is learned.

## THE MYTH OF ABILITY

An enduring myth of mathematics education is the view that some learners can do mathematics while others cannot (Mighton, 2003). There is no evidence at all for a 'mathematical brain' that some are born with and others are not (Dehaene, 2011). All learners, without exception, are able to learn mathematics and we can all learn to do mathematics better. It is indeed the case that some learners appear to acquire mathematics concepts effortlessly while others require explicit, carefully structured teaching. In some cases, this may be due to brain injury or dysfunction (dyscalculia) or differences in brain development. More commonly, mathematics learning difficulties can be attributed to *learned* difficulties. In the past, students may have been described as lacking ability to learn mathematics whereas more recent research has identified many possible factors that may make learning mathematics more difficult for some students. Faragher (2011, p.144) lists these as:

~ Beliefs learners hold about themselves as learners and beliefs teachers hold about learners (Rosenthal & Jacobsen, 1969)

- ~ Socio-economic status (Dowling, 1998; Emerson, Graham, McCulloch, Blacher, Hatton & Llewellyn, 2008) and power relations (Diversity in Mathematics Education Center for Learning and Teaching, 2007)
- ~ Type of mathematics activity (particularly influencing gender differences) (Boaler, 1997; Burton, 1995; Vale, 2002)
- ~ School structures and groupings, e.g. streaming (Linchevski & Kutscher, 1998; Zevenbergen, 2005)

In the early years, it is critical that teachers communicate (in action as well as words) to young learners and their parents that mathematics is an important area of human endeavour and that all can enjoy learning the discipline. One of the principles underlying the *Early Years Learning Framework for Australia* is the importance of high expectations: 'Children progress well when they, their parents and educators hold high expectations for their achievement in learning' (DEEWR, 2009, p.12). When students have difficulties learning mathematics, the challenge is for the teacher to find ways of teaching concepts to achieve understanding.

**CRITICAL REFLECTION QUESTION**

Do you believe that all learners can learn mathematics? What were your experiences? If you had difficulties, have you been encouraged to understand that you may not have been taught in a way that helped you learn?

## GENDER DIFFERENCES

A persistent misconception is that boys are more likely to be good at mathematics than girls. This was the prevailing view until the latter part of the twentieth century, when feminist scholarship in the early 1980s led to a change in thinking from 'What's wrong with the girls?' to 'What's wrong with the curriculum?' (Forgasz, Leder & Vale, 2000). Position statements, such as that by the Australian Association of Mathematics Teachers (AAMT, 1990), led to changes in the way mathematics was presented in textbooks and other curriculum material. There was a greater understanding about teaching methods that led to the exclusion and alienation of girls. Particularly damning was research indicating that most students seem to dislike studying mathematics in secondary school, however, it was more socially acceptable for girls to withdraw or take lower level mathematics than it was for boys.

For the next twenty years, Australia made steady progress in the attainment of mathematics by girls as measured on international tests such as the Trends In Mathematical And Science Study (TIMSS) and the Program For International

Student Assessment (PISA). Unfortunately, in recent testing, the gains appear to have been lost (Forgasz & Hill, 2013). It would appear necessary to revisit the strategies that have proved successful in supporting the learning of girls. These include 'collaborative learning, discussion in small and whole-class groups, using applications of mathematics to social contexts, making contexts clear ... and including contexts that would appeal to girls and boys' (Faragher, 2011, pp.156–157).

Teachers and parents are very influential in the formation of learners' attitudes about mathematics. It is critical that all who teach young children are convinced that boys and girls are equally capable of being successful at learning mathematics and that they convey that belief to learners in their charge.

**FIGURE 19.2** BOX CREATIONS

*Photo: Kathy Cologon*

## CULTURAL ASSUMPTIONS

Cultural differences have intrigued mathematics education researchers (Nunes, 1992). We can learn much from studying how mathematics is learnt around the world and fascinating research exists from countries such as the Netherlands (especially from the Freudental Institute) (Freudenthal, 1991, van den Heuvel-Panhuizen, 2012), Germany, Japan and Singapore (Clarke, Keitel & Shimizu, 2006, Ng & Lee, 2009), in addition to English speaking countries to where Australians have traditionally referred.

In recent years, considerable interest has focused on Indigenous Australians' learning of mathematics. Early writers observed that some Aboriginal languages did not have counting words and from that assumed that mathematics was not developed, or perhaps was even impossible to learn in those cultures. Unfortunately, that myth persists and indicates a grave misconception about the nature of mathematics in general and in Indigenous cultures in particular. Mathematics is more than number, as we have already noted. Researchers with a richer view of mathematics (Harris, 1980; Jones, Kershaw & Sparrow, 1995) have identified and described the way mathematics is understood and practised in tribal Indigenous Australian cultures.

Ethnomathematics is a branch of mathematics education research that studies the way mathematics is understood and learnt in non-Western cultures. In appreciating the cultural basis of mathematics, it is easier to value the potential for learners from culturally and linguistically diverse groups when we are teaching.

With young children, it is important to focus on vocabulary when introducing new concepts in mathematics. It is also critical to value the mathematics and ways of learning of students from diverse cultural groups. Seeking advice from community elders or cultural groups is likely to be useful. Recognising there are differences in learning encourages sensitivity.

---

## GEOMETRY IN ABORIGINAL CULTURE

Spatial awareness and location are important aspects of geometry. Harris (1980) cited a dramatic description of the ability of Australian Aboriginal hunters to keep track of their origin (such as their vehicle) while chasing a kangaroo. This directional ability is based around a compass and rather than using left or right, directions are given as compass points. Left and right are not as practical and depend on the frame of reference—is it my left or your left?

All children can learn to follow direction by compass points. Young Aboriginal children are reported to learn these words while their parents are still carrying them. For those of us who have not grown up being taught in this manner, thinking of direction in this way can be very challenging. It is possible to retrain ourselves. Practise by regularly finding north. When driving, rather than thinking, 'left turn', challenge yourself to determine the compass direction. Visualise a street directory with north facing up.

---

**CRITICAL REFLECTION QUESTIONS**

Are you convinced that there are cultural differences in learning and doing mathematics? Do you believe there is a perception that some cultural groups are more able at mathematics than others? How could you counter these opinions?

## Inclusive mathematics teaching practices

Young children learn a great deal from each other, as well as their teachers. When children are surrounded by classmates who have something to teach them they are likely to thrive. Research in the field of mathematics education has indicated the importance of the opportunity to learn mathematics from other children in the class. In the past, many classrooms featured children learning mathematics in isolation and silence. With the development of theories of social constructivism such as by Vygotsky and Cobb (Beswick, 2011; Cobb, 1994) came changes in our understanding of how learners best learn mathematics. According to these theories, learners actively construct their knowledge from interacting with their world. Vygotsky was central to identifying the important role of others in learning. These theories have been moulded with research about how mathematicians work (Schoenfeld, 1992). Mathematicians actively engage in problem solving, often in collaboration with colleagues. As a result, approaches to teaching mathematics in schools over the last half century have focused on explicit teaching of problem solving in collaborative classrooms where learners engage in communities of practice.

For many children, the early years in school are a time of coming to understand the world of the classroom. This is a new social setting and for those of us who can hardly remember a time when we have not been in a classroom, it can be difficult to understand just how much there is to learn about how to behave and interact. When teaching children who abscond from the classroom or leave activities within the room, it can seem they would be better served by learning in other settings. However, there is a great deal to be gained from patiently persisting with encouraging children to learn in inclusive settings. Young children learn from copying others. As they grow older, if they have been supported to understand the expectations of the classroom, they need less and less focus on behaviour modification and more attention can be directed towards learning.

Many parents and teachers may be concerned that learners who do not acquire key mathematics concepts in the early years will never be able to progress in later years. This view can lead teachers to become very anxious about learners who do not appear to be engaging with classroom activities and to consider alternative settings, including special schooling. Fortunately, recent research suggests these concerns may be unfounded. Evidence is mounting that learners, regardless of prior experiences, can engage with year level content (the curriculum set for the school year level) that has been modified as required (Browder & Spooner, 2006; Faragher, 2014).

## CASE STUDY 19.1

### Catching the maths in the moment

The powerful role of inclusive mathematics education was seen in a case study documented by Clarke and Faragher (2004). The teacher and her preschool class, including children with complex needs, were part of a larger research study exploring effective numeracy teaching in the early years of schooling. The project had identified a sample of teachers who were demonstrably effective, as defined by the growth in mathematics achievement of their students. The case study aimed to identify practices that were contributing to the effectiveness of the teacher.

I observed the teacher for a day as she taught her young children. At the end of the first session, we walked together to the staffroom and she apologised for not having done any mathematics. What she meant was that disruptions had prevented her from teaching the mathematics lesson she had planned. What struck me, though, was how much vicarious mathematics had been taught.

The teacher was able to 'catch the maths in the moment'. Her focus with her young students was to help them learn the procedures of a classroom. The morning session involved mat time, where the children were encouraged to sit in a semicircle around the teacher while they talked about the calendar, the day's activities and so forth. The teacher awarded a star for the child who behaved the most appropriately during mat time. This common activity was turned into a powerful opportunity to reinforce important mathematics concepts in the early years by the introduction of a simple rule written at the top of the star chart: '5 stars = a prize'. The teacher knew that 'benchmarks to five' is a key concept in the early childhood mathematics curriculum. The children day after day were working out how many more stars they needed to win a prize. This chart also provided an opportunity for the children to practise counting—some in ones and one of the more advanced children in fives. The teacher knew the mathematical development of her students and was able to ask targeted questions to the children. The learners who were still learning to count by ones were able to see modelled a faster way to count, even though they could not do this themselves as yet.

### ENGAGING WITH YEAR LEVEL CURRICULUM

Mathematics has been regarded as hierarchical but this is not necessarily the case.

1. Consider a topic, for example, operating with negative numbers. What are the prerequisite knowledge and skills a student needs?

2. What supports would be required (include the use of a calculator) for a learner who does not have these prerequisites?
3. Which of these prerequisites might be learned along with new material?

Answer these questions before reading on.

Negative numbers are an extension of the number line. Adults with robust number sense have an intact mental number line that indicates the relative position of any number. The more mathematics a person does, the more numbers that become incorporated into their mental number line. Learners need an awareness of the relative position of numbers, including zero. Let us consider a learner in the early secondary years who has not mastered calculation with whole numbers (zero and positive counting numbers). Learners can be introduced to operating with negative numbers and in the process can learn or reinforce their understanding of whole numbers.

Suppose we wish them to learn to add and subtract positive or negative integers. An example could be -3 + 4.

One approach could be:

- Have a number line constructed on card and laminated. This could range from -10 to 10.
- Teach students to find the first number and, using a green whiteboard marker, draw a starting dot at -3 on the number line.
- + Means 'move to the right'.
- Count together and at the same time, draw 4 jumps along the number line (remember you are counting the jumps, not the numbers). In our example, you would end at +1.
- With a red whiteboard marker, draw a finishing dot at +1.
- Write down the answer.

The same approach can be used to revise simple whole number additions such as 6+2.

Another approach uses a calculator. Calculators should be used in conjunction with number lines. Use a scientific calculator where possible. Note that most scientific calculators distinguish between minus and negative. 'Negative' can be thought of as an adjective. It describes the number, so negative 3 is the number located 3 places to the left of the zero. The symbol is a superscript. In contrast, 'minus' is a verb. It indicates an operation on a number. The symbol for 'minus' is written in the centre of the space.

To enter -3 + 4 on a scientific calculator, keystrokes could be +/- 3 + 4 =. The model's manual (usually on the internet if it has been misplaced) will give required steps.

---

# Teaching aspects of the mathematics curriculum

Some years ago now, when my daughter was born with Down syndrome, I went searching for the way to teach her mathematics. I was looking for the special trick or technique that I was sure was out there. Perhaps I should not have been surprised to learn it did not exist. There is no 'one right way' to teach or learn mathematics. All learners need many different approaches. The more connections we have, the more we understand concepts and so teachers need to have a repertoire of techniques and strategies for any mathematics topic. Many books are available that provide strategies for teaching mathematics to learners in the early childhood and primary years (see for example, Siemon et al., 2011; Van de Walle, 2004). Using a range of approaches based on the techniques found helpful for children in general, will assist those with mathematics learning difficulties. In addition, we do know that learning mathematics is more effective if the following principles are followed:

- Use a variety of senses in demonstrating concepts. In particular, identify opportunities to focus on visual representations. Many children with intellectual disabilities find auditory communication a relative weakness. This can be due to the additional presence of a hearing impairment or working memory limitations, which rely on auditory input. Visual representations can include printed words and symbols and not just pictures.
- Provide opportunities for learners to communicate their understanding. This can take many forms such as symbols, number lines showing calculation paths (see the box above), a sentence written by them in a reflection book (or recorded by an assistant) or a short video clip taken as they work. These records can then be used to reinforce concepts and understanding as well as serving to communicate with families.
- Focus on the 'big ideas' of the discipline. Syllabus documents, such as the Australian Curriculum: Mathematics, give guidance to teachers about the important concepts of the discipline across the school years. Through this, teachers are able to identify key ideas that form the basis for learning in future years, and also which topics are relatively minor and can be de-emphasised if necessary, to allow sufficient time for consolidation and practice.
- Teach understanding of 'why' rather than just 'how'. For example, if children are learning to find the area of a rectangle, they should learn not just how to apply the formula 'length x width' but also why the rule finds the area. There are many activities that they can do to understand why, including covering an area with squares and counting how many squares there are. They learn that it is easier to count how many squares across (length) and multiply that by how many rows there are (width).

- Provide opportunities for learners to solve problems. Here, problems are mathematics questions where the solution path is not already known. For example, if you already know the solution to finding the area of a rectangle, and you are asked to find the area of a rectangle with sides 12cm and 10cm, this would be an exercise for you. Alternatively, if you were asked to find how many different rectangles you could draw with an area of 120cm$^2$ and sides with whole number lengths, this may be a problem for you if you do not know the solution path to follow. Learners with intellectual disabilities tend not to be given the opportunity to undertake problem solving (Bottge, 2001; Geary, 2004) but there is evidence that they can (Sullivan, 2007; Sullivan, Mousley & Zevenbergen, 2006). Use **enabling prompts**—scaffolded support to assist learners unable to make a start or when they become stuck—and **extending prompts**—challenges to encourage learners to explore the task further.

**enabling prompts:** Involve scaffolded support to assist learners unable to make a start or when they become stuck.

**extending prompts:** Challenges to encourage learners to explore the task further.

## FOCUSING ON PROPERTIES OF SHAPES

An important concept in geometry is an appreciation that shapes are labelled according to their properties. For example, a three-sided shape with three angles is called a triangle. It does not matter what the orientation of the shape is, it is still a triangle. That means there is no such thing as an 'upside down' triangle. Initially, young children learn to label shapes by their appearance. A young child will only call a square a square when it has its base placed horizontally.

Some strategies to assist children learn to label triangles according to their properties include:

- Have many different shapes made out of different materials readily available for children to explore;
- Ensure shapes are oriented in many directions on posters or other displays, not just with the base horizontal;
- Ensure words are used to label shapes on visual displays;
- Use correct terminology when referring to shapes. Avoid 'upside down triangles', 'half a triangle';
- Trace around triangles, counting the sides as you go. Alternatively, colour the sides with different colours;
- Use pegboards and rubber bands to make different triangles. Pegboards can be made at home by hammering nails on a board to make a grid pattern. Alternatively, they are readily available from teaching supply shops;

Many children commence school with a robust understanding of the labels of simple shapes such as triangles. These children need the opportunity to extend their learning rather than just have it reinforced. They may not be aware of the importance of properties when giving a name to a shape. Teachers can use a range of shapes, including irregular ones (those where the sides are not the same length or the angles are different sizes) for the activities above. Those in the class who know labels for simple shapes such as triangles and squares can be introduced to more complex shapes such as trapeziums or hexagons while other learners can be investigating the concepts using simpler shapes.

**FIGURE 19.3** SHAPE, LIGHT AND COLOUR

*Photo: Kathy Cologon*

## Assessing learning in mathematics

Australian mathematics education in recent years has seen a great interest in assessing development of mathematics concepts in the early years. A number of researchers have developed task-based interviews to assess learning (Bobis et al., 2005). An example is the Early Numeracy Interview developed in Victoria. This assessment follows a protocol where the interviewer (usually the class teacher) follows a script and asks a child a series of increasingly difficult questions. Once the child is unsuccessful, the interviewer asks no further questions in that series, instead moving to a new area. Teachers can gain a very rich understanding of the development of the child and their mathematical reasoning underlying their responses. Importantly, teachers are able to determine what is needed to assist learners to move to the next stage of development of the concepts. As discussed elsewhere in this book (for example in Chapters 11, 17, 21 and 25), observation and naturalistic assessment are key to supporting learning.

For learners with specific learning difficulties, there can be value in assessments being undertaken by psychologists who may be able to identify the cause of learning difficulties as well as offering suggestions for supporting a learner in their development. For day to day learning, however, it is very important for the class teacher to undertake assessment of learning. This is the case for the previously discussed task-based mathematics interviews. Through sitting with a child, watching them and listening to their explanations, the

**FIGURE 19.4** ART IN MATHS!

*Artwork by Kaitlyn*

teacher gains considerable insight into the understandings of the learner as well as the learner's misconceptions. Strategic planning can then focus lessons on countering misconceptions and moving learners to next stages.

Assessment of and for learning is an important part of a teacher's work. It is essential for informing parents and subsequent teachers. Families of children in the early years should be provided with descriptions of what their child can do, what they are working on and where they are headed next with respect to mathematics. Numerical or letter grades are less helpful and can detract from the verbal description.

## Implications for professionals and paraprofessionals in early years settings

The early years sets the path for education across the lifespan. Educators in this context have a critical role in establishing effective patterns for the learning of mathematics through school and beyond. This is a daunting responsibility, but there are some fairly straightforward and easily established principles, which are discussed below.

*All early years educators need a positive outlook,* with a belief that all learners can and should learn mathematics. Sometimes educators must challenge parents who were not successful with mathematics when they were at school and who assume their child will also not succeed. Children are most likely to be successful if they are surrounded by adults who expect them to enjoy mathematics and to do well at its study.

*Active planning to include all learners* is essential. When I began teaching, I was told to 'teach to the middle'. This was hardly helpful advice. On the other hand, it is not possible to prepare individual lessons for all the children in every class. Differentiation of the program is what is required. Finding good open-ended tasks and then planning enabling and extending prompts is critical for good planning for inclusive classrooms (an excellent source of mathematics problems can be found in Downton, Knight, Clarke & Lewis, 2006).

*Good teaching and the right support will enhance the learning of all students.* Accommodations made are likely to assist many learners in the class. As teachers become more experienced, they build a resource collection of lessons and ideas that can be reused. When faced with planning adjustments for a learner, it is helpful to consider other learners in the class who may also benefit. All of us need more than one way to understand a concept.

*Involvement of paraprofessionals in planning* helps build a team approach and ensures that consistent teaching occurs. Explanation of concepts in the planning stage should be undertaken to ensure all in the teaching team have clarified any misconceptions and all are aware of key points for learners and likely areas of difficulty.

*Involvement of paraprofessionals in mathematics lessons* can be very effective, although responsibility for the learning of the children in the class remains with the professional teacher who may use additional classroom assistance in a variety of ways. Under the direction of the class teacher, paraprofessionals who have been involved in the planning process may work with small groups, including students requiring additional challenge and stimulation, as well as those having difficulty learning. Sometimes, they may supervise the majority of the class, allowing the class teacher to work with a small group, perhaps undertaking task-based assessments. Over support of children is to be avoided (Giangreco, Edelman, Luiselli, & MacFarland, 1997).

## Implications for working with families

Other chapters in this book provide detailed guidance for early years educators when working with families (see Chapters 5 and 9). When considering mathematics education, some additional factors may exist. Some parents may have had a negative schooling experience, particularly with mathematics, and this can have a significant impact on their views of how effective they feel they can be in supporting their child's learning. Many will feel much more confident with literacy, particularly reading stories, than they do with supporting mathematics learning. Early years educators can assist by providing examples of what parents can do. A series of pamphlets have been produced by the New South Wales Department of Education and Communities and are available for free download from the Department's website (see the websites section at the end of this chapter). Some schools have run parent nights where they have demonstrated approaches to teaching and offered suggestions for parents to help their children (Clarke, Faragher & Gaffney, in press).

Parents often take the role of 'case-managers' and may be able to provide invaluable information about how their child learns and what they have already accomplished. Providing opportunities to keep parents up to date with what is being taught in the classroom can allow parents to reinforce concepts at home. A brief email at the end of the day or on a Friday afternoon about what has been covered and what is coming up can be very appreciated by parents.

**CASE STUDY 19.2**

## Communicating with families

Recently I was asked by a school in a remote centre to provide assistance to staff teaching a young girl with an intellectual disability. The teachers were particularly concerned that the mother did not seem to have a lot of contact with the school and they felt she was not accessing support, which could assist her parenting.

It was fortuitous that on the day of my visit to the school, the mother was attending the community breakfast barbeque. A short mother-to-mother conversation revealed she was very much supported, but through the internet rather than the school. For whatever reason, communication with the school had become limited and the teachers drastically underestimated the extent of information the mother had about her daughter's disability and how to help her learn.

Good communication between parents and schools is vital. Many parents can be particularly fearful of mathematics. As for any relationship, if problems with communication arise, all efforts need to be expended to remediate the situation. This could involve trying alternative approaches, such as casual conversations at community barbeques, or sending emails or photographs home, ensuring positive events are depicted. Sometimes it might be necessary to change the staff members making contact with the parents. Also, it could be useful to review the communication approaches previously made. The relationship is likely to be strained if contact with parents has been limited to advising of the child's shortcomings, or problems. Look for ways to communicate to parents that indicates their child is appreciated and welcome.

**CRITICAL REFLECTION QUESTIONS**

1. What does your personal experience allow you to bring to the inclusion of young children in mathematics classrooms?
2. What strategies have you experienced that have been used to restore relationships when communication has broken down?

*Rhonda Faragher*

## Conclusion

This chapter has introduced readers to the important role of early years professionals and paraprofessionals in establishing inclusive mathematics education. A lifelong love of mathematics can be fostered in the early years of a child's life, building on a natural interest in exploring a fascinating world. All learners—especially those with intellectual disabilities—have a right to engage with rich mathematics. Inclusive mathematics education practices rely on an ability to adjust teaching for the needs of learners. In this chapter, it has been argued that mathematics is accessible to all through the use of strategies that have been shown to be effective, such as the use of enabling and extending prompts. Surely one of the most rewarding experiences for a teacher is being able to see a child learn mathematics as a result of adjustments they have made. May you experience that reward!

# FOR FURTHER REFLECTION

1. What is the purpose of mathematics education? Explain the connection between mathematics, numeracy and the importance of school mathematics for lifelong quality of life.
2. List some strategies that are helpful for enhancing the learning of mathematics by all learners. Consider strategies of use for individuals with specific needs.
3. Write a letter to a new teaching assistant that explains your approach to classroom planning, how you intend to involve the teaching assistant in the work of the classroom and your approach to working with families.

## WEBSITES

www.curriculumsupport.education.nsw.gov.au/primary/mathematics/numeracy/parents/

A website of the New South Wales Department of Education and Communities featuring a range of pamphlets for parents to help children with mathematics.

http://nrich.maths.org

A website containing a vast collection of resources for supporting the mathematical experiences of *all* learners.

http://maths300.esa.edu.au

A website with a collection of lessons across the full range of mathematics and across the year levels. Rich tasks with detailed teacher guidance offer enabling and extending prompts as well as ready-to-use lesson resources.

## REFERENCES


Australian Association of Mathematics Teachers (AAMT). (1990). *A national statement on girls and mathematics.* Adelaide: Author.

Australian Curriculum Assessment & Reporting Authority (ACARA). (2010). *The Australian curriculum: Mathematics.* Retrieved from www.australiancurriculum.edu.au/Mathematics/Rationale

Beswick, K. (2011). Learning mathematics. In D. Siemon, K. Beswick, K. Brady, J. Clark, R. Faragher & E. Warren (Eds), *Teaching mathematics. Foundations to middle years.* (pp.46–65). South Melbourne: Oxford University Press.

Bobis, J., Clarke, B., Clarke, D.M., Thomas, G., Wright, R., Young-Loveridge, J. & Gould, P. (2005). Supporting teachers in the development of young children's mathematical thinking: Three large scale cases. *Mathematics Education Research Journal, 16*(3), 27–57. doi:10.1007/BF03217400

Bottge, B.A. (2001). Reconceptualizing mathematics problem solving for low-achieving students. *Remedial and Special Education, 22*(2), 102–112. doi:10.1177/074193250102200204

Browder, D. M. & Spooner, F. (Eds). (2006). *Teaching language arts, math, & science to students with significant cognitive disabilities.* Baltimore, MA: Brookes.

Clarke, B. & Faragher, R. (2004). Possibilities not limitations: Teaching special needs children. In B. Clarke, D.M. Clarke, G. Emanuelsson, B. Johansson, D.V. Lambdin, F.K. Lester, A. Wallby & K. Wallby (Eds), *International perspectives on learning and teaching mathematics* (pp.379–394). Goteborg: National Center for Mathematics Education.

Clarke, B., Faragher, R. & Gaffney, M. (in press). Engaging school communities with numeracy. In M. Gaffney & R. Faragher (Eds), *Leading developments in student numeracy—A guide for schools and systems.* Melbourne: ACER.

Clarke, D.J., Keitel, C., & Shimizu, Y. (Eds). (2006). *Mathematics classrooms in twelve countries: The insider's perspective.* Rotterdam, The Netherlands: Sense.

Cobb, P. (1994). Where is the mind? Constructivist and sociocultural perspectives on mathematical development. *Educational Researcher, 23*(7), 13–20. doi:10.3102/0013189X023007013

Council of Australian Governments Human Capital Working Group. (2008). *National numeracy review report.* Canberra, ACT: COAG.

Dehaene, S. (2011). *The Number Sense. How the mind creates mathematics.* (Revised and Expanded edn). New York: Oxford University Press.

Department of Education, Employment and Workplace Relations (DEEWR). (2009). *Belonging, being & becoming: The early years learning framework for Australia*. Canberra ACT: Commonwealth of Australia.

Downton, A., Knight, R., Clarke, D. & Lewis, G. (2006). *Mathematics assessment for Learning: Rich tasks & work samples*. Melbourne: Mathematics Teaching and Learning Centre, Australian Catholic University.

Faragher, R. (2011). Diversity. In D. Siemon, K. Beswick, K. Brady, J. Clark, R. Faragher & E. Warren (Eds), *Teaching mathematics. Foundations to middle years.* (pp.142–165). South Melbourne: Oxford University Press.

Faragher, R. (2014). Learning mathematics in the secondary school—possibilities for students with Down syndrome. In B. Clarke & R. Faragher (Eds), *Educating learners with Down syndrome: Research and practice for children and adolescents* (pp.174–192). London, UK: Taylor Francis.

Faragher, R.M. & Brown, R.I. (2005). Numeracy for adults with Down syndrome: It's a matter of quality of life. *Journal of Intellectual Disability Research, 49*(10), 761–765. doi:10.1111/j.1365-2788.2005.00747.x

Forgasz, H. & Hill, J. (2013). Factors implicated in high mathematics achievement. *International Journal of Science and Mathematics Education, 11*(2), 481–499. doi:10.1007/s10763-012-9348-x

Forgasz, H., Leder, G.C. & Vale, C. (2000). Gender and mathematics: Changing perspectives. In K. Owens & J. Mousley (Eds.), *Mathematics education research in Australasia: 1996–1999* (pp.305–340). Turramurra, NSW: MERGA.

Freudenthal, H. (1991). *Revisiting mathematics education.* Dordrecht, The Netherlands: Kluwer.

Geary, D. C. (2004). Mathematics and learning disabilities. *Journal of Learning Disabilities, 37*(1), 4–15. doi:10.1177/00222194040370010201

Giangreco, M.F., Edelman, S.W., Luiselli, T.E. & MacFarland, S.Z.C. (1997). Helping or hovering. Effects of instructional assistant proximity on students with disabilities. *Exceptional Children, 64*(1), 7–18. Retrieved from http://journals.cec.sped.org/ec/

Harris, P. (1980). *Measurement in tribal aboriginal communities*. Darwin, NT: Northern Territory Department of Education.

Jones, K., Kershaw, L. & Sparrow, L. (1995). *Aboriginal children learning mathematics.* Perth, WA: Mathematics, Science and Technology Education Centre, Edith Cowan University.

Mankiewicz, R. (2000). *The story of mathematics*. London: Cassell.

Mighton, J. (2003). *The myth of ability.* Toronto: House of Anansi Press Inc.

Monari Martinez, E. (1998). Teenagers with Down syndrome study algebra in high school. *Down Syndrome Research and Practice, 5*(1), 34–38. doi:10.3104/case-studies.73

Monari Martinez, E. & Benedetti, N. (2011). Learning mathematics in mainstream secondary schools: Experiences of students with Down's syndrome. *European Journal of Special Needs Education, 26*(4), 531–540. doi:10.1080/08856257.2011.597179

Ng, S.F. & Lee, K. (2009). The Model Method: Singapore children's tool for representing and solving algebraic word problems. *Journal for Research in Mathematics Education, 40*(3), 282–313.

Nunes, T. (1992). Ethnomathematics and everyday cognition. In D.A. Grouws (Ed.), *Handbook of research on mathematics teaching and learning.* (pp.557–574). New York: Macmillian.

Rosen, M. & Oxenbury, H. (1989). *We're going on a bear hunt.* New York: Margaret K. McElderry Books.

Rynders, J. & Horrobin, J. (1990). Always trainable? Never educable? Updating educational expectations concerning children with Down's syndrome. *American Journal on Mental Retardation, 95*, 77–83. Retrieved from http://aaiddjournals.org/loi/ajmr.1

Schoenfeld, A.H. (1992). Learning to think mathematically: Problem solving, metacognition, and sense making in mathematics. In D.A. Grouws (Ed.), *Handbook of research on mathematics teaching and learning.* (pp.334–370). New York: Macmillan.

Siemon, D., Beswick, K., Brady, K., Clark, J., Faragher, R. & Warren, E. (Eds). (2011). *Teaching mathematics. Foundations to middle years*. Melbourne, Vic: Oxford University Press.

Steen, L.A. (Ed.). (2001). *Mathematics and democracy. The case for quantitative literacy.* National Council on Education and the Disciplines. Retrieved from www.maa.org/sites/default/files/pdf/QL/MathAndDemocracy.pdf

Sullivan, P. (2007). Teaching mixed ability mathematics classes. In S. Close, D. Corcoran & T. Dooley (Eds), *Proceedings of second national conference on research in mathematics education.* (pp.372–383). Dublin: MEI2.

Sullivan, P., Mousley, J. & Zevenbergen, R. (2006). Teacher actions to maximize mathematics learning opportunities in heterogeneous classrooms. *International Journal of Science and Mathematics Education, 4*, 117–143. doi:10.1007/s10763-005-9002-y

United Nations. (2006). *Convention of the rights of persons with disabilities*. Retrieved from: www.un.org/disabilities/convention/conventionfull.shtml

United Nations. (1948). *Universal Declaration of Human Rights*. Retrieved from: www.un.org/en/documents/udhr/

van den Heuvel-Panhuizen, M. (2012). Forty years of working on mathematics education, seeing mathematics as a human activity for all—The Freudenthal Institute. In International Group of Experts on Science and Mathematics Education Policies (Ed.), *Challenges in basic mathematics education* (pp.56–60). Paris: UNESCO.

Van de Walle, J.A. (2004). *Elementary and middle school mathematics: Teaching developmentally.* (5th edn). Boston, MA: Pearson.

# 20 Engaging All Children through the Arts

*Cathy Nutbrown and Peter Clough*

CHAPTER OVERVIEW

This chapter will focus on ways in which early years practitioners can support and encourage the inclusion of all young children through the arts.

Learning goals for this chapter include:

- Understanding the importance of the arts to all human beings, including all young children;
- Being aware of a framework for working in the arts with young children;
- Knowing ways of engaging young children in the arts, and about arts-based learning experiences.

KEY TERMS AND CONCEPTS

documentation

humanity

ORIM-arts framework

# Introduction

Engaging in creative arts experiences is important for the sheer joy it can bring, as well as on account of the self and shared expression that can be enabled through creative processes. Creative arts experiences have also been shown to impact on cognitive, social and emotional development. This chapter argues for, and discusses ways of, facilitating the participation of all young children (and their families) in inclusive creative arts experiences, with particular emphasis on including children who experience disablement. First we shall outline something of the importance of the arts for all people, before focusing specifically on their importance in young children's development. We shall then explain a framework, developed at the University of Sheffield, England, for working with young children in the arts. This will be followed by some rich examples of young children using the arts before we offer some suggestions for arts-based learning experiences.

In England, and many other contexts across the world, we have seen reductions in funding for the Arts, year on year, risking a narrowing of opportunity for children and their families to enjoy the arts in their leisure time. The Arts are suffering in the early years and beyond. The arts, so far as education is concerned, are often regarded with lesser value, and perhaps something to be kept for leisure time.

**humanity:** All human beings, or the quality of being human.

Our premise in this chapter is that the Arts are essential to our **humanity**, and as such should be central, not peripheral, to learning and development of people of all ages and abilities.

Cultures, communities and curricula are by definition exclusive; we know things by their characteristics and by the boundaries of those features; we group things and we group people, for example, by religion, age, geography, role; we classify and we recognise what lies outside those classifications; were we unable to exclude, we would be different kinds of beings. Cultures, then, communities and curricula are as exclusive as they are inclusive.

We have set out a series of simple theses of inclusive policies and projects. The theses are (Nutbrown & Clough, 2013, pp.7–8):

- Inclusion has an operational rather than conceptual focus.
- Inclusion is always in a 'state of becoming'.
- Inclusion can/must only be known by its outcomes, not by its rhetoric.
- There are as many versions of inclusion as there are people to be included.
- Cultures, communities and curricula are, by definition, exclusive.
- Inclusion must not be imposed from without, but developed in partnership with those who seek it.
- Inclusion is ultimately about how people treat each other.

Put simply, it is what we *do* and *how* we include that matters, and curricula—in this chapter arts curricula in particular—must be developed to include and partner with children and families who are to be included; as discussed in Chapter 1, ultimately this is about being human.

## The importance of the arts to all human beings

> Viewing the species Homo sapiens as it evolves and expresses a behaviour of art is a way of understanding ourselves and the modern condition humane (Dissanayake, 1990, p.xi).

Human beings around the world have always made art; from ancient times civilizations have left tangible traces of their own aesthetic relationship to their environments. The arts are central to human life, and people around the world draw, sing, dance and tell stories because it is part of the condition of being human (Dissanayake, 1990, 1995, 2000; Eisner, 2002), and it has long been argued that the arts can strongly influence the human affective (Charlesworth, 1982). Historically we can see this in, for example, the paintings and intricately crafted artefacts of the Minoan Empire in the temple at Knossos, Crete; the cave paintings of Chauvet-Pont-d'Arc, France; Ancient Egyptian paintings and artefacts; five thousand-year-old sculptures in the painted galleries of the Hal Saflieni Hypogeum, Malta; and the numerous depictions of the prehistoric Navajo deity Kokopelli found in thousand-year-old rock art, in the south western deserts and mountains of the USA.

All these (and so many more) depict the battles, beliefs, fears, lives and loves of their creators. Storytelling too, is essential to the human condition, and traditions of storying have evolved in every single culture as a sine qua non of its identity (the Travellers of Ireland, the Native American Indians, the Aboriginal peoples of Australia and the folk tales of Norway are just some examples from many). Stories and arts forms, often passing on traditions and advice from earlier generations, and from one generation to the next have been told throughout humanity's ages (Brown, 1991; Murdock, 1945). 'All peoples tell stories', and the passing on of those stories through oral telling, dance, music, drawings and models, down through time has been an important factor in creating and sustaining cultures, and sometimes in terms of physical survival (Sugiyama, 2001, p.235).

Discussing the innateness of the arts to human beings, Dissanayake (2001) suggests that infants are born with *aesthetic incunabula*, a sort of 'swaddling', which makes emotional effects of the arts discernible from the earliest months. The human need to seek out and organise through the aesthetic is what Clough

(2002) calls an 'aesthetic attending': the way in which, as a condition of being in the world, we attend—through the senses—to the 'objects' we encounter:

> Aesthetic attending to something is not a special or a marginal case peculiar to (self-conscious) artists, but one which can be systematically developed … because it is the very foundation of intelligence (Clough, 2002, p.85).

The youngest of human beings engage with the world first through an innate aesthetic attending, through their senses; babies are sensory beings, open to sensory exploration of everything they encounter (Goldschmeid & Jackson, 1999; Trevarthen, 1984). Therefore we can say that, from birth, we humans are 'wired' with a compulsion to seek experiences that smell, taste, feel, sound or look pleasing to us, because each of our senses craves satisfaction.

**FIGURE 20.1** PAINTING FOR PLEASURE

*Artwork by Charbel*

## The importance of the arts to all young children

Our argument in this chapter is that because human beings carry such aesthetic attending through their lives—always with the need for the sensory stimuli and satisfaction that can be found in many of the arts—then education must pay due regard to the human need, in *all* young children, for aesthetics. To satisfy this innate human condition in the early years of learning, curricula need to offer inclusive possibilities for young children, whatever their (dis)ability, to engage in and enjoy the arts. This argument is not simply an academic or historical one—as discussed throughout this book, it is also a matter of rights.

The United Nations Convention on the Rights of the Child, Article 31 states:

> ~ That every child has the right to rest and leisure, to engage in play and recreational activities appropriate to the age of the child and to participate freely in cultural life and the arts.
>
> ~ That member governments shall respect and promote the right of the child to participate fully in cultural and artistic life and shall encourage the provision of appropriate and equal opportunities for cultural, artistic, recreational and leisure activity (United Nations, 1989, n.p.).

This chapter considers how through arts-based learning experiences, young children might be better equipped 'to participate in cultural and artistic life'. Our argument is threefold: first, *all* human beings need the arts for their holistic development; second, (from an English viewpoint at least) that the value and practice of arts-based learning has yet to be widely accepted, articulated and developed in the early years; and third, arts-based learning in the early years requires a stronger conceptual basis.

> The arts and artistry as sources of improved educational practice are considered, at best, a fall-back position, a court of last resort, something you retreat to when there is no science to provide guidance (Eisner 2004, p.1).

Elliot Eisner's (2004) vision of how a pedagogy of the arts might inform education, in contrast to the 'fall-back position' as described in the quote above, offers a 'social vision of what schools can be' (p.13).

A demise of the arts in many schools (National Advisory Committee on Creative, Cultural Education [NACCCE], 1999; Chapman, 2004) has occurred in response to worries over underachievement in English and Maths (often termed 'the basics'). However, developments in Scandinavia (Barratt, 2006; Hopperstad 2008a, 2008b; Pramling Samuelsson, Carlsson, Isson, Pramling & Wallerstedt, 2009) in Northern Italy, (ReggioChildren, 1995) and in Melbourne, Australia (Deans & Brown, 2005) show how a focus on the arts can enhance children's learning both in the arts and other aspects of their development.

The work of Reggio Emilia (Filippini & Vecchi, 1996) has long demonstrated how an arts-based curriculum and the involvement of experienced artists as well as teachers, can give rise to many forms and focuses of learning in the early years, where pedagogues talk of 'special rights' not 'special needs' (for a critique of this terminology see Chapter 3) and where inclusion of all children is expected.

In Sweden, a physical environment and adult involvement stimulating and enabling children's dramatic play, has been shown to enhance young children's imaginations and involvement (Lindqvist, 2001). Studies and projects in the UK have confirmed that the youngest children can respond to, and enjoy, participation in the arts. Initiatives in art galleries and museums designed especially for young children and their parents have shown how artist involvement can open up new avenues for young children to explore and enjoy the arts (Eckhoff, 2008; Hancock & Cox, 2002; MacRae, 2007).

The importance of talk and storytelling in early years settings has been shown continually to be central to all areas of learning (Harrett, 2002; Thompson, 1990); something the ancient civilisations and indigenous communities of Australia, Ireland, New Zealand, Peru and the USA for example, have long known. Recent arts-based learning projects have shown that the involvement of artists can enhance the early years curriculum (Brown, Benedette, & Armistead, 2010, Gillespie, 2006).

The arts enhance early years curricula, not simply by promoting children's ability in traditionally established areas of learning and development but also in those lesser mentioned, but centrally important, areas of life (Dissanayake, 1990, 2000; Eisner, 2004). Young children need the arts to help them learn central lessons in life (Gardner, 1990; Eisner, 2002) such as how to communicate ideas, collaborate with others, persist with a problem, deal with disappointment, and enjoy the support of peers and adults (Nutbrown & Jones, 2006).

Seeing the possibilities of song, dance, music, drama, paint, sculpture and storytelling for enhanced teaching and learning is not new. Valuing of the aesthetic can be traced in the work of Comenius, Rousseau, Froebel and Pestalozzi, where rhyme, verse, song and storytelling were regarded as important to young children's development. Inclusion of the arts in curricula also helps young children to develop vital aesthetic tendencies, which are so much part of their humanity (Dewey, 1902; Gardner, 1989; Dissanayake, 1995; Eisner, 2002). The art forms that young children thus encounter are 'merely' more sophisticated expressions that model and gently nurture their own striving to express, showing the nascent artist how her early marks and mouldings and makings and movements rightfully belong in the cultural world in which she is taking her place as a citizen.

Therefore, we could say that children engage spontaneously in the arts because it is a most natural thing for them to do. Their *Aesthetic Incunabulae* (Dissanayake, 2001) means that to the best of their ability, babies suck, grasp, gaze, move, and babble; and many toddlers readily dance or move to music, clap to a tune and speak with unmistakeable tunefulness in their voice (Lamont, 2008; Marsh, 2004, 2010). Children do these things because there is a natural impulse to do so; they are sensory beings, and thus need to learn and grow and develop in environments that satisfy such innate desires.

On the whole, in England, young children's experiences of the arts have not been nurtured in ways that would support their art-attuned development; these have been much neglected. As far back as the 1950s Kellogg (1955) noted the way in which kindergarten teachers devalued drawing. Children's schematic developments through movement, speech and graphic representations have often been poorly nourished through a narrow curriculum where opportunities for play are limited (Nutbrown, 2006). Their opportunity to create from their own imaginations has been limited to small corners of their preschool settings known as 'the creative area' and their holistic development has often been stunted in the drive to promote literacy and numeracy to the detriment of the arts and play (Anning & Edwards, 2003).

Internationally, research into aspects of arts-based learning often focuses more specifically on the practice of elements of particular skills in the arts. In music, for example, the emphasis often is on playing an instrument or singing (Young, 2005), and developing repertoire and skill (Barrett, 2006, 2009; Young, 2008) rather than the experience and more holistic development and understanding of music per se (Young, 2008) for which we are 'wired from birth' (Trehub, 2003, p.3). We know little about the place of dance in early years curricula (Bannon & Sanderson, 2000), and the use of poetry, dance and graphic arts in the early years appear to be 'means to ends'. Such art forms are sometimes used as vehicles through which other things are taught, rather than experiences of learning in their own right (Brown et al., 2010). This is what Pramling Samuelsson et al. (2009) refer to as 'music for children' or 'children's music' rather than music integrated with other elements of the arts (Jordan-Decarbo & Nelson, 2002). Central to this chapter is how the early learning of all young children can be supported by a clear conceptualisation of their experiences of the arts. As Pramling Samuelsson et al. (2009, p.132) put it,

> The arts are foundational constituents of early schooling. They deserve to be taken seriously as forms of knowledge in themselves that children should be given opportunities for developing their knowledge of. Hence, we argue for the importance of helping children, thorough pedagogy, to develop domain-intrinsic knowing of the arts, rather than merely using the arts as means for developing art-extrinsic knowing. Learning in preschool and the first years of primary school cannot only be matters of mathematics, reading and writing. That is too limited a view of human capabilities and cultural life.

Pramling Samuelsson et al. (2009) argue that since many teachers do not themselves 'practise' any art form—be it painting, dance, making or listening attentively to music—they do not necessarily have these aspects of life experience to underpin their sharing with children. They argue that professional development is essential for teachers to teach the aesthetic arts meaningfully, in order to promote instances

> Where the arts, or aesthetics, are regarded as goals in themselves, and not just as means for something else (for example to achieve social ability or support emotional development) .... and where meta-cognitive talk is brought into a learning situation (Pramling Samuelsson et al., 2009, p.127).

**FIGURE 20.2** MAKING ART TOGETHER

## A framework for working in the arts with all young children

Pramling Samuelsson et al. (2009) focused largely on teachers' interactions with children around skills in three elements of the arts: music, dance and poetry. Writing from a Swedish perspective, they note

> The aesthetic subjects have always had a place in education for children in the early years. Teaching and learning for children in preschool, kindergarten and primary school have relied upon the creative subjects in making children aware of the world around them and of their own creative and artistic competencies—even though emergent reading, writing and mathematics have lately been seen as more important (p.119).

Pramling Samuelsson et al. (2009) argue for a theoretical framework for teaching the arts based on developmental pedagogy. They too note the lack of studies on learning music, poetry and dance in the early years and use examples of teachers creating opportunities for children to imagine to argue for the importance of 'talk' as part of their tripartite developmental pedagogy framework. MacRae (2007, p.169) argues that 'we should not be afraid to use "art language" with children, but we should not insist on pre-specified vocabulary as evidence of their knowledge.'

Nyland, Ferris and Dunn (2008) report of a music program based in the well known Early Learning Centre in Melbourne, Australia, which promotes the arts with the aim of supporting the image of the child as 'creative, capable and inquisitive'. What the Melbourne Early Learning Centre and those in Reggio Emilia offer are ideas and practices that are helpful in articulating a theoretical basis for *all* children's arts-based learning. Early years education needs a thorough conceptualisation of such an approach, and for arts-based learning opportunities to be conceptually grounded so that *all* children's learning in such contexts can flourish.

## A conceptual framework: Opportunities, Recognition, Interaction and Models

### THE ORIM-ARTS FRAMEWORK

A UK study has suggested that adults can provide four things in order to support children's development, by providing Opportunities, Recognition, Interaction and a Model for their children (Hannon, 1995; Nutbrown, Hannon & Collier 1996). Adults provide many opportunities for children to do things in everyday life, like events, materials, toys, equipment, space and time. We can see such *opportunities* as a set of 'permissions' to do things. Children need *recognition*, acknowledgment of their achievements, and adults to show recognition in many ways: praising efforts, telling others what the child has done, celebrating their successes, taking photographs, taking an interest in and displaying their work. Children need *interaction* with adults who spend time with them, supporting, explaining, endorsing, talking about what they are doing and challenging them to do more. Adults interact with children in many different ways: by talking, demonstrating, tutoring, involving children in real tasks and projects and playing games. Through such interactions adults can enable children to progress from what they can do now with help to becoming more independent in the future (Vygotsky, 1978). Adults can act as powerful *models*; children imitate what they see in everyday life. Young children learn through the adult models they see, including family members, adults in preschool, television characters and personalities.

These four adult roles (opportunities, recognition, interaction, model) were originally conceptualised in the ORIM framework, first developed in relation to parents supporting their children's early literacy development (Hannon, 1995; Hannon & Nutbrown, 1997; Nutbrown, Hannon, & Morgan, 2005). The ORIM framework has since been used in practice to support parents of young children who wanted to do more to help their young children's early literacy development.[1] By focusing on the four key roles parents can play, alongside elements of early literacy, the ORIM framework helped to make more explicit the support parents could offer their children. This framework has since been usefully adapted to focus on other aspects of learning: the training of early years practitioners, the development of self-esteem in young children and on adult community literacy (Fagan, 2000; Rigo-Toth & Ure, 2000; Roberts, 2001). Most recently, it has been adapted as a tool for arts-based learning in the early years

(Nutbrown & Jones, 2006).[2] The four adult roles that make up ORIM can be explored and exploited in relation to adult roles beyond those of the parent and in relation to the arts; combining these together with key strands of development in the arts gives the **ORIM-Arts framework**.

**FIGURE 20.3** THE ORIM-ARTS FRAMEWORK

| | | STRANDS OF DEVELOPMENT IN THE ARTS | | | |
|---|---|---|---|---|---|
| | | Materials and experiences | Imagination | Skills | Talk about the Arts |
| SETTINGS and ARTISTS | Opportunities | | | | |
| CAN | Recognition | | | | |
| PROVIDE | Interaction | | | | |
| | Model | | | | |

**ORIM-Arts framework:** Adult roles providing Opportunities, Recognition, Interaction and a Model for development in the arts.

The ORIM-Arts framework (Figure 20.3) maintains the four key adult roles, adapting them for settings and artists whereby they can provide Opportunities, Recognition, Interaction and a Model of artists and users of the arts. The four strands of the ORIM-Arts Framework focus attention on: *materials and experiences, imagination, skills*, and *'talk about the arts'. Materials and experiences* refers to the wide range of possibilities that can be offered to children—this can range from enjoying the tickle of a feather on your face to rolling in swathes of fabric, to using equipment now available through new technologies to make or respond to sound, to listening to a visiting string quartet or jazz band. *Imagination* in the ORIM framework refers to everything that can be made available to help children imagine—this might be story, music, graphic or tactile stimuli, a performance by a dancer or singer, watching an artist make his/her own work, an idea offered by a child or an adult. There are points where adults need to support children's development in specific *skills*, so that they can further develop in the arts. The extent to which skills can be nurtured and the nature of those skills will vary and the same is the case when it comes to *'talk about the arts'.* While all adults should, we argue, be using the language of the arts with the children they work with, the extent to which children are able to use this language for themselves, verbally or by signing, will vary (see Chapter 23 for an exploration of using augmentative and alternative communication to support inclusion).

Figure 20.4 shows the framework used to document some arts experiences with two- to five-year-old children.

**FIGURE 20.4** USING THE ORIM FRAMEWORK TO DOCUMENT SOME ARTS EXPERIENCES WITH 2–5 YEAR OLD CHILDREN

| | MATERIALS AND EXPERIENCES | IMAGINATION | SKILLS | TALK ABOUT THE ARTS |
|---|---|---|---|---|
| Opportunities | | | Ashaq (5:4) led the drawing around Tariq (5:5). Ashaq was very gentle as he drew around him. They both helped to draw around Zara (5:3). Bailey (5:7) watched and waited for his turn. Each time they discussed what size paper they would need. The children worked in large scale, listening to Moya's suggestions about techniques and working together to ensure they fitted all their bodies on the large sheets of paper. | |
| Recognition | The children were fascinated by the ocean drum. Abigail put her nose really close to the surface of the drum. She watched the little balls roll from side to side. Noah began to beat a repeated rhythm. Ashley's mum encouraged him, 'Well done, really good!' | Katie showed the children a stuffed fox. They began asking questions and making comments about him:<br>'Has he got a wet nose?'<br>'Why is his mouth open?'<br>'We went in the wolf's tummy.'<br>'He's scary.'<br>'Not really scary.'<br>'He's come from the zoo.' | | |
| Interaction | | | Molly (2:11) pointed to the stuffed fox. Moya invited her to draw. Molly sat on Moya's knee to draw the fox. Molly pointed at the fox with some chalk, Charlotte (3:9) helped by passing Molly colours. Molly made a range of marks on the paper while looking at the fox. Moya and Charlotte's interaction with Molly ensured that she was included in this experience. | Moya helped Charlotte to focus on observing colour by drawing her attention, quite specifically, to different parts of the duck and encouraging her to look for the detail in the many different colours of its feathers. |
| Model | | | Moya (the graphic artist) lay on the floor and began to draw a stuffed squirrel. Maisie (3:4) joined her, using paper of the same colour and pencils. She too lay down—mirroring Moya's pose—and the two drew together, side by side. | |

# Examples of engaging young children in the arts

In this section we relate three examples of engaging young children in the arts, to demonstrate the potential of inclusive practices.

## CASE STUDY 20.1

### James and the string quartet: The 'sound' of 'touch'

Karen Furber is Principal of Tenby St Nursery, a setting of some 56 children with a total of 22 practitioners. Situated in a large city in the North of England marked by industrial collapse and high unemployment, its reputation as an exciting and caring centre has thrived for more than forty years.

> Karen: James was just four when his mum first brought him to Tenby St and we soon became quite concerned that he seemed to be so withdrawn from everything and all the other children. I spoke to his mum about this, but she herself wasn't concerned; her other children (Mikey, then 7 and David, then 10) had been like that, she said, 'self-contained but not unhappy'. We have a policy [at the nursery] that we don't use labels, we don't seek them and we try to dissuade parents from bringing them in, so we were quite happy to avoid any notion of, well, Asperger's or anything which might have been easy to think ... but I did speak to [the Educational Psychologist] who did an informal observation and saw no immediate cause for further referral ... I was relieved about that, because you do worry, don't you? But also because of what happened later .... We have an arrangement with the Music Department at [the local College] who send different students every Wednesday afternoon, and we have Musical Play for an hour and then they and the children do a little concert. Well one week we had a quartet—you know, two violins and a viola and a cello—and James just couldn't take his eyes off the cello; if he could he'd have got into it he would, honestly! He just stood by it all afternoon, and the student encouraged him to keep his hand on the body of it. Well, it's not rocket science, as they say: call it just any old multi-sensory experience or just the sheer animal pleasure of vibrating with those low low notes ... fantastic! So whatever it was it was a result, it was a ... a sign of engagement. And then James—who really didn't show much sign of taking notice of anything—would be there on Wednesday after lunch, and he's set out the music stands and chairs and stuff. Oh and there was a terrible kerfuffle one week when the quartet wouldn't come and it was just a pianist, I mean only a pianist by herself ... Well—he wouldn't have it at first and he went back to the main door as if willing the quartet to turn up ... But y'know in the end Mandy his key person persuaded him to come in and he sort-of leaned against the piano and smiled and .... If we didn't believe in little steps—however little, sometimes so little that they don't even look like movement at all—well if we didn't believe in little steps we wouldn't be doing this job, would we?

The overriding theme in the example above is the sheer pleasure that can be derived from experiencing the arts close hand, and the importance of providing for young children high quality experiences with which they can closely engage in ways which are most meaningful to them.

**CRITICAL REFLECTION QUESTIONS**

Think about James' experience.

1. How in your practice would you encourage children to engage in their own individual ways with musical instruments?
2. How might the children you work with benefit from close up experiences with live music?
3. What other close up engagement in the arts can you develop for the children in your setting?
4. How would you ensure that such arts experiences are inclusive of all children in your setting?

Live Music Now (LMN), a charity established by Yehudi Menuhin, the US-born virtuoso violinist and teacher, aims to bring the 'joy and inspiration of live music to those who have limited access to conventional music-making' (www.livemusicnow.org.uk). The work of LMN shows how music can support the social, emotional, physical and educational development of those (often underprivileged) children and adults who participate in its projects, leading to social cohesion, teamwork, participation, confidence, communication, positive mental and physical health, and social justice.

**FIGURE 20.5** AUSLAN FOR *SING*

*Photos: Dinah Cocksedge*

CASE STUDY 20.2

## Hands and Voices Choir: Signing and singing for all

One example of LMN work involved creating the very first school singing and signing choir in the region, through a project delivered by LMN and Accessible Arts and Media's Hands and Voices Choir.

An LMN musician, a trainer who himself experiences disablement, and his mentor, worked with more than thirty pupils over ten weeks. Children in the newly formed choir developed their singing and signing skills and built up a repertoire of music, which varied from rock and roll to a new composition written by the pupils themselves.

The Makaton communication program was central to the project. Unlike British Sign Language (or Auslan—Australian Sign Language), which is a complete language, Makaton focuses on key words within the text, enabling anyone to learn the signs quite quickly (see discussion of Key Word Sign, formerly Makaton, in Australia in Chapter 23).

The project drew to a close with a celebratory showcase performance featuring the new school choir and the Hands and Voices Choir (the UK's first singing and signing choir).

*(With thanks to LMN for permission to include this example)*

CRITICAL REFLECTION QUESTIONS

1. Consider the ways in which signing might enable more children and their families to engage in choral singing.
2. How might all children use signing in inclusive settings?
3. Think about whether working towards an inclusive performance can be facilitated by local musicians and or organisations similar to LMN.

In the following example we can see how storytelling and drama can promote inclusive practices in an early years setting.

CASE STUDY 20.3

## Mr Winkle on Sausage Street and the Baby Jesus: Storying towards inclusion

*Buttercups and Daisies* is a small, privately-owned setting (approximately twenty-five children) in a leafy suburb of a medium-sized city in the East Midlands of the UK. Among other features, it is well known as a setting that readily welcomes all children from the community, including some with a variety of learning difficulties and disablements. The manager, Dave Walliams—the only male on the staff, and one of only seven male Early Years Educators in the city—is a former bank manager.

Dave: Jarry Tarr is a storyteller—a 'FableSmith' on her business card—whom we employed through ESCAPE! [Erith & Scarsdale Community Arts Programme in Education]. I have to say that everything about her is stunning! Her virulent red hair, her silver Doc Martens, a face and hands full of jewellery and other ironmongery and a sort-of clown's bib-and-braces suit of patchwork ... but as near a true magician as you could imagine ... I think that the staff were a bit wary of her, and wary of what parents might say, but the children had no such concerns—they just climbed on her, took her straight in to their hearts, I think .... She did a story one day by just picking up the Telephone Directory and leafing through it and she said to the children 'Who's on this page, then?' and one of them would say something like ... 'Mr Winkle' and she'd say, 'Well, well! How did you know that? And do you know what his address is?' And someone would say ... er ... 'Sausage Street' and she'd say 'Sausage Street indeed! Shall we ring him?' and she'd take out her phone and have this one-sided conversation with Mr Winkle, and she'd somehow bring all the children's names into it .... like 'What's that Mr Winkle? How's Sara Cornwell? She's very well and she's got her new pink jeans on!' Well, you can imagine the children were just enthralled. And eventually when they discovered the trick—as it were—she got some of them to have the one-sided, the improvised conversation ... and that takes some doing ....

[Jarry] did a play with the 4–5 age group, which turned out to be a Nativity in Nottingham! Mary and Joseph turning up at the Notty [a local hotel, the Nottingham Arms] but the Landlord did actually have some spare rooms and the play's all about what happened when they came down to breakfast the next morning with a baby ... And among these were some young children some with quite complex learning difficulties, but they knew exactly what that play was about, what the issues were ... and could describe their 'character' ... now by anyone's standards that's quite a sophisticated process to objectify that make-believe character ... There was a bit I'll always remember when a scene wasn't going very well in rehearsal and Jarry said, 'What's Joseph thinking, Andrew?' and Andrew said, 'Miss he's thinking "Eh, I've got myself into a right mess 'ere:" ...' Priceless!

**CRITICAL REFLECTION QUESTIONS**

1. Consider how professional storytellers or other creative arts practitioners can contribute to building arts practice in your setting.
2. Discuss the importance of adopting an inclusive attitude to involvement of children whose complex difficulties might at first lead you to believe that it will be difficult for them to participate.
3. Think about how you can offer new and different opportunities to children who have few or no experiences of drama or production.

# Suggestions for arts-based learning experiences

We suggest that it is essential that arts-based learning experiences offered to young children are planned, led and run by those who are themselves experienced in working with the arts and young children. We are particularly convinced of the value and contribution of artists themselves engaging in their arts with young children in early years and community settings. While experienced early years teachers and other professionals can certainly give children good arts experiences that will support their learning and development, the evidence suggests that professional artists can add to this and create rich opportunities for young children to have meaningful encounters within the arts.

**FIGURE 20.6** DOCUMENTING CHILDREN'S ENGAGEMENT IN THE ARTS

*Source: Nutbrown and Jones (2006)*

**documentation:** The collection of artefacts that demonstrate and provide a record of learning.

*Observation* is an important part of understanding young children's learning in the arts. Figure 20.6 shows how observations and photographs can be combined to generate insightful **documentation** of children's engagement.

Of course, creative practitioners will find their own routes to and through creative arts-based learning. However, in the spirit of learning from each other the following guidelines offer suggestions as to how artists might be involved in developing arts-based learning initiatives.

For artists, collaboration and communication is essential. On one project (Nutbrown, 2013; Nutbrown & Jones, 2006) where artists spent time in residence in early years settings, artists were quoted as saying:

> It is essential not to be precious about ideas and to allow children and practitioners to take you on journeys you would never have predicted.
>
> It's very difficult to structure sessions in the way that you would for older groups and I felt a lot of my own personal development was in adjusting to the needs and expressions of this age group.

This points to the need for shared professional development where artists and early years professionals can work, think, plan and reflect together. Early years professionals also had suggestions and reflections, feeling that greater involvement in planning would have helped them. One suggested that they could have offered more ideas:

> How are you going to use that idea? How are you going to put it into your own practice?

And another enthused:

> I'd say really get involved in planning work alongside the artist as much as you can—learn from their ideas and techniques.

Above all it is partnership that brings out the best work; this includes

- Planning together;
- Having clarity about roles and responsibilities;
- Being clear about how many children can be involved at once;
- Artists sharing their aims and plans for sessions with practitioners;
- Having agreements about workspace and storage;
- Practitioners sharing ideas, wants and concerns with artists;
- Providing clear information for parents;
- When working with ORIM there needs to be freedom to interpret and adapt;
- Allowing space for children to take a lead in developments;
- Recognising that artists are artists, practitioners are practitioners and together they can make a wonderful partnership;
- Debriefing at the end of each session;
- Making observations and taking photographs to discuss with each other and with the children and parents;
- Recognising that children's individual needs and interests are paramount—everyone working with them needs to keep them central, and practitioners need to adapt provision to ensure inclusivity.

## Conclusion

In this chapter we have aimed to show how *all* young children can benefit from experience of and engagement in the arts according to their ability. We have illustrated how responsive, respectful and creative practitioners can attune themselves to young children's artistic endeavours, and, with knowledge of the children they work with, can build inclusive and creative, arts-based learning communities where (dis)ability does not inhibit engagement with various art forms, whether made by others or by the children themselves. To this end, Article 31 of the United Nations *Convention on the Rights of the Child* applies to *all* children. To paraphrase and extend the words of the Convention (United Nations, 1989),

> *Every* child has the right to rest and leisure, to engage in play and recreational activities appropriate to their age *and ability* and to participate freely in cultural life and the arts.

And:

> Member governments shall respect and promote the right of *all children* to participate fully in cultural and artistic life and encourage the provision of appropriate and *equal opportunities* for *all children to experience* cultural, artistic, recreational and leisure activity.

# FOR FURTHER REFLECTION

Many of the sources cited in this chapter will provide further and deeper reading material. As starters we suggest you begin with the following three books if you want to explore and reflect on this topic further:

Dissanayake, E. (2000). *Art and intimacy: How the arts began.* Seattle, WA: University of Washington Press.

Eisner, E.W. (2002). *The arts and the creation of the mind.* New Haven, CD: Yale University Press.

Nutbrown, C. & Clough, P. (2013). *Inclusion in the Early Years: Critical analyses and enabling narratives* (2nd edn). London: Sage.

## WEBSITES

www.thepoint.org.uk/article/daring-discoveries

Here you can learn more about the background and outcomes of the Daring Discoveries project where the ORIM Arts framework was first developed and explored. You can also download a book about the project.

More on ORIM and how to join the ORIM network is to be found at www.real-online.group.shef.ac.uk/orim-network.html

## NOTES

1 For more information see www.real-online.group.shef.ac.uk.

2 More information is available at www.real-online.group.shef.ac.uk/orim-arts.html.

## REFERENCES

Anning, A. & Edwards, A. (2003). Language and literacy learning. In J. Devereaux and L. Miller (Eds). *Working with children in the early years* (pp.47–59). London: David Fulton/Open University.

Bannon, F. & Sanderson, P. (2000). Experience every moment: Aesthetically significant dance education. *Research in Dance Education, 1*(1), 9–26. doi:10.1080/14647890050006550

Barrett, M.S. (2006). Inventing songs, inventing worlds: The 'genesis' of creative thought and activity in young children's lives. *International Journal of Early Years Education, 14*(3), 201–20. doi:10.1080/09669760600879920

Barrett, M.S. (2009). Sounding lives in and through music: A narrative inquiry of the 'every-day' musical engagement of a young child. *Journal of Early Childhood Research, 7*(2), 115–34. doi:10.1177/1476718X09102645

Brown, E.D. (1991). *Human universals*. New York: McGraw-Hill.

Brown, E.D., Benedette, E. & Armistead, M.E. (2010). Arts enrichment and school readiness for children at risk. *Early Childhood Research Quarterly, 25,* 112–24. Retrieved from www.journals.elsevier.com/early-childhood-research-quarterly/

Chapman, L.H. (2004). No child left behind in art? *Arts Education Policy Review, 106*, 3–17. doi:10.3200/AEPR.106.2.3-20

Charlesworth, E.A. (1982). Music, psychology and psychotherapy. *The Arts in Psychotherapy, 9*, 191–202. Retrieved from www.journals.elsevier.com/the-arts-in-psychotherapy/

Clough, P. (2002). *Narratives and fictions in educational research*. Buckingham: Open University Press.

Deans, J. & Brown, R. (2005). Reflection, renewal and relationship building: An on-going journey in early childhood arts education. *Contemporary Issues in Early Childhood,* 9(4), 339–53. doi:10.2304/ciec.2008.9.4.339

Dewey, J. (1902). *The educational situation*. Chicago, IL: University of Chicago Press.

Dissanayake, E. (1990). *What is art for?* Seattle, WA: University of Washington Press.

Dissanayake, E. (1995). *Homo aestheticus*. Seattle, WA: University of Washington Press.

Dissanayake, E. (2000). *Art and intimacy: How the arts began.* Seattle, WA: University of Washington Press.

Dissanayake, E. (2001). Aesthetic incunabula. *Philosophy and Literature, 25*, 335–46. doi:10.1353/phl.2001.0026

Eckhoff, A. (2008). The importance of art viewing experiences in early childhood visual arts: The exploration of a master art teacher's strategies for meaningful early arts experiences. *Early Childhood Education Journal, 35*, 463–72. doi:10.1007/s10643-007-0216-1

Eisner, E.W. (2002). *The arts and the creation of the mind.* New Haven, CD: Yale University Press.

Eisner, E.W. (2004). What can education learn from the arts about the practice of education? *International Journal of Education and the Arts, 5*(4), 12–7. Retrieved from www.ijea.org/v5n4/

Fagan, W.T. (2000). Family literacy: Fives steps to success. *Literacy Today, 24*(26) 4–6.

Filippini, T., & Vecchi, V. (1996). *The hundred languages of children: The exhibit.* Reggio Emilia: Reggio Children.

Gardner, H. (1989). The key in the key slot. *Journal of Aesthetic Education, 23*(1), 141–58. Retrieved from www.press.uillinois.edu/journals/jae.html

Gardner, H. (1990). *Art education and human development: An essay commissioned by the J. Paul Getty Center for Education in the Arts, Occasional Paper* 3. Los Angeles: The J. Paul Getty Museum.

Gillespie, A. (2006). Children, art and artists. *Early Education, 24*(3), 5–7.

Goldschmeid, E. & Jackson, S. (1999). *People under three.* London: Routledge.

Hancock, R. & Cox, A. (2002). 'I would have worried about her being a nuisance': Workshops for children under three and their parents at Tate Britain. *Early Years, 22*(2), 118–23. doi:10.1080/09575140220151459

Hannon, P. (1995). *Literacy, home and school: Research and practice in teaching literacy with parents.* London: Falmer Press.

Hannon, P. & Nutbrown, C. (1997). Teachers' use of a conceptual framework for early literacy education with parents. *Teacher Development, 1*(3), 405–20. doi:10.1080/13664539700200031

Harrett, J. (2002). Young children talking: An investigation into the personal stories of key stage one infants. *Early Years, 22*(1), 19–26. doi:10.1080/09575140120111481

Hopperstad, M. (2008a). Relationships between children's drawing and accompanying peer interaction in teacher-initiated drawing sessions. *International Journal of Early Years Education, 16*(2), 133–50. doi:10.1080/09669760802044844

Hopperstad, M. (2008b). How children make meaning through drawing and play. *Visual Communication, 7*(1), 77–96. doi:10.1177/1470357207084866

Jordan-Decarbo, J. & Nelson, J.A. (2002). Music and early childhood education. In R. Colwell and C. Richardson (Eds). *The new handbook of research on music teaching and learning* (pp.210–42). NY: Oxford University Press.

Kellogg, R. (1955). *What children scribble and why.* USA: Golden Gate Kindergarten Association in San Francisco.

Lamont, A. (2008). Young children's musical worlds: Musical engagement in 3.5-year-olds. *Journal of Early Childhood Research, 6*(3), 247–61. doi:10.1177/1476718X08094449

Lindqvist, G. (2001). When small children play: How adults dramatise and children create meaning. *Early Years, 21*(1), 7–14. doi:10.1080/09575140123593

MacRae, C. (2007). Using sense to make sense of art: Young children in art galleries. *Early Years, 27*(2), 159–70. doi:10.1080/09575140701425290

Marsh, J. (2004). The techno-literacy practices of young children. *Journal of Early Childhood Research, 2*(1), 51–66. doi:10.1177/1476718X0421003

Marsh, J. (2010). Young children's play in online virtual worlds. *Journal of Early Childhood Research, 8*(1), 23–39. doi:10.1177/1476718X09345406

Murdock, G.P. (1945). The common denominator of cultures. In R. Linton (Ed.) *The science of man in the world crisis* (pp.123–42). New York: Columbia University Press.

National Advisory Committee on Creative, Cultural Education (NACCCE). (1999). *All our futures: Creativity, culture and education.* Report to the Secretary of State for Education and Employment and the Secretary of State for Culture, Media and Sport. London: HMSO.

Nutbrown, C. (2006). *Threads of thinking: Young children learning and the role of early education.* [3rd edn]. London: Sage.

Nutbrown, C. (2013) Conceptualising arts based learning in the early years. *Research Papers in Education, 28*(2), 239–263. doi:10.1080/02671522.2011.580365

Nutbrown, C. & Clough, P. (2013). *Inclusion in the Early Years: Critical analyses and enabling narratives* [2nd edn]. London: Sage.

Nutbrown, C. & Jones, H. (2006). *Daring discoveries: Arts-based learning in the early years.* Doncaster: Creative Partnerships/Darts.

Nutbrown, C., Hannon, P. & Collier, S. (1996). *Early literacy education with parents: A framework for practice.* Sheffield: The REAL Project/University of Sheffield, Sheffield University Television.

Nutbrown, C., Hannon, P. & Morgan, A. (2005). *Early literacy work with families: Policy, practice and research.* London: Sage.

Nyland, B., Ferris, J. & Dunn, L. (2008). Mindful hands, gestures as language: Listening to children. *Early Years,* 28(1), 73–80. doi:10.1080/09575140701846552

Pramling Samuelsson, I., Carlsson, M.A., Isson, B., Pramling, N. & Wallerstedt, C. (2009). The art of teaching children in the arts: Music, dance and poetry with children aged 2–8 years old. *International Journal of Early Years Education, 17*(2), 119–36. doi:10.1080/09669760902982323

ReggioChildren. (1995). *Le Fantane: Da un progetto per la construczione di u Luna Park degli uccellini [The Fountains:*

*From a project for the construction of an amusement park for birds]*. Reggio Emilia: Reggio Children.

Rigo-Toth, R. & Ure, C. (2000). Evaluating literacy in the preschool: A review of Hannon's ORIM framework. *International Journal of Learning, 7*(2), 27–31. Retrieved from http://ijl.cgpublisher.com/product/pub.30/prod.4

Roberts, R. (2001). *PEEP voices: A five year diary*. Oxford: PEEP.

Sugiyama, M.S. (2001). Narrative theory and function: Why evolution matters. *Philosophy and Literature, 25*, 233–50. doi:10.1353/phl.2001.0035

Thompson, C.M. (1990). 'I make a mark': The significance of talk in young children's artistic development. *Early Childhood Research Quarterly, 5*, 215–32. Retrieved from www.journals.elsevier.com/early-childhood-research-quarterly/

Trehub, S. (2003). Toward a developmental psychology of music. In G. Avanzini, C. Faienza, D. Minciacchi, L. Lopez & M. Majno (Eds). *The neurosciences and music: Annals of the New York academy of sciences* (pp.402–13). New York: New York Academy of Sciences, Vol. 999.

Trevarthen, C. (1984). Emotions in infancy: Regulators of contact and relationships with persons. In K. Scherer & P. Ekman (Eds). *Approaches to emotion* (pp.129–570). Hillsdale, NJ: Erlbaum.

United Nations. (1989). *Convention on the rights of the child*. New York: United Nations. Retrieved from www.unicef.org/crc/

Vygotsky, L.S. (1978). *Mind and society*. Cambridge, MA: Harvard University Press.

Young, S. (2005). Changing tune: Reconceptualizing music with under three year olds. *International Journal of Early Years Education, 13*(3), 289303. doi:10.1080/09669760500295987

Young, S. (2008). Collaboration between 3- and 4-year-olds in self-initiated play on instruments. *International Journal of Educational Research, 47*, 3–10. Retrieved from www.journals.elsevier.com/international-journal-of-educational-research/

# 21 Why Does the Moon Change Shape?: Inclusive Science and Technology in the Early Years

*Camilla Gordon and Kate Highfield*

CHAPTER OVERVIEW

This chapter will focus on the development of inclusive practices in science and technology, with a focus of how this can occur in integrated practice, such as project-based investigations. The chapter will explore inclusive practices in science learning, as well as potential uses of technology in supporting the engagement of young children who experience disability.

Learning goals for this chapter include:

- Exploring practical and pedagogic decisions educators make when engaging children in science and scientific investigations and projects;
- Considering the roles and affordances of technology as a tool in an inclusive context;
- Identifying opportunities for play and investigation to support scientific thinking;
- Examining the role of 'academic' and 'intellectual' goals in science and technology.

KEY TERMS AND CONCEPTS

project-based investigations

science

scientific processes

technology

# Introduction

Why does the moon change shape? Are there little people living in our TV? How does the Sydney Harbour Bridge stay up? Problem solving and evidence-based decision-making are essential components of learning and engaging with the world. Inclusive **science** and **technology** experiences enable all children to develop their capacity for asking and answering questions, identifying a 'problem' and proposing a solution. We use a range of tools to do this, including technologies. With the continuing growth of new technologies in the world today, it is essential that teachers be well equipped to explore and deliver inclusive experiences for all children, including children who experience disability, particularly where technology has potential for supporting the engagement of children who experience disability.

**science:** In schools science is considered as a distinct curriculum area. Here we define science as children's understanding of the world around them, their place within it and the interconnection of all things living and non-living.

**technology:** All tools used to facilitate engagement, explore content and document children's actions and construction of knowledge. Technology includes tools such as digital microscopes, interactive whiteboards and tablet technologies.

The focus of this chapter is how all children can be included into science and technology experiences in early years prior-to-school and school settings. We will begin by emphasising the role of a learning community in the construction of scientific knowledge, presenting a range of examples from practice and exploring technologies that can be used to support learning and engagement in science. Here we examine the curriculum area of science, presenting a perspective that young children are natural scientists, constantly investigating and exploring their worlds and integrating science with technology. This focus area is recognised at all levels of education, particularly in the key documents for prior-to-school and school. The *Early Years Learning Framework for Australia* (Department of Education, Employment and Workplace Relations [DEEWR], 2009) is specifically inclusive, embracing 'being', 'belonging' and 'becoming' for all children. Within this document the scientific approach, specifically the activity of investigation, is foundational. Further, the Australian Curriculum and Assessment Reporting Authority's (ACARA) national curriculum promotes equity and aims to be seen 'as a curriculum for all learners' (ACARA, 2013, para. 3).

When we examine technology use we draw on the Early Years Learning Framework's (DEEWR, 2009) definition of technology as 'much more than computers and digital technologies … These products extend beyond artefacts designed and developed by people and include processes, systems, services and environments' (DEEWR, 2009, p.46). This definition reflects a notion of 'high' and 'low' technologies as used by Siraj-Blatchford and Siraj-Blatchford (2006) and acknowledges both technological artefacts, such as computers and digital technologies, as well as technology as an iterative process. Here technology is proposed not as a subject in its own right but as a tool to promote learning, as a tool to facilitate engagement, explore content and document children's actions and construction of knowledge.

## Science and technology in perspective

Science is not only for all people and all ages, regardless of ability or disability; science is at the core of human existence. On planet Earth no action or reaction of the living or non-living is devoid of its scientific derivation or consequence. Physics controls and decides how we move and breathe and exist; chemistry predetermines how we grow and eat; astronomy is the core of all the sciences since our planet resulted from the supernova death of a star and the birth of a Solar System. Growing up, all children quickly become aware of the limitations placed on them by the physics of their environment, especially by gravity and the principles of balance, and testing these limitations is the function of childhood. So science is universal inquiry regardless of who is practising it. As explored in Chapters 1 and 2, we cannot afford to see children in terms of 'special' and 'normal'; children are individuals, each with their unique capabilities and ways of understanding. If disability is seen as an abnormality then we will practise the strategies of special education (Ballard, 2013). The authors would suggest that instead, scientific exploration should be experiential and cultivated through children's interests, burgeoning knowledge and motivation—we do not all engage in learning in the same way. The tools for learning and experimenting in science are technological and logistical, and always adaptable.

Technology provides the tools of connectivity with science, digital tools to enhance learning, to engage with new ideas or concepts that can't be replicated in the classroom. For example, technology affords children the opportunity of travelling through space, virtually meeting with astronauts or examining the molecular structure of key elements. When used well, technology is a facilitator of learning and a tool for documentation within the classroom learning community. While the success of any classroom hugely depends on the values and belief systems of those who teach and administer, success also requires community within the classroom—citizenship and belonging. Building a science and technology inclusive early years community involves accepting the integrated nature of subject, student and environment, a place where learning takes place within family, within the classroom and within the outside community. It involves changing the values and beliefs of exclusion and embracing full participation of all peoples, regardless of gender, wealth or ability. This way, science and technology learning becomes part of a multilayered system that caters for all children and creates a broad, inclusive society.

## The inclusive science classroom

Science learning and the practice of scientific techniques changes little with the physical, intellectual or behavioural ability of the children. As explored throughout this book, we adopt a perspective on inclusion where all children, regardless of their abilities are perceived as active meaning-makers. As discussed in Chapter 2, children who experience disability face barriers to doing and being. Our position here is that all contexts—be they classrooms, playgroups or informal learning opportunities (such as museums and observatories)—can be a place of learning for all children, and removing barriers to doing and being is an essential part of the early years professional's role.

Most mass education systems, which involve the teaching of children in large groups such as formal school, tend to have an expectation of conformity and a propensity to teaching in pre-determined, linear trajectories. There is often concern within the prescriptive classroom that behaviour and cognitive skills need to be uniform. This is exclusionary and creates the very difficult requirement for children to 'fit' within this approach. The hardest part of a day for any of us is that time when we are expected to be someone we are not. It is our job as educators to re-configure our classroom contexts, to re-evaluate the prescriptive context to enable all learners the opportunity to engage.

Science is an ideal curriculum area for inclusive practice—an opportunity to revise expectations of linear learning and prescribed goals. Science learning ideally requires investigation and discovery. It supports curiosity, experimentation and invention. Science, the subject within a school curriculum, must be integrally bound to scientific pedagogy—because science teaching is in many ways an art. The effective science teacher is a facilitator of learning about

**FIGURE 21.1** THE SCIENCE EXPERIMENT

*Artwork by Kaitlyn*

how the world works. Good science teaching is in every way inclusive and socially constructivist.

Katz describes the differences between *academic* and *intellectual* curriculum goals, with academic goals as the pre-set curriculum and skills and intellectual goals focusing on 'reasoning, hypothesizing, predicting, the quest for understanding and conjecturing, as well as the development and analysis of ideas' (2010, p.2). Science provides opportunities to engage children in the development of intellectual skills, particularly when learning is rich and meaningful.

## The inclusive technology classroom

To describe a classroom as 'an inclusive technology classroom' is somewhat of an anathema, as it implies technology is a separate curriculum area. Instead we propose a technological classroom, where Information and Communication Technology (ICT) is used as a tool to facilitate engagement for all children. Technologies are included to augment learning, as a tool to enable new forms of multi-modal communication and as a resource for engaging with the scientific community beyond the classroom. Many forms of technology, such as iPads and tablet games, are, by their nature, engaging—these tools are suggested as useful for practising specific skills and developing fluency, but also as opportunities to investigate the world, zooming in on images and capturing investigations. Given this notion, this chapter does not promote a separate technology classroom, but rather it suggests a classroom, with appropriate technological resources, used effectively to facilitate engagement. Exemplars are provided in this chapter to demonstrate some of the ways that technologies can be integrated in science learning.

## The role of the environment in science and technology

The Reggio Emilia approach has long examined the idea of a child having three teachers: the teacher, the child and the environment (Strong-Wilson & Ellis, 2007). In science learning this is particularly true, with the environment playing an integral role in prompting, enticing and facilitating learning. A great deal of effort goes into the planning and provision of a science-learning environment. In configuring rich learning opportunities for children, a science-learning environment aims to be one which reflects the stories of those who live in it and provides work spaces where children can return to ideas and projects, spaces without specific boundaries, and which entice children to return and rediscover. Moments of discovery immediately become opportunities to share. There is openness to conflict and other points of view, of arguing, sharing and untangling ideas. Waiting for the child is the key—allowing children to be involved in the process rather than supplying activities and answers (Milikan, 2003). Here the environment is not just a space for learning, but an essential participant in learning.

In provisioning the environment inclusively, providing a range of materials is not enough; the teacher also needs to ensure access to those resources. For example, if the teacher provides building and construction materials, these need to be accessible by all children. When resourcing the environment, effective teachers will consider both the collection of tools, furniture and artefacts as well as the allocation and placement of space. Here, space is needed to enable ongoing learning and deeper investigation. For example, block play provides opportunity for children to explore a range of skills including investigation, problem solving, spatial concepts and development or engineering skills through construction. However, to extend this to enable development of intellectual goals, sustained engagement must be facilitated. Hence, the teacher must not only provide the blocks, but also provide space for building and construction, a stable area that promotes ongoing investigation and analysis of ideas.

**CASE STUDY 21.1**

## A table for blocks

Mathew, aged five, is an active participant in his kindergarten classroom. He is a popular class member with a bright, sunny smile that lights up the room. Mathew is diagnosed with autism and sometimes struggles with mobility in the classroom, particularly when sitting down on the floor. He enjoys routine and particularly enjoys challenging himself in block constructions, building tall structures and working with peers, co-playing to balance blocks and build bridges. At times Mathew becomes frustrated, particularly when he is asked to finish building before he sees his project as complete.

Mathew's teacher noted his active engagement with the blocks. She carefully documented his learning in this context and noted the barriers he faced. Without fuss she added a low table to the block area, enabling a stable and more easily accessible area for Mathew and his peers to use the blocks. The teacher also added a digital photo frame, with images of block constructions previously made by the children and images of famous bridges and towers from around the world. The table and digital photo frame facilitated prolonged engagement, provoking reflection and providing a safe space for ongoing projects to be continued in the busy classroom.

CRITICAL REFLECTION QUESTIONS

1. Reflect on the example of block play above. What language do teachers use to extend play and what language should be used to inspire **scientific processes**?
2. In block play children are engaging with a number of engineering skills. How can teachers facilitate engagement for children with limited mobility?
3. What activities, questions or tools can be used to promote deep learning and facilitate extended engagement?

**scientific processes:** The range of activities that children use to acquire science knowledge such as: questioning, investigating, reasoning, communication, designing and observing.

In the case study above, the teacher can be seen considering the needs of the child, and modifying the environment to facilitate engagement. These minor modifications present the opportunity both to extend learning and to enable all children's engagement. The inclusion of the table was particularly key here, helping Mathew overcome physical barriers to engagement. Block play, while enabling Mathew to engage with academic skills such as counting, measuring and comparing, also facilitated intellectual skills of problem solving and reasoning. Here, by facilitating Mathew's participation, along with that of

**FIGURE 21.2** BLOCK PLAY

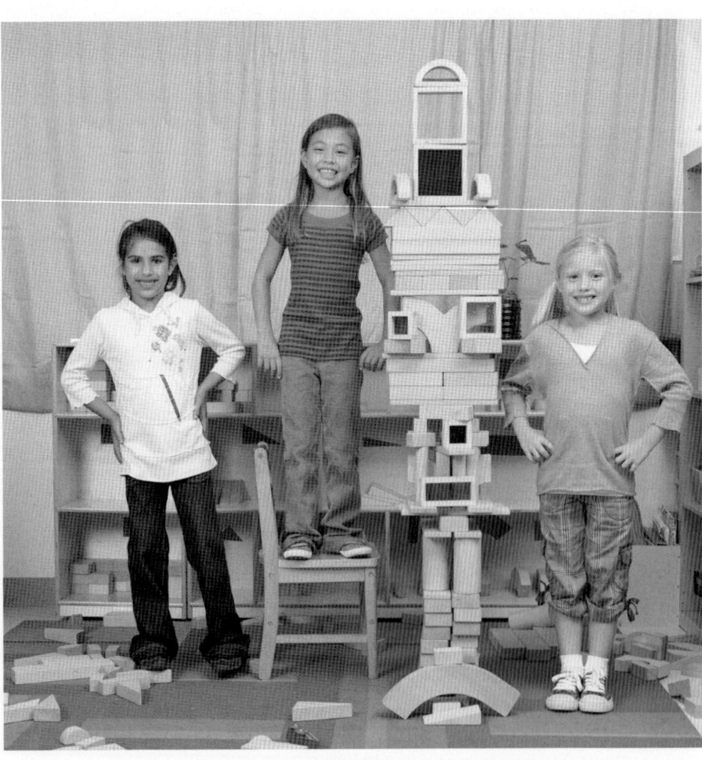

his peers, the teacher also extended the children's engagement into social and emotional realms.

As mentioned earlier, the environment can be considered children's third teacher, In viewing it this way, we move beyond the physical space and resources to also account for those who are using this space. Here educators are active participants, modelling engagement and facilitating dispositions of learning in groups. For young learners, science and technology understandings do not occur in laboratories. They are stimulated within the course of everyday discovery and are within the reach of all children regardless of ability, stature or disposition. Children greatly benefit from the learning of the children around them—such learning stems from the development and the ecology of the inclusive classroom. A constructed knowledge of science may thus be viewed as a set of socially negotiated understandings based on collaborative and individual interactions with complex data, and over time. Much of good teaching practice involves small group activities, peer associations and collaborative deliberations. However, for some children, solitude can also be calming and can facilitate learning. When a child who experiences difficulty with social interaction is alone there is no social impairment (Attwood, 2004; Kutscher & Attwood, 2007). It is in these complex and apparently contradictory needs of learners that the art of science and technology teaching comes into play, with the role of the teacher integral in any learning community.

**FIGURE 21.3** THE HUMAN SKELETON

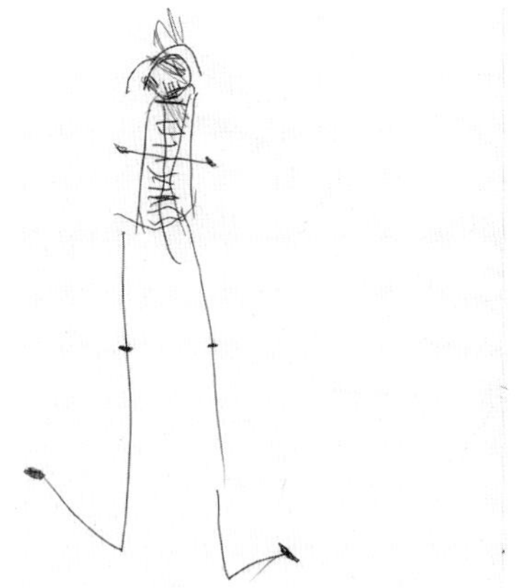

This is Gracie's skeleton, drawn scientifically by feeling the different bones in her body.
*Artwork by Grace*

# The role of the teacher in science and technology

## TEACHER AS PEDAGOGIC LEADER

Practical and pedagogic decisions that educators make when engaging children in science determine the extent of learning that is possible. It is constantly emphasised that children learn better in an active environment where learning is practical; where each child can work at a pace suitable to their interest and ability; and where learning is cooperative and collaborative. In the very early years, science and technology is playful, and when learning is embedded in day-to-day recreation and activity there is time for children to think and wonder within the framework of what Vygotsky called the intermental and the intramental, where learning is social first and then transformed to embedded understanding (Hedegaard, 2001). Quality teaching provides children with a flexible environment in which there is the time and motivation to embed themselves.

Planning science learning for a classroom of diverse children should not be difficult. Most science can be deconstructed into stages of understanding and broken down into smaller steps or embellished as needed. A drop of water can be explained in its molecular conformation, its shape or its movement, and as such can be understood at many stages and ages. An 18-month-old child may see water as a facilitator for movement—it makes a surface slippery; at ten years of age water becomes one of the many factors which create or inhibit friction. Knowing how to teach these stages of science is a vital skill for catering to the variety of ability levels found in the classroom.

Early research by Inhelder and Piaget (1958) elicits that the particular thinking of young children is likely to be transductive, that is, seeing relationships between things that are not related; and inductive, that is, making assumptions based on observation or function. Concrete and practical learning needs to precede abstraction, and is critical to allow for advancement of scientific thinking. Here the science educator makes key decisions and ensures that science and technology experiences are both frequent and continuous. Further, these experiences are revisited and re-evaluated, open-ended and bursting with opportunities for further exploration. Only when this is the case are science and technology truly practiced, understood and available to all children.

As the teacher assumes the role of the pedagogic leader this frequently means that they are planning lessons and activities, collecting resources and building their content knowledge. Often these actions place the teacher in the role of leader, demonstrating science and imparting their knowledge. However, teachers can also focus on sharing leadership roles and enabling students to share their knowledge.

**CASE STUDY 21.2**

## Informal learning opportunities

Charlie is eight years old and is attending an informal science club, exploring astronomy. He *loves* to learn—he is very intelligent, highly gifted, he works particularly well on his own and by himself and is often assumed to have Asperger syndrome. Previously, when Charlie walked into a room, he appeared not to be aware of the other children. Initially the other children in this setting neither talked to him nor acknowledged his presence, though they all knew him. He often began to talk to me (his teacher) without regard for the fact that I may be talking.

Charlie's astronomy knowledge is huge and peppered with alternative frameworks and misconceptions, though much of it is scientifically accurate and memorised. He states his knowledge with confidence and assurance, though when corrected quietly withdraws as if to consider the new information. In the classroom, Charlie is intensely absorbed when he is discovering for himself or when he is following his own agenda.

One of the distinguishing characteristics of Charlie is the intensity and focus of his interest in science, especially astronomy. In our informal astronomy group I stand back and ask Charlie to teach the children. I prepare special projects for him. He can do this if he doesn't have to look at the other children and if I am standing next to him (as we would if having a conversation together). When the other children realised that I regarded Charlie's knowledge as unique and useful he was given an elevated status among our group. The other children listened to him and welcomed his intervention—this was particularly so when I asked him to talk to share his knowledge with them.

CRITICAL REFLECTION QUESTIONS

1. How can teachers cater for children who at times, like Charlie, benefit from working alone?
2. What is the role of informal science in a formal classroom context?
3. Here the teacher has an understanding of Charlie as an individual and has goals for his learning. How would you inspire scientific thinking for Charlie?

The fact that intellectual development can be advanced through education leads to an important suggestion, first made by Vygotsky (1962) and later by Luria (1979), that the level of children's ability should be assessed by what they can do given adult help. A fundamental feature of human intelligence is our capacity to learn through instruction, and scientific perceptions are within the grasp of all children if structured to the right level.

However purveyors of instruction need not only be teachers or adults. As seen in the above case study, Charlie was the instructor. The educational model of kids teaching kids supports the Reggio Emilia philosophy (Dahlberg, Moss & Pence, 1999; Malaguzzi, 1996) and is a substantial part of a program established to stimulate environmental leadership (http://www.kidsteachingkids.com.au/).

## TEACHER AS DOCUMENTER

Inclusive teaching is a fundamental and professional skill for all educators and requires sensitivity and knowledge about children both as individuals and as a group. Documentation unlocks meaning, providing a new view of the child's meaning-making. It also provides a basis for studying the dynamics of the group. In documentation, the understanding accrued is far greater than could be found in any formal assessment. It involves continuous and slow assessment of children, without judgment, and total involvement in teaching, accepting there needs to be a shift in emphasis from teaching to learning (Inan, Trundle. & Kantor, 2010). Pedagogical documentation makes learning visible and captures the stories of the children's classroom experiences. Documentation then becomes a tool for teacher research, reflection, collaboration and decision-making (Katz & Chard, 1996).

The school curriculum historically evolved using a separate subject structure, which required students to focus on developing one framework at a time—one schema that is isolated from the others. Science, the source of the greatest motivation for the children in the scenarios shared in this chapter, is relegated

### CASE STUDY 21.3

### Knowing your children: The role of documentation

Jacob is seven years old. He is diagnosed with Attention Deficit Hyperactivity Disorder (ADHD) and is medicated. In Grade 1 Jacob was very confined to the requirements of the whole class. His teacher justified this by saying '[h]e has to learn to conform'. Jacob talks all the time, which sometimes interferes with the activities in the classroom. His mind is bright and his personality 'bubbly', but he is unable to control his need to intervene in conversation, or correct the teacher. 'I know that!' he will call out, and then give a dissertation on the subject. Jacob yearns to know both 'more' and 'different', but this is not supported in a classroom where conformity, rather than inclusion, is valued.

However, in Grade 2, his teacher was more experienced and employed different strategies, beginning the year by learning all he could about Jacob, his family and about ADHD. He visited

Jacob's home, spoke to his parents and began to structure his classroom for the children he was teaching. He learnt that, contrary to the assumption that children labelled with ADHD are unable to stay focused at a task, Jacob is fascinated by science, especially astronomy, and can remain riveted to a learning opportunity. Experience has shown that conformity—the expectation that all the children will behave in a roughly uniform way—is an unsuitable scenario and an unnecessary requirement (Richards, 2010). In Grade 2, Jacob was not required to conform but to participate on the level of his capability and to learn. For Jacob's teacher the challenge was always to find the engagement within the learning—where is the stimulus, the motivation? Jacob's teacher found getting to know Jacob very helpful. Jacob is stimulated by books that are highly visual and scientific, together with paints, pencils and papers. These often allow him to settle and become involved in drawing, colouring or representing understandings that he gleans from reading and interpreting the visual medium.

What is so important to remember is that children 'are individuals with personal profiles depicting interests and needs that are unique to each one' (Baum & Olenchak, 2002). Jacob's new teacher applied changes based on his developing understanding of Jacob, and his perception of the other children in the class. Each lesson was divided into small group work. Children moved from group to group but the numbers in each group were small enough for good communication. Science is Jacob's great love, so science became a major focus—science integrated with mathematics, science integrated with literacy, science integrated with PDHPE. Jacob was finally learning well and not disrupting the class ... as much. The other children were far more accepting also. Understanding Jacob made a great deal of difference.

**CRITICAL REFLECTION QUESTIONS**

1. In what ways does understanding children as individuals determine how to facilitate science learning?
2. When presented with a large class size how can structure and flexible learning be integrated to enable children to pursue goals for learning?

to a part of a day or a week. In the scenario above this teacher changed this and in doing so removed barriers that were preventing his student's learning. When students apply reason they tend to draw from the knowledge and emotions within a single organised pattern of thought. For children who have an embedded interest in one area, it is logical to assume that other experiences are not drawn upon because those experiences exist in different schema. These children subsequently disengage from the educational process. The inclusive early years professional needs to embrace different needs of learners to connect the schema that instils the greatest motivation with others that don't—this can involve, for example, teaching literacy through science, or mathematics through science.

Children also have the potential to act as documenters of learning, developing strategies for inclusion by documenting learning in ways that allow others, also, to participate. In Case study 21.4, the children take on the task of documentation to enable both class members and visitors to the room to understand the investigations.

**CASE STUDY 21.4**

## Technology as a tool: Facilitating engagement for all children

Denise attends a long day care centre. She is four years old and has been at the same centre since she was six months. Denise is a capable communicator and a kind friend, loved by her peers and staff alike. Denise has a congenital vision disorder and while she maintains some vision in one eye, this is diminishing and she is expected to be educationally blind in a few years.

In Denise's classroom the children have been exploring insects that they've found in the garden. The teacher, after noting this interest, has brought the science inside and, working with the children, has developed a science table. This table has a collection of resources including an insect habitat for phasmids (commonly referred to as stick insects), an ant farm and a range of books and posters to support the children's construction of knowledge in this area. The teacher has also placed a large screen and a digital microscope on the table. This hand-held microscope is displayed on the screen and enables all children, including Denise, to investigate the small insects. Denise also uses an iPad in a similar way, taking photos of objects then using the iPad to zoom the image and see details.

Most of the children in this class have been in the centre for a long time and know each other well. They've developed skills in describing what they see and with support from the teacher they often use descriptive language to explain the things they observe. The descriptive language skills and the teacher's scaffolding of this process have been beneficial both for Denise, who has been enabled to participate more fully, and for her peers.

**CRITICAL REFLECTION QUESTIONS**

1. In what ways can children with a visual impairment be assisted to engage freely in a classroom? (See also Chapter 22)
2. Here a range of technologies are presented as tools to facilitate engagement. What other tools would enable Denise to think scientifically?

In this scenario, Denise and her peers are taking a role in documenting observations. They are using descriptive language to explain what they are seeing, both extending their own skills and vocabulary as well as helping to overcome barriers for Denise. If the teacher were to simply leave the children to do this, Denise might not be able to fully participate; however the use of multiple strategies, including the use of technology as a facilitative tool, assists Denise's engagement.

In this scenario the teacher has used technology as an assistive tool. As discussed in Chapter 23, there is long-standing and broad-ranging literature on the use of technology in this way (for example, see Campbell, Milbourne, Dugan, & Wilcox, 2006 or Marchel, Fischer, & Clarke, 2014). Increasingly we're seeing mainstream tools, particularly touch devices such as tablets, smart phones and iPads, used in this way. Here apps can be used to facilitate language, for example Prologue2go (www.assistiveware.com/product/proloquo2go) is commonly suggested as an augmentative and alternative communication tool. Alternatively, mobile touch screens, with the capacity to zoom in on images and content, can be used to assist children with vision concerns. Further, apps such as Explain Everything (www.explaineverything.com) can be used to enable children to communicate ideas through images simple animations and recorded voices, thereby overcoming fine motor or written language barriers.

In school gardening learning could also be supported by technology, for example through documentation of plant growth and student learning (for example using digital cameras and documenting growth through time-lapse

**CASE STUDY 21.5**

## Project-based investigation: Gardening

In Australia, children often spend a great deal of their free time outdoors, while much of the school day is spent indoors. To emphasise the need for nature-based learning, Johnson (2012) looks at ways in which gardening, specifically the school garden, has been interpreted in Western society. She proposes that a reconceptualised version of school gardening could promote inclusive education and 'support new pedagogical approaches to ecological and play-based knowledge' (p.581). Gardening supports all the criteria for good science learning—it is hands on, active, it encourages skill development and knowledge of ethical issues, and it engages children in taking responsibility in holistic and authentic projects. The practical skill of gardening stimulates scientific knowledge, as children need to ask questions such as:

- Will this soil grow my plants?
- How much water do these plants and seeds need?
- Is there enough sunlight?

Gardening is a fun practical play opportunity, and is available and suitable for all ages and abilities. It can be as easily structured for children under five years as it can with older primary children. It encourages cooperation and collaboration and engages children emotionally. Garden-based projects have potential to explore and develop both academic and intellectual skills, while facilitating problem solving and investigation. These ideas incorporate both science and technology and require teachers to explore with children ways to extend understanding and investigate technological solutions that extend engagement for all age groups. Examples of this might be finding the most efficient way to move water to the plants; and devising the best design for the garden plot to facilitate access by all children; and working out how to provide sunlight for both tall and short plants. This is science and technology at its best!

**CRITICAL REFLECTION QUESTIONS**

1. What nature-based projects can be developed in and outside of the classroom, and how can these assist in creating inclusivity?
2. What are the special scientific features of gardening that will stimulate children to explore and investigate?
3. This **project-based investigation** provides an example where technology could be integrated through the design process. What are iterative design processes and how can this process be inclusive?

**project-based investigations:** Rich units of study that cross multiple curriculum areas. They enable students to question and investigate areas of learning in depth.

photography, making movies of the experience etc.) and as a research tool. Apps such as Insect Orders (by Lucid Mobile) or Nature Gate (by NatureGate Ltd) provide learners with fast access to information, which can then be shared with peers. Gardening provides limitless opportunities for science learning and projects linked to science and technology curricula.

# Conclusion

This chapter has begun to explore the curriculum area of science and technology, examining how these curriculum areas can be addressed inclusively. The chapter has presented a range of case studies, classroom scenarios where the teacher has made informed decisions to facilitate engagement of all children. These scenarios have also exemplified the use of technology as a supporting tool for learning—rather than as a distinct subject or curriculum focus.

The chapter, through its examples, has also focused on the role of the teacher, examining the teacher's function as a pedagogic leader and facilitator of learning. This multi-faceted role is important, the role of knowing children as individuals; of knowing what goals they are pursuing, and of knowing how to inspire children to think scientifically.

## FOR FURTHER REFLECTION

Ask yourself:

1. What education do I need to fulfil the role of inclusive science educator?
2. How can I provide appropriate resources to promote scientific thinking for teachers and students in the setting where I work?
3. How can I use what I have learnt here to build a climate of acceptance within the early years setting?
4. What actions am I going to pursue, in my work setting, to strengthen my skills as a science educator?
5. How can I use technology to share information, extending learning documentation and reflective practice?

## WEBSITES

www.commonsensemedia.org/educators and www.commonsensemedia.org/reviews

Common Sense Media present a range of tools for educators using media and technology in their classroom. This site also presents reviews of apps, games and resources that will assist educators in making decisions when using technologies.

www.howstuffworks.com/

This is an excellent website for gaining information and knowledge about almost everything. Search this site for details on the mechanisms of physics and chemistry in straightforward language and practical steps. Though some information is geared to the older learner, there is a search slot that allows for all sorts of questions,such as 'Where did the moon come from?' and 'Where does water come from?' This site is invaluable when children ask questions and the answer is unknown!

www.newton.dep.anl.gov

One way to find answers is to, simply, log onto the Internet and ask your question. It is very likely that the question has been asked before and the answer is immediately available. The Newton website, *Ask a Scientist*, is a good resource.

http://science.nasa.gov/ask-a-scientist

This site is also 'Ask a Scientist' but covers a number of science fields: http://science.nasa.gov/ask-a-scientist.

## REFERENCES


Australian Curriculum and Reporting Authority (ACARA). (2013). *Student Diversity.* Retrieved from www.acara.edu.au/curriculum/student_diversity/student_diversity.html

Attwood, A. (2004). *Exploring feelings: Cognitive behaviour therapy to manage anxiety.* Future Horizons: Arlington, Texas.

Ballard, K. (2013). Thinking in another way: Ideas for sustainable inclusion. *International Journal of Inclusive Education. 17*(8), 762–775. doi:10.1080/13603116.2011.602527

Baum, S.M. & Olenchak, F.R. (2002). The alphabet children: GT, ADHD, and more. *Exceptionality, 10* (2), 77–91. doi:10.1207/S15327035EX1002_3

Campbell, P., Milbourne, S., Dugan, L. & Wilcox, M. (2006). A review of evidence on practices for teaching young children to use assistive technology devices. *Topics in Early Childhood Special Education, 2*(3), 3–13. doi:10.1177/02711214060260010101

Dahlberg, G., Moss, P. & Pence, A. (1999). *Beyond quality in early childhood education and care: Postmodern perspectives.* London: Falmer Press.

Department of Education, Employment and Workplace Relations (DEEWR). (2009). *Belonging, being and becoming: The early years learning framework for Australia.* Retrieved from: www.deewr.gov.au/Earlychildhood/Policy_Agenda/Quality/Documents/Final%20EYLF%20Framework%20Report%20-%20WEB.pdf

Hedegaard, M. (2001). *Learning and child development.* Aarhus: Aarhus Universitetsforlag.

Inan, H.Z., Trundle, K.C. & Kantor, R. (2010). Understanding natural sciences education in a Reggio Emilia-inspired preschool. *Journal of Research in Science Teaching, 47*(10), 1186–1208. doi:10.1002/tea.20375

Inhelder, B. & Piaget, J. (1958). *The growth of logical thinking from childhood to adolescence.* New York: Basic Books.

Johnson, S. (2012). Reconceptualising gardening to promote inclusive education for sustainable development, *International Journal of Inclusive Education, 16*(5–6), 581–596. doi:10.1080/13603116.2012.655493

Katz, L.G. (2010). STEM in the early years. Early childhood research and practice. *Collected Papers from the SEED (STEM in Early Education and Development) Conference.* Retrieved from ecrp.uiuc.edu/beyond/seed/index.html

Katz, L.G., & Chard, S.C. (1996). The contribution of documentation to the quality of early childhood education, *ERIC Digest*. Urbana, IL: ERIC Clearinghouse on Elementary and Early Childhood Education.

Kutscher, M.L. & Attwood., A. (2007). *Kids in the syndrome mix.* London: Jessica Kingsley Publishers.

Luria, A.R. (1979). *The making of mind.* Cambridge, MA: Harvard University Press.

Malaguzzi, L. (1996). The right to environment. In T. Filippini and V. Vecchi, *The hundred languages of children: The exhibit.* Reggio Emilia: Reggio Children.

Marchel, M., Fischer, T. & Clarke, D. (2014). *Assistive technology for children and youth with disabilities.* New Jersey: Pearson, Higher Ed.

Milikan, J. (2003). *Reflections: Reggio Emilia principles within Australian contexts.* Castle Hill, NSW: Pademelon Press.

Richards, C. (2010). *Can we make space for children's decision-making? Perspectives on educational policy. Children as decision makers in education.* Continuum International Publishing Group Retrieved from www.uea.ac.uk/polopoly_fs/1.146042!Children_as_decision_makers.pdf

Siraj-Blatchford, I. & Siraj-Blatchford, J. (2006). *A guide to developing the ICT curriculum for early childhood education.* London: Trentham Books.

Strong-Wilson, T., & Ellis, J. (2007). Children and place: Reggio Emilia's environment as third teacher. *Theory into Practice, 46*(1), 40–7. doi:10.1080/00405840709336547

Vygotsky, L.S. (1962). *Thought and language.* Cambridge, MA: MIT press.

SECTION 6

# Facilitating Inclusion

# 22 Including Children with Sense Impairments in the Early Years

*Paul Pagliano*

CHAPTER OVERVIEW

This chapter will focus on including children with sense impairments in the early years.

Learning goals for this chapter include:

- Understanding the senses and the essential role they play in development and learning;
- Understanding how children use their senses, particularly vision and hearing, how these senses are assessed, and how these sense impairments are categorised;
- Being aware of how sense impairments of vision and hearing may impact on development, social interaction and learning;
- Knowing ways of maximising development, social interaction and learning within an inclusive setting.

KEY TERMS AND CONCEPTS

educationally blind

educationally deaf

hard of hearing

low vision

sense impairment

# Introduction

The senses are the basis of development and learning. If a child doesn't have senses then the brain won't receive valuable stimulation. The senses are the way a child accesses information about their internal selves or about the outside world. As early years professionals we therefore must be continually checking whether the children in our care are using their senses in the best ways they possibly can to engage in the learning activities we are offering (Winter, 2010).

**sense impairment:** When additional support is required beyond what is usually provided in order for a child to effectively learn through the senses.

All children use their sense experiences to construct their understanding of themselves and the outside world. In the early years, vision and hearing are particularly important for development and learning; however the other senses also play significant roles—often in unexpected ways. For that reason, in this chapter we will not only be learning about how to include children with **sense impairments** in the early years, we will also be learning about the vital role all the senses play in development and learning.

**FIGURE 22.1** CHILDREN DRIVING IN THE CAR TOGETHER

*Photo: Dinah Cocksedge*

# The senses and the essential role they play in development and learning

All early years professionals must clearly understand the role the senses play in development and learning if they are to provide the most appropriate services to support individual child development. Furthermore, as a bonus, the better we understand the role the senses play, the better we will all be at designing experiences that engage children through the senses in more interesting, targeted, effective and efficient ways. The term sensory impairment is often thought to be synonymous with vision and hearing. To break the hegemony and to be more inclusive this chapter uses the term sense impairment.

The child accesses stimulation through the senses; to be more precise, through a set of six different types of sense receptors. The child has hundreds of millions of sense receptors. They respond to body position, chemical stimuli, light, mechanical stress or strain, temperature and tissue damage. A sense organ consists of a group of similar sense receptors that work together to access a particular type of sense information. The receptors convert the sense information into electrical activity, which then travels along the nerves to the brain, where it is processed to form part of an overall pool of experience that is available for future reference.

Sensing comprises two interconnected actions: sense acuity and sensory processing. Sense acuity entails accessing stimulation, converting it into a type of electrical energy and posting it to the brain. Sensory processing involves receiving the electrical energy, detecting it, recognising it, and differentiating it in increasingly more sophisticated ways. As the process becomes more efficient and effective, these two sets of actions combine to take on an anticipatory role called predictive coding (Pagliano, 2012). Past sense experiences modulate current sense perceptions in both overt and covert ways.

With predictive coding, the central, peripheral and autonomic nervous systems team up to become 'an engine of prediction' (Clark, 2011, p.1). This means we can use anticipation to orchestrate sense acuity, sensory processing, perception, thought and action, all at the same time, and at progressively more purposeful and interrelated levels of intensity and precision.

Sense perception is not linear. Early years professionals need to be aware of three complicating factors. The first relates to predictive coding being strongly influenced by the affective. Young children are much more likely to repeat sense experiences that are gratifying and less likely to re-engage in sense experiences that provide no reward, lack meaning or are perceived as unpleasant. This means the affective adds another layer where children can experience differences with the senses: sense acuity, sensory processing, and the psycho-emotional.

The second complication is the idea that the senses do not work in isolation. Children are multisensory beings and their senses work together. As Calvert, Spence and Stein (2004, p.xi) explain,

> There can be no doubt that our senses are designed to function in concert and that our brains are organized to use the information they derive from their various sensory channels cooperatively in order to enhance the probability that objects and events will be detected rapidly, identified correctly, and responded to appropriately.

In actual fact there is no such thing as an isolated sense experience. For example, the vestibular system provides us with a sense of balance so without the vestibular sense, vision cannot be stabilised.

This leads us to the third complication. Some senses predominantly work at a subconscious level while others function at a more conscious level. Those that mostly function at the subconscious level are the senses of interoception. These senses provide information about what is happening inside the body: proprioception (muscle spindles, Golgi tendon organs), and the vestibular (which provides information about movement and head position and is important for balance and spatial awareness). With up to ninety per cent of the brain's energy devoted to posture alone, it is easy to understand why the senses of interoception tend to operate at a more subconscious level. If they didn't, this sense information would completely drown out other sense information.

Those senses that function more readily at a conscious level are the senses of exteroception. These senses, for example touch, taste, smell, hearing and vision, provide information about what is happening outside the body. Children need this information to enable them to purposefully occupy themselves in the world around them. Yet, even the senses of exteroception only give prominence to sense information considered to be particularly relevant and important at that moment in time. Therefore, superfluous exteroception sense information also slips into the subconscious. For example after a while children generally cease to hear the clock ticking or do not think about how their clothes feel; that is, unless there is some reason for them to focus on the clock ticking or their clothes are just too uncomfortable to ignore. Also, some children with 'autistic like' tendencies may report ongoing heightened awareness of sensory information that others may assume slips into subconsciousness.

When children's senses work well together they provide coordinated information about where the body begins and ends, and its position in space. Without this collaboration their senses would lack meaning. This is because the meaning comes from the context provided by the senses working in combination. The senses of exteroception provide the senses of interoception with essential foundation information for them to function. To return to our example, the vestibular aligns with vision to help us move our head in compensatory ways, thereby ensuring the visual image on the retina is stable.

The early years professional must therefore be particularly alert to the ways all children use all their senses and regularly share pertinent information regarding individual functioning. Where differences in the senses are identified, an initial overall examination by the child's family doctor might result in a referral to a paediatrician, a physiotherapist, occupational therapist, or speech and language pathologist for further assessment.

As the majority of our conscious perceptions relate to hearing and vision, and therefore to development and learning, challenges associated with these senses are the principal focus of this chapter. Hearing plays a critical role in the acquisition of speech and language and vision plays a vital role in social development and learning. Children who are blind or deaf experience the world in novel ways. This means they will have particular strengths that are different to those of other children. These must be recognised, acknowledged and nurtured. We will now consider these senses in greater detail.

## How children use their vision and hearing

Hearing starts with the pinna, the visible part of the ear, funnelling sound waves down the external auditory canal to the middle ear. In the middle ear, little bones called the ossicles and the oval window convert those waves into vibrations. These pressure waves then travel to the cochlea, located in the inner ear, where they are converted into neural impulses and sent along the auditory nerve to the brain for processing.

Vision begins when light enters the eye through the pupil, a black hole in the iris. The iris is the coloured part of the eye that expands to make the pupil smaller in bright light and contracts to make the pupil larger in dim light. Light travels through the lens, where it is focused onto the retina at the back of the eye. Two types of photoreceptors, rods and cones, convert light into electrical impulses that travel along the optic nerve to the brain. The rods convert dim light and the cones convert coloured light. The refracted light enters the retina upside down so the image must be turned up the right way by the brain.

The best learning environments are created for children when the designer takes particular account of the child's perspective. You do this by first recognising that the child's perspective is going to be very different to your own. Even though you might be in exactly the same environment as the child, the way the child experiences that environment is going to be influenced by their age, their stage of development, their unique set of prior experiences, their sense acuity, their sensory processing ability, and the types of psycho-emotional environments the child inhabits. Each child is therefore going to have a subtly different perspective to every other child, with the differences becoming more pronounced if the child has a sense impairment that relates to hearing or vision, and even more pronounced if other challenges are also involved.

Both hearing and vision are considered from an educational standpoint as existing along an ability continuum, from typical sense acuity (the majority of the population) through to mild concerns (widespread, but easily correctable), to impairment (less frequent, and persists even after correction). Here the word 'impairment' is used to indicate two things: that the child still has a sensory difference even after the best correction possible, and as a consequence of this sense difference, the child requires additional, more specialised support than that usually provided to the other children.

## Assessing and categorising vision and hearing

**hard of hearing:** Possessing some hearing that is accessible for learning.

**educationally deaf:** Possessing insufficient hearing accessible for learning, so the majority of learning must occur through other senses.

Mild hearing and vision differences in young children are difficult to identify because without assistance the young child has no way to make comparisons. For each child using their own frame of reference, what they hear and see is 'normal'. Early years professionals therefore must be astutely observant of the child's auditory and visual functioning, and this observation needs to be ongoing.

With hearing, the impairment end of the continuum goes from **hard of hearing**, where there is some functional hearing for learning, through to **educationally deaf**, where there is an absence of functional hearing available for learning. The early years professional is most interested in whether the child has sufficient hearing for it to be a useful channel for learning, particularly communication, or whether the child must predominantly learn through other sense channels, principally vision.

Young children with hearing impairment are referred to an ear, nose and throat specialist (otorhinolaryngologist), who examines the health of these organs and conducts surgery. An audiologist, a non-medical practitioner, measures hearing using an audiometer and prescribes hearing aids. In audiometry, hearing for each ear is plotted separately on an audiogram comprising an XY grid where the X-axis represents pitch measured in Hertz (Hz) and the Y-axis represents loudness measured in Decibels (dB) (see Figure 22.2).

**FIGURE 22.2** AUDIOGRAM

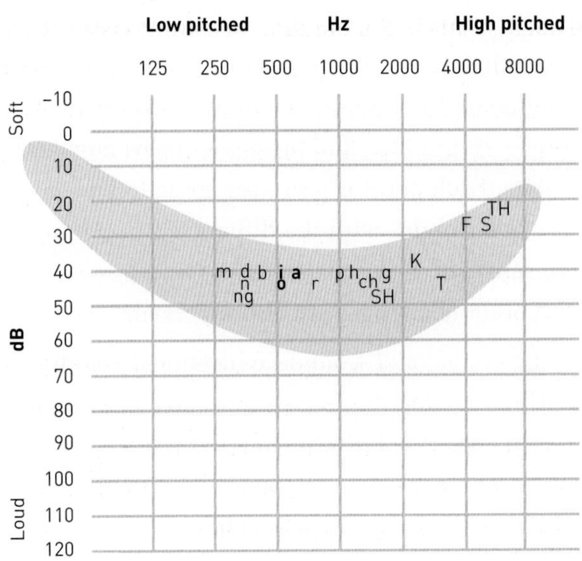

The majority of human speech occurs between 300 and 5000 Hz and 15 and 60 dB, so any hearing loss that covers these levels will cause difficulties with spoken communication. The most common differences are high frequency sounds like 's' in plurals, tenses and word endings. Hearing aids are designed to support the particular needs of the user by amplifying those tones they find difficult to hear and blocking out background noise. Hearing aids amplify sounds up to the human pain threshold (120 dB), but personal discomfort may occur at considerably lower levels.

With vision, the impairment end of the continuum continues from **low vision**, where there is some functional vision for learning, through to **educationally blind**, where there is an absence of functional vision for learning. Here the early years professional is interested in whether the child has sufficient vision for it to be a useful channel for learning or whether the child must learn predominantly through other sense channels, chiefly hearing and touch. As with hearing there are many things to consider.

**low vision:** Possessing some vision accessible for learning.

**educationally blind:** Possessing insufficient vision accessible for learning so majority of learning must occur through other senses.

Young children with vision impairment are referred to an eye specialist (ophthalmologist) who checks the health of the eye and conducts surgery. An optometrist, a non-medical practitioner, assesses vision and prescribes glasses, contact lenses and other low vision aids such as a monocular miniscope-telescope. Skills accomplished by one eye are called monocular skills and those requiring the coordination of both eyes are called binocular skills. Stereopsis (depth perception) is an important binocular skill. When making decisions about whether the child has sufficient vision it is important to be aware that there are two different types of vision—peripheral or general vision and central or fine vision.

Children have a large visual field, which expands with age (140 degrees vertically, 180 degrees horizontally) but the majority of this vision is general in nature. Such vision enables them to see shapes and get around safely but does not allow them to see details: this is the function of central vision. Central vision is like shining a spotlight on something. The child sees the parts that are best lit more clearly. Central vision is necessary for fine work like reading and writing. As well as testing a child's visual field, general and central vision, the optometrist will assess distance visual acuity, near visual acuity, colour vision, straightness of the eyes (heterophoria), focusing skills (accommodation, fusional vergence, near point of convergence), and eye movements (saccades, tracking).

About one in a thousand babies have a congenital hearing impairment. The impairment is identified through the automated auditory brainstem response test given to newborn babies once they are 12 hours old. This painless, risk-free test immediately determines whether the baby has a hearing difference. Congenital causes of hearing impairment include genetic factors, prenatal infections, toxins and prematurity. Another one in a thousand children acquire hearing impairment sometime after birth. Causes of acquired hearing impairment include infections, trauma, drugs and excessive exposure to noise.

An additional consideration regarding acquired hearing impairment is whether it was acquired pre- or post-lingually. Not acquiring speech and language before developing hearing impairment is a significant disadvantage. Another consideration is the presence of additional impairments, with over one third of children with hearing impairments having additional impairments.

Hearing impairment is divided into four types: conductive, sensorineural, central, and mixed (Roberson, Byrne-Haberm, & Robertson, 2013). Each type relates to a different part of the ear. Conductive hearing impairment is caused by a blockage in the middle ear that muffles and distorts the sound. Usually the middle ear is filled with air. With otitis media (inflammation of the middle ear), a respiratory infection blocks this flow of air so the middle ear fills with liquid. Otitis media is widespread in the early years, especially in Indigenous children. This blockage can cause fluctuating hearing differences where the child might hear clearly one day and experience considerable difficulty the next. Early medical treatment is recommended to alleviate the earache and in extreme cases a grommet may be inserted to drain the fluid. A preventive measure during flu season involves teaching children to breathe, blow and wipe their nose, and to jump up and down to promote drainage and air flow.

Sensorineural hearing impairment indicates damage to the cochlea in the inner ear. This can result in deafness. Damage to the cochlea may be bypassed by a cochlear implant. Research indicates that the best results for cochlear implants are achieved when the implant is inserted before the child reaches two years of age. In such cases the implant may move the child along the continuum from educationally deaf to hard of hearing, which means that hearing can become one of the senses the child uses for learning. Many in the Deaf community strongly object to cochlear implants for very young children, arguing that the child is not involved in the decision-making and implants threaten Deaf culture and language.

Hearing aids may provide additional support and can be prescribed even to children with a cochlear implant. Usually young children are given the simpler and easier to maintain behind-the-ear (BTE) hearing aids. They can also be connected to hearing assistive technology systems using FM (frequency modulated) devices. These comprise a microphone and transmitter worn by the speaker and a receiver worn by the child. As FM devices enable sound to be wirelessly transmitted over distance from one person to another, irrelevant background noise is substantially reduced.

The term 'central hearing impairment' is used to refer to damage to the auditory nerve or to the auditory cortex in the brain. The word 'mixed' is used to refer to a combination of both conductive and sensorineural hearing impairments.

Regarding vision in the early years, up to 25 per cent of children will experience a vision difference of some kind, yet only about one third of this population will have their eyes checked by an ophthalmologist or optometrist. Common eye conditions to be aware of include:

- A refractive error (myopia—nearsightedness, hyperopia—far sightedness, or a mixture of both, in which case the child will experience considerable difficulty with depth perception);
- Amblyopia (one eye is doing most of the work);
- Strabismus (misaligned eyes);
- Conjunctivitis (infection);
- Allergy (dust, sun, smoke);
- Altered colour vision.

The majority of these conditions are easily corrected with glasses or medical attention, except colour vision. Possible strategies to help the child with differences in colour vision include helping the child to understand what colours they can see, what colours they find difficult to distinguish, knowing basic colour rules and explicitly naming the colours of drawing implements.

The prevalence of vision impairment in young children is about two in one thousand with low vision and three in ten thousand being educationally blind in developed countries, and 15 in ten thousand in underdeveloped countries (Gilbert & Awan, 2003). At least 50 per cent of those with vision impairment have additional impairments. As with children with hearing impairments, the presence of additional impairments is largely due to advances in modern medicine where children with complicated conditions are living longer. The presence of additional impairments may pose challenges for the child's learning, so these children may require more highly specialised assistance. Some children have a condition called cerebral vision impairment (CVI), where visual performance is directly related to neurological functioning (Dutton & Bax, 2010).

# How sense impairments may impact on development, social interaction and learning

Extreme caution is recommended when making generalisations about how sense impairment may impact on development, social interaction and learning. One needs to ask how those generalisations were made, whether they were the result of making comparisons between children with sense impairments and those without sense impairments, and whether they are stated in terms of deficits. Focusing on deficits can negatively impact on expectations, and they offer few positive guides for promoting learning.

The individualised approach takes on board the broad general principles of child development and reconsiders them from the perspective of the individual child. These general principles include:

- In child development all the domains (physical, social, emotional and cognitive) are interrelated. For example, 12-month-old Henry's world expands as he becomes more mobile;
- Child development tends to occur in a cumulative process where later skills and abilities are built on earlier ones. For example, baby Angela builds on her learned ability to control her breathing in order to support her vocal development;
- Intra- and inter-individual differences influence the rates of child development. For example, many girls are often taller than boys around puberty;
- Early experiences can either promote or delay development, with some experiences having greater benefit if they occur in more optimal periods than others. For example, Ted, who has hearing impairment and a cochlear implant, may acquire oral language skills at an earlier age than Simon, who does not have an implant;
- Advances in development occur through play, practice and extension activities. For example, Susan, who has vision impairment, will need to be explicitly taught how to play using her other senses. This is because she is not able to visually copy other children;
- Children experience the world in different ways but learn best within a context where their needs are met and they feel safe and valued. For example, Jenny, who is both deaf and blind, learnt that crocodiles have legs while touching a taxidermist's specimen at the museum when under the expert supervision of her early years professional;
- Ideally all major sense impairments are identified as early as possible. It is also recommended that an individualised family service plan is prepared to guide and promote the coordination of specialist services and to ensure these purposefully fit in with early years services (see Chapter 11).

To achieve this more individual understanding of child development we must extensively consult with key stakeholders and experts to find out the pertinent details for each individual child. For instance, what do you know about the child's family—who they are, where they live, their socio-economic status, the language(s) they speak, any cultural, religious or belief systems one needs to be aware of, and whether they have any relatives with, or prior experience of, sense impairments.

Another useful idea regarding development is to consider what is a fair consequence of the sense impairment. To be able to make this kind of assessment it is necessary to have a more in-depth understanding of the senses and their possible impact on development.

Some aspects of sense impairment may interfere with early bonding between the baby and the parent. Lack of eye contact in the baby with vision impairment, or a lack of response to the mother's voice in the baby with hearing impairment, may subtly and negatively impact on the way the mother and/or father interacts with the baby. Early diagnosis and support to help the parents better understand what is happening offer the opportunity for parents to find other ways to bond. For the baby with vision impairment this will focus on smell, touch and voice whereas for the baby with hearing impairment this will focus on smell, touch and sight. Another factor that can negatively impact on bonding is prematurity, when the baby spends long periods of time in a humidicrib. Once again deliberate measures need to be introduced early to promote more natural bonding. For example, under direction of the health care professional, lie baby on your chest for lots of skin on skin contact, tune in by closely observing what sense experiences are calming or distressing, explicitly imitate baby's actions and use these to gradually build a sense communication repertoire. Interact as often as possible ensuring your actions are calm, soothing, gentle, consistent and mutually appreciated.

Before talking about the impact of hearing impairment on communication it is important to distinguish between communication (the exchange of information), speech (oral communication) and language (the code or system the child uses to communicate). The moment one hears the words 'hearing impairment' one wonders whether there will be a negative impact on the early acquisition of communication skills. This, however, is not always the case. Approximately one in ten children who are educationally deaf have parents who are also deaf. These children are therefore likely to be born into a Deaf culture and be introduced to sign language from birth (Lane, Hoffmeister, Bahan & Machemer, 2013). (As noted in Chapter 3, lower-case 'd' e.g. deaf denotes impairment whereas capital 'D' as in Deaf denotes culture). This means the Deaf child's communication development will be at a similar level to that of hearing children. Other children may have a cochlear implant early in their life, and this may also greatly assist their communication development.

Most children with hearing impairment, however, will find the acquisition of speech and language a great challenge. Delayed communication development may then have serious knock-on effects in social and emotional development. According to Yoshinaga-Itano, Coulter and Thomson (2001), children who receive early education services from before six months of age are 2.6 times more likely to acquire 'normative' language skills. This groundbreaking research was instrumental in the worldwide adoption of hearing testing at birth.

A major role of the early years professional is to support the family of the child with hearing impairment, while they explore which communication options will best suit their child and their family. This can be complicated and controversial, as different people have strongly held and diverse points of view regarding which option is best. Naturally those who can hear are generally biased towards the power and importance of spoken language, whereas many who are deaf value their own Deaf culture and sign language. With so much emphasis on inclusion and diversity nowadays, there is increasing opportunity to go beyond making either/or decisions. Bilingual education incorporating signed and spoken languages creates many opportunities to value multiple means of communication.

The child with vision impairment faces a different but similar set of challenges. As up to eighty per cent of learning is thought to be visual (American Optometric Association, 2010) having vision impairment also poses a serious challenge to accessibility to information. Ferrell (2000) identified possible developmental milestones where there could be delays. These are: reaching for and touching an object, sitting alone without support, feeding self, crawling, walking, dressing, talking, toileting, using stairs, and reflecting on a past event. The following section now focuses on what you can do to promote optimum development.

## Maximising the child's development, social interaction and learning within an inclusive setting

Sense impairments are impairments of accessibility. Much of the early years professional's work then is to ensure the child with sense impairments has equal opportunities to access information. To do this professionals must learn how to think in visual ways so activities are meaningful for the child with hearing impairment. The same applies for children with vision impairments except now the professional must learn how to think in non-visual ways.

It takes considerable time and self-discipline to learn these skills. One teacher began to teach herself by wearing a blindfold for 15 minutes each night and keeping a diary. Another did the same, only she wore a noise cancellation headphone. It is important though to acknowledge that these are merely simulations, experienced out of context. You can return to your usual way of accessing information by simply removing the device, so the experience is exaggerated. The child with sense impairment will have developed many well-integrated visual or auditory skills that take more effort than merely wearing a blindfold or a noise cancellation headphone.

When working with a young child one must consider the child's immediate needs within the larger contexts of the whole child, the child's whole family, and the child's whole life. Being aware of these three broad contexts is especially important because it is easy to over-focus on a particular learning task and lose sight of how the task fits into the big picture. For example, Wolffe (2012) reminds us that career concepts for all children begin in early years, so children with sense impairments similarly need role models to help them develop career concepts, such as adults with sense impairment who have responsible jobs in the community.

Strategies to ensure the professional maintains an awareness of these different contexts include:

- *Involve the family.* The individualised family services plan (IFSP) and the individual education plan (IEP) provide frameworks for stakeholders to work together to support the child and the family in a consistent and well-coordinated manner (see Chapters 11 and 12). The family must be given parity and be framed as part of the solution (see Chapter 9). Team members may include an advisory teacher: hearing (a teacher specialising in support in the area of hearing) and a speech language pathologist who supports the communication needs of children with hearing impairments, or an an advisory teacher: vision (a teacher specialising in support for children with vision impairment) and an orientation and mobility instructor who supports the travel needs of children with vision impairments. In Australia the way these services are provided will differ in each state and territory. Children with sense impairment also receive specialised instruction in areas in addition to those in the regular curriculum. For children with vision impairment these areas are called the expanded core curriculum, and include areas such as Braille, listening skills, orientation and mobility, social skills, independent living skills and use of assistive technology. For children with hearing impairments, areas include communication (speech, sign, language and listening skills), literacy, social skills and use of assistive technology.
- *Inclusion.* With inclusion the emphasis is on the child's right to gain an education in the 'regular' education setting and to engage in equitable learning opportunities and play activities. The teacher supports inclusion by focusing on the learning potential of the child, building on what the child can do, and approaching learning challenges by considering how responsive the curriculum is to the child's learning needs and making pedagogical changes

as needed. If the setting or the approach does not meet the needs of the particular child then changes need to be made to accommodate the child's needs. Support services are available. For example, the Royal Institute for Deaf and Blind Children's Teleschool provides expert education and therapy services to support children throughout regional and remote Australia using high quality videoconferencing.

Professionals work together with families to consistently ensure children achieve learning outcomes that demonstrate accessibility, equal opportunity, self-sufficiency and children's highest potential.

- *Curriculum differentiation.* Professionals change the learning environment by making it child-centred, by altering what children learn, how they learn and how they demonstrate that learning.
- *Use the senses you have.* Ensure children with sense impairment use the senses they have to the best of their ability. Encourage children who are hard of hearing to use their hearing whenever possible and teach them how to use their hearing more effectively and efficiently. Encourage children with low vision to use their vision whenever possible and teach them how to use their vision more effectively and efficiently.
- *Maintain high expectations.* The general rule is to have the same high expectations for all children, and aim to have each child consistently work at their highest potential.
- *Independence.* Ensure children independently demonstrate their own learning. There is a real danger that children with sense impairments are given too much assistance and are overprotected. Sometimes the child is so used to being helped they actively elicit assistance from others: their parents, siblings, peers, teacher aides and even teachers. Remember every time you do something for the child with a sense impairment you steal from them the opportunity for them to do it for themselves. Also be particularly alert to how you model your interactions, because the other children will copy you and interact in the same way in the classroom and in the playground. Instead of doing the activity for the child provide a verbal orientation for the child with vision impairment and a visual orientation for the child with hearing impairment. Whenever the child appears confused or becomes disengaged repeat the orientation and the task instruction. Be precise in your communication and construct the communication from the child's perspective. This requires resoluteness and patience but it will be worth it in the end.
- *Choose learning activities that are level appropriate* (match task difficulty with the child's ability) *and age appropriate* (make certain the type of task is suitable for the child's age and experience).

- Ensure that the child has the necessary *prerequisites for learning* (what basic concepts *must* the child know to be able to make progress with this particular task?).

As the world for the child with hearing impairment is going to be very visual the early years professional must learn how to modify all classroom interactions so they are visually authentic. Remember children with hearing impairment learn to communicate by speech-reading so make certain the child can see people's faces, especially their lips, and make a practice of not talking about the child in public. The same applies for the child with vision impairment who relies heavily on hearing.

The child with hearing impairment may use a variety of different approaches to communicate. These will be informed by the amount of functional hearing available to the child. Higher levels of functional hearing will result in the child using an oral approach with speech-reading as a support. If greater emphasis needs to be placed on the child developing language proficiency then the oral may be further supplemented with signs, particularly finger spelling. Finger spelling involves the representation of letters of the alphabet using either two hands (British) or one hand (American). Despite the two-hand system being favoured in Australia the one hand system is also often used. An even more intense oral approach is cued speech, which uses hand shapes to inform speech production and clarify sounds that might otherwise be missed. In Australia, children who are educationally deaf may be taught using Auslan, the Australian sign language of the Deaf community. Auslan is a language in its own right.

**FIGURE 22.3** AUSLAN FOR *CAMEL*

*Photo: Dinah Cocksedge*

A few simple rules when communicating with a child with a hearing impairment are: check hearing aids, reduce background noise, make certain the child is watching you, speak in regular grammatical sentences with regular pace, be aware of the ear the child hears with (where relevant) and what frequencies the child can most easily hear, draw attention to difficult sounds, match sound to meaning using visual links, and play listening games. Also encourage others to follow your lead regarding how to communicate. Another valuable strategy is to explicitly teach vocabulary before a lesson so the child is well prepared.

If the child with vision impairment explores the environment through touch the information is built up sequentially, from the part to the whole (Cavitt & Gwise, 2013). If that child uses hearing often the child has no way of knowing what is making the sound or understanding how a particular sound might relate to another sound. Sense information is fragmented. It lacks cohesion. On the other hand, vision instantly unites large amounts of information. With vision the person can move from the whole to explore particular parts in context. There is a much greater level of cohesion. The sheer volume of information that comes through vision is just not available through any of the other senses. Vision impairment greatly reduces opportunities for incidental learning so this missed learning needs to occur in other ways. Vision also provides lots of confirmatory information. It provides continuous feedback to the child, and lots of redundant information that helps to ensure that associations are accurate and meaningful. As the child with vision impairment misses out on this kind of support when trying to construct meaning out of their senses, experiences can be much more difficult. The role of the early years professional is therefore pivotal. For example, greater cohesion could be achieved by regularly providing an audio description of pertinent components of the early years setting as an introduction and follow-up to each activity. Children who are educationally blind may learn Braille—a tactual system of reading and writing. They will also learn to read through listening, especially when using computers and other forms of technology with speech output.

**CASE STUDY 22.1**

## Working together for inclusion

Four-year-old Annette is a vivacious, outgoing child who's well liked by her peers. She was born with an eye condition that's resulted in very low vision, even after correction. Annette needs to hold the picture storybook 5cm from her eyes to be able to see it. This makes it impossible for Louise, her teacher, to be able to read from the same book during group activities. Louise therefore has two copies, one for Annette and one for everyone else. Annette loves story time and when everyone talks about the pictures she uses her magnifying glass to see the same details. Sometimes Annette even notices things the other children miss, but that's probably because Louise always gives her the book the night before to check it out. Her friends get confused and often think Annette can see just like them. After all she seems to be able to find them in the playground and she plays catchy. 'How do you find us, Annette?' asked her friend Julie one day. Annette replied, 'When everyone arrives in the morning I look at what you're all wearing. That helps me to make clever guesses.' Annette's becoming quite confident at making guesses and she doesn't even mind if sometimes she makes mistakes.

CRITICAL REFLECTION QUESTION

If you were working with Annette, how might you further extend on her developing confidence to facilitate her inclusion within the early years setting?

Jim's excited because he's just about to start Year 1. He has a moderate hearing impairment, so he wasn't eligible for a cochlear implant. His hearing aids make a positive difference. His preschool teacher from last year has specially prepared a report for Jim's new teacher. She said: 'Jim's very good with concrete words like house, car and truck, but he has difficulty with more abstract words like before, after and jealous. I therefore try to anticipate any new concepts we might be learning and make sure I explicitly teach them before we do it in class. I have a checklist of key basic concepts and regularly go over them with Jim. This emphasis on anticipation seems to help a lot. Overall, Jim tends to use simpler words than those used by his peers. Also he makes more mistakes with plurals, tenses and possessives and he does sometimes speak more loudly than everyone else. Jim understands this and when I use a turning the dial sign he will lower his volume. Mostly I've been focusing on Jim's message rather than over-emphasising perfect speech. This has helped him gain confidence with the other boys in the playground. Jim particularly likes visual games like playing soccer and cricket. He's so good at these sports I'm hoping it'll help him make lots of friends into the future. Let me know if I can be of further assistance.'

CRITICAL REFLECTION QUESTION

If you were Jim's new teacher, how might this information be helpful? What other information would you like to know?

# Conclusion

This chapter focuses on including children with sense impairments in early years settings, particularly children with vision and hearing impairments. The senses play an essential role in development and learning. Sensing comprises two interconnected actions: sense acuity and sensory processing. These actions combine to take on an anticipatory role called predictive coding. Predictive coding uses prediction to manage how children perceive sense experiences. The senses work best when they are multisensory and sense experiences are deemed to be gratifying. The senses of interoception operate at a more subconscious level to support the senses of exteroception that work at a more conscious level. Sense impairment is divided into hearing impairment (hard of hearing and educationally deaf) and vision impairment (low vision and educationally blind). It is best to avoid making broad generalisations when considering how hearing and vision impact on the child's development, social interaction and learning, and to focus more on how it all impacts on the individual child. This enables the provision of education that takes many other factors into account. The early years professional maximises the child with sense impairment's development, social interaction and learning within an inclusive setting by involving the family, using curriculum differentiation, encouraging the child to use the senses they have, maintaining high expectations, and focusing on the child developing independence.

## FOR FURTHER REFLECTION

1. A digital sound meter is an instrument for measuring environmental sounds. They are easily available in electronic stores or as a 0.99 cent smart phone app. Use the sound meter to measure the noise level in your early years setting (or in your home or workplace). Reflect on the level of background noise and identify ways this might be reduced. Investigate how to sound proof particularly troublesome noise sources.
2. Conduct an audit of lighting and glare for your early years setting (or your home or workplace), both inside and outside, at different times during the day, and during different weather conditions. Suggest strategies that would enable you to have more control over lighting and glare.
3. Prepare an audio description of your bedroom. Remember to start from the whole and then focus in on the pertinent parts. Ask a friend to give you feedback on your audio description as to whether they would be able to navigate the room without using their vision.

## WEBSITES

www.aussieeducator.org.au

Aussie Educator provides an Australian perspective to education. Click Home > Education > Specific Areas > Special Education then Hearing or Vision Impairment—The site includes comprehensive details about professional associations, key education sites, hearing/vision technology, and other information.

www.trinity.edu/org/sensoryimpairments/index.htm

'Teaching students with sensory impairments: Strategies for mainstream teachers' is a site developed for Australian, New Zealander and American teachers that focuses on helpful strategies for teachers to include children with sensory impairments.

## REFERENCES


American Optometric Association. (2010). *School aged vision: 6 to 18 years of age.* Retrieved from www.aoa.org/x9451.xml

Calvert, G., Spence, C. & Stein, B. (Eds). (2004). *The handbook of multisensory processes.* Cambridge, MA: MIT Press.

Cavitt, W. & Gwise, T. (2013). *A blind child's pathway to learning: Developing cognition without sight.* Bloomington, IN: AuthorHouse.

Clark, A. (2011). *Predictive coding. What scientific concept would improve everybody's cognitive toolkit?* Retrieved from www.edge.org/q2011/q11_6.html

Dutton, G. & Bax, M. (Eds). (2010). *Visual impairment in children due to damage to the brain.* London: Max Keith Press.

Ferrell, K. (2000). Growth and development of young children. In M.C. Holbrook & A.J. Koenig (Eds). *Foundations of education: Vol. 1. History and theory of teaching children and youths with visual impairment* (pp.111–134). (2nd edn). New York, NY: AFB Press.

Gilbert, C. & Awan, H. (2003). Blindness in children: Half of it is avoidable, and suitable cost effective interventions are available. *British Medical Journal, 327*(7418), 760–761. doi:10.1136/bmj.327.7418.760

Lane, H., Hoffmeister, R., Bahan, B. & Machemer, C. (2013). *A journey into the Deaf world.* San Diego, CA: Dawn Sign Press.

Pagliano, P. (2012). *The multisensory handbook: A guide for children and adults with sensory learning disabilities.* London: David Fulton (Routledge).

Roberson, J., Byrne-Haberm, S. & Robertson, K. (2013). *Hear for life: Dr. Joe's guide to your child's hearing loss.* East Palo Alto, CA: Let Them Hear Foundation.

Winter, P. (2010). *Engaging families in the early childhood development story: Neuroscience and early childhood development. Summary of selected literature and key messages for parenting.* Carlton South, Vic: Education Services Australia Ltd., MCEECDYA. Retrieved from www.mceecdya.edu.au/verve/_resources/ECD_Story-Neuroscience_and_early_childhood_dev.pdf

Wolffe, K. (2012). *Career counseling for people with disabilities: A practical guide to finding employment* (2nd edn). Austin, TX: PRO-ED.

Yoshinaga-Itano, C., Coulter, D. & Thomson, V. (2001). Developmental outcomes of children with hearing loss born in Colorado hospitals with and without universal newborn hearing screening programs. *Seminars in Neonatology, 6*(6), 521–529. doi:10.1053/siny.2001.0075

# 23 Inclusion of Children through Augmentative and Alternative Communication Supports

*Teresa Iacono and Kathy Cologon*

CHAPTER OVERVIEW

Society in general privileges spoken language and narrow understandings of communication. This chapter will explain Augmentative and Alternative Communication (AAC) systems and ways of enabling participation through inclusive approaches to language and communication.

Learning goals for this chapter include:

- Identifying the right to communication for all children and the implications this has for early years practice;
- Exploring practical and philosophical considerations for early years professionals using AAC;
- Considering the importance of strengths-based, naturalistic, embedded, child and family-centred approaches to AAC;
- Developing an understanding of how AAC can support the quality provision of academic and social inclusion in early years settings.

KEY TERMS AND CONCEPTS

Augmentative and Alternative Communication (AAC)

dynamic assessment

incidental teaching

Participation Model

# Introduction

Sharing and exchanging thoughts and ideas, emotions, needs, likes and dislikes are all part of everyday communication. Society in general privileges spoken language and narrow understandings of communication. However, humans communicate with each other in many different ways every day. Everyone can communicate, whether or not that person can speak, write or read. For some individuals, including young children who have impairments that impact on their speech and language development, modes of communication that provide an alternative to, or supplement, spoken language may need to be established to facilitate effective communication (Cologon & McNaught, 2014).

Along with international covenants, the *Australian Curriculum*, the *Australian Professional Standards for Teachers*, the *National Quality Framework* and the *Australian Early Years Learning Framework* (ACARA, 2012; ACECQA, 2011; AITSL, 2011; DEEWR, 2009) all recognise the importance of (a) providing support to ensure that all children can communicate effectively and participate, and (b) the key role of teachers and other early years professionals in responding to student diversity and ensuring the participation of all students as learners. Reflecting on the importance of being able to communicate and be heard draws into sharp focus the need to fulfil this aspect of the early years professional's role.

Unsurprisingly then, providing support to ensure all children can participate and communicate is also critical to upholding basic human rights, as articulated in the *Convention on the Rights of the Child* (UNCRC) (United Nations, 1989) and the *Convention on the Rights of Persons with Disabilities* (UNCRPD) (United Nations, 2006). The words of a group of adults who live with communication impairments illustrates important considerations in upholding these rights:

> We are used to people saying we cannot communicate, but of course they are wrong. In fact we have powerful and effective ways of communicating and we usually have many ways to let you know what it is we have in mind. Yes, we have communication difficulties, and some of those are linked with our impairment. But by far the greater part of our difficulty is caused by 'speaking' people not having the experience, time or commitment to try to understand us or to include us in everyday life. You can imagine how tough this can be (SCOPE UK, 2002, pp.1–2).

The right to freedom of expression (Article 13 UNCRC & Article 21 UNCRPD) can be violated if opportunities are not provided for using multiple modes of communication. As noted in SCOPE UK (2002, p.2), 'we can't have proper consultation about our views unless people enable us to "be heard", and we cannot access information if it is not properly available to us in formats we can use and respond to.' Denying the opportunity to communicate beyond basic needs can also result in a violation of the right to freedom from inhuman or degrading treatment (Article 37 UNCRC, Article 15 UNCRPD):

> Consider how degrading and inhuman it is for year after year to go by without anyone really trying to communicate with you, except maybe just about your basic needs. If no-one takes the time to find out what you are thinking, or assists you to express your views, or just chat with others, this is treating you as if you were not a full human being (SCOPE UK, 2002, p.2).

While these words come from a group of adults, these considerations are just as important in regards to children. In order to take seriously the rights and dignity of every child, all early years professionals must consider ways of supporting effective communication. Providing such support may seem daunting, but is essential in light of the barriers experienced by children when communication partners (all those around a child who communicate with him/her) lack knowledge or commitment to engage in or facilitate shared communication (Kent-Walsh & Light, 2003; Myers, 2007). Therefore, supporting effective communication is a key focus for all early years professionals. In this chapter we will provide information as a starting point to assist in developing knowledge and understanding of **Augmentative and Alternative Communication (AAC)** strategies that can be implemented in early years settings.

**Augmentative and Alternative Communication (AAC)**: Symbols, aids, strategies and techniques that enhance communication for people with complex communication needs (American Speech-Language Hearing Association, 1991). AAC facilitates choice, participation and social inclusion (Beukelman & Mirenda, 2013).

## Augmentative and Alternative Communication

AAC involves the use of aided and unaided strategies. Unaided AAC strategies include gestures and manual signs. For children with communication difficulties, manual signs from the sign language of the host country are used to reflect core or key words of a sentence that are simultaneously spoken by the teacher. This approach, known as *Key Word Sign* in Australia, has evolved from the Makaton Vocabulary from the UK—whereby manual signs are taught according to a pre-determined vocabulary (Grove & Walker, 1990). In Australia, Key Word Sign borrows signs from Auslan (the language of the Australian Deaf community), which are produced along with spoken language.

Aided AAC strategies include low (or light) and high technology systems. Low-tech systems include simple devices that enable the production of brief messages, such as a greeting or request produced by activating a single switch device to generate speech output. Other low-tech systems include those requiring only a communication board, book or cards. High-tech systems include dedicated electronic communication devices, or software that can be

**FIGURE 23.1** AUSLAN FOR *MOON*

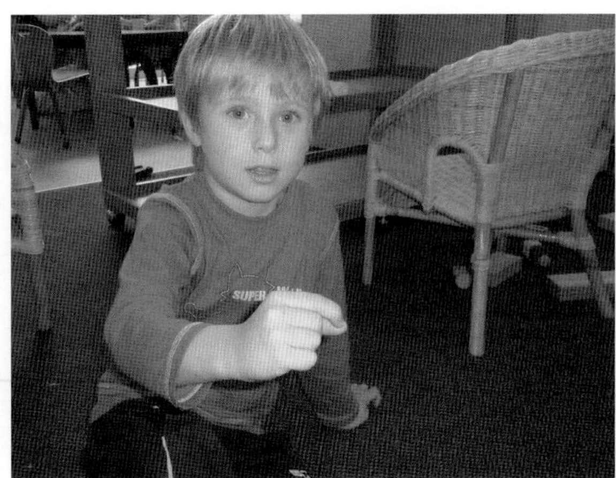

*Photo: Dinah Cocksedge*

incorporated into computers (or other devices) to allow use of the same device for communication, as well as for other functions (e.g. word processing or electronic games). Up until recently, high-tech options have relied on specialised technology developed for people who have complex communication needs, hence, given the relatively small market, high costs. As noted in Chapter 21, more recently, mainstream devices, in particular mobile devices such as phones and tablets that are internet enabled, have provided children who experience disability the opportunity to use the same technology used by their peers who do not experience disability, but with applications developed to meet their needs (Flores et al., 2012; Kagohara et al., 2013).

The range of AAC options available can create confusion about which to choose, and much has been written about the advantages and disadvantages of each (Sigafoos & Iacono, 1993; Wilkinson & Hennig, 2007). Manual signs, for example, require no external device, and so can be more convenient, but they rely on others to know and use them. Also, there can be a tendency to think that sophisticated high-tech devices are preferable, but children require support to learn how to access various pages of symbols using a menu system, and adults, such as parents and teachers, need to know how to program appropriate messages and vocabulary, as well as how to troubleshoot when there are technical problems. Such advantages and disadvantages need to be considered when developing AAC systems. Important considerations include the preferences of the child and the child's family, as well as the child's current abilities across areas relevant to the use of AAC needs and contexts (e.g. cognition, language, literacy, fine motor skills, forming a capability profile) (Beukelman & Mirenda, 2013). Hence, decisions need to be made about each AAC component, which may comprise more than one form of AAC, so they can come together as an integrated whole. These components are (a) the symbols, which are the methods used to represent key concepts, and include gestures, manual signs, real objects, parts or miniatures of objects, photographs, and drawings or other picture types, and written words; (b) aids (where relevant), which are the physical objects on which the symbols appear; (c) strategies that enable the child to use the system, such as through direct instruction, modelling, or incidental teaching; and (d) techniques used to transmit messages, including signing, selecting symbols on a keyboard through direct touching/pointing or using a switch to enable scanning and then selection of symbols. A key principle is that the best AAC solution is likely to be multimodal: that is, comprising various forms of AAC, as well as making use of the child's existing communication skills, such as speech or speech approximations, vocalisations and gestures.

## Underlying philosophies

As discussed in Chapter 2, the social model of disability shifts the focus from impairment to the disabling social effects arising from action or inaction by society, often motivated by negative attitudes or poor understanding within communities. Practices within AAC have been strongly influenced by the social model of disability, most especially in the form of the **Participation Model** of assessment. The Participation Model, described in detail by Beukelman and Mirenda (2013), provides a guide that extends usual assessment practices beyond the abilities and communication needs of the individual with complex communication needs, to consideration of his/her participation patterns against requirements in the setting. This process involves consideration of four key aspects: What are the communication needs and participation patterns required? What barriers are currently preventing participation? What changes (intervention) could be planned and made to eliminate these barriers through the incorporation of AAC? And, once these changes are implemented, evaluation of how effective these changes were and consideration of further adaptations to improve participation. In this way, interventions that include AAC can be developed to maximise the child's current and future communication strategies, simultaneously creating environments and contexts that enhance communication opportunities and success.

Participation Model: The participation model involves analysing or assessing the participation requirements of a particular task or experience to determine what AAC support is required to facilitate inclusion (Beukelman & Mirenda, 2013).

**CASE STUDY 23.1**

## Beginning the process of inclusion through AAC supports

Julie is four years old. She has Down syndrome and has been attending an early intervention program for the last two years. As part of this early intervention, Julie has been using manual signs, and picture-based AAC topic boards have been available in both indoor and outdoor areas. As part of a transition to school program, Julie will spend a year attending a regular preschool. Her parents, early intervention teacher, speech pathologist, and occupational therapist comprise the assessment team for Julie. They request a meeting at the preschool to observe the social and physical environment, and to discuss how to facilitate Julie's inclusion. Attending the meeting are the preschool Director and teachers in the four-year-old program. The assessment team make note that the classroom includes small activity areas, which are varied from week to week. Some of these activity areas have pictures, but none that will assist Julie to participate fully in the play or social activities in which the other children participate. The lack of supports presents possible barriers to Julie's inclusion and learning. Also, the preschool Director and teachers express concern about Julie's use of manual signs, given that no-one in the preschool understands sign; they are also concerned that the other children may start to use them, and Julie will over-rely on them resulting in them all becoming lazy in their speech. The lack of skill in manual sign and lack of knowledge about their impact on speech in the preschool present potential knowledge and attitudinal barriers to Julie's inclusion.

**dynamic assessment:** An approach to assessment that focuses on potential for learning (Hasson & Joffe, 2007), and in which the child and adult participate actively together.

Iacono and Caithness (2009) extended the Participation Model for children and adults with ASD. They considered the influence of family-centred practice (see Chapter 9), and how **dynamic assessment** strategies can inform interventions to build on current learning strengths and preferences, within social interactions in the child's daily routines. The Participation Model is potentially useful to all children with communication difficulties, including, but not limited to, those who may benefit from AAC (e.g. those whose are learning English as a new language). In particular, and key within the Participation Model, family members, teachers, speech pathologists and others who have a role to play in assessing communication and participation, work as a team to develop consensus about how best to meet the child's current and future communication needs. In this way, barriers to participation can be identified and strategies developed to ameliorate them. Such strategies must address knowledge, concerns and practical limitations across environments, with home and school providing powerful learning contexts, especially when an inclusive approach that incorporates AAC is used (Iacono, 1999). Such inclusive approaches take advantage of naturally occurring opportunities that can be integrated into everyday interactions.

**FIGURE 23.2** ASSESSING DYNAMICALLY!

*Photo: Viki Demetriou*

### CASE STUDY 23.1

*Continued*

Julie's speech pathologist and occupational therapist provide the preschool Director and staff with results of a recent assessment of Julie's skills and functioning within the early intervention classroom. They provide details of her progress in communication, including her increased vocabulary, produced using either speech or manual sign. They also demonstrate her improved ability to engage in symbolic and, recently, interactive play, and her increased participation in group activities through appropriate turn-taking and contributions. In addition, they provide information about the use of manual sign as a form of AAC, drawing from research demonstrating the positive impact of AAC on language development and interaction with peers. They acknowledge that it can be difficult to suddenly introduce AAC across all classroom activities. They and the teachers decide to start by developing a plan in which picture supports can be prepared for one of the activity areas planned for the first week of Julie's attendance. This support includes assistance in identifying pictured vocabulary for a topic board for the activity area, and teaching the teachers and the whole group five key word signs that would be used frequently: three of these are likely to be used across situations (*help, my turn, want*).

A key underlying philosophy of the Participation Model is inclusion in general educational programs (Beukelman & Mirenda, 2013). Children who use AAC face particular barriers to developing expressive language and learning to read. For young children who use AAC, true inclusion relies on having

(a) access to appropriate AAC systems for use in integrated language activities throughout the day and across school and home settings; (b) teachers who know how to support the use of AAC, including modelling AAC communication and providing support and instruction to peers in interacting with the child using AAC; (c) participation in emergent reading activities and reading instruction that utilises AAC as appropriate; and (d) their families being involved in assessment, goal setting and intervention as can be accommodated in relation to family situations and competing demands (Myers, 2007; Sturm & Clendon, 2004).

## AAC and early years teachers

As early years professionals, teachers in early years settings have key roles in contributing to (a) dynamic assessment of children's abilities to learn from supports provided within day-to-day interactions; and (b) implementing child-directed naturalistic interventions that incorporate AAC. Iacono and Caithness (2009) noted the value of using dynamic assessments of young children's communication within learning contexts. Such assessment involves observing the child's performance with and without assistance. As an example, the frequency with which a child directs requests and comments to other children using speech, sign or a picture board without support from an adult can be compared to when the adult provides a gestural and/or spoken prompt (e.g. partial production of a sign, or suggesting that the child 'tell' another child). The child's response to such supports informs intervention by identifying those strategies that best increase the child's communication. Further, using such real-life situations indicates what AAC supports may be needed—such as whether the child may also need a picture-based communication board. Integrating assessment into everyday teaching situations sets up an assess-teach-reassess process, ensuring an ongoing process of review.

### CASE STUDY 23.1

*Continued*

The plan for Julie's inclusion within the preschool setting activities includes strategies for the teachers to keep track of Julie and the other children's communication and play interactions. The teachers decide to use a system of observation and recording similar to one they use regularly. They will also note Julie's responses to their spoken and gestural prompts to use the topic board (e.g. saying 'Tell me what you want' or pointing to the topic board), and to their models of manual signs. This contributes to the ongoing dynamic assessment process that will inform modifications to existing support strategies or use of further ones.

Early years settings provide rich environments for inclusive teaching strategies. A well-known and evidence-based approach is **incidental teaching.** Early research demonstrated that children can develop both pre-language (Yoder, Warren, Kim & Gazdag, 1994) and early language skills (Warren, 1992) when incidental opportunities throughout the day are used to teach targeted skills. Most importantly, these teaching opportunities occur when children direct activities, as this ensures they are engaged and attentive, and therefore most likely to learn from models and supports provided by adults and other children (Kaiser, Ostrosky & Alpert, 1993).

**incidental teaching:** A naturalistic intervention that makes use of teachable moments throughout the child's day through relationship-based engagement (Iacono, 1999; Stahmer, Akshoomoff & Cunningham, 2011).

Play has been found to be a particularly powerful medium for incidental teaching or shared engagement in teachable moments (Hyun & Marshall, 2003; Jung, 2013). The creation of communication opportunities has been found effective in enhancing child initiations, but only when adults respond to the child's communicative attempts (Yoder, Warren, McCathren & Leew, 1998). Naturalistic interventions that make use of incidental teaching strategies, within responsive environments, can also incorporate AAC. Such naturalistic interventions include creating situations that increase the need for a child to initiate communication (e.g. asking a child to stir a cake mix and providing all that is needed except the spoon, but having a card with a picture of a spoon that enables the child to request the spoon) (Iacono, 1999). Such approaches enhance the potential for AAC to be embedded within early years activities (Johnston, McDonnell, Nelson & Magnavito, 2003), increasing the frequency of meaningful teaching moments.

The potential for environments to be responsive to child communication attempts and to provide required environmental supports relies on all communication partners. As children develop their play skills, they interact increasingly with other children, who can be supported to provide models and prompts, and perhaps most importantly, to be responsive to communication attempts. A small but growing body of research examining peer involvement in AAC intervention demonstrates that engaging peers inclusively in learning to use AAC strategies and supports can be effective in increasing reciprocal communication and social interactions, as well as in promoting more positive views of AAC (Myers, 2007; Fisher & Shogren, 2012). Fisher and Shogren (2012) conducted a review of 13 studies involving children in early years and upper primary settings; they found that even after only a few intervention sessions, children with and without AAC needs demonstrated increased use of AAC strategies for communication and social engagement. However, the analysis demonstrated the importance of taking an inclusive approach to implementing AAC strategies (Fisher & Shogren, 2012). These findings are notable, as they demonstrate improvements in communication when involving peers in the implementation of AAC strategies. Not only that, but they show positive outcomes for social interactions (e.g. commenting, requesting turns in a game, play initiations, conversation), rather than for only requests for basic needs or wants. A restricted focus on simple requests, unfortunately, can often be the primary intervention targets for young children who use AAC, thus the many purposes of communication are neglected. According to early work by Light (1988), the functions of communication extend beyond requests to satisfy needs and wants, to include transfer of information, social closeness and social etiquette. There are meaningful opportunities for children to use AAC for these varied functions in both home and early years settings.

### CASE STUDY 23.1

*Continued*

Noting Julie's enjoyment of imaginative play within the early intervention setting, her early intervention and preschool teachers worked to integrate AAC into an activity corner with a theme of a sandwich shop. There was a counter, till, toy money, plates, pretend bread and possible sandwich fillings, and food wraps. They created a topic board with the following vocabulary: *sandwich, cut, lettuce, tomato, cheese, butter, how much*. The teachers learnt the manual signs for *help, my turn, want, yum, butter* (action word). On the first day that Julie attended the preschool, the teacher introduced Julie and another child to the activity corner. She assigned them roles, with Julie as the shop assistant and the other child, George, as the customer. The teacher prompted George to tell Julie what he wanted for his lunch, showing him the topic board. George said, 'I want to buy a sandwich please,' and pointed to the picture for sandwich. The teacher modelled for Julie the question, 'What do you want on the sandwich,' signing *want* and pointing to the picture on topic board. She observed that Julie pointed to the picture of the sandwich. It was not until it was her turn to be the customer that she was observed to sign *want*, while also producing a spoken approximation, which the teacher thought sounded like 'you wa'?' for 'you want?' She noted these observations on her recording sheet.

## Research support for AAC

There is much research to demonstrate the problems that occur when young children do not receive appropriate AAC systems and supports, or when opportunity barriers impede participation. Sturm and Clendon (2004), for example, reviewed studies demonstrating the difficulties experienced by children who rely on AAC across various communication domains. These difficulties included (a) delays in the linguistic areas of phonology, semantics, grammatical word endings and syntax; (b) limited functions (in particular, being restricted to simple requests); (c) taking a respondent role in interactions, rendering the child a passive communicator; and (d) restricted experiences with discourse in the classroom (Sturm & Clendon, 2004). Further, much early research has demonstrated the high levels of illiteracy among adults who use AAC, which have been attributed to a lack of early emergent reading experiences or direct instruction (Koppenhaver, Evans, & Yoder, 1991), with limited range and quality of opportunities and lack of time provided to engage with literacy experiences creating major barriers (Hetzroni, 2004; Myers, 2007). Other factors contributing to limited literacy development, as identified in a seminal study by Light and McNaughton (1993), include low parental or teacher expectations about reading potential, a tendency to focus on expressive communication and skills in basic functioning at the expense of reading instruction, and barriers to taking on active roles in joint reading activities, especially for those with physical impairments (Light, Binger & Kelford Smith, 1994).

Fortunately, there is a research base that increasingly has addressed these challenges. According to Iacono (2004), this research has included evaluation of different forms of AAC, such as aided versus unaided (Schlosser & Sigafoos, 2006; Wendt, 2009), as well as assessment of the design features of aided systems, such as different forms of speech output produced by high-tech speech generating (voice output) devices (Drager, Clark-Serpentine, Johnson & Roeser, 2006). Research has also addressed the effectiveness of implementing various forms of AAC in increasing children's communication skills. Iacono (2004) noted that much of this research has been in the form of single-case designs. These designs are well suited to determining the effectiveness of interventions for individuals and avoid the need to form groups of children with similar characteristics. Certainly, children who stand to benefit from AAC have varied skills. Reviews of this research base have indicated that the evidence is largely suggestive rather than conclusive about positive outcomes, because of faults with study designs, such as failure to control for potential biases in the data (Schlosser & Sigafoos, 2006; Schlosser & Wendt, 2008; Wendt, 2009).

Despite problems with many studies, research can inform the implementation of AAC supports within early years settings. Research has demonstrated that young children can benefit from the use of various forms of AAC, not only to learn functional communication skills (Ganz, Davis, Lund, Goodwyn & Simpson, 2012; Johnston et al., 2003), but also to develop language skills, including in expressive and receptive domains (e.g. Taylor & Iacono, 2003; van der Shuit, Segers, van Balkom, Stoep & Verhoeven, 2010), and to learn to read and write (Sturm & Clendon, 2004). Furthermore, research has demonstrated that needs for various forms of AAC will change as young children develop communication skills. The Picture Exchange Communication System (PECS), for example, has been found effective in teaching young children diagnosed with ASD to initiate interactions, but less effective for developing language skills (Ganz et al., 2012). Once children have gained basic functional communication, they may benefit from the addition of other AAC systems, requiring a re-evaluation of a child's communication profile and needs, in line with suggestions for ongoing and dynamic assessment to ensure that children's current and future needs are considered (Iacono & Caithness, 2009).

In terms of early years settings, research demonstrates positive outcomes when teachers participate in goal setting and implementing AAC, and when evidence-based early intervention strategies are used (Johnston et al., 2003; van der Shuit et al., 2010). Johnston et al. (2003), for example, drew on evidence of the effectiveness of naturalistic teaching embedded within classroom activities. They taught three young children with developmental delays and multiple impairments to use functional communication. Individualised AAC systems were used to address each child's goals identified during assessment. For example, to request turns in a game the AAC system used comprised a single switch voice output device for two children and a graphic symbol (picture) for the third. Intervention included creating communication opportunities by arranging the environment, ensuring adults and peers were responsive to communication attempts, while allowing time for the child to initiate communication, providing models and guidance, and ensuring naturalistic consequences when the desired behaviour was observed (for example the opportunity for a turn in the game). All three children demonstrated increases in their functional communication, using their AAC systems and/or spoken language.

An additional outcome of the study by Johnston et al. (2003) was that the children increased their active participation in classroom activities through increased communication, including through the use of speech. The authors argued this was an important finding given that teachers were often concerned that AAC would inhibit speech development because of a learnt dependency on modalities sometimes perceived to be easier than speech. This concern has been discussed frequently in the AAC literature (Cress & Marvin, 2003), with Australian early childhood speech pathologists noting that parental concern about AAC impeding speech can act as barriers to intervention (Iacono & Cameron, 2009). This fear has not been supported by the research literature, which has shown that AAC can support speech development, most likely because it facilitates successful communication (Millar, Light, & Schlosser, 2006; Schlosser & Wendt, 2008). Cress and Marvin (2003) noted that as children develop spoken language, they might use AAC only when communication breakdowns occur, thus naturally moving towards speech but supplementing with AAC as needed. Consequently, introducing AAC to young children who need assistance with communication, and more specifically speech and language development, will assist rather than impede development and is therefore strongly recommended (Branson & Demchak, 2009; Cress & Marvin, 2003; Dunst, Meter & Hamby, 2011). The concerns raised by parents and teachers about AAC can pose opportunity barriers (Beukelman & Mirenda, 2013), but these can be overcome through a family-centred and team-based approach, whereby unbiased and accurate information is provided and consensus is reached about goals and how best to achieve them.

## CASE STUDY 23.1

*Continued*

The preschool teachers observed that when Julie was in other activity areas, she used speech approximations to request items, or her turn in a game, but the other children did not understand her. At these times, she would use the manual signs for *want* and *my turn*, which some, but not all, children understood and responded to. They also noticed that she did not have vocabulary to make comments, and would sometimes scream when there was a change in classroom activities. The teachers decided to provide opportunities for the other children to learn to use manual signs, including modelling *want* and *my turn* at snack and lunch times, and when outside playing with equipment. They also developed a generic communication board, which had vocabulary based on comments they had heard from the other children, including 'I like that,' 'Yuck,' and 'Did you see that!' They made multiple copies of this board, and placed them strategically around the inside and outside areas. They also provided models for signs and gestures to reflect the same messages: Thumbs up for *like*, thumbs down for *yuck*, and the manual sign for *see* + pointing. To assist with transitions, they developed a calendar board, which comprised pictures of the activities that were to occur throughout the day (e.g. play in activity areas, music, snack time, outside play, rest time). They found that if they showed Julie the day's activities at the beginning of the day, and then just prior to each transition, she did not scream. Now that they were using the AAC strategies with all the children, the teachers observed that the other children seemed more willing to initiate interactions with Julie, using speech, manual signs and/or the picture boards, which they also used in interactions with each other and the teachers. In turn, Julie was seen to respond to the children's initiations with various modes, such as speech approximations, which she supplemented with a manual sign or by pointing to a board. Finally, Julie started to initiate requests for turns in play using the boards or manual signs.

The knowledge and attitudes of early years professionals in implementing AAC is critical to ensure ongoing use of AAC as supports to inclusion. Kent-Walsh and Light (2003) interviewed 11 teachers in the United States who had used AAC. These teachers considered that the following factors contributed to the successful incorporation of AAC into general educational settings: (a) honest and open communication; (b) teacher competence in using the AAC system; (c) ensuring sufficient time for planning, which required collaboration and effective time management; (d) recognising the humanity of children at all times; (e) ensuring all children were included in all activities; (f) carefully considering the match between the requirements of the activity and the AAC supports used; and (g) taking an inclusive approach, including informing peers throughout the process. These teacher recommendations are consistent with the Participation Model.

## Matching AAC to learner characteristics

In accordance with the social model of disability, a primary consideration in implementing AAC is children's individual strengths, which can provide the basis for supporting development and informing teaching practice. Hence, assessment and intervention are child-, rather than diagnosis-focused. This principle does not preclude developing understanding of particular challenges faced by children who share the same diagnosis. For example, children with Down syndrome may need support to communicate the understanding that they have through their expressive language (Chan & Iacono, 2001). Children with this profile, regardless of whether or not they have Down syndrome, have been found to benefit from AAC, which enables them to demonstrate underlying symbolic ability in a non-speech form of communication (Taylor & Iacono, 2003).

The dynamic assessment approach facilitates understanding of how a child learns and particular challenges faced. Some children, when provided with a model of a signed word, for example, may not imitate the model immediately, but nonetheless may be observed to watch the model and then, later, produce it in an appropriate context; others may imitate it immediately. Such differences in terms of immediate versus delayed imitation reflect individual learning styles; both forms of imitation can lead to improved skills (Iacono, 1992). Differences in learning style may account for why some interventions may be effective for some, but not all children who share a diagnosis. The use of PECS is a case in point. PECS has been a favoured AAC intervention for young children diagnosed with ASD because of a belief that people with ASD are visual learners (Iacono & Caithness, 2009; Iacono & Cameron, 2009). While many children have been found to benefit from PECS, some have not (Ganz et al., 2012). The implication is that AAC interventions must be individualised according to children's skills, strengths and preferences, regardless of any label or diagnosis. Iacono and Caithness (2009) argued that assessment for AAC should be comprehensive, with clinicians, teachers and families working to identify children's learning profiles, including their preference for various forms of AAC (e.g. manual sign, graphic symbols, voice output). Inclusion of a dynamic assessment approach also provides information on strategies that assist a child to develop new skills (Iacono & Caithness, 2009).

# From research to practice

Early years teachers are significant communication partners and facilitators for children. For children with complex communication needs, early years teachers play a crucial role in ensuring that AAC systems are chosen to meet a child and family's needs and preferences, and that intervention strategies address individual learning profiles within inclusive settings. As acknowledged within the Participation Model, early years teachers bring to the assessment team critical information about the social and environmental setting in which a child will spend a large part of every day. They are often the link between other early years professionals, such as speech pathologists and occupational therapists, and families, and are well situated to reduce potential access barriers and increase participation opportunities.

In particular, teachers are integral to dispelling myths and misconceptions about AAC use with young children (Cress & Marvin, 2003; Romski & Sevcik, 2005). By integrating AAC into early years settings, teachers can demonstrate the value of providing visual supports for transitions across activities, social interactions, and language comprehension and expression, which can benefit all children within those settings. In this way, AAC can become an accepted, valued and everyday part of early years experiences, thereby reducing the fears of families and other teachers of a possible stigmatising effect (Iacono & Cameron, 2009). The use of AAC by peers also has the potential to facilitate comprehension within interactions and improve attitudes towards the use of AAC, and teachers can assist peers to engage inclusively with each other using AAC (Fisher & Shogren, 2012). Inclusive AAC environments create contexts in which children develop symbolic skills in both play and communication (Taylor & Iacono, 2003). AAC can be used to support communication as a starting point to empowering children to be active communication partners, and facilitating their development of expressive and receptive communication and literacy skills, thereby providing essential foundations for ongoing academic learning.

**FIGURE 23.3** COMMUNICATION PARTNERS

*Photo: Kathy Cologon*

The design of AAC systems requires in-depth understanding and current knowledge of AAC, which can be difficult in light of continuous developments, particularly in high-tech systems. Decisions about the design features to include in a child's AAC system can be made most effectively through a team-based approach, in which early years professionals work together. For example speech pathologists and occupational therapists can provide information on available options, and the demands that these options may place on families and teachers (Goldbart & Marshall, 2004; Kent-Walsh & Light, 2003). The success of such a team-based approach relies on AAC professionals being able to provide support to teachers who are willing to learn about the use of the systems, and about how to support families and children in their use. Teachers and speech pathologists have reported barriers in terms of time needed to learn about and implement AAC systems (Iacono & Cameron, 2009; Kent-Walsh & Light, 2003). Still, positive experiences have been reported by teachers (Kent-Walsh & Light, 2003), therapists (Iacono & Cameron, 2009), and families (Goldbart & Marshall, 2004; Myers, 2007) in terms of skill development, participation and self-esteem of children who use AAC; this supports the argument for perseverance, which can best be achieved by a collaborative, team-based approach. Further, such an approach can support families to overcome unfounded concerns that AAC will inhibit their children's speech (Cress & Marvin, 2003; Iacono & Cameron, 2009; Romski & Sevcik, 2005). As teachers gain experience in supporting children who use AAC, they can reassure families about its benefits in supporting language and social interactions, without detrimental effects on speech. Of course, for some children who may not develop speech, AAC access becomes even more crucial to supporting communication, and thereby learning and inclusion.

From an instructional perspective, teachers are in the best position to maximise communication and learning opportunities. Their role in organising, supporting other adults and children, and participating in a child's environment means teachers can ensure that frequent daily interactions can become teachable moments (Hyun & Marshall, 2003; Jung, 2013). These high frequency and meaningful teaching opportunities create powerful contexts for learning by children with complex communication needs, thereby improving skill development and their generalisation across a child's daily settings (Iacono, 1999). Consequently, providing interventions within meaningful activities and natural contexts is considered a key principle for language interventions (Kaiser & Roberts, 2011).

The understanding of future teachers about AAC was explored in a recent Australian study, in which 196 pre-service early years teachers shared their recommendations regarding using Key Word Sign as a form of AAC within early years settings (Cologon, in preparation). Participants completed a Key Word Sign workshop and planned and implemented AAC in early years experiences. Participants reported beliefs that Key Word Sign was important for supporting communication development, with a focus on language comprehension and expressive communication. Participants also reported perceived benefits of Key Word Sign for facilitating inclusive practices through (a) reducing barriers and ensuring participation of all children; (b) accommodating for individual learning styles, including multi-modal and multi-sensory learning; (c) valuing diversity in children and diverse forms of communication; and (d) supporting a sense of belonging. In implementing Key Word Sign, participants recommended naturalistic and inclusive use within everyday learning experiences, such as play, literacy activities, small-group learning activities, and music and singing experiences. Participants also recommended modelling of signs within the environment through everyday conversations, routines and transitions. The support of visual aids was recommended as an effective approach. Involving all staff and families and providing evidence-based and accessible information was perceived to be important for the successful implementation of AAC.

## Conclusion

AAC provides a powerful means of overcoming barriers so as to enable inclusion of children with complex communication needs. Teachers play a crucial role in ensuring the successful use of AAC by children within these settings. In doing so, teachers can reduce *barriers to doing*, as discussed in Chapter 2. Additionally, recognising and valuing multiple forms of communication and incorporating these inclusively into early years practice may contribute to improved attitudes towards AAC use, thus reducing *barriers to being*. Early years professionals have much to contribute to a collaborative assessment and intervention process, thereby creating environments that support all children to flourish through interactions that promote communication development within social and play-based interactions.

# FOR FURTHER REFLECTION

1. Take a moment and think about how important it is to you to be able to communicate.
   a. In your day today how many times have you engaged with some form of communication?
   b. What communicative interactions will you have over the course of a week?
   c. What difference would it make to your week if those around you could not recognise your communicative efforts?
   d. With all this in mind, consider the implications for early years professionals in working with children, particularly children who use AAC to communicate?
2. Building on these reflections, and what have you learnt through reading this chapter, consider:
   a. How might you support children to communicate through AAC inclusively in early years settings?
   b. What might be some key considerations in introducing AAC into an early years setting?

## WEBSITES

www.auslan.org.au
   Auslan signbank containing a searchable dictionary with a video of each sign

www.ridbc.org.au/resources/auslan_tutor.asp
   Auslan Key Word Sign App (for iPads and iPhones) from the Royal Institute for Deaf and Blind Children

www.visualaidsforlearning.com
   Downloadable visual aids to support communication

www.scopevic.org.au/index.php/site/resources
   A range of downloadable resources to support communication are available from the SCOPE Victoria website.

www.everyonecommunicates.org/aaclinks.html
   Resources to support the use of augmentative and alternative communication systems

## REFERENCES

American Speech-Language Hearing Association. (1991). *Report: Augmentative and alternative communication*. ASHA, 33(Suppl. 5), 9–12. Retrieved from www.asha.org/

Australian Children's Education and Care Quality Authority (ACECQA). (2011). *Guide to the National Quality Standards*. Canberra: ACECQA. http://acecqa.gov.au/Uploads/files/National%20Quality%20Framework%20Resources%20Kit/2-DE_03_National%20Quality%20Standard_v8_Secn1.pdf

Australian Curriculum, Assessment and Reporting Authority (ACARA). (2012). *Australian Curriculum*. Sydney: ACARA. Retrieved from www.australiancurriculum.edu.au

Australian Institute for Teaching and School Leadership (AITSL). (2011). *The national professional standards for teachers*. Retrieved from www.teacherstandards.aitsl.edu.au/static/docs/AITSL_National_Professional_Standards_for_Teachers_Final_110511.pdf

Beukelman, D. & Mirenda, P. (2013). *Augmentative and alternative communication: Supporting children and adults with complex communication needs* (4th edn). Baltimore: Paul H. Brookes.

Branson, D. & Demchak, M. (2009). The use of Augmentative and Alternative Communication methods with infants and toddlers with disabilities: A research review. *AAC: Augmentative & Alternative Communication, 25*(4), 274–286. doi:10.3109/07434610903384529

Chan, J. & Iacono, T. (2001). Gesture and word production in children with Down syndrome. *Augmentative and Alternative Communication, 17*, 73–87. doi:0743-4618/01/1702-0073

Cologon, K., & McNaught, M. (2014). Early intervention for literacy learning. In L. Arthur, J. Ashton, & B. Beecher (Eds) *Diverse literacies and social justice: Implications for practice* (pp.146–165). Melbourne: Australian Council for Educational Research.

Cress, C. & Marvin, C. (2003). Common questions about AAC services in early intervention. *Augmentative and Alternative Communication, 19*(4), 254–272. doi:10.1080/07434610310001598242

Department of Education, Employment and Workplace Relations (DEEWR). (2009). *Belonging, being, becoming: The early years learning framework for Australia.* Canberra, ACT: Commonwealth of Australia. Retrieved from http://foi.deewr.gov.au/system/files/doc/other/belonging_being_and_becoming_the_early_years_learning_framework_for_australia.pdf

Drager, K., Clark-Serpentine, E., Johnson, K. & Roeser, J. (2006). Accuracy of repetition of digitized and synthesized speech for young children in background noise. *American Journal of Speech-Language Pathology, 15*, 155–164. doi:10.1044/1058-0360(2006/015)

Dunst, C. J., Meter, D. & Hamby, D.W. (2011). Influences of sign and oral language interventions on the speech and oral language production of young children with disabilities. *CELL Reviews, 4*(4), 1–20. Retrieved from www.earlyliteracylearning.org/cellreviews/cellreviews_v4_n4.pdf

Fisher, K.W. & Shogren, K.A. (2012). Integrating Augmentative and Alternative Communication and peer support for students with disabilities: A social-ecological perspective. *Journal of Special Education Technology, 27*(2), 23–39. Retrieved from www.tamcec.org/wp-content/uploads/2009/06/JSET-272.pdf#page=27

Flores, M., Musgrove, K., Renner, S., Hinton, V., Strozier, S., Franklin, S. & Hil, D. (2012). A comparison of communication using the Apple iPad and a picture-based system. *Augmentative & Alternative Communication, 28*(2), 74–84. doi:101.3109/07434618.2011.644579

Ganz, J., Davis, J., Lund, E., Goodwyn, F. & Simpson, R. (2012). Meta-analysis of PECS with individuals with ASD: Investigation of targeted versus non-targeted outcomes, participant characteristics, and implementation phase. *Research in Developmental Disabilities, 33*, 406–418. doi:10.1016/j.ridd.2011.09.023

Goldbart, J. & Marshall, J. (2004). 'Pushes and pulls' on the parents of children who use AAC. *Augmentative and Alternative Communication*, 20, 194–208. doi:10.1080/07434610400010960

Grove, N. & Walker, M. (1990). The Makaton vocabulary: Using manual signs and graphic symbols to develop interpersonal communication. *Augmentative and Alternative Communication, 6*, 15–28. doi:10.1080/07434619012331275284

Hasson, N. & Joffe, V. (2007). The case for Dynamic Assessment in speech and language therapy. *Child Language Teaching and Therapy 23*(1), 9–25. doi:10.1177/0265659007072142

Hetzroni, O.E. (2004). AAC and literacy. *Disability & Rehabilitation, 26*(21–22), 1305–1312. doi:10.1080/09638280412331280334

Hyun, E. & Marshall, J.D. (2003). Teachable-moment-oriented curriculum practice in early childhood education. *Journal of Curriculum Studies, 35*(1), 111–127. doi:10.1080/00220270210125583

Iacono, T. (1992). Augmented communicators and individual differences in language learning. *Augmentative and Alternative Communication, 8*, 33–40. Retrieved from http://informahealthcare.com/loi/aac/

Iacono, T. (1999). Language intervention in early childhood. *International Journal of Disability, Development, and Education, 46*, 383–420. doi:10.1080/103491299100560

Iacono, T. (2004). The evidence base in augmentative and alternative communication. In S. Reilly, A. Perry & J. Douglas (Eds), *Evidence-based practice in speech pathology.* (pp.288–313). London: Wiley.

Iacono, T. & Caithness, T. (2009). Assessment issues. In P. Mirenda & T. Iacono (Eds), *Autism and augmentative and alternative communication* (pp.23–48). Baltimore: Paul H. Brookes.

Iacono, T. & Cameron, M. (2009). Australian speech-language pathologists' perceptions and experiences of augmentative and alternative communication in early childhood intervention. *Augmentative and Alternative Communication, 25*, 236–249. doi:10.3109/07434610903322151

Johnston, S., McDonnell, A., Nelson, C. & Magnavito, A. (2003). Teaching functional communication skills using augmentative and alternative communication in inclusive settings. *Journal of Early Intervention, 25*(4), 263–280. doi:10.1177/105381510302500403

Jung, J. (2013). Teachers' roles in infants' play and its changing nature in a dynamic group care context. *Early Childhood Research Quarterly, 28*, 187–198. doi:10.1016/j.ecresq.2012.05.001

Kagohara, D., van der Meer, L., Ramdoss, S.M.O.R., Lancioni, G., Davis, T., Sigafoos, J. (2013). Using iPods and iPads in teaching programs for individuals with developmental disabilities: A systematic review. *Research in Developmental Disabilities, 34*(1), 147–156. doi:10.1016/j.ridd.2012.07.027

Kaiser, A., Ostrosky, M. & Alpert, C. (1993). Training teachers to use environmental arrangement and milieu teaching with nonvocal preschool children. *Journal of The Association for Persons with Severe Handicaps, 18*, 188–199. Retrieved from http://tash.org/about/publications/

Kaiser, A.P. & Roberts, M.Y. (2011). Advances in early communication and language intervention. *Journal of Early Intervention, 33*(4), 298–309. doi:10.1177/1053815111429968

Kent-Walsh, J.E. & Light, J.C. (2003). General education teachers' experiences with inclusion of students who use augmentative and alternative communication. *Augmentative and Alternative Communication, 19*(2), 104–124. Retrieved from http://informahealthcare.com/loi/aac/

Koppenhaver, D., Evans, D. & Yoder, D. (1991). Childhood reading and writing experiences of literate adults with severe speech and motor impairments. *Augmentative and Alternative Communication, 7*, 20–33. Retrieved from http://informahealthcare.com/loi/aac/

Light, J. (1988). Interaction involving individuals using augmentative and alternative communication systems: State of the art. *Augmentative and Alternative Communication, 4*, 66–82. Retrieved from http://informahealthcare.com/loi/aac/

Light, J., Binger, C. & Kelford Smith, A. (1994). Story reading interactions between preschoolers who use AAC and their mothers. *Augmentative and Alternative Communication, 10*, 255–268. Retrieved from http://informahealthcare.com/loi/aac/

Light, J. & McNaughton, D. (1993). Literacy and augmentative and alternative communication (AAC): The expectations and priorities of parents and teachers. *Topics in Language Disorders, 13*, 33–46. doi:00011363-199302000-00005

Millar, D., Light, J. & Schlosser, R. (2006). The impact of augmentative and alternative communication on the speech production of individuals with developmental disabilities: A research review. *Journal of Speech, Language, and Hearing Research, 49*, 248–264. doi:10.1044/1092-4388(2006/021)

Myers, C. (2007). 'Please listen, it's my turn': Instructional approaches, curricula and contexts for supporting communication and increasing access to inclusion. *Journal of Intellectual & Developmental Disability*, 32(4), 263–278. doi:10.1080/13668250701693910

Romski, M.A. & Sevcik, R. (2005). Augmentative communication and early intervention: Myths and realities. *Infants and Young Children, 18*(3), 174–185. doi:10.1097/00001163-200507000-00002

Schlosser, R. & Sigafoos, J. (2006). Augmentative and alternative communication interventions for persons with developmental disabilities: Narrative review of comparative single-subject experimental studies. *Research in Developmental Disabilities, 27*(1), 1–29. doi:10.1016/j.ridd.2004.04.004

Schlosser, R. & Wendt, O. (2008). Effects of augmentative and alternative communication intervention on speech production in children with autism: A systematic review. *American Journal of Speech-Language Pathology, 13*(3), 212–230. doi:10.1044/1058-0360(2008/021)

SCOPE UK. (2002). *The good practice guide, for support workers and personal assistants working with disabled people with communication impairments*. Essex Coalition of Disabled People/Scope Research Department, London. Retrieved from www.scope.org.uk/sites/default/files/pdfs/Communication/Scope_guide_for_PAs.pdf

Sigafoos, J. & Iacono, T. (1993). Selecting augmentative and alternative communication devices for persons with severe disabilities: Some factors for educational teams to consider. *Australian and New Zealand Journal of Developmental Disabilities, 18*(3), 133–146. Retrieved from http://cirrie.buffalo.edu/database/journals/2130/

Stahmer, A.C., Akshoomoff, N. & Cunningham, A.B. (2011). Inclusion for toddlers with autism spectrum disorders: The first ten years of a community program. *Autism, 15*(5), 625–641. doi:10.1177/1362361310392253

Sturm, J. & Clendon, S. (2004). Augmentative and alternative communication, language, and literacy: Fostering the relationship. *Topics in Language Disorders, 24*(1), 76–91. doi:10.1097/00011363-200401000-00008

Taylor, R. & Iacono, T. (2003). AAC and scripting activities to facilitate communication and play. *Advances in Speech-Language Pathology, 5*, 79–94. doi:10.1080/14417040510001669111

United Nations. (1989). *Convention on the rights of the child.* New York: United Nations General Assembly. Retrieved from www.ohchr.org/en/professionalinterest/pages/crc.aspx

United Nations. (2006). *Convention of the rights of persons with disabilities.* Retrieved from www.un.org/disabilities/convention/conventionfull.shtml

van der Shuit, M., Segers, E., van Balkom, H., Stoep, J. & Verhoeven, L. (2010). Immersive communication intervention for speaking and non-speaking children with intellectual disabilities. *Augmentative & Alternative Communication, 26*(3), 203–220. doi:10.3109/07434618.2010.505609

Warren, S. (1992). Facilitating basic vocabulary acquisition with milieu teaching procedures. *Journal of Early Intervention, 16*, 235–251. doi:10.1177/105381519201600304

Wendt, O. (2009). Research on the use of manual signs and graphic symbols in autism spectrum disorders: A systematic review. In P. Mirenda & T. Iacono (Eds), *Autism and augmentative and alternative communication* (pp.83–140). Baltimore: Paul H. Brookes.

Wilkinson, K.M. & Hennig, S. (2007). The state of research and practice in augmentative and alternative communication for children with developmental/intellectual disabilities. *Mental Retardation and Developmental Disabilities Research Reviews, 13*(1), 58–69. doi:10.1002/mrdd.20133

Yoder, P., Warren, S., Kim, K. & Gazdag, G. (1994). Facilitating prelinguistic communication skills in young children with developmental delay II: Replication and extension. *Journal of Speech and Hearing Research, 37*, 841–851. Retrieved from http://jslhr.asha.org/

Yoder, P., Warren, S., McCathren, R. & Leew, S. (1998). Does adult responsivity to child behavior facilitate communication development? In A. Wetherby, S. Warren & J. Reichle (Eds), *Transitions in prelinguistic communication* (pp.39–58). Baltimore: Paul H. Brookes.

# 24 (Un)Becoming Behaviour

*Linda J. Graham*

CHAPTER OVERVIEW

This chapter will focus on the role of teachers in supporting children who experience difficulties in early years settings and who engage in disruptive behaviour.

Learning goals for this chapter include:

- Understanding how challenging behaviour develops and what can happen if it remains unaddressed;
- Developing the ability to analyse student behaviour;
- Understanding how to interpret common behaviours and how to avoid misperceptions;
- Being aware of ways to develop alternative approaches that are respectful of difference.

KEY TERMS AND CONCEPTS

Attention Deficit Hyperactivity Disorder (ADHD)
expressive and receptive language
Oppositional Defiance Disorder (ODD)
Theory of Mind (ToM)

# Introduction

Teachers frequently rate disruptive behaviour among their greatest areas of concern (Scruggs & Mastropieri, 1996; Loreman, Florin & Sharma, 2007). Research finds however that disruptive student behaviour is often viewed as a consequence of individual student deficit, which obscures the contribution made by curriculum, pedagogy and schooling structures (Graham, 2008; Sullivan, Johnson, Owens & Conway, 2014). Such individualisation promotes a perception that the problem is the aberrant student and that once the 'problem' is treated—often by way of withdrawal, suspension or exclusion—everything will be as it should be (Slee, 1995).

Let me quickly make the point that this tends not to work out well in practice and there are at least two reasons why. The first is that the departure of our main protagonists leaves us—their teachers—with no incentive to modify curriculum, to improve our own instructional behaviour, or to address exclusionary school cultures. Secondly, the removal of one difficult student can sometimes highlight students whose behaviour has previously been masked by the teacher's chief distractor. In other words, school- and classroom-based factors that work to alienate students remain unquestioned and unaddressed, ready to work against future candidates. While the outcomes in terms of suspension, exclusion and early school leaving tend to emerge in the secondary years, my research with students aged nine to 16 years with severely disruptive behaviour has found that the majority began disliking school in the early years: junior primary. Chronic learning difficulties (in reading, writing and/or mathematics) also began early; however, these students reported a cycle of inadequate support leading to disengagement, growing frustration and violent outbursts triggering successive long-term suspensions and referrals to separate settings. As reported by one principal of a behaviour school, this cycle began very early for some:

> I had one boy here—I'm sure I've had more, but this one, his first long-term suspension was two hours into kindergarten. So if you start kindergarten, in two hours you've got a long-term suspension, if you've already got problems, you're not going to get any better after four weeks away from school.

Despite the failure of exclusion to comprehensively address problem behaviour, it is an increasingly common approach. Take Australia's largest school system, the New South Wales (NSW) government school sector, as an example. Despite evidence that school suspension is the most robust predictor of special education placement and later school failure (Skiba, Poloni-Staudinger, Simmons, Feggins-Assiz & Choong-Geun, 2005), the total number of long suspensions (5–20 days) issued by government schools in NSW increased by 36 per cent between 2006 and 2011 (Beauchamp, 2012). Of these, 15 per cent were for primary school aged children (Beauchamp, 2012). Over the same six-year period, there was a 16.2 per cent increase in enrolments in separate special educational settings, fuelled mainly by the exclusion of students described as having emotional and behavioural difficulties (Graham & Sweller, 2011).

Citing the NSW government's own assertion that these increases should be 'attributed to initiative funding rather than growth in student numbers', Graham, Sweller and Van Bergen (2010, p.243) argue that these shifts reflect growth in placement availability, resulting from the construction of 'nearly 100 specialist facilities to support students with disruptive behaviour, including 35 behaviour schools, 22 suspension centres and 40 tutorial centres' (p.243). These settings are similar to Pupil Referral Units (PRUs) in England except that they are fully government-owned and -operated. They fulfil much the same function as PRUs in that they service disaffected students who live in communities marked by school residualisation, high unemployment, concentrated social housing and limited infrastructure.

> Students 'whose behaviour can no longer be supported in their home schools' (DEC, 2011, p.1) are referred to schools specialising in intensive behaviour support for an intended maximum of 12 months. Unless the student has been expelled, their home school enrolment is maintained on a partial (or part-time) basis so that the student may spend four days in the behaviour school and one day back in their home school environment. Theoretically, as time goes by, the number of days spent attending the home school will increase as the student's behaviour improves (Granite & Graham, 2012, p.43).

Although initially developed as a short-term intervention model (Conway, 2006), a NSW government commissioned review of behaviour schools and tutorial centres has reported that enrolments of up to four years in duration are not uncommon (Inca Consulting, 2009). Recent analysis of government school enrolment trends also suggests that, rather than returning to mainstream schools, students with disruptive behaviour may be graduating from less to more restrictive settings, for example from support classes in early primary (K–4) to behaviour schools in upper primary (Year 5) to juvenile detention in the middle years of secondary school (Graham et al., 2010). Surveys of young people in detention centres support these findings with over 40 per cent of inmates reporting that they spent considerable time in special schools and support classes prior to being incarcerated (NSW Department of Juvenile Justice, 2003). Unfortunately, longitudinal studies have shown that young people who end up in these settings rarely make a successful return to mainstream education (Bouhours, 2006; Bradley, Doolittle & Bartolotta, 2008; Lane, Wehby, Little & Cooley, 2005). More often than not, their next stop is adult prison and a life of crime and dysfunction, which then tends to be visited upon their own children and grandchildren in the most corrosive form of cyclical disadvantage (Vinson, 2007).

Worryingly, it appears that some educators believe that the removal of difficult students can be expedited by *not* treating the presenting issues, or as described by one primary school principal, '...you've got to demonstrate that you've tried things, and—hey, we all know about "trying things". You can set things up to fail, if you know what I mean?' (Graham & Spandagou, 2011, p.232). Exclusion, however, is counterproductive as children are simply removed from a setting where their needs were not being served and this does nothing to improve the quality and fit of the pedagogy within that setting. Neither is there any guarantee that their needs will be better served elsewhere, as specialised settings typically focus on behaviour and because they cannot offer a high quality academic curriculum, student learning continues to suffer (Lane et al., 2005). The end result is that some young children never receive the understanding or support they so desperately need. While their exclusion may solve a problem for individual schools and teachers, early learning and behavioural difficulties can become viciously entrenched if not tackled with appropriate and timely interventions.

For example, we know that behaviours associated with learning and language difficulties are often ignored or misinterpreted as behavioural, adjustment, and/or attentional issues (Lindsay & Dockerell, 2000; Ripley & Yuill, 2005; Graham, 2008). We know that many young people who enter the juvenile detention system began school with poor self-regulation and language difficulties (Snow & Powell, 2008). We also know that early and sustained intervention can disrupt negative trajectories (Freiberg, Homel & Branch, 2010). Given the relationships between early language and learning difficulties, disruptive behaviour and later school failure, this chapter will outline some common characteristics to look out for and what individual teachers can do (or not do) to make a difference in the lives of sometimes difficult but always deserving children and young people.

## Analysing behaviour

Disruptive behaviour has meaning. It is not simply a manifestation of personality or character, as it is often taken to be. Rather, disruptive behaviour is an action in reaction. Watch a group of primary-school-aged children who have been asked to sit in a group to listen to the teacher read a story. Invariably, some will begin to fidget and others will attempt to disrupt their peers. Why? This is not hard to answer, as reading behaviour in this scenario is easy enough.

Few stories are engaging enough to capture the interest of *all* children. Maybe some of our class have receptive language difficulties and find it hard to understand the story. It might be late afternoon and our fidgeters may be hungry or tired …

There can be many reasons. But, watch enough classroom activity over time and at least one thing becomes clear: our champion fidgeters tend to be boys and the same boys tend to pop up in each observational session. Some might say that this suggests a problem with the individual, but inclusive early years professionals take a different view. In this situation we would consider whether we are asking these particular children to do something that they find too difficult to do *and* whether we might be contributing to the problem through our own pedagogical choices. In other words, is their behaviour *situational*, in the sense that it changes depending on the context? In that case, what can we do to alter the context and therefore change the dynamics to improve student outcomes?

**FIGURE 24.1** LISTENING

*Artwork by Joshua*

Let us consider the following scenario—developed from observations conducted as part of a research project investigating the increase in diagnosis of special educational needs in New South Wales government schools—and question how one student's behaviour might be situational and can therefore be analysed as an *interaction*: an action in reaction that could be anticipated and thereby prevented.

CASE STUDY 24.1

## A lesson in the foundations

It is 3.05pm and the end of a hot and humid school day at the beginning of the Foundation year. Through the classroom windows, 20 excited children can see their parents and younger siblings waiting to pick them up. Although aware that the bell had already rung, Mrs Freeman calls her class to attention by asking them to line up at the door in height order. Some smaller children immediately move to the front of the line but jostling and arguing arises at the rear. Mrs Freeman calls out, 'Those of you who are still and quiet will be allowed to go home when I call your name.' She stands waiting and then after a minute, approvingly calls the names of the children—mainly girls—who are standing patiently at the front of the line.

By this point, even the children who had managed to form an orderly group in the middle of the line are beginning to get restless, waving to their family members outside or turning to admonish the heaving scrum behind them. Mrs Freeman is fast running out of quiet students to select and shouts loudly, '*No one* will be going home if I don't have silence!' This threat is enough to get the attention of her meeker students but three boys arguing between themselves at the back of the line do not appear to hear her.

Frustrated and not a little embarrassed, Mrs Freeman releases the rest of the students and instructs the three boys to lift each of the stray classroom chairs onto the tables to enable the cleaners to vacuum underneath. She then turns to begin cleaning the board. Jack, who is not yet five years old and who was recently diagnosed and medicated for ADHD, rushes and accidentally nudges one chair with another, causing it to fall and bump Oscar on the way down. Oscar cries out loudly, accusing Jack of doing it 'on purpose'. The frazzled Mrs Freeman turns from the board to shout '*Jack*! Leave him alone and *do* as you are told!' Jack, tired, frustrated and humiliated, throws his chair in no particular direction and runs from the classroom crying.

The next day, Jack is given a two-day suspension for 'not following directions' and 'not respecting property'. His account of events in the Principal's office is halting and muddled, mainly featuring the protest 'I didn't do it!' Jack returns from suspension with a reputation for lying and a record of violent behaviour. Six months later, after two more suspensions, he is transferred to a behaviour support class in a new school 3km further from his home.

### CRITICAL REFLECTION QUESTIONS

While teachers talk about using 'teachable moments' (Hyun & Marshall, 2003) and the Foundation year has long been known as a period that focuses on socialisation, there is an appropriate time, place and method for everything. The average school day is packed with such moments; however, when working with young children especially, careful reflection is required to ensure that we choose and use those moments well. The following questions might help us to consider what the teacher in the above scenario may have been trying to teach her class, whether Jack's rushed approach to the chair task could have been anticipated, and ultimately, whether his reaction is a result of a series of interactions between Jack, Oscar and Mrs Freeman, or whether it was something unique to Jack:

1. What was Mrs Freeman attempting to teach her students by asking them to line up in height order?

*Linda J. Graham*

2. Are some children going to be better at this than others?
3. Which children may have difficulty doing this?
   a. Young children who have not yet developed the skills to self-regulate;
   b. Tired children;
   c. Children who can see their family waiting outside;
   d. All of the above?
4. Will some of these children 'get it wrong' every time? What might be the effect of always getting it wrong?
5. What perceptions may teachers develop about such students? What perceptions may these students develop of themselves?
6. Are there other times during the school day when lining up in height order might be more appropriate?
7. Why might Jack have been rushing? Could this be anticipated? What might he learn from this experience? Is Jack's learning experience likely to have a positive or negative effect?
8. What are the side effects of stimulant medication and what time of day might these be in full force?
9. Why did Jack react so emotionally to the statement, 'Leave him alone and *do* as you are told!'?
10. What might he have meant by 'I didn't do it'? How might Jack's statement relate to the accusation that he wasn't doing as he was told?
11. Jack's muddled and halting account of events was taken as evidence of evasion and dishonesty: what alternative explanations might there be?
12. How might the situation have been handled differently?
13. Is the value of the 'teachable moment' merely in the opportunity that presents itself (the arising of the 'teachable' concept) or is its value contingent on the teachability of the moment (the opportunity + children's receptiveness)?

## Supporting learning, language and behaviour

Children who experience difficulties in school and with learning often share certain subtle characteristics. Many find it hard to regulate their emotions and their actions. For example, they tend to be the children who blurt out answers before putting their hands up. Sadly, the answers are often wrong because—in their bid to be first—they have either not waited for the whole question or not taken the time to think their answer through. This is not because they are seeking to disrupt but because they are all too aware of their limitations compared to the 'smart kids' who generally get in first and who tend to get all the praise.

Although it is impossible to box children who experience behavioural difficulties into neat categories, it is relatively easy to spot them in a group. This is because they tend not to blend in and they generally cannot help but stand out.

For example, some have poor spatial awareness and only vague perceptions of personal space—other than knowing that they like their own! In their desire to be a part of things, to be the first at doing something or to be the best at *anything*, they can inadvertently crowd others and bump or distract. This all happens without malicious intent but because they didn't mean to bump or distract, an accusal is perceived as an insult. Tempers flare and aggrievement sets in.

Some children with learning, language and behavioural difficulties can be quick to anger and some are physical in response. And many do not sound convincing when it comes to explaining how a fight started or how something got broken. But, they are also children who can be desperate for approval and acceptance, children who want to receive that approving nod or smile but have no idea how to get it (Graham et al., 2010). Incidentally, this is often the driving motivation behind their unbidden provision of the wrong answer. Knowing and understanding this is key to working with complicated little people in a proactive and strategic way. In what follows, I will describe some characteristics to look out for, explain how these characteristics play out and what effect they have for the children involved. We will begin with language.

**CASE STUDY 24.2**

## 'Racehorsing'[1]

At just 24 months of age, Olivia was a precocious toddler with a 300-word vocabulary, a range that is more typical of a 36-month-old. Although it may sound immodest, my husband and I attributed this prodigious talent to her parentage. So did her paediatrician, who dryly observed that a mother who had studied literature and a father who was a journalist had not necessarily produced a genius. Apparently, it is common for verbose parents to produce verbose children.

Imagine our collective surprise, just six months later, when our two-and-half-year-old began putting her words together in very novel ways. Rather than constructing sentences using individual words, Olivia would string together chunks, many of which had been used in other contexts and memorised for later use. While this was not always obvious to the layperson, it was clear to those who knew her well, including her early childhood teacher, Jennie. Olivia began attending speech therapy at the age of three, however, her difficulties with **expressive language** and especially sequencing—or what can otherwise be referred to as narrative discourse—have continued.

For example, when she was nine, one of Olivia's most interesting chunked phrases was, 'You shouldn't have tooken'. Paradoxically, this meant, 'You should take' but only someone who knew her well knew that. Eventually, these phrases disappeared from her everyday lexicon but others soon emerged. As a family, we have come to look forward to each new addition, as these phrases are a part of what makes Olivia who she is and we love everything about her. For example, at the age of 13, she started using the term 'racehorsing' when she really meant 'horseracing'. Even now, and at least once a week, we collapse into laughter as she comes out with yet another 'racehorsing moment'—one that usually involves an extremely long and mystifying recount of something that happened or something she has read that ends up making sense only to her.

Olivia has learned to accept that she has difficulty in this area and takes ownership at these moments by laughing and saying, 'I just went racehorsing again, didn't I?' However, while she is good-natured about it, her experiences over the years have highlighted to me just how hard it is for children with language difficulties—even mild ones—to succeed at school. For example, she is very reluctant to call attention to herself by asking questions out loud in class. And, although she is a good reader and has the **receptive** vocabulary of a 17-year-old, her difficulties with expressive language and sequencing play into her written work as well. Her essays—usually involving intricately developed characters, highly descriptive words and elaborate plots—are a joyous but convoluted stream of consciousness of which Joyce would be proud. These difficulties affect her endeavours across all curriculum areas and, not surprisingly, the rules and structure of maths have made it her greatest foe.

Language also made making friends very difficult when Olivia was very little because it was hard to find the right words at the right time. This left her trying to enter conversations with lines memorised from movies or running up and pushing other children instead of asking whether they would like to play 'chasings'. These strategies usually ended badly but luckily three-year-old Olivia had an ally. Her early childhood teacher, Jennie, used to carefully structure cooperative play experiences that would give Olivia some experience of imaginative play but which wouldn't place too much of a linguistic burden on her. She also teamed Olivia up with other children whom she thought would be good mentors and took care to watch for signs of emotional distress. I often think of that wonderful teacher as I watch and listen to my now teenage daughter navigate the highs and lows of the adolescent world and marvel at how balanced and calm she now seems in relation to some of her more worldly peers. She still finds it hard to find the right words at the right time but, because she received the right support at the right time, having expressive language difficulties has had far less impact on her than it may otherwise have.

**expressive and receptive language:** The term 'expressive' relates to language production and 'receptive' relates to language comprehension. Receptive and expressive language difficulties can occur singly or in unison and are often grouped under the term Specific Language Impairment (SLI).

Unfortunately, receptive and expressive language difficulties are not well understood in schools and the 'symptoms' are often misinterpreted or ignored. Researchers in the field of speech/language pathology warn that because some six to 13 per cent of children entering school have language difficulties that go undetected by their teacher, a significant number of children 'may not receive the additional assistance they need to achieve academic benchmarks, and risk falling behind their peers' (Antoniazzi, Snow & Dickson-Swift, 2010, p.249). These researchers also argue that language difficulties—which can affect young people's interpretation and understanding of questions, as well as the coherence and perceived authenticity of their verbal accounts—have significant implications for how young offenders are interviewed by police and authority figures, and for how their stories are taken as evidence.

The same logic applies to the investigation and treatment of incidents within schools. When asked to explain 'their side of the story', children with language difficulties invariably fall short. Their halting verbal explanations are often taken as confirmation of mistruth. This is a common response to children who experience difficulties with language and learning. There are signs to look out for though and careful observation can reveal what is really going on. Listed below are some common characteristics of language impairment, which have been paired with equally common perceptions. Next to these are alternative explanations for these behaviours and some suggestions to support such children in the classroom:

**TABLE 24.1** COMMON BEHAVIOURS, PERCEPTIONS AND ALTERNATIVE ROUTES TO SUCCESS

| Common behaviours | Common perception | Alternative explanations | Pedagogical remedy |
|---|---|---|---|
| Consistently misses steps in set tasks | Not paying attention | ~ Receptive language difficulties;<br>~ Difficulty with abstract reasoning;<br>~ Under-developed working memory. | ~ Explain task using short, concrete sentences;<br>~ Avoid cognitive overload; no more than two brief instructions at a time;<br>~ Speak clearly and at a measured pace;<br>~ Provide a step-by-step (written) task guide;<br>~ Check understanding;<br>~ Constantly reiterate task objectives and steps;<br>~ Pair with a supportive buddy. |
| Emotional and angry outbursts (with or without physical aggression) | Anger management issues<br><br>Mental health problems<br><br>Poor parenting | ~ Expressive language difficulties;<br>~ Unable to explain or defend themselves verbally;<br>~ May be getting teased or bullied by other children. | ~ Anticipate and intervene by distracting and redirecting;<br>~ Collaboratively develop a private code for a 'chill-out' pass and reward the child for using it;<br>~ Provide a safe, simple alternative physical response strategy; e.g. 'Turn around, fold your arms and walk away';<br>~ Ensure that all staff are aware of these strategies and encourage the child to seek adult support when needed. |

(Continued)

| Common behaviours | Common perception | Alternative explanations | Pedagogical remedy |
|---|---|---|---|
| Poorly written work: ordering awry, spelling mistakes, little output | Not paying attention<br><br>Lack of effort | ~ Receptive language difficulties: unsure of task requirements;<br>~ Expressive language difficulties: problems with sequencing;<br>~ Has difficulty with 'Theory of Mind'. | If instructions were verbal, see above.<br><br>If instructions were written:<br>~ Ensure they are clear, concise and easy to understand;<br>~ Avoid clutter, use simple fonts, space out;<br>~ Keep it neat, use tables;<br>~ Scaffold sequencing by stepping out the task process and order required. |
| Incoherent recall of events, avoids eye contact | Not telling the truth | ~ Expressive language difficulties;<br>~ Poor working memory;<br>~ Has difficulty with 'Theory of Mind'. | ~ Avoid placing child into a 'he said/ she said' situation with other children present;<br>~ Take aside quietly and ask gently 'what happened'—*wait* patiently for the full response, don't accuse and don't badger;<br>~ Stick to the concrete and avoid asking 'why' or other questions that rely on abstract reasoning or inference. |

**CRITICAL REFLECTION QUESTIONS**

1. How else might difficulties with receptive or expressive language present?
2. What other alternative explanations for these common behaviours can you think of?
3. Are there other pedagogical solutions that might work in these instances?

**Theory of Mind (ToM):** A term that is used to describe the ability to impute mental states (emotions, intentions, knowledge and wants) to others (Baron-Cohen, Leslie & Frith, 1985).

Expressive language difficulties often manifest in written work too. Children who have trouble recounting oral narratives can experience the same difficulty with written narratives. The sequence of events in their stories may be jumbled and their meaning can lack clarity. But language difficulties may not be the only issue. One thing to consider when working with children with language, learning and behavioural difficulties—or indeed any children—is whether the child thinks like you do because if they do not then expectations based on that assumption are unreasonable. This introduces the importance of **'Theory of Mind'**.

## Theory of Mind

It is evident from the ways in which we ask young children to look at and infer meaning from the pictures in a story book, to this typical question about a novel from the Australian Year 7 English curriculum, that the ability to impute mental states to others is an assumed skill in schools (Michaels, n.d., p.8):

> In the novel Parvana, a young girl 'is persuaded to disguise herself as a "boy" to help a family of women who are now isolated and vulnerable without a man. She becomes her dead brother Hossain and this causes pain for her mother'.
>
> Imagine that you 'are Parvana after the first day she disguised herself as Hossain and write a diary entry that reflects on the experience and her feelings and hopes for the future'.

For some young people this is difficult to do, but their inability to convincingly place their self in the shoes of another does not necessarily mean that they did not read the book. These issues usually show up in tests of comprehension but there is a difference between types of comprehension that can indicate difficulties relating to ToM as opposed to those resulting from basic reading difficulties. For example, if the student is relatively accurate at simple comprehension tasks that require them to read a passage and nominate what time the character boarded the train or what clothes they were wearing and who they were going to visit, the chances are that these children will be able to tell us. If however, we ask *why* the character was going to visit that person and how they *felt* about it, children who experience difficulties with ToM will fall short.

ToM is most often associated with autism spectrum disorders and assessed diagnostically using false belief tests. The most widely known of these is the Sally-Anne Test, where an experimenter acts out a story about two dolls, Sally and Anne. Each doll is placed facing a lidded container: a basket and a box. The experimenter names the dolls for the child and then checks that the child has understood which doll is which. The child is then told that Sally has hidden a marble in the basket while the other doll (Anne) is watching. Sally then leaves the room and can no longer 'see' the basket. While Sally is away, Anne takes the marble and hides it in the box. Sally then 'returns' and the experimenter asks the child three questions:

1. 'Where will Sally look for her marble?' (this is the *belief question* and the correct answer is 'in the basket');
2. 'Where is the marble really?' (this is the *reality question* and the correct answer is 'in the box');
3. 'Where was the marble in the beginning?' (this is the *memory question* and the correct answer is 'in the basket').

If the child realises that Sally does not know what has occurred in her absence then they will say that Sally should look in the basket and not in the box. However, if the child is unable to impute what *should* be in Sally's mind, then they will say that Sally should look in the box. Children generally acquire the ability to impute mental states to others from four to six years of age; however, some may not fully acquire this ability at all.[2] The consequences for misunderstanding are immense and not just from the child's perspective. Interestingly, research has indicated that children who experience behavioural difficulties may also experience difficulty with ToM (Walker, 2005); however, the general perception of their behaviour is that it is *intentional.* I have a different view. Let me demonstrate how ToM can present itself in behavioural terms and what the implications can be through another story. This case study draws on personal experience; however to protect the identities of those involved and to illustrate certain points, both the story and the characters have been fictionalised.

**CASE STUDY 24.3**

## Tom & ToM

Yvette was visiting her sister, Karly, and her nephews, Tom and Harry. She hardly knew her nephews as Yvette had lived in another country since the eldest was a year old. Her sister, their mother, had a big work function on, which involved an overnight stay and Yvette agreed to babysit Tom and Harry for the night. She was a bit nervous about doing so because 10-year-old Tom had been diagnosed with Asperger syndrome some years prior and she wasn't sure that she'd be able to handle him. But, because the event was important to her sister, she agreed, thinking 'Well, kids are kids—he couldn't be that different to mine!'

Her sister, Karly, left just before midday, telling Yvette not to worry about cooking dinner and to just order some pizza. As she'd heard that children on the autism spectrum could be particular about food, Yvette made sure to check which type of pizza Tom liked. Karly said he'd be fine with BBQ Meatlovers. Later that evening, after a long afternoon of games in the pool and adjudicating fights between the two siblings—one of which had resulted in a scary meltdown by Tom—Yvette decided against going out for pizza and ordered from the local pizza restaurant online. When it arrived, Tom was extremely angry that his pizza had 'green stuff' (finely chopped parsley) and that it didn't look like 'his' BBQ Meatlovers. Although Yvette was troubled by his rudeness, she realised that she should have checked with Karly as to where she usually ordered Tom's pizza.

The evening grew more difficult as Yvette struggled to reason with Tom over bedtime. When she finally succeeded in getting him to stay in his room, he called angrily from his doorway that he needed to sleep with the light on. Tired and frustrated, Yvette switched his bedroom light on only to be met with a howl of rage: 'No, no, no!! That's wrong!' Close to tears, Yvette went to Tom's younger brother and asked him whether Tom slept with the light on but Harry said no. Remembering that some children with Asperger syndrome have a need for routine and difficulty with communication, Yvette finally went in to Tom and said, 'Tom darling, I don't live here and so I don't know what to do. You need to use your words and tell me how mum does it.' Tom looked at her witheringly but cooperated by explaining that he slept with the *bathroom* light on and that the bathroom door needed to be held open with a prop, so that the light could shine into his room at night.

With that problem sorted, Yvette sat and thought about what had taken place that day, noting with interest that logic appeared to quickly defuse Tom's anger. She went to bed exhausted but determined to try out this new approach. She didn't have to wait long. Early the next morning Tom approached Yvette to ask her to cook his porridge. Gingerly, she agreed and began to prepare it, following the instructions on the back of the packet. When it was ready, she showed Tom the porridge and asked him, 'Is this okay? Would you like me to cook it a bit more?' He agreed and so she cooked it until it was a little less runny. Upon receiving his breakfast, Tom looked at her incredulously and said abruptly 'Where's the milk?'

Taking a deep breath, Yvette replied calmly, 'Tom, remember I don't live here, so I don't know how mum does things. You need to use your words and tell *me* how you like it so that I know what to do'. Tom nodded slowly as he processed this information. Suddenly his eyes lit up as if it had finally dawned on him as to why Yvette was not doing anything 'right'. 'Yvette, Mum puts milk on top. Can you please put some milk on top for me?'

### CRITICAL REFLECTION QUESTIONS

Earlier I made the point of questioning whether a particular child thinks like you do and noted that the consequences for misunderstanding are immense. The following reflection questions aim to unpack the implications and to consider how this situation could have been better approached:

1. What could Karly have done or provided to support Yvette before leaving?
2. Why did Tom look at Yvette witheringly and why might his initial response have been anger?
3. What do you think could be the consequence for Tom from lack of understanding by
   a. His peers?
   b. His teachers?
   c. Other parents?

There are other ways in which difficulties with ToM can manifest, affecting children's educational performance and school experience. Like students with expressive language difficulties, children who have difficulty with ToM may submit written work that lacks logical sequence, exhibits poor introduction to new characters or events, and generally misses detail essential for understanding. This can be because the child expects the reader to have the same knowledge that they do and they write accordingly—without inserting the implicit codes that many people realise are necessary to bring someone else onto the same page as us. In other words, the written work produced by children who have difficulty with ToM can be characterised by the same missing elements that are highlighted by the Sally-Anne test. Simply understanding where a child is coming from helps us to work out ways of supporting them. Intuitive pedagogical methods are more successful with children who experience difficulties in school and with learning because we minimise misunderstanding and confrontations, which helps to avoid rejection and alienation.

**Attention Deficit Hyperactivity Disorder (ADHD)** and **Oppositional Defiance Disorder (ODD)**: Two of three disruptive behaviour disorders listed in the Diagnostic and Statistical Manual for Mental Disorders (DSM) published by the American Psychiatric Association.

Imagine what it must be like to go through life with adults who continually misjudge your intentions, your effort, your character and your meaning. From the overtired four-year-old with poor spatial awareness who eagerly rushes to do what he is told and inadvertently knocks a chair off a table that bumps his friend, to the frustrated 10-year-old who simply cannot understand why this woman whom he has only met twice before refuses to do important everyday routines correctly: neither child is acting intentionally but, in 'regular' schools, the consequences for both will often be the same as if they were. Sadly, both Jack and Tom have experienced repeated suspension and both have ended up in separate special educational settings. In the process, each child has come to know that they are somehow 'different' and that this difference is 'bad'. This can have profoundly negative effects over time. In my research with older students enrolled in behaviour schools, I met a teenage version of Jack and Tom, whom I shall call James. Although James said that he didn't have much hope for his future because he knew he was 'screwed', he had a different perspective on who had the 'disability'. Like many of the students we interviewed, he offered significant insight as to what teachers could do to better support children and young people like himself.

**CASE STUDY 24.4**

## A different take ...

James is an intelligent boy who was first diagnosed with **Attention Deficit Hyperactivity Disorder (ADHD)** at the age of five and enrolled in a support class not long thereafter. He moved from support class to support class—picking up two more diagnoses (**Oppositional Defiance Disorder** and anxiety) somewhere along the way. After his mother relinquished care to the Department of Community Services, James entered an adolescent psychiatric unit at the age of 11. During his time in hospital, James was diagnosed with Asperger syndrome and medicated with five psychoactive medications, including anti-psychotics, anti-depressants, anti-coagulants, anti-convulsives and stimulants, all of which he still takes even though he doesn't want to. After six months in the ward, James was enrolled in a behaviour school but as he refused to attend, he was sent back to a support class in a 'regular' high school. It was in this class that we finally met up with him. James knew that he was 'different' to other kids but he was adamant that he was not intrinsically 'bad'—more that he'd never been given a chance and that he found it hard to make himself understood:

Linda: Do you think that adults listen to you?

James: Not that much, but some do.

Linda: Some do and some don't. OK, so the ones that do, how come they do and how come others don't?

James: They don't have feeling. They don't really understand. At least that's my way of thinking.

Linda: Yeah.

James: It's their brain, that's how I see it ...

Linda: What could teachers do differently?

James: Hear them out and actually give them a chance.

Linda: Right, OK. If they did this, do you think you'd ...

James: I'd be damn well surprised.

Linda: Yeah? Do you think you'd do a bit better at school if they listened to you?

James: Yeah, definitely.

Linda: And heard you out? What difference would that make to you?

James: That day one, they'd probably see my whole record changed, hopefully.

## Conclusion

Inclusive education embraces flexibility. We use terms like 'adjustments' and 'accommodations' to reflect this stance; however, being inclusive is about more than modifying materials or expectations. Curriculum, assessment, stairs and seating arrangements are not the only aspects of schooling that need adjusting. In fact, our own behaviour and the assumptions that underpin it can be the most alienating factors. Children who experience difficulty in schools and with learning can learn to overcome or at least endure those aspects of the curriculum that they find challenging. Much harder for most is dealing with the negative perceptions of others: the teacher who doesn't listen, the peers who tease or reject, and the parent who judges. The problem is that these experiences have hardening effects over time. Children who constantly experience failure and rejection learn to expect it. They become guarded and angry but instead of taking the time to understand why and responding inclusively, the adults in their lives react punitively. In this chapter we have examined alternative approaches that work because they begin from an understanding of the child as opposed to the assumptions of adults. While no one method works with all children and there is no magic wand, deliberative planning and careful reflection can help to identify and neutralise triggers, so that you can make a difference in the lives of the children and young people who most need it.

*Linda J. Graham*

## FOR FURTHER REFLECTION

A common perception reported in surveys of teacher attitudes is that children with a disability, particularly those with challenging behaviour, do not belong in 'regular' schools. But, as this chapter has highlighted, problem behaviours can be addressed with the use of relatively simple strategies developed and honed by reflective teachers who know and understand their own students. Given what we have learned about some child characteristics and ways to work with them rather than against them, let us now reconsider the issue of inclusion for children with challenging behaviour by asking:

1. How might children like Jack, Tom and James be successfully included and what types of adjustments are necessary?
2. If children like Jack, Tom and James were successfully included, would that school cease to be a 'regular' school?
3. What does this suggest about the use of terms like 'regular'? On what assumptions are such terms based?

## NOTES

1 This section is lovingly dedicated to my now 15-year-old daughter—with her permission—whose fractious relationship with the English language has taught me to always listen to and interpret what children are trying to say before making judgment or taking action.

2 For example, the original researchers found that only 14 per cent of children with Down syndrome and 15 per cent of typically developing children failed the belief question, compared to 80 per cent of children with autism (Baron-Cohen, et al., 1985).

## REFERENCES


Antoniazzi, D., Snow, P. & Dickson-Swift, V. (2010). Teacher identification of children at risk for oral language impairment in the first year of school. *International Journal of Speech Language Pathology, 12*(3), 244–252. Retrieved from www.speechpathologyaustralia.org.au/publications/international-journal-of-speech-language-pathology.

Baron-Cohen, S., Leslie, A.M. & Frith, U. (1985). Does the autistic child have a 'theory of mind'? *Cognition*, 21, 37–46. doi:10.1016/0010-0277(85)90022-8

Beauchamp, T. (2012). *Addressing high rates of school suspension.* UnitingCare Policy Research Paper. Retrieved from www.becausechildrenmatter.org.au/wp-content/uploads/AddressingHighRatesOfSchoolSuspension.pdf

Bouhours, T. (2006). *The Journey of the excluded: Schooling and crime in the exclusive society.* (Unpublished PhD thesis), Griffith University, Brisbane.

Bradley, R., Dolittle, J. & Bartolotta, R. (2008). Building on the data and adding to the discussion: The experiences and outcomes of students with emotional disturbance. *Journal of Behavioural Education, 17*(1), 4–23. doi:10.1007/s10864-007-9058-6

Conway, R. (2006). Students with emotional and behavioural disorders: An Australian perspective, *Preventing School Failure, 50*(2), 15–21. doi:10.3200/PSFL.50.2.15-20

Freiberg, K., Homel, R. & Branch, S. (2010). Circles of care. *Family Matters, 84*, 28–34. doi:10.1093/bjsw/bcq010

Graham, L.J., (2008). Drugs, labels and (p)ill-fitting boxes: ADHD and children who are hard to teach. *Discourse: studies in the cultural politics of education, 29*(1), 85–106. doi:10.1080/01596300701801377

Graham, L.J. & Spandagou, I. (2011). From Vision to Reality: The views of primary school principals on inclusive education. *Disability & Society, 26*(1), 223–237. doi:10.1080/09687599.2011.544062

Graham, L.J. & Sweller, N. (2011). The Inclusion Lottery: Who's in and who's out? Tracking inclusion and exclusion in New South Wales government schools. *International Journal of Inclusive Education, 15*(1), 941–953. doi:10.1080/13603110903470046

Graham, L.J., Sweller, N. & Van Bergen, P. (2010). Detaining the usual suspects: Charting the use of segregated settings in New South Wales government schools. *Contemporary Issues in Early Childhood, 11*(3), 234–248. doi:10.2304/ciec.2010.11.3.234

Granite, E. & Graham, L.J. (2012). Remove, rehabilitate, return? The use and effectiveness of behaviour schools in New South Wales, Australia. *International Journal on School Disaffection, 9*(1), 39–50. Retrieved from www.trentham-books.co.uk/acatalog/The_International_Journal_on_School_Disaffection.html

Hyun, E. & Marshall, J.D. (2003). Teachable-moment-oriented curriculum practice in early childhood education. *Journal of Curriculum Studies, 35*(1), 111–127. doi:10.1080/00220270210125583

Inca Consulting. (2009). *Behaviour schools/learning centres appraisal report, NSW Department of Education and Training 2009.* GIPA-11-145.

Lane, K.L., Wehby, J.H., Little, M.A. & Cooley, C. (2005). Students educated in self-contained classes and self-contained schools: Part II—How do they progress over time? *Behavioral Disorders, 30*(4), 363–374. Retrieved from www.ccbd.net/

Lindsay, G. & Dockerell, J. (2000). The behaviour and self-esteem of children with specific speech and language difficulties. *British Journal of Educational Psychology*, 70, 583–601. doi:10.1348/000709900158317

Loreman, T., Forlin, C. & Sharma, U. (2007). An international comparison of pre-service teacher attitudes to inclusive education. *Disability Studies Quarterly, 27*(4), Society for Disability Studies, www.dsq-sds.org/_articles_html/2007/fall/dsq_v27_04_2007_fall_fs_02_loreman.htm, pp.1–13.

Michaels, W. (n.d.). *Teachers notes: Parvana* (p.11). Retrieved from www.allenandunwin.com/_uploads/BookPdf/TeachersNotes/9781865086941.pdf

NSW Department of Juvenile Justice. (2003). *Young people in custody health survey: Key findings report.* Sydney: Author. Retrieved from www.justicehealth.nsw.gov.au/about-us/publications/ypichs.pdf

Ripley, K. & Yuill, N. (2005). Patterns of language impairment and behaviour in boys excluded from school. *British Journal of Educational Psychology*, 75, 37–50. doi:10.1348/000709905X27696

Scruggs, T. & Mastropieri, M.A. (1996). Teacher perceptions of mainstreaming/inclusion 1958–1995: A research synthesis. *Exceptional Children, 63,* 59–74. Retrieved from http://journals.cec.sped.org/ec/

Skiba, R.J., Poloni-Staudinger, L., Simmons, A.B., Feggins-Azziz, L.R. & Choong-Geun, C. (2005). Unproven links: Can poverty explain ethnic disproportionality in special education? *Journal of Special Education, 39*(3), 130–144. doi:10.1177/00224669050390030101

Slee, R. (1995). *Changing theories and practices of discipline.* Falmer Press: London.

Snow, P.C. & Powell, M.B. (2008). Oral language competence, social skills, and high risk boys: What are juvenile offenders trying to tell us? *Children and Society*, 22, 16–28. doi:10.1111/j.1099-0860.2006.00076.x

Sullivan, A.M., Johnson, B., Owens, L. & Conway, R. (2014). Punish them or engage them? Teachers' views of unproductive student behaviours in the classroom. *Australian Journal of Teacher Education, 39*(6), 43–56. doi:10.14221/ajte.2014v39n6.6

Vinson, T. (2007). *Dropping off the edge: The distribution of disadvantage in Australia.* Melbourne: Jesuit Social Services.

Walker, S. (2005). Gender differences in the relationship between young children's peer-related social competence and individual differences in theory of mind. *The Journal of Genetic Psychology, 166*(3), 297–312. doi:10.3200/GNTP.166.3.297-312

# 25 Extending and Enriching Children's Learning

*Kerry Hodge*

CHAPTER OVERVIEW

This chapter will focus on ensuring that all children are engaged in their educational programs and continue to learn new knowledge and skills.

Learning goals for this chapter include:

- Avoiding assumptions about a child's capabilities;
- Developing a range of strategies to assess children's strengths, interests and needs;
- Understanding the importance of appropriate challenge in learning;
- Planning for extension and enrichment in everyday practice;
- Ensuring appropriate extension when children have exceptional strengths.

KEY TERMS AND CONCEPTS

enrichment

exceptional strengths

extension

masking factors

# Introduction

The education of children outside the home is largely organised according to age, yet within any inclusive playroom or classroom there will be a range of developmental levels and achievement. It is unrealistic to assume that all children of the same age are developmentally similar and can be taught in the same way. Children have their own profiles of strengths, interests and needs, often uneven across domains (Clark, 2002). These arise from inherited abilities and temperament; environmental circumstances that include culture, family and educator input; and the element of chance (Gagné, 2003). As discussed in Chapters 2 and 3, there is little reality in the concept of a 'normal' or 'typical' child of a particular age.

Educators, then, have a daunting task: to identify and extend the abilities of individual children within the dynamics of a group. They do this within the parameters of a curriculum framework that may have expected outcomes based on age or grade.

Whatever the curriculum in place, its dimensions can be thought of as *content* (what is learned), *process* (what the educator and children do in teaching and learning), *product* (the tangible and intangible outcomes of learning) and the *learning environment* (the setting, both physical and psychological) (Maker, 1986; Maker & Schiever, 1995). When educators plan to extend children's learning, modifications to, or differentiation of, these dimensions may be required. While all domains of development and learning are acknowledged as important and interdependent—and any child can have remarkable strengths in any one (or more) of these domains—the focus of this chapter will be on learning in the intellectual domain. Approaches to curriculum differentiation will be presented to assist educators in enriching and extending the learning of all children, including when strengths are exceptional.

# Assessing children's current knowledge, skills and interests

In order to extend children's learning it is important for educators to know from where they are extending, that is, to assess what children already know and can do, and how they respond to challenge (Brimijoin, Marquissee, & Tomlinson, 2003). There are a number of strategies to facilitate collection of the information needed in a dynamic and ongoing assessment process. Strategies may differ between prior-to-school and school settings.

## ASSESSMENT IN THE PRIOR-TO-SCHOOL YEARS

Assessment strategies in early years settings usually involve observation as children interact with people, ideas and materials (Fleet & Patterson, 2011) and are most meaningful when embedded in the curriculum and part of everyday experiences (Arthur, Beecher, Death, Dockett & Farmer, 2012). This means that often educators are teaching and assessing simultaneously while joining in children's play, for example (Gronlund, 2010), or talking with them (Siraj-Blatchford & Sylva, 2004). There are many ways to document children's strengths, needs and interests, with a focus on individuals and groups (Arthur et al.). These include narrative approaches that describe what the child or group is doing (e.g. Arthur, 2010; Coates, Thompson & Shimmin, 2008); transcriptions of children's talk; collections of children's products; and visual representations using photographs, video-recordings and sketches. Inspiration from the Reggio Emilia approach (Edwards, Gandini, & Forman, 1998) has led to combinations of these methods, which Carr (2001) called 'learning stories'. Creating simple concept maps using objects and pictures is another way to assess understandings and misunderstandings (Birbili, 2006). Assessment may target quite precise outcomes based on analysis of steps involved towards mastery of skills, especially when a child has an impairment (Pretti-Frontczak & Bricker, 2004).

While these documentations make learning visible to educators, children and families (Dahlberg, Moss, & Pence, 1999), it is important to view assessment as one part of a larger process. A very important step is the educator's reflection on what this information means for the child's future learning experiences (Arthur et al., 2012; Fleet & Patterson, 2011).

## ASSESSMENT IN THE SCHOOL YEARS

In the school years, where the curriculum is prescribed and structured on specific learning outcomes, children have their own 'entry points' into that structure and rates of progression through it (Tomlinson, 2003). Within an age group the entry points and pace of learning can be extremely diverse. The within-grade range in literacy and/or numeracy in large primary school samples have been estimated to cover at least four years, with the gap only increasing with age (Gagné, 2005). In many foundation year classes in Australia the age range is widening as many parents choose to delay their child's entry, particularly for their sons (Edwards, Taylor, & Fiorini, 2011). Whether an increasing age range corresponds to a widening developmental range is not clear.

In schools paper-and-pencil tests are often used in assessment, although ongoing observation as children engage in learning experiences provides essential information (Arthur et al., 2012). Published or educator-made tests require items sufficiently easy and difficult to enable each child to show the extent of their understanding (Howell & Nolet, 2000). Additional ways to assess include the following: direct questioning of children; group discussions, creating a concept map of understandings (Brimijoin et al., 2003; Helm & Katz, 2001); and asking children to represent their knowledge through a drawing or diagram (Hertzog & Klein, 2005). In recent years many Australian schools have implemented a systematic individual assessment of children's literacy and numeracy skills as they enter the first year of school, which acknowledges that children arrive at school with prior learning (Bobis, 2002). However, this practice has drawn criticism, especially if children who would benefit from school are deemed 'not ready' and are denied entry (Arthur et al., 2012).

### *Potential masking factors*

There are factors to be considered when assessing children and interpreting information. **Masking factors** can create bias or stereotyping—conscious or unconscious—which influences educators' expectations of what children can achieve and their plans for teaching and learning.

**masking factors:** These conceal the extent of children's abilities, leading to lower educator expectations. These factors may pertain to the child, the family and the educational setting.

When a child is diagnosed with an impairment that alters his or her learning in some way (such as a physical disability, sensory impairment, autism spectrum disorder or a specific learning difficulty), the tendency is for educators to focus only on the limitations and not expect any particular strengths, which may actually be exceptional (Henderson, 2001; Kalbfleisch & Iguchi, 2008; Karnes & Johnson, 1986). Children with both impairments and exceptional strengths are described as 'gifted and learning disabled' or 'twice-exceptional' (Kalbfleisch & Iguchi), and they need extension of their strengths alongside attention to their areas of need (Brody & Mills, 1997). Karnes, Schwedel and Linnemeyer (1982) described a preschool program for children with a range of mild and moderate impairments. Through early observations in the natural setting, children were assessed for evidence of advanced skill in intellectual, creative, leadership, academic, performing arts or psychomotor abilities. High ratings led to further assessment and an educational program addressing both areas of need and exceptional strengths.

Children's temperaments and actions can adversely influence educators' judgments of their abilities. Hesitant children are often underestimated (Gordon & Thomas, 1967), and an introverted child might avoid unwanted attention by using remarkable skills only when unobserved (Wright & Coulianos, 1991). Careless work or resistance to participate can be interpreted as low ability or disruptive behaviour rather than a sign of impatience with insufficient challenge and pace (Diezmann & Watters, 1997; Valpied, 2005). On the other hand, perfectionist tendencies lead some highly competent children to prefer easy work, thereby hiding their capabilities (Hodge & Kemp, 2006). Other reasons that children may deliberately hide their advanced abilities, such as fluent reading when entering school, include wanting to fit in with perceived teacher expectations and do what others are doing (Gross, 1999) or to find social acceptance (Gross, 1998). Sometimes children from minority cultures conceal their abilities in order to avoid 'acting white', thereby preserving their cultural affiliations (Borland, 2004; Chaffey, 2008).

Family factors can lead to underestimation when viewed one-dimensionally or inaccurately. Stereotypically negative views of cultural, racial or linguistic minority groups can prevent educators from noticing children's strengths (Maker, 1996). Biased perceptions of economically disadvantaged communities and low expectations for their children can also mask strengths that may reach an exceptional degree (Borland 2004).

The learning environment itself, including what the educator does and says when teaching, can limit children's opportunities to show what they know and can do. If activities, tasks and materials are selected with a narrow range of expectations in mind and encourage only this narrow range of responses from children, abilities beyond will not easily be recognised (Hertzog, 1998). When varying degrees of challenge are built into everyday learning experiences for all children, an alert educator will notice the range of responses and perhaps be surprised by how much is already understood (Sutherland, 2008).

**exceptional strengths**: A child who is gifted is 'one who performs or has the potential to perform at a level significantly beyond his or her age peers and whose unique abilities and characteristics require special provision' (Harrison, 2003, p.8).

## ASSESSING THE EXTENT OF CHILDREN'S STRENGTHS

While educators want to build on all prior learning, it is very important to know when a child has an **exceptional strength** (is gifted) in an academic or developmental domain.

**FIGURE 25.1** SINGING THE ALPHABET

*Photo: Kathy Cologon*

The aim here is not to isolate or label the child as exceptional but to ensure an appropriate match to learning needs (Matthews & Foster, 2006). Otherwise, children can develop negative attitudes to school and learning, become disruptive, withdraw, or simply conform to low expectations and underachieve (Valpied, 2005).

Particular observable learning characteristics or dispositions can alert educators to the potential for advanced learning and the need for extension. Research over several decades has revealed the following characteristics associated with high intellectual ability: reasoning ability, impressive short- and long-term memory that is organised well for easy retrieval, curiosity and searching for understanding, extensive vocabulary, love of challenge (or avoidance if being an instant expert is not assured), unusually long concentration span and persistence when interested, and an early interest and skill in symbol systems like reading or mathematics (Koshy & Robinson, 2006; Porter, 2005). An individual child would have a cluster of these characteristics rather than all of them and may have higher reasoning ability and interest in one academic area than another, for example in reading and not in mathematics (Koshy & Robinson, 2006). Awareness of these characteristics can alert educators to twice-exceptional children (Karnes & Johnson 1986).

Testing can reveal the extent of a child's academic strengths. Sometimes a child is so advanced, rarely making an error even on difficult items in class tests, that a norm-referenced test may be helpful to determine what the level of instruction should be. Usually given by an educational psychologist, a norm-referenced test—commonly of reading or mathematics—measures the child's achievement against a large sample of children of the same age who represent a range of abilities in that domain (Anastasi & Urbina, 1997). It provides scores as a percentile or an age/grade equivalent (Salvia, Ysseldyke & Bolt, 2010). A child may require accommodations, such as the use of an augmentative and alternative communication system (see Chapter 23), in order to have every opportunity to attempt the test items (Salvia et al., 2010). When a child scores at the ceiling of the age-appropriate test, a norm-referenced test designed for older children can give a more accurate assessment (Assouline, 2003).

Children below school age may be given norm-referenced academic tests alongside an IQ test if early entry to school is being considered (Proctor, Feldhusen & Black, 1988). Although there are problems associated with testing very young children, when a child seems comfortable and motivated the score can be credible, and can be used with informal sources of information in educational decision making (Robinson & Robinson, 1992).

Information from parents is a very important contribution when building a picture of any child's educational needs. Children do not necessarily behave similarly in the education setting and at home, and parents see their child's approach to a wider range of situations and people (Karnes & Johnson, 1986). Even if unsure how advanced their child is, parents are able to describe what their children can do (Hodge & Kemp, 2000). Some parents of children with advanced development are reluctant to initiate discussion of their child's strengths for fear of appearing 'pushy' (Porter, 2008). When all parents are invited to tell about their children's strengths as well as any developmental concerns, educators have an opportunity to know each child better (Margrain, 2010).

### UNCOVERING CHILDREN'S INTERESTS

Knowing children's interests allows educators to employ these in engaging and challenging children in their learning (Koshy, 2002). Parents can provide information when the setting provides little opportunity for interests to be revealed. Children's interests can be intensely focused from as early as 18 months of age and last for years, occupying a large proportion of the child's attention, play and conversation (DeLoache, Simcock, & Macari, 2007). Boys are more likely to develop intense interests, which are likely to be gender-stereotyped (DeLoache et al.) or involved in acquiring deep conceptual knowledge that could predispose them towards science learning (Chapter 21; Johnson, Alexander, Spencer, Leibham & Neitzel, 2004). Sustained interests are associated with higher cognitive abilities and parental consistency, interest in educational activities and provision of related materials and time for free play (Johnson et al.).

## Extension and enrichment

**extension** and **enrichment**: *Extension* concerns depth of learning, with level of difficulty tailored to individual children; *enrichment* is the widening of content beyond the usual curriculum.

The terms **extension** and **enrichment** are often used in education. Braggett (1994) contended that extension and enrichment are twin concepts and not easily separated in practice. For example, if a primary school class is visiting a furniture factory for the first time (enrichment), existing skills and understanding may be extended through such processes as comparing the costs of bus and train travel, brainstorming questions to ask the manager, predicting what machinery might be used and sketching that machinery onsite, making a map of the factory, and writing thank you letters. Extension only occurs, however, when these tasks are deepening the level of learning for individual children, not giving practice in skills already mastered.

Braggett's (1994) explanation of extension chimes with Vygotsky's idea of the zone of proximal development (ZPD; Vygotsky, 1978) whereby teaching is aimed at an achievable level just beyond the child's current skills and understanding. Based on ongoing assessment, the level of challenge is important—not too easy, not too difficult—and should be part of the planning process (Koshy, 2002). While enrichment builds breadth of understanding in all children, it may be especially important for children from economically disadvantaged communities where families' capacities to introduce new experiences and materials to children's lives are sometimes limited (Tomlinson, 2005). Enrichment is also an opportunity to discover and explore new interests.

Some aspects of curriculum process and learning environment apply to extension in both prior-to-school and school settings. An obvious process is educators' planning for experiences and tasks that will encourage children to think. Bloom's Taxonomy of Educational Objectives, revised by Anderson and Krathwohl (2001), is one model often used to encourage increasingly demanding levels of thought, from 'lower level' remembering, understanding, and applying of knowledge to the higher levels of analysing, evaluating and creating. Educators can select tasks and questions from this taxonomy at levels relevant to children in their classes.

In the learning environment, psychological elements can impact on learning dispositions. Dispositions have been defined as 'participation repertoires from which a learner recognises, selects, edits, responds to, resists, searches for and constructs learning opportunities' (Carr, 2001, p.21). Educators can facilitate positive dispositions in many ways, including helping children to view their abilities as expandable. Dweck and colleagues (e.g. Dweck & Molden, 2005) have hypothesised that people view their abilities as either able to grow (an 'incremental' mindset) or as fixed (an 'entity' mindset). This theory implies that if adults express encouragement and feedback in terms of each child's ability to grow in competence towards mastery, children are more likely to develop positive dispositions towards learning, including accepting unfamiliar or challenging experiences and viewing errors as opportunities for learning. Praise for effort towards specific accomplishments (e.g. 'I saw you practising those spelling words and now you know them all') rather than global praise (e.g. 'You're so clever') will help this growth mindset to develop (Sutherland, 2008).

Although the learning needs of each child are unique, it does not follow that each child is taught individually! Flexible grouping of children according to complementary interests, strengths and needs may increase opportunities for educators to better scaffold learning for individuals and facilitate social relationships among children (Reid, 2002).

## EXTENDING AND ENRICHING LEARNING IN THE PRIOR-TO-SCHOOL SETTING

In the prior-to-school years the curriculum is usually based on learning outcomes across developmental areas. This is the case in the Australian Early Years Learning Framework (EYLF) (DEEWR, 2009), in which the broad

**FIGURE 25.2** ENGAGING THROUGH INTERESTS

*Photo: Kerry Hodge*

outcomes are that children will have a strong sense of identity and wellbeing, be connected with and contribute to their world, and become confident and involved learners who communicate effectively. Some early years curricula, such as England's Early Years Foundation Stage curriculum (Department for Education, 2012), add outcomes in academic areas. A variety of curriculum approaches used in Australian prior-to-school settings are compatible with the practices and learning outcomes of the EYLF (Arthur et al., 2012).

For many decades, play and exploration have been the foundation of learning for young children, enabling development across intellectual, physical, social and emotional domains (Gronlund, 2010). Learning through play remains as a key practice in the EYLF (DEEWR, 2009), and early years professionals and academics fiercely defend a play-based approach when they fear that school-like curriculum content and processes could be 'pushed down' to the prior-to-school years (Arthur et al., 2012).

Young children's learning through play and exploration is not left to chance; educators assess in a variety of ways and plan to extend each child's learning through play and other experiences, as well as capitalising on spontaneous 'teachable moments' as they arise (DEEWR, 2009, p.15). Teaching is intentional, but it is also responsive to children. Findings from the Effective Provision of Pre-School Education (EPPE) project indicated that the settings most effectively assisting children towards a good start to school provided a balance of experiences: educator-initiated and child-initiated (Sylva, Melhuish, Sammons, Siraj-Blatchford, Taggart & Elliot, 2003).

Child-initiated experiences such as play are enriched and extended when educators observe children playing, allow sufficient time for real engagement and sensitively scaffold children towards higher levels of play (Gronlund, 2010). According to Gronlund, educators can complicate children's play and provoke deeper thinking with excursions, books, more or fewer materials, and short-term flexible groupings. They can add documentation and playfully incorporate literacy and numeracy skills related to the play. Children's thinking and communication skills can be extended when they are involved in designing and setting up their environment and in naming areas (Sutherland, 2008). The learning environment is enriched when open-ended materials are accessible and children are allowed to use them in unexpected ways (Coates et al., 2008; Kolbe, 2007). Materials related to children's interests invite sustained involvement (Arthur et al., 2012).

Educators also initiate learning experiences with the intention of extending the learning of individual children and groups. Inquiry-based approaches like that from Reggio Emilia (Edwards et al., 1998) and the project approach (Helm & Katz, 2001) are examples of provision in which educators and children together investigate meaningful questions and document the process. Flexible groupings can be created to extend and enrich learning based on common interests. A large London nursery school, Chelsea Open Air, grouped three- to five-year-old children across the setting daily for story time, bringing together children of varying ages but assessed as having similar levels of concentration (Hodge, 2012). In addition, interest-related excursions into the community occurred for small groups (Hodge).

Intentional teaching usually involves educators in talk, and the quality of that talk influences quality of learning. The EPPE project (Sylva et al., 2003) showed that 'sustained shared thinking' was a feature of settings where children's intellectual development was highest. This was defined as 'an effective pedagogic interaction, where two or more individuals "work together" in an intellectual way to solve a problem, clarify a concept, evaluate activities, or extend a narrative' (Sylva et al., n.p.). Both child and educator must get involved and contribute, and the interaction must extend thinking (Sylva et al.).

Questioning is an opportunity to provide appropriate levels of challenge but has been commonly used to manage children (Siraj-Blatchford & Manni, 2008) or to seek feedback or facts (Massey, 2004) rather than to encourage higher levels of thought or debate (Bayley, 2002). Asking higher-order questions during storybook reading can extend already-competent thinkers (Walsh & Kemp, 2013). Educators, however, tend to ask more challenging questions when reading informational books than when reading fiction (Zucker, Justice, Piasta & Kaderavek, 2010).

### *When very young children's strengths are exceptional*

As conceptualised by Gagné (2003), the strengths of very young children can be exceptional for their age (indicating giftedness) in one or more developmental domains. The need to adjust usual practices in response to advanced development has become more visible since quality framework documents for Australian prior-to-school settings have included 'children who are gifted or have special talents' among children who 'will require or benefit from specific considerations or adaptations' (Australian Children's Education & Care Quality Authority [ACECQA], 2011, p.202). Harrison's (2005) research showed that even in infancy some children require play opportunities and interactions considered more appropriate for an older child.

The evidence base for responding appropriately to giftedness in children below school age is very limited (Koshy & Robinson, 2006). Most recommendations for wise practice come from authors who have worked with groups of young children who are gifted intellectually and revolve around responding to and extending the characteristics that make these children different in the first place (Maker, 1986). Maker proposed that there is much in the generic early years curriculum that is beneficial for children who are gifted—experiences that allow participation at the child's level and encouragement to respond at the highest possible level. She added that special efforts should be made to modify the curriculum when there is insufficient challenge. Harrison's (2005) view that children who are gifted seek complexity and connection to their world suggests that curriculum approaches that emphasise inquiry are especially suited to extending the learning of these children (Barbour & Shaklee, 1998; Hertzog, 2008).

Play remains a legitimate activity for children with advanced development. In play the child can explore interests and introduce satisfying complexity, although some children may not want to join in complicated scenarios or mature themes (Harrison, 2005) and adults may be preferred play partners (Murphy, 2007). Grant (2004) provided learning experiences based on science or art during the play period and followed up later with interested children, finding that the high number of children self-selecting for the extension activities prompted educators to reflect on the degree of challenge they had been offering. At Chelsea Open Air nursery school, children showing readiness for abstract thought were led through philosophical thinking using concrete objects and pictures (Hodge, 2012).

Some—but not all—young children with advanced intellectual development have advanced academic skills or interests before school (Hodge & Kemp, 2000). Some develop a fascination with symbol systems in reading (Margrain, 2010) or mathematics (Pletan, Robinson, Berninger & Abbott, 1995). Hertzog (2008) recommended that the child's interest should guide the educator regarding the level the child is ready for and gave the example of a child learning numerals 1 to 100 because of his interest in a speedometer. Wadlington and Burns (1993) suggested time and measurement as abstract concepts that could engage a young child who is gifted in mathematics. Children who read early require a range of reading materials related to their interests (Harrison, 2003; Hodge & Kemp, 2002).

Some children who are gifted may 'outgrow' the prior-to-school setting by the age of four and be keen to develop their academic skills and socialise with older children in school. Although educators may be hesitant about early entry to school, the evidence is strong for positive outcomes provided that certain criteria are met (Diezmann, Watters, & Fox, 2001; Proctor et al., 1988). Regardless of early or on-time entry, sharing of information about the child's learning in the prior-to-school setting at the time of transition to school facilitates appropriate extension in school (Whitton, 2005). This can complement any assessment conducted in the early weeks of the child's Foundation class (Arthur et al., 2012).

## EXTENDING AND ENRICHING LEARNING IN THE SCHOOL SETTING

Braggett (1994) proposed that extension and enrichment occur within and around the curriculum in response to individual children's learning needs. Curriculum in schools is usually quite prescribed, both in the scope and sequence of content and in the time parameters for mastering content. The Australian Curriculum (Australian Curriculum Assessment and Reporting Authority [ACARA], 2013) has three dimensions. In addition to the academic *learning areas,* there are seven *general capabilities* that are addressed through the learning areas—literacy, numeracy, information communication technology capability, critical and creative thinking, personal and social capability, ethical understanding and intercultural understanding. Arthur et al. (2012) noted a reduced focus on processes such as inquiry and meaning making. A third dimension encompasses the *cross-curriculum priorities* of Aboriginal and Torres Strait Islander histories and culture, Asia and Australia's engagement with Asia, and sustainability. These are envisaged as 'opportunities to add depth and richness to student learning in content elaborations' (ACARA, 2013, n.p.), although it is unclear whether children's interests outside the curriculum would be welcomed. While these three curriculum dimensions appear to offer ample depth and breadth, it is difficult, so early in the implementation of this new curriculum, to know how it will support extension and enrichment.

Although the Australian Curriculum specifies content and achievement standards for children at each year level, schools appear to have some flexibility

**CASE STUDY 25.1**

## Extension and enrichment for Robbie

New to the preschool, Robbie walked through each play area commenting, 'I can do that' or 'That's boring'. However, he was hesitant to join new experiences or groups of children, often observing first. Robbie's extensive vocabulary, very quick grasp of meanings in stories and skill with puzzles on the computer suggested to his educator, Jenny, that his intellectual abilities were advanced. Since he had completed the hardest puzzles and spending all his time on the computer was not an option, Jenny asked Robbie's mother about his favourite pastimes at home for clues to engaging him and extending his learning. Hearing that Robbie regarded pretend play and action songs as too babyish, loved word and board games and was fascinated by the universe and numbers, Jenny was able to gather resources and plan.

Robbie loved sharing the joke books and information texts on space with his educators whose conversations and questioning helped him towards higher levels of thinking. Other children joined in with enthusiasm and unexpected skill in completing dot-to-dot puzzles, playing Scrabble and playing a computer-based dictionary game. At first Jenny needed to be involved until they became more competent and helped each other. Robbie became friends with one of these children and taught her how to play the Hangman spelling game. Robbie also discovered a new interest when a parent demonstrated how to paint Chinese characters.

Through Robbie, Jenny learned that for some children, extension requires input from parents, different resources and new ways of interacting. Intentional extension and enrichment for one child enhanced the learning of several children and created new, mutually beneficial relationships in the group. All the learning outcomes of the EYLF were being addressed.

in selecting the teaching processes that best engage children in learning that content. Some schools will develop whole-school approaches (e.g. a particular scheme of levelled readers), and sometimes an educational system will make decisions to be applied in many schools. However, the individual educator generally has some freedom to choose processes, related products and the classroom learning environment.

Research in the USA by Reis, Westberg, Kulilowich, Caillard, Hébert, Plucker, et al. (1993) found that during whole-class teaching most educators adjusted their teaching pace to the learning pace of around the twenty-fifth percentile of the class (top of the bottom quarter). It is important, then, that strategies are developed to differentiate for variation in children's skill level and pace. Montgomery (1996) described two approaches to providing appropriate challenge across the class through 'tiered activities': (a) differentiation of inputs in the form of activities of various levels of difficulty within a topic, for which children are targeted or self-select; and (b) differentiation of outcomes as children attempt a task set for everyone and respond at their own levels of capability.

Mathematics is a learning area where levels of difficulty are clear and careful assessment can determine appropriate inputs. This has prompted Bobis (2002) to question the use of one level of mathematics textbook within primary classes. Mathematical learning is enriched by discussions and encouragement of children to justify their solutions and listen to multiple viewpoints (Bobis, 2002; Perry, McConney, Flevares, Mingle & Hamm, 2011). Mathematical games that explicitly address curriculum content can increase children's task engagement and promote task-related talk (Bragg, 2012).

In reading, within-class grouping commonly occurs in Australian schools and enables differentiating inputs. Reid (2002) advised that, while it takes time to develop groups and have them working effectively, the benefits of being able to observe individual children and scaffold learning are clear. Brimijoin et al. (2003) described strategies for increasing the independence of children working in groups, including step-by-step task cards and agreed signals for the urgency of need for assistance. Choice in reading materials and learning companions can improve children's engagement (Davis, 2010; Hertzog, 1998). Access to informational texts can spark enthusiasm, especially for boys (Mantzicopoulos & Patrick, 2011). In other learning areas, differentiated outcomes will be more appropriate, although children may choose to stay within their comfort zone (Hertzog, 1998).

### *Extending exceptional strengths in school*

As noted previously, children who are gifted share some learning characteristics (Koshy & Robinson, 2006; Porter, 2005). According to Tomlinson (1996), they can make larger leaps in learning and work with more complex ideas and resources in their area of strength. Rogers' (2007) synthesis of research evidence suggested that children with these characteristics need the following responses from educators: challenge daily in their areas of strength, access to advanced content, and the opportunity to work independently in their area of strength and passion. This is supported in the Australian Curriculum, which recognises the right to rigorous, relevant and engaging learning activities for children who are gifted, allows flexibility for more depth and breadth, and permits access to content from higher-grade levels (ACARA, 2013).

Access to advanced content can take various forms, including higher-grade work done in class while peers work at a lower level, early entry to school, and skipping one or more grades (Rogers, 2007). According to Gross, Urquhart, Doyle, Juratowitch and Matheson (2011), Australian educators are generally positive about grade-skipping on academic terms and accelerated children are happy, but educators' doubts linger about the social-emotional outcomes. There is, however, ample evidence of short-term and long-term benefits, even for multiple grade skips (Colangelo, Assouline, & Gross, 2004; Hoogeveen, van Hell, & Verhoeven, 2012).

Working independently in an area of strength and interest requires that children have the time and the skills to do so. A process called 'curriculum compacting' can provide the time. It involves pre-testing and then eliminating any content already known (Reis et al., 1993). In Rogers' (2007) synthesis it was deemed a highly effective strategy, and children appreciate it too (Stamps, 2004). Reis et al. (1993) found that educators could eliminate 40 to 50 per cent of content for children who were gifted. Independent learning skills can be taught explicitly so that the time 'bought' by compacting the curriculum is used productively, although time with the educator is also needed (Winebrenner, 2001).

To extend children who are gifted in reading, educators need to offer advanced materials across varied genres, teach strategies for critical reading and comprehension, and provide appropriately challenging and interesting reading-related activities (Moore, 2005; Wood, 2009). Lack of appropriate challenge over time can lead to avoidance when even mild challenge is reintroduced (Reis & Boeve, 2009).

Choice and open-ended tasks, important for all children, appear to be powerful factors in engaging children who are gifted (Alexander & Schnick, 2008). When children in inclusive classes were permitted to choose how to complete open-ended tasks, they took more time, engaged more deeply, consulted more sources of information and elaborated more (Hertzog, 1998). The opportunity to enter competitions offers children the chance to strive for personal achievement or to work collaboratively while solving challenging problems (Bicknell, 2008).

Actually providing challenge and extending learning, however, may be difficult for educators without support; studies in the USA, for example, found that few adjustments were made for children who were gifted in inclusive primary classrooms (Westberg, Archambault, Dobyns & Slavin, 1993). Dimitriadis' (2012) case study of four schools in the UK found that educators provided enrichment but not necessarily greater depth for children who had advanced mathematical skills, because the children needed frequent scaffolding with new material and the educators themselves sometimes lacked the subject knowledge required. With the appropriate skills, resources and support, educators can be highly effective in providing extension and enrichment to children who have an exceptional strength without isolating them or excluding other children who would benefit from these provisions.

CASE STUDY 25.2

## 'Numbers girl'

Hannah had always been a 'numbers girl'. As a toddler she noticed numbers everywhere. By age four she could name all the numerals from one to 100 in her Snakes and Ladders game. Although learning to read was an enjoyable challenge when she started school, 'easy peasy' mathematics was a huge disappointment, relieved only by trying the maths homework of her older sister (who disapproved). Hannah remained well behaved in school, but by the beginning of Year 1 her frustration was boiling over at home. When Hannah's mother asked her teacher for more mathematical challenge, the school's response was this: another teacher prepared a selection of work weekly for Hannah to collect from the school office and return after completion at home. Her work was always marked, but she had no interaction with this teacher. In class she was expected to do the same maths work as the other children.

**CRITICAL REFLECTION QUESTIONS**

1. Were Hannah's opportunities for learning in mathematics equitable?
2. What messages was Hannah getting about her learning needs and her schooling?
3. If you were Hannah's Year 1 teacher how would you have approached the task of extending her mathematical learning in class?
4. What other options did the school have in this situation? Would these disadvantage other members of the school community; could they bring advantages?

# Conclusion

To teach children inclusively, early years professionals can develop a range of strategies to uncover each child's knowledge, skills and interests in order to extend and enrich learning accordingly. Awareness of possible assumptions about children and their families can assist educators to view any child, including one with an impairment, as having strengths to be extended. Although extension and enrichment will unfold differently in prior-to-school and school settings, the principles of providing appropriate challenge by adjusting the curriculum content, process, products and learning environment for individual children where possible, are similar. Unusual approaches may be needed when identifying and extending strengths that are exceptional.

*Kerry Hodge*

# FOR FURTHER REFLECTION

1. How might children develop a fixed/entity or growth/incremental mindset about their abilities? What does this mean for your interactions with children, including those with an impairment?
2. When you meet a child with an impairment, do you focus on the limitations only? How could you discover strengths that may lie hidden? Who else might know?
3. What kinds of support do early years professionals need to extend and enrich the learning of children identified as gifted in inclusive classrooms? How can this support be provided in early years settings?
4. If you were to teach a Foundation (first year of school) class next year and were attending a meeting for parents of four-year-old children about transition to school, consider your response—and any assumptions you might be making—to parents who ask about the following issues:
   a. Delaying entry so the child will be among the oldest in the Foundation class;
   b. A child who is eligible and eager to begin academic learning but will be among the youngest of the class;
   c. A child who is already reading (not memorising) books.

## WEBSITES

www.austega.com/gifted/

Austega is a collection of resources and links to information about giftedness, parents' perspectives and school provisions, mostly from an Australian perspective.

www.aaegt.net.au/

The Australian Association for the Education of the Gifted and Talented (AAEGT) provides online resources as well as links for families and educators, including links to the policies of Australian state and territory departments of education and to state/territory organisations offering support.

https://education.arts.unsw.edu.au/about-us/gerric/

The Gifted Education, Research, Resource and Information Centre (GERRIC) at the University of New South Wales, Sydney provides professional development options and publications for educators.

www.education.vic.gov.au/childhood/professionals/learning/Pages/gtmakedifference.aspx

*Making a difference for young gifted and talented children* was developed by the Department of Education and Early Childhood Development (DEECD) Victoria in 2013 to assist educators and parents to engage and challenge children aged 0–8 whose development is advanced for their age. It covers understanding and identifying giftedness, learning opportunities and resources, working with families and transition to school.

## REFERENCES


Alexander, J.M. & Schnick, A.K. (2008). Motivation. In J.A. Plucker & C.M. Callahan (Eds), *Critical issues and practices in gifted education: What the research says* (pp.423–447). Waco, TX: Prufrock Press.

Anastasi, A. & Urbina, S. (1997). *Psychological testing* (7th edn). Upper Saddle River, NJ: Prentice-Hall International.

Anderson, L. & Krathwohl, D.A. (2001). *Taxonomy for learning, teaching and assessing: A revision of Bloom's Taxonomy of Educational Objectives*. New York: Longman.

Arthur, L. (2010). *The early years learning framework: Building confident learners*. Canberra: Early Childhood Australia.

Arthur, L., Beecher, B., Death, E., Dockett, S. & Farmer, S. (2012). *Programming and planning in early childhood settings* (5th edn). Melbourne: Thomson.

Assouline, S.G. (2003). Psychological and educational assessment of gifted children. In N. Colangelo & G.A. Davis (Eds), *Handbook of gifted education* (3rd edn, pp.124–145). Boston: Allyn & Bacon.

Australian Children's Education and Care Quality Authority (ACECQA). (2011). *Guide to the national quality standard*. Retrieved from www.acecqa.gov.au/national-quality-framework

Australian Curriculum Assessment and Reporting Authority (ACARA). (2013). Retrieved from www.acara.edu.au/curriculum/curriculum.html

Barbour, N. & Shaklee, B. (1998). Gifted education meets Reggio Emilia: Visions for curriculum in gifted education for young children. *Gifted Child Quarterly, 42,* 228–237. doi:10.1177/001698629804200406

Bayley, R. (2002). Thinking skills in the early years. *Gifted Education International, 16,* 248–260. doi:10.1177/026142940201600308

Bicknell, B. (2008). Gifted students and the role of mathematics competitions. *Australian Primary Mathematics Classroom, 13*(4), 16–20. Retrieved from hwww.aamt.edu.au/Webshop/Entire-catalogue/Australian-Primary-Mathematics-Classroom

Birbili, M. (2006). Mapping knowledge: Concept maps in early childhood education. *Early Childhood Research and Practice, 8*(2), no pagination. Retrieved from http://ecrp.uiuc.edu/v8n2/birbili.html

Bobis, J. (2002). Is school ready for my child? *Australian Primary Mathematics Classroom, 7*(4), 4–8. Retrieved from www.aamt.edu.au/Webshop/Entire-catalogue/Australian-Primary-Mathematics-Classroom

Borland, J. (2004). *Issues and practices in the identification and education of gifted students from under-represented groups*. Storrs, CT: National Research Center on the Gifted and Talented, University of Connecticut.

Bragg, L.A. (2012). The effect of mathematical games on on-task behaviours in the primary classroom. *Mathematics Education Research Journal, 24*(4), 385–401. Retrieved from http://hdl.handle.net/10536/DRO/DU:30049400

Braggett, E.J. (1994). *Developing programs for gifted students: A total-school approach*. Melbourne: Hawker Brownlow Education.

Brimijoin, K., Marquissee, E. & Tomlinson, C.A. (2003). Using data to differentiate instruction. *Educational Leadership, 60*(5), 70–73. Retrieved from www.ascd.org/publications/educational-leadership.aspx

Brody, L.E. & Mills, C.J. (1997). Gifted children with learning disabilities: A review of the issues. *Journal of Learning Disabilities, 30,* 282–296. Retrieved from http://ldx.sagepub.com/

Carr, M. (2001). *Assessment in early childhood settings: Learning stories*. London: Sage.

Chaffey, G. (2008). Is gifted education a necessary ingredient in creating a level playing field for Indigenous children in education? *Australasian Journal of Gifted Education, 17*(1), 38–39. Retrieved from www.aaegt.net.au/index.htm

Clark, B. (2002). *Growing up gifted* (6th edn). Upper Saddle River, NJ: Pearson Education.

Coates, D., Thompson, W. & Shimmin, A. (2008). Using learning journeys to develop a challenging curriculum for gifted children in a nursery (kindergarten) setting. *Gifted and Talented International, 23*(1), 97–104. Retrieved from www.gifted-children.com.au/world_council_for_gifted_and_talented_children

Colangelo, N., Assouline, S.G. & Gross, M. (2004). *A nation deceived: How schools hold back America's brightest* (Vol. 1). Iowa City, IA: Belin-Blank Center. Retrieved from www.accelerationinstitute.org/nation_deceived/

Dahlberg, G., Moss, P. & Pence, A. (1999). *Beyond quality in early childhood education and care: Postmodern perspectives*. London: Falmer Press.

Davis, L. (2010). Toward a lifetime of literacy: The effect of student-centres and skills-based reading instruction on the experiences of children. *Literacy Teaching and Learning, 15*(1, 2), 53–79. Retrieved from http://readingrecovery.org/rrcna/journals/ltl-archive

DeLoache, J.S., Simcock, G. & Macari, S. (2007). Planes, trains, automobiles—and tea sets: Extremely intense interests in very young children. *Developmental Psychology, 43*(6), 1579–1586. doi:10.1037/0012-1649.43.6.1579

Department for Education. (2012). *2013 early years foundation handbook*. London: Author. Retrieved from http://media.education.gov.uk/assets/files/pdf/2/2013_eyfs_handbook.pdf

Department of Education, Employment and Workplace Relations (DEEWR). (2009). *Belonging, being and becoming: The early years learning framework for Australia*. Canberra: DEEWR.

Diezmann C.M. & Watters, J.J. (1997). Bright but bored: Optimising the environment for gifted children. *Australian Journal of Early Childhood, 22*(2), 17–21. Retrieved from www.earlychildhoodaustralia.org.au/australian_journal_of_early_childhood/about_ajec.html

Diezmann C.M., Watters, J.J. & Fox, K. (2001). Early entry to school in Australia: Rhetoric, research and reality. *Australasian Journal of Gifted Education, 10*(2), 5–18. Retrieved from www.aaegt.net.au/index.htm

Dimitriadis, C. (2012). How are schools in England addressing the needs of mathematically gifted children in primary classrooms? A review of practice. *Gifted Child Quarterly, 56,* 59–72. doi:10.1177/0016986211433200

Dweck, C.S. & Molden, D.C. (2005). Self theories: Their impact on competence motivation and acquisition. In A.J. Elliot & C.S. Dweck (Eds), *Handbook of competence and motivation* (pp.122–140). New York: Guilford Press.

Edwards, B., Taylor, M. & Fiorini, M. (2011). Who gets the 'gift of time' in Australia? Exploring delayed primary school entry. *Australian Review of Public Affairs, 10*(1), 41–60. Retrieved from www.australianreview.net/journal/v10/n1/edwards_etal.html

Edwards, C., Gandini, L. & Forman, G. (Eds) (1998). *The hundred languages of children* (2nd edn). Greenwich, CN: Ablex.

Fleet, A. & Patterson, C. (2011). *Seeing assessment as a stepping stone: Thinking in the context of the EYLF.* Canberra: Early Childhood Australia.

Gagné, F. (2003). Transforming gifts into talents: The DMGT as a developmental theory. In N. Colangelo & G.A. Davis, *Handbook of gifted education* (3rd edn, pp.60–74). Boston: Allyn & Bacon.

Gagné, F. (2005). From noncompetence to exceptional talent: Exploring the range of academic achievement within and between grade levels. *Gifted Child Quarterly, 49,* 139–153. doi:10.1177/001698620504900204

Gordon, E.M. & Thomas, A. (1967). Children's behavioral style and the teacher's appraisal of their intelligence. *Journal of School Psychology, 5,* 292–300. Retrieved from www.journals.elsevier.com/journal-of-school-psychology/

Grant, A. (2004). Picasso, physics and coping with perfectionism: Aspects of an early childhood curriculum for gifted preschoolers. *Journal of Australian Research in Early Childhood Education, 11*(2), 61–69. Retrieved from www.education.monash.edu/research/conferences/arece/

Gronlund, G. (2010). *Developmentally appropriate play: Guiding young children to a higher level.* St Paul, MN: Redleaf Press.

Gross, M.U.M. (1998). The 'me' behind the mask: Intellectually gifted students and the search for identity. *Roeper Review, 20*(3), 167–174. doi:10.1080/02783199809553885

Gross, M.U.M. (1999). Small poppies: Highly gifted children in the early years. *Roeper Review, 21*(3), 207–214. Retrieved from www.tandfonline.com/loi/uror20

Gross, M.U.M., Urquhart, R., Doyle, J., Juratowitch, M. & Matheson, G. (2011). *Releasing the brakes for high-ability learners: Administrator, teacher and parents attitudes and beliefs that block or assist the implementation of school policies on academic acceleration.* Sydney: Gifted Education Research, Resource and Information Centre, University of New South Wales. Retrieved from http://gerric.arts.unsw.edu.au/media/File/1_Releasing_the_Brakes_Overview_A4__Nov2011.pdf

Harrison, C. (2003). *Giftedness in early childhood* (3rd edn). Sydney: GERRIC, University of NSW.

Harrison, C. (2005). *Young gifted children: Their search for complexity and connection.* Exeter: INSCRIPT.

Helm, J.H. & Katz, L. (2001). *Young investigators: The project approach in the early years.* New York: Teachers College Press.

Henderson, L.M. (2001). Asperger's syndrome in gifted individuals. *Gifted Child Today, 24*(3), 28–34. Retrieved from http://gct.sagepub.com/

Hertzog, N. (1998). Open-ended activities: Differentiation through learner responses. *Gifted Child Quarterly,* 42, 212–227. doi:10.1177/001698629804200405

Hertzog, N. (2008). *Early childhood gifted education.* Waco: TX: Prufrock Press.

Hertzog, N. & Klein, M. (2005). Beyond gaming: A technology explosion in early childhood classrooms. *Gifted Child Today, 28*(3), 24–31, 65. Retrieved from http://gct.sagepub.com/

Hodge, K.A. (2012). When a child's development is advanced: Program directions from the literature and the field. In P. Whiteman & K. De Gioia (Eds), *Perspectives, places and practices* (pp.187–202). Newcastle upon Tyne: Cambridge Scholars.

Hodge, K.A. & Kemp, C.R. (2000). Exploring the nature of giftedness in preschool children. *Journal for the Education of the Gifted, 24,* 46–73. Retrieved from http://jeg.sagepub.com/

Hodge, K.A. & Kemp, C.R. (2002). The role of an invitational curriculum in the identification of giftedness in young children. *Australian Journal of Early Childhood, 27*(1), 33–38. Retrieved from www.earlychildhoodaustralia.org.au/australian_journal_of_early_childhood/about_ajec.html

Hodge, K.A. & Kemp, C.R. (2006). Recognition of giftedness in the early years of school: Perspectives of teachers, parents, and children. *Journal for the Education of the Gifted, 30,* 164–204. Retrieved from http://jeg.sagepub.com/

Hoogeveen, L., van Hell, G. & Verhoeven, L. (2012). Social-emotional characteristics of gifted accelerated and non-accelerated students in the Netherlands. *British Journal of Educational Psychology, 82,* 585–605. doi:10.1111/j.2044-8279.2011.02047.

Howell, K.W. & Nolet, V. (2000). *Curriculum-based evaluation: Teaching and decision making.* Belmont, CA: Wadsworth.

Johnson, K.E., Alexander, J.M., Spencer, S., Leibham, M.E. & Neitzel, C. (2004). Factors associated with the early emergence of intense interests within conceptual domains. *Cognitive Development, 19,* 325–343. doi:10.1016/j.cogdev.2004.03.001

Kalbfleisch, M.L. & Iguchi, C.M. (2008). Twice-exceptional learners. In J.A. Plucker & C.M. Callahan (Eds), *Critical issues and practices in gifted education: What the research says* (pp.707–719). Waco, TX: Prufrock Press.

Karnes, M.B. & Johnson, L.J. (1986). Identification and assessment of gifted/talented handicapped and nonhandicapped children in early childhood. In J.R. Whitmore (Ed.), *Intellectual giftedness in young children: Recognition and development* (pp.35–54). New York: The Haworth Press.

Karnes, M.B., Shwedel, A.M. & Linnemeyer, S.A. (1982). The young gifted/talented child: Programs at the University of Illinois. *Elementary School Journal, 82*(5), 195–213. Retrieved from www.press.uchicago.edu/ucp/journals/journal/esj.html

Kolbe, U. (2007). *Rapunzel's supermarket: All about young children and their art* (2nd ed.). Byron Bay, NSW: Peppinot Press.

Koshy, V. (2002). *Teaching gifted and talented children 4–7: A guide for teachers.* London: David Fulton.

Koshy, V. & Robinson, N.M. (2006). Too long neglected: Gifted young children. *European Early Childhood*

*Education Research Journal, 14*(2), 113–126. doi:10.1080/13502930285209951

Maker, C.J. (1986). Suggested principles of gifted preschool curricula. *Topics in Early Childhood Special Education* 6(1), 62–73. doi:10.1177/027112148600600109

Maker, C.J. (1996). Identification of gifted minority students: A national problem, needed changes and a promising solution. *Gifted Child Quarterly, 40,* 41–50. doi:10.1177/001698629604000106

Maker, C.J. & Schiever, S.W. (1995). *Teaching models in education of the gifted* (3rd edn). Austin, TX: PRO-ED.

Mantzicopoulos, P. & Patrick, H. (2011). Reading picture books and learning science: Engaging young children with informational text, *Theory Into Practice, 50*, 269–276. doi:10.1080/00405841.2011.607372

Margrain, V. (2010). Parent-teacher partnership for gifted early readers in New Zealand. *International Journal about Parents in Education, 4*(1), 39–48. Retrieved from www.ernape.net/ejournal/index.php/IJPE

Massey, S.L. (2004). Teacher–child conversation in the preschool classroom. *Early Childhood Education Journal, 31*, 227–231. doi:10.1023/B:ECEJ.0000024113.69141.23

Matthews, D.J. & Foster, J.F. (2006). Mystery to mastery: Shifting paradigms in gifted education. *Roeper Review, 28*(2), 64–69. Retrieved from www.tandfonline.com/loi/uror20

Montgomery, D. (1996). *Educating the able*. London: Cassell.

Moore, M. (2005). Meeting the educational need of young gifted readers in the regular classroom. *Gifted Child Today, 28*(4), 40–47, 65. Retrieved from http://gct.sagepub.com/

Murphy, C. (2007). How do young children who are gifted play in an early childhood centre setting? *New Zealand Research in Early Childhood Education Journal, 10*, 191–198. Retrieved from www.childforum.com/research/research-journal-articles-reviewed-ece.html

Perry, M., McConney, M., Flevares, L.M., Mingle, L.A. & Hamm, J.V. (2011). Engaging first graders to participate as students of mathematics. *Theory Into Practice, 50*, 293–299. doi:10.1080/00405841.2011.607388

Pletan, M., Robinson, N., Berninger, V. & Abbott, R. (1995). Parents' observations of Kindergartners who are advanced in mathematical reasoning. *Journal for the Education of the Gifted, 19,* 30–44. Retrieved from http://jeg.sagepub.com/

Porter, L. (2005). *Gifted young children* (2nd edn). Sydney: Allen & Unwin.

Porter, L. (2008). *Teacher–parent collaboration: Early childhood to adolescence*. Melbourne: Australian Council for Educational Research.

Pretti-Frontczak, K. & Bricker, D. (2004). *An activity-based approach to early intervention* (3rd edn). Baltimore: Paul H. Brookes.

Proctor, T., Feldhusen, J. & Black, K. (1988). Guidelines for early admission to elementary school. *Psychology in the Schools, 25*, 41–43. doi:10.1002/1520-6807(198801)25:1<41::AID-PITS2310250107>3.0.CO;2-J

Reid, J. (2002). *Managing small-group learning.* Sydney: Primary English Teaching Association.

Reis, S.M. & Boeve, H. (2009). How academically gifted elementary, urban students respond to challenge in an enriched, differentiated reading program. *Journal for the Education of the Gifted, 33*(2), 203–240. Retrieved from http://jeg.sagepub.com/

Reis, S., Westberg, K., Kulilowich, J., Caillard, F., Hébert, T., Plucker, J., et al. (1993). *Why not let high ability students start school in January? The curriculum compacting study.* Storrs, CT: The National Research Center of the Gifted and Talented.

Robinson, N.M. & Robinson, H. (1992). The use of standardized tests with young gifted children. In P.S. Klein & A.J. Tannenbaum (Eds), *To be young and gifted* (pp.141–170). Norwood, NJ: Ablex.

Rogers, K. (2007). Lessons learned about educating the gifted and talented: A synthesis of the research on educational practice. *Gifted Child Quarterly, 51*, 382–396. Retrieved from gcq.sagepub.com/

Salvia, J., Ysseldyke, J.E. & Bolt, S. (2010). *Assessment: In special and inclusive education.* Belmont, CA: Cengage Learning.

Siraj-Blatchford, I. & Manni, L. (2008). 'Would you like to tidy up now?' An analysis of adult questioning in the English Foundation Stage. *Early Years, 28*(1), 5–22. doi:10.1080/09575140701842213

Siraj-Blatchford, I. & Sylva, K. (2004). Researching pedagogy in English pre-schools. *British Educational Research Journal, 30*, 713–730. doi:10.1080/0141192042000234665

Stamps, L. (2004). The effectiveness of curriculum compacting in first grade classrooms. *Roeper Review, 27*(1), 31–41. Retrieved from www.tandfonline.com/loi/uror20

Sutherland, M. (2008). *Developing the gifted and talented young learner.* London: Sage.

Sylva, K., Melhuish, E., Sammons, P., Siraj-Blatchford, I., Taggart, B. & Elliot, K. (2003). *The Effective Provision of Pre-school Education (EPPE) project: Findings from the pre-school period.* Research Brief No. RBX15-03. London: Department for Education and Skills.

Tomlinson, C.A. (1996). Good teaching for one and all: Does gifted education have an instructional identity? *Journal for the Education of the Gifted, 20*(2), 155–174. Retrieved from http://jeg.sagepub.com/

Tomlinson, C.A. (2003). Deciding to teach them all. *Educational Leadership, 61*(2), 6–11. Retrieved from www.ascd.org/publications/educational-leadership.aspx

Tomlinson, C.A. (2005). Quality curriculum and instruction for highly able students. *Theory into Practice, 44*(2), 160–166. Retrieved from www.jstor.org/stable/3497034

Valpied, J. (2005). The flip side of giftedness: Interactions between gifted characteristics and school responses. *Australasian Journal of Gifted Education, 14*(2), 12–26. Retrieved from www.informit.com.au/products/productdetails.aspx?id=1323-9686&container=IELHSS

Vygotsky, L. (1978). *Mind in society: The development of higher psychological processes.* Cambridge, MA: Harvard University Press.

Wadlington, E. & Burns, J.M. (1993). Math instructional practices within preschool/Kindergarten gifted programs. *Journal for the Education of the Gifted, 17*(1), 41–52. Retrieved from http://jeg.sagepub.com/

Walsh, R.L. & Kemp, C.R. (2013). Evaluating interventions for young gifted children using single-subject methodology: A preliminary study. *Gifted Child Quarterly, 57*, 110–120. doi:10.1177/0016986212466259

Westberg, K.L., Archambault, F.X., Jr., Dobyns, S.M. & Salvin, T.J. (1993). *An observational study of instructional and curricular practices used with gifted and talented students in regular classrooms* (RM93104). Storrs, CT: University of Connecticut, The National Research Center on the Gifted and Talented.

Whitton, D. (2005). Transition to school for gifted children. *Australian Journal of Early Childhood, 30*(3), 27–31. Retrieved from www.earlychildhoodaustralia.org.au/australian_journal_of_early_childhood/about_ajec.html

Winebrenner, S. (2001). *Teaching gifted kids in the regular classroom: Strategies and techniques every teacher can use to meet the academic needs of the gifted and talented.* Minneapolis, MN: Free Spirit Publishing.

Wood, P.F. (2009). Growing young gifted readers. *Understanding our Gifted, 21*(3), 6–8. Retrieved from www.ourgifted.com/understanding-our-gifted/

Wright, L. & Coulianos, C. (1991). A model program for precocious children: Hollingworth Preschool. *Gifted Child Today, 14*(5), 24–29. Retrieved from http://gct.sagepub.com/

Zucker, T.A., Justice, L.M., Piasta, S.B. & Kaderavek, J.N. (2010). Preschool teachers' literal and inferential questions and children's responses during whole-class shared reading. *Early Childhood Research Quarterly, 25*, 65–83. doi:10.1016/j.ecresq.2009.07.001

# 26 Constructing Inclusion: Putting Theory into Practice

*Kathy Cologon*

CHAPTER OVERVIEW

In this book we have considered key practical and philosophical elements in facilitating inclusive early years experiences. As discussed throughout, inclusion is an ongoing process that requires reflection and renewal, as well as systemic change. In this chapter I will draw together key issues regarding moving from rhetoric to reality in inclusive early years education.

Learning goals for this chapter include:

- Understanding inclusive education as an ongoing process;
- Reflecting on the importance of leadership for bringing about inclusive education in reality;
- Considering a starting point for becoming more inclusive within early years settings;
- Developing an understanding of an affirmative model of disability and considering the implications for inclusion in the early years—including and beyond processes of disablement;
- Recognising the significance of inclusive representations in media and popular culture;
- Engaging with resistance theory and the importance of resistance to dominant discourse in bringing about inclusive education in everyday reality.

KEY TERMS AND CONCEPTS

affirmation model of disability

conscientização

othering

praxis

# Inclusive education: Rhetoric to reality

'Inclusive education is about providing the best possible education for all' (Armstrong & Barton, 2008, p.11). As explored throughout this book, inclusive education involves 'embracing human diversity and welcoming all children and adults as equal members of an educational community. This involves valuing and supporting the full participation of all people *together* within mainstream educational settings' (Cologon, 2013a, p.6, emphasis added). However, inclusive education 'is a process of *construction*, and not something which can be simply "delivered"' (Plaisance, 2008, p.37, emphasis original)

Inclusive education is an approach to education that is free from discriminatory beliefs, attitudes and practices and requires recognising and upholding the rights of all people (Cologon, 2013a). It involves understanding diversity as an everyday part of all human environments and interactions and as a rich resource (Cologon, 2013a). To bring this to a reality requires acknowledging that we are all equally human and putting this recognition into action in everyday practical ways to 'ensure all children and adults belong, participate and flourish' (Cologon, 2013a, p.6).

In my lifetime alone, many important leaps forward have occurred on the journey towards greater inclusion. However, there is also a long way yet to go before the right to inclusive education is genuinely realised in Australia. 'The notion that there is one way to teach any group of children is both problematic and untrue, as it denies the individuality of all children and the diversity within any group' (Cologon, 2013a, p.33). Bringing about inclusive education in reality requires *fundamental change* in culture, policy and practice. But it is also possible.

**CASE STUDY 26.1**

## Inclusion: 'The way we live together'

I have been fortunate to conduct some recent research in Italy—a country where segregated 'special' education ended in 1977. The 1977 legislation that brought this about recognised the danger in providing the option to exclude and segregate, and therefore asserted the need to have education *together* as the *only* possibility. Consequently, since 1977 all children in Italy have gone to school together in the same schools, and grown up together.

On account of this legislation it is no longer possible in Italy to decide that a child cannot attend a particular school—that the accommodations required would be 'unreasonable', that the child is 'too disabled' to go to a mainstream school. There are no 'mainstream' or 'regular' and 'special' schools in Italy—there are just schools—for *everyone*.

Now of course Italy has its own challenges, including fewer financial resources than a relatively wealthy country such as Australia. However, the existence of the option to exclude children is no longer one of the challenges that Italy faces—and hasn't been for some decades now.

In Italy I interviewed teachers, school principals and students in preschools, primary schools and a high school. I would like to share an experience in an Italian high school. This story comes from a recent paper of mine (Cologon, 2013b).

In the high school I visited, among other people, I was fortunate to interview the student representative (similar to a 'school captain' in Australia but elected by student vote only). Before interviewing him I was told that this student is considered by many teachers to be rebellious and difficult to teach and that he may not choose to speak to me.

At this time, he had called a student strike at the school. During a student strike all staff and students attend school, but the students mainly hold classes for each other. Teachers hold classes if the students invite them to. When I interviewed the student representative, he had just concluded teaching a class on tattoo design to a group of enthusiastic peers. I will call him Renaldo.

Wearing a leather jacket and surrounded by a posse of other students, Renaldo greeted me—not with any disrespect, but with a perceptible air of indifference. It was clear that I was to know that he was a person of great importance and authority (a super-cool dude really)—and that I should count myself lucky to be speaking with him.

At the start of the interview Renaldo wanted to ask me some questions about Australia (including about surfing and about what was happening with the footballer Alessandro Del Piero at Sydney FC). He also wanted to ask me about education in Australia.

After hearing that in Australia we have schools where only children labelled 'disabled' or 'disordered' attend, his whole demeanour shifted. The 'tough guy' bravado was replaced with the strength and conviction of a leader as he earnestly sought to convince me of the importance of inclusion for *all* from the very beginning of education. He used many examples of his friends—a diverse group—and he also used examples of his teachers, including the fact that inclusion was much harder for some of his older teachers as they did not grow up together—they lived through segregation of people who experienced disability.

Renaldo argued that: '[I]n general people are very insensitive and don't care, but if educated together from the beginning ... If students are educated together from very young ... then they care for each other. If from the beginning then there are many possibilities.' He emphasised the importance of inclusion from the early years onwards—something that he had experienced as a reality throughout his life. He also emphasised the need to understand inclusion as being about more than education settings, arguing that *'... inclusion is about the whole of life—the way we live together as people for the whole of life.'*

As discussed throughout this book, inclusive education is the right of every child. The realisation of this right requires considerable effort and leadership at every level—from systemic change through to everyday interactions between one person and another. Changes in attitudes and cultural understandings of 'difference', 'diversity' and 'disability' are a key aspect of this transformation. This necessitates an ongoing cycle of *reflection and action* for change (**praxis**), involving openness to reconsidering current attitudes and practices and a willingness to *genuinely* listen to each other—including listening to children and young people.

**praxis:** 'Reflection and action upon the world in order to transform it' (Freire, 1970, p.33).

## CASE STUDY 26.2

### Danny's message

Danny Dickson is an advocate for *Children with Disability Australia*, the peak organisation representing children who experience disability in Australia. Danny gave the following speech to his Year 7 class for International Day of People With Disability:

> It is International Day Of People With Disability on the 3rd December. I'm Danny Dickson and I want you to think for one minute about disability and about your attitudes.
>
> Don't roll your eyes, don't mock people, don't tease, don't bully. You're better than that. Aren't you? No matter what. It's not OK. It's about respect. I will feel better and you will feel better too.
>
> Maybe you need to stop and rethink your attitude to disability. Disability is a different ability. You may have called someone with a disability 'not normal' or 'a retard', which I don't want you to do. Also, people often use this word to put someone down. Disability does not mean less ability.
>
> Many people with disability have made great contributions globally. Stephen Hawking, Franklin Roosevelt, Kurt Fearnley and Christopher Reeve are just four such people, and there are many more. Many people's efforts to advance the rights of people with disability go unnoticed.
>
> So I just wanted to take this opportunity to try and encourage you to think about disability and some of the things that are happening in Australia to celebrate disability as being an important part of the community.
>
> In your school, in your workplace, in your home think before you act, think before you talk. Don't bully or disrespect someone with disability. Look at things from another perspective. Celebrate everyone in your community. It will enrich us all.

**CRITICAL REFLECTION QUESTIONS**

1. What do Danny's and Renaldo's stories tell you about inclusive education?
2. Consider some of the barriers that Danny draws attention to that exist in the parallel systems of segregated and mainstream education in Australia, compared with the education of all children together in Italy. How might these impact on attitudes of students and staff towards inclusive education?
3. Consider Renaldo's reflections on the importance of the early years. If children are not educated together from the start of life, what messages does this send to them? What does segregation teach children about themselves and each other?
4. Danny and Renaldo demonstrate leadership for inclusion. Why are leaders needed in bringing about inclusion in reality?
5. Leadership occurs at many different levels. Consider the ways in which you can be (or are) a leader and how you can use your leadership capacity to facilitate inclusion in the early years.

Bringing about inclusion in education involves working to ensure that the supports that are required—including professional development and support for the development of inclusive attitudes—are fully provided. It is important to consider barriers to inclusion and gaps between stated and enacted policy within each setting (Westwood & Graham, 2003). However, even in the face of the exclusionary structures that we exist within, becoming an inclusive setting may be closer than you think. Ainscow (2007, p.6) argues that

> *Schools know more than they use* and the logical starting point for development [of inclusivity] is with a detailed analysis of existing arrangements. This allows good practices to be identified and shared, whilst, at the same time, drawing attention to ways of working that may be creating barriers to the participation and learning of some students. However ... the focus must not only be on practice; it must also address and sometimes challenge the thinking behind existing ways of working.

Whether in schools, preschools or childcare settings, inclusive education is not something entirely new or unknown—inclusive education is just 'good teaching'. But creating an inclusive culture does require active awareness of the practices in place and what underpins them, and openness to continual change and improvement.

## Breaking barriers to inclusion

Attitudes towards inclusion have been identified as a key barrier to or facilitator of inclusion. The attitudes and beliefs of early years professionals about the value of inclusion and their confidence in their ability to teach all children have been identified as keys to the success of inclusive early years education (Cologon, 2012).

**CRITICAL REFLECTION QUESTIONS**

As Ainscow (2007) argues, developing an inclusive setting needs to start with reviewing current practices and resources. The following questions provide a starting point:

1. What are the current strengths of the setting?
2. What positive practices are currently occurring that can be identified and shared?
3. What current practices may be creating barriers to participation for some children?
4. What are the underlying assumptions or attitudes underpinning current practice?
5. Who attends the setting currently and who does not—why don't they?

**FIGURE 26.1** PLAYING WITH FRIENDS

*Artwork by Lucas*

In Chapter 2, we explored medical model and social model understandings of disability. These ideas also apply to diverse notions of 'difference'. As discussed throughout the book, medical model understandings of disability can also be referred to as a 'tragedy model' or a 'personal tragedy theory of disability' (French & Swain, 2004).

French and Swain (2004, p.34) write, 'In the personal tragedy theory, disability, or rather impairment—which is equated with disability—is thought to strike individuals at random, causing suffering and blighting lives. This view is so dominant, so prevalent and so infused throughout media representations, language, cultural beliefs, research, policy and professional practice', that it permeates attitudes and representations at all levels of society and is used as a justification for ableist efforts to eradicate or 'normalise' people with designated impairments (French & Swain, 2004). For example, abortion on account of 'risk' of impairment is barely challenged and forced sterilisation is still practised

**FIGURE 26.2** ENJOYING THE GREAT OUTDOORS

*Photo: Alison Wilson*

(French & Swain, 2004). The ableist and mistaken view that people who experience disability 'cannot be happy, or enjoy an adequate quality of life, lies at the heart of this response' (French & Swain, 2004, p.34). Whereas, in reality '[n]obody can predict the amount of tragedy or happiness a person will experience in life and yet people feel confident to make such predictions about [people who experience disability]. The inherent assumption is that [people who experience disability] want to be other than as they are, even though this would mean a rejection of identity' (French & Swain, 2004, p.38).

As discussed in Chapter 2, from a medical or tragedy model perspective, it is assumed that 'problems' that a person encounters result from impairment or 'difference', rather than from the social imposition of disability and stigma. Additionally, it is assumed that such a thing as 'normal' exists and that people who experience 'difference' and 'disability' want to be 'normal' (see Chapter 3).

People who are deemed 'different' in some way, including people who experience disability, 'are subjected to many disabling expectations, for example, to be "independent", "normal", to "adjust" and "accept" their situation. It is these expectations that can cause unhappiness: rather than the impairment [or other "difference"] itself' (French & Swain, 2004, p.34). Unfortunately, this medical model, and its tragedy understanding of difference and disability, is very prevalent even today—as a general rule it is based on fear, whether conscious or subconscious—and in '**othering**'. Sadly, in order to belong or be included, as humans, we learn to privilege the existing power of the

**othering:** The stigmatising process of creating an 'other' who we perceive to be different to ourselves, and in some sense lesser or inferior—the creation of a 'them' and 'us'.

*Kathy Cologon*

'normal', which reinforces the construct of an 'other' who is excluded. Thus we create 'them' and 'us', or 'disabled' and 'non-disabled', rather than accepting and acknowledging that we are all equally human and share a vast array of human diversity. Consequently, we are generally conditioned to approach disability from an ableist, tragedy model perspective.

If inclusive education is to become a reality for the children and families we work with, then resisting the medical, tragedy model is an ongoing challenge that we must each face—regardless of our own experiences. To resist this model we need to seek to understand the reality of how 'difference' and 'disability' are constructed in society and work to eradicate all forms of discriminatory attitudes, beliefs and practices.

For early years professionals, this includes working to resist and eradicate the belief that it is OK to exclude someone because they have a disability label. Consequently, we need to reject notions of 'special' education for 'special' people and move beyond this towards genuine inclusive education. While challenging, the exciting part of this is that, in questioning our own beliefs, we can develop a deeper understanding of the social construction of 'difference' and 'disability' and resist the tragedy, medical model view. In doing so, early years professionals have the opportunity to break the cycle of intergenerational ableism, racism, sexism, genderism, classism, homophobia, transphobia, ageism and discrimination in relation to religion and belief/non-belief.

## Towards an affirmative model of 'difference' and 'disability'

A non-tragic view of 'difference' and 'disability', rather than being about 'the problem', is about difference and 'disability as a positive personal and collective identity… [with] people leading fulfilled and satisfying lives' (Swain & French, 2000, p.571). From this basis Swain and French (2000) propose an **affirmative model of disability**. The affirmative model of disability not only recognises the social construction of disability, but builds on this towards understanding 'a non-tragic view of disability and impairment which encompasses positive social identities, both individual and collective' (Swain & French, 2000, p.569). This thinking can also be applied when considering the stigmatisation of people who have been labelled with any 'difference'.

**affirmative model of disability:** '[A] non-tragic view of disability and impairment which encompasses positive social identities, both individual and collective' (Swain & French, 2000, p.569).

An affirmative model not only challenges us to erase the idea that impairment is a tragedy, but to move to the idea that impairment can be positive. It highlights the fact that people with impairments, or any other labelled 'difference', can enjoy being who they are and have positive identities—including in relation to their impairments or other 'differences'. People who experience disability worldwide are increasingly 'creating positive images of themselves and are

**FIGURE 26.3** MAKING MUSIC TOGETHER

*Photo: Kathy Cologon*

demanding the right to be the way they are—to be equal but different' (French & Swain, 2004, p.38). This is at the core of an affirmative model.

As explored in Chapter 2, children who participated in research by Connors and Stalker (2003; 2007) did not consider their impairments to be a tragedy and when asked if they could change anything about their lives, their impairment was not what they wished to change. Similarly, Mason (2000, p.8) writes of not viewing her impairment as a 'tragedy' and of not wanting to be 'cured'—and about the shock this revelation caused those around her:

> [A]t my special school, I remember one of the care staff loudly telling me that I should never give up hope because one day doctors would find a cure for my affliction, and I loudly told her that I did not want to be 'cured'. I remember this incident because of the utter disbelief this statement caused among all the [people who did not experience disability] present, and the delight this statement caused amongst my friends [who experience disability]. The school decided that I had 'The Wrong Attitude' and that I should indeed go to Lourdes so that Jesus, the Virgin Mary and St. Bernadette could sort me out.

As French and Swain (2004) argue, the medical tragedy model view of disability is disabling in itself. A tragedy/medical model view of disability denies the enjoyment of the living of life on the one hand and at the same time denies the experiences and realities of a disabling society (French & Swain, 2004). By contrast, '[t]he affirmation of positive identity challenges the tyranny of the personal tragedy theory of disability and impairment' (French & Swain, 2004, p.39).

Holliday Willey (1999, p.96) shares: 'I do not wish for a cure to Asperger's syndrome. What I wish for is a cure for the common ill that pervades too many lives, the ill that makes people compare themselves to a normal that is measured in terms of perfect and absolute standards, most of which are impossible for anyone to reach.'

**CASE STUDY 26.3**

## An affirmation model and children's literature

In Chapter 3, we explored issues relating to language and power, and the messages we convey, intentionally and unintentionally, through the language and terminology we use. This is also true of the messages conveyed through images and other representations within popular culture. Ideas, understandings and social trends are expressed through this medium. Both representation and *lack* of representation of particular groups of people can convey messages and reflect the views of society.

There are many forms of representation. Media, movies, television shows, advertisements, toys and children's literature are some examples of places where representations are made, or can be blatantly absent. Critically reflecting on these representations (or lack thereof) is useful for understanding social change and culture, and for understanding and reflecting on our own views and on where we find others' representations challenging. As early years professionals, these critical reflections on representations are an essential part of reflective practice.

Niland (2013, p.36) writes that '[p]icture books enable children to experience the worlds of others, through engaging with fictional characters and narratives. These vicarious imaginary experiences play a part in forming children's understandings of social values.' Inclusive social values can be fostered by representing humans in all our diversity (Cologon, 2013a). One aspect of this human diversity is impairment, upon which disablement is based (see Chapter 2):

> While it is common to advocate for 'disability awareness' as part of the efforts towards inclusion, this tends to be interpreted to mean awareness of characteristics associated with disability labels. A critical aspect of working towards inclusion does in fact involve 'disability awareness'—that is, resisting dominant normative narratives or understandings of disability. Supporting children and teachers to genuinely develop disability awareness opens possibilities for actively reducing the barriers that result in the experience of disability for many children (Cologon, 2013a, p.41).

Focusing on representation of d/Deaf characters in children's literature, Brittain (2004, n.p.) outlines 'the six pitfalls of disability fiction'. These are:

- Portraying the character with an impairment as 'other' than human:
  - Showing the character as otherworldly in a negative or positive sense—extremely 'evil' or extremely 'good';
  - Likening the character to vegetable matter;
  - Forging links between the character and animals.

- Portraying the character with an impairment as 'extra-ordinary':
  - The character's ordinary humanity is not described but is represented either as a negative or positive stereotype.
- The 'second fiddle' phenomenon:
  - The character with an impairment is neither the central character within the narrative nor fully developed, merely serving to bring the central character/s to a better understanding of themselves or disability.
- Lack of realism and accuracy in the portrayal of the impairment:
  - The author neglects to properly research a particular impairment, resulting in inaccuracy of portrayal.
- The outsider:
  - The character with an impairment is portrayed as a figure of alienation and social isolation.
- Happy endings?
  - The author fails to see a happy and fulfilled life being a possibility for a character with an impairment.

Research with early years professionals has found that reviewing and reflecting on children's literature creates a powerful opportunity to be challenged and can inspire us to resist the dominant medical/tragedy model view of 'difference' and 'disability' (Cologon, 2013c).

**CRITICAL REFLECTION ACTIVITIES**

1. Go to your local library or bookstore and review the selection of children's books available. Who is represented and who is not? What model of 'disability' and 'difference' is presented in the books available? What messages are conveyed through the presence or absence of images of diversity? How can you challenge and resist dominant representations and ideas by using books?
2. Review Brittain's (2004) 'six pitfalls of disability fiction'. Consider a children's book that incorporates representations of culture, gender, impairment and disability. Reflect on the way the characters are portrayed through the storyline and illustrations and compare this with Brittain's list. Does the book provide positive or negative representation? Would you recommend the book for use with children? Why or why not? How might you approach using the book to ensure it facilitates inclusion and supports an affirmative model of 'disability' and 'difference'?
3. Read *Ziba came on a boat* by Lofthouse and Ingpen (2007), *The Little Refugee* by Do, Do and Whatley (2011), *My Friend Isabelle* by Woloson and Gough (2003) and *Susan Laughs* by Willis and Ross (1999). Consider the ways in which these books can be used to support the development of an affirmative model of human diversity. How do these books represent an affirmative model? What challenges do they present?

It is clear that moving towards an affirmative model of 'difference' and 'disability' is an important component of moving from rhetoric to the reality of inclusive education. The question then becomes, how do we get from the currently pervasive medical/tragedy model to the affirmation model? Two of the key (and interlinked) components to this process are, first, engaging with the social model and seeking to understand it (see Chapter 2), and, second, actively resisting the dominant medical/tragedy model.

## Inclusive education: Engaging in resistance

> To surmount the situation of oppression, people must first critically recognize its causes, so that through transforming action they can create a new situation, one which makes possible the pursuit of a fuller humanity. But the struggle to be more fully human has already begun in the authentic struggle to transform the situation (Freire, 1970, p.29).

In Chapter 5, we explored ways in which families resist stigma in the form of ableism and disablism. In this chapter we build on this by considering resistance theory and what this has to offer us in moving towards an affirmation model of 'difference' and 'disability'.

Resistance theory has been explored by a number of theorists and philosophers, notably Foucault, Freire, Giroux, Aronowitz and bell hooks (among others). Freire (1970, p.39) writes that

> The radical, committed to human liberation, does not become the prisoner of a 'circle of certainty' within which reality is also imprisoned. On the contrary, the more radical the person is, the more fully he or she enters into reality so that, knowing it better, he or she can better transform it. This individual is not afraid to confront, to listen, to see the world unveiled.

This statement contains some important ideas that are essential to resisting dominant discourse, and therefore to inclusive education. However, it is helpful to unpack its meaning. Firstly, when Freire refers to being 'radical', this is not in the sense of an accusation (in the way that radical is sometimes used) or a call to extremism. Instead, it is about being radical enough in our thinking to be able to 'think outside the box'; to be able to think *for ourselves* and therefore, to question the status quo rather than unquestioningly following dominant discourses. Being radical, in the sense that Freire uses it, means engaging in critical thinking and critical reflection with a view to social justice (praxis) (Freire, 1998). As Giroux (2001) argues, this critical consciousness, a concept that Freire refers to as **conscientização**, coupled with valuing and intentionally striving towards social transformation with the goal of removing or reducing domination and oppression, is essential to resistance.

**conscientização:** Recognising and questioning the processes of power that underpin and perpetuate dominant beliefs and practices, thus developing a social consciousness and reflecting and acting upon this consciousness (Freire, 1970).

For early years professionals and researchers, being radical in this sense is essential to our everyday roles. We need to be able to be flexible and reflective in our thinking and see possibilities beyond what has always been done or how it has always been done. Given that inclusion requires radical thinking, it is also essential to inclusive education.

Freire's notion of resisting the 'circle of certainty' is important if we are to work towards an affirmation model of 'difference' and 'disability'. Given that the tragedy/medical model view of disability is so pervasive, staying within the 'circle of certainty' in this case would mean being enculturated into medical model thinking and accepting without question this medical/tragedy model view. Similarly, in the nineteenth century staying within the 'circle of certainty' in Australia (and elsewhere) would have included accepting that women are the property of their husbands and should not be given access to equal education, and into the twentieth century, believing that women should not vote (Oldfield, 1992) (Australian Aboriginal women were not given the vote until 1962).

From the 'circle of certainty' the cycle of stigmatisation that excludes and marginalises people continues, thus detracting from the experience of life for all humans.

Staying within the 'circle of certainty' can be tempting though. As humans we tend to want simple answers and the comfort of certainty. Questioning what is presented to us as certain can be uncomfortable at times, both as individuals and when we challenge those around us. In large and small ways, though, questioning the 'circle of certainty' is key to progress. The 'circle of certainty' leaves no room for change, rather it is a self-fulfilling and self-reinforcing cycle.

While inclusive education has been explored, discussed, debated and progress has been made over a considerable period of time now, in the context of education as a whole, inclusive education is still a new phenomenon. This means that bringing it into reality requires questioning—or breaking—the 'circle of certainty'. Freire writes of the importance of conscientização—'learning to perceive social, political, and economic contradictions, and to take action against the oppressive elements of reality' (Freire, 1970, p.35). Thus, as Freire argues, it is essential to be unafraid (or to conquer the fear) of questioning, examining, confronting ourselves and others and unveiling taken-for-granted, common 'truths'.

In engaging with these challenging ideas, there are two key aspects that I would like to highlight. Firstly, as Foucault (1991, 2002) argued, critical thinking is essential to challenging structures of domination, such as those that (re)produce stigma and prevent the realisation of inclusion. Foucault (1991, pp.11–12) emphasised the importance of 'shaking up habits, ways of acting and thinking, of dispelling commonplace beliefs, of taking a new measure of rules and institutions' coupled with taking action—conscientização.

Secondly, engaging in this process of critical consciousness requires challenging the perpetuation of the notion of 'special' teachers being required for 'special' children, which results in (re)production of exclusion, inequality and restricted participation, and undermines the confidence of 'mainstream' teachers to teach all children. Challenging this 'circle of certainty' and questioning the validity of the notion of 'special' education is essential if ableism (and all forms of stigma) is to be disestablished and thus inclusion is to become genuinely possible. It is also essential if early years professionals are to develop confidence that they can, indeed, be inclusive and that the system can and should be inclusive.

This is not to suggest that specialist early years professionals do not have an important role in bringing about inclusive education. The role of a wide range of early years professionals, including physiotherapists, speech therapists, occupational therapists and early intervention specialists, for example, is of considerable importance in supporting teachers in successfully including children in the early years. However, this support needs to be implemented from a non-ableist (non-tragic) perspective and in such a way as to assist the teacher in including the child, rather than creating micro-exclusion (see Chapter 1).

Understanding inclusion involves deconstructing the myth of 'normal' and moving from medical/tragedy model thinking towards recognising the social construction of 'difference' and 'disability' (stigmatisation)—and finally towards an affirmation model. This requires resistance to the 'circle of certainty', resistance to the tragedy/medical model and resistance to structures of domination that perpetuate these forms of discrimination and oppression.

Resistance requires being prepared to ask ourselves questions about what we believe and why. It requires us to reflect on our own practices and to be ready to consider that there is always more than one way of doing something, of participating and ultimately more than one way of being and becoming. 'True reflection leads to action … when the situation calls for action, that action will constitute an authentic praxis only if its consequences become the object of critical reflection' (Freire, 1970, p.48). For early years professionals, this openness to and engagement with resistance necessarily leads to day-to-day action towards greater inclusion in everyday moments within practice.

Resisting the medical/tragedy model view and ableist thinking makes it possible to see that we can all be equal but different. Through this we can create the space for inclusion—a space that is increasingly free of stigmatised thinking and practices as we continue to resist and move closer to an affirmation model.

This is not an easy task though—for anyone. Resistance can be 'difficult and painful/isolating/exhausting/draining/discouraging/disheartening' (Broderick, Reid & Valle, 2006, cited in Broderick et al., 2012, p.831). It can result in 'conflict or disequilibrium between our own convictions and beliefs and bureaucratic special education discourses and practices' (Broderick et al., 2012, p.831). And yet, it can also be rewarding and ultimately transforming—for ourselves and for the children, families and colleagues with whom we work.

**CASE STUDY 26.4**

## Inclusion in action

In my research with colleagues in Timor Leste, I was fortunate to spend time in a preschool with a teacher who I will call Maria. Maria runs a preschool for 25 children aged four to six years in a remote rural area of Timor Leste. Maria was selected by the village to run the preschool; she received 10 days of teacher education and is unpaid. In addition to ongoing impacts of the history of conflict, natural disasters and high levels of poverty in Timor Leste, Maria faces many practical everyday challenges in her role. However, she is a dedicated teacher with a strong commitment to the rights of all children to play and learn together.

Maria emphasised the need to raise awareness in the community about the importance of early years education. She raised concerns regarding young children's lack of access to the preschool and about similar issues in school attendance. The children all walk to the preschool, often across long distances over mountainous, dangerous terrain. This prevents many children from attending, particularly very young children due to safety concerns, and children who cannot walk this distance are not able to attend. Maria also shared that many children cannot attend as they are needed by their families to assist with farming.

Maria raised concerns about the lack of opportunity for children who experience disability to attend, noting that there are many children who experience disability in the village and surrounding areas. However, there is considerable stigma regarding disability and Maria shared that most children are hidden away to avoid stigma. Stigma and marginalisation of the Timorese indigenous population (a historically marginalised group of Timorese people) and language barriers were other factors leading to exclusion. Maria noted that there are multiple languages spoken within this community, but the community members do not speak Portuguese, which is the language that teachers are required to teach and report in.

Maria argued that teachers in Timor Leste require education regarding inclusive education. She also shared her concerns regarding the lack of materials for the preschool (for example a lack of books and drawing/writing/painting materials); serious issues with malnutrition; high infant and child mortality; lack of food for the children (including at the preschool); lack of clean water and toilet facilities; and the need for health care.

Clearly Maria faces many challenges. Nonetheless, she has been developing this preschool community for eight years and is aware of the importance of inclusion in the early years. As a reflective teacher, Maria expresses a strong commitment to social justice and inclusion.

Maria welcomes all children into this setting, including children who are marginalised due to their background or due to impairment, and actively advocates for the right of every child to attend and participate fully. Maria emphasises the need for building relationships with the children and their families, as well as working to raise awareness of the importance of the early years within the community.

*Kathy Cologon*

Rather than seeking to change children to 'fit' to the setting, Maria adapts materials and experiences, using small group, play-based experiences to support the children in their learning and development. One example of this is the incorporation of an improvised sign language that Maria has devised with the children (in Timor Leste, there is not a national sign language) so that they can all communicate together, including with one child who is deaf. In making up their own sign language that they can all understand, Maria and the children have avoided perpetuating barriers to doing and being for one student. Additionally, Maria has made visual supports to assist with communication and has created a colour-coding system that she uses to let the children know which small group to join for each activity. This way, the children can follow the colours—not just spoken instructions—as they move between activities. Using a range of visuals (incorporating multiple languages) to accompany all activities, Maria also uses the mother-tongue languages of the community while teaching the children the official languages little by little.

Maria walks to collect many children on her way to and from preschool every day in order to make the journey safe and encourage the children to attend. She engages the children in creative work with local and recycled materials, making resources to support their learning and development through play-based experiences.

Clearly there are many challenges for this community, but Maria recognises that all children can learn and have the right to participate. She embraces the diversity of the children in her community and seeks to provide flexible approaches and experiences and actively reflect on her practices in order to continue to increase inclusion. Through her actions Maria is playing a transformative role in increasing inclusion across this community.

### CRITICAL REFLECTION QUESTIONS

1. Reading Maria's story, consider the notion of resistance and the concepts of praxis and conscientização. In what ways is Maria engaging in these processes? Why are these concepts important for everyday early years practice?
2. Consider some of the barriers that Maria faces in her situation. What similar barriers might you experience? What barriers are different? How might attitudes impact on inclusion?
3. Reflecting on Maria's concerns and practices, what understanding of inclusion does Maria demonstrate? What qualities does Maria demonstrate that are important to inclusive education?
4. Concerns about lack of resources and professional development are frequently raised across the world as barriers to inclusion. Consider these concerns in light of Maria's context. What can you learn from Maria in terms of your own inclusive practice?

**CRITICAL REFLECTION QUESTIONS**

1. Consider the notion of a 'circle of certainty' and the role of resistance in being an inclusive early years professional.
2. Reflect on the idea of an affirmation model. What is challenging about an affirmation model? What is exciting about it? What does it mean for you in your life and your practice?
3. How can and will you create the conditions to continue to explore these ideas and find support for your own resistance?

As discussed above, inclusive education is a human right for all children. However, human rights don't just belong in conventions. As Eleanor Roosevelt argued (see Chapter 1), human rights are realised in the living out of the everyday between human beings. Inclusion is a broad concept that reaches into every corner of shared human existence. Inclusive education is one important aspect of this—and inclusive education is a process that has great potential for transformation towards a more inclusive society. Inclusive education is, as Roger Slee (2011) suggests, a necessary condition for the realisation of the democratic project.

# Conclusion

Writing of his childhood in his book *The Words* (*Les Mots*), the great French philosopher John Paul Sartre provides what could be viewed as an eloquent justification for inclusion and inclusive education. Reflecting on our shared humanity, Sartre concludes that he, like all of us, is simply: '[a] whole man, made of all men, worth all of them, and any one of them worth him' (Sartre, 1964, p.158).

It is, in the end, about equality. We are not the same. We are *all* different. Recognising that every person is of equal value and acting upon this in our everyday interactions with each other is what inclusion is about. For an early years professional, this means ensuring equitable access to, and participation in, education and care for every child, every day, and making sure that each and every person is always welcome and valued—whoever they may be.

# FOR FURTHER REFLECTION

1. Having reflected throughout the book, how would you now define:
   a. Disability;
   b. Difference;
   c. Diversity; and
   d. Inclusion.
2. Considering inclusive education as fundamental to quality education, and a basic human right for all children, how does this inform your philosophy of early years education?
3. Going forward, how will your understanding of inclusion, the importance of resistance to the dominant medical/tragedy model, and the ways in which resistance opens possibilities, influence your practice?

## WEBSITES

http://dsq-sds.org/article/view/841/1016
*Disability Studies Quarterly* is a freely available online, peer-reviewed disability studies journal

www.winchester.ac.uk/academicdepartments/EnglishCreativeWritingandAmericanStudies/Documents/w4cJune2013Diversity.pdf
*Write4Children: The International Journal for the Practice and Theories of Writing for Children and Children's Literature*. This is a special issue on diversity in children's literature.

www.childreninthepicture.org.uk
*Children in the picture*. This provides information about a research project focused on including characters who experience disability in children's books. Includes an image bank of inclusive illustrations.

http://www.edizionianicia.it/store/content/category/13-italian-journal-of-disability-studies
The *Italian Journal of Disability Studies* is a freely available online, peer-reviewed disability studies journal with papers in Italian and English.

www.cda.org.au
*Children with Disability Australia*. This is the peak representative body for children who experience disability in Australia. The website provides information and resources for advocating for children who experience disability.

## REFERENCES


Ainscow, M. (2007). Taking an inclusive turn. *Journal of Research in Special Educational Needs, 7*(1), 3–7. doi:10.1111/j.1471-3802.2007.00075.x

Armstrong, F. & Barton, L. (2008). Policy, experience and change and the challenge of inclusive education: the case of England. In L. Barton and F. Armstrong (Eds) *Policy, experience and change: Cross-cultural reflections on inclusive education* (pp.5–18). UK: Springer Science.

Brittain, I. (2004). An examination into the portrayal of deaf characters and deaf issues in picture books for children. *Disability Studies Quarterly, 24*(1). Retrieved from http://dsq-sds.org/article/view/841/1016

Broderick, A.A., Hawkins, G., Henze, S., Mirasol-Spath, C., Pollack-Berkovits, R. Prozzo Clune, H., Skovera, E. & Steel, C. (2012). Teacher counter narratives: Transgressing and 'restorying' disability in education, *International Journal of Inclusive Education, 16*(8), 825–842. doi:10.1080/13603116.2010.526636

Cologon, K. (2012). Confidence in their own ability: Postgraduate early childhood students examining their attitudes towards inclusive education. *International Journal of Inclusive Education, 16*(11), 1155–1173. doi:10.1080/13603116.2010.548106

Cologon, K. (2013a). *Inclusion in education: Towards equality for students with disability*. Children with Disability Australia, Issues Papers. Retrieved from www.cda.org.au/_literature_159457/Issues_Paper_on_Inclusion_-_PDF

Cologon, K. (2013b). Recognising our shared humanity: Human rights and inclusive education in Italy and Australia. *Italian Journal of Disability Studies, 1*(1). 151–169. Retrieved from www.edizionianicia.it/docs/Rivista_Vol1_N1.pdf - page=151.

Cologon, K. (2013c). Growing up with 'difference': Inclusive education and the portrayal of characters who experience disability in children's literature. *Write4Children: The International Journal for the Practice and Theories of Writing for Children and Children's Literature, 4*(2), 100–120. Retrieved from www.winchester.ac.uk/academicdepartments/EnglishCreativeWritingandAmericanStudies/Documents/w4cJune2013Diversity.pdf#page=100

Connors, C. & Stalker, K. (2003). *The views and experiences of disabled children and their siblings: A positive outlook*. London: Jessica Kingsley.

Connors, C. & Stalker, K. (2007). Children's experiences of disability: Pointers to a social model of childhood disability. *Disability & Society, 22*(1), 19–33. doi:10.1080/09687590601056162

Do, A., Do, S. & Whatley, B. (2011). *The little refugee*. Sydney: Allen & Unwin.

Foucault, M. (1991). *Remarks on Marx: Conversations with Duccio Trombadori*. New York: Semiotext(e) (Original work published 1981).

Foucault, M. (2002). *Power*. London: Penguin.

French, S. & Swain, J. (2004). Whose tragedy? Towards a personal non-tragedy view of disability. In J. Swain, S. French, C. Barnes & C. Thomas, *Disabling barriers—enabling environments* (pp.34–40). London: Sage.

Freire, P. (1970). *Pedagogy of the oppressed*. New York: Continuum International.

Freire, P. (1998). *Pedagogy of freedom: Ethics, democracy, and civic courage*. Maryland: Rowman & Littlefield Publishers, Inc.

Giroux, H.A. (2001). *Theory and resistance in education: Towards a pedagogy for the opposition*. Westport, CT: Bergin & Garvey.

Holliday Willey, L. (1999). *Pretending to be normal: Living with Asperger's syndrome*. London: Jessica Kingsley.

Lofthouse, L. & Ingpen, R. (2007). *Ziba came on a boat*. Victoria: Penguin.

Mason, M. (2000). *Incurably human*. London: Working Press.

Niland, A. (2013). Waiting for Hugo: Writing picture books about children with autism. *Write4Children: The International Journal for the Practice and Theories of Writing for Children and Children's Literature, 4*(2), 36–44. Retrieved from www.winchester.ac.uk/academicdepartments/EnglishCreativeWritingandAmericanStudies/Documents/w4cJune2013Diversity.pdf#page=36

Oldfield, A. (1992). *Woman suffrage in Australia*. Melbourne: Cambridge University Press.

Plaisance, E. (2008). The integration of 'disabled' children in ordinary schools in France: A new challenge. In L. Barton & F. Armstrong (Eds), *Policy, experience and change: Cross-cultural reflections on inclusive education* (pp.37–51). London, UK: Springer.

Sartre, J.P. (1964). *Les Mots*, translated by Irene Clephane. London: Penguin

Slee, R. (2011). *The irregular school: Exclusion, schooling and inclusive education*. Abingdon, Oxon: Routledge.

Swain, J., & French, S. (2000). Towards an affirmation model of disability. *Disability & Society, 15*(4), 569–582, doi:10.1080/09687590050058189

Westwood, P., & Graham, L. (2003). Inclusion of students with special needs: Benefits and obstacles perceived by teachers in New South Wales and South Australia. *Australian Journal of Learning Disabilities, 8*(1), 3–15. doi:10.1080/19404150309546718

Willis, J. & Ross, T. (2000). *Susan laughs*. Sydney: Random House.

Woloson, E. & Gough, B. (2003) *My friend Isabelle*. Bethesda: Woodbine House.

# Glossary

**ABLEISM**

'Discriminatory and exclusionary practices that result from the perception that being able-bodied is superior to being disabled, the latter being associated with ill health, incapacity, and dependence. Like racism, ableism directs structural power relations in society, generating inequalities located in institutional relations and social processes' (McLean, 2008, p.607).

**ABORIGINAL ELDER**

A respected person in the Aboriginal community who has a deep understanding, experience and knowledge of culture. Elders are often called upon to give guidance and to share knowledge within their local community, and to represent their communities locally, nationally and internationally. Elders are referred to as Aunty or Uncle as a sign of respect.

**ABORIGINAL IDENTITY**

'An Aboriginal or Torres Strait Islander person is a person of Aboriginal or Torres Strait Islander descent, who identifies as an Aboriginal or Torres Strait Islander and is accepted as such in the community in which he or she lives. Dodson (1994) states that this definition was first put forward in the constitutional section of the Department of Aboriginal Affairs report on the review of the administration of the working definition for Aboriginal and Torres Strait Islander people, Canberra 1981' (Forrest, 1998, p.101). This formal definition is accepted by most Aboriginal and Torres Strait Islander communities. Importantly it focuses on the social/community construction of Aboriginality rather than relying on physical appearance or particular lifestyles.

**ABORIGINAL PERSPECTIVES**

Aboriginal Perspectives Across the Curriculum (APAC) is a project that aims to broaden and deepen students' and teachers' understanding of Aboriginal cultures and ways of being. Teaching APAC will assist all students to be able to look at the world from an Aboriginal viewpoint and understand the different Aboriginal points of view on a range of issues such as reconciliation, social justice and equality (Government of Western Australia, 2010).

**ADAPTATION OF THE CURRICULUM**

Changes in the educational environment including the content, delivery and assessment of learning, and the physical and social environment, made to provide equal opportunity of access. Adaptation of the curriculum may or may not involve different outcomes to those set for an age group. Different countries, education jurisdictions and systems use different terms to describe and categorise the types of adaptation of curriculum. In the context of the *DDA 1992* and the *DSE 2005* the term adjustment is used to describe necessary measures taken to provide a student with a disability access to the curriculum *on the same basis as* students without a disability.

**ADAPTATIONS**

Changes to activities or the environment to meet the presenting needs of the child. This may require reviewing and reassessing goals and objectives in consultation with the child, the family and health professionals.

**AFFIRMATIVE MODEL OF DISABILITY**

'[A] non-tragic view of disability and impairment which encompasses positive social identities, both individual and collective ... grounded in the benefits of lifestyle and life experience of being impaired and disabled. This view has arisen in direct opposition to the dominant personal tragedy model of disability and impairment, and builds on the liberatory imperative of the social model' (Swain & French, 2000, p.569).

**AGENCY**

'[B]eing able to make choices and decisions, to influence events and to have an impact on one's world' (DEEWR, 2009, p.45).

**ASSESSMENT FOR LEARNING**

As outlined in the EYLF, this is 'the process of gathering and analysing information as evidence about what children know, can do and understand. It is part of an ongoing cycle that includes planning, documenting and evaluating children's learning' (DEEWR, 2009, p.17).

**ASYLUM SEEKER**

A refugee whose claims have not been formally processed, and therefore whose refugee status has not been officially determined.

**ATTENTION DEFICIT HYPERACTIVITY DISORDER (ADHD) AND OPPOSITIONAL DEFIANCE DISORDER (ODD)**

Two of three disruptive behaviour disorders listed in the Diagnostic and Statistical Manual for Mental Disorders (DSM) published by the American Psychiatric Association.

**ATTRIBUTE**

A characteristic of an object that can be measured, e.g. length, mass, colour.

**AUGMENTATIVE AND ALTERNATIVE COMMUNICATION (AAC)**

Symbols, aids, strategies, and techniques that enhance communication for people with complex communication needs (American Speech-Language Hearing Association, 1991). AAC facilitates choice, participation and social inclusion (Beukelman & Mirenda, 2013).

**AUTHENTIC/INAUTHENTIC**

These definitions as opposites are often used to define Aboriginality using a colonial framework. For example authentic Aboriginal people are positioned as living a 'traditional' lifestyle in isolated communities in Central or Northern Australia and are dark skinned. Fair-skinned Aboriginal people living in areas such as Victoria are more likely to be viewed as inauthentic, in being totally assimilated or absent.

**BELONGING**

'Knowing where and with whom you belong ... Belonging acknowledges children's interdependence with others and the basis of relationships in defining identities' (DEEWR, 2009, p.7)

**BIOLOGICAL THEORIES OF GENDER DEVELOPMENT**

Based on scientific interpretations, these argue that gender differences and inequities are inevitable, unchangeable and natural.

**CHILD-LED DISASTER RISK REDUCTION (CLDRR)**

A community-based, child-centred approach to DRR that acknowledges the capacity of children to improve the safety of their communities. CLDRR actively supports children in working individually and in groups to bring about positive DRR outcomes (Lopez et al., 2012; Martin 2010; Mitchell, Haynes, Hall, Wei, & Oven, 2008).

**CHILD RIGHTS-BASED APPROACH**

Humanitarian organisations that apply such an approach use the principles of child rights to plan, implement, manage and monitor emergency responses with the goal to strengthen the rights of children (Save the Children, 2002).

**CHRONIC HEALTH CONDITION**

A health condition that continues for a considerable time, has persistent consequences, requires ongoing hospitalisations, has a poor prognosis and impacts on quality of life.

**CONSCIENTIZAÇÃO**

Recognising and questioning the processes of power that underpin and perpetuate dominant beliefs and practices, thus developing a social consciousness and reflecting and acting upon this consciousness (Freire, 1970).

**CONTINUITY**

Implies that there is a relatively smooth and gradual shift, rather than abrupt major change, as a child and family transition from one setting to another. It does not imply that practices in both settings are necessarily identical.

**COPING STRATEGIES**

Behaviours that were adaptive in a child's traumatic environment but which are not appropriate in different contexts.

**COURTESY STIGMA**

Stigma felt by those around the stigmatised person (Goffman, 1963).

**CULTURAL PERSPECTIVE**

The set of values, beliefs and practices that characterise the behaviours and priorities of a group of people.

**CULTURALLY AND LINGUISTICALLY DIVERSE (CALD)**

A term often applied in policy contexts to describe groups of people whose languages, beliefs, customs and daily practices may differ from those of the 'mainstream'. In applying this term, it is critically important not to generalise within or across groups of people. Individuals from the same ethnic group, for example, may hold vastly different beliefs if they do not subscribe to the same religious faith. In the same vein, individuals from different ethnic backgrounds may, on the other hand, share fundamental values.

**CURRICULUM DIFFERENTIATION**

Encompasses different models and approaches aiming to provide teaching and learning experiences to students with diverse abilities in the same class, recognising their background knowledge, interests and preferences in learning.

**DISABLISM**

'The social imposition of avoidable restrictions on the life activities, aspirations and psycho-emotional well-being of people categorised as "impaired" by those deemed "normal". Disablism is social-relational in character and constitutes a form of social oppression in contemporary society—alongside sexism, racism, ageism, and homophobia. As well as enacted in person-to-person interactions, disablism may manifest itself in institutionalised and other socio-structural forms' (Thomas, 2012, p.211).

**DISASTER RISK REDUCTION (DRR)**

Working to reduce risks and strengthen supports to mitigate the impact of disasters (Hayden & Cologon, 2011).

**DIVERSITY DOLLS**

Adapted from Barbette Brown's work with persona dolls, these are specifically designed dolls used with children to talk about issues of diversity and inclusion (Brown, 2001).

**DOCUMENTATION**

The collection of artefacts that demonstrate and provide a record of learning.

**DYNAMIC ASSESSMENT**

An approach to assessment that focuses on potential for learning (Hasson & Joffe, 2007), and in which the child and adult participate actively together. It is consistent with Vygotsky's notion of the zone of proximal development. Dynamic assessment contrasts with static assessment in that, rather than focusing on static achievement levels, it focuses on *potential for learning* (Hasson & Joffe, 2007). Consequently, within dynamic assessment, the child and adult participate actively together. Dynamic assessment involves a strengths-based approach considering learning potential, rather than deficit, and involves a responsive approach to the child.

**EARLY CHILDHOOD DEVELOPMENT IN EMERGENCIES (ECDIE)**

ECDiE takes on a comprehensive approach that is critical to supporting the holistic wellbeing of young children. It considers the development of the whole child and promotes an integrated response to supporting children in emergencies. An integrated response links the standard emergency response sectors of health, nutrition, water and sanitation and hygiene (WASH), education, and child protection in an effort to support a young child's holistic development.

**EARLY YEARS**

Throughout this book, this term is used to encompass early childhood (prior-to-school) and primary school settings.

**EARLY YEARS PROFESSIONAL**

Throughout this book, this term refers to all professionals involved in early years education and care in a range of roles and settings, including teachers and allied health professionals, for example.

**EDUCATION FOR ALL (EFA)**

A global movement (supported by governments around the world and international agencies such as UNESCO, UNICEF, The World Bank, Save the Children and others) committed to ensuring that *all* citizens in *all* societies can benefit from basic education. The movement is guided by six specific goals, which focus particularly on ensuring access to groups of people who may be at risk of exclusion from education.

**EDUCATIONALLY BLIND**

Possessing insufficient vision accessible for learning so the majority of learning must occur through other senses.

**EDUCATIONALLY DEAF**

Possessing insufficient hearing accessible for learning, so the majority of learning must occur through other senses.

**EFFECTIVE HELP-GIVING**

Having good technical knowledge and skills, positive attitudes and behaviours, the ability to share decisions and actions with families, and a willingness to collaborate to ensure that goals are achieved.

**ENABLING PROMPTS**

Involve scaffolded support to assist learners unable to make a start or when they become stuck.

**ENACTED STIGMA**

The experience of discrimination (Goffman, 1963).

**EPIGENETIC LEGACY OF DISADVANTAGE**

Adverse experiences impact on the genome in ways that are then inherited by descendants. See the section entitled 'The underpinning neurobiology of trauma' on page 305.

**EUPHEMISMS**

Words that are used with the intention of being less blunt or direct when a topic or term is considered embarrassing, rude or unpleasant.

**EXCEPTIONAL STRENGTHS**

A child who is gifted is 'one who performs or has the potential to perform at a level significantly beyond his or her age peers and whose unique abilities and characteristics require special provision' (Harrison, 2003, p.8).

**EXPRESSIVE AND RECEPTIVE LANGUAGE**

The term 'expressive' relates to language production and 'receptive' relates to language comprehension. Receptive and expressive language difficulties can occur singly or in unison and are often grouped under the term Specific Language Impairment (SLI).

**EXTENDING PROMPTS**

Challenges to encourage learners to explore the task further.

**EXTENSION AND ENRICHMENT**

*Extension* concerns depth of learning, with level of difficulty tailored to individual children; *enrichment* is the widening of content beyond the usual curriculum.

**FAMILY-CENTRED PRACTICE**

A set of values, attitudes and approaches to providing services for children with disabilities and their families.

**FAMILY–PROFESSIONAL PARTNERSHIP**

Professionals working respectfully alongside parents and other family members, helping families achieve their goals for their child and/or family.

**FELT STIGMA**

The fear of enacted stigma and feelings of shame on account of being stigmatised (Goffman, 1963).

**FEMINIST POSTSTRUCTURALIST THEORIES OF GENDER DEVELOPMENT**

Argue that identity is multiple, contingent, shifting and political and that identities are not fixed or complete. Gender identities can be performed in multiple ways. Gender, sexuality, culture, 'race', class, ability and religion all intersect and cannot be separated when exploring identities. Feminist post-structuralist theories also examine how power is produced and exercised within the local context (e.g. the classroom) to examine how 'the gendered social order is structured and regulated' (Blaise, 2005, p.15).

**FOUNDATION YEAR**

The first year of formal schooling. 'Prep' or 'preparatory' is the title of the school foundation year in some Australian state jurisdictions. The foundation year has titles such as reception or kindergarten in other Australian states and other countries.

**HARD OF HEARING**

Possessing some hearing that is accessible for learning.

**HEGEMONY**

The 'domination of one group over another' (Gramsci, 1971 cited in Blaise, 2005, p.21). In relation to gender this means that there are dominant ways of performing gender that are seen as natural and desirable.

**HUMANITY**

All human beings, or the quality of being human.

**INCIDENTAL TEACHING**

A naturalistic intervention that makes use of teachable moments throughout the child's day through relationship-based engagement (Iacono, 1999; Stahmer, Akshoomoff, & Cunningham, 2011).

**INCLUSIVE EDUCATION**

Involves embracing human diversity and valuing and supporting the belonging and full participation of all people together (Cologon, 2013a). This includes upholding the rights of all children and providing education free from discriminatory beliefs and attitudes. Inclusive education is an ongoing process that requires examining beliefs and developing and putting into action inclusive values, policies and practices.

**INDIVIDUAL FAMILY SERVICE PLAN (IFSP)**

A planning process and document centred on mobilising resources to support children and families. IFSP outcomes are focused on the child and family.

**INDIVIDUALISED EDUCATION PLAN (IEP)**

A planning process and document focused on supporting a child's education inclusion.

**INDIVIDUALISED PLANNING**

Processes and practices used to develop educational programs for individual students based on their strengths, needs and interests. These processes and practices may vary depending on the setting, level of education and individual students. In schools, commonly a formalised individual plan is used to develop, record, review and report such planning.

**INDIVIDUALISED PRACTICE**

Treating every child and family member as a unique individual and using help-giving practices that are customised to meet each family's needs and priorities.

**INDIVIDUALISED TEACHING**

Teaching that recognises the individuality, or uniqueness, of every learner and therefore the need to teach children in a way that matches their individual strengths, interests, knowledge and needs. Individualised teaching is also sometimes referred to as differentiated teaching, acknowledging the importance of using teaching approaches and materials that are differentiated to suit the context and individual child. Individualised teaching involves meeting children where they are and scaffolding them to continue in a positive trajectory of development. This requires a flexible and responsive approach to teaching and is intended to support all children to flourish.

**INTEGRATION**

Involves attendance at a 'mainstream' setting, part-time or full-time, with needs-based practical accommodations to facilitate participation, but without change to the setting.

**INTERCULTURAL EDUCATION**

Goes beyond education *about* cultural and linguistic diversity to engage educators and children in challenging stereotypes and racism in order to develop more culturally inclusive attitudes and behaviours.

**INTER-DISCIPLINARY**

In inter-disciplinary work, professionals work together (for example, to develop service plans), but maintain professional boundaries.

**INTERGENERATIONAL SKILLS AND KNOWLEDGES**

Aboriginal Elders as knowledge holders and as educators of children and younger adults are central in transmitting skills and knowledges across the generations in Aboriginal communities. Such 'intergenerational skills and knowledges' represent the multiple knowledges and understandings that are fundamental for Aboriginal children to make meaning of who they are in relation to the past, present and the future. Intergenerational skills and knowledges include Aboriginal ways of understanding interactions and relationships not just with human beings, but also with the land, animals and the vast spaces above, below and all around us. Storytelling as Aboriginal pedagogy is central to this process and therefore essential to Aboriginal identity.

**INTERNATIONAL CONVENTION**

An international human rights document which, unlike a declaration, is legally binding. Conventions are supported by protocols to facilitate their implementation by signatory countries.

**INTERVENTION PROGRAMS**

Programs that are usually designed to meet specific needs—this may be for children perceived to have difficulties, or they can be concerned with a particular curriculum or behaviour goal. They are more often for individuals or small groups than universal; they can be delivered by regular or additional staff, and are often evaluated.

**LITERATE CITIZENSHIP**

Being valued and supported as an active and developing participant in the literate world of any given community (Kliewer, 2008).

### LOW VISION

Possessing some vision accessible for learning.

### MACRO-EXCLUSION IN EDUCATION

When children are denied education or excluded from general education settings and segregated into 'special' schools, classes or units for all or some of the time (Cologon, 2013a).

### MAINSTREAMING

The placement of children together within the same setting, but without making adjustments or adaptations to facilitate inclusion.

### MASKING FACTORS

These conceal the extent of children's abilities, leading to lower educator expectations. These factors may pertain to the child, the family and the educational setting.

### MEDICAL MODEL OF DISABILITY

Holds that disability exists within a person, that it is impairment or is caused by impairment, that it is a tragedy, and that the person needs to be 'fixed' and 'cured' (Cologon, 2013; Thomas 2004; WHO, 2002). A medical model of disability is also known as a charity, or tragedy model of disability.

### MEDICAL PLAY

Play that uses real or pretend medical equipment and supplies to help children understand and express their feelings and fears about hospitals and medical procedures. It also allows them to practise new skills and understandings.

### MICRO-EXCLUSION IN EDUCATION

When physical presence or placement alone is misunderstood as inclusion. Micro-exclusion is exclusion within activities or settings that are considered to be inclusive and occurs when a child is present but segregated in the sense of participating in a different curriculum with different staff members, or is removed for some of the time to receive support.

### MODES OF COMMUNICATION

Channels of communication such as writing, drawing, using technology, speech, gesture, gaze and posture.

### MULTICULTURALISM

Often used to refer to the Australian Government's Multicultural Policy. 'Multiculturalism' reflects acknowledgment that Australia is made up of, celebrates and embraces cultural diversity. Importantly, multiculturalism reflects a policy commitment to a 'just, inclusive and socially cohesive society where everyone can participate in the opportunities that Australia offers' (Government of Australia, 2011, p.5)

### MULTI-DISCIPLINARY

In multi-disciplinary work, professionals from different disciplines work individually, alongside one another, rather than *with* one another.

### NATIONAL CURRICULUM

A common program of learning areas or subjects, skills and capabilities that aims to provide uniformity and consistency of content and standards within a state, regardless of any other differences and variations in the education systems and sectors of different jurisdictions.

### NATURAL DISASTER

A natural event or a series of events that disrupts the basic fabric and functioning of a society or community. Disasters may result in high casualties, loss of infrastructure and essential services, and loss of livelihoods beyond the capacity of the affected society or community. A family's assets and material belongings may be destroyed leaving households impoverished and displaced. Families may be forced to relocate in the aftermath of a disaster. Children exposed to internal displacement may face a number of specific risks such as separation from their families, child trafficking and a host of other child protection concerns.

**NON-DIRECTIVE**

This is about not leading the child directly, not working to prescribed patterns or structures, but being responsive to the child and to emerging possibilities. This is not the same as just leaving children to it. Non-directive teachers are still guided by overall principles, such as valuing play and valuing children's own ideas, and they are often sensitively observing and responding to individual children.

**NUMERACY**

The *use* of mathematics in the contexts of daily life.

**OPPORTUNITY**

Circumstances, a situation or an occasion that makes it possible to do something, achieve a goal or develop.

**ORIM-ARTS FRAMEWORK**

Adult roles providing Opportunities, Recognition, Interaction and a Model for development in the arts.

**OTHERING**

The stigmatising process of creating an 'other' who we perceive to be different to ourselves, and in some sense lesser or inferior.

**PARTICIPATION**

Being involved and taking part, through action, along with others.

**PARTICIPATION MODEL**

The participation model involves analysing or assessing the participation requirements of a particular task or experience to determine what AAC support is required to facilitate inclusion (Beukelman & Mirenda, 2013).

**PERSON-FIRST LANGUAGE**

Naming the person before the use of a label. For example, a person with chronic illness.

**PHONIC DECODING**

Phonics, which builds on phonological awareness, is the process of actively teaching relationships between graphemes (letters) and phonemes (sounds) and how they are used to make up words in reading and spelling.

**PHONOLOGICAL AWARENESS**

Phonological awareness can be defined as an individual's ability to consciously focus on the sound structure of language. For example, identifying syllables in a spoken word.

**PLAY-BASED ASSESSMENT**

Involves evaluating children's developmental skills, social interactions, learning approaches and so on in the natural context of play.

**PLAY-BASED LEARNING**

A playful context for learning in which children enjoy themselves, and are self-motivated and actively engaged.

**POSTCOLONIAL/ISM**

A time and space that represents the end of colonial occupation politically, and yet is traversed by practices that are constantly challenging and challenged by colonial domination (Young, 2001; 2003).

**PRAXIS**

'Reflection and action upon the world on order to transform it' (Freire, 1970, p.33).

**PROJECT-BASED INVESTIGATIONS**

Rich units of study that cross multiple curriculum areas. They enable students to question and investigate areas of learning in depth.

**PSYCHOSOCIAL SUPPORT**

Protecting or promoting psychosocial wellbeing and development for children and their families (IASC, 2007).

**REASONABLE ADJUSTMENT**

An adaptation to assist a child with disability to participate in education, while balancing the interests of others and ensuring the validity of assessment outcomes.

**RECOGNISED CONTRIBUTION**

Contributions made by a person or group that are recognised and valued by those around them.

**REFUGEE**

The 1951 Refugee Convention establishing the United Nations High Commissioner for Refugees (UNHCR) spells out that a refugee is someone who 'owing to a well-founded fear of being persecuted for reasons of race, religion, nationality, membership of a particular social group or political opinion, is outside the country of his nationality, and is unable to, or owing to such fear, is unwilling to avail himself of the protection of that country' (UNHCR, 2013, para. 3).

**RELATIONSHIP-BASED APPROACH**

An approach to professional interactions that emphasises a deep concern with mutual understanding and 'interest' in each other's perspectives/priorities. Moore (2007, p.5) describes such relationships as characterised by nine key features: Attunement; Responsiveness; Clear communication; Managing communication breakdowns; Emotional openness; Understanding one's own feelings; Empowerment; Moderate challenges; and Building coherent narratives.

**RIGHTS FRAMEWORK**

A framework used for observing, interpreting and planning. It focuses on strengths and children's agency, using a strengths-based, ecological approach.

**SCIENCE**

In schools science is considered as a distinct curriculum area. Here we define science as children's understanding of the world around them, their place within it and the interconnection of all things living and non-living.

**SCIENTIFIC PROCESSES**

The range of activities that children use to acquire science knowledge such as: questioning, investigating, reasoning, communication, designing and observing.

**SENSE IMPAIRMENT**

When additional support is required beyond what is usually provided in order for a child to effectively learn through the senses.

**SERVICE SUPPORT PLAN (SSP)**

A planning process and document centred on staff goals and needs, with a view to enhancing staff capacity to support inclusion.

**SHADOW ASSISTANT**

A support educator who focuses on one child (e.g. a child with a disability) to offer substantial individual assistance throughout the day.

**SOCIAL MODEL OF DISABILITY**

The social model has largely been developed and promoted by people who experience disability, particularly within the disability rights movement in the UK. It holds that disability is a socially created problem, brought about by unaccommodating attitudes, physical and social environments, not a problem within an individual, and that it demands a political response (WHO, 2002, p.9).

**SOCIAL RELATIONAL UNDERSTANDING OF DISABILITY**

Suggests that disability is always socially situated, and arises from social interaction between people with ascribed impairments and people without, with the former being constructed as 'second rate'. These interactions can occur at a person-to-person or institutional scale. The social relational understanding also suggests that there are parallels between racism and sexism and the social relationships that bring disability into being (Thomson, 1999, 2001, 2007).

**SOCIAL SUPPORT**

Any type of assistance provided by a member of someone's close personal network that positively helps the recipient.

**SOCIALISATION THEORIES OF GENDER DEVELOPMENT**

Argue that children construct their gender identity through their interactions with their social world. Children are viewed as passively absorbing what it means to be a boy or a girl through observations of their environments and then modelling and imitating gender behaviours based on their observations (Blaise, 2005).

**SOCIOCULTURAL CONTEXT**

The combination of social and cultural factors such as the resources, customs, beliefs and attitudes associated with the individual's social, ethnic, cultural or religious group; the context begins very close to the child in the family, and extends to their school, neighbourhood, nationality and ethnicity.

**SUBITISING**

The process of recognising the number of objects in a group without counting them. (From the Italian word *subito*, meaning 'suddenly'.)

**TECHNOLOGY**

All tools used to facilitate engagement, explore content and document children's actions and construction of knowledge. Technology includes tools such as digital microscopes, interactive whiteboards and tablet technologies.

**THEORY OF MIND (TOM)**

A term that is used to describe the ability to impute mental states (emotions, intentions, knowledge and wants) to others (Baron-Cohen, Leslie, & Frith, 1985).

**TRANS-DISCIPLINARY**

In trans-disciplinary work, the most recent iteration of inter-professional work in early intervention and also the most collaborative, professionals work across professional boundaries.

**UNIVERSAL DESIGN FOR LEARNING (UDL)**

It is structured around three principles that recognise the diverse ways that children learn by providing multiple means of representation, action and expression and engagement. Each principle includes a number of guidelines and each guideline has a number of checkpoints. The aim of the UDL is to design a curriculum that is inclusive of all learners.

**UNREASONABLE OR UNJUSTIFIABLE HARDSHIP**

Demonstrated when catering for a child's needs would require extraordinary and unmanageable changes to facilities, staffing or education services that are beyond reasonable service resources or available funding sources.

**VERTICAL AND HORIZONTAL TRANSITIONS**

Vertical transitions mark a distinct uni-directional shift from one service to another (e.g. transition into an ECEC service or into school). Horizontal transitions occur regularly within a day or week (e.g. between an education program and a therapy program), between segments of a program day in the one setting (e.g. mat time to free play) or sometimes within a year (e.g. changing centres or schools for children who are geographically mobile).

# Index